Teach Yourself
VISUAL C++® 5

in 21 Days
Fourth Edition

Teach Yourself
VISUAL C++ ® 5
in 21 Days
Fourth Edition

Ori Gurewich
Nathan Gurewich

SAMS
PUBLISHING

201 West 103rd Street
Indianapolis, Indiana 46290

Publisher and President   Richard K. Swadley
Publishing Manager   Greg Wiegand
Director of Editorial Services   Cindy Morrow
Director of Marketing   Kelli S. Spencer
Assistant Marketing Managers   Kristina Perry, Rachel Wolfe

Acquisitions Editor
Christopher Denny

Development Editor
Fran Hatton

Production Editor
Nancy Albright

Indexer
Christine Nelsen

Technical Reviewer
Matt Butler

Editorial Coordinator
Katie Wise

Technical Edit Coordinator
Lynette Quinn

Resource Coordinator
Deborah Frisby

Editorial Assistants
Carol Ackerman
Andi Richter
Rhonda Tinch-Mize

Cover Designer
Tim Amrhein

Book Designer
Gary Adair

Copy Writer
David Reichwein

Production Team Supervisors
Brad Chinn
Charlotte Clapp

Production
Jena Brandt
Jeanne Clark
Tim Osborn
Ian Smith
Andrew Stone

Teach Yourself
VISUAL C++® 5
in 21 Days
Fourth Edition

Ori Gurewich
Nathan Gurewich

201 West 103rd Street
Indianapolis, Indiana 46290

Publisher and President   Richard K. Swadley
Publishing Manager   Greg Wiegand
Director of Editorial Services   Cindy Morrow
Director of Marketing   Kelli S. Spencer
Assistant Marketing Managers   Kristina Perry, Rachel Wolfe

Acquisitions Editor
Christopher Denny

Development Editor
Fran Hatton

Production Editor
Nancy Albright

Indexer
Christine Nelsen

Technical Reviewer
Matt Butler

Editorial Coordinator
Katie Wise

Technical Edit Coordinator
Lynette Quinn

Resource Coordinator
Deborah Frisby

Editorial Assistants
Carol Ackerman
Andi Richter
Rhonda Tinch-Mize

Cover Designer
Tim Amrhein

Book Designer
Gary Adair

Copy Writer
David Reichwein

Production Team Supervisors
Brad Chinn
Charlotte Clapp

Production
Jena Brandt
Jeanne Clark
Tim Osborn
Ian Smith
Andrew Stone

Overview

Appendixes

Contents

Appendixes

Acknowledgments

We would like to thank Chris Denny, the acquisitions editor of this book; Fran Hatton, the development editor; and Nancy Albright, the production editor.

We would also like to thank Matt Butler, the technical editor of the book, and all the other people at Sams Publishing who contributed to this book.

Thanks also to Microsoft Corporation, which supplied us with technical information and various betas and upgrades of the software product.

About the Authors

Ori Gurewich and Nathan Gurewich are well-known authors of several best-selling books about Visual C++, Visual Basic for Windows, C/C++ programming, multimedia programming, database design and programming, and other topics.

Ori Gurewich holds a bachelor's degree in electrical engineering from Stony Brook University, Stony Brook, New York. His background includes working as a senior software engineer and a software consultant engineer for companies developing professional multimedia and Windows applications. He is an expert in the field of PC programming and network communications and has developed various multimedia algorithms for the PC. Ori Gurewich can be contacted by e-mail at the following address:

```
Ori_Gurewich@msn.com
```

Nathan Gurewich holds a master's degree in electrical engineering from Columbia University, New York, and a bachelor's degree in electrical engineering from Hofstra University, Long Island, New York. Since the introduction of the PC, he has been involved in the design and implementation of commercial software packages for the PC. He is an expert in the field of PC programming and in providing consulting services on programming, local and wide area networks, database management and design, and software marketing. Nathan Gurewich can be contacted by e-mail at the following address:

```
Nathan_Gurewich@msn.com
```

Tell Us What You Think!

As a reader, you are the most important critic and commentator of our books. We value your opinion and want to know what we're doing right, what we could do better, what areas you'd like to see us publish in, and any other words of wisdom you're willing to pass our way. You can help us make strong books that meet your needs and give you the computer guidance you require.

Do you have access to CompuServe or the World Wide Web? Then check out our CompuServe forum by typing GO SAMS at any prompt. If you prefer the World Wide Web, check out our site at http://www.mcp.com.

NOTE

> If you have a technical question about this book, call the technical support line at 317-581-3833.

As the publishing manager of the group that created this book, I welcome your comments. You can fax, e-mail, or write me directly to let me know what you did or didn't like about this book—as well as what we can do to make our books stronger. Here's the information:

FAX: 317-581-4669

E-mail: programming_mgr@sams.samspublishing.com

Mail: Greg Wiegand
          Sams Publishing
          201 W. 103rd Street
          Indianapolis, IN 46290

Introduction

Using Visual C++ to Develop Professional Windows Applications

Welcome to the fascinating world of programming powerful, professional Windows applications with the Microsoft Visual C++ 5 package.

Windows is currently the most popular operating system for the PC; consequently, almost all vendors ship their PCs with a mouse and the Windows operating system already installed. In this book, *Teach Yourself Visual C++ 5 in 21 Days*, you'll learn how to develop state-of-the-art Windows applications by using the Visual C++ package. This means you'll have to write code using the C/C++ programming language—but don't worry! Even if you've never used C/C++ before, you'll be able to use this book. Why? Because this book comes with a tutorial in Appendixes A, B, and C that teaches you C/C++ quickly. As you'll soon see, you'll write your first Windows program with Visual C++ in Chapter 1 of this book!

Why Use Windows? Why Use Visual C++?

There are several reasons why Windows has become so popular in a relatively short time:

☐ *Device-independent programs.* Windows lets you write device-independent programs. This means that while you're writing the application, you don't have to concern yourself with what type of printer, mouse, monitor, keyboard, sound card, CD-ROM drive, or other devices your users own. Your application will work fine, no matter what hardware your users have. So does this mean, for example, that your user can have *any* sound card? Not at all! It is your user's responsibility to install the sound card into his or her PC. During the installation, Windows asks the user to install the appropriate drivers, then either accepts or rejects the sound card. Windows will accept the sound card if the hardware and the software (drivers) your user received from the sound card vendor were used according to Windows requirements. Once Windows accepts the sound card, the Windows applications you write should work with that sound card. The same applies for other devices, such as the printer, the monitor, and the CD-ROM drive.

☐ *Pre-installed code.* A lot of code is already installed in your user's PC. Once Windows is installed, the PC contains much Windows-related software. This code exists on your PC (the developer's PC) and on your users' PCs. This means that before you even start writing the first line of code yourself, your user already has more than half your program in his or her PC! Not only do you not have to write this code, you don't even have to distribute that code to your users.

☐ *Standard user interface.* The user-interface mechanism is the same for all Windows applications. Without reading your application's documentation, your users know how to execute your application, they can use the icon on the corner of the application's window to minimize the window, they know the meaning of the OK and Cancel buttons, they know what the About dialog box is, and they understand many other features of your program before you even start writing it!

These reasons for using Windows are applicable no matter what programming language you use for developing the application. Why should you use Visual C++ for writing Windows applications and not "regular" C with the SDK (Software Developer's Kit) for Windows? The answer to this question is provided in the following sections.

What Is Visual C++?

The *C++* in this book's title means you have to use C/C++ for writing the code. However, this book assumes no previous C/C++ experience. That's why the book includes a tutorial (see Appendixes A, B, and C). During the course of this book, you will learn all the C++ techniques you need to write professional, powerful Windows applications.

Now that you know the meaning of the *C++* in *Visual C++,* what does *Visual* mean? It means you'll accomplish many of your programming tasks by using the keyboard and the mouse to visually design and write your applications. You'll select controls such as pushbuttons, radio buttons, and scrollbars with the mouse, drag them to your application's window, and size them—and you'll be able to see your application as you build it (this is called *design time*). In other words, you'll be able to see what your application will look like before you execute it. This is a great advantage because it saves you considerable time (you can see your application without compiling/linking it), and you can change your mind about the placement and size of edit boxes, pushbuttons, and other objects simply by using the mouse.

ClassWizard: What Is That?

The most powerful feature of Visual C++ is a "wizard" called *ClassWizard.* ClassWizard writes code for you! In the industry, this type of program is often referred to as a *CASE (computer-aided software engineering) program.* Of course, ClassWizard is not a magic program—you have to tell it what you want it to write for you. For example, suppose you visually placed a pushbutton in your application's window with the mouse. Once you have placed the button, you want to write code that's executed when the user clicks that button. This is the time to use ClassWizard. By choosing various options in ClassWizard's window, you tell ClassWizard to prepare all the overhead code. ClassWizard responds by preparing all the overhead code and then showing you where to insert your own code. Therefore, your job is to write your code in the area ClassWizard prepared. In addition to ClassWizard, Visual C++ is equipped with other wizards, such as the AppWizard. You'll learn about all these wizards during the course of this book.

What Are ActiveX Controls?

One of the main advantages of using Visual C++ 5 is the ability to use ActiveX controls (also called OCX controls). ActiveX controls are pieces of software that you can easily "plug" into your Visual C++ programs. In modern modular programming (such as Visual C++), the trend is to "pick up" ActiveX controls and plug them into your programs. ActiveX controls let you perform sophisticated and powerful operations quickly. In Chapters 18, 19, and 20, "Creating Your Own ActiveX Control (Parts I, II, and III)," you'll learn how to design your own ActiveX controls.

In this book, you'll also learn how to use ActiveX controls to implement multimedia programs that include animation and sound.

Conventions Used in This Book

The following typographic conventions are used in this book:

- [ ] Statements, functions, variables, events, and any text you type or see on the screen appear in a `computer` typeface.

- [ ] *Italics* highlight technical terms when they first appear in the text and are sometimes used to emphasize important points.

- [ ] Code that you type yourself appears in a **bold computer** typeface. This book also sets off code that you enter with these "flags":

```
/////////////////////////
// MY CODE STARTS HERE
/////////////////////////

.............................
... Your code appears here ...
.............................

/////////////////////////
// MY CODE ENDS HERE
/////////////////////////
```

Visual C++ Is Fun

Visual C++ is an interesting, fun package to use because it lets you develop sophisticated Windows applications in a short time. So relax and prepare yourself for a pleasant journey!

Week 1

At a Glance

In Week 1, you'll realize that Visual C++ is very easy to use. Yes, on the first day of this week you'll jump into the Visual C++ water! You'll actually write your first Visual C++ program.

On the second day, you'll learn how to write a Visual C++ program that uses the edit box control and the check box control. You'll learn how to visually create a dialog box that uses these controls and how to attach code to their events.

On the third day, you'll learn how to use ActiveX controls. You'll learn what ActiveX controls are and how to incorporate them into your Visual C++ programs.

1

2

3

4

5

6

7

On the fourth day, you'll learn how to detect and use mouse operations from within your Visual C++ programs. In particular, you'll learn how to create a program that lets the user draw with the mouse. You'll also learn how to detect which keys are pressed on the keyboard.

On the fifth day, you'll learn how to design menus and incorporate them into your Visual C++ programs.

On the sixth day, you'll learn how to create and use predefined and custom-made dialog boxes.

On the seventh day, you'll learn how to create programs that draw graphics. You'll also learn how to install and use a timer.

Day **1**

Writing Your First Visual C++ Application

Today you'll write your first Visual C++ program! This involves two steps:

- The visual design step
- The code-writing step

In the *visual design step*, you design the appearance of your program. You use the Visual C++ tools to place various objects (such as pushbuttons, scroll bars, radio buttons, and so on) in your programs' windows. During the visual design step, you don't write any code.

In the *code-writing step*, you write code using the Visual C++ text editor and the C++ programming language.

The Hello.EXE Program

In this chapter, you'll write a Visual C++ program called Hello.EXE. Before you start writing it, however, let's first specify what the Hello.EXE program should look like and what it should do:

■ When you start the Hello.EXE program, its window should look like the one shown in Figure 1.1.

Figure 1.1.

The window of the Hello.EXE program.

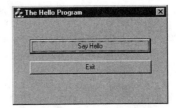

■ The Hello.EXE program includes two pushbuttons: Say Hello and Exit. When you click the Say Hello button, a HELLO message box appears. (See Figure 1.2.)

Figure 1.2.

The HELLO message box.

☐ To close the HELLO message box, click its OK button. Then click the Exit pushbutton to terminate the Hello.EXE program.

Now that you know what the Hello.EXE program should look like and how it should behave, you can start designing it. In the following sections, you'll design the Hello.EXE program by following step-by-step instructions.

Creating a Directory for the Hello.EXE Program Files

Before you start creating the project file and program files of the Hello.EXE program, first create a directory on your hard drive where the Hello.EXE files will reside.

☐ Use the Windows Explorer of Windows 95 to create the directory C:\TYVCPROG \PROGRAMS\CH01.

Creating the Project of the Hello.EXE Program

The first thing you have to do when you start a new Visual C++ program is create the project of the program. To create the project of the Hello.EXE program, follow these steps:

☐ Start Visual C++. The icon of the Visual C++ program resides in the Microsoft Visual C++ 5 program group. (See Figure 1.3.)

Figure 1.3.
Executing Visual C++.

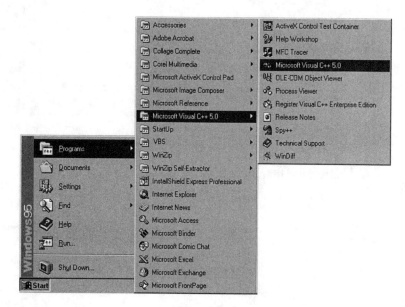

After you execute Visual C++, its main window appears, as shown in Figure 1.4. (Depending on the desktop setting of your Visual C++, the window of your Visual C++ might look a little different from the one shown in Figure 1.4.)

NOTE

In Figure 1.4, the title of the window is Microsoft Developer Studio. You write and maintain your Visual C++ programs by using the Microsoft Developer Studio. The names "Developer Studio" and "Visual C++" are interchangeable; however, all the steps in the following sections and throughout this book will use "Visual C++" instead of "Developer Studio."

Figure 1.4.

The main window (desktop) of Visual C++.

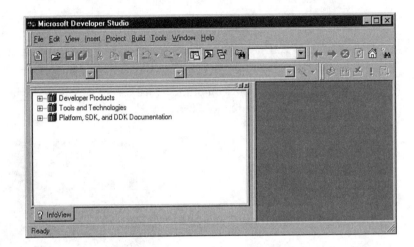

Now create the project of the Hello.EXE program:

☐ Select New from the File menu of Visual C++.

Visual C++ responds by displaying the New dialog box. (See Figure 1.5.)

Figure 1.5.

The New dialog box.

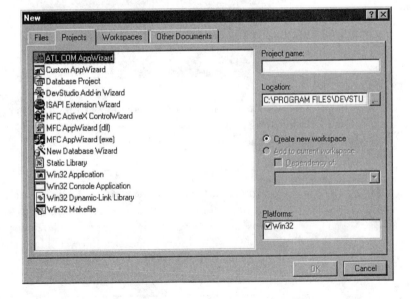

☐ As shown in Figure 1.5, make sure that the Projects tab of the New dialog box is selected.

☐ Select MFC AppWizard (exe) in the New dialog box.

By selecting MFC AppWizard (exe), you are telling Visual C++ that you want to create an EXE program.

☐ Type Hello in the Project name box of the New dialog box.

By typing Hello in the Project name box, you are telling Visual C++ that you want your project to be called Hello.

☐ Click the small button that is located to the right of the Location box (the button that has three dots (...) as its caption) and then select the C:\TYVCPROG\PROGRAMS\CH01\ directory from the dialog box that pops up.

By selecting the C:\TYVCPROG\PROGRAMS\CH01\ directory you are telling Visual C++ that you want the files of the Hello project to be under the C:\TYVCPROG\PROGRAMS\CH01\ directory.

You have finished specifying the project type, project name, and project location for the Hello.EXE program. Your New dialog box should now look like the one shown in Figure 1.6.

Figure 1.6.

Specifying the project type, project name, and project location.

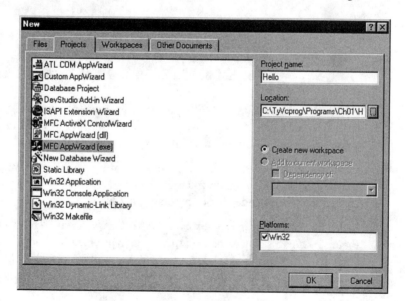

☐ Click the OK button of the New dialog box.

Visual C++ responds by displaying the MFC AppWizard - Step 1 dialog box. (See Figure 1.7.)

Figure 1.7.

The MFC AppWizard - Step 1 dialog box.

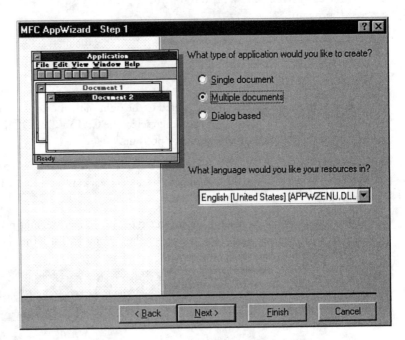

What is MFC AppWizard? *MFC AppWizard* is a powerful "wizard" that writes the skeleton code of your program for you. Instead of writing overhead code every time you start writing a new program, you can use MFC AppWizard to write it for you.

In the following steps, you'll use the dialog boxes of MFC AppWizard to specify various characteristics of the program you want to create. Once you are done, MFC AppWizard will create the skeleton code of your program for you.

MFC AppWizard currently displays the MFC AppWizard - Step 1 dialog box shown in Figure 1.7. In this dialog box, you specify the type of application you want to create and the language you would like to use for the program's resources.

☐ Click the "Dialog based" radio button of the MFC AppWizard - Step 1 dialog box.

By selecting the Dialog based radio button, you are telling MFC AppWizard that you want to create a *dialog-based program*, which means that the main window of the Hello program is a dialog box. As you saw earlier in Figure 1.1, the Hello.EXE program's main window should be a dialog box with two pushbuttons: Say Hello and Exit.

☐ Leave the Language combo box at the default setting: English [United States] (APPWZENU.DLL).

Your MFC AppWizard - Step 1 dialog box should now look like the one shown in Figure 1.8.

Figure 1.8.
The MFC AppWizard - Step 1 dialog box.

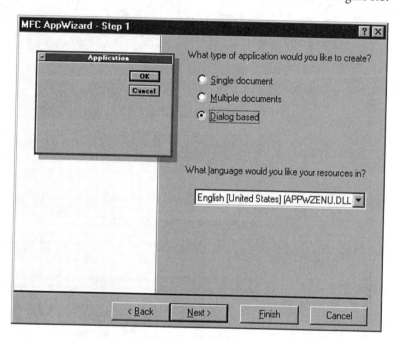

☐ Click the Next button to advance to the next MFC AppWizard dialog box.

The MFC AppWizard - Step 2 of 4 dialog box appears. (See Figure 1.9.)

As you can see, the MFC AppWizard - Step 2 of 4 dialog box lets you specify whether various features should be included in the program. This dialog box also lets you specify the title of the program's dialog box (that is, the title of the main window).

☐ Set the MFC AppWizard - Step 2 of 4 dialog box as shown in Figure 1.10. Leave all the check boxes at the default settings and set the title of the dialog box to The Hello Program.

☐ Click the Next button to advance to the next MFC AppWizard dialog box.

The MFC AppWizard - Step 3 of 4 dialog box appears. (See Figure 1.11.)

Figure 1.9.

*The MFC
AppWizard - Step 2
of 4 dialog box.*

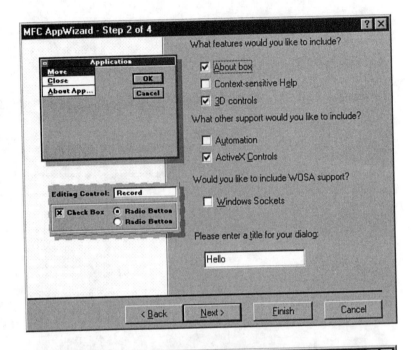

Figure 1.10.

*Setting the MFC
AppWizard - Step 2
of 4 dialog box.*

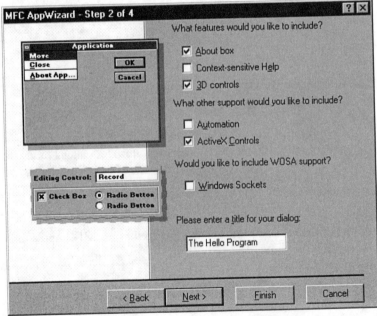

Figure 1.11.

The MFC AppWizard - Step 3 of 4 dialog box.

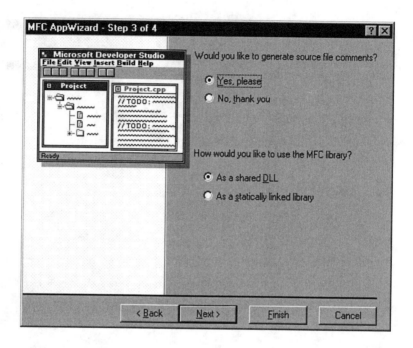

As you can see, the MFC AppWizard - Step 3 of 4 dialog box asks you two questions:

1. Would you like to generate source file comments?
2. How would you like to use the MFC library?

☐ Answer the two questions as shown in Figure 1.11.

By using the settings shown in Figure 1.11, you are specifying the following:

1. When MFC AppWizard creates the skeleton code of the program for you, it will include comments. Including comments in the skeleton files will help you understand the code that MFC AppWizard writes for you (in case you want to review it).

2. The program that MFC AppWizard creates for you will use a dynamic link library (DLL), not a statically linked library. Using a DLL gives you the advantage of having a smaller EXE file.

   ☐ Click the Next button to advance to the next MFC AppWizard dialog box.

   The MFC AppWizard - Step 4 of 4 dialog box appears. (See Figure 1.12.)

Figure 1.12.
*The MFC
AppWizard - Step 4
of 4 dialog box.*

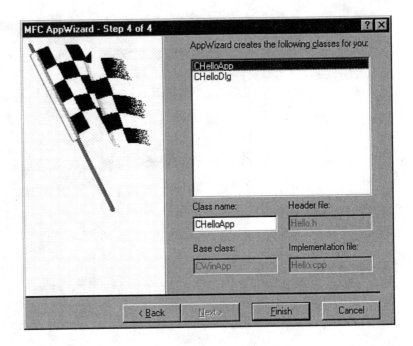

As you can see, the MFC AppWizard - Step 4 of 4 dialog box tells you what classes and files MFC AppWizard will create for you. You don't have to change any of the settings in this dialog box.

☐ Click the Finish button to tell MFC AppWizard to create the project and skeleton files of the Hello program.

The New Project Information dialog box appears. (See Figure 1.13.)

The New Project Information dialog box summarizes all the specifications you made in the previous steps.

☐ Click the OK button of the New Project Information dialog box.

Visual C++ responds by creating all the skeleton files of the Hello program in the directory C:\TYVCPROG\PROGRAMS\CH01\HELLO. Finally, the Visual C++ window appears, as shown in Figure 1.14.

Figure 1.13.

The New Project Information dialog box.

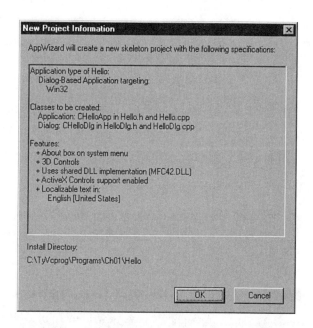

Figure 1.14.

The Visual C++ window after creating the project of the Hello program.

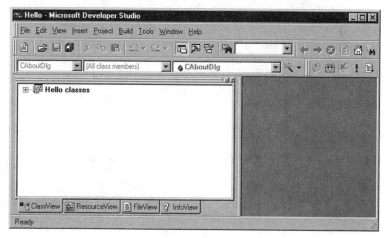

NOTE

Depending on Visual C++'s desktop settings, your Visual C++ desktop may look different from the window shown in Figure 1.14.

The dialog box at the left side of the window, which contains the text Hello classes, is called the Project Workspace dialog box. If you don't see the Project Workspace dialog box in your Visual C++ desktop, select Workspace from the View menu of Visual C++.

You'll learn about the Project Workspace dialog box (what it is and how to use it) later in this chapter.

As shown in Figure 1.14, the title of your Visual C++ window is now Hello - Microsoft Developer Studio. The Hello in the title indicates that you are currently working on the Hello project.

Compiling and Linking the Hello Program

Believe it or not, although you haven't written a single line of code yet, you already have a working Windows program. The skeleton code that MFC AppWizard wrote for you actually does something. To see this code in action, you need to compile and link the Hello program and then execute it.

Follow these steps to compile and link the Hello program:

☐ Select Set Active Configuration from the Build menu of Visual C++.

Visual C++ responds by displaying the Set Active Project Configuration dialog box. (See Figure 1.15.)

Figure 1.15.

The Set Active Project Configuration dialog box.

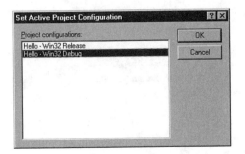

You use the Set Active Project Configuration dialog box to specify how Visual C++ will generate the EXE file of the project. If you set the Set Active Project Configuration dialog box to Win32 Debug (as in Figure 1.15), Visual C++ will generate an EXE file with the code lines needed for debugging. However, if you set the Set Active Project Configuration dialog box to Win32 Release, no debugging code will be embedded in the EXE file.

☐ Select Hello - Win32 Release in the Default Project Configuration dialog box, then click the OK button.

Although you haven't written a single line of code yet, try compiling and linking the program at this early stage of the development.

To create the Hello.EXE file, do the following:

☐ Select Build Hello.EXE from the Build menu.

Visual C++ responds by compiling and linking the files of the Hello program and creating the Hello.EXE file.

NOTE

In the preceding step, you were instructed to compile and link the Hello program by selecting Build Hello.EXE from the Visual C++ Build menu. You can also compile and link the program by selecting Rebuild All from the Build menu.

When you select Build Hello.EXE from the Build menu, only the files changed since the last time you compiled the program are compiled. When you select Rebuild All from the Build menu, all the program files are compiled (whether or not the files were changed since the last compilation).

Sometimes, your project may go out of sequence and Visual C++ will "think" that files that need to be compiled should not be compiled. In such cases, you can force Visual C++ to compile all the files by selecting Rebuild All from the Build menu.

☐ Select Execute Hello.EXE from the Build menu to execute the Hello.EXE program.

Visual C++ responds by executing the Hello.EXE program. The main window of the Hello.EXE program appears, as shown in Figure 1.16.

Figure 1.16.

*The main window of
the Hello.EXE
program.*

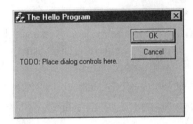

As you can see, the skeleton code that MFC AppWizard wrote for you created a simple EXE program whose main window contains two pushbuttons (OK and Cancel) and displays the text TODO: Place dialog controls here.

Notice that the title of the program's window is The Hello Program, which you specified in the MFC AppWizard - Step 2 of 4 dialog box. (Refer to Figure 1.10.)

The Hello.EXE program also includes an About dialog box, because you used Step 2 of the MFC AppWizard to include an About dialog box in the program. (Refer to Figure 1.10.) To see the About dialog box of the Hello.EXE program, follow these steps:

☐ Open the System menu of the Hello.EXE program by clicking the small icon at the upper-left corner of the application window.

  The Hello.EXE program responds by displaying its system menu. (See Figure 1.17.)

Figure 1.17.

*The system menu of
the Hello.EXE
program.*

☐ Select About Hello from the system menu.

  The Hello.EXE program responds by displaying the About Hello dialog box. (See Figure 1.18.)

☐ Close the About dialog box by clicking its OK button.

☐ Terminate the Hello.EXE program by clicking the × icon at the upper-right corner of the program's window.

Figure 1.18.

*The About Hello
dialog box.*

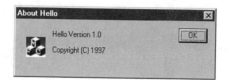

As you have just seen, the skeleton code that MFC AppWizard wrote for you produced a working Windows program. Of course, at this point the Hello.EXE program does not look and behave like you want it to. In the following sections, you'll use the Visual C++ tools to customize the Hello.EXE program until it looks and behaves like you want it to.

NOTE

In the preceding steps, you executed the Hello.EXE program by selecting Execute Hello.EXE from the Visual C++ Build menu.

The Hello.EXE program is a regular Windows EXE file, so you can also execute it directly from Windows just as you execute any other Windows EXE file (for example, by using Windows Explorer).

Visual C++ placed the Hello.EXE file in your C:\TYVCPROG\PROGRAMS\CH01\HELLO\RELEASE directory because you set the default project configuration to Win32 - Release before compiling and linking the files of the Hello project. If you had set the default project configuration to Win32 - Debug, Visual C++ would have placed the Hello.EXE file in the Debug subdirectory— C:\TYVCPROG\PROGRAMS\CH01\HELLO\DEBUG.

The Visual Implementation of the Hello.EXE Program

As discussed at the beginning of this chapter, writing a Visual C++ program involves two steps: the visual design step and the code-writing step. You'll now perform the visual design step. You'll use the visual design tools of Visual C++ to customize the main window of the Hello.EXE program until it looks like the one shown in Figure 1.1.

Take a look at the desktop of Visual C++. Your Visual C++ desktop should currently look like the one shown in Figure 1.19.

Figure 1.19.
The Visual C++
desktop with the
Project Workspace
dialog box of the
Hello project.

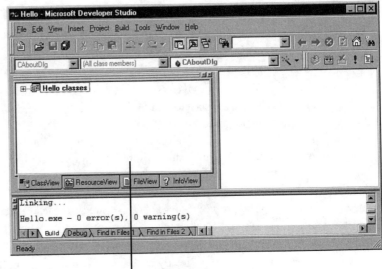

The Project Workspace dialog box of the Hello program

As shown in Figure 1.19, the dialog box at the left side of the Visual C++ window is called the Project Workspace dialog box. Remember to select Workspace from the View menu if you don't see the Project Workspace dialog box.

As its name implies, the Project Workspace dialog box is the place for managing all aspects of your project. For example, you can use the Project Workspace dialog box to view a list of all your project files or to open any of your project files.

As shown in Figure 1.19, the bottom of the Project Workspace dialog box has four tabs: ClassView, ResourceView, FileView, and InfoView. The ClassView tab lets you view and edit the project's classes. The ResourceView tab lets you view and edit the project's resources (for example, dialog boxes, menus, icons, BMP pictures). You use the ResourceView tab for the visual design of your program. The FileView tab lets you view and edit any of the project files. The InfoView tab lets you access the documentation (help files) of Visual C++.

Right now you want to customize the visual aspect of the Hello.EXE program, so you need to use the ResourceView tab:

☐ Click the ResourceView tab of the Project Workspace dialog box.

Your Project Workspace dialog box should now look like the one shown in Figure 1.20.

Figure 1.20.
*Selecting the
ResourceView tab.*

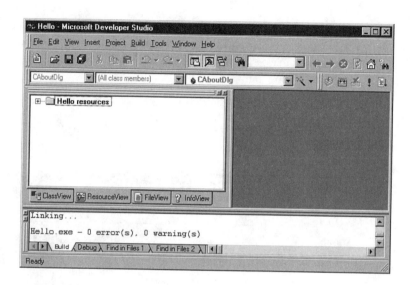

As shown in Figure 1.20, the Project Workspace dialog box displays the text Hello resources.

☐ Double-click the Hello resources item to list all the resources of the Hello project (or click
the + icon to the left of the Hello resources item).

*Visual C++ responds by expanding the Hello resources item to list several subitems. (See
Figure 1.21.)*

Figure 1.21.
*Expanding the Hello
resources item.*

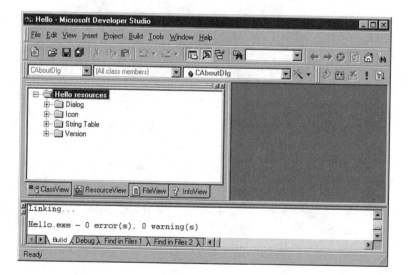

As shown in Figure 1.21, the subitems under the Hello resources item are various resources types: Dialog, Icon, String Table, and Version. Right now, your objective is to visually design the dialog box that serves as the main window of the Hello program. Therefore, you have to expand the Dialog item:

☐ Double-click the Dialog item (or click the + icon to the left of the Dialog item).

   Visual C++ responds by expanding the Dialog item—two subitems are listed beneath it. (See Figure 1.22.)

Figure 1.22.

*Expanding the
Dialog item.*

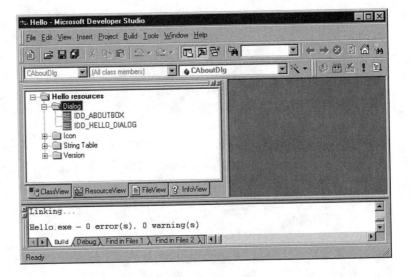

As you can see, there are two subitems under the Dialog item: IDD_ABOUTBOX and IDD_HELLO_DIALOG. As you might have guessed, IDD_ABOUTBOX is the ID of the Hello program's About dialog box, and IDD_HELLO_DIALOG is the ID of the dialog box that serves as the main window of the Hello program.

☐ Double-click the IDD_HELLO_DIALOG item to customize the dialog box serving as the Hello program's main window.

   Visual C++ responds by displaying the IDD_HELLO_DIALOG dialog box in design mode, ready for you to customize. (See Figure 1.23.)

As you can see, the IDD_HELLO_DIALOG dialog box contains three controls: an OK pushbutton, a Cancel pushbutton, and the text TODO: Place dialog controls here. Your objective is to customize the IDD_HELLO_DIALOG dialog box so that it will look like the one shown in Figure 1.1.

Figure 1.23.

*The
IDD_HELLO_DIALOG
dialog box in design
mode (before
customization).*

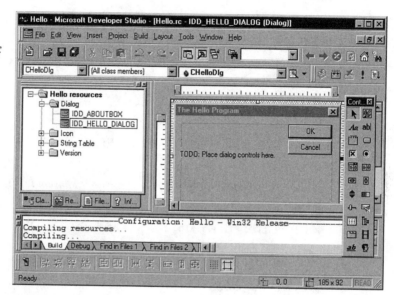

NOTE

In the following steps, you will customize the
IDD_HELLO_DIALOG dialog box. While you work on the
IDD_HELLO_DIALOG dialog box, you will find it more convenient
to view the IDD_HELLO_DIALOG dialog box in Full Screen mode.
When you view a dialog box in Full Screen mode, the entire area of
the screen is dedicated to the purpose of viewing and editing the
dialog box.

To view the IDD_HELLO_DIALOG dialog box in Full Screen mode,
do the following:

☐ While the IDD_HELLO_DIALOG dialog box is selected, select Full
Screen from the View menu.

*Visual C++ responds by displaying the IDD_HELLO_DIALOG
dialog box in Full Screen mode.*

To cancel the Full Screen mode, do the following:

☐ Press the Esc key on your keyboard.

Visual C++ responds by canceling the Full Screen mode.

Begin the customization by deleting the OK pushbutton, deleting the Cancel pushbutton, and deleting the TODO: Place dialog controls here. text:

☐ Click the OK pushbutton in the IDD_HELLO_DIALOG dialog box, then press the Delete key.

Visual C++ responds by removing the OK button from the IDD_HELLO_DIALOG dialog box.

☐ Click the Cancel pushbutton in the IDD_HELLO_DIALOG dialog box, then press the Delete key.

Visual C++ responds by removing the Cancel button from the IDD_HELLO_DIALOG dialog box.

☐ Click the text TODO: Place dialog controls here. in the IDD_HELLO_DIALOG dialog box, then press the Delete key.

Visual C++ responds by removing the text TODO: Place dialog controls here. *from the IDD_HELLO_DIALOG dialog box.*

Your IDD_HELLO_DIALOG dialog box is now empty. (See Figure 1.24.)

Figure 1.24.
The IDD_HELLO_DIALOG dialog box after removing the controls.

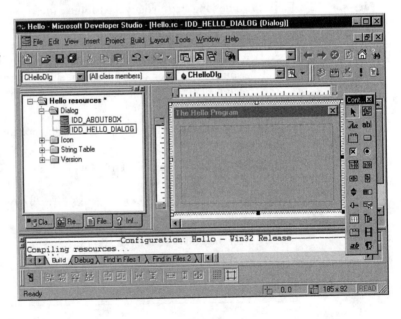

In the following steps, you'll place two pushbutton controls in the IDD_HELLO_DIALOG dialog box; to do this, you'll use the Controls toolbar of Visual C++. (See Figure 1.25.)

Figure 1.25.

The Controls toolbar of Visual C++.

NOTE

If you do not see the Controls toolbar on your Visual C++ desktop, do the following:

☐ Select Customize from the Tools menu of Visual C++.

Visual C++ will respond by displaying the Customize dialog box.

☐ Select the Toolbars tab of the Customize dialog box and make sure the Controls check box has a check mark in it. If it doesn't, click it to place a check mark in it.

☐ Close the Customize dialog box by clicking its Close button.

Visual C++ will respond by displaying the Controls toolbar.

If you still have problems locating the Controls toolbar, display the IDD_HELLO_DIALOG dialog box in Full Screen mode (that is, select Full Screen from the View menu). Remember, to cancel the Full Screen mode, press the Esc key.

Follow these steps to place a pushbutton in the IDD_HELLO_DIALOG dialog box:

☐ Click the pushbutton tool, shown in Figure 1.26, in the Controls toolbar of Visual C++.

Figure 1.26.

The pushbutton tool in the Controls toolbar.

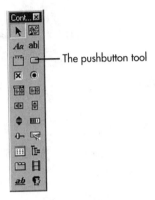

The pushbutton tool

☐ Now click in the IDD_HELLO_DIALOG dialog box where you want the pushbutton control to appear.

> *Visual C++ responds by placing a pushbutton control at the point where you clicked the mouse. (See Figure 1.27.)*

Figure 1.27.

Placing a pushbutton control in the IDD_HELLO_DIALOG dialog box.

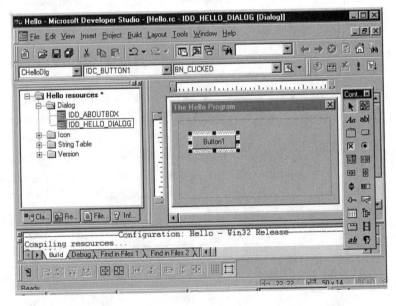

The pushbutton caption is currently Button1. As shown in Figure 1.1, it should be Say Hello. Here is how you change the pushbutton caption:

☐ Right-click on the Button1 pushbutton control (that is, place the mouse cursor over the pushbutton and click the mouse's right button).

Visual C++ responds by displaying a pop-up menu next to the Button1 control. (See Figure 1.28.)

Figure 1.28.

The pop-up menu displayed after you right-click the Button1 control.

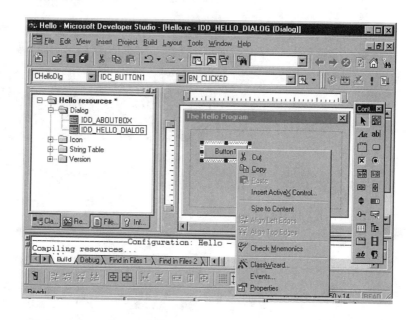

☐ Select Properties from the pop-up menu.

Visual C++ responds by displaying the Push Button Properties dialog box. (See Figure 1.29.)

As shown in Figure 1.29, the Caption box contains the text Button1. Here is how you change the caption:

☐ Click in the Caption box and replace the text Button1 with the text Say Hello.

Your Push Button Properties dialog box should now look like the one shown in Figure 1.30.

Figure 1.29.
The Push Button
Properties dialog box.

Figure 1.30.
Changing the caption
to Say Hello.

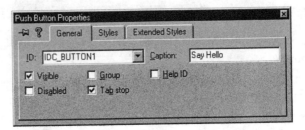

☐ Close the Push Button Properties dialog box by clicking the ✕ icon at the upper-right corner of the window.

Your IDD_HELLO_DIALOG dialog box should now look like the one shown in Figure 1.31—the pushbutton's caption is Say Hello.

Figure 1.31.
The pushbutton's
new caption.

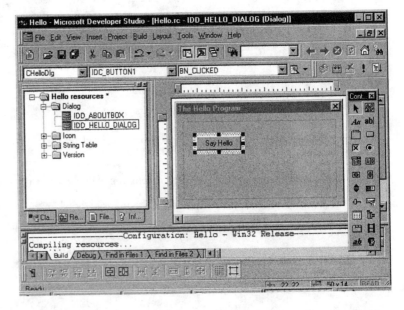

As shown in Figure 1.1, the Say Hello button should be wider than it is in Figure 1.31. Here is how you change the width of the Say Hello button:

☐ Make sure the Say Hello button is selected (by clicking it), then drag any of the handles on the button's right edge to the right until the button is the desired width. (The handles are the solid black squares on the rectangle enclosing the button.)

Similarly, to increase the height of the Say Hello button, do the following:

☐ Make sure the Say Hello button is selected, then drag any of the handles on the bottom edge of the button downward until the button is the desired height.

The enlarged Say Hello button is shown in Figure 1.32.

Figure 1.32.

Enlarging the Say Hello button.

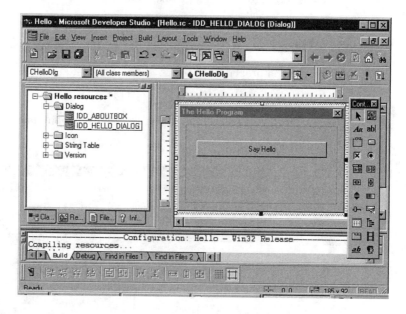

You can also move the Say Hello button to any location in the dialog box by clicking the button and dragging it with the mouse.

When you placed the button in the dialog box, Visual C++ automatically assigned IDC_BUTTON1 as a default ID for the button. However, you should change the button's ID to make it easier to identify it as the ID for the Say Hello button (for example, IDC_SAYHELLO_BUTTON). Here is how you do that:

☐ Right-click the Say Hello button, then select Properties from the pop-up menu.

Visual C++ responds by displaying the Push Button Properties dialog box. (Refer to Figure 1.29.)

☐ Click in the ID box and replace the text IDC_BUTTON1 with the text IDC_SAYHELLO_BUTTON.

From now on, Visual C++ will refer to the Say Hello button as IDC_SAYHELLO_BUTTON.

You are almost done with the visual design of the IDD_HELLO_DIALOG dialog box. As shown back in Figure 1.1, the dialog box should also contain an Exit pushbutton. Follow these steps to add the Exit pushbutton:

☐ Place a new button in the dialog box by clicking the pushbutton tool in the Controls toolbar, then clicking anywhere in the IDD_HELLO_DIALOG dialog box.

☐ Move the new button below the Say Hello button by clicking and dragging it.

☐ Make the new button the same size as the Say Hello button by dragging its handles.

Now change the properties of the new button as follows:

☐ Right-click the new button and select Properties from the pop-up menu.

☐ Set the Caption property to Exit.

☐ Set the ID property to IDC_EXIT_BUTTON.

Your IDD_HELLO_DIALOG dialog box should now look like the one shown in Figure 1.33.

Figure 1.33.
The
IDD_HELLO_DIALOG
dialog box with the
Say Hello and Exit
pushbuttons.

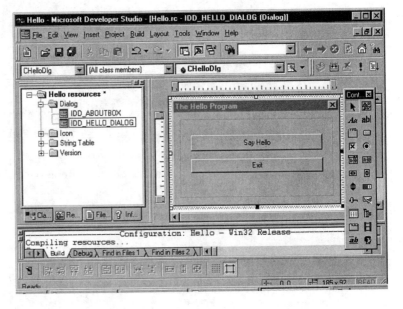

Congratulations! You have finished the visual design of the Hello program.

☐ Save your work by selecting Save All from the File menu.

Seeing Your Visual Design in Action

Although you haven't written any code yet, you have finished the visual design of the Hello.EXE program. To see your visual design in action, follow these steps:

☐ Select Build Hello.EXE from the Build menu.

> *Visual C++ responds by compiling and linking the Hello program.*

Once Visual C++ finishes compiling and linking the program, you can execute the program:

☐ Select Execute Hello.EXE from the Build menu.

> *Visual C++ responds by executing the Hello.EXE program. The main window of Hello.EXE appears, as shown in Figure 1.34.*

Figure 1.34.

The main window of the Hello.EXE program.

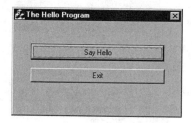

As you can see, the main window of the Hello.EXE program (the IDD_HELLO_DIALOG dialog box) appears just as you designed it—with a Say Hello pushbutton and an Exit pushbutton.

☐ Click the Say Hello and Exit buttons.

As you can see, nothing happens when you click the Say Hello and Exit buttons. That's because you haven't attached any code to them. You'll attach code to these buttons in the following sections.

☐ Terminate the Hello.EXE program by clicking the ✕ icon at the upper-right corner of the program's window.

Attaching Code to the Say Hello Pushbutton

As you have seen, at this point nothing happens when you click the Say Hello and Exit pushbuttons. In this section, you'll attach code to the Say Hello pushbutton so the program will do what it's supposed to do when you click the button. In the next section, you'll attach code to the Exit pushbutton.

When you click the Say Hello pushbutton, the Hello.EXE program should display a HELLO message box. (Refer to Figure 1.2.) Follow these steps to attach code to the Say Hello button:

☐ Select ClassWizard from the View menu.

Visual C++ responds by displaying the MFC ClassWizard dialog box. (See Figure 1.35.)

Figure 1.35.

The MFC ClassWizard dialog box.

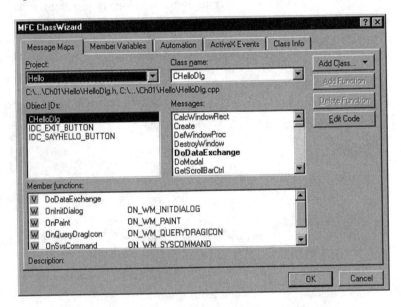

What is ClassWizard? ClassWizard is another powerful wizard that lets you attach code to the controls of your program very easily. In the following steps, you'll use ClassWizard to attach code to the Say Hello pushbutton.

As shown in Figure 1.35, the top of ClassWizard's dialog box has five tabs: Message Maps, Member Variables, Automation, ActiveX Events, and Class Info.

☐ Make sure the Message Maps tab is selected.

☐ Make sure the Class name drop-down list box at the top of the ClassWizard dialog box is set to CHelloDlg.

The CHelloDlg class is the class associated with the IDD_HELLO_DIALOG dialog box (the main window of the Hello program). This class was created for you by MFC AppWizard when you created the Hello project. Because the Say Hello button is in the IDD_HELLO_DIALOG dialog box, the code you attach to the Say Hello pushbutton will be written in the CHelloDlg class.

You will now use ClassWizard to write the code that's automatically executed when the user clicks the Say Hello pushbutton. Here is how you do that:

☐ Select IDC_SAYHELLO_BUTTON in the Object IDs list box of the ClassWizard dialog box.

Your MFC ClassWizard dialog box should now look like the one shown in Figure 1.36.

Figure 1.36.

Selecting the IDC_SAYHELLO_BUTTON item in the Object IDs list box.

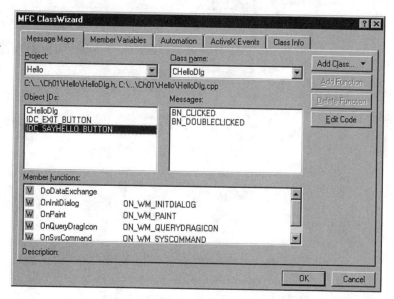

In the preceding step, you selected the IDC_SAYHELLO_BUTTON object because you want to attach code to the Say Hello pushbutton (recall that IDC_SAYHELLO_BUTTON is the ID you assigned to the Say Hello button).

The Messages list box (to the right of the Object IDs list) lists messages representing events associated with the currently selected object. As shown in Figure 1.36, there are two possible events (messages) associated with the IDC_SAYHELLO_BUTTON pushbutton: BN_CLICKED and BN_DOUBLECLICKED. BN_CLICKED represents the event "the user clicked the pushbutton"; BN_DOUBLECLICKED represents the event "the user double-clicked the pushbutton."

You want to attach code to the event "the user clicked the Say Hello pushbutton." You have already selected IDC_SAYHELLO_BUTTON in the Object IDs list box, so now you need to perform this step:

☐ Select the BN_CLICKED item in the Messages list box.

Your MFC ClassWizard dialog box should now look like the one shown in Figure 1.37—the IDC_SAYHELLO_BUTTON is selected in the Object IDs list box, and BN_CLICKED is selected in the Messages list box.

Figure 1.37.

Selecting the
BN_CLICKED *event of*
the
IDC_SAYHELLO_BUTTON
button.

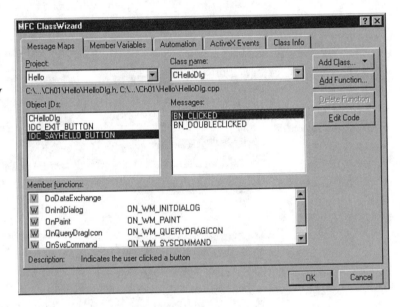

Next, you have to tell ClassWizard to add the function corresponding to the event you just selected. This function is executed automatically when the user clicks the Say Hello button. Here is how you do that:

☐ Click the Add Function button of ClassWizard.

ClassWizard responds by displaying the Add Member Function dialog box. (See Figure 1.38.)

As shown in Figure 1.38, ClassWizard suggests naming the new function OnSayhelloButton.

☐ Click the OK button to accept the default name that ClassWizard suggests.

ClassWizard responds by adding the function OnSayhelloButton() to the Hello program. This function will be automatically executed when the user clicks the Say Hello pushbutton.

Figure 1.38.

The Add Member Function dialog box.

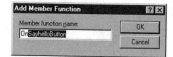

ClassWizard wrote only the code that declares the OnSayhelloButton() function and the skeleton of the function. It is your job to write the code in the OnSayhelloButton() function. To do that, follow these steps:

☐ Click the Edit Code button of ClassWizard.

ClassWizard responds by opening the file HelloDlg.cpp with the function OnSayhelloButton() ready for you to edit. (See Figure 1.39.)

NOTE

If you wish, you can view the HelloDlg.cpp file in Full Screen mode. When you view a file in Full Screen mode, the entire area of the screen is dedicated to the purpose of viewing and editing the file.

To view the HelloDlg.cpp file in Full Screen mode, do the following:

☐ While the window of the HelloDlg.cpp file is selected, select Full Screen from the View menu.

Visual C++ responds by displaying the Hellodlg.cpp file in Full Screen mode.

To cancel the Full Screen mode, do the following:

☐ Press the Esc key on your keyboard.

Visual C++ responds by canceling the Full Screen mode.

☐ Write code in the OnSayhelloButton() function so that it will look like this:

```
void CHelloDlg::OnSayhelloButton()
{

// TODO: Add your control notification handler code here

/////////////////////////
// MY CODE STARTS HERE
/////////////////////////

MessageBox("Hello! This is my first Visual C++ program.");

/////////////////////////
// MY CODE ENDS HERE
/////////////////////////

}
```

Figure 1.39.

The
OnSayhelloButton()
function, ready for
editing.

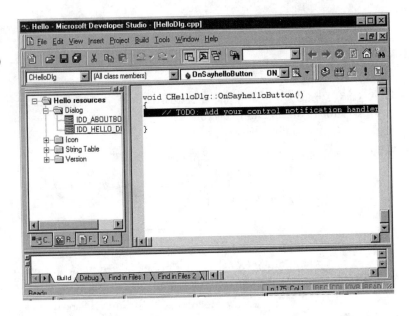

☐ Save your work by selecting Save All from the File menu.

As you have just seen, when you use MFC ClassWizard to attach code to a control, you type your code in a skeleton of the function that ClassWizard writes for you.

To make it easy for you to distinguish between code that Visual C++ wrote for you and code that you type yourself, the following convention is used in this book:

Code that you type yourself is presented in the following manner:

```
/////////////////////////
// MY CODE STARTS HERE
/////////////////////////


. . . . . . . . . . . . . . . . . . . . . . . . . .
... Your code appears here ...
. . . . . . . . . . . . . . . . . . . . . . . . . .


/////////////////////////
// MY CODE ENDS HERE
/////////////////////////
```

> The MY CODE STARTS HERE and MY CODE ENDS HERE comments will help you distinguish between code that Visual C++ wrote for you and code that you typed.

The code you typed in the `OnSayhelloButton()` function is very simple (one line):

```
MessageBox("Hello! This is my first Visual C++ program.");
```

It uses the `MessageBox()` function to display a message box with the text `Hello! This is my first Visual C++ program.`

To see the code you attached to the Say Hello pushbutton in action, follow these steps:

☐ Select Build Hello.EXE from the Build menu.

   Visual C++ responds by compiling and linking the Hello program.

Once Visual C++ finishes compiling and linking the program, you can execute it:

☐ Select Execute Hello.EXE from the Build menu.

   Visual C++ responds by executing the Hello.EXE program. The main window of Hello.EXE appears, as shown in Figure 1.34.

☐ Click the Say Hello pushbutton.

As expected, the Hello.EXE program responds by displaying a HELLO message box. (See Figure 1.40.) The code you attached to the Say Hello pushbutton is working!

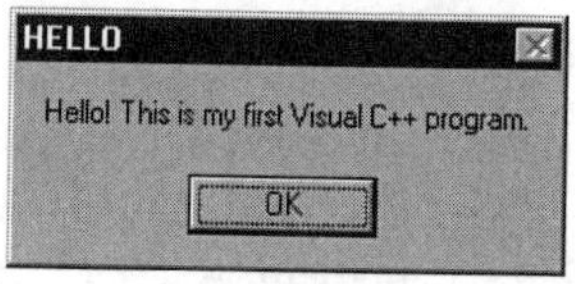

Figure 1.40.

Displaying the HELLO message box.

☐ Close the HELLO message box by clicking its OK button.

☐ Try to click the Exit pushbutton.

Of course, nothing happens when you click the Exit pushbutton because you haven't attached code to it yet. You'll attach code to the Exit pushbutton in the following section.

☐ Terminate the Hello.EXE program by clicking the ✕ icon at the upper-right corner of the program's window.

Attaching Code to the Exit Pushbutton

At this point, nothing happens when the user clicks the Exit pushbutton. In this section, you'll attach code to the Exit pushbutton so that the Hello.EXE program will terminate when the user clicks this button. Follow these steps to attach code to the Exit pushbutton:

☐ Select ClassWizard from the View menu of Visual C++.

> *Visual C++ responds by displaying the MFC ClassWizard dialog box. (Refer to Figure 1.35.)*

☐ Make sure the Message Maps tab is selected.

☐ Make sure the Class name drop-down list box at the top of the ClassWizard dialog box is set to CHelloDlg.

In the preceding step, you were instructed to select the CHelloDlg class in the ClassWizard dialog box because you're going to attach code to the Exit pushbutton, which is in the IDD_HELLO_DIALOG dialog box. The IDD_HELLO_DIALOG dialog box is associated with the CHelloDlg class. Therefore, the code you attach to the Exit pushbutton will be written in the CHelloDlg class.

☐ Select IDC_EXIT_BUTTON in the Object IDs list of the ClassWizard dialog box (because you are attaching code to the Exit pushbutton).

☐ Select BN_CLICKED in the Messages list box to attach code to the BN_CLICKED event of the Exit pushbutton.

Your MFC ClassWizard dialog box should now look like the one shown in Figure 1.41—IDC_EXIT_BUTTON is selected in the Object IDs list box, and BN_CLICKED is selected in the Messages list box.

By selecting IDC_EXIT_BUTTON in the Object IDs list box and BN_CLICKED in the Messages list box, you are specifying that you want to attach code to the event "the user clicked the Exit pushbutton." That is, you want to attach code to the Click event of the Exit pushbutton.

Next, tell ClassWizard to add the function corresponding to the event you just selected. This function is executed automatically whenever the user clicks the Exit button. Here is how you do that:

☐ Click the Add Function button of ClassWizard.

> *ClassWizard responds by displaying the Add Member Function dialog box. ClassWizard suggests naming the new function OnExitButton.*

Figure 1.41.

*Selecting
IDC_EXIT_BUTTON
in the Object IDs list
box and BN_CLICKED
in the Messages
list box.*

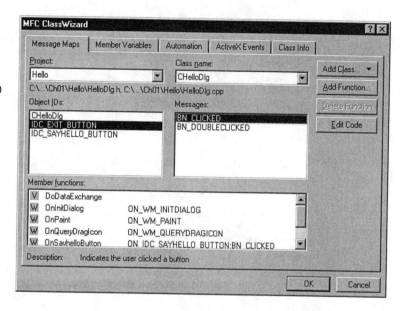

☐ Click the OK button of the Add Function dialog box to accept the default name that ClassWizard suggests.

> *ClassWizard responds by adding the function* OnExitButton() *to the Hello program. This function will be executed automatically when the user clicks the Exit pushbutton.*

To write code in the OnExitButton() function, do the following:

☐ Click the Edit Code button of ClassWizard.

> *ClassWizard responds by opening the file Hello.cpp with the function* OnExitButton() *ready for you to edit.*

☐ Write code in the OnExitButton() function so that it will look like this:

```
void CHelloDlg::OnExitButton()
{
// TODO: Add your control notification handler code here

/////////////////////////
// MY CODE STARTS HERE
/////////////////////////

OnOK();

/////////////////////////
// MY CODE ENDS HERE
/////////////////////////

}
```

NOTE

In the preceding step, you are instructed to type this statement:

```
OnOK();
```

Notice that both the O and the K in OnOK() are uppercase. Visual C++ is case-sensitive. If, for example, instead of typing OnOK(), you type OnOk(), you'll get a compiling error.

☐ Save your work by selecting Save All from the File menu.

The code you typed in the OnExitButton() function is very simple (one line):

```
OnOK();
```

This statement closes the IDD_HELLO_DIALOG dialog box of the Hello program by calling the OnOK() member function of the CHelloDlg class. The OnOK() member function works like an OK button—it closes the dialog box. Because the IDD_HELLO_DIALOG dialog box serves as the main window of the Hello program, closing it by calling the OnOK() function terminates the program.

NOTE

The reason you can call the OnOK() member function of the CHelloDlg class from the OnExitButton() function is that OnExitButton() is also a member function of the CHelloDlg class. Recall that when you added the OnExitButton() function by using ClassWizard, you specified that the class name is CHelloDlg, as shown in Figure 1.41.

The OnOK() function is actually a member function of the MFC class CDialog. When Visual C++ created the CHelloDlg class for you, Visual C++ derived the CHelloDlg class from the MFC class CDialog. Therefore, the CHelloDlg class inherited the OnOK() member function from its parent, CDialog.

To see the code you attached to the Exit pushbutton in action, follow these steps:

☐ Select Build Hello.EXE from the Build menu.

Visual C++ responds by compiling and linking the Hello program.

Once Visual C++ finishes compiling and linking the program, you can execute it:

☐ Select Execute Hello.EXE from the Build menu.

Visual C++ responds by executing the Hello.EXE program. The main window of Hello.EXE appears, as shown in Figure 1.34.

☐ Click the Exit pushbutton.

As expected, the Hello.EXE program responds by terminating. The code you attached to the Exit pushbutton is working!

Customizing the Icon of the Hello.EXE Program

The icon of the Hello.EXE program is the small picture at the upper-left corner of the program's window. The Hello program's icon is currently the default icon that Visual C++ created when you generated the skeleton of the program. (See Figure 1.42.)

Figure 1.42.
The default icon created for the Hello.EXE program.

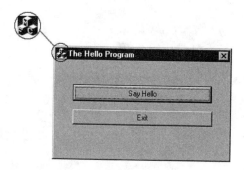

You can change the default icon that Visual C++ created for the program as follows:

☐ Select the ResourceView tab of the Project Workspace dialog box.

NOTE

If for some reason the Project Workspace dialog box is not open on the Visual C++ desktop, you can display it by selecting Workspace from the View menu.

☐ In the Project Workspace dialog box, expand the Icon item by double-clicking it, then double-click the IDR_MAINFRAME item listed under the Icon item. (See Figure 1.43.)

Figure 1.43.

Selecting the
IDR_MAINFRAME
item.

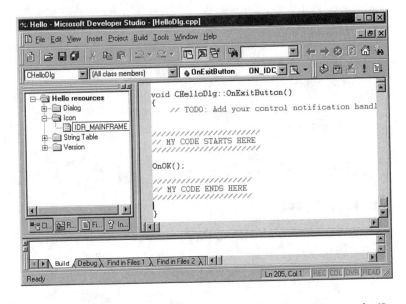

Visual C++ responds by displaying the icon of the Hello.EXE program in design mode. (See Figure 1.44.)

Figure 1.44.

The icon of the
Hello.EXE program
in design mode.

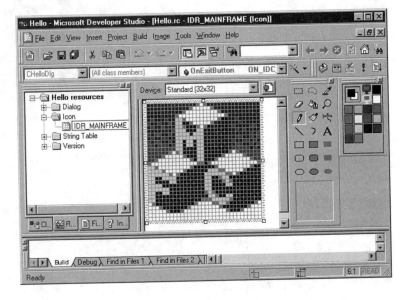

You can now use the Graphics toolbar and Colors toolbar of Visual C++ to replace the default picture of Hello.EXE's icon with your own drawing. The Graphics and Colors toolbars of Visual C++ are shown in Figure 1.45.

Figure 1.45.

The Graphics and Colors toolbars of Visual C++.

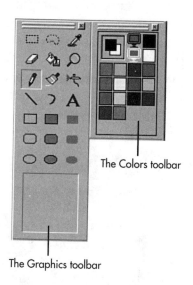

The Colors toolbar

The Graphics toolbar

 NOTE

If you do not see the Graphics toolbar or Colors toolbar on your Visual C++ desktop, do the following:

☐ Select Customize from the Tools menu of Visual C++.

Visual C++ will respond by displaying the Customize dialog box.

☐ Select the Toolbars tab of the Customize dialog box, and make sure the Graphics check box and Colors check box have check marks in them. If they don't, click them to place a check mark.

☐ Close the Customize dialog box by clicking its Close button.

 NOTE

You use the Graphics toolbar and the Colors toolbar of Visual C++ just as you use similar toolbars in other drawing programs. For example, you can use the eraser tool of the Graphics toolbar to erase the drawing.

Remember, you can display the icon in full-screen mode by selecting Full Screen from the View menu. To cancel the full-screen mode, press the Esc key.

NOTE

Figure 1.46 shows the icon of the Hello.EXE program in design mode after the default drawing has been replaced with a simple drawing of the word Hello.

Once you finish customizing the icon of the Hello program, you can see your visual design in action by compiling and linking the Hello project and then executing the Hello.EXE program.

Figure 1.46.

The icon of the Hello.EXE program in design mode (after customization).

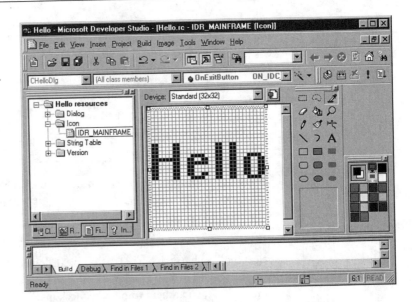

Opening an Old Project

Suppose you work on the Hello project for a while, then you quit Visual C++, and sometime later you want to resume working on the Hello project. In this case, you would have to start Visual C++ and load the Hello project. The following step-by-step tutorial illustrates how to open an old Visual C++ project:

☐ Quit Visual C++ by selecting Exit from the File menu.

In the preceding step, you are instructed to quit Visual C++ so that you'll get a real "feel" for starting Visual C++ and opening an old project.

☐ Start Visual C++ as you did in the beginning of this chapter (refer to Figure 1.3).

The Visual C++ desktop appears.

To open the Hello project, do the following:

☐ Select Open Workspace from the File menu.

Visual C++ responds by displaying the Open Workspace dialog box.

☐ Use the Open Workspace dialog box to select the C:\TYVCProg\Programs \CH01\Hello\Hello.dsw project workspace file.

Visual C++ responds by opening the Project Workspace of the Hello program.

You can now use the ResourceView tab of the Project Workspace dialog box to customize the resources of the Hello program, just as you did at the beginning of this chapter.

An alternative way for opening a recent project that you worked with is to select Recent Workspaces from the File menu. When you do that, Visual C++ displays a list of projects that you worked with recently. You can then open the desired project by selecting it from the list.

Following a Properties Table

In this chapter, you have been instructed to perform the visual design of the Hello.EXE program by following detailed step-by-step instructions. However, in subsequent chapters, instead of using step-by-step instructions, you'll be instructed to perform the visual design of the programs by following a *properties table*.

Table 1.1 is a typical example of a properties table. This table is the properties table of the IDD_HELLO_DIALOG dialog box of the Hello.EXE program.

Table 1.1. The properties table of the IDD_HELLO_DIALOG dialog box.

Object	Property	Setting
Dialog Box	**ID**	**IDD_HELLO_DIALOG**
Push Button	**ID**	**IDC_SAYHELLO_BUTTON**
	Caption	Say Hello
Push Button	**ID**	**IDC_EXIT_BUTTON**
	Caption	Exit

Following a properties table to design a dialog box is easy. All you have to do is place the listed controls in the dialog box and set their properties as specified in the table.

Summary

In this chapter, you have written your first Visual C++ program. You have learned that writing a Visual C++ program involves two steps: the visual design step and the code-writing step.

As you have seen, performing the visual design of your program with Visual C++ is easy. You use the ResourceView tab of the Project Workspace dialog box to open the resource you want to customize (for example, a dialog box) and then use the Visual C++ tools to perform your visual design.

Once you finish the visual design, you attach code to the controls you created during the visual design by using ClassWizard.

Q&A

Q The About dialog box that Visual C++ created for the Hello.EXE program is nice (see Figure 1.18). However, I'd like to customize this dialog box. For example, I'd like to include my own copyright notice in this dialog box. How do I do that?

A You can customize the About dialog box that Visual C++ created for the Hello.EXE program just as you customized the IDD_HELLO_DIALOG dialog box. Here is how you do that:

☐ Open the project workspace of the Hello program (if it's not open already). You open the project workspace by selecting Open Workspace from the File menu, then selecting the C:\TYVCProg\Programs\CH01\Hello\Hello.dsw workspace file.

☐ If you do not see the Project Workspace dialog box in your desktop, select Workspace from the View menu.

☐ Select the ResourceView tab of the Project Workspace dialog box, expand the Hello resources item, expand the Dialog item, and finally double-click the IDD_ABOUTBOX item under the Dialog item.

> *Visual C++ responds by displaying the About dialog box of the Hello program in design mode.*

You can now use the Controls toolbar to customize the About dialog box. For example, you can use the static text tool of the Controls toolbar to add your own text to the About dialog box. The static text tool is shown magnified in Figure 1.47.

Figure 1.47.

The static text tool in the Controls toolbar.

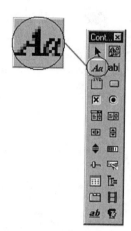

You place the static text control in the dialog box the same way you placed the pushbutton control: click the static text tool in the Controls toolbar, then click in the dialog box.

To set the text of the static text control, right-click the static text control in the dialog box, select Properties from the pop-up menu, then set the Caption property of the control to the desired text.

Q **The main window of the Hello.EXE program has an × icon at its upper-right corner, but it does not include the Minimize and Maximize boxes that many Windows programs have. How can I change the main window of the Hello.EXE program so that it includes the Minimize and Maximize boxes?**

A To add Minimize and Maximize boxes to the main window of the Hello.EXE program (the IDD_HELLO_DIALOG dialog box), set the Maximize box and Minimize box properties of the IDD_HELLO_DIALOG dialog box to TRUE. Here is how you do that:

☐ Open the project workspace of the Hello program (if it's not open already) by selecting Open Workspace from the File menu, then selecting the C:\TYVCProg\Programs\CH01\Hello\Hello.dsw workspace file.

☐ If you don't see the Project Workspace dialog box in your desktop, select Project Workspace from the View menu.

☐ Select the ResourceView tab of the Project Workspace dialog box, expand the Hello resources item, expand the Dialog item, and finally double-click the IDD_HELLO_DIALOG item under the Dialog item.

Visual C++ responds by displaying the IDD_HELLO_DIALOG dialog box in design mode.

You need to change the Maximize box and Minimize box properties of the
IDD_HELLO_DIALOG dialog box. Here is how you do that:

☐ Right-click the mouse in any free area—not occupied by a control—in the
IDD_HELLO_DIALOG dialog box.

☐ Select Properties from the pop-up menu.

Visual C++ responds by displaying the Dialog Properties dialog box.

☐ Select the Styles tab of the Dialog Properties dialog box. (See Figure 1.48.)

Figure 1.48.
*The Styles tab of the
Dialog Properties
dialog box.*

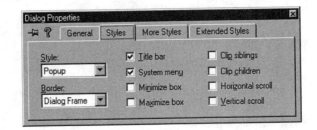

☐ Place a check mark in the Minimize box and Maximize box check boxes.

That's it! Your IDD_HELLO_DIALOG dialog box now includes the Maximize
and Minimize boxes. (See Figure 1.49.)

Figure 1.49.
*The
IDD_HELLO_DIALOG
dialog box with the
Maximize and
Minimize boxes.*

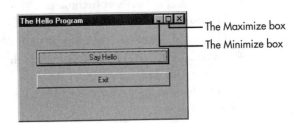

The Maximize box
The Minimize box

Quiz

1. What are the two steps in the design process of a Visual C++ program?

2. What is a dialog-based program?

3. Describe the steps you take to open the IDD_HELLO_DIALOG dialog box of the
Hello program so you can visually customize it.

4. What is ClassWizard?

Exercise

The main window of the Hello.EXE program currently has two pushbuttons in it: Say Hello and Exit. Add a third pushbutton called Beep to the main window of the program. Attach code to the BN_CLICKED event of the Beep pushbutton so that the PC will beep when the user clicks this button.

Hint: This is the statement that causes the PC to beep:

```
MessageBeep((WORD)-1);
```

Quiz Answers

1. The two steps in the design process of a Visual C++ program are the visual design step and the code-writing step.

2. A dialog-based program is a program whose main window is a dialog box.

3. To open the IDD_HELLO_DIALOG dialog box in design mode, do the following:

   ☐ Select the ResourceView tab of the Project Workspace dialog box, expand the Hello resources item, expand the Dialog item, and finally double-click the IDD_HELLO_DIALOG item under the Dialog item.

   Visual C++ will respond by displaying the IDD_HELLO_DIALOG dialog box in design mode.

4. ClassWizard is a powerful "wizard" that enables you to attach code to controls very easily. For example, in the Hello program, you used ClassWizard to attach code to the Click events of the Say Hello and Exit pushbuttons.

Exercise Answer

To add the Beep pushbutton, follow these steps:

☐ Open the project workspace of the Hello program by selecting Open Workspace from the File menu, then selecting the C:\TYVCProg\Programs\CH01\Hello\Hello.dsw workspace file.

☐ If you do not see the Project Workspace dialog box in your desktop, select Workspace from the View menu.

☐ Select the ResourceView tab of the Project Workspace dialog box, expand the Hello resources item, expand the Dialog item, and finally double-click the IDD_HELLO_DIALOG item under the Dialog item.

Visual C++ responds by displaying the IDD_HELLO_DIALOG dialog box in design mode.

☐ Place a new pushbutton control in the IDD_HELLO_DIALOG dialog box.

☐ Right-click the new pushbutton control, select Properties from the pop-up menu, then set the properties of the new pushbutton as follows:

```
ID: IDC_BEEP_BUTTON
Caption: Beep
```

Remember, choose Full Screen from the View menu to display the IDD_HELLO_DIALOG dialog box in full-screen mode and enlarge the dialog box by dragging its handles.

Now attach code to the Click event of the Beep pushbutton as follows:

☐ Select ClassWizard from the View menu.

Visual C++ responds by displaying the MFC ClassWizard dialog box.

☐ Make sure the Message Maps tab is selected.

☐ Make sure the Class name drop-down list box at the top of the ClassWizard dialog box is set to CHelloDlg.

In the preceding step, you were instructed to select the CHelloDlg class in the ClassWizard dialog box to attach code to the Beep pushbutton; the Beep pushbutton is in the IDD_HELLO_DIALOG dialog box, which is associated with the CHelloDlg class. Therefore, the code you attach to the Beep pushbutton will be written in the CHelloDlg class.

☐ Select IDC_BEEP_BUTTON in the Object IDs list of the ClassWizard dialog box to attach code to the Beep pushbutton.

☐ Select BN_CLICKED in the Messages list box to attach code to the BN_CLICKED event of the Beep pushbutton.

By selecting IDC_BEEP_BUTTON in the Object IDs list box and BN_CLICKED in the Messages list box, you are specifying that you want to attach code to the event "the user clicked the Beep pushbutton."

☐ Click the Add Function button of ClassWizard.

ClassWizard responds by displaying the Add Member Function dialog box. ClassWizard suggests naming the new function OnBeepButton.

☐ Click the OK button of the Add Function dialog box to accept the default name that ClassWizard suggests.

ClassWizard responds by adding the function OnBeepButton() *to the Hello program. This function will be executed automatically whenever the user clicks the Beep pushbutton.*

To write the code in the OnBeepButton() function, do the following:

☐ Click the Edit Code button of ClassWizard.

ClassWizard responds by opening the file HelloDlg.cpp, with the function OnBeepButton() *ready for you to edit.*

☐ Write code in the OnBeepButton() function so that it will look like this:

```
void CHelloDlg::OnBeepButton()
{
// TODO: Add your control notification handler code here

/////////////////////////
// MY CODE STARTS HERE
/////////////////////////

MessageBeep((WORD)-1);

/////////////////////////
// MY CODE ENDS HERE
/////////////////////////

}
```

☐ Save your work by selecting Save All from the File menu.

The code you typed in the OnBeepButton() function is very simple (one line):

MessageBeep((WORD)-1);

This statement causes the PC to beep through the PC speaker. To see (and hear) the Beep pushbutton in action, follow these steps:

☐ Select Build Hello.EXE from the Build menu.

Visual C++ responds by compiling and linking the Hello program.

Once Visual C++ finishes compiling and linking the program, you can execute it:

☐ Select Execute Hello.EXE from the Build menu.

Visual C++ responds by executing the Hello.EXE program. The main window of Hello.EXE appears.

☐ Click the Beep pushbutton.

As expected, the Hello.EXE program responds by beeping. The code you attached to the `Click` *event of the Beep pushbutton is working!*

☐ Terminate the Hello.EXE program by clicking its Exit pushbutton.

Day 2

Controls, Properties, and Events

In the previous chapter, you wrote a Visual C++ program that uses the pushbutton control. You learned how to place a pushbutton control in a dialog box and how to attach code to the `BN_CLICKED` event of the pushbutton control.

In this chapter, you'll get experience with other controls. You'll learn how to write a Visual C++ program that uses the edit box control and the check box control. You'll learn how to visually design a dialog box that uses these controls and how to attach code to the events of these controls.

The Test.EXE Program

In this chapter, you'll write a Visual C++ program called Test.EXE, which illustrates how to write Visual C++ programs that use two popular Windows controls: the edit box and the check box. But before you start writing the Test.EXE program, first specify what it should look like and what it should do:

■ When you start the Test.EXE program, its window should look like the one shown in Figure 2.1.

Figure 2.1.

The window of the Test.EXE program.

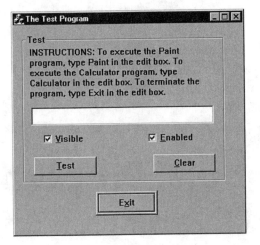

■ The window of the Test.EXE program includes several controls: a static text control with instructions text, an edit box, two check boxes (Visible and Enabled), and three pushbuttons (Test, Clear, and Exit). (A static text control is used for displaying text.)

■ As specified by the instructions text, if you type the word Paint in the edit box, the Test program executes the Windows Paint program. If you type the word Calculator in the edit box, the Test program executes the Windows Calculator program. And if you type the word Exit in the edit box, the Test program terminates. You don't have to press Enter after typing the word. As soon as you type the last letter of the word, Test.EXE responds by executing the appropriate program.

■ When you click the Test button, the Test.EXE program displays the text This is a test! in the edit box. (See Figure 2.2.) When you click the Clear button, the Test.EXE program clears the edit box.

Figure 2.2.

Displaying text in Test.EXE's edit box.

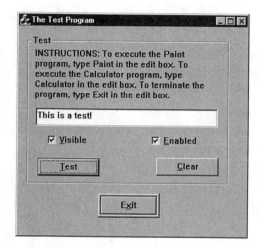

■ As shown in Figure 2.1, the Visible and Enabled check boxes have check marks in them when you start the program. When you remove the check mark from the Visible check box, the edit box becomes invisible. (See Figure 2.3.) To make the edit box visible again, place a check mark in the Visible check box.

Figure 2.3.

Removing the check mark from the Visible check box.

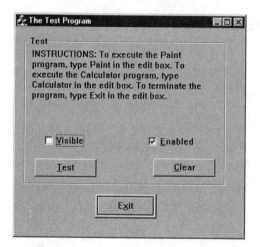

■ When you remove the check mark from the Enabled check box, the edit box becomes disabled. The text is dimmed, and you can't change its value. (See Figure 2.4.) To enable the edit box again, place a check mark in the Enabled check box.

Figure 2.4.

Removing the check mark from the Enabled check box.

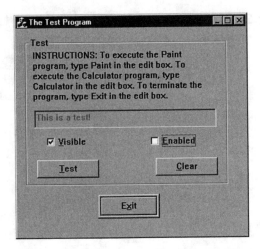

- When you click the Exit pushbutton, the Test.EXE program terminates.

Now that you know what the Test.EXE program should look like and what it should do, you can start designing this program.

Creating the Project of the Test.EXE Program

Follow these steps to create the project and skeleton files of the Test.EXE program:

☐ Use the Windows Explorer of Windows 95 to create the directory C:\TYVCPROG\ PROGRAMS\CH02.

☐ Start Visual C++.

☐ Select New from the File menu.

    Visual C++ responds by displaying the New dialog box.

☐ Select the Projects tab of the New dialog box.

☐ Select MFC AppWizard(exe) from the list of project types.

☐ Type Test in the Project Name box.

☐ Click the button that is located on the right of the Location box and select the C:\TYVCPROG\PROGRAMS\CH02 directory.

☐ Click the OK button.

    Visual C++ responds by displaying the MFC AppWizard - Step 1 window.

☐ Set the MFC AppWizard - Step 1 window as shown in Figure 2.5 to create a dialog-based application.

Figure 2.5.

The MFC AppWizard - Step 1 window.

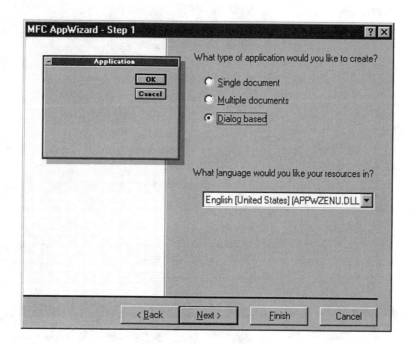

☐ Click the Next button of the Step 1 window.

Visual C++ responds by displaying the MFC AppWizard - Step 2 of 4 window.

☐ Set the MFC AppWizard - Step 2 of 4 window as shown in Figure 2.6 to set the dialog box's title to The Test Program.

☐ Click the Next button.

Visual C++ responds by displaying the Step 3 of 4 window.

☐ Set the Step 3 of 4 options as shown in Figure 2.7.

☐ Click the Next button.

Visual C++ responds by displaying the Step 4 of 4 window. (See Figure 2.8.)

Figure 2.6.

*The MFC
AppWizard - Step 2
of 4 window.*

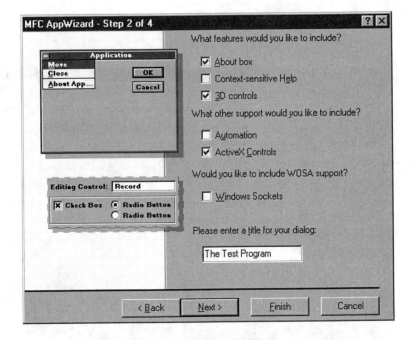

Figure 2.7.

*The MFC
AppWizard - Step 3
of 4 window.*

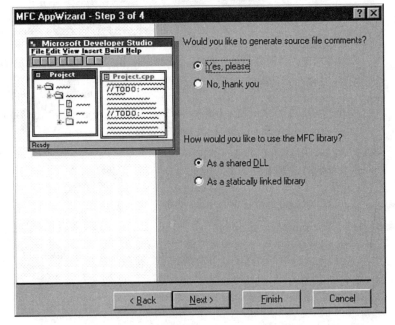

Figure 2.8.

*The MFC
AppWizard - Step 4
of 4 window.*

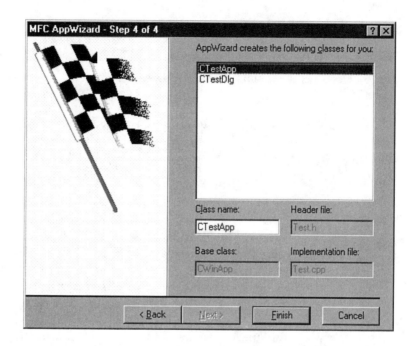

☐ Click the Finish button.

> *Visual C++ responds by displaying the New Project Information window.*

☐ Click the OK button of the New Project Information window.

☐ Select Set Active Configuration from the Build menu of Visual C++.

> *Visual C++ responds by displaying the Set Active Project Configuration dialog box.*

☐ Select Test - Win32 Release in the Default Project Configuration dialog box, then click the OK button.

That's it! You've finished creating the project file and skeleton files of the Test program.

The Visual Design of the Test Program

You'll now visually design the dialog box that serves as the main window of the Test program (the IDD_TEST_DIALOG dialog box).

☐ Select Workspace from the View menu.

☐ Select the ResourceView tab of the Project Workspace window.

☐ Expand the Test resources item.

☐ Expand the Dialog item.

☐ Double-click the IDD_TEST_DIALOG item.

Visual C++ responds by displaying the IDD_TEST_DIALOG dialog box in design mode.

☐ Delete the OK button, Cancel button, and text in the IDD_TEST_DIALOG dialog box.

☐ Design the IDD_TEST_DIALOG dialog box according to Table 2.1. When you finish designing the dialog box, it should look like Figure 2.9.

NOTE

Table 2.1 instructs you to place several controls in the IDD_TEST_DIALOG dialog box and to set certain properties of these controls. If you forgot how to place controls in a dialog box or how to set the properties of controls, refer to Chapter 1, "Writing Your First Visual C++ Application." After you set the properties of a certain control in the dialog box, resize the control if necessary. For example, after you set the properties of the INSTRUCTIONS static text control as instructed by Table 2.1, you will have to resize this static text control so that all the text that you typed will be visible. Recall that you resize a control by dragging its handles.

If you don't see the Controls toolbar on your Visual C++ desktop, select Customize from the Tools menu, select the Toolbars tab of the Customize dialog box, and place a check mark in the Controls check box.

If you aren't sure whether a certain tool in the Controls toolbar is the right tool, do the following:

☐ Place the mouse cursor over the tool in the Controls toolbar.

Visual C++ will respond by displaying a small yellow caption that shows the tool's name. For example, if you move the mouse cursor over the tool of the edit box control, Visual C++ will display a yellow caption with the text Edit Box.

Remember, you can display the IDD_TEST_DIALOG dialog box in full-screen mode by selecting Full Screen from the View menu. To cancel the full-screen mode, press the Esc key.

Table 2.1. The properties table of the IDD_TEST_DIALOG dialog box.

Object	Property	Setting
Dialog Box	ID	**IDD_TEST_DIALOG**
	Caption	The Test Program
	Font	System, Size 10 (General tab)
	Minimize box	Checked (Styles tab)
	Maximize box	Checked (Styles tab)
Group Box	ID	**IDC_STATIC**
	Caption	Test
Static Text	ID	**IDC_STATIC**
	Caption	INSTRUCTIONS: To execute the Paint program, type Paint in the edit box. To execute the Calculator program, type Calculator in the edit box. To terminate the program, type Exit in the edit box.
Edit Box	ID	**IDC_TEST_EDIT**
Check Box	ID	**IDC_VISIBLE_CHECK**
	Caption	&Visible
Check Box	ID	**IDC_ENABLED_CHECK**
	Caption	&Enabled
Push Button	ID	**IDC_TEST_BUTTON**
	Caption	&Test
Push Button	ID	**IDC_CLEAR_BUTTON**
	Caption	&Clear
Push Button	ID	**IDC_EXIT_BUTTON**
	Caption	E&xit
	Client edge	Checked (Extended Styles tab)
	Static edge	Checked (Extended Styles tab)
	Modal frame	Checked (Extended Styles tab)

2

Figure 2.9.

Customizing the
IDD_TEST_DIALOG
dialog box.

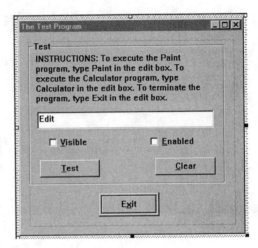

The following list explains, in more detail, how to use the properties table for the IDD_TEST_DIALOG dialog box:

1. The first object listed in Table 2.1 is the IDD_TEST_DIALOG dialog box itself. You set its Minimize box and Maximize box properties to Checked as follows:

   ☐ Right-click any free area in the dialog box and select Properties from the pop-up menu.

   ☐ Select the Styles tab of the Dialog Properties dialog box and place a check mark in the Minimize box and Maximize box check boxes.

   After you place a check mark in the Minimize box and Maximize box check boxes, the IDD_TEST_DIALOG dialog box will have a Minimize box and a Maximize box in the upper-right corner. During runtime, you can use these boxes to minimize or maximize the dialog box.

2. Table 2.1 instructs you to set the Font property of the IDD_TEST_DIALOG dialog box to System, Size 10. You do that as follows:

   ☐ Right-click any free area in the dialog box and select Properties from the pop-up menu.

   ☐ Select the General tab of the Properties dialog box, click the Font button, and set the font to System, Size 10.

   The Font property of the dialog box specifies the font type and size used for the text of all the controls you'll place in the dialog box.

3. The second object listed in Table 2.1 is a group box control. The group box control is used for cosmetic reasons only. In Figure 2.9, the group box control is

the frame enclosing the Instructions static text control, the edit box control, the Visible and Enabled check box controls, and the Test and Clear pushbutton controls. Set the Caption property of the group box control to Test by following these steps:

☐ Right-click the frame of the static text control and select Properties from the pop-up menu.

☐ After you place the group box control in the dialog box, you can move it to any location by dragging its frame. You can also set its size by dragging its handles.

4. The Caption properties of the check box controls and pushbutton controls include the *&* character. For example, Table 2.1 specifies that the Caption property of the Exit pushbutton should be E&xit. The *&* character before the *x* underlines the letter *x* in E&xit. This means that during the execution of the program, pressing Alt+X produces the same results as clicking the Exit button.

5. Use the Extended Styles tab of the properties dialog box to set the Client edge, Static edge, and Modal frame properties of the Exit pushbutton control to Checked. These properties affect only the visual appearance of the control. Once you set them, you'll see their effects on the pushbutton.

You've finished the visual design of the IDD_TEST_DIALOG dialog box. To see your visual design in action, follow these steps:

☐ Select Build Test.EXE from the Build menu.

☐ Select Execute Test.EXE from the Build menu.

Visual C++ responds by executing the Test.EXE program. The main window of Test.EXE appears, as shown in Figure 2.10.

Figure 2.10.

The main window of the Test.EXE program.

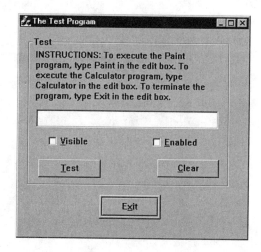

As you can see, the main window of the Test.EXE program (the IDD_TEST_DIALOG dialog box) appears just as you designed it.

☐ Experiment with the controls in the program's window.

As you can see, you can type in the edit box, you can check and uncheck the check boxes, and you can click the pushbuttons. Of course, none of the controls are doing what they're supposed to do because you haven't attached any code yet. You'll attach code to the controls later in this chapter.

☐ Terminate the Test.EXE program by clicking the × icon at the upper-right corner.

Attaching Variables to the Edit Box and Check Box Controls

In this section, you need to attach variables to the edit box control and to the two check box controls so you can use the variables to access these controls when you write the program's code. These variables are used for reading and writing data to and from the controls.

Follow these steps to attach a variable to the IDC_TEST_EDIT edit box control:

☐ Select ClassWizard from the View menu.

   Visual C++ responds by displaying the MFC ClassWizard dialog box.

☐ Select the Member Variables tab of the MFC ClassWizard dialog box. (See Figure 2.11.)

Figure 2.11.

Selecting ClassWizard's Member Variables tab.

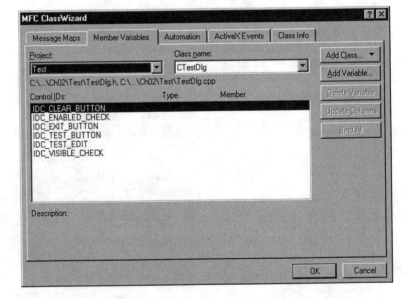

2

☐ Make sure that the Class name drop-down list box is set to CTestDlg.

The CTestDlg class is the class associated with the IDD_TEST_DIALOG dialog box, which serves as the main window of the Test program. Because you are attaching a variable to a control in the IDD_TEST_DIALOG dialog box, the variable will be a data member of the CTestDlg class.

☐ Select IDC_TEST_EDIT in the Object IDs list to attach a variable to the IDC_TEST_EDIT edit box.

☐ Click the Add Variable button.

Visual C++ responds by displaying the Add Member Variable dialog box. (See Figure 2.12.)

Figure 2.12.

The Add Member Variable dialog box.

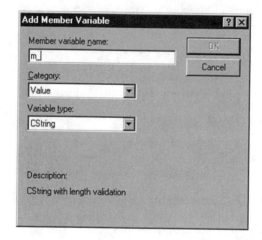

☐ Set the Add Member Variable dialog box as follows:

Member variable name:	m_TestEdit
Category:	Value
Variable type:	CString

☐ Click the OK button of the Add Member Variable dialog box.

You've now attached a variable to the IDC_TEST_EDIT edit box control.

NOTE

In the preceding steps, you attached a variable of type CString to the IDC_TEST_EDIT edit box. CString is an MFC class specifically designed for storing and manipulating strings of characters. You can store a string in a variable of type CString and then use the member functions of the CString class to manipulate the string.

Next, attach a variable to the IDC_VISIBLE_CHECK check box control:

☐ Select IDC_VISIBLE_CHECK in the Object IDs list box, click the Add Variable button, then set the Add Member Variable dialog box as follows:

Member variable name:	m_VisibleCheck
Category:	Value
Variable type:	BOOL

☐ Click the OK button of the Add Member Variable dialog box.

Finally, attach a variable to the Enabled check box control:

☐ Select IDC_ENABLED_CHECK in the Object IDs list box, click the Add Variable button, then set the Add Member Variable dialog box as follows:

Member variable name:	m_EnabledCheck
Category:	Value
Variable type:	BOOL

☐ Click the OK button of the Add Member Variable dialog box.

☐ Click the OK button of the MFC ClassWizard dialog box.

So, putting it all together, you attached a variable of type CString to the IDC_TEST_EDIT edit box and named it m_TestEdit. When you write the program code, you'll use this variable to read and write strings into the IDC_TEST_EDIT edit box.

You attached a variable of type BOOL to the IDC_VISIBLE_CHECK check box and named it m_VisibleCheck. When you write the program code, you'll use this variable to access the IDC_VISIBLE_CHECK check box.

You also attached a variable of type BOOL to the IDC_ENABLED_CHECK check box and named it m_EnabledCheck. When you write the program code, you'll use this variable to access the IDC_ENABLED_CHECK check box.

All these variables are data members of the CTestDlg class (the class associated with the IDD_TEST_DIALOG dialog box). In the following sections, you'll write code that makes use of these variables.

Writing Code That Initializes the Dialog Box Controls

When you start a dialog-based program, you want some of the controls in the program's main window to have certain initial settings. For example, in the Test.EXE program, you want the

Visible and Enabled check boxes to have check marks in them. (Refer to Figure 2.1.) Follow these steps to write the code that initializes the Visible and Enabled check boxes:

☐ Select ClassWizard from the View menu.

Visual C++ responds by displaying the MFC ClassWizard dialog box.

☐ Select the Message Maps tab of ClassWizard.

☐ Use the ClassWizard dialog box to make the following selection:

Class name:	CTestDlg
Object ID:	CTestDlg
Message:	WM_INITDIALOG

Your MFC ClassWizard dialog box should now look like Figure 2.13.

Figure 2.13.
Selecting the
WM_INITDIALOG
event with
ClassWizard.

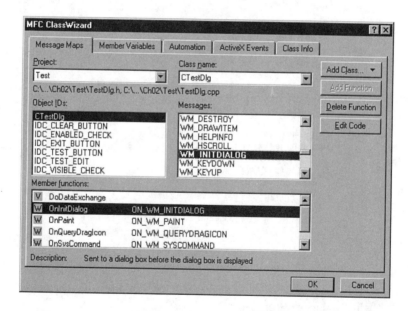

As its name implies, WM_INITDIALOG is the event "initialize the dialog box." Therefore, the code you attach to the WM_INITDIALOG event is responsible for initializing the dialog box.

☐ Click the Edit Code button of ClassWizard.

Visual C++ responds by opening the file TestDlg.cpp with the function OnInitDialog() *ready for you to edit.*

The `OnInitDialog()` function already has some code written by Visual C++. You'll type your own code below this comment line:

```
// TODO: Add extra initialization here
```

☐ Write the following code in the `OnInitDialog()` function:

```
BOOL CTestDlg::OnInitDialog()
{
CDialog::OnInitDialog();
...
...
...

// TODO: Add extra initialization here

/////////////////////////
// MY CODE STARTS HERE
/////////////////////////

// Set the variable of the IDC_VISIBLE_CHECK
// check box to TRUE.
m_VisibleCheck = TRUE;

// Set the variable of the IDC_ENABLED_CHECK
// check box to TRUE.
m_EnabledCheck = TRUE;

// Update the screen.
UpdateData(FALSE);

/////////////////////////
// MY CODE ENDS HERE
/////////////////////////

return TRUE;   // return TRUE  unless you set the focus
               // to a control
}
```

☐ Save your work by selecting Save All from the File menu.

The first statement you typed in the `OnInitDialog()` function sets the variable `m_VisibleCheck` to a value of TRUE:

```
m_VisibleCheck = TRUE;
```

The `m_VisibleCheck` variable is of type BOOL (boolean), which means it can have a value of either TRUE or FALSE. By setting `m_VisibleCheck` to TRUE, you are specifying that you want the IDC_VISIBLE_CHECK check box to have a check mark in it. If you want to remove a check mark from a check box, set the variable to FALSE.

The next statement sets the variable `m_EnabledCheck` to a value of TRUE:

```
m_EnabledCheck = TRUE;
```

By setting `m_EnabledCheck` to TRUE, you are specifying that you want the IDC_ENABLED_CHECK check box to have a check mark in it.

At this point, the variables of the two check box controls are updated with the values you want the controls to display. However, the controls themselves aren't yet updated with the values of the variables. To actually transfer the values of the variables into the controls (to display onscreen), you need to use the `UpdateData()` function with FALSE as its parameter. Therefore, the last statement you typed in the `OnInitDialog()` function updates the screen with the new values of the variables:

```
// Update the screen.
UpdateData(FALSE);
```

After the preceding statement is executed, the current contents of the variable `m_VisibleCheck` will be transferred into the IDC_VISIBLE_CHECK check box, and the current contents of the variable `m_EnabledCheck` will be transferred into the IDC_ENABLED_CHECK check box.

NOTE

> To write code that sets the value of a control, you need to set the value of the variable attached to the control and then call the `UpdateData()` function with its parameter set to FALSE.
>
> For example, suppose you have a dialog box with a check box control whose ID is IDC_MY_CHECK and a variable attached called `m_MyCheck`. The following code places a check mark in the IDC_MY_CHECK check box control:
>
> ```
> // Set the variable of the IDC_MY_CHECK check box to TRUE.
> m_MyCheck = TRUE;
>
> // Transfer the variable into the control.
> // (i.e. update the screen).
> UpdateData(FALSE);
> ```
>
> The following code removes the check mark from the IDC_MY_CHECK check box control:
>
> ```
> // Set the variable of the IDC_MY_CHECK check box to FALSE.
> m_MyCheck = FALSE;
>
> // Transfer the variable into the control.
> // (i.e. update the screen).
> UpdateData(FALSE);
> ```

To see the initialization code you typed in the OnInitDialog() function in action, follow these steps:

☐ Select Build Test.EXE from the Build menu.

☐ Select Execute Test.EXE from the Build menu.

Visual C++ responds by executing the Test.EXE program. The main window of Test.EXE appears, as shown in Figure 2.14.

Figure 2.14.

The main window of the Test.EXE program.

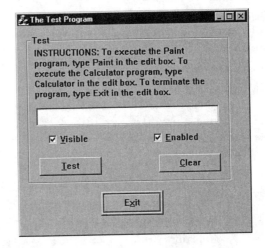

As you can see, the initialization code you wrote in the OnInitDialog() function works! Both the Visible check box and the Enabled check box have check marks in them.

☐ Terminate the Test.EXE program by clicking the × icon at the upper-right corner.

Attaching Code to the BN_CLICKED Event of the Exit Pushbutton

At this point, when you click the Exit pushbutton, nothing happens. In this section, you'll attach code to the BN_CLICKED event of the Exit pushbutton so the program will do what it's supposed to do—terminate the Test.EXE program. Remember, the BN_CLICKED event occurs when you click the control.

Follow these steps to attach code to the BN_CLICKED event of the Exit pushbutton:

☐ Select ClassWizard from the View menu.

Visual C++ responds by displaying the MFC ClassWizard dialog box.

☐ Select the Message Maps tab of ClassWizard.

☐ Use the ClassWizard dialog box to select the following event:

Class name:	CTestDlg
Object ID:	IDC_EXIT_BUTTON
Message:	BN_CLICKED

Your MFC ClassWizard dialog box should now look like Figure 2.15.

Figure 2.15.

Selecting the BN_CLICKED event of the IDC_EXIT_BUTTON pushbutton.

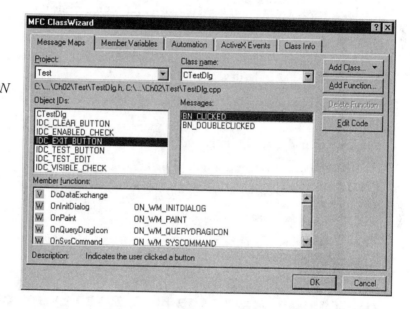

☐ Click the Add Function button of ClassWizard and name the new function OnExitButton.

☐ Click the Edit Code button of ClassWizard.

Visual C++ responds by opening the file TestDlg.cpp with the function OnExitButton() ready for you to edit.

☐ Write the following code in the OnExitButton() function:

```
void CTestDlg::OnExitButton()
{
// TODO: Add your control notification handler code here

////////////////////////
// MY CODE STARTS HERE
////////////////////////
```

```
// Terminate the program.
OnOK();

//////////////////////
// MY CODE ENDS HERE
//////////////////////

}
```

☐ Save your work by selecting Save All from the File menu.

The code you typed in the OnExitButton() function is made up of a single statement:

```
OnOK()
```

This statement terminates the program by calling the OnOK() function, which terminates the program by closing the dialog box.

To see the code you attached to the BN_CLICKED event of the Exit pushbutton in action, follow these steps:

☐ Select Build Test.EXE from the Build menu.

☐ Select Execute Test.EXE from the Build menu.

Visual C++ responds by executing the Test.EXE program.

☐ Click the Exit pushbutton.

As expected, the Test.EXE program responds by terminating. The code you attached to the Exit pushbutton is working!

Attaching Code to the BN_CLICKED Event of the Test Pushbutton

When you click the Test pushbutton, the Test.EXE program should display the text This is a test! in the IDC_TEST_EDIT edit box. (Refer to Figure 2.2.) Follow these steps to attach code to the BN_CLICKED event of the Test pushbutton that performs this task:

☐ Select ClassWizard from the View menu.

Visual C++ responds by displaying the MFC ClassWizard dialog box.

☐ Select the Message Maps tab of ClassWizard.

☐ Use the ClassWizard dialog box to select the following event:

Class name:	CTestDlg
Object ID:	IDC_TEST_BUTTON
Message:	BN_CLICKED

☐ Click the Add Function button of ClassWizard and name the new function OnTestButton.

☐ Click the Edit Code button of ClassWizard.

Visual C++ responds by opening the file TestDlg.cpp with the function OnTestButton() *ready for you to edit.*

☐ Write the following code in the OnTestButton() function:

```
void CTestDlg::OnTestButton()
{
// TODO: Add your control notification handler code here

/////////////////////////
// MY CODE STARTS HERE
/////////////////////////

// Fill the variable of the IDC_TEST_EDIT edit box
// with the text: "This is a test!".
m_TestEdit = "This is a test!";

// Update the screen.
UpdateData(FALSE);

/////////////////////////
// MY CODE ENDS HERE
/////////////////////////

}
```

☐ Save your work by selecting Save All from the File menu.

The code you typed in the OnTestButton() function is made up of two statements. The first statement fills the m_TestEdit variable attached to the IDC_TEST_EDIT edit box with the string "This is a test!":

```
m_TestEdit = "This is a test!";
```

The second statement updates the screen:

```
UpdateData(FALSE);
```

As discussed earlier, calling the UpdateData() function with its parameter set to FALSE updates the dialog box controls with the values of the variables attached to the controls. So after the preceding statement is executed, the text This is a test! will be displayed in the IDC_TEST_EDIT edit box.

To see the code you attached to the BN_CLICKED event of the Test pushbutton in action, follow these steps:

☐ Select Build Test.EXE from the Build menu.

☐ Select Execute Test.EXE from the Build menu.

Visual C++ responds by executing the Test.EXE program.

☐ Click the Test pushbutton.

As expected, the Test.EXE program responds by displaying the text This is a test! *in the IDC_TEST_EDIT edit box.*

☐ Terminate the Test.EXE program by clicking the Exit button.

Attaching Code to the BN_CLICKED Event of the Clear Pushbutton

When you click the Clear pushbutton, the Test.EXE program should clear the IDC_TEST_EDIT edit box. Follow these steps to attach code to the BN_CLICKED event of the Clear pushbutton that performs this task:

☐ Select ClassWizard from the View menu.

Visual C++ responds by displaying the MFC ClassWizard dialog box.

☐ Select the Message Maps tab of ClassWizard.

☐ Use the ClassWizard dialog box to select the following event:

Class name:	CTestDlg
Object ID:	IDC_CLEAR_BUTTON
Message:	BN_CLICKED

☐ Click the Add Function button of ClassWizard and name the new function OnClearButton.

☐ Click the Edit Code button of ClassWizard.

Visual C++ responds by opening the file TestDlg.cpp with the function OnClearButton() *ready for you to edit.*

☐ Write the following code in the OnClearButton() function:

```
void CTestDlg::OnClearButton()
{
// TODO: Add your control notification handler code here

/////////////////////////
// MY CODE STARTS HERE
/////////////////////////

// Fill the variable of the IDC_TEST_EDIT edit box
// with NULL.
m_TestEdit = "";
```

```
// Update the screen.
UpdateData(FALSE);

/////////////////////////
// MY CODE ENDS HERE
/////////////////////////

}
```

☐ Save your work by selecting Save All from the File menu.

The code you typed in the OnClearButton() function is made up of two statements. The first statement fills the m_TestEdit variable attached to the IDC_TEST_EDIT edit box with a NULL string:

```
m_TestEdit = "";
```

The second statement updates the screen so that the new value of the m_TestEdit variable will be transferred to the IDC_TEST_EDIT edit box:

```
UpdateData(FALSE);
```

To see the code you attached to the BN_CLICKED event of the Clear pushbutton in action, follow these steps:

☐ Select Build Test.EXE from the Build menu.

☐ Select Execute Test.EXE from the Build menu.

Visual C++ responds by executing the Test.EXE program.

☐ Type something in the edit box.

☐ Click the Clear button.

As expected, the Test.EXE program responds by clearing the text you typed in the edit box— the edit box is filled with a NULL string.

☐ Terminate the Test.EXE program by clicking the Exit button.

Attaching Code to the BN_CLICKED Event of the Visible Check Box

When you remove the check mark from the Visible check box, the Test.EXE program should hide the IDC_TEST_EDIT edit box from view; when you check the Visible check box, the Test.EXE program should make the IDC_TEST_EDIT edit box visible. You'll now attach code to the BN_CLICKED event of the Visible check box that performs these tasks.

NOTE

> The BN_CLICKED event of a check box control occurs when you place or remove a check mark in the check box.

Follow these steps to attach code to the BN_CLICKED event of the Visible check box:

☐ Select ClassWizard from the View menu.

Visual C++ responds by displaying the MFC ClassWizard dialog box.

☐ Select the Message Maps tab of ClassWizard.

☐ Use the ClassWizard dialog box to select the following event:

Class name:	CTestDlg
Object ID:	IDC_VISIBLE_CHECK
Message:	BN_CLICKED

☐ Click the Add Function button of ClassWizard and name the new function OnVisibleCheck.

☐ Click the Edit Code button of ClassWizard.

Visual C++ responds by opening the file TestDlg.cpp with the function OnVisibleCheck() ready for you to edit.

☐ Write the following code in the OnVisibleCheck() function:

```
void CTestDlg::OnVisibleCheck()
{
// TODO: Add your control notification handler code here

/////////////////////////
// MY CODE STARTS HERE
/////////////////////////

// Update the variables of the controls
// (the screen contents are transferred
// to the variables of the controls).
UpdateData(TRUE);

// If the IDC_VISIBLE_CHECK check box is checked, make
// the IDC_TEST_EDIT edit box visible. Otherwise, hide the
// IDC_TEST_EDIT edit box.
if (m_VisibleCheck==TRUE)
    GetDlgItem(IDC_TEST_EDIT)->ShowWindow(SW_SHOW);
else
    GetDlgItem(IDC_TEST_EDIT)->ShowWindow(SW_HIDE);

/////////////////////////
// MY CODE ENDS HERE
/////////////////////////

}
```

2

☐ Save your work by selecting Save All from the File menu.

The first statement you typed in the OnVisibleCheck() function updates the variables of the controls with the current contents of the screen:

```
UpdateData(TRUE);
```

When you call the UpdateData() function with its parameter set to TRUE, the current values of the controls on the screen are transferred to the variables attached to the controls.

> **NOTE**
>
> When you call the UpdateData() function with its parameter set to TRUE, you update the variables:
>
> ```
> UpdateData(TRUE);
> ```
>
> That is, you transfer the current contents of the onscreen controls into the variables attached to the controls.
>
> When you call the UpdateData() function with its parameter set to FALSE, you update the screen:
>
> ```
> UpdateData(FALSE);
> ```
>
> That is, you transfer the current values of the variables attached to the controls to the onscreen controls.

The first statement you typed in the OnVisibleCheck() function transfers the current contents of the controls onscreen into the variables attached to the controls:

```
UpdateData(TRUE);
```

After the preceding statement is executed, the variable m_VisibleCheck is filled with the current value of the IDC_VISIBLE_CHECK check box. If you place a check mark in the IDC_VISIBLE_CHECK check box, m_VisibleCheck will be filled with the value TRUE; if you remove the check mark, m_VisibleCheck will be filled with the value FALSE.

The remaining code you typed in the OnVisibleCheck() function uses an if...else statement to evaluate the m_VisibleCheck variable:

```
if (m_VisibleCheck==TRUE)
   GetDlgItem(IDC_TEST_EDIT)->ShowWindow(SW_SHOW);
else
   GetDlgItem(IDC_TEST_EDIT)->ShowWindow(SW_HIDE);
```

If the IDC_VISIBLE_CHECK check box is currently selected, the preceding if condition is satisfied and the statement under the if is executed:

```
GetDlgItem(IDC_TEST_EDIT)->ShowWindow(SW_SHOW);
```

This statement uses the ShowWindow() function to make the IDC_TEST_EDIT edit box visible. When the parameter of ShowWindow() is set to SW_SHOW, the control is made visible.

If, however, the IDC_VISIBLE_CHECK check box is not selected, the statement under the else is executed:

```
GetDlgItem(IDC_TEST_EDIT)->ShowWindow(SW_HIDE);
```

This statement uses the ShowWindow() function to make the IDC_TEST_EDIT edit box invisible. When the parameter of ShowWindow() is set to SW_HIDE, the control is hidden.

Notice that in the preceding statements, the ShowWindow() function is being executed on this expression:

```
GetDlgItem(IDC_TEST_EDIT)
```

The GetDlgItem() function returns a pointer to the control whose ID is supplied as the function's parameter. For example, GetDlgItem(IDC_TEST_EDIT) returns a pointer to the IDC_TEST_EDIT edit box control. Therefore, the following statement will hide the IDC_TEST_EDIT edit box control from view:

```
GetDlgItem(IDC_TEST_EDIT)->ShowWindow(SW_HIDE);
```

To summarize, here is how the code in the OnVisibleCheck() function works: When you check or uncheck the Visible check box, its BN_CLICKED event occurs, and the OnVisibleCheck() function is automatically executed. If you check the Visible check box, the code in the OnVisibleCheck() function makes the IDC_TEST_EDIT edit box visible; if you uncheck it, however, the code in the OnVisibleCheck() function hides the IDC_TEST_EDIT edit box from view.

To see the code you attached to the BN_CLICKED event of the Visible check box in action, follow these steps:

☐ Select Build Test.EXE from the Build menu.

☐ Select Execute Test.EXE from the Build menu.

Visual C++ responds by executing the Test.EXE program.

☐ Experiment with the Visible check box.

As expected, the Test.EXE program shows or hides the IDC_TEST_EDIT edit box when you check and uncheck the Visible check box.

☐ Terminate the Test.EXE program by clicking the Exit button.

Attaching Code to the BN_CLICKED Event of the Enabled Check Box

When you uncheck the Enabled check box, the Test.EXE program should disable the IDC_TEST_EDIT edit box; conversely, when you check the Enabled check box, the Test.EXE program should enable the IDC_TEST_EDIT edit box. You'll attach the code that performs these tasks to the BN_CLICKED event of the Enabled check box.

☐ Just as you did for the Visible check box, choose ClassWizard from the View menu, select ClassWizard's Message Maps tab, and select the following event in the ClassWizard dialog box:

Class name:	CTestDlg
Object ID:	IDC_ENABLED_CHECK
Message:	BN_CLICKED

☐ Click the Add Function button, name the new function OnEnabledCheck, and click the Edit Code button.

Visual C++ responds by opening the file TestDlg.cpp with the function OnEnabledCheck() *ready for you to edit.*

☐ Write the following code in the OnEnabledCheck() function:

```
void CTestDlg::OnEnabledCheck()
{
// TODO: Add your control notification handler code here

/////////////////////////
// MY CODE STARTS HERE
/////////////////////////

// Update the variables of the controls.
// (the screen contents are transferred
// to the variables of the controls).
UpdateData(TRUE);

// If the IDC_ENABLED_CHECK check box is checked, enable
// the IDC_TEST_EDIT edit box. Otherwise, disable the
// IDC_TEST_EDIT edit box.
if (m_EnabledCheck==TRUE)
   GetDlgItem(IDC_TEST_EDIT)->EnableWindow(TRUE);
else
   GetDlgItem(IDC_TEST_EDIT)->EnableWindow(FALSE);

/////////////////////////
// MY CODE ENDS HERE
/////////////////////////

}
```

☐ Select Save All from the File menu to save your work.

The code in the `OnEnabledCheck()` function works the same way as the code in the `OnVisibleCheck()` function. When you check or uncheck the Enabled check box, its `BN_CLICKED` event occurs, and the `OnEnabledCheck()` function is automatically executed. The first statement in the `OnEnabledCheck()` function updates the variables of the controls with the current onscreen contents:

```
UpdateData(TRUE);
```

After this statement is executed, the `m_EnabledCheck` variable is filled with the current value of the IDC_ENABLED_CHECK check box. Therefore, placing a check mark in the Enabled check box fills `m_EnabledCheck` with the value TRUE. The remaining code uses an `if...else` statement to evaluate the `m_EnabledCheck` variable:

```
if (m_EnabledCheck==TRUE)
    GetDlgItem(IDC_TEST_EDIT)->EnableWindow(TRUE);
else
    GetDlgItem(IDC_TEST_EDIT)->EnableWindow(FALSE);
```

If the Enabled check box is checked, the preceding `if` condition is satisfied and the statement under the `if` is executed:

```
GetDlgItem(IDC_TEST_EDIT)->EnableWindow(TRUE);
```

This statement uses the `EnableWindow()` function to enable the IDC_TEST_EDIT edit box. When the parameter of the `EnableWindow()` function is set to TRUE, the control is enabled.

If the Enabled check box isn't checked, then the statement under the `else` is executed. When the parameter of `EnableWindow()` is set to FALSE, the control is disabled:

```
GetDlgItem(IDC_TEST_EDIT)->EnableWindow(FALSE);
```

The `EnableWindow()` function is being executed on the following expression:

```
GetDlgItem(IDC_TEST_EDIT)
```

The `GetDlgItem(IDC_TEST_EDIT)` returns a pointer to the IDC_TEST_EDIT edit box control. So, the following statement disables the IDC_TEST_EDIT edit box control:

```
GetDlgItem(IDC_TEST_EDIT)->EnableWindow(FALSE);
```

To see the code you attached to the `BN_CLICKED` event of the Enabled check box in action, follow these steps:

☐ Select Build Test.EXE from the Build menu.

Visual C++ responds by compiling and linking the Test.EXE program.

☐ Select Execute Test.EXE from the Build menu.

Visual C++ responds by executing the Test.EXE program.

☐ Experiment with the Enabled check box, then click the Exit button to terminate the Test.EXE program.

As expected, when you check and uncheck the Enabled check box, the Test.EXE program enables and disables the IDC_TEST_EDIT edit box.

2

Attaching Code to the EN_CHANGE Event of the Edit Box Control

The EN_CHANGE event of an edit box control occurs when you change the contents of the edit box by entering or deleting characters. In this section, you'll attach code to the EN_CHANGE event of the IDC_TEST_EDIT edit box. This code will perform the following three tasks:

☐ Execute the Windows Paint program when you type Paint in the edit box.

☐ Execute the Windows Calculator program when you type Calculator in the edit box.

☐ Terminate the program when you type Exit in the edit box.

Follow these steps to attach code to the EN_CHANGE event of the IDC_TEST_EDIT edit box:

☐ Select ClassWizard from the View menu, select ClassWizard's Message Maps tab, and select the following event in the ClassWizard dialog box:

Class name:	CTestDlg
Object ID:	IDC_TEST_EDIT
Message:	EN_CHANGE

☐ Click the Add Function button, name the new function OnChangeTestEdit, and click the Edit Code button.

Visual C++ responds by opening the file TestDlg.cpp with the function OnChangeTestEdit() ready for you to edit.

☐ Write the following code in the OnChangeTestEdit() function:

```
void CTestDlg::OnChangeTestEdit()
{
// TODO: If this is a RICHEDIT control, the control
// will not send this notification unless you modify
// CDialog::OnInitDialog() function to send the
// EM_SETEVENTMASK message to the control with the
// ENM_CHANGE flag ORed into the lParam mask.
```

```
// TODO: Add your control notification handler code here

/////////////////////////
// MY CODE STARTS HERE
/////////////////////////

// Update the variables of the controls.
UpdateData(TRUE);

// Fill the variable UpperValue with the uppercase string
// of the IDC_TEST_EDIT edit box.
CString UpperValue;
UpperValue = m_TestEdit;
UpperValue.MakeUpper();

// If the user typed Paint in the edit box, execute the
// Paint program (pbrush.exe) and clear the IDC_TEST_EDIT
// edit box.
if (UpperValue=="PAINT")
   {
   system("pbrush.exe");
   m_TestEdit="";
   UpdateData(FALSE);
   }

// If the user typed Calculator in the edit box, execute the
// Calculator program (calc.exe) and clear the IDC_TEST_EDIT
// edit box.
if (UpperValue=="CALCULATOR")
   {
   system("calc.exe");
   m_TestEdit="";
   UpdateData(FALSE);
   }

// If the user typed Exit in the edit box, terminate
// the program and clear the IDC_TEST_EDIT
// edit box.
if (UpperValue=="EXIT")
   {
   OnOK();
   }

/////////////////////////
// MY CODE ENDS HERE
/////////////////////////

}
```

☐ Save your work by selecting Save All from the File menu.

The first statement in the OnChangeTestEdit() function updates the variables of the controls with the current onscreen contents:

```
UpdateData(TRUE);
```

After this statement is executed, the m_TestEdit variable of the IDC_TEST_EDIT edit box is filled with the current value of the IDC_TEST_EDIT edit box. For example, if you type the word Hello in the IDC_TEST_EDIT edit box, m_TestEdit will be filled with the string "Hello".

These are the next three statements:

```
// Fill the variable UpperValue with the uppercase string
// of the IDC_TEST_EDIT edit box.
CString UpperValue;
UpperValue = m_TestEdit;
UpperValue.MakeUpper();
```

This statement creates a variable called UpperValue of type CString:

```
CString UpperValue;
```

This statement fills the variable UpperValue with the value of the m_TestEdit variable:

```
UpperValue = m_TestEdit;
```

Recall that when you attached the m_TestEdit variable to the IDC_TEST_EDIT edit box, you specified that m_TestEdit is of type CString. Therefore, the variable UpperValue holds the contents of the IDC_TEST_EDIT edit box.

The next statement executes the MakeUpper() member function of the CString class on the UpperValue variable:

```
UpperValue.MakeUpper();
```

As its name implies, the MakeUpper() function converts the string's lowercase characters to uppercase characters. For example, if the variable initially contained the string "Hello", the MakeUpper() function would convert the variable to hold the string "HELLO". Therefore, if you type Paint in the edit box at this point, UpperValue is filled with the string "PAINT".

The remaining code you typed in the OnChangeTestEdit() function uses three if statements to evaluate the UpperValue variable:

```
// If the user typed Paint in the edit box, execute the
// Paint program (pbrush.exe) and clear the IDC_TEST_EDIT
// edit box.
if (UpperValue=="PAINT")
    {
    system("pbrush.exe");
    m_TestEdit="";
    UpdateData(FALSE);
    }

// If the user typed Calculator in the edit box, execute the
// Calculator program (calc.exe) and clear the IDC_TEST_EDIT
```

```
// edit box.
if (UpperValue=="CLOCK")
    {
    system("calc.exe");
    m_TestEdit="";
    UpdateData(FALSE);
    }

// If the user typed Exit in the edit box, terminate
// the program and clear the IDC_TEST_EDIT
// edit box.
if (UpperValue=="EXIT")
    OnOK();
```

If the uppercase conversion of what you typed in the IDC_TEST_EDIT edit box is "PAINT", the condition of the first if statement is satisfied and the following three statements are executed:

```
system("pbrush.exe");
m_TestEdit="";
UpdateData(FALSE);
```

This statement uses the system() function to execute the EXE file of the Paint program (PBRUSH.EXE):

```
system("pbrush.exe");
```

In the preceding statement, the full pathname of the program is not specified. Therefore, the system() function will execute the PBRUSH.EXE file in your \WINDOWS directory.

The next two statements fill the IDC_TEST_EDIT edit box with a NULL string:

```
m_TestEdit="";
UpdateData(FALSE);
```

This is done so that after Test.EXE executes the Paint program, the IDC_TEST_EDIT edit box will be cleared.

If the uppercase conversion of what you typed in the IDC_TEST_EDIT edit box is "CALCULATOR", the condition of the second if statement is satisfied and the following three statements are executed:

```
system("calc.exe");
m_TestEdit="";
UpdateData(FALSE);
```

This statement executes the EXE file of the Calculator program (CALC.EXE):

```
system("calc.exe");
```

These two statements clear the IDC_TEST_EDIT edit box:

```
m_TestEdit="";
UpdateData(FALSE);
```

2

If the uppercase conversion of what you typed in the IDC_TEST_EDIT edit box is "EXIT", the condition of the third if statement is satisfied and the following statement is executed to terminate the program:

```
OnOK();
```

To see the code you attached to the EN_CHANGE event of the IDC_TEST_EDIT edit box in action, follow these steps:

☐ Select Build Test.EXE from the Build menu.

☐ Select Execute Test.EXE from the Build menu.

Visual C++ responds by executing the Test.EXE program.

☐ Type Paint in the IDC_TEST_EDIT edit box.

The Test.EXE program responds by executing the Windows Paint program.

☐ Terminate the Paint program.

☐ Type Calculator in the IDC_TEST_EDIT edit box.

The Test.EXE program responds by executing the Windows Calculator program.

☐ Terminate the Calculator program.

☐ Type Exit in the IDC_TEST_EDIT edit box.

The Test.EXE program responds by terminating.

Summary

In this chapter, you have gained some experience with controls and you have written a program that uses the edit box control, the check box control, and the pushbutton control.

As you have seen, writing a program that uses a control amounts to placing the control in the dialog box, setting the control's properties, and attaching code to the events of the control.

Q&A

Q During the design of the Test program, I attached a variable to the edit box control and to the check box controls. But I didn't have to attach variables to the pushbutton controls. Why not?

A You attached variables to the edit box and check box controls so you could write code that reads and writes values to and from these controls. In the case of the pushbutton control, you don't have to read and write values to or from this control (because a pushbutton does not have text in it to be read or written into).

Q **The Test.EXE program illustrates how to disable or enable and hide or show an edit box control. What about other controls? What code do I have to write to disable or enable and hide or show controls such as pushbuttons, check boxes, and so on?**

A With other types of controls, you use the same code you used with the edit box control. For example, suppose your program includes a pushbutton control whose ID is IDC_MY_BUTTON. The following statements illustrate how to disable or enable and hide or show the IDC_MY_BUTTON pushbutton:

```
// Hide the IDC_MY_BUTTON pushbutton.
GetDlgItem(IDC_MY_BUTTON)->ShowWindow(SW_HIDE);

// Make the IDC_MY_BUTTON pushbutton visible.
GetDlgItem(IDC_MY_BUTTON)->ShowWindow(SW_SHOW);

// Disable the IDC_MY_BUTTON pushbutton.
GetDlgItem(IDC_MY_BUTTON)->EnableWindow(FALSE);

// Enable the IDC_MY_BUTTON pushbutton.
GetDlgItem(IDC_MY_CONTROL)->EnableWindow(TRUE);
```

Quiz

1. Explain what the following statement does:

   ```
   UpdateData(FALSE);
   ```

2. Explain what the following statement does:

   ```
   UpdateData(TRUE);
   ```

3. Suppose your program includes an edit box control whose ID is IDC_MY_EDIT and you attached a variable of type CString called m_MyEdit to the IDC_MY_EDIT edit box. Describe what the following code does:

   ```
   m_MyEdit = "Hello";
   UpdateData(FALSE);
   ```

4. Suppose your program includes a check box control whose ID is IDC_MY_CHECK and you attached a variable of type BOOL called m_MyCheck to the IDC_MY_CHECK check box. Describe what the following code does:

   ```
   m_MyCheck = TRUE;
   UpdateData(FALSE);
   ```

5. Suppose your program includes an edit box control whose ID is IDC_MY_EDIT and you attached a variable of type CString called m_MyEdit to the IDC_MY_EDIT edit box. Describe what the following code does:

```
UpdateData(TRUE);
MessageBox(m_MyEdit);
```

6. When does the BN_CLICKED event of a check box control occur?
7. When does the EN_CHANGE event of an edit box control occur?
8. Explain how to make a control visible and invisible during runtime.
9. Explain how to make a control enabled and disabled during runtime.

Exercise

Currently, when you type Paint in the edit box of the Test.EXE program, it executes the Windows Paint program. When you type Calculator in the edit box, the Test.EXE program executes the Windows Calculator program, and when you type Exit in the edit box, the Test.EXE program terminates.

Add code to the Test.EXE program so that when you type Beep in the edit box, your PC will beep.

Hint: This is the statement that causes the PC to beep:

```
MessageBeep((WORD)-1);
```

Quiz Answers

1. The following statement updates the controls onscreen (in the dialog box) with the current values of the variables attached to the controls:

```
UpdataData(FALSE);
```

After the preceding statement is executed, the values of the variables attached to the controls are transferred to the corresponding controls onscreen.

2. The following statement updates the variables attached to the controls with the current values of the controls themselves:

```
UpdataData(TRUE);
```

After the preceding statement is executed, the current settings of the controls onscreen are transferred to the corresponding variables attached to the controls.

3. The following statement fills the m_MyEdit variable of the IDC_MY_EDIT edit box with the string "Hello":

```
m_MyEdit = "Hello";
```

This statement transfers the contents of the m_MyEdit variable to the IDC_MY_EDIT edit box:

```
UpdateData(FALSE);
```

The preceding two statements display the text Hello in the IDC_MY_EDIT edit box.

4. The following statement fills the m_MyCheck variable of the IDC_MY_CHECK check box with the value TRUE:

```
m_MyCheck = TRUE;
```

And this statement transfers the contents of the m_MyCheck variable to the IDC_MY_CHECK check box:

```
UpdateData(FALSE);
```

When a value of TRUE is transferred to a check box control, a check mark is placed in the check box, so the preceding two statements place a check mark in the IDC_MY_CHECK check box.

5. The following statement transfers the current contents of the IDC_MY_EDIT edit box control into the m_MyEdit variable attached to the control:

```
UpdateData(TRUE);
```

And this statement displays a message box with the contents of the m_MyEdit variable:

```
MessageBox(m_MyEdit);
```

The preceding two statements display a message box showing the current contents of the IDC_MY_EDIT edit box.

6. The BN_CLICKED event of a check box control occurs when you place or remove a check mark in the check box control.

7. The EN_CHANGE event of an edit box control occurs when you change the contents of the edit box.

8. To hide or show a control, you can use the ShowWindow() function. For example, suppose you have a control whose ID is IDC_MY_CONTROL. To hide the IDC_MY_CONTROL control, execute the ShowWindow() function as follows:

```
GetDlgItem(IDC_MY_CONTROL)->ShowWindow(SW_HIDE);
```

To make the IDC_MY_CONTROL control visible, execute the ShowWindow() function as follows:

```
GetDlgItem(IDC_MY_CONTROL)->ShowWindow(SW_SHOW);
```

9. To enable and disable a control, you can use the `EnableWindow()` function. For example, suppose you have a control whose ID is IDC_MY_CONTROL. To disable the IDC_MY_CONTROL control, execute the `EnableWindow()` function as follows:

```
GetDlgItem(IDC_MY_CONTROL)->EnableWindow(FALSE);
```

To enable the IDC_MY_CONTROL control, execute the `EnableWindow()` function as follows:

```
GetDlgItem(IDC_MY_CONTROL)->EnableWindow(TRUE);
```

Exercise Answer

To enhance the Test.EXE program so you can make your PC beep when you type `Beep` in the edit box control, add the following code to the end of the `OnChangeTestEdit()` function in the TestDlg.cpp file:

```
// If the user typed Beep in the edit box, beep and
// clear the IDC_TEST_EDIT edit box.
if (UpperValue=="BEEP")
   {
   MessageBeep((WORD)-1);
   m_TestEdit="";
   UpdateData(FALSE);
   }
```

After you add this code to the end of the `OnChangeTestEdit()` function, it will look like this:

```
void CTestDlg::OnChangeTestEdit()
{
// TODO: If this is a RICHEDIT control, the control
// will not send this notification unless you modify
// CDialog::OnInitDialog() function to send the
// EM_SETEVENTMASK message to the control with the
// ENM_CHANGE flag ORed into the lParam mask.

// TODO: Add your control notification handler code here

////////////////////////////
// MY CODE STARTS HERE
////////////////////////////

// Update the variables of the controls.
UpdateData(TRUE);

// Fill the variable UpperValue with the uppercase string
// of the IDC_TEST_EDIT edit box.
CString UpperValue;
UpperValue = m_TestEdit;
UpperValue.MakeUpper();
```

2

```
// If the user typed Paint in the edit box, execute the
// Paint program (pbrush.exe) and clear the IDC_TEST_EDIT
// edit box.
if (UpperValue=="PAINT")
   {
   system("pbrush.exe");
   m_TestEdit="";
   UpdateData(FALSE);
   }

// If the user typed Clock in the edit box, execute the
// Clock program (clock.exe) and clear the IDC_TEST_EDIT
// edit box.
if (UpperValue=="CLOCK")
   {
   system("clock.exe");
   m_TestEdit="";
   UpdateData(FALSE);
   }

// If the user typed Exit in the edit box, terminate
// the program and clear the IDC_TEST_EDIT
// edit box.
if (UpperValue=="EXIT")
   {
   OnOK();
   }

// If the user typed Beep in the edit box, beep and
// clear the IDC_TEST_EDIT edit box.
if (UpperValue=="BEEP")
   {
   MessageBeep((WORD)-1);
   m_TestEdit="";
   UpdateData(FALSE);
   }

////////////////////////
// MY CODE ENDS HERE
////////////////////////

}
```

To see (and hear) the code you added to the OnChangeTestEdit() function in action, follow these steps:

☐ Select Build Test.EXE from the Build menu.

☐ Select Execute Test.EXE from the Build menu.

Visual C++ responds by executing the Test.EXE program.

☐ Type Beep in the edit box.

> *As expected, the Test.EXE program responds by beeping and clearing the edit box. Type* Beep *once again in the edit box, and your PC will beep again.*

☐ Terminate the Test.EXE program by clicking its Exit pushbutton or by typing Exit in the edit box.

2

Day **3**

Using ActiveX Controls

In the previous two chapters, you wrote Visual C++ programs that use standard Visual C++ controls. In this chapter, you'll learn what ActiveX controls are and how to use them in your Visual C++ programs.

What Is an ActiveX Control?

The standard Visual C++ controls you've used in the previous two chapters are in the Controls toolbar (for example, the pushbutton control, the check box control, the edit box control, and so on). A control has both properties and events. For example, the pushbutton control has the Caption property and the BN_CLICKED event. The code you attach to a control's event is executed automatically when the event occurs. When you attach code to the BN_CLICKED event of a pushbutton, for example, this code is automatically executed whenever you click the pushbutton.

Wouldn't it be nice if you could use other controls (made by third-party vendors) in addition to Visual C++ standard controls? Well, that's what ActiveX controls are all about. An *ActiveX control* is a file with the extension OCX (for example, MyButton.OCX). Visual C++ and other visual programming languages enable you to incorporate the ActiveX control into your program and use it just as you use standard Visual C++ controls. You can place ActiveX controls in your program's dialog boxes, set the properties of ActiveX controls, and attach code to the events of ActiveX controls.

When you use an ActiveX control in your program, the ActiveX file typically resides in the \WINDOWS\SYSTEM directory. An ActiveX control is like a dynamic linked library (DLL)—it's linked to your program dynamically.

ActiveX controls extend Visual C++'s out-of-the-box features. They enable you to easily write sophisticated, state-of-the-art programs. In Chapter 21, "Sound, Animation, and DirectX," you'll learn how to use ActiveX controls for creating programs that include sound and animation. You'll also learn about an ActiveX control that enables you to incorporate DirectX technology for writing 3D Virtual Reality programs.

In this chapter, you'll learn how to add an ActiveX control, already included with Visual C++, to your Visual C++ program and how to use this control in the program.

The MyCal.EXE Program

In this chapter, you'll write a Visual C++ program called MyCal.EXE that illustrates how to write a Visual C++ program that uses an ActiveX control. The MyCal.EXE program uses the Calendar ActiveX control. As implied by its name, the Calendar ActiveX control helps you write programs that display a calendar. The Calendar ActiveX control is included with Visual C++; its filename is MSCAL.OCX.

NOTE

If your edition of Visual C++ does not include the MSCAL.OCX file, you will not be able to implement the program of this chapter. Nevertheless, it is recommended that you browse through this chapter. This way you'll see that using an ActiveX control is the same as using the standard Visual C++ controls (for example, the pushbutton control) that you have used in the previous two chapters.

3

Before you start writing the MyCal.EXE program, first specify what the MyCal.EXE program should look like and what it should do:

- When you start the MyCal.EXE program, its window should look like the one shown in Figure 3.1.

Figure 3.1.

The window of the MyCal.EXE program.

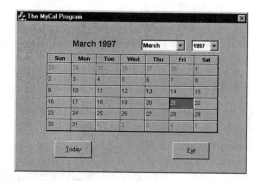

- The window of the MyCal.EXE program displays a calendar control and two pushbuttons: Today and Exit.
- You can use the calendar control to select a desired year and month, and the calendar control will display the appropriate calendar page of the selected month.
- When you click the Today button, the calendar will initialize itself to display the month of today's date and today's date will be highlighted in the calendar.
- When you click the Exit button, the program will terminate.

Now that you know what the MyCal.EXE program should look like and what it should do, you can start creating it.

Creating the Project of the MyCal.EXE Program

Follow these steps to create the project and skeleton files of the MyCal.EXE program:

☐ Create the directory C:\TYVCPROG\PROGRAMS\CH03 and start Visual C++.

☐ Select New from the File menu.

   Visual C++ responds by displaying the New dialog box.

☐ Select the Projects tab of the New dialog box.

☐ Select MFC AppWizard(exe) from the list of project types.

☐ Type MyCal in the Project Name box.

☐ Click the button that is located on the right of the Location box and select the C:\TYVCPROG\PROGRAMS\CH03 directory.

☐ Click the OK button.

Visual C++ responds by displaying the MFC AppWizard Step 1 window.

☐ In the Step 1 window, choose the option to create a dialog-based application, then click the Next button.

Visual C++ responds by displaying the MFC AppWizard - Step 2 of 4 window.

☐ In the Step 2 window, set the title of the dialog box to The MyCal Program and make sure the ActiveX Controls check box is checked. (See Figure 3.2.) When you're done, click the Next button.

Figure 3.2.
The MFC
AppWizard - Step 2
of 4 window.

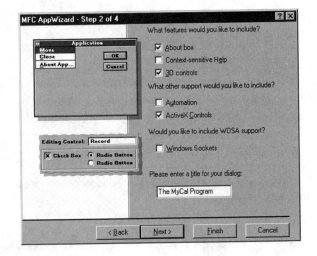

 NOTE

> Make sure the ActiveX Controls check box is checked, as shown in Figure 3.2, because the program you're creating will use an ActiveX control.

Visual C++ responds by displaying the Step 3 of 4 window.

☐ In the Step 3 window, leave the options at their default settings and then click the Next button.

Visual C++ responds by displaying the Step 4 of 4 window.

☐ In the Step 4 window, notice that AppWizard created the CMyCalApp and CMyCalDlg classes for you.

☐ Click the Finish button.

   Visual C++ responds by displaying the New Project Information window.

☐ Click the OK button.

   Visual C++ responds by creating the project file and skeleton files for the MyCal application.

☐ Select Set Active Configuration from the Build menu.

   Visual C++ responds by displaying the Set Active Project Configuration dialog box.

☐ Select MyCal - Win32 Release in the Set Active Project Configuration dialog box, then click the OK button.

That's it! You've finished creating the project and skeleton files of the MyCal program.

Copying the Calendar ActiveX Control to Your Windows System Directory

As discussed earlier, the MyCal.EXE program will use the Calendar ActiveX control. Thus, you need to copy the Calendar ActiveX control to your Windows system directory. The filename of the Calendar ActiveX control is MSCAL.OCX.

NOTE

If you are using Windows 95 and you installed Windows 95 in the C:\WINDOWS directory, your Windows system directory is C:\WINDOWS\SYSTEM.

If you are using Windows NT and you installed Windows NT in the C:\WINNT directory, your Windows system directory is C:\WINNT\SYSTEM32 (*not* C:\WINNT\SYSTEM).

You may already have the MSCAL.OCX file in your Windows system directory (because Visual C++ or another program already installed this file for you).

☐ Use the Windows Explorer program to copy the MSCAL.OCX file from the \DEVSTUDIO\VC\REDIST\OCX directory of the Visual C++ CD-ROM into your Windows system directory. If you are using Windows 95, your Windows system directory is C:\WINDOWS\SYSTEM. If you are using Windows NT, your Windows system directory is C:\WINNT\SYSTEM32.

Registering the Calendar ActiveX Control

Before you can use the Calendar ActiveX control, you have to register it with Windows. The Test Container program that is included with Visual C++ is used to register and test ActiveX controls. Follow these steps to register the Calendar ActiveX control:

☐ Select ActiveX Control Test Container from the Tools menu of Visual C++.

Visual C++ responds by running the Test Container program, as shown in Figure 3.3.

Figure 3.3.

The Test Container program.

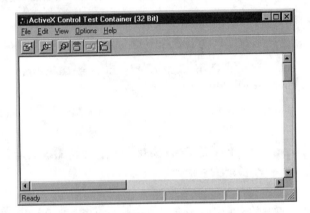

☐ If you have problems starting the Test Container program from Visual C++, you can start it directly from Windows:

☐ Click the Start button of Windows, select Programs, select Microsoft Visual C++ 5, and finally select ActiveX Control Test Container.

☐ Select Register Controls from the File menu of Test Container.

Test Container responds by displaying the Controls Registry dialog box. (See Figure 3.4.)

The Controls Registry dialog box lists all the ActiveX controls currently registered in your Windows system. To register the Calendar ActiveX control, do the following:

☐ Click the Register button of the Controls Registry dialog box.

Test Container responds by displaying the Register Controls dialog box. (See Figure 3.5.)

Figure 3.4.

The Controls Registry dialog box.

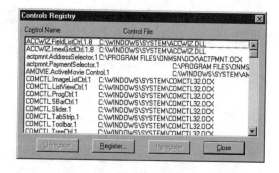

Figure 3.5.

The Register Controls dialog box.

☐ Use the Register Controls dialog box to select the file C:\WINDOWS\SYSTEM\ MSCAL.OCX, then click the Open button. (If you are using Windows NT, you have to select the C:\WINNT\SYSTEM32\MSCAL.OCX file.)

Test Container responds by registering the Calendar ActiveX control and then displaying the Controls Registry dialog box again.

☐ You can verify that the Calendar ActiveX control is registered by looking for the filename C:\WINDOWS\SYSTEM\MSCAL.OCX in the Control File column:

Control Name	*Control File*
MSCAL.Calendar.7	C:\WINDOWS\SYSTEM\MSCAL.OCX

This item is shown highlighted in Figure 3.6.

☐ Click the Close button, then select Exit from Test Container's File menu to end the Test Container program.

Now that the Calendar ActiveX control is registered, you can incorporate it into the MyCal.EXE program, as described in the following sections.

Figure 3.6.

The MSCAL.OCX
file listed in the
Controls Registry.

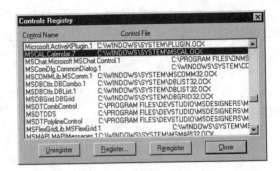

The Visual Design of the MyCal Program

You'll now visually design the dialog box that serves as the main window of the MyCal program (the IDD_MYCAL_DIALOG dialog box):

☐ Select the ResourceView tab of the Project Workspace window.

☐ Expand the MyCal resources item, expand the Dialog item, and double-click the IDD_MYCAL_DIALOG item.

Visual C++ responds by displaying the IDD_MYCAL_DIALOG dialog box in design mode.

☐ Delete the OK button, Cancel button, and text in the IDD_MYCAL_DIALOG dialog box.

Before you can place a Calendar control in the IDD_MYCAL_DIALOG dialog box, you first have to add the Calendar ActiveX control to the MyCal project. Here is how you do that:

☐ Select Add to Project from the Project menu.

Visual C++ responds by opening the Add to Project submenu next to the Project menu.

☐ Select Components and Controls from the Add to Project submenu. (See Figure 3.7.)

Visual C++ responds by displaying the Components and Controls Gallery dialog box. (See Figure 3.8.)

Figure 3.7.

Selecting Components and Controls from the Add to Project submenu.

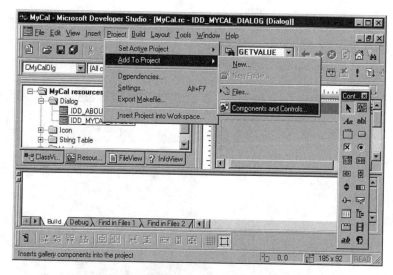

Figure 3.8.

The Components and Controls Gallery dialog box.

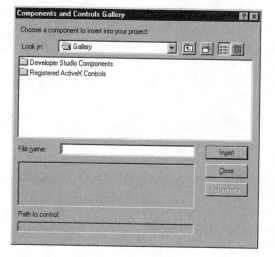

☐ In the Components and Controls Gallery dialog box, double-click the Registered ActiveX
Controls item.

Visual C++ responds by displaying all the registered ActiveX controls. (See Figure 3.9.)

Figure 3.9.

*Displaying all the
registered ActiveX
controls in the
Components and
Controls Gallery
dialog box.*

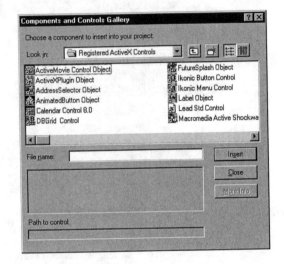

☐ Select the Calendar Control 8.0 item, then click the Insert button of the Components and
Controls Gallery dialog box.

*Visual C++ responds by displaying a small confirmation message box asking whether you
want to insert the component that you selected to the project. (See Figure 3.10.)*

Figure 3.10.

*The confirmation
message box that
asks you whether
you want to insert the
selected component
to the project.*

☐ Click the OK button of the confirmation message box.

Visual C++ responds by displaying the Confirm Classes dialog box. (See Figure 3.11.)

Figure 3.11.

The Confirm Classes dialog box.

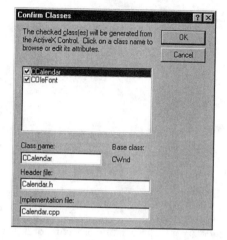

The Confirm Classes dialog box displays the names of the classes that Visual C++ will add to the MyCal project in order to add the Calendar ActiveX control.

☐ Click the OK button of the Confirm Classes dialog box.

> *Visual C++ responds by adding the Calendar ActiveX control to the MyCal project and by redisplaying the Components and Controls Gallery dialog box.*

☐ Click the Close button of the Components and Controls Gallery dialog box.

That's it! You completed adding the Calendar ActiveX control to the MyCal project. From now on, you can use the Calendar ActiveX control in the MyCal project just as you use standard Visual C++ controls (for example, the pushbutton control). That is, you can place the Calendar ActiveX control in the IDD_MYCAL_DIALOG box, set the properties of the Calendar ActiveX control, and attach code to the events of the Calendar ActiveX control.

Take a look at your Controls toolbar. As shown in Figure 3.12, your Controls toolbar now contains the tool of the Calendar ActiveX control.

NOTE

> If you don't see the Controls toolbar on your Visual C++ desktop, select Customize from the Tools menu, select the Toolbars tab of the Customize dialog box, and place a check mark in the Controls check box.

Figure 3.12.

*The tool of the
Calendar ActiveX
control in the
Controls toolbar.*

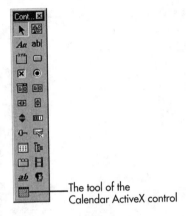

—— The tool of the
    Calendar ActiveX control

You'll now place a Calendar ActiveX control in the IDD_MYCAL_DIALOG dialog box:

☐ Click the tool of the Calendar ActiveX control in the Controls toolbar and then click in
the IDD_MYCAL_DIALOG dialog box.

*Visual C++ responds by placing the Calendar control in the IDD_MYCAL_DIALOG
dialog box at the point where you clicked the mouse. (See Figure 3.13.)*

NOTE

Remember, for your convenience you can display the
IDD_MYCAL_DIALOG dialog box in full-screen mode by selecting
Full Screen from the View menu. To cancel the full-screen mode, press
the Esc key.

Figure 3.13.

*The Calendar ActiveX
control in the
IDD_MYCAL_DIALOG
dialog box.*

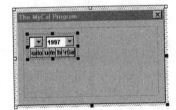

You can now treat the Calendar ActiveX control just as you treat a standard Visual C++
control. You can drag it with the mouse to move it, you can size it by dragging its handles,
and you can set its properties by right-clicking the control and selecting Properties from the
pop-up menu.

☐ Enlarge the height and width of the IDD_MYCAL_DIALOG dialog box by dragging its
bottom edge downward and its right edge to the right.

☐ Enlarge the Calendar ActiveX control (by dragging its bottom handle downward and its right handle to the right) until it looks as shown in Figure 3.14.

Figure 3.14.

The Calendar ActiveX control in the IDD_MYCAL_DIALOG dialog box after increasing the size of both the IDD_MYCAL_DIALOG dialog box and the Calendar ActiveX control.

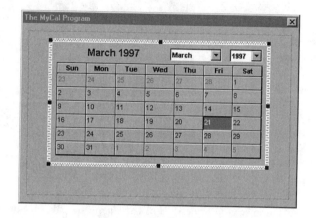

☐ Design the IDD_MYCAL_DIALOG dialog box by using the specifications in Table 3.1. When you're done, the dialog box should look like the one shown in Figure 3.15.

Table 3.1. The properties table of the IDD_MYCAL_DIALOG dialog box.

Object	Property	Setting
Dialog Box	ID	IDD_MYCAL_DIALOG
	Caption	The MyCal Program
Calendar Control	ID	IDC_CALENDAR1
Push Button	ID	IDC_TODAY_BUTTON
	Caption	&Today
Push Button	ID	IDC_EXIT_BUTTON
	Caption	E&xit

Keep the following points in mind as you're using Table 3.1:

■ The first object listed in Table 3.1 is the IDD_MYCAL_DIALOG dialog box itself. By default, the dialog box does not have a Minimize box and a Maximize box in its upper-right corner. If you wish, you can add a Minimize box and a Maximize box to the dialog box as follows:

☐ Right-click any free area in the dialog box and select Properties from the pop-up menu.

Figure 3.15.

The IDD_MYCAL_DIALOG dialog box in design mode after customization.

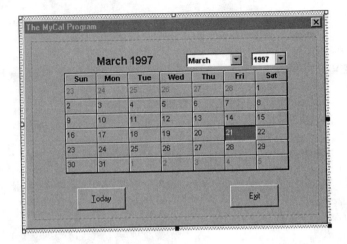

☐ Select the Styles tab of the Properties dialog box and place a check mark in the Minimize box and Maximize box check boxes.

After you place a check mark in the Minimize box and Maximize box check boxes, the IDD_MYCAL_DIALOG dialog box will have a Minimize box and a Maximize box in its upper-right corner. During runtime, you can use them to minimize or maximize the dialog box.

■ The second object listed in Table 3.1 is the Calendar control. You set the properties of the Calendar control just as you set the properties of any other control. That is, right-click the control and select Properties from the pop-up menu.

■ Table 3.1 instructs you to set the ID property of the Calendar control to IDC_CALENDAR1, which is the default ID that Visual C++ assigned to the control. Of course, if you wish, you can use any other name for the ID.

You've finished the visual design of the IDD_MYCAL_DIALOG dialog box. To see it in action, follow these steps:

☐ Select Build MyCal.EXE from the Build menu.

> **NOTE**
>
> When you select Build MyCal.EXE from the Build menu, only the files that have been changed since the last time you compiled the program are compiled. However, sometimes your project may go out of sequence and Visual C++ will "think" that files needing to be compiled shouldn't be compiled. As a result, the linker may fail. In such cases, you can force Visual C++ to compile all the files by selecting Rebuild All from the Build menu.

☐ Select Execute MyCal.EXE from the Build menu.

Visual C++ responds by executing the MyCal.EXE program. The main window of MyCal.EXE appears, as shown in Figure 3.16.

Figure 3.16.

The main window of the MyCal.EXE program.

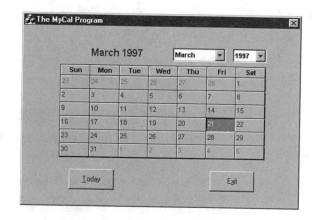

As you can see, the main window of the MyCal.EXE program (the IDD_MYCAL_DIALOG dialog box) looks just as you designed it.

☐ Experiment with the calendar by selecting different months and different years using the month list box and year list box at the top-right corner of the calendar control.

As you can see, the calendar displays the appropriate calendar page per your selections. For example, Figure 3.17 shows the calendar after the year 1900 and the month of January were selected.

☐ Terminate the MyCal.EXE program by clicking the × icon at the upper-right corner of the program's window.

Figure 3.17.

Displaying a calendar page for the month of January 1900.

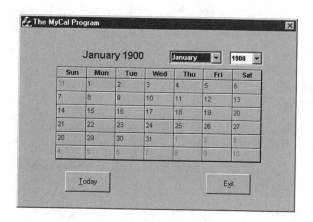

Attaching a Variable to the Calendar Control

You'll now attach a variable to the Calendar control, so you can use the variable later to write code that accesses the properties of the Calendar control. Follow these steps to attach a variable to the IDC_CALENDAR1 Calendar control:

☐ Select ClassWizard from the View menu.

   Visual C++ responds by displaying the MFC ClassWizard dialog box.

☐ Select the Member Variables tab of the MFC ClassWizard dialog box. (See Figure 3.18.)

Figure 3.18.

Selecting the Member Variables tab of ClassWizard.

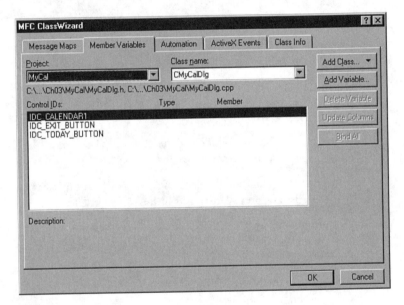

☐ Make sure that the Class name list box is set to CMyCalDlg.

The CMyCalDlg class is associated with the IDD_MYCAL_DIALOG dialog box (the main window of the MyCal program). Because you're going to attach a variable to a control in the IDD_MYCAL_DIALOG dialog box, the Class name list box should be set to CMyCalDlg. As a result, the variable that you'll attach to the control will be a data member of the CMyCalDlg class.

☐ Select IDC_CALENDAR1 in the Object IDs list to attach a variable to the IDC_CALENDAR1 Calendar control, then click the Add Variable button.

   Visual C++ responds by displaying the Add Member Variable dialog box shown in Figure 3.19.

Figure 3.19.

The Add Member Variable dialog box.

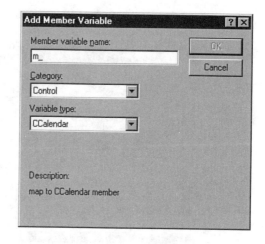

☐ Set the Add Member Variable dialog box as follows:

Member variable name:	`m_cal`
Category:	`Control`
Variable type:	`CCalendar`

☐ Click the OK button of the Add Member Variable dialog box, then click the OK button of the ClassWizard dialog box.

You've finished attaching a variable to the IDC_CALENDAR1 Calendar control!

Putting it all together, you have attached a variable of type `CCalender` to the IDC_CALENDAR Calendar control and named it `m_cal`. In the following sections, you'll write the code of the MyCal.EXE program and use the `m_cal` variable to access the properties of the Calendar control.

Writing the Code That Initializes the Calendar Control

You'll now write the code that initializes the IDC_CALENDAR1 Calendar control. You'll attach this initialization code to the WM_INITDIALOG event of the IDD_MYCAL_DIALOG dialog box, which is the event "initialize the dialog box." Follow these steps to attach code to the WM_INITDIALOG event of the IDD_MYCAL_DIALOG dialog box:

☐ Select ClassWizard from the View menu, select the Message Maps tab, and use the ClassWizard dialog box to select the following event:

Class name:	`CMyCalDlg`
Object ID:	`CMyCalDlg`
Message:	`WM_INITDIALOG`

Your MFC ClassWizard dialog box should now look like the one shown in Figure 3.20.

Figure 3.20.

Selecting the
WM_INITDIALOG
event.

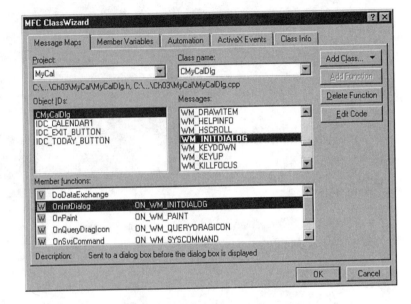

☐ Click the Edit Code button of ClassWizard.

> *Visual C++ responds by opening the file MyCalDlg.cpp with the function* OnInitDialog()
> *ready for you to edit. Remember, you can view and edit code in full-screen mode (select Full
> Screen from the View menu and press Esc to cancel the full-screen mode).*

The OnInitDialog() function already has some code written by Visual C++. You'll type your
own code below this comment line:

```
// TODO: Add extra initialization here
```

☐ Write the following code in the OnInitDialog() function:

```
BOOL CMyCalDlg::OnInitDialog()
{
CDialog::OnInitDialog();
...
...
...

// TODO: Add extra initialization here

/////////////////////////
// MY CODE STARTS HERE
/////////////////////////
```

3

```
// Set the date of the calendar control to today's date.
m_cal.Today();

////////////////////////
// MY CODE ENDS HERE
////////////////////////

return TRUE;  // return TRUE  unless you set the focus
              // to a control
}
```

☐ Save your work by selecting Save All from the File menu.

The code you typed in the OnInitDialog() function is made up of a single statement:

```
m_cal.Today();
```

The preceding statement executes the Today() function on the m_cal variable you attached to the IDC_CALENDAR1 Calendar control. As implied by its name, the Today() function (a member function of the CCalendar class) sets the date of the Calendar control to today's date. Because the OnInitDialog() function is automatically executed whenever the program starts, from now on, upon starting the program, the calendar will display today's date (that is, the calendar will display today's month and today's year, and today's day of month will be selected in the calendar).

NOTE

The initialization code that you wrote in the OnInitDialog() function sets the date of the calendar control to today's date. Thus, whenever the user starts the MyCal.EXE program, the calendar will display today's date. For example, if the user will run the program on January 1, 1999, upon starting the program, the calendar control will display the date of January 1, 1999.

Had you not written this initialization code, upon starting the program, the calendar control would have always displayed the original date on which you placed the Calendar control in the IDD_MYCAL_DIALOG dialog box.

To see the initialization code you typed in the OnInitDialog() function in action, follow these steps:

☐ Select Build MyCal.EXE from the Build menu.

☐ Select Execute MyCal.EXE from the Build menu.

Visual C++ responds by executing the MyCal.EXE program. As expected, the calendar appears with today's date displayed.

3

☐ Terminate the MyCal.EXE program by clicking the × icon at the upper-right corner of the program's window.

Attaching Code to the BN_CLICKED Event of the Exit Pushbutton

When you click the Exit pushbutton, the MyCal.EXE program should terminate. Follow these steps to attach code to the BN_CLICKED event of the Exit pushbutton:

☐ Select ClassWizard from the View menu, select the Message Maps tab, and use the ClassWizard dialog box to select the following event:

Class name:	CMyCalDlg
Object ID:	IDC_EXIT_BUTTON
Message:	BN_CLICKED

☐ Click the Add Function button, name the new function OnExitButton, and click the Edit Code button.

Visual C++ responds by opening the file MyCalDlg.cpp with the function OnExitButton() *ready for you to edit.*

☐ Write the following code in the OnExitButton() function:

```
void CMyCalDlg::OnExitButton()
{
// TODO: Add your control notification handler code here

/////////////////////////
// MY CODE STARTS HERE
/////////////////////////

// Terminate the program.
OnOK();

/////////////////////////
// MY CODE ENDS HERE
/////////////////////////

}
```

☐ Save your work by selecting Save All from the File menu.

The code in the OnExitButton() function is made up of a single statement that terminates the program:

```
OnOK()
```

Recall from Chapter 2, "Controls, Properties, and Events," that the OnOK() function terminates the program by closing the dialog box.

To see the code you attached to the BN_CLICKED event of the Exit pushbutton in action, follow these steps:

☐ Select Build MyCal.EXE from the Build menu.

☐ Select Execute MyCal.EXE from the Build menu.

Visual C++ responds by executing the MyCal.EXE program.

☐ Click the Exit pushbutton.

As expected, the MyCal.EXE program responds by terminating.

Attaching Code to the BN_CLICKED Event of the Today Pushbutton

When the user clicks the Today button, you want the calendar control to display today's date. You'll now attach code to the BN_CLICKED event of the Today pushbutton. Follow these steps to attach code to the BN_CLICKED event of the Today pushbutton:

☐ Select ClassWizard from the View menu, select the Message Maps tab, and use the ClassWizard dialog box to select the following event:

Class name:	CMyCalDlg
Object ID:	IDC_TODAY_BUTTON
Message:	BN_CLICKED

☐ Click the Add Function button, name the new function OnTodayButton, then click the Edit Code button.

Visual C++ responds by opening the file MyCalDlg.cpp with the function OnTodayButton() ready for you to edit.

☐ Write the following code in the OnTodayButton() function:

```
void CMyCalDlg::OnTodayButton()
{
// TODO: Add your control notification handler code here

/////////////////////////
// MY CODE STARTS HERE
/////////////////////////

// Set the date of the calendar control to today's date.
m_cal.Today();
```

```
///////////////////////
// MY CODE ENDS HERE
///////////////////////
```

　　}

☐ Save your work by selecting Save All from the File menu.

The code you typed in the `OnTodayButton()` function is identical to the code that you wrote earlier in the `OnInitDialog()` function. It uses the `Today()` member function of the `CCalendar` class to set the calendar to today's date:

```
m_cal.Today();
```

The MyCal.EXE program is now finished! To see the code you attached to the `BN_CLICKED` event of the Today pushbutton, follow these steps:

☐ Select Build MyCal.EXE from the Build menu.

☐ Select Execute MyCal.EXE from the Build menu.

　　Visual C++ responds by executing the MyCal.EXE program.

☐ Use the calendar to select a date other than today's date.

☐ Click the Today pushbutton.

　　As expected, the MyCal.EXE program responds by setting the calendar's date to today's date.

☐ Terminate the MyCal.EXE program by clicking the Exit button.

Summary

In this chapter, you learned how to incorporate an ActiveX control into your Visual C++ programs. Using an ActiveX control is similar to using a standard Visual C++ control: You place the control in a dialog box, set its properties, and attach code to its events.

Q&A

Q In the MyCal.EXE program, I didn't attach any code to the events of the Calendar ActiveX control. Does the Calendar ActiveX control have events? If so, how do I attach code to its events?

A Yes, the Calendar ActiveX control has events. You can attach code to its events just as you attach code to events of standard Visual C++ controls—use the Message Maps tab of ClassWizard.

To see a list of the events of the Calendar ActiveX control, follow these steps:

☐ Open the project of the MyCal.EXE program if it's not open already. (Select Open Workspace from the File menu, then select the C:\TYVCPROG\PROGRAMS\ CH03\ MYCAL\MYCAL.DSW file.)

☐ Select ClassWizard from the View menu, select the Message Maps tab, and use the ClassWizard dialog box to make the following selection:

Class name: CMyCalDlg
Object ID: IDC_CALENDAR1

Your ClassWizard dialog box should now look like the one shown in Figure 3.21—all the events of the Calendar control are listed in the Messages list box.

Figure 3.21.
Listing the events of the Calendar ActiveX control.

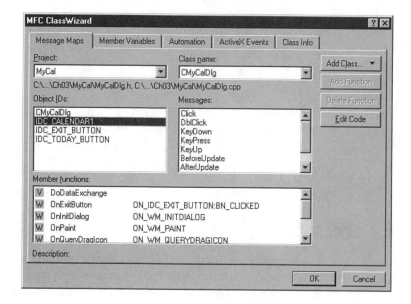

As shown in Figure 3.21, the Calendar control has events associated with it. Some of the names of these events are self-explanatory. For example, the Click event occurs when you click the control, and the DblClick event occurs when you double-click the control.

Q What code do I write to make an ActiveX control invisible?

A To make an ActiveX control invisible, you can execute the ShowWindow() function on the variable you attached to the control. For example, in the MyCal.EXE program, the following statement makes the Calendar control invisible:

```
m_cal.ShowWindow(SW_HIDE);
```

Similarly, the following statement makes the Calendar control visible:

```
m_cal.ShowWindow(SW_SHOW);
```

Q Why would I ever want to make an ActiveX control invisible?

A In some cases, you may want your programs to use the functions of a certain ActiveX control, but not want the user to see the ActiveX control. When you make the ActiveX control invisible, the user won't see it, but your program can use the properties and events of the control.

Quiz

1. An ActiveX control has the extension OCX (for example, MyControl.OCX).

    a. True
    b. False

2. The filename of the ActiveX control used in the MyCal.EXE program is MSCAL.OCX.

    a. True
    b. False

3. Suppose the variable attached to the Calendar ActiveX control is called `m_MyCalendar`. Describe what the following statement does:

```
m_MyCalendar.Today();
```

Exercise

Currently, when you double-click the Calendar control in the MyCal.EXE program, nothing happens. Enhance the MyCal.EXE program so that when you double-click the Calendar control, the program displays a message box that displays the text: `"You double-clicked the calendar!"`.

Quiz Answers

1. True

2. True

3. This statement sets the date in the Calendar ActiveX control to today's date.

Exercise Answer

To enhance the MyCal.EXE program so that when you double-click the Calendar control, the program displays a message box showing the text "You double-clicked the calendar!", do the following:

☐ Attach code to the DblClick event of the IDC_CALENDAR1 control. The code will consist of a single statement:

```
MessageBox("You double-clicked the calendar!");
```

3

Day **4**

The Mouse and the Keyboard

In this chapter, you'll learn how to write Visual C++ programs that use the mouse and the keyboard. In particular, you'll create the Draw and MyKey programs.

The Draw Program

The Draw program illustrates how you can write a program that uses the mouse for drawing. But before writing the Draw program yourself, let's first review its specifications:

- When you start the program, the window shown in Figure 4.1 appears.
- When you move the mouse while holding down the left mouse button, the Draw program draws according to your mouse movements. Figure 4.2 shows how you can use the Draw program to write something.

Figure 4.1.
*The window of the
Draw program.*

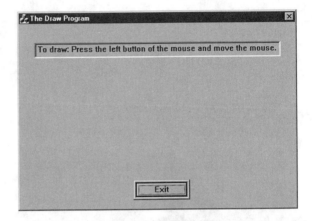

Figure 4.2.
*Writing with the
Draw program.*

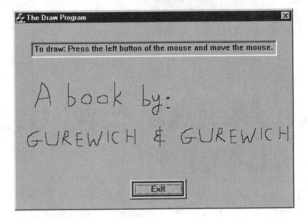

■ When you click the Draw program's Exit button, the Draw program terminates.

In the following sections you'll write the Draw program.

Creating the Project of the Draw Program

Follow these steps to create the project of the Draw program:

☐ Create the C:\TYVCPROG\PROGRAMS\CH04 directory, start Visual C++, and select
New from the File menu.

   Visual C++ responds by displaying the New dialog box.

☐ Select the Projects tab of the New dialog box.

☐ Select MFC AppWizard(exe) from the list of project types.

☐ Type Draw in the Project Name box.

☐ Click the button that is located on the right of the Location box and select the C:\TYVCPROG\PROGRAMS\CH04 directory.

☐ Click the OK button.

Visual C++ responds by displaying the MFC AppWizard - Step 1 window.

☐ In Step 1 of the MFC AppWizard, click the "Dialog based" radio button (because you want to create a dialog-based application), then click the Next button to advance to the Step 2 window.

☐ In Step 2 of the MFC AppWizard, place a check mark in the About box and 3-D controls check boxes and enter the title Draw for the dialog box. When you're done, click the Next button to advance to the Step 3 window.

☐ In Step 3 of the MFC AppWizard, select the "Yes, please" radio button (because you want Visual C++ to generate source file comments) and the "As a shared DLL" radio button. Click the Next button to advance to the Step 4 window.

☐ Click the Finish button of the Step 4 window, then click the OK button of the New Project Information dialog box.

☐ Select Set Active Configuration from the Build menu.

Visual C++ responds by displaying the Set Active Project Configuration dialog box.

☐ Set the project to Draw Win32 - Release.

That's it! You've finished creating the Draw project.

The Visual Design of the Draw Program

You'll now visually design the window of the Draw program with the following steps:

☐ Select Workspace from the View menu to display the Project Workspace window, then select the ResourceView tab of the Project Workspace window. Next, expand the Draw resources item, expand the Dialog item, and double-click the IDD_DRAW_DIALOG item.

Visual C++ responds by displaying the IDD_DRAW_DIALOG dialog box in design mode.

☐ Delete the OK and Cancel buttons and the TODO static text of the IDD_DRAW_DIALOG dialog box.

☐ Design the IDD_DRAW_DIALOG dialog box according to Table 4.1. When you finish designing the dialog box, it should look like Figure 4.1.

4

Table 4.1. The properties table of the IDD_DRAW_DIALOG dialog box.

Object	Property	Setting
Dialog Box	**ID**	**IDD_DRAW_DIALOG**
	Caption	The Draw Program
	Font	System, Size 10
Push Button	**ID**	**IDC_EXIT_BUTTON**
	Caption	Exit
	Client edge	Checked (Extended Styles tab)
	Static edge	Checked (Extended Styles tab)
	Modal frame	Checked (Extended Styles tab)
Static Text	**ID**	**IDC_INSTRUCTION_STATIC**
	Align Text	Center (Styles tab)
	Static edge	Checked (Extended styles tab)
	Client edge	Checked (Extended styles tab)
	Caption	To Draw: Press the left button of the mouse and move the mouse

Attaching Code to the BN_CLICKED Event of the Exit Button

You'll now attach code to the BN_CLICKED event of the Exit button:

☐ Select ClassWizard from the View menu.

Visual C++ responds by displaying the MFC ClassWizard dialog box.

☐ Select the Message Maps tab and use the ClassWizard dialog box to select the following event:

        Class name: CDrawDlg
        Object ID: IDC_EXIT_BUTTON
        Message: BN_CLICKED

☐ Click the Add Function button, name the new function OnExitButton, and click the Edit Code button.

Visual C++ responds by opening the file DrawDlg.cpp with the function OnExitButton() ready for you to edit.

☐ Write the following code in the `OnExitButton()` function:

```
void CDrawDlg::OnExitButton()
{
// TODO: Add your control notification handler code here

//////////////////////////
// MY CODE STARTS HERE
//////////////////////////

// Terminate the program
OnOK();

//////////////////////////
// MY CODE ENDS HERE
//////////////////////////

}
```

Attaching Code to the WM_MOUSEMOVE Event of the Dialog Box

You'll now attach code to the WM_MOUSEMOVE event of the dialog box, which is automatically executed when you move the mouse:

☐ Select ClassWizard from the View menu, select the Message Maps tab, and use the ClassWizard dialog box to select the following event:

Class name:	CDrawDlg
Object ID:	CDrawDlg
Message:	WM_MOUSEMOVE

☐ Click the Add Function button to create the new function OnMouseMove, then click the Edit Code button.

Visual C++ responds by opening the file DrawDlg.cpp with the function OnMouseMove() *ready for you to edit.*

☐ Write the following code in the `OnMouseMove()` function:

```
void CDrawDlg::OnMouseMove(UINT nFlags, CPoint point)
{
// TODO: Add your message handler code here and/or call
// default

//////////////////////////
// MY CODE STARTS HERE
//////////////////////////
```

4

```
if ( (nFlags & MK_LBUTTON) == MK_LBUTTON )
{

// Create a dc object
CClientDC   dc(this);

// Draw a pixel
dc.SetPixel(point.x,
            point.y,
            RGB(0,0,0) );


} //end of if

/////////////////////////
// MY CODE ENDS HERE
/////////////////////////

CDialog::OnMouseMove(nFlags, point);
}
```

☐ Select Save All from the File menu to save your work.

The code you typed in the OnMouseMove() function is an if statement:

```
if ( (nFlags & MK_LBUTTON) == MK_LBUTTON )
{

/// This code is executed, provided that
/// the mouse was moved while the left
/// button of the mouse is pressed down.

}
```

The OnMouseMove() function is executed whenever you move the mouse over the dialog box. The first parameter of the OnMouseMove() function is nFlags, which indicates whether certain keyboard keys (such as Ctrl and Shift) and mouse buttons were pressed while the mouse was moved.

The & operation (bitwise AND operation) examines whether the left mouse button is pressed down while the mouse is moved; if it is, the code under the if statement is executed.

NOTE

If you are unfamiliar with the bitwise AND operation, note the following:

Suppose that MyFlag is equal to 00111111—it consists of 8 bits. You want to determine whether the rightmost bit is equal to 0 or 1. You can make this determination as follows (assuming that RIGHT_MOST is a constant equal to 00000001):

```
if ( (MyFlag & RIGHT_MOST) == RIGHT_MOST )
{
// This code is executed, provided that the rightmost
```

```
// bit of MyFlag is equal to 1.
}
```

Therefore, when you use AND on 00111111 with 00000001, the result is 00000001:

```
00111111 & 00000001 = 00000001
```

In a similar manner, you can perform the AND operation to determine the value of any bit location in MyFlag. For example, if 3RD_FROM_RIGHT is a constant equal to 00000100, you can determine whether the third bit from the right of MyFlag is equal to 1 as follows:

```
if ( (MyFlag & 3RD_FROM_RIGHT ) == 3RD_FROM_RIGHT )
{
// This code is executed, provided that the 3rd bit from
// the right of MyFlag is equal to 1.
}
```

Therefore, the code under the if statement is executed when you move the mouse while the left button is held down.

The code you typed under the if statement creates a device context object:

```
CClientDC  dc(this);
```

You can think of the *device context* (dc) as an imaginary screen that resides in memory. Once you create the dc, you can draw into it as if it were a regular screen. You can draw pixels, lines, geometrical shapes, and so on. Whatever you draw in the dc is transferred to the real screen.

The next statement you typed draws a pixel in the dc:

```
dc.SetPixel(point.x,
            point.y,
            RGB(0,0,0) );
```

The dc is an imaginary screen in memory, but if you could look at it now, you'd see a pixel drawn in it. The SetPixel() function draws the pixel at the location specified by the first and second parameters of the SetPixel() function. point.x is the horizontal coordinate of the mouse cursor, and point.y is the vertical coordinate. For example, if point.x is equal to 100 and point.y is equal to 200, the pixel will be drawn 100 pixels to the right of the window's left edge and 200 pixels below the window's top edge.

But what are the values of point.x and point.y? The second parameter of the OnMouseMove() function is point, which holds the coordinates of the mouse cursor at the time the OnMouseMove() function is executed. Therefore, the SetPixel() function draws the pixel at the location of the mouse cursor.

The third parameter of the SetPixel() function is the returned value of the RGB() function, which indicates the color of the pixel that SetPixel() draws.

The *R* in RGB stands for red, the *G* stands for green, and the *B* stands for blue. The RGB() function has three parameters: the first indicates the amount of red in the resulting color, the second indicates the amount of green, and the third indicates the amount of blue. You can generate any color by "mixing" the red, green, and blue colors. For example, to indicate the color red, use RGB(255,0,0).

Each color can have a maximum value of 255 and a minimum value of 0. RGB(255,0,0) is red because the value for red is at its maximum and the green and blue amounts are 0. Similarly, RGB(0,255,0) is green, and RGB(0,0,255) is blue.

You should recognize two additional colors by inspecting the RGB() function. White is represented by RGB(255,255,255), the maximum amounts of red, green, and blue. Black is generated as RGB(0,0,0), the result of no red, green, or blue. Therefore, the third parameter of SetPixel() indicates that the pixel should be drawn in black.

Drawing a Picture Point by Point

To see your code in action, follow these steps:

☐ Compile and link the Draw program.

☐ Execute the Draw program.

☐ While holding the left mouse button down, drag the mouse.

Draw responds by drawing pixels according to the mouse movement.

☐ Practice with the Draw program, then click the Exit button to terminate it.

Checking the Mouse Status

The OnMouseMove() function is executed when you move the mouse, but your PC can't respond to every mouse movement. Why? Because if your CPU was busy executing the OnMouseMove() function in response to every mouse movement, it couldn't perform any other tasks. Instead of executing the OnMouseMove() function every time the mouse is moved, Windows checks the mouse cursor location periodically. If the mouse cursor is at a different location than it was during the previous check, then a *flag* is set indicating the mouse was moved. The new coordinates of the mouse cursor, as well as key presses and button clicks, are noted and saved.

When the OnMouseMove() function is executed, the point parameter indicates the coordinates of the mouse cursor during the last position check, and nFlags indicates the status of certain keys and mouse buttons. Remember that the CPU can perform other tasks between executions of the OnMouseMove() function. However, if you move the mouse quickly, the OnMouseMove() function won't be executed for each new location of the mouse during the movement. You can prove it to yourself as follows:

☐ Execute the Draw program and move the mouse as shown in Figure 4.3—begin by moving the mouse slowly, then increasing the speed of your mouse movement.

Figure 4.3.

Varying your mouse movement speed.

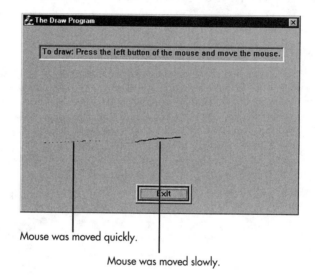

Mouse was moved quickly.

Mouse was moved slowly.

There are many points on the right side of the window shown in Figure 4.3. Why? Because you moved the mouse very slowly, the OnMouseMove() function was executed many times. Each execution of OnMouseMove() causes a pixel to be drawn at the new mouse location.

When the mouse was moved very quickly, only a few points were drawn along its path. Why? Because the OnMouseMove() function was executed only a few times during the mouse movement.

Enhancing the Draw Program

If you've ever drawn with Paint (Windows 95 and Windows NT) or Paintbrush (Windows 3.1x), you might have noticed that, unlike the Draw program, the lines drawn when you move the mouse are solid. In the Draw program, you have to move the mouse very slowly to draw a solid line. In this section, you'll try enhancing your Draw program so it performs more like Paint or Paintbrush.

You're going to attach code that makes it seem as though the lines are drawn according to the mouse movement—the same trick used by Paint and Paintbrush. The code will connect the points with straight lines. It will look as though the program draws lines at each point along the mouse path, but in reality, the program simply "connects the dots" drawn by the Draw program. If you move the mouse very quickly along the path shown in Figure 4.4, you would expect the program to draw the line along that path. Because the mouse was moved very quickly, however, the resulting line looks very different than it should. (The same situation occurs when using programs such as Paint and Paintbrush.)

Figure 4.4.

Drawing by connecting the dots.

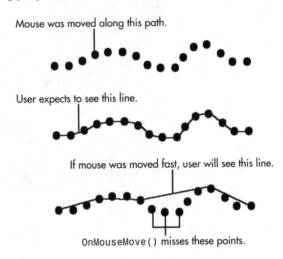

To connect the pixels with lines, the OnMouseMove() function needs to know the previous coordinates of the mouse. You'll now declare two member variables, m_PrevX and m_PrevY, which will be used to hold the coordinates of the mouse cursor.

☐ Display the DrawDlg.h file by opening the Project Workspace, clicking the FileView tab, expanding the Header Files item, and double-clicking the DrawDlg.h item.

☐ Add the declaration of the m_PrevX and m_PrevY member variables to the CDrawDlg class declaration (in the DrawDlg.h file) as follows:

```
// DrawDlg.h : header file
//
...
...
...
/////////////////////////////////////////////////////
// CDrawDlg dialog

class CDrawDlg : public CDialog
{
// Construction
```

4

```
public:
    CDrawDlg(CWnd* pParent = NULL);   // standard constructor

/////////////////////////
// MY CODE STARTS HERE
/////////////////////////

int m_PrevX;
int m_PrevY;

/////////////////////////
// MY CODE ENDS HERE
/////////////////////////

    ...
    ...
    ...
};
```

☐ Modify the OnMouseMove() function in the DrawDlg.cpp file:

```
void CDrawDlg::OnMouseMove(UINT nFlags, CPoint point)
{
// TODO: Add your message handler code here
// and/or call default

/////////////////////////
// MY CODE STARTS HERE
/////////////////////////

if ( (nFlags & MK_LBUTTON) == MK_LBUTTON )
{

// Create a dc object
CClientDC  dc(this);

// Draw a pixel
// dc.SetPixel(point.x,
//             point.y,
//             RGB(0,0,0) );

dc.MoveTo(m_PrevX, m_PrevY);
dc.LineTo(point.x, point.y);

m_PrevX = point.x;
m_PrevY = point.y;

}

/////////////////////////
// MY CODE ENDS HERE
/////////////////////////

CDialog::OnMouseMove(nFlags, point);
}
```

The code you typed first comments out the SetPixel() function:

```
// Draw a pixel
// dc.SetPixel(point.x,
//             point.y,
//             RGB(0,0,0) );
```

Then the MoveTo() and LineTo() functions are executed:

```
dc.MoveTo(m_PrevX, m_PrevY);
dc.LineTo(point.x, point.y);
```

To draw a line, you use the MoveTo() function to indicate the starting point. The coordinates of the line's starting point are the previous coordinates of the mouse cursor. Then you execute the LineTo() function; its parameters indicate the line's endpoint, which is the current coordinates of the mouse cursor.

You also updated the m_PrevX and m_PrevY member variables with the current mouse cursor coordinates; the next time the OnMouseMove() function is executed, the m_PrevX and m_PrevY variables are updated:

```
m_PrevX = point.x;
m_PrevY = point.y;
```

NOTE

The previous coordinates of the mouse (m_PrevX and m_PrevY) were declared as *data member variables* to maintain the values of m_PrevX and m_PrevY during the life of the program. OnMouseMove() updates the values of m_PrevX and m_PrevY. After the execution of OnMouseMove(), the values of m_PrevX and m_PrevY are not lost—they are updated on the next execution of OnMouseMove.

☐ Compile, link, and execute the Draw program.

☐ Draw something with the Draw program.

As you can see in Figure 4.5, now the dots are connected with straight lines.

☐ Experiment with the Draw program, then click its Exit button to terminate the program.

Figure 4.5.

Connecting the dots with straight lines.

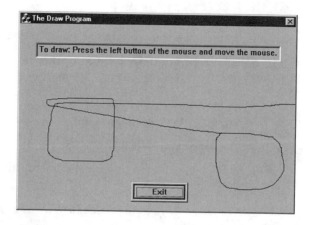

Revising the Draw Program

Did you notice that there's something wrong with the current version of Draw? The program always draws a straight line as the first line that is drawn. Why is this happening? In OnMouseMove() you added code that connects the previous mouse location with the current mouse location. The previous mouse coordinates are m_PrevX and m_PrevY, but when you start the program, m_PrevX and m_PrevY aren't updated yet. You might also notice that you can't draw two separate circles like the ones shown in Figure 4.6, because when you start drawing the second circle, a straight line will connect the last point of the first circle to the first point of the second circle.

Figure 4.6.

Drawing two circles with the Draw program.

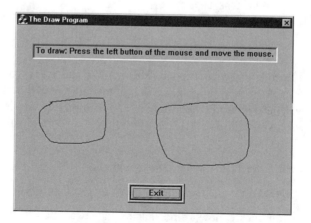

To solve the problems of the Draw program, you need to attach code to the WM_LBUTTONDOWN event, which occurs when you press the left mouse button.

☐ Select ClassWizard from the View menu, select the Message Maps tab, and use the ClassWizard dialog box to select the following event:

Class name:	CDrawDlg
Object ID:	CDrawDlg
Message:	WM_LBUTTONDOWN

☐ Click the Add Function button to create the new function OnLButtonDown, then click the Edit Code button.

Visual C++ responds by opening the file DrawDlg.cpp with the function OnLButtonDown() *ready for you to edit.*

☐ Write the following code in the OnLButtonDown() function:

```
void CDrawDlg::OnLButtonDown(UINT nFlags, CPoint point)
{
// TODO: Add your message handler code here
// and/or call default

//////////////////////////
// MY CODE STARTS HERE
//////////////////////////
m_PrevX = point.x;
m_PrevY = point.y;
//////////////////////////
// MY CODE ENDS HERE
//////////////////////////

CDialog::OnLButtonDown(nFlags, point);
}
```

The code you typed updates the m_PrevX and m_PrevY member variables. Note that the OnLButtonDown() function has the same parameters as the OnMouseMove() function. The point parameter indicates the current mouse position when the left mouse button is pressed. Now, when you start drawing, the m_PrevX and m_PrevY variables are updated with the current mouse position.

☐ Build and execute the Draw program.

☐ Draw the two circles shown previously in Figure 4.6.

As you can see, now it's possible to draw two separate circles. When you start drawing the second circle, you press the left mouse button down at the first point of the second circle. This causes the execution of the OnLButtonDown() function, which updates m_PrevX and m_PrevY with the coordinates of the first point of the second circle.

☐ Experiment with the Draw program, then click the Exit button to terminate the program.

The MyKey Program

The Draw program demonstrates how you can attach code to the MouseMove and LButtonDown events. You can also attach code to keyboard events. The MyKey program demonstrates how to do this, but before you start designing the program, let's review its specifications:

■ When you start the MyKey program, the window shown in Figure 4.7 appears.

Figure 4.7.

The MyKey program.

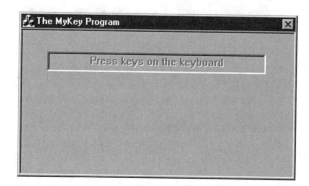

■ When you press a key on the keyboard, a message box displays the values of various flags representing the key that was pressed.

Creating the MyKey Project

You'll now create the MyKey project with the following steps:

☐ Start Visual C++, then select New from the File menu.

> *Visual C++ responds by displaying the New dialog box.*

☐ Select the Projects tab of the New dialog box.

☐ Select MFC AppWizard(exe) from the list of project types.

☐ Type MyKey in the Project Name box.

☐ Click the button that is located on the right of the Location box and select the C:\TYVCPROG\PROGRAMS\CH04 directory.

☐ Click the OK button.

> *Visual C++ responds by displaying the MFC AppWizard - Step 1 window.*

☐ Click the "Dialog based" radio button of the Step 1 window to create a dialog-based application, then click the Next button to advance to the Step 2 window.

☐ In Step 2 of the MFC AppWizard, select the options for an About box and 3-D controls and enter the title MyKey for the dialog box. When you're done, click the Next button to advance to the Step 3 window.

☐ In Step 3 of the MFC AppWizard, select the "Yes, please" radio button (because you want Visual C++ to place comments) and the "As a shared DLL" radio button. Then click the Next button to advance to the Step 4 window.

☐ Click the Finish button of the Step 4 window, then click the OK button of the New Project Information dialog box.

> *Visual C++ responds by creating the MyKey project and all its associate files.*

☐ Select Set Active Configuration from the Build menu.

> *Visual C++ responds by displaying the Set Active Project Configuration dialog box.*

☐ Set the project to MyKey Win32 - Release.

That's it! You've finished creating the MyKey project.

The Visual Design of the MyKey Program

You'll now visually design the window of the MyKey program:

☐ Select Workspace from the View menu, click the ResourceView tab of the Project Workspace window, expand the MyKey resources item, expand the Dialog item, and finally double-click the IDD_MYKEY_DIALOG item.

> *Visual C++ responds by displaying the IDD_MYKEY_DIALOG dialog box in design mode.*

☐ Delete the OK, Cancel, and TODO text in the IDD_MYKEY_DIALOG dialog box.

☐ Design the IDD_MYKEY_DIALOG dialog box according to Table 4.2. When you finish designing the dialog box, it should look like Figure 4.7.

Table 4.2. The properties table of the IDD_MYKEY_DIALOG dialog box.

Object	Property	Setting
Dialog Box	**ID**	**IDD_MYKEY_DIALOG**
	Caption	The MyKey Program
	Font	System, Size 10
	Client edge	Checked (Extended Styles tab)
	Static edge	Checked (Extended Styles tab)

4

Object	Property	Setting
Static Text	ID	IDC_INSTRUCTION_STATIC
	Caption	Press keys on the keyboard
	Align text	Center (Styles tab)
	Client edge	Checked (Extended Styles tab)
	Static edge	Checked (Extended Styles tab)
	Disabled	Checked (General)

Attaching Code to the Keyboard Events

You'll now attach code that's executed when you press keys on the keyboard:

☐ Select ClassWizard from the View menu, select the Message Maps tab, and use the ClassWizard dialog box to select the following event:

Class name:	CMyKeyDlg
Object ID:	CMyKeyDlg
Message:	WM_KEYDOWN

☐ Click the Add Function button to create the new function OnKeyDown(), then click the Edit Code button.

Visual C++ responds by opening the file MyKeyDlg.cpp with the function OnKeyDown() *ready for you to edit.*

☐ Write the following code in the OnKeyDown() function:

```
void CMyKeyDlg::OnKeyDown(UINT nChar, UINT nRepCnt, UINT nFlags)
{
// TODO: Add your message handler code here
// and/or call default

//////////////////////////
// MY CODE STARTS HERE
//////////////////////////

char   strnChar[10];
char   strnRepCnt[10];
char   strnFlags[10];

CString  strKeyPressed;

itoa(nChar,    strnChar,   10);
itoa(nRepCnt,  strnRepCnt, 10);
itoa(nFlags,   strnFlags,  10);
```

4

```
strKeyPressed = (CString)"You pressed the key: " +
                "\n" +
                "nChar=" +
                strnChar +
                "\n" +
                "nRepCnt=" +
                strnRepCnt +
                "\n" +
                "nFlags="+
                strnFlags;

MessageBox(strKeyPressed);


/////////////////////////
// MY CODE ENDS HERE
/////////////////////////

CDialog::OnKeyDown(nChar, nRepCnt, nFlags);
}
```

Take a look at the parameters of the OnKeyDown() function:

```
void CMyKeyDlg::OnKeyDown(UINT nChar, UINT nRepCnt, UINT nFlags)
{
...
...
...
}
```

The first parameter of OnKeyDown() is nChar, which specifies the code of the pressed key. The second parameter, nRepCnt, represents the number of times the key was pressed down repeatedly. For example, if you hold the A key down and keep pressing it, the nRepCnt parameter of the OnKeyDown() function holds the number of times the PC considers the A key pressed. The third parameter of the OnKeyDown() function is nFlags, which specifies a number representing special keys (such as the Alt key, the function keys, and so on).

The code you typed declares three strings:

```
char  strnChar[10];
char  strnRepCnt[10];
char  strnFlags[10];
```

They will hold the strings corresponding to the nChar, nRepCnt, and nFlags parameters.

Then you declared the strKeyPressed variable as a variable of type CString:

```
CString  strKeyPressed;
```

Next, you update the strKeyPressed variable with a string that will be displayed when you press a key on the keyboard. The nChar parameter is converted to a string as follows:

```
itoa(nChar, strnChar, 10);
```

NOTE

Use the `itoa()` function to convert a number to a string. For example, to convert the number `MyNumber` to a string named `sNumber`, first declare the `sNumber` as a string:

```
char   sNumber[5];
```

In the preceding statement, five characters were allocated to the `sNumber` string. Then you can use the `itoa()` function to update the `sNumber` string as follows:

```
itoa(sNumber, Number, 10);
```

The third parameter of the `itoa()` function is `10` because you are specifying that the number supplied as the second parameter of `itoa()` is a decimal number.

You then convert the `nRepCnt` and `nFlags` numbers to strings as follows:

```
itoa(nRepCnt, strnRepCnt, 10);
itoa(nFlags,  strnFlags,  10);
```

Now that the three parameters of the `OnKeyDown()` function are stored as strings, you can update the `strKeyPressed` string as follows:

```
strKeyPressed = (CString)"You pressed the key: " +
                "\n" +
                "nChar=" +
                strnChar +
                "\n" +
                "nRepCnt=" +
                strnRepCnt +
                "\n" +
                "nFlags="+
                strnFlags;
```

`\n` is the line-feed character.

Finally, you display the `strKeyPressed` string with the `MessageBox()` function as follows:

```
MessageBox(strKeyPressed);
```

(The `\n` character you inserted in the `strKeyPressed` string causes the string to be displayed on multiple lines.)

☐ Build and execute the MyKey program.

☐ Press a key on your keyboard, and notice that the message box displays the contents of the `OnKeyDown()` function's parameters corresponding to the pressed key.

☐ Experiment with the MyKey program, then click the × icon at the upper-right corner to terminate the MyKey program.

NOTE

> It's important to note that you were instructed to disable the static text control in the MyKey window during design time. Why? Because you want the messages that correspond to pressing the keys to reach the IDD_MYKEY_DIALOG dialog box and be processed by the OnKeyDown() function. If the dialog box contains an enabled control, the messages corresponding to the key press will reach the control that has keyboard focus (instead of reaching the OnKeyDown() function of the IDD_MYKEY_DIALOG dialog box).

Summary

In this chapter, you have designed and executed the Draw program, a program that uses the mouse for drawing. As you have seen, the Draw program uses the OnMouseMove() function to execute code whenever you move the mouse. The Draw program also uses the OnLButtonDown() function, a function executed whenever you press the left mouse button.

You have also designed and executed the MyKey program, a program that detects which keys you pressed on the keyboard.

Q&A

Q Are there other mouse messages I can use?

A Yes. In this chapter, you have learned about the WM_MOUSEMOVE message (generated whenever you move the mouse) and the WM_LBUTTONDOWN message (generated whenever you press the left mouse button). Other messages you may find useful are the WM_LBUTTONDBLCLK message (generated whenever you double-click the mouse) and the LBUTTONUP message (generated whenever you release the left mouse button). Use ClassWizard to examine the messages associated with the IDD_DRAW_DIALOG dialog box and notice other mouse-related messages, such as WM_RBUTTONUP and WM_RBUTTONDOWN.

Q Are there other keyboard messages I can use?

A In this chapter, you use the WM_KEYDOWN message (generated whenever you press a key on the keyboard). Use ClassWizard to examine other keyboard-related messages of the IDD_MYKEY_DIALOG dialog box. For example, the WM_KEYUP message is generated when a key is released.

Quiz

1. The OnKeyDown() function is executed whenever you press:
   a. The left mouse button
   b. A key on the keyboard
   c. None of the above

2. nChar is the parameter of the OnKeyDown() function, and the ASCII code of the *A* character is 65. When you press the A key, nChar is equal to what?

3. RGB(0,0,255) represents the color _____.

4. RGB(123,211,98) represents the color _____.

Exercises

1. What code will you write that is executed whenever the second bit from the right of a variable called HerFlag is equal to 1? Assume that a constant is declared as 2ND_FROM_RIGHT and that this constant is equal to 00000010.

2. Modify the Draw program so that it will draw thick red lines when you draw with the mouse. *Note:* New information is introduced in the answer of this exercise. Follow the steps presented there.

Quiz Answers

1. b
2. 65
3. Blue
4. I don't know whether this color has a name, but it's a mixture of red, green, and blue (the color is actually green with some yellow in it).

Exercise Answers

1. Here is the code that accomplishes this:

```
if ( (HerFlag & 2ND_FROM_RIGHT) == 2ND_FROM_RIGHT)
{
// This code is executed whenever the second
// bit from the right of HerFlag is equal
// to 1.
}
```

2. The Draw program draws lines (in the `OnMouseMove()` function) by using the `LineTo()` function as follows:

```
dc.LineTo(point.x, point.y);
```

But what color will be used for drawing the line? And what is the thickness of the line that will be drawn with the `LineTo()` function? Because you didn't specify any particular pen, the default pen will be used, which is a solid black pen that is 1 pixel wide.

☐ Modify the `OnMouseMove()` function:

```
void CDrawDlg::OnMouseMove(UINT nFlags, CPoint point)
{
// TODO: Add your message handler code here
// and/or call default

/////////////////////////
// MY CODE STARTS HERE
/////////////////////////

if ( (nFlags & MK_LBUTTON) == MK_LBUTTON )
{

// Create a dc object
CClientDC dc(this);

// Create a new pen (solid, 10 pixels, red).
CPen NewPen(PS_SOLID,
            10,
            RGB(255,0,0) );

// Select the pen.
dc.SelectObject(&NewPen);

// Draw a pixel
// dc.SetPixel(point.x,
//             point.y,
//             RGB(0,0,0) );

dc.MoveTo(m_PrevX, m_PrevY);
dc.LineTo(point.x, point.y);

m_PrevX = point.x;
m_PrevY = point.y;

}

/////////////////////////
// MY CODE ENDS HERE
/////////////////////////

CDialog::OnMouseMove(nFlags, point);
}
```

4

The code you added creates a new pen called NewPen of type CPen:

```
// Create a new pen (solid, 10 pixels, red).
CPen NewPen(PS_SOLID,
            10,
            RGB(255,0,0) );
```

The new pen is declared as a solid red pen, 10 pixels wide.

Then the SelectObject() function is executed to apply the new pen:

```
// Select the pen.
dc.SelectObject(&NewPen);
```

It's not enough to declare the new pen. You must also put the new pen in use by executing the SelectObject() function.

The rest of the code in the OnMouseMove() function remains the same:

```
dc.MoveTo(m_PrevX, m_PrevY);
dc.LineTo(point.x, point.y);
```

The line will be drawn as a solid red line that is 10 pixels wide.

☐ Build and execute the program.

☐ Use the mouse to draw and notice that the lines are solid red and 10 pixels wide. (See Figure 4.8.)

Figure 4.8.

Using the enhanced version of the Draw program.

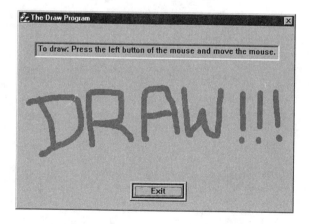

Day 5

Menus

So far, you've written programs without menus. In this chapter, you'll learn how to add a menu to your Visual C++ program.

The Speed.EXE Program

In this chapter, you'll write a program called Speed.EXE that illustrates how to write a Visual C++ program that includes a menu. Before you start writing the Speed.EXE program, let's first specify what the Speed.EXE program should look like and what it should do:

- When you start the Speed.EXE program, its window should look like the one in Figure 5.1.

- As shown in Figure 5.1, the window of the Speed.EXE program contains an edit box where you can type a numeric value. The Speed.EXE program also includes two pop-up menus: File and Help. (See Figures 5.2 and 5.3.)

Figure 5.1.

*The window of the
Speed.EXE program.*

Figure 5.2.

*The File menu of the
Speed.EXE program.*

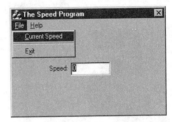

Figure 5.3.

*The Help menu of the
Speed.EXE program.*

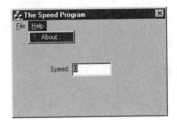

■ When you select Current Speed from the File menu, the program displays a
message box showing the numeric value specified in the edit box. When you select
About from the Help menu, the program displays an About dialog box. (See Figure 5.4.)

Figure 5.4.

*The About Speed
dialog box of the
Speed.EXE program.*

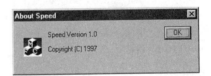

■ When you select Exit from the File menu, the program terminates.

Now that you know what the Speed.EXE program should look like and what it should do,
start creating this program.

Creating the Project of the Speed.EXE Program

Follow these steps to create the project and skeleton files of the Speed.EXE program:

☐ Create the directory C:\TYVCPROG\PROGRAMS\CH05, start Visual C++, and select New from the File menu of Visual C++.

   Visual C++ responds by displaying the New dialog box.

☐ Select the Projects tab of the New dialog box.

☐ Select MFC AppWizard(exe) from the list of project types.

☐ Type Speed in the Project Name box.

☐ Click the button that is located on the right of the Location box and select the C:\TYVCPROG\PROGRAMS\CH05 directory.

☐ Click the OK button.

   Visual C++ responds by displaying the MFC AppWizard - Step 1 window.

☐ In the Step 1 window, choose the option to create a dialog-based application, then click the Next button.

☐ In Step 2, enter The Speed Program as the title of the dialog box. Make sure the buttons for "About box" and "3D controls" are selected, then click the Next button.

☐ In Step 3, choose the "Yes, please" radio button to generate comments and the "As a shared DLL" radio button, then click the Next button.

☐ In Step 4, notice that AppWizard has created the CSpeedApp and CSpeedDlg classes for you. Click the Finish button.

   Visual C++ responds by displaying the New Project Information window.

☐ Click the OK button.

   Visual C++ responds by creating the Speed project and all its associate files.

☐ Select Set Active Configuration from the Build menu.

   Visual C++ responds by displaying the Set Active Project Configuration dialog box.

☐ Set the project to Speed Win32 - Release.

That's it! You've finished creating the Speed project.

5

Creating the Menu of the Speed Program

Follow these steps to create the menu of the Speed program:

☐ Select Workspace from the View menu, select the ResourceView tab of the Project
Workspace window, and expand the Speed resources item.

Your Project Workspace window should now look like Figure 5.5.

Figure 5.5.

*The Project
Workspace
window with
the ResourceView
tab selected.*

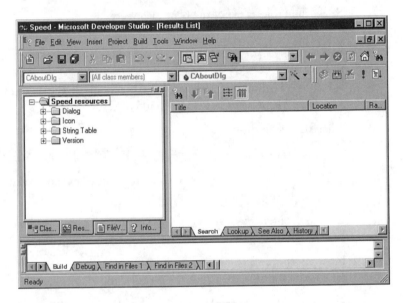

As shown in Figure 5.5, the project of the Speed program currently includes four types of
resources: Dialog, Icon, String Table, and Version. However, you want to design a menu, so
you need to insert a menu resource to the project. Here is how you do that:

☐ Right-click the Speed resources item in the Project Workspace window and select Insert
from the pop-up menu.

> *Visual C++ responds by displaying the Insert Resource dialog box. (See Figure 5.6.)*

☐ Select Menu, then click the New button of the dialog box.

> *Visual C++ responds by inserting a new blank menu in the project and displaying it in design
> mode, ready for you to edit. (See Figure 5.7.)*

Figure 5.6.

The Insert Resource dialog box.

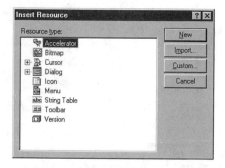

Figure 5.7.

Inserting a new blank menu in design mode.

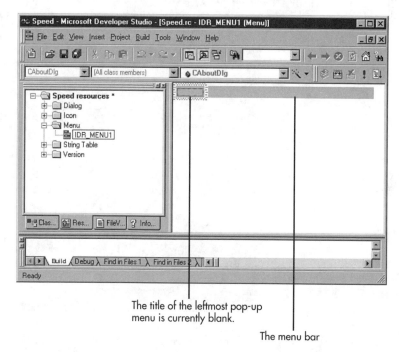

The title of the leftmost pop-up menu is currently blank.

The menu bar

As you can see in Figure 5.7, the title of the Visual C++ window includes the text IDR_MENU1 (Menu). This means that the menu Visual C++ created for you has the ID IDR_MENU1. The menu bar is currently blank; you'll be customizing it until it looks like the one shown in Figures 5.2 and 5.3. The leftmost side of the menu bar has a small blank rectangle surrounded by black dots. This rectangle represents the title of the leftmost pop-up menu of the menu bar. Follow these steps to set its title to File:

☐ Double-click the leftmost rectangle of the menu bar.

Visual C++ responds by displaying the Menu Item Properties dialog box. (See Figure 5.8.)

Figure 5.8.

Displaying the Menu Item Properties dialog box.

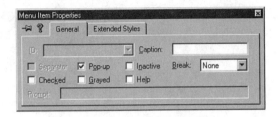

☐ Set the Caption field to &File.

Notice as you type in the Caption field that the title of the leftmost pop-up menu changes accordingly. Your menu bar should now look like the one shown in Figure 5.9.

Figure 5.9.

Setting the title of the leftmost pop-up menu to File.

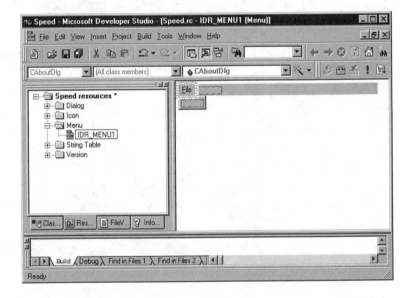

The *F* in "File" is underlined because you prefixed File with the & character. Consequently, the File pop-up menu will open when you press Alt+F on the keyboard during runtime.

As shown in Figure 5.9, there's now a small empty rectangle under the File menu title. This rectangle represents the caption of the first menu item of the File menu. (If you don't see this rectangle on your screen, click the File title.) To set the caption of the first item in the File pop-up menu, do the following:

☐ Double-click the blank rectangle under the File title.

Visual C++ responds by opening the Menu Item Properties dialog box again so you can set the caption of the first menu item of the File pop-up menu.

☐ Set the Caption field to &Current Speed.

Your IDR_MENU1 menu should look like the one in Figure 5.10. The caption of the first menu item is now set to Current Speed.

Figure 5.10.

Setting the caption of the first File menu item to Current Speed.

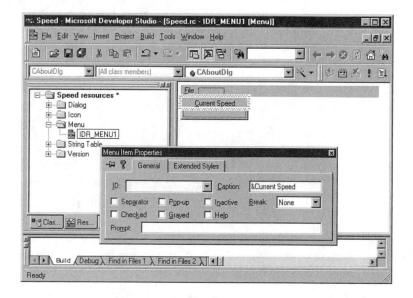

The *C* in "Current Speed" is prefixed with the & character. During runtime, you can press C on the keyboard to select the Current Speed menu item when the File pop-up menu is open.

As shown in Figure 5.10, the Menu Item Properties dialog box also has an ID field. However, you don't have to set the ID of the menu item. Visual C++ will automatically assign an ID for each menu item you add to the pop-up menu. To make sure Visual C++ automatically assigned an ID to the Current Speed menu item, do the following:

☐ Double-click the Current Speed item of the File pop-up menu.

Visual C++ responds by opening the Menu Item Properties dialog box again. (See Figure 5.11.)

As you can see, Visual C++ assigned ID_FILE_CURRENTSPEED as an ID for the Current Speed menu item. (You can't see the last *D* in ID_FILE_CURRENTSPEED because the ID field isn't wide enough.)

5

Figure 5.11.

*Checking the ID of
the Current Speed
menu item.*

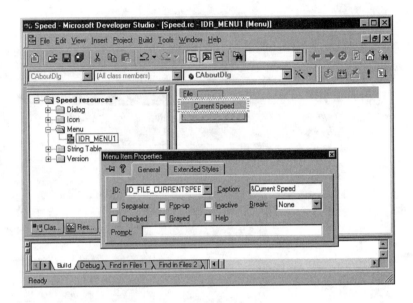

The next menu item to add to the File pop-up menu is a separator bar. As shown in Figure 5.2, there's a separator bar between the Current Speed menu item and the Exit menu item. To add the separator bar, do the following:

☐ Double-click the blank rectangle under the Current Speed menu item.

    Visual C++ responds by again displaying the Menu Item Properties dialog box so you can add a separator bar.

☐ Place a check mark in the Separator check box. (See Figure 5.12.)

    Visual C++ responds by inserting a separator bar below the Current Speed menu item.

The last menu item to add is the Exit menu item. Follow these steps to add the Exit menu item to the File pop-up menu:

☐ Double-click the blank rectangle under the separator bar of the File pop-up menu.

    Visual C++ responds by again displaying the Menu Item Properties dialog box so you can set the caption of File's third menu item.

☐ Set the Caption field to E&xit.

The File pop-up menu is finished! Your IDR_MENU1 menu should now look like the one shown in Figure 5.13.

Figure 5.12.
*Adding a
separator bar.*

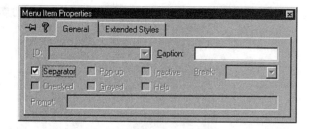

Figure 5.13.
*The IDR_MENU1
menu after finishing
the File pop-up menu.*

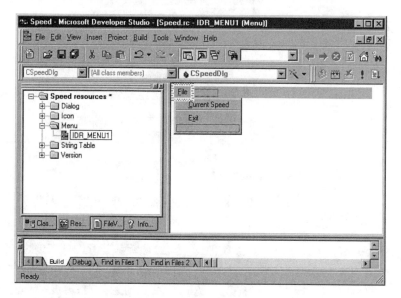

5

As shown in Figure 5.3, the menu of the Speed.EXE program should also include a Help pop-up menu; follow these steps to add one:

☐ Double-click the small rectangle on the menu bar to the right of the File pop-up menu title.

☐ Set the Caption field in the Menu Item Properties dialog box to &Help.

Your IDR_MENU1 menu should now look like the one shown in Figure 5.14.

As shown in Figure 5.3, the Help pop-up menu should include only one menu item: About. Follow these steps to add the About menu item to the Help pop-up menu:

☐ Double-click the blank rectangle under the Help title.

Visual C++ responds by again displaying the Menu Item Properties dialog box so you can set the caption of Help's first menu item.

Figure 5.14.

Setting the title of the second pop-up menu to Help.

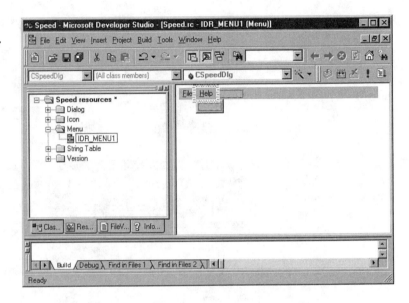

☐ Set the Caption field to &About...

That's it! You've finished the Help pop-up menu of the IDR_MENU1 menu. (See Figure 5.15.)

Figure 5.15.

Adding the About menu item.

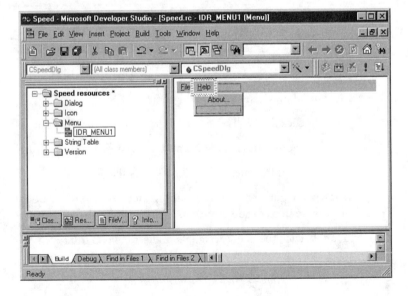

The last thing to do before you've finished the design of the IDR_MENU1 menu is to associate the IDR_MENU1 menu with a class. Here is how you do that:

☐ Select ClassWizard from the View menu.

Visual C++ responds by displaying the Adding a Class dialog box. (See Figure 5.16.)

Visual C++ displays the Adding a Class dialog box because you're working on the IDR_MENU1 menu, which isn't currently associated with any class.

Figure 5.16.

The Adding a Class dialog box.

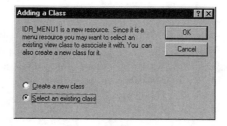

☐ Select the "Select an existing class" radio button in the Adding a Class dialog box, then click the OK button.

Visual C++ responds by displaying the Select Class dialog box. (See Figure 5.17.)

Figure 5.17.

The Select Class dialog box.

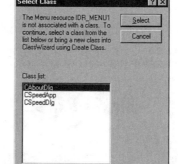

☐ Select the CSpeedDlg class in the Class List box, then click the Select button. (Note: Do not use the default setting of CAboutDlg shown in Figure 5.17. Instead, select the CSpeedDlg item, then click the Select button.)

Visual C++ responds by displaying the MFC ClassWizard dialog box. (See Figure 5.18.)

Figure 5.18.

*The MFC
ClassWizard
dialog box.*

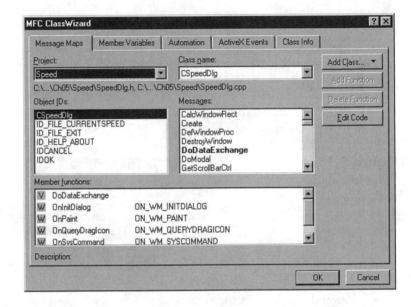

☐ Click the OK button of the MFC ClassWizard dialog box.

That's it! You've finished associating the IDR_MENU1 menu with a class.

Why did you associate the IDR_MENU1 menu with the CSpeedDlg class and not with another class? Because the CSpeedDlg class is associated with the IDD_SPEED_DIALOG dialog box that serves as the program's main window. Therefore, the code you attach later to the menu items of the IDR_MENU1 menu can access member functions and data members associated with the IDD_SPEED_DIALOG dialog box.

The Visual Design of the IDD_SPEED_DIALOG Dialog Box

In the previous section, you designed the IDR_MENU1 menu and associated it with the CSpeedDlg class. In this section, you'll visually design the IDD_SPEED_DIALOG dialog box—the main window of the program. You'll place controls in the dialog box and attach the IDR_MENU1 menu to the dialog box by following these steps:

☐ Select the ResourceView tab of the Project Workspace window.

☐ Expand the Speed resources item, expand the Dialog item, and double-click the IDD_SPEED_DIALOG item.

   Visual C++ responds by displaying the IDD_SPEED_DIALOG dialog box in design mode.

☐ Delete the OK button, Cancel button, and text in the IDD_SPEED_DIALOG dialog box.

☐ Place a static text control in the IDD_SPEED_DIALOG dialog box and set its Caption property to Speed:.

☐ Place an edit box control in the IDD_SPEED_DIALOG dialog box and set its ID to IDC_SPEED_EDIT.

Your IDD_SPEED_DIALOG dialog box should now look like the one in Figure 5.19.

Figure 5.19.

The IDC_SPEED_DIALOG dialog box after customization.

To finish the visual design of IDD_SPEED_DIALOG, attach the IDR_MENU1 menu you designed earlier to the IDD_SPEED_DIALOG dialog box. Here is how you do that:

☐ Right-click any free area in the IDD_SPEED_DIALOG dialog box and select Properties from the pop-up menu.

Visual C++ responds by displaying the Dialog Properties dialog box. (See Figure 5.20.)

Figure 5.20.

The Dialog Properties dialog box.

5

Use the Menu drop-down list under the Caption field to select the menu you want to attach to the dialog box:

☐ Click the down-arrow next to the Menu drop-down list and select the IDR_MENU1 menu.

Your Dialog Properties dialog box should now look like the one in Figure 5.21.

Figure 5.21.

Setting the Menu drop-down list to IDR_MENU1.

☐ Save your work by selecting Save All from the File menu.

You've finished the visual design of the IDD_SPEED_DIALOG dialog box, and you attached the IDR_MENU1 menu to the IDD_SPEED_DIALOG dialog box. To see your visual design in action, follow these steps:

☐ Select Build Speed.EXE from the Build menu.

☐ Select Execute Speed.EXE from the Build menu.

> *Visual C++ responds by executing the Speed.EXE program. The main window is shown in Figure 5.22.*

Figure 5.22.

The main window of the Speed.EXE program.

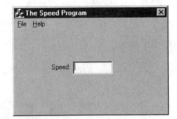

As you can see, the main window of the Speed.EXE program is just as you designed it—it includes the text Speed: and an edit box control, and the menu you designed is attached.

☐ Experiment with the File menu and the About menu. (Refer to Figures 5.2 and 5.3.)

Of course, when you select a menu item, nothing happens because you haven't attached code to the menu items yet. You'll attach code to the menu items later in this chapter.

☐ Terminate the Speed.EXE program by clicking the × icon located at the top-right corner of the program's window.

Attaching a Variable to the Edit Box Control

You need to attach a variable to the IDC_SPEED_EDIT edit box control so that when you write the program's code, you can use this variable to read the contents of the edit box control.

To do this, follow these steps:

☐ Select ClassWizard from the View menu.

☐ In the Member Variables tab of ClassWizard, make the following selections:

> Class name: CSpeedDlg
> Control ID: IDC_SPEED_EDIT

☐ Click the Add Variable button and set the variable as follows:

> Variable name: m_SpeedEdit
> Category: Value
> Variable type: int

☐ Click the OK button of the Add Member Variable dialog box.

Your MFC ClassWizard dialog box should now look like the one shown in Figure 5.23.

Figure 5.23.

Attaching the m_SpeedEdit variable to the edit box.

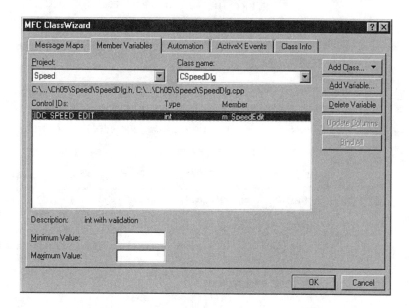

Because you specified the m_SpeedEdit variable as type int (numeric), Visual C++ lets you specify the minimum value and maximum value for the variable.

☐ Set the Minimum Value and Maximum Value fields at the bottom of the ClassWizard dialog box as follows:

> Minimum Value: 0
> Maximum Value: 100

These settings mean that during runtime, you can type values only in the range from 0 to 100 in the IDC_SPEED_EDIT edit box.

☐ Click ClassWizard's OK button.

Attaching Code to the EN_CHANGE Event of the Edit Box Control

You'll now attach code to the EN_CHANGE event of the IDC_SPEED_EDIT edit box, which occurs when you change the contents of the edit box by entering or deleting characters.

☐ Select ClassWizard from the View menu. In the Message Maps tab, select the following event:

Class name:	CSpeedDlg
Object ID:	IDC_SPEED_EDIT
Message:	EN_CHANGE

☐ Click the Add Function button, name the new function OnChangeSpeedEdit, and click the Edit Code button.

Visual C++ responds by opening the file SpeedDlg.cpp with the function OnChangeSpeedEdit() *ready for you to edit.*

☐ Write the following code in the OnChangeSpeedEdit() function:

```
void CSpeedDlg::OnChangeSpeedEdit()
{
// TODO: If this is a RICHEDIT control, the control will
// not send this notification unless you modify
// CDialog::OnInitDialog() function to send the
// EM_SETEVENTMASK message to the control with the
// ENM_CHANGE flag ORed into the lParam mask.

// TODO: Add your control notification handler code here

/////////////////////////
// MY CODE STARTS HERE
/////////////////////////

// Update the variable of the IDC_SPEED_EDIT.
UpdateData(TRUE);

/////////////////////////
// MY CODE ENDS HERE
/////////////////////////

}
```

☐ Save your work by selecting Save All from the File menu.

The single statement you typed in the OnChangeSpeedEdit() function updates the variables of the controls with the controls' current contents:

```
UpdateData(TRUE);
```

Therefore, after the preceding statement is executed, the m_SpeedEdit variable will be updated with the value you enter in the IDC_SPEED_EDIT edit box.

Attaching Code to the Current Speed Menu Item of the File Menu

You'll now attach code to the Current Speed menu item of the File menu that will display a message box with the current value entered in the IDC_SPEED_EDIT edit box:

☐ Display the IDR_MENU1 menu in design mode by double-clicking the IDR_MENU1 item in the Project Workspace window or by selecting Speed.rc-IDR_MENU1[Menu] from the Window menu.

☐ Select ClassWizard from the View menu. In the Message Maps tab, select the following event:

Class name:	CSpeedDlg
Object ID:	ID_FILE_CURRENTSPEED
Message:	COMMAND

Your ClassWizard dialog box should now look like the one shown in Figure 5.24.

The COMMAND event of a menu item occurs when you select that menu item. Therefore, the code you'll attach to the COMMAND event of the Current Speed menu item will be automatically executed whenever you select the Current Speed menu item.

☐ Click ClassWizard's Add Function button, name the new function OnFileCurrentspeed, then click the Edit Code button.

> *Visual C++ responds by opening the file SpeedDlg.cpp with the function* OnFileCurrentspeed() *ready for you to edit.*

☐ Write the following code in the OnFileCurrentspeed() function:

```
void CSpeedDlg::OnFileCurrentspeed()
{

// TODO: Add your command handler code here
```

5

```
//////////////////////////
// MY CODE STARTS HERE
//////////////////////////

// Convert the numeric value of m_SpeedEdit into a string.
char strSpeed[15];
itoa(m_SpeedEdit, strSpeed, 10);

// Display the speed.
MessageBox(strSpeed);

//////////////////////////
// MY CODE ENDS HERE
//////////////////////////

}
```

Figure 5.24.

Selecting the COMMAND *event of the Current Speed menu item.*

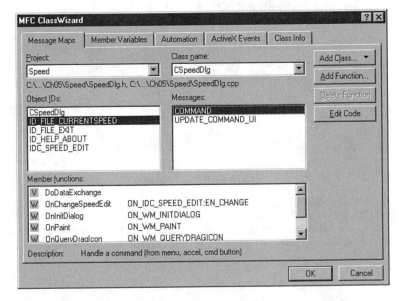

☐ Save your work by selecting Save All from the File menu.

The first two statements you entered in the OnFileCurrentspeed() function convert the integer value stored in the m_SpeedEdit variable into a string:

```
char strSpeed[15];
itoa(m_SpeedEdit, strSpeed, 10);
```

The next statement uses the MessageBox() function to display the string value:

```
MessageBox(strSpeed);
```

To see the code you attached to the Current Speed menu item in action, follow these steps:

☐ Select Build Speed.EXE from the Build menu.

☐ Select Execute Speed.EXE from the Build menu.

Visual C++ responds by executing the Speed.EXE program.

☐ Type any integer value from 0 to 100 in the edit box.

☐ Select Current Speed from the File menu of the Speed.EXE program.

As expected, the Speed.EXE program responds by displaying a message box with the value you typed in the edit box.

☐ Close the message box by clicking its OK button.

☐ Terminate the Speed.EXE program by clicking the × icon located at the top-right corner of the program's window.

Attaching Code to the Exit Menu Item of the File Menu

You'll now attach code to the Exit menu item of the File menu. Follow these steps:

☐ Display the IDR_MENU1 menu in design mode.

☐ Select ClassWizard from the View menu. In the Message Maps tab, select the following event:

Class name:	CSpeedDlg
Object ID:	ID_FILE_EXIT
Message:	COMMAND

☐ Click the Add Function button, name the new function OnFileExit, and click the Edit Code button.

Visual C++ responds by opening the file SpeedDlg.cpp with the function OnFileExit() ready for you to edit.

☐ Write the following code in the OnFileExit() function:

```
void CSpeedDlg::OnFileExit()
{
// TODO: Add your command handler code here
```

5

```
////////////////////////
// MY CODE STARTS HERE
////////////////////////

// Terminate the program.
OnOK();

////////////////////////
// MY CODE ENDS HERE
////////////////////////

}
```

☐ Save your work by selecting Save All from the File menu.

The single statement you typed in the OnFileExit() function terminates the program by calling the OnOK() function. Recall from previous chapters that the OnOK() function terminates the program by closing the dialog box.

To see the code you attached to the Exit menu item in action, follow these steps:

☐ Select Build Speed.EXE from the Build menu.

☐ Select Execute Speed.EXE from the Build menu.

Visual C++ responds by executing the Speed.EXE program.

☐ Select Exit from the File menu of the Speed.EXE program.

As expected, the Speed.EXE program responds by terminating.

Attaching Code to the About Menu Item of the Help Menu

You'll now attach code to the About menu item of the Help menu. This code will display the About dialog box of the Speed.EXE program. Follow these steps:

☐ Display the IDR_MENU1 menu in design mode.

☐ Select ClassWizard from the View menu. In the Message Maps tab, select the following event:

Class name:	CSpeedDlg
Object ID:	ID_HELP_ABOUT
Message:	COMMAND

☐ Click the Add Function button, name the new function OnHelpAbout, and click the Edit Code button.

   Visual C++ responds by opening the file SpeedDlg.cpp with the function OnHelpAbout() *ready for you to edit.*

☐ Write the following code in the OnHelpAbout() function:

```
void CSpeedDlg::OnHelpAbout()
{

// TODO: Add your command handler code here

/////////////////////////
// MY CODE STARTS HERE
/////////////////////////

// Create an object of class CAboutDlg
CAboutDlg dlg;

// Display the About dialog box.
dlg.DoModal();

/////////////////////////
// MY CODE ENDS HERE
/////////////////////////

}
```

☐ Save your work by selecting Save All from the File menu.

The first statement you entered in the OnHelpAbout() function creates an object called dlg of class CAboutDlg:

```
CAboutDlg dlg;
```

The CAboutDlg class was created by Visual C++ when you created the project and skeleton files of the program. This class is associated with the About dialog box that Visual C++ created for you.

The second statement displays the About dialog box by executing the DoModal() member function on the dlg object:

```
dlg.DoModal();
```

As its name implies, the DoModal() function displays the dialog box as a modal dialog box. This means that while the dialog box is displayed, you cannot make other windows of the program active.

5

The Speed.EXE program is finished! To see the code you attached to the About menu item in action, follow these steps:

☐ Select Build Speed.EXE from the Build menu.

☐ Select Execute Speed.EXE from the Build menu.

Visual C++ responds by executing the Speed.EXE program.

☐ Select About from the Help menu of the Speed.EXE program.

As expected, the Speed.EXE program responds by displaying the About dialog box.

☐ Close the About dialog box by clicking its OK button.

☐ Terminate the Speed.EXE program by selecting Exit from its File menu.

Summary

In this chapter, you have learned how to incorporate a menu into a dialog-based program. You have learned how to design a menu, how to associate the menu with the class of the dialog box serving as the program's main window, how to attach the menu to the dialog box, and how to attach code to the menu items.

Q&A

Q In the Speed.EXE program, I associated the IDR_MENU1 menu with the CSpeedDlg class. Why the CSpeedDlg class and not another class?

A The CSpeedDlg class is the class associated with the IDD_SPEED_DIALOG dialog box, the main window of the Speed.EXE program. Because you associate the IDR_MENU1 with the CSpeedDlg class, when you attach code to the menu items, the code can access data members and member functions of the CSpeedDlg class. This means that the code you attach to the menu items can access the data members attached to the controls of the IDD_SPEED_DIALOG dialog box.

Quiz

1. A separator bar is a horizontal line that separates menu items.
   a. True
   b. False

2. When does the COMMAND event of a menu item occur?

3. Suppose you add a new menu item to the IDR_MENU1 menu of the Speed.EXE program, and its ID is ID_MY_MENUITEM. Describe the steps needed to attach code to the ID_MY_MENUITEM menu item.

Exercise

Enhance the Speed.EXE program by adding a new menu item to the Help menu of the Speed program and setting its caption to Say Hello. Attach code to the Say Hello menu item so that the program will display a Hello message box when you select this menu item.

Quiz Answers

1. True

2. The COMMAND event of a menu item occurs when you select the menu item.

3. To attach code to the ID_MY_MENUITEM menu item of the Speed.EXE program, do the following:

   ☐ Display the IDR_MENU1 menu in design mode.

   ☐ Select ClassWizard from the View menu. In the Message Maps tab, select the following event:

Class name:	CSpeedDlg
Object ID:	ID_MY_MENUITEM
Message:	COMMAND

   ☐ Click the Add Function button, name the new function OnMyMenuitem, and click the Edit Code button.

   ☐ Write code in the OnMyMenuitem() function. This code will be automatically executed whenever you select the ID_MY_MENUITEM menu item.

Exercise Answer

To add the Say Hello menu item to the Help menu of the Speed.EXE program, do the following:

☐ Display the IDR_MENU1 menu in design mode.

☐ Click the Help menu title in the IDR_MENU1 menu bar.

5

☐ Click the small blank rectangle under the About menu item of the Help pop-up menu.

   Visual C++ responds by displaying the Menu Item Properties dialog box, so you can set the caption of the new menu item.

☐ Set the Caption field to &Say Hello.

Next, attach code to the Say Hello menu item:

☐ Make sure the IDR_MENU1 menu is currently displayed by double-clicking the IDR_MENU1 item in the Project Workspace window.

☐ Select ClassWizard from the View menu. In the Message Maps tab, select the following event:

Class name:	CSpeedDlg
Object ID:	ID_HELP_SAYHELLO
Message:	COMMAND

☐ Click the Add Function button, name the new function OnHelpSayhello, and click the Edit Code button.

☐ Write the following code in the OnHelpSayhello() function:

```
void CSpeedDlg::OnHelpSayhello()
{
// TODO: Add your control notification handler code here

//////////////////////////
// MY CODE STARTS HERE
//////////////////////////

// Display a Hello message box.
MessageBox("Hello");

//////////////////////////
// MY CODE ENDS HERE
//////////////////////////

}
```

Day **6**

Dialog Boxes

In this chapter, you'll learn how to create and display dialog boxes from within your Visual C++ programs and how to use predefined and custom-made dialog boxes.

Types of Dialog Boxes

You can display two types of dialog boxes:

- Predefined dialog boxes
- Custom-made dialog boxes

Predefined dialog boxes are also called *message boxes*. Their appearance has already been defined, so you can make only minor changes to them. Custom-made dialog boxes, on the other hand, are dialog boxes you define and design, so you have full control over their appearance and behavior.

The *MyMsg* Program

You'll now design and create the MyMsg program, a program that uses predefined dialog boxes. Before creating the MyMsg program, let's review its specifications:

■ When you execute the program, the window shown in Figure 6.1 appears.

Figure 6.1.

The window of the MyMsg program.

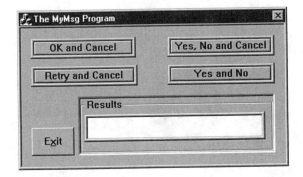

■ You can click any of the four buttons in the upper portion of the window to display various message boxes. For example, after clicking the Yes and No button, the message box shown in Figure 6.2 appears. The edit box shown in Figure 6.1 will display the name of the button you clicked. You can click the other buttons to experiment with other message boxes that have different icons and buttons.

Figure 6.2.

The message box displayed after clicking the Yes and No button.

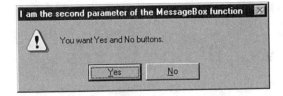

Creating the Project of the *MyMsg* Program

You'll now create the project of the MyMsg program:

☐ Create the C:\TYVCPROG\PROGRAMS\CH06 directory.

☐ Start Visual C++ and select New from the File menu.

Visual C++ responds by displaying the New dialog box.

☐ Select the Projects tab of the New dialog box.

☐ Select MFC AppWizard(exe) from the list of project types.

☐ Type MyMsg in the Project Name box.

☐ Click the button that is located on the right of the Location box and select the C:\TYVCPROG\PROGRAMS\CH06 directory.

☐ Click the OK button.

>   *Visual C++ responds by displaying the MFC AppWizard - Step 1 window.*

☐ In Step 1, select the Dialog Based option to create a dialog-based application, then click the Next button.

☐ In Step 2, use the default settings and enter MyMsg as the title for the dialog box. When you're done, click the Next button.

☐ In Step 3, use the default settings and click the Next button.

☐ In Step 4, notice that AppWizard has created the CMyMsgApp and CMyMsgDlg classes for you. Click the Finish button, then click the OK button of the New Project Information window.

☐ Select Set Active Configuration from the Build menu, then select the MyMsg - Win32 Release item.

That's it! Visual C++ has created the MyMsg project and all its associated files.

The Visual Design of the MyMsg Program

You'll now visually design the main window of the MyMsg program by following these steps:

☐ In the Project Workspace window, click the ResourceView tab and expand the MyMsg resources item, then expand the Dialog item. Finally, double-click the IDD_MYMSG_DIALOG item.

>   *Visual C++ responds by displaying the IDD_MYMSG_DIALOG dialog box in design mode.*

☐ Delete the OK button, the Cancel button, and the TODO text from the IDD_MYMSG_DIALOG dialog box.

☐ Design the IDD_MYMSG_DIALOG dialog box according to Table 6.1. When you finish, it should look like Figure 6.1.

6

Table 6.1. The properties table of the IDD_MYMSG_DIALOG dialog box.

Object	Property	Setting
Dialog Box	**ID**	**ID_MYMSG_DIALOG**
	Caption	The MyMsg Program
	Font	System, Size 10 (General tab)
	Client edge	Checked (Extended Styles tab)
	Static edge	Checked (Extended Styles tab)
Push Button	**ID**	**IDC_EXIT_BUTTON**
	Caption	E&xit
Push Button	**ID**	**IDC_OKCANCEL_BUTTON**
	Caption	OK and Cancel
	Client edge	Checked (Extended Styles tab)
	Static edge	Checked (Extended Styles tab)
	Modal frame	Checked (Extended Styles tab)
Push Button	**ID**	**IDC_YESNO_BUTTON**
	Caption	Yes and No
	Client edge	Checked (Extended Styles tab)
	Static edge	Checked (Extended Styles tab)
	Modal frame	Checked (Extended Styles tab)
Push Button	**ID**	**IDC_YESNOCANCEL_BUTTON**
	Caption	Yes, No and Cancel
	Client edge	Checked (Extended Styles tab)
	Static edge	Checked (Extended Styles tab)
	Modal frame	Checked (Extended Styles tab)
Push Button	**ID**	**IDC_RETRYCANCEL_BUTTON**
	Caption	Retry and Cancel
	Client edge	Checked (Extended Styles tab)
	Static edge	Checked (Extended Styles tab)
	Modal frame	Checked (Extended Styles tab)

Object	Property	Setting
Group Box	**ID**	**IDC_RESULTS_STATIC**
	Caption	Results
	Client edge	Checked (Extended Styles tab)
	Static edge	Checked (Extended Styles tab)
Edit Box	**ID**	**IDC_RESULTS_EDIT**
	Multiline	Checked (Styles tab)
	Client edge	Checked (Extended Styles tab)
	Static edge	Checked (Extended Styles tab)
	Modal frame	Checked (Extended Styles tab)
	Align text	Centered (Styles tab)

Attaching a Variable to the Edit Box

You'll now attach a variable to the IDC_RESULTS_EDIT edit box:

☐ Select ClassWizard from the View menu.

☐ In the Member Variables tab of ClassWizard, make the following selection:

Class name: `CMyMsgDlg`

Control ID: `IDC_RESULTS_EDIT`

☐ Click the Add Variable button and set the variable as follows:

Variable name: `m_ResultsEdit`

Category: `Value`

Variable type: `CString`

☐ Click the OK button of the Add Member Variable dialog box, then click the OK button of ClassWizard.

Attaching Code to the Exit Button

You'll now attach code to the `BN_CLICKED` event of the Exit button:

☐ Select ClassWizard from the View menu.

6

☐ In the Message Maps tab of ClassWizard, select the following event:

Class name:	CMyMsgDlg
Object ID:	IDC_EXIT_BUTTON
Message:	BN_CLICKED

☐ Click the Add Function button, name the new function `OnExitButton`, and click the Edit Code button.

Visual C++ responds by opening the file MyMsgDlg.cpp with the function `OnExitButton()` *ready for you to edit.*

☐ Write the following code in the `OnExitButton()` function:

```
void CMyMsgDlg::OnExitButton()
{
// TODO: Add your control notification handler code here


/////////////////////////
// MY CODE STARTS HERE
/////////////////////////

// Terminate the program
OnOK();

/////////////////////////
// MY CODE ENDS HERE
/////////////////////////

}
```

Attaching Code to the BN_CLICKED Event of the OK and Cancel Button

You'll now attach code to the BN_CLICKED event of the IDC_OKCANCEL_BUTTON button:

☐ Select ClassWizard from the View menu.

☐ In the Message Maps tab of ClassWizard, select the following event:

Class name:	CMyMsgDlg
Object ID:	IDC_OKCANCEL_BUTTON
Message:	BN_CLICKED

☐ Click the Add Function button, name the new function OnOkcancelButton, and click the Edit Code button.

Visual C++ responds by opening the file MyMsgDlg.cpp, with the function OnOkcancelButton() *ready for you to edit.*

☐ Write the following code in the OnOkcancelButton() function:

```
void CMyMsgDlg::OnOkcancelButton()
{
// TODO: Add your control notification handler code here

/////////////////////////
// MY CODE STARTS HERE
/////////////////////////

int iResults;

iResults =
MessageBox
    (
    "You want Ok and Cancel buttons.",
    "I am the second parameter of the MessageBox function",
    MB_OKCANCEL + MB_ICONSTOP
    );

if (iResults==IDOK)
{
m_ResultsEdit = "You clicked the OK button!";
UpdateData(FALSE);
}


if (iResults==IDCANCEL)
{
m_ResultsEdit = "You clicked the Cancel button!";
UpdateData(FALSE);
}

/////////////////////////
// MY CODE ENDS HERE
/////////////////////////

}
```

The code you typed declares an integer variable:

```
int iResults;
```

The iResults variable will hold an integer corresponding to the button you clicked in the message box displayed by the MyMsg program.

6

The `MessageBox()` function is then executed as follows:

```
iResults =
  MessageBox
    (
    "You want Ok and Cancel buttons.",
    "I am the second parameter of the MessageBox function",
     MB_OKCANCEL + MB_ICONSTOP
     );
```

The returned value from `MessageBox()` is assigned to the `iResults` variable. Later in this function, you'll use `if` statements to examine the value of `iResults`.

The `MessageBox()` function has three parameters. The first is a string that appears in the message box, the second is a string that appears as the caption of the message box, and the third parameter of `MessageBox()` is the following:

```
MB_OKCANCEL + MB_ICONSTOP
```

`MB_OKCANCEL` is a constant that tells the `MessageBox()` function to display two buttons in the message box: the OK button and the Cancel button. `MB_ICONSTOP` is a constant that tells the `MessageBox()` function to display the Stop icon in the message box.

The `MessageBox()` function returns an integer, which is assigned to the `iResults` variable. A series of two `if` statements is then executed to examine the value of `iResults`. The code under the first `if` statement is executed if you click the OK button of the message box:

```
if (iResults==IDOK)
{
m_ResultsEdit = "You clicked the OK button!";
UpdateData(FALSE);
}
```

The code under the preceding `if` statement updates the `m_ResultsEdit` variable (the variable of the edit text box); then the edit box is updated with the `UpdateData()` function.

Therefore, the edit box displays text telling you that you clicked the OK button. The code under the second `if` statement is executed if you click the Cancel button of the message box:

```
if (iResults==IDCANCEL)
{
m_ResultsEdit = "You clicked the Cancel button!";
UpdateData(FALSE);
}
```

The code under the second `if` statement is similar to the code under the first `if` statement, except that it displays this text:

```
"You clicked the Cancel button!";
```

☐ Select Save All from the File menu to save your work.

☐ Build and execute the MyMsg program.

☐ Click the OK and Cancel button.

MyMsg responds by displaying the message box shown in Figure 6.3.

Note that the × icon is displayed in the message box, because the third parameter of the `MessageBox()` function contains the `MB_ICONSTOP` constant. Also, the message box contains the OK and Cancel buttons, because the third parameter of the `MessageBox()` function indicates OK and Cancel buttons.

Figure 6.3.

The message box displayed after you click the OK and Cancel buttons.

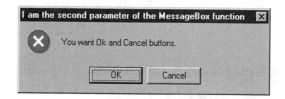

☐ Click the OK button of the message box.

MyMsg responds by updating the edit box, as shown in Figure 6.4.

Figure 6.4.

The text displayed after you click the OK button of the message box.

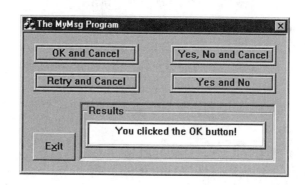

☐ Click the OK and Cancel button.

MyMsg responds by displaying the message box shown in Figure 6.3.

☐ Click the Cancel button of the message box.

MyMsg responds by updating the edit box with a string telling you that you clicked the Cancel button of the message box. (See Figure 6.5.)

☐ Experiment with the MyMsg program, then click the Exit button to terminate the program.

Figure 6.5.
*The text displayed
after you click the
Cancel button of the
message box.*

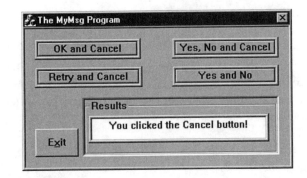

Attaching Code to the BN_CLICKED Event of the Yes, No and Cancel Button

You'll now attach code to the BN_CLICKED event of the IDC_YESNOCANCEL_BUTTON button:

☐ Select ClassWizard from the View menu.

☐ In the Message Maps tab of ClassWizard, select the following event:

Class name:	CMyMsgDlg
Object ID:	IDC_YESNOCANCEL_BUTTON
Message:	BN_CLICKED

☐ Click the Add Function button, name the new function OnYesnocancelButton, and click the Edit Code button.

Visual C++ responds by opening the file MyMsgDlg.cpp, with the function OnYesnocancelButton() *ready for you to edit.*

☐ Write the following code in the OnYesnocancelButton() function:

```
void CMyMsgDlg::OnYesnocancelButton()
{
// TODO: Add your control notification handler code here

//////////////////////////
// MY CODE STARTS HERE
//////////////////////////

int iResults;

iResults =
     MessageBox (
```

```
        "You want Yes, No, and Cancel buttons.",
        "I am the second parameter of the MessageBox function",
         MB_YESNOCANCEL + MB_ICONINFORMATION

                        );

    if (iResults==IDYES)
    {
    m_ResultsEdit = "You clicked the Yes button!";
    UpdateData(FALSE);
    }


    if (iResults==IDNO)
    {
    m_ResultsEdit = "You clicked the No button!";
    UpdateData(FALSE);
    }


    if (iResults==IDCANCEL)
    {
    m_ResultsEdit = "You clicked the Cancel button!";
    UpdateData(FALSE);
    }


    //////////////////////
    // MY CODE ENDS HERE
    //////////////////////

    }
```

The code you typed is similar to the code in the OnOkcancelButton() function, except that this is the third parameter of the MessageBox() function:

```
MB_YESNOCANCEL + MB_ICONINFORMATION
```

The preceding constants mean that the message box includes the Yes, No, and Cancel buttons (MB_YESNOCANCEL) and that the icon displayed in the message box is the Information icon (MB_ICONINFORMATION). Also, the first parameter of the MessageBox() function displays text indicating that you clicked the IDC_YESNOCANCEL_BUTTON button:

```
iResults =
    MessageBox (

    "You want Yes, No, and Cancel buttons.",
    "I am the second parameter of the MessageBox function",
     MB_YESNOCANCEL + MB_ICONINFORMATION

                        );
```

6

A series of three if statements is executed. The code under the first if statement is executed if you clicked the Yes button:

```
if (iResults==IDYES)
{
m_ResultsEdit = "You clicked the Yes button!";
UpdateData(FALSE);
}
```

The code under the second if statement is executed if you clicked the No button:

```
if (iResults==IDNO)
{
m_ResultsEdit = "You clicked the No button!";
UpdateData(FALSE);
}
```

The code under the third if statement is executed if you clicked the Cancel button:

```
if (iResults==IDCANCEL)
{
m_ResultsEdit = "You clicked the Cancel button!";
UpdateData(FALSE);
}
```

☐ Select Save All from the File menu to save your work.

☐ Build and execute the MyMsg program.

☐ Click the Yes, No, and Cancel buttons and make sure the MyMsg program is working properly. For example, when the message box is displayed, click the Yes button of the message box. The edit box of the MyMsg main window should contain text confirming that you clicked the Yes button.

☐ Experiment with the MyMsg program, then click its Exit button to terminate the program.

Attaching Code to the BN_CLICKED Event of the Retry and Cancel Button

You'll now attach code to the BN_CLICKED event of the IDC_RETRYCANCEL_BUTTON button:

☐ Select ClassWizard from the View menu.

☐ In the Message Maps tab of ClassWizard, select the following event:

Class name:	CMyMsgDlg
Object ID:	IDC_RETRYCANCEL_BUTTON
Message:	BN_CLICKED

☐ Click the Add Function button, name the new function `OnRetrycancelButton`, and click the Edit Code button.

Visual C++ responds by opening the file MyMsgDlg.cpp, with the function `OnRetrycancelButton()` *ready for you to edit.*

☐ Write the following code in the `OnRetrycancelButton()` function:

```
void CMyMsgDlg::OnRetrycancelButton()
{
// TODO: Add your control notification handler code here

//////////////////////////
// MY CODE STARTS HERE
//////////////////////////

int iResults;

iResults =
     MessageBox (

     "You want Retry and Cancel buttons.",
     "I am the second parameter of the MessageBox function",
      MB_RETRYCANCEL + MB_ICONQUESTION

                   );

if (iResults==IDRETRY)
{
m_ResultsEdit = "You clicked the Retry button!";
UpdateData(FALSE);
}


if (iResults==IDCANCEL)
{
m_ResultsEdit = "You clicked the Cancel button!";
UpdateData(FALSE);
}

//////////////////////////
// MY CODE ENDS HERE
//////////////////////////

}
```

The code you typed is similar to the code in the previous section. Note that now the parameters of the `MessageBox()` function are as follows:

```
iResults =
     MessageBox (

     "You want Retry and Cancel buttons.",
     "I am the second parameter of the MessageBox function",
      MB_RETRYCANCEL + MB_ICONQUESTION

                   );
```

6

The constant MB_ICONQUESTION, part of the third parameter of MessageBox(), causes the Question icon to appear in the message box. The MB_RETRYCANCEL constant, also part of the third parameter of MessageBox(), causes the MessageBox() function to display the Retry and Cancel buttons.

A series of two if statements is then executed. The code under the first if statement is executed if you clicked the Retry button:

```
if (iResults==IDRETRY)
{
m_ResultsEdit = "You clicked the Retry button!";
UpdateData(FALSE);
}
```

The code under the second if statement is executed if you clicked the Cancel button:

```
if (iResults==IDCANCEL)
{
m_ResultsEdit = "You clicked the Cancel button!";
UpdateData(FALSE);
}
```

☐ Select Save All from the File menu to save your work.

☐ Build and execute the MyMsg program.

☐ Click the Retry and Cancel button and make sure the MyMsg program works properly. For example, when the message box is displayed, click its Retry button. The edit box of the MyMsg main window should contain text confirming you clicked the Retry button.

☐ Experiment with the MyMsg program, then click its Exit button to terminate the program.

Attaching Code to the BN_CLICKED Event of the Yes and No Button

You'll now attach code to the BN_CLICKED event of the IDC_YESNO_BUTTON button:

☐ Select ClassWizard from the View menu.

☐ In the Message Maps tab of ClassWizard, select the following event:

Class name:	CMyMsgDlg
Object ID:	IDC_YESNO_BUTTON
Message:	BN_CLICKED

☐ Click the Add Function button, name the new function OnYesnoButton, and click the Edit Code button.

Visual C++ responds by opening the file MyMsgDlg.cpp, with the function OnYesnoButton() *ready for you to edit.*

☐ Write the following code in the OnYesnoButton() function:

```
void CMyMsgDlg::OnYesnoButton()
{
// TODO: Add your control notification handler code here

////////////////////////
// MY CODE STARTS HERE
////////////////////////

int iResults;

iResults =
    MessageBox (

  "You want Yes and No buttons.",
  "I am the second parameter of the MessageBox function",
  MB_YESNO + MB_ICONEXCLAMATION

            );

if (iResults==IDYES)
{
m_ResultsEdit = "You clicked the Yes button!";
UpdateData(FALSE);
}


if (iResults==IDNO)
{
m_ResultsEdit = "You clicked the No button!";
UpdateData(FALSE);
}


////////////////////////
// MY CODE ENDS HERE
////////////////////////

}
```

6

The code you typed is similar to the code in previous sections. The message box is displayed as follows:

```
iResults =
    MessageBox (

  "You want Yes and No buttons.",
  "I am the second parameter of the MessageBox function",
  MB_YESNO + MB_ICONEXCLAMATION

            );
```

The third parameter of MessageBox() indicates that the Exclamation icon (MB_ICONEXCLAMATION) will be displayed and the Yes and No button will be included in the message box (MB_YESNO).

A series of two if statements is executed. The code under the first if statement is executed if you clicked the Yes button of the message box:

```
if (iResults==IDYES)
{
m_ResultsEdit = "You clicked the Yes button!";
UpdateData(FALSE);
}
```

The code under the second if statement is executed if you clicked the No button of the message box:

```
if (iResults==IDNO)
{
m_ResultsEdit = "You clicked the No button!";
UpdateData(FALSE);
}
```

☐ Select Save All from the File menu to save your work.

☐ Build and execute the MyMsg program.

☐ Click the Yes and No button and check that the MyMsg program works properly. For example, when the message box is displayed, click its Yes button. The edit box of the MyMsg main window should display text confirming you clicked the Yes button.

☐ Experiment with the MyMsg program, then click its Exit button to terminate the program.

NOTE

> You can also add *modality constants* to the third parameter of the MessageBox(). If you do not specify a modality constant, the default is used, which is MB_APPLMODAL. This makes the message box a modal dialog box, meaning you can't switch to other windows in the same application unless you first close the message box.
>
> Another option is MB_SYSTEMMODAL, a constant that makes the message box a system modal, which means you can't switch to another window of any application unless the message box is closed.

The MyCus Program

The MyMsg program illustrated how to display predefined message boxes. An alternative method for displaying dialog boxes is to use custom-made dialog boxes, illustrated in the

MyCus program. Before starting to design the MyCus program, let's review its specifications:

■ When you start the MyCus program, the window shown in Figure 6.6 appears.

Figure 6.6.
The main window of
the MyCus program.

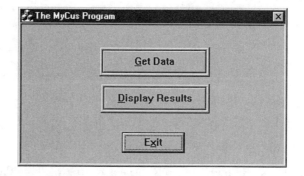

■ When you click the Get Data button, the MyCus program displays the custom-made dialog box shown in Figure 6.7. You can then enter data into the edit box.

Figure 6.7.
The Custom-Made
Dialog box.

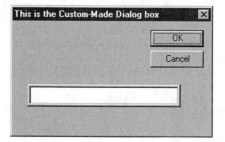

■ When you close the custom-made dialog box, the main window of the MyCus program appears again. You can then click the Display Results button to display the text you entered in the edit box of the custom-made dialog box.

For example, if you typed the text This is a test in the edit box of the custom-made dialog box, the message box displayed after clicking the Display Results button is shown in Figure 6.8.

Figure 6.8.
The message box
displayed after
clicking the Display
Results button.

Creating the Project of the MyCus Program

Create the project of the MyCus program as follows:

☐ Close the current open project workspace (if any) by selecting Close Workspace from the File menu of Visual C++.

☐ Select New from the File menu of Visual C++.

   Visual C++ responds by displaying the New dialog box.

☐ Select the Projects tab of the New dialog box.

☐ Select MFC AppWizard(exe) from the list of project types.

☐ Type MyCus in the Project Name box.

☐ Click the button that is located on the right of the Location box and select the C:\TYVCPROG\PROGRAMS\CH06 directory.

☐ Click the OK button.

   Visual C++ responds by displaying the MFC AppWizard - Step 1 window.

☐ In Step 1, select the Dialog based option to create a dialog-based application, then click the Next button.

☐ In Step 2, use the default settings and enter MyCus as the dialog box title. When you're done, click Next.

☐ In Step 3, use the default settings, then click Next.

☐ In the Step 4 window, notice that AppWizard created the CMyCusApp and CMyCusDlg classes for you. Click the Finish button, then click the OK button of the New Project Information window.

☐ Select Set Active Configuration from the Build menu, then select the MyCus - Win32 Release item.

That's it! Visual C++ has created the MyCus project and all its associated files.

The Visual Design of the MyCus Program

You'll now visually design the main window of the MyCus program:

☐ In the Project Workspace window, click the ResourceView tab and expand the MyCus resources item, then expand the Dialog item. Finally, double-click the IDD_MYCUS_DIALOG dialog box.

6

Visual C++ responds by displaying the IDD_MYCUS_DIALOG dialog box in design mode.

☐ Delete the OK button, Cancel button, and TODO text.

☐ Design the IDD_MYCUS_DIALOG dialog box according to Table 6.2. When you finish designing the dialog box, it should look like Figure 6.6.

Table 6.2. The properties table of the IDD_MYCUS_DIALOG dialog box.

Object	Property	Setting
Dialog Box	**ID**	**IDD_MYCUS_DIALOG**
	Caption	The MyCus Program
	Font	System, Size 10
	Client edge	Checked (Extended Styles tab)
	Static edge	Checked (Extended Styles tab)
Push Button	**ID**	**IDC_EXIT_BUTTON**
	Caption	E&xit
Push Button	**ID**	**IDC_GETDATA_BUTTON**
	Caption	&Get Data
	Client edge	Checked (Extended Styles tab)
	Static edge	Checked (Extended Styles tab)
	Modal frame	Checked (Extended Styles tab)
Push Button	**ID**	**IDC_DISPLAYRESULTS_BUTTON**
	Caption	Display &Results
	Client edge	Checked (Extended Styles tab)
	Static edge	Checked (Extended Styles tab)
	Modal frame	Checked (Extended Styles tab)

Attaching Code to the BN_CLICKED Event of the Exit Button

You'll now attach code to the BN_CLICKED event of the Exit button:

☐ Select ClassWizard from the View menu.

☐ In the Message Maps tab of ClassWizard, select the following event:

```
Class name:   CMyCusDlg
Object ID:    IDC_EXIT_BUTTON
Message:      BN_CLICKED
```

☐ Click the Add Function button, name the new function OnExitButton, then click the Edit Code button.

> *Visual C++ responds by opening the file MyCusDlg.cpp, with the function* OnExitButton() *ready for you to edit.*

☐ Write the following code in the OnExitButton() function:

```
void CMyCusDlg::OnExitButton()
{
// TODO: Add your control notification handler code here

//////////////////////////
// MY CODE STARTS HERE
//////////////////////////

OnOK();

//////////////////////////
// MY CODE ENDS HERE
//////////////////////////

}
```

The code you typed terminates the program.

The Visual Design of the Custom-Made Dialog Box

Currently, the MyCus program has two dialog boxes: the IDD_MYCUS_DIALOG dialog box, which serves as the main window of the MyCus program, and the IDD_ABOUTBOX dialog box, which is the About box of the MyCus program. To display the About dialog box, the user has to click the small icon at the upper-left corner of the window, then select About from the system menu that pops up.

You'll now add a third dialog box to the MyCus program that will be displayed when the user clicks the Get Data button:

☐ In the Project Workspace window, click the ResourceView tab and expand the MyCus resources item, then the Dialog item. Make sure there are two dialog boxes items under the Dialog item (IDD_ABOUTBOX and IDD_MYCUS_DIALOG).

☐ Right-click the Dialog item.

> *Visual C++ responds by displaying a pop-up menu.*

☐ Select Insert Dialog from the menu.

> *Visual C++ responds by inserting another dialog box to the MyCus project. The ID of the new dialog box is IDD_DIALOG1.*

Follow these steps to customize the IDD_DIALOG1 dialog box:

☐ Right-click anywhere inside the IDD_DIALOG1 dialog box, select Properties from the menu that pops up, and change the ID property from IDD_DIALOG1 to IDD_CUSTOM_DIALOG.

☐ Set the Caption property of the IDD_CUSTOM_DIALOG to This is the Custom-Made Dialog box.

NOTE

When you create programs in this book, you are typically instructed to create dialog-based programs, in which a dialog box serves as the main window of the program. For example, IDD_MYCUS_DIALOG is a dialog box that serves as the main window of the MyCus program. Furthermore, you're instructed to delete the TODO text, OK button, and Cancel button of the dialog box.

However, the IDD_CUSTOM_DIALOG dialog box is displayed after clicking a button in the IDD_MYCUS_DIALOG dialog box. The IDD_CUSTOM_DIALOG dialog box serves as a dialog box for getting user's input. Typically, such a dialog box needs the OK button and the Cancel button, so don't delete its OK and Cancel buttons.

Placing an Edit Box in the Custom-Made Dialog Box

You'll now place an edit box in the IDD_CUSTOM_DIALOG dialog box:

☐ Place an edit box control in the IDD_CUSTOM_DIALOG dialog box.

☐ Set the ID property of the edit box to IDC_MYDATA_EDIT.

☐ Set the following properties of the edit box (for cosmetic reasons):

Property	Setting
Client edge	Checked (Extended Styles tab)
Static edge	Checked (Extended Styles tab)
Modal frame	Checked (Extended Styles tab)

6

Associating the Custom-Made Dialog Box with a Class

Dialog boxes have to be associated with classes. For example, the IDD_MYCUS_DIALOG is associated with the CMyCusDlg class, which Visual C++ added when the program and skeleton files of the project were created. CMyCusDlg was created as a derived class from the CDialog class, which has many useful member functions. Therefore, CMyCusDlg will inherit these member functions.

Follow these steps to verify that CMyCusDlg is indeed a derived class of CDialog:

☐ Select the IDD_MYCUS_DIALOG item in the Project Workspace window.

☐ Double-click the IDD_MYCUS_DIALOG item to display the IDD_MYCUS_DIALOG dialog box in design mode.

☐ Right-click in a free area in the dialog box and select ClassWizard from the menu that pops up.

Visual C++ responds by displaying the MFC ClassWizard window.

☐ Click the Class Info tab.

Visual C++ responds by displaying the Class Info tab, shown in Figure 6.9.

Figure 6.9.

The Class Info tab.

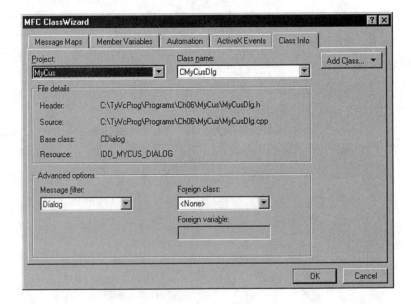

As you can see from Figure 6.9, the base class of CMyCusDlg is indeed CDialog.

You'll now create a class for the IDD_CUSTOM_DIALOG dialog box, using CDialog as the base class:

☐ Close the MFC ClassWizard window.

☐ Double-click the IDD_CUSTOM_DIALOG item under the Dialog item in the Project Workspace window.

Visual C++ responds by displaying the IDD_CUSTOM_DIALOG dialog box in design mode.

☐ Select ClassWizard from the View menu.

Instead of displaying the MFC ClassWizard window, Visual C++ responds by displaying the Adding a Class window, shown in Figure 6.10, because the IDD_CUSTOM_DIALOG dialog box doesn't have a class associated with it yet.

Figure 6.10.

The Adding a Class window.

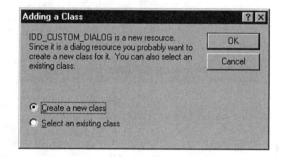

☐ Make sure the "Create a new class" button is selected, then click the OK button.

Visual C++ responds by displaying the New Class window, shown in Figure 6.11.

Figure 6.11.

The New Class window.

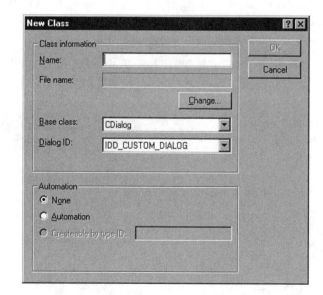

☐ Set the Name box under "Class information" to CCustDlg and make sure the Base class list box is set to CDialog. (See Figure 6.12.)

Figure 6.12.

Setting the class name of IDD_CUSTOM_DIALOG to CCustDlg.

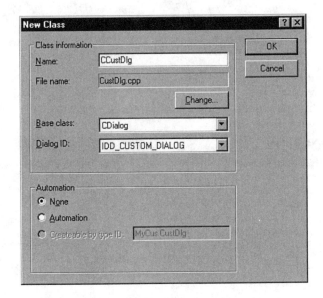

Whenever Visual C++ creates a class, it creates two files associated with the class. For example, when Visual C++ created the CMyCusDlg class for the IDD_MYCUS_DIALOG dialog box, it created the MyCusDlg.cpp and MyCusDlg.h files. So, if you named the class of IDD_CUSTOM_DIALOG CCustDlg, what are the names of the .cpp and .h files that Visual C++ will create? This is how you find out:

☐ Click the Change button of the Create New Class window.

Visual C++ responds by displaying the Change Files dialog box, shown in Figure 6.13.

Figure 6.13.

The Change Files dialog box.

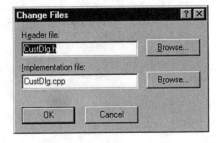

As shown in Figure 6.13, the two files associated with the CCustDlg class are CustDlg.h and CustDlg.cpp.

☐ Click the OK button of the Change Files dialog box.

☐ Click the Create button of the Create New Class window.

Visual C++ responds by opening the MFC ClassWizard window.

☐ Click the OK button to close the MFC ClassWizard window.

Attaching a Variable to the Edit Box of IDD_CUSTOM_DIALOG

During the visual design of the IDD_CUSTOM_DIALOG dialog box, you added the IDC_MYDATA_EDIT edit box. You'll now attach a member variable to this edit box:

☐ Select ClassWizard from the View menu.

☐ In the Member Variables tab of ClassWizard, set the Class name to CCustDlg and select the IDC_MYDATA_EDIT item.

The MFC ClassWizard window should now look like the one shown in Figure 6.14.

Figure 6.14.

Attaching a member variable to the IDC_MYDATA_EDIT edit box.

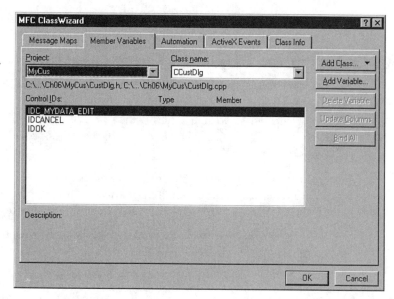

☐ Click the Add Variable button and select the following options in the Add Member Variable dialog box:

Variable name:	m_MyDataEdit
Category:	Value
Variable type:	CString

Your Add Member Variable dialog box should now look like Figure 6.15.

Figure 6.15.
Adding the
`m_MyDataEdit`
member variable.

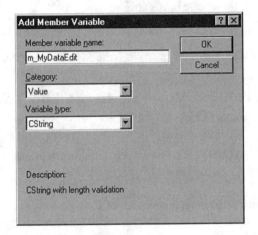

☐ Click the OK button of the Add Member Variable dialog box.

☐ Click the OK button of the MFC ClassWizard window.

Creating an Object of Class `CCustDlg`

You have visually designed the IDD_CUSTOM_DIALOG dialog box and associated it with the `CCustDlg` class. In this section and the next, you'll write code in the `CMyCusDlg` class (the MyCusDlg.cpp and MyCusDlg.h files)—the class associated with the main window of the program, the IDD_MYCUS_DIALOG dialog box. This code will be responsible for displaying the IDD_CUSTOM_DIALOG dialog box.

First create the `m_dlg` object, an object of class `CCustDlg`. What does it mean to create an object `m_dlg` of class `CCustDlg`? It means you'll create a dialog box whose visual appearance is the same as the IDD_CUSTOM_DIALOG dialog box. Follow these steps to create the `m_dlg` object:

☐ In the Project Workspace window, click the FileView tab, expand the MyCus Files item, then expand the Header Files item, and finally double-click the MyCusDlg.h item.

Visual C++ responds by opening the MyCusDlg.h file.

☐ Insert the following code in the `CMyCusDlg` class declaration (in the MyCusDlg.h file):

```
class CMyCusDlg : public CDialog
{
// Construction
public:
```

```
            CMyCusDlg(CWnd* pParent = NULL);

//////////////////////////
// MY CODE STARTS HERE
//////////////////////////

CCustDlg m_dlg;

//////////////////////////
// MY CODE ENDS HERE
//////////////////////////

...
...
...


};
```

The preceding code declares m_dlg as a data member of the CMyCusDlg class, because you want m_dlg to be visible from any member function of the CMyCusDlg class. For example, when you attach code to the BN_CLICKED event of the buttons in IDD_MYCUS_DIALOG, you'll be able to use m_dlg from within your code.

You declared m_dlg as an object of class CCustDlg. Although you know that CCustDlg is the class associated with the IDD_CUSTOM_DIALOG dialog box, the compiler doesn't. Therefore, when the compiler compiles the MyCusDlg.cpp file and encounters CCustDlg, you'll get a compiling error!

Remember that when you created the CCustDlg class, the CustDlg.h file was created. (Refer to Figure 6.13.) In fact, Visual C++ declared the CCustDlg class in the CustDlg.h file. To avoid compiling errors, all you have to do is use the #include statement as follows:

☐ Add the #include statement at the beginning of the MyCusDlg.h file:

```
// MyCusDlg.h : header file
//

//////////////////////////
// MY CODE STARTS HERE
//////////////////////////

#include "CustDlg.h"

//////////////////////////
// MY CODE ENDS HERE
//////////////////////////

...
...
...
```

6

Attaching Code to the BN_CLICKED Event of the Get Data Button

You'll now attach code to the BN_CLICKED event of the IDC_GETDATA_BUTTON button. When you click this button, the IDD_CUSTOM_DIALOG dialog box should appear.

☐ Select ClassWizard from the View menu.

☐ In the Message Maps tab of ClassWizard, select the following event:

Class name:	CMyCusDlg
Object ID:	IDC_GETDATA_BUTTON
Message:	BN_CLICKED

☐ Click the Add Function button, name the new function OnGetdataButton, and click the Edit Code button.

Visual C++ responds by opening the file MyCusDlg.cpp, with the function OnGetdataButton() *ready for you to edit.*

☐ Write the following code in the OnGetdataButton() function:

```
void CMyCusDlg::OnGetdataButton()
{
// TODO: Add your control notification handler code here

//////////////////////////
// MY CODE STARTS HERE
//////////////////////////


// Display the IDD_CUSTOM_DIALOG dialog box
m_dlg.DoModal();

//////////////////////////
// MY CODE ENDS HERE
//////////////////////////

}
```

The code you typed displays the m_dlg dialog box as a modal dialog box:

```
m_dlg.DoModal();
```

 NOTE

A *modal dialog box* must be closed before you can switch to another window in the same application. For example, you can click the Get Data button to display the custom-made dialog box. Once the custom-made dialog box is displayed, you cannot return to the main window of the application unless you close the custom-made dialog box.

Attaching Code to the BN_CLICKED Event of the Display Results Button

You'll now attach code to the IDC_DISPLAYRESULTS_BUTTON of the IDD_MYCUS_DIALOG dialog box:

☐ Select ClassWizard from the View menu.

☐ In the Message Maps tab of ClassWizard, select the following event:

Class name:	CMyCusDlg
Object ID:	IDC_DISPLAYRESULTS_BUTTON
Message:	BN_CLICKED

☐ Click the Add Function button, name the new function OnDisplayresultsButton, and click the Edit Code button.

> *Visual C++ responds by opening the file MyCusDlg.cpp, with the function* OnDisplayresultstButton() *ready for you to edit.*

☐ Write the following code in the OnDisplayresultsButton() function:

```
void CMyCusDlg::OnDisplayresultsButton()
{
// TODO: Add your control notification handler code here

//////////////////////////
// MY CODE STARTS HERE
//////////////////////////


// Display the data that the user entered
MessageBox(m_dlg.m_MyDataEdit);

//////////////////////////
// MY CODE ENDS HERE
//////////////////////////

}
```

The code you typed displays a message box:

```
MessageBox( m_dlg.m_MyDataEdit );
```

Note how the text of the edit box is provided as the parameter of the MessageBox() function—m_MyDataEdit is the member variable you attached to the IDC_MYDATA_EDIT edit box in IDD_CUSTOM_DIALOG. Therefore, the text of the edit box is denoted as follows:

```
m_dlg.m_MyDataEdit
```

6

☐ Build and execute the MyCus program.

☐ Click the Get Data button.

    MyCus responds by displaying the custom-made dialog box.

☐ Type something in the edit box, then click the OK button of the custom-made dialog box.

☐ Click the Display Results button.

    MyCus responds by displaying a message box showing the text you typed in the edit box of the custom-made dialog box.

☐ Experiment with the MyCus program, then click the Exit button to terminate it.

Summary

In this chapter, you have designed and created two programs:

- MyMsg, a program that uses predefined dialog boxes.
- MyCus, a program that uses a custom-made dialog box.

As you've seen, using predefined dialog boxes is easier, but you have limited control over their appearance and behavior. On the other hand, you can go to the trouble of designing your own custom-made dialog boxes, which means more work, but also more control over how the dialog boxes look and what they do.

Q&A

Q Should I use predefined dialog boxes or custom-made dialog boxes?

A It depends on the particular application you are developing. For example, suppose you are prompting the user with a message such as `insert diskette into disk drive a:`, then `click the OK button`. This is a simple instruction to the user, so a predefined dialog box is appropriate.

However, if your program needs to accept some data from the user (such as checking or unchecking a check box, setting a radio button, and so on), you'll have to use a custom-made dialog box that lets the user enter the data.

Q The MyCus program uses the following `MessageBox()` function to display a message box:

```
MessageBox( m_dlg.m_MyDataEdit );
```

I thought that the MessageBox() function had three parameters. What happened to the other two parameters?

A The MessageBox() function does have three parameters. If you supply only the first parameter, the message box will appear with no icon, and its caption will be the same as the program name. (Refer to Figure 6.8.) When you're developing applications, you should supply the second and third parameters of the MessageBox() function. However, during the study of Visual C++, you'll find that the MessageBox() function can frequently be used to display values for the purpose of debugging and understanding the material. In these cases, when the MessageBox() function is used for the sole purpose of displaying values, there's no need to supply the second and third parameters.

Quiz

1. You can close the custom-made dialog box by clicking its OK button or its Cancel button. What is the difference between these two methods of closing the custom-made dialog box in the MyCus program?

2. Why were you instructed not to delete the OK and Cancel buttons of the custom-made dialog box of the MyCus program?

Exercise

Enhance the MyCus program so that when the user clicks the Exit button, the program does not immediately terminate. Rather, the program displays a message box asking users if they really want to terminate the program.

Quiz Answers

1. You can answer this question by performing the following experiment:
   - ☐ Start the MyCus program.
   - ☐ Click the Get Data button.
   - ☐ Type Testing!!! in the edit box.
   - ☐ Click the OK button of the custom-made dialog box.
   - ☐ Now click the Get Data button again.

6

As you can see, the edit box contains the text Testing!!!. In other words, because you previously closed the custom-made dialog box by clicking its OK button, the value you typed in the edit box is maintained.

☐ Click the Get Data button again, and in the edit box of the custom-made dialog box, type NOT TESTING!!!.

☐ Click the Cancel button of the custom-made dialog box.

☐ Click the Get Data button.

As you can see, the edit box contains the text Testing!!! because you previously closed the custom-made dialog box by clicking its Cancel button. Therefore, the text you typed in the edit box is not maintained; the old value that existed in the edit box is maintained.

2. Data attached to controls in the IDD_CUSTOM_DIALOG dialog box will maintain its value if you click the OK button of the custom-made dialog box. If you click the Cancel button, the value of the controls in the IDD_CUSTOM_DIALOG dialog box remain as they were the last time the IDD_CUSTOM_DIALOG dialog box was closed with the OK button.

Exercise Answer

Add the following code in the OnExitButton() function (in the MyCusDlg.cpp file):

```
void CMyCusDlg::OnExitButton()
{
// TODO: Add your control notification handler code here

/////////////////////////
// MY CODE STARTS HERE
/////////////////////////

int iResult =
MessageBox ( "Exit?",
            "Are you sure you want to exit?",
            MB_YESNO+MB_ICONQUESTION);

if (iResult == IDYES)
    {
    OnOK();
    }

/////////////////////////
// MY CODE ENDS HERE
/////////////////////////

}
```

The code you typed displays a message box whenever the user clicks the Exit button. The message box includes a Yes button and a No button. If the user clicks the No button, the code under the `if` statement is not executed. If the user clicks the Yes button, the code under the `if` statement is executed. This code terminates the program.

6

Day **7**

Graphics and Drawings

In this chapter, you'll learn how to create programs that draw graphics and how to install and use a timer.

The Graph Program

The Graph program illustrates how to use graphics drawing in your Visual C++ programs. Before creating the Graph program yourself, let's review its specifications:

- When you execute the Graph program, the window shown in Figure 7.1 appears.

- The Graph program continuously draws a circle with a varying radius. The radius of the circle increases, reaches its maximum, and then decreases. When the radius of the circle reaches its minimum value, the whole process starts over again.

- When you click the Draw Graphics button, the dialog box shown in Figure 7.2 is displayed.

Figure 7.1.
The window of the Graph program.

Figure 7.2.
The Set Graph dialog box.

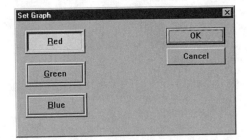

■ You can then select a color from the dialog box. For example, if you select the Blue button and then click the OK button, the circle will be drawn in blue.

■ While the Set Graph dialog box is displayed, the circle in the main window of the program should keep changing its radius. (See Figure 7.3.) However, the new color you select should be applied only after you click the OK button.

Figure 7.3.
While the Set Graph dialog box is displayed, the Graph program keeps animating the circle.

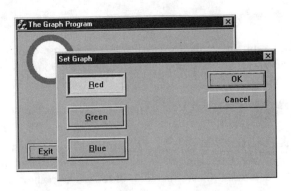

Now that you know what the Graph program should do, start by creating the program's project.

Creating the Project of the Graph Program

Follow these steps to create the project of the Graph program:

☐ Create the C:\TYVCPROG\PROGRAMS\CH07 directory.

☐ Start Visual C++ and select New from the File menu.

Visual C++ responds by displaying the New dialog box.

☐ Select the Projects tab of the New dialog box.

☐ Select MFC AppWizard(exe) from the list of project types.

☐ Type Graph in the Project Name box.

☐ Click the button that is located on the right of the Location box and select the C:\TYVCPROG\PROGRAMS\CH07 directory.

☐ Click the OK button.

Visual C++ responds by displaying the MFC AppWizard Step 1 window.

☐ In the Step 1 window, choose the option to create a dialog-based application, then click the Next button.

☐ In the Step 2 window, use the default settings and enter Graph as the title for the dialog box. When you're done, click the Next button.

☐ In the Step 3 window, use the default settings, then click the Next button.

☐ In the Step 4 window, notice that AppWizard has created the CGraphApp and CGraphDlg classes for you. Click the Finish button to display the New Project Information window, then click the OK button of the New Project Information window.

Visual C++ responds by creating the Graph project and all its skeleton files.

☐ Select Set Active Configuration from the Build menu and then select the Graph - Win32 Release option. Finally, click the OK button of the Set Active Project Configuration dialog box.

That's it—Visual C++ has created the project of the Graph program.

The Visual Design of the Graph Program

You'll now visually design the main window of the Graph program:

☐ In the Project Workspace, click the ResourceView tab, expand the Graph resources item, and expand the Dialog item. Finally, double-click the IDD_GRAPH_DIALOG item.

Visual C++ responds by displaying the IDD_GRAPH_DIALOG dialog box in design mode.

7

☐ Delete the OK button, Cancel button, and TODO text in the IDD_GRAPH_DIALOG dialog box.

☐ Set up the IDD_GRAPH_DIALOG dialog box according to Table 7.1. When you finish, it should look like the one in Figure 7.4.

Table 7.1. The properties table of the IDD_GRAPH_DIALOG dialog box.

Object	Property	Setting
Dialog Box	ID	**IDD_GRAPH_DIALOG**
	Caption	The Graph Program
	Font	System, Size 10
	Client edge	Checked (Extended Styles tab)
	Static edge	Checked (Extended Styles tab)
Push Button	ID	**IDC_EXIT_BUTTON**
	Caption	E&xit
Push Button	ID	**IDC_DRAWGRAPHICS_BUTTON**
	Caption	&Draw Graphics...
	Client edge	Checked (Extended Styles tab)
	Static edge	Checked (Extended Styles tab)
	Modal frame	Checked (Extended Styles tab)

Figure 7.4.

The IDD_GRAPH_DIALOG dialog box in design mode.

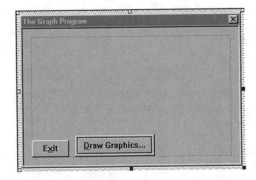

Attaching Code to the BN_CLICKED Event of the Exit Button

You'll now attach code to the BN_CLICKED event of the Exit button:

☐ Select ClassWizard from the View menu.

☐ In the Message Maps tab of ClassWizard, select the following event:

Class name:	CGraphDlg
Object ID:	IDC_EXIT_BUTTON
Message:	BN_CLICKED

☐ Click the Add Function button of ClassWizard, name the new function OnExitButton, then click the Edit Code button.

Visual C++ responds by opening the file GraphDlg.cpp with the function OnExitButton() *ready for you to edit.*

☐ Write the following code in the OnExitButton() function:

```
void CGraphDlg::OnExitButton()
{
// TODO: Add your control notification handler code here

/////////////////////////
// MY CODE STARTS HERE
/////////////////////////

OnOK();

/////////////////////////
// MY CODE ENDS HERE
/////////////////////////

}
```

The code you typed terminates the program when you click the Exit button.

Installing a Timer

The Graph program uses a *timer,* which is a software mechanism that generates the WM_TIMER event at regular time intervals. Your program's code will set the frequency at which the WM_TIMER event will occur. For example, if you set the interval of the timer to 500 milliseconds (0.5 seconds), the WM_TIMER event will occur every 500 milliseconds, as will the code you attach to the WM_TIMER event.

Here is how you install a timer:

☐ Select ClassWizard from the View menu.

☐ In the Message Maps tab of the ClassWizard window, select the following event:

Class name:	CGraphDlg
Object ID:	CGraphDlg
Message:	WM_INITDIALOG

7

☐ Click ClassWizard's Edit Code button.

Visual C++ responds by opening the file GraphDlg.cpp with the function `OnInitDialog()` *ready for you to edit.*

☐ Write the following code in the `OnInitDialog()` function:

```
BOOL CGraphDlg::OnInitDialog()
{

...
...
...

// TODO: Add extra initialization here

/////////////////////////
// MY CODE STARTS HERE
/////////////////////////

// Install a system timer.
int iInstallResult;

iInstallResult = SetTimer(1,
                         500,
                         NULL);

if (iInstallResult == 0 )
{

MessageBox ("cannot install timer!");

}

/////////////////////////
// MY CODE ENDS HERE
/////////////////////////

return TRUE;
// return TRUE  unless you set the focus to a control
}
```

The `OnInitDialog()` function is automatically executed when you start the program.

The code you typed first declares a variable:

```
int iInstallResult;
```

Then the `SetTimer()` function is executed:

```
iInstallResult = SetTimer(1,
                         500,
                         NULL);
```

The `SetTimer()` function has three parameters. The first parameter is the ID of the timer, which you declared as `Timer 1`. The second parameter indicates the interval at which the `WM_TIMER` event will occur; you specified every 500 milliseconds. The third parameter specifies the address of a function that will be executed every 500 milliseconds. Because you supplied `NULL` as the third parameter, this means you didn't specify a function; therefore, the `WM_TIMER` event will be executed every 500 milliseconds. (You'll attach code to the `WM_TIMER` event later in this chapter.)

An `if` statement is then executed to examine the returned value of `SetTimer()`:

```
if (iInstallResult == 0 )
{

MessageBox ("cannot install timer!");

}
```

If the returned value of `SetTimer()` is equal to `0`, it means that the timer was not installed.

NOTE

It's very important to use an `if` statement to examine the returned value of `SetTimer()`. Why? Because depending on the particular system you are using, you can install only a finite number of timers on your PC. Suppose that before executing the Graph program, the user already executed several other programs that use a timer, and the PC had exceeded the number of timers that can be installed. In that case, the Graph program's `SetTimer()` function will fail to install an additional timer.

In that situation, you should display a message box saying that the Graph program cannot be executed because other programs are using the timers. Your message box should suggest closing some of the programs that are running, then starting the Graph program again.

NOTE

Once a timer is installed, you can remove it by executing the `KillTimer()` function. For example, to write code that removes the timer at the exit point of the program, do the following:

☐ Select ClassWizard from the View menu.

☐ In the Message Maps tab of the ClassWizard window, select the following event:

7

Class name:	CGraphDlg
Object ID:	CGraphDlg
Message:	WM_DESTROY

☐ Add the OnDestroy() function, then edit it in the GraphDlg.cpp file as follows:

```
void CGraphDlg::OnDestroy()
{
    CDialog::OnDestroy();

// TODO: Add your message handler code here

/////////////////////////
// MY CODE STARTS HERE
/////////////////////////

KillTimer(1);

/////////////////////////
// MY CODE ENDS HERE
/////////////////////////

}
```

Note that the parameter of the KillTimer() function is the ID of the timer you installed.

The OnDestroy() function is executed when the IDD_GRAPH_DIALOG dialog box is about to be destroyed. For example, when the user clicks the Exit button, the program terminates, but the OnDestroy() function is executed before the program is terminated. Similarly, if the user clicks the × icon on the upper-right corner of the window, the program terminates, and again, OnDestroy() is executed prior to the program's termination.

Testing the Timer

Before proceeding with the Graph program, make sure the timer has been installed and is working as expected:

☐ Select ClassWizard from the View menu.

☐ In the Message Maps tab of the ClassWizard window, select the following event:

Class name:	CGraphDlg
Object ID:	CGraphDlg
Message:	WM_TIMER

☐ Click the Add Function button, then click the Edit Code button.

Visual C++ responds by opening the file GraphDlg.cpp with the function OnTimer() *ready for you to edit.*

☐ Write the following code in the OnTimer() function:

```
void CGraphDlg::OnTimer(UINT nIDEvent)
{
// TODO: Add your message handler code
// here and/or call default

/////////////////////////
// MY CODE STARTS HERE
/////////////////////////

MessageBeep((WORD)-1);


/////////////////////////
// MY CODE ENDS HERE
/////////////////////////


CDialog::OnTimer(nIDEvent);
}
```

The code you typed causes the PC to beep. And because you set the interval of the timer to 500 milliseconds, this code will be executed every 500 milliseconds.

☐ Build and execute the Graph program.

As you can hear, the PC beeps every 500 milliseconds.

☐ Terminate the Graph program by clicking its Exit button.

Before proceeding with the Graph program, remove the code that causes the PC to beep:

☐ Comment out the MessageBeep() statement in the OnTimer() function (in the GraphDlg.cpp file) as follows:

```
void CGraphDlg::OnTimer(UINT nIDEvent)
{
// TODO: Add your message handler code here
// and/or call default
```

7

```
/////////////////////////
// MY CODE STARTS HERE
/////////////////////////

//// MessageBeep((WORD)-1);


/////////////////////////
// MY CODE ENDS HERE
/////////////////////////

CDialog::OnTimer(nIDEvent);
}
```

Later in this chapter, you'll add additional code to the OnTimer() function.

☐ Build and execute the Graph program to make sure the PC does not beep every 500 milliseconds.

The WM_PAINT Event

What is the WM_PAINT event? Suppose you are covering the window of the Graph program with another window. Then you expose the Graph program's window by removing the other application's window, which means the area that was covered by the other application has to be "repainted." What does Windows do about this? Instead of repainting the area, Windows generates the WM_PAINT event. It is your job to repaint the window whenever the WM_PAINT event occurs. Windows also generates the WM_PAINT event whenever the window of the Graph program needs to be repainted. For example, suppose you drag Graph's window so that half the window is outside the screen, then drag it back into the screen again. In such a case, the window of the Graph program has to be repainted. Again, Windows will not repaint Graph's window, but Windows will generate the WM_PAINT event so that the code you attached to the WM_PAINT event will be executed.

You'll now type code that demonstrates the need for WM_PAINT:

☐ Select ClassWizard from the View menu.

☐ In the Message Maps tab of the ClassWizard window, select the following event:

Class name:	CGraphDlg
Object ID:	IDC_DRAWGRAPHICS_BUTTON
Message:	BN_CLICKED

☐ Click the Add Function button, name the new function OnDrawgraphicsButton, and click the Edit Code button.

Visual C++ responds by opening the file GraphDlg.cpp with the function OnDrawgraphicsButton() *ready for you to edit.*

☐ Write the following code in the `OnDrawgraphicsButton()`function:

```
void CGraphDlg::OnDrawgraphicsButton()
{
// TODO: Add your control notification handler code here

////////////////////////////
// MY CODE STARTS HERE
////////////////////////////

// Create a DC object
CClientDC dc(this);

// Create a new pen
CPen MyNewPen;

MyNewPen.CreatePen (PS_SOLID,
                    10,
                    RGB(255,0,0) );


// Select the new pen.
CPen*  pOriginalPen;
pOriginalPen = dc.SelectObject(&MyNewPen);


CRect MyRectangle (20,
                   10,
                   120,
                   110);

// Draw the circle
dc.Ellipse (&MyRectangle);

// Return the original pen
dc.SelectObject(pOriginalPen);

////////////////////////////
// MY CODE ENDS HERE
////////////////////////////

}
```

The code you typed is executed when you click the Draw Graphics button.

First, a device context is created:

```
// Create a DC object
CClientDC dc(this);
```

Next, a new pen is created that's solid red and 10 pixels wide:

```
// Create a new pen
CPen MyNewPen;

MyNewPen.CreatePen (PS_SOLID,
                    10,
                    RGB(255,0,0) );
```

7

The new pen is selected:

```
// Select the new pen.
CPen*  pOriginalPen;
pOriginalPen = dc.SelectObject(&MyNewPen);
```

Note that once the new pen is selected, it replaces the current pen. The returned value of `SelectObject()` is a pointer to the original pen.

Next, a rectangle object is created:

```
CRect MyRectangle (20,
                   10,
                   120,
                   110);
```

The rectangle is declared so that its upper-left corner is 20 pixels to the right of the window's left edge and 10 pixels below the window's upper edge. The rectangle's lower-right corner is 120 pixels to the right of the window's left edge and 110 pixels below the window's upper edge.

An ellipse is then drawn:

```
// Draw the circle
dc.Ellipse (&MyRectangle);
```

The parameter of the `Ellipse()` function is the rectangle you declared. Therefore, the ellipse is drawn so that the rectangle encloses the ellipse. Because the rectangle you declared is a square, the ellipse is a circle.

Finally, the original pen is selected:

```
// Return the original pen
dc.SelectObject(pOriginalPen);
```

The first question in the Q&A section at the end of this chapter discusses the parameter and returned value of the `SelectObject()` function.

☐ Build and execute the Graph program.

The window of the Graph program appears, as shown in Figure 7.5.

☐ Click the Draw Graphics button.

Graph responds by drawing a circle so it's enclosed by an imaginary rectangle with the coordinates specified by the `MyRectangle` object you created and supplied as the parameter of the `Ellipse()` function. (See Figure 7.6.)

Figure 7.5.

When you start the Graph program now, no circle is drawn.

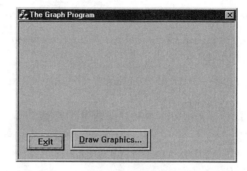

Figure 7.6.

After you click the Draw Graphics button, a circle is drawn.

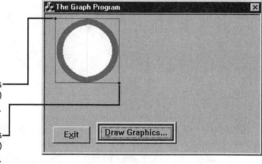

This point is 20 pixels from the left and 10 pixels from the top.

This point is 120 pixels from the left and 110 pixels from the top.

Follow these steps to demonstrate why you need the WM_PAINT event:

☐ Drag the Graph program's window to the left so that half the circle is outside the screen. (See Figure 7.7.)

Figure 7.7.

Dragging the Graph program's window to the left so that half the circle is outside the screen.

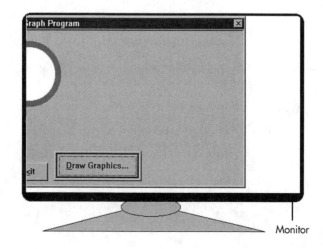

Monitor

7

☐ Drag the Graph program's window to the right so you can see the entire window again.

As shown in Figure 7.8, now only half the circle is shown. The half that was outside the screen has not been redrawn.

☐ Terminate the Graph program by clicking its Exit button.

Figure 7.8.

After returning the window to its original position, the section of the circle that was outside the screen is not redrawn.

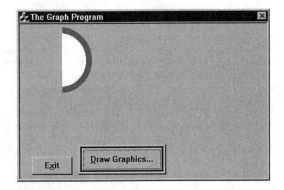

Naturally, your first impression is that something is wrong with Windows! But actually, there is nothing wrong with Windows. Windows did notice that the window of Graph needs to be repainted and generated the WM_PAINT message. Here's how you verify that happened:

☐ Select ClassWizard from the View menu.

☐ In the Message Maps tab of the ClassWizard window, select the following event:

Class name:	CGraphDlg
Object ID:	CGraphDlg
Message:	WM_PAINT

☐ Click ClassWizard's Edit Code button.

Visual C++ responds by opening the file GraphDlg.cpp with the function OnPaint() *ready for you to edit.*

☐ Write the following code in the OnPaint() function:

```
void CGraphDlg::OnPaint()
{
    if (IsIconic())
    {
        ...
        ...
        ...
    else
    {
```

```
/////////////////////////
// MY CODE STARTS HERE
/////////////////////////

MessageBeep((WORD)-1);

/////////////////////////
// MY CODE ENDS HERE
/////////////////////////
  ...
  ...
  ...
      }
  }
```

NOTE

Typically, Visual C++ inserts the following text so you'll know where to type your own code:

`// TODO: Add your control notification handler code here`

In the current version of Visual C++, the TODO text does not appear in the OnPaint() function, so make sure you type the preceding code as instructed under the else statement.

The code you typed makes the PC beep when Windows generates the WM_PAINT event.

☐ Build and execute the Graph program.

☐ Drag Graph's window to the left, as shown in Figure 7.7, and release the mouse button. Then drag the window back to its original location.

As you can hear, the PC beeps. Windows noticed that Graph's window needed to be repainted, and the WM_PAINT event occurred.

☐ Experiment with the Graph program, then click its Exit button to terminate the program.

Writing Repainting Code

Now that you're convinced the window needs to be redrawn in the OnPaint() function, add the repaint code:

☐ Modify the code of the OnPaint() function:

```
void CGraphDlg::OnPaint()
{
    if (IsIconic())
    {
        ...
```

7

```
          ...
          ...
          else
          {
//////////////////////////
// MY CODE STARTS HERE
//////////////////////////

/// MessageBeep((WORD)-1);

OnDrawgraphicsButton();

//////////////////////////
// MY CODE ENDS HERE
//////////////////////////
          ...
          ...
          ...
          }
}
```

The code you added comments out the `MessageBeep()` function:

```
/// MessageBeep((WORD)-1);
```

Then the `OnDrawgraphicsButton()` function is executed:

```
OnDrawgraphicsButton();
```

Whenever Graph's window needs to be repainted, Windows will generate the `WM_PAINT` event and the `OnPaint()` function will be executed. The code you typed in the `OnPaint()` function calls the `OnDrawgraphicsButton()` function. Recall that the `OnDrawgraphicsButton()` function is the function that you attached to the `BN_CLICKED` event of the Draw Graphics button (the function that draws a circle). Thus, whenever Graph's window needs to be repainted, the circle will be drawn.

☐ Build and execute the Graph program to make sure that the window is repainted when needed and that the full circle is drawn.

☐ Click the Exit button of the Graph program to terminate the program.

Modifying the `OnPaint()` Function

In the previous section, you did the redrawing in `OnPaint()` by executing the `OnDrawgraphicsButton()` function. However, later in this chapter, you'll add additional code in the `OnDrawgraphicsButton()` function that you won't want to be executed every time the `WM_PAINT` event occurs. So, modify the code in the `OnPaint()` function:

☐ Modify the code in the `OnPaint()` function (in the GraphDlg.cpp file) as follows:

```
void CGraphDlg::OnPaint()
{
    if (IsIconic())
    {
    ...
    ...
    ...
    else
    {
/////////////////////////
// MY CODE STARTS HERE
/////////////////////////

//// MessageBeep((WORD)-1);

//// OnDrawgraphicsButton();


// Create a DC object
CPaintDC dc(this);

// Create a new pen
CPen MyNewPen;

MyNewPen.CreatePen (PS_SOLID,
                    10,
                    RGB(255,0,0) );


// Select the new pen.
CPen*  pOriginalPen;
pOriginalPen = dc.SelectObject(&MyNewPen);


CRect MyRectangle (20,
                   10,
                   120,
                   110);


dc.Ellipse (&MyRectangle);

// Return the original pen
dc.SelectObject(pOriginalPen);

/////////////////////////
// MY CODE ENDS HERE
/////////////////////////
    ...
    ...
    ...
    }
}
```

7

The code you typed comments out the execution of `OnDrawgraphicsButton()`:

```
//// OnDrawgraphicsButton();
```

You then created a `dc` object as follows:

```
// Create a DC object
CPaintDC dc(this);
```

The rest of the code is identical to the code in the `OnDrawgraphicsButton()` function:

```
// Create a new pen
CPen MyNewPen;

MyNewPen.CreatePen (PS_SOLID,
                    10,
                    RGB(255,0,0) );


// Select the new pen.
CPen*  pOriginalPen;
pOriginalPen = dc.SelectObject(&MyNewPen);

CRect MyRectangle (20,
                   10,
                   120,
                   110);

dc.Ellipse (&MyRectangle);

// Return the original pen
dc.SelectObject(pOriginalPen);
```

☐ Build and execute the Graph program.

☐ Drag the window of the Graph program and verify that the code in the `OnPaint()` function repaints the window properly.

☐ Click the Exit button of the Graph program to terminate the program.

The Visual Design of the IDD_CUSTOM_DIALOG Dialog Box

You'll now design the IDD_CUSTOM_DIALOG dialog box, which will be displayed when you click the Draw Graphics button:

☐ In the Project Workspace, click the Resource View tab, expand the Graph resources item, then expand the Dialog item.

As you can see, the Graph program currently has two dialog boxes: IDD_GRAPH_DIALOG (the main window of the Graph program) and IDD_ABOUTBOX (the About dialog box).

☐ Right-click the Dialog item.

Visual C++ responds by displaying a menu.

☐ Select Insert Dialog from the menu.

Visual C++ responds by inserting a dialog box to the project with the default ID of IDD_DIALOG1.

☐ Set the ID property of the new dialog box to IDD_CUSTOM_DIALOG.

☐ Set the IDD_CUSTOM_DIALOG dialog box according to Table 7.2. When you finish designing the dialog box, it should look like the one shown in Figure 7.2.

Table 7.2. The properties table of the IDD_CUSTOM_DIALOG dialog box.

Object	Property	Setting
Dialog Box	**ID**	**IDD_CUSTOM_DIALOG**
	Caption	Set Graph
	Font	System, Size 10
Radio Button	**ID**	**IDC_RED_RADIO**
	Caption	&Red
	Group	Checked (General tab)
	Push-like	Checked (Styles tab)
	Client edge	Checked (Extended Styles tab)
	Static edge	Checked (Extended Styles tab)
	Modal frame	Checked (Extended Styles tab)
Radio Button	**ID**	**IDC_GREEN_RADIO**
	Caption	&Green
	Group	Not Checked (General tab)
	Push-like	Checked (Styles tab)
	Client edge	Checked (Extended Styles tab)
	Static edge	Checked (Extended Styles tab)
	Modal frame	Checked (Extended Styles tab)

7

continues

Table 7.2. continued

Object	Property	Setting
Radio Button	**ID**	**IDC_BLUE_RADIO**
	Caption	&Blue
	Group	Not Checked (General tab)
	Push-like	Checked (Styles tab)
	Client edge	Checked (Extended Styles tab)
	Static edge	Checked (Extended Styles tab)
	Modal frame	Checked (Extended Styles tab)

Keep the following points in mind while you're designing the IDD_CUSTOM_DIALOG dialog box:

- When designing the IDD_CUSTOM_DIALOG dialog box, do *not* delete the OK and Cancel buttons, as you usually do.

- Table 7.2 instructs you to place three radio buttons in the IDD_CUSTOM_DIALOG dialog box. Make sure you place them in sequential order: first the IDC_RED_RADIO radio button, then the IDC_GREEN_RADIO radio button, and finally the IDC_BLUE_RADIO radio button. When you finish placing the three radio buttons, select Resource Symbols from the View menu and make sure the ID numbers of the radio buttons are sequential numbers.

- As instructed by Table 7.2, don't forget to set the Group property of the IDC_RED_RADIO radio button to Checked.

- Checking the Push-like property of the radio buttons makes them look like pushbuttons. However, because the three radio buttons belong to the same group, only one radio button can be pushed down at any given time. Consequently, these three controls are still "regular" radio buttons, except that they look different from conventional radio buttons. This was done for cosmetic reasons and to demonstrate the Push-like property of the radio buttons in Visual C++.

☐ Select Save All from the File menu to save your work.

Attaching a Variable to the Radio Buttons

You'll now attach a variable to the radio buttons you placed in the IDD_CUSTOM_DIALOG dialog box.

☐ Right-click the IDD_CUSTOM_DIALOG dialog box to display a menu, then select the ClassWizard item.

Visual C++ responds by displaying the Adding a Class dialog box, because IDD_CUSTOM_DIALOG does not have a class of its own yet.

☐ Make sure the "Create a new class" radio button is selected, then click the OK button of the Adding a Class dialog box.

Visual C++ responds by displaying the New Class dialog box.

☐ Set the Name box to CSetDlg and the base class to CDialog.

☐ Click the Change button to display the Change Files dialog box. Notice that the name of the files associated with the new CSetDlg class you are creating are SetDlg.cpp and SetDlg.h.

☐ Close the Change Files dialog box, then click the OK button of the New Class dialog box.

Visual C++ responds by creating the CSetDlg class of the IDD_CUSTOM_DIALOG dialog box, and the MFC ClassWizard window appears.

☐ Make sure the Class name box of the MFC ClassWizard window is set to CSetDlg. Then click the Member Variables tab of the MFC ClassWizard window, select the IDC_RED_RADIO item, and click the Add Variable button.

Visual C++ responds by displaying the Add Member Variable dialog box.

☐ Set the options listed below:

Variable name:	m_RedRadio
Category:	Value
Variable type:	int

☐ Click the OK button of the Add Member Variable dialog box.

Visual C++ responds by adding a member variable to the radio buttons.

Therefore, when m_RedRadio is equal to 0, the Red radio button is selected; when it's equal to 1, the Green radio button is selected; and when it's equal to 2, the Blue radio button is selected.

Creating an Object of Class CSetDlg

In the previous sections, you created the class CSetDlg. This class is derived from CDialog, and the IDD_CUSTOM_DIALOG dialog box is associated with the CSetDlg class. The two files

7

associated with the CSetDlg class are SetDlg.cpp and SetDlg.h. You'll now create an object m_dlg of class CSetDlg:

☐ In the declaration of the CGraphDlg class (in the GraphDlg.h file), add code that creates an object called m_dlg of class CSetDlg as follows (*note:* to open the GraphDlg.h file, display the Project Workspace window, click the FileView tab, expand the Graph files item, expand the Header Files item, and finally, double-click the GraphDlg.h item):

```
class CGraphDlg : public CDialog
{
// Construction
public:
CGraphDlg(CWnd* pParent = NULL);

///////////////////////
// MY CODE STARTS HERE
///////////////////////

CSetDlg m_dlg;

///////////////////////
// MY CODE ENDS HERE
///////////////////////

...
...
...
};
```

The code you typed creates an object m_dlg of class CSetDlg. However, when the compiler compiles the GraphDlg.h file, it won't know the meaning of CSetDlg. You need to use the #include statement in the declaration of the CSetDlg class, which is in the file SetDlg.h.

☐ At the beginning of the GraphDlg.h file, add the #include statement as follows:

```
// GraphDlg.h : header file
//

///////////////////////
// MY CODE STARTS HERE
///////////////////////

#include "SetDlg.h"

///////////////////////
// MY CODE ENDS HERE
///////////////////////
...
...
...
```

Modifying the Code of the BN_CLICKED Event of the Draw Graphics Button

You'll now modify the code in the BN_CLICKED event of the Draw Graphics button:

☐ Select ClassWizard from the View menu.

☐ In the Message Maps tab of the ClassWizard window, select the following event:

Class name:	CGraphDlg
Object ID:	IDC_DRAWGRAPHICS_BUTTON
Message:	BN_CLICKED

☐ Click the Edit Code button of ClassWizard.

> *Visual C++ responds by opening the file GraphDlg.cpp with the function* OnDrawgraphicsButton() *ready for you to edit.*

☐ Modify the code in the OnDrawgraphicsButton() function as follows:

```
void CGraphDlg::OnDrawgraphicsButton()
{
// TODO: Add your control notification handler code here

/////////////////////////
// MY CODE STARTS HERE
/////////////////////////

m_dlg.DoModal();

/////////////////////////
// MY CODE ENDS HERE
/////////////////////////

}
```

After deleting the code you previously typed in this function, you typed the following statement, which displays the m_dlg object (the IDD_CUSTOM_DIALOG dialog box):

```
m_dlg.DoModal();
```

Although you haven't finished the Graph program, let's look at some of the code you typed in action:

☐ Select Save All from the File menu to save your work.

☐ Build and execute the Graph program.

☐ Click the Draw Graphics button.

> *Graph responds by displaying the IDD_CUSTOM_DIALOG dialog box. Note that, initially, none of the radio buttons is selected.*

7

☐ Experiment with the radio buttons of the IDD_CUSTOM_DIALOG dialog box. Notice that only one pushbutton-like radio button can be selected at any given time. When you're done, terminate the Graph program.

Initializing the Radio Buttons

As you saw in the previous section, when you start the Graph program, none of the radio buttons is selected. You'll now add code that makes the Red radio button the selected button:

☐ In the Message Maps tab of the ClassWizard window, select the following event:

Class name:	CGraphDlg
Object ID:	CGraphDlg
Message:	WM_INITDIALOG

☐ Click the Edit Code button of ClassWizard.

Visual C++ responds by opening the file GraphDlg.cpp file with the function OnInitDialog() *ready for you to edit.*

☐ Write the following code in the OnInitDialog() function:

```
BOOL CGraphDlg::OnInitDialog()
{
...
...
...

// TODO: Add extra initialization here

/////////////////////////
// MY CODE STARTS HERE
/////////////////////////

// Install a system timer.
int iInstallResult;

iInstallResult = SetTimer(1,
                          500,
                          NULL);

if (iInstallResult == 0 )
{

MessageBox ("cannot install timer!");

}

// Select the Red radio button
m_dlg.m_RedRadio = 0;
```

```
/////////////////////////
// MY CODE ENDS HERE
/////////////////////////

return TRUE;
// return TRUE  unless you set the focus to a control
}
```

The code you added makes the Red radio button the selected button:

```
// Select the Red radio button
m_dlg.m_RedRadio = 0;
```

☐ Select Save All from the File menu.

☐ Build and execute the Graph program.

☐ Click the Draw Graphics button.

> *Graph responds by displaying the IDD_CUSTOM_DIALOG dialog box with the Red radio button selected.*

☐ Experiment with the Graph program, then click the Exit button to terminate it.

Adding Member Variables to the `CGraphDlg` Class

You'll now add two member variables to the `CGraphDlg` class so they will be visible from any of the class's member functions:

☐ In the declaration of the `CGraphDlg` class, add the declarations of the `m_Radius` and `m_Direction` member variables as follows:

```
class CGraphDlg : public CDialog
{
// Construction
public:
CGraphDlg(CWnd* pParent = NULL);
// standard constructor

/////////////////////////
// MY CODE STARTS HERE
/////////////////////////

CSetDlg m_dlg;

int m_Radius;
int m_Direction;

/////////////////////////
// MY CODE ENDS HERE
/////////////////////////
```

7

```
...
...
...

};
```

The code you typed declares two member variables as follows:

```
int m_Radius;
int m_Direction;
```

Initializing the Values of m_Radius and m_Direction

You'll now write code that initializes the values of m_Radius and m_Direction:

☐ Select ClassWizard from the View menu.

☐ In the Message Maps tab of the ClassWizard window, select the following event:

Class name:	CGraphDlg
Object ID:	CGraphDlg
Message:	WM_INITDIALOG

☐ Click the Edit Code button of ClassWizard.

Visual C++ responds by opening the file GraphDlg.cpp file with the function OnInitDialog() *ready for you to edit.*

☐ Write the following code in the OnInitDialog() function:

```
BOOL CGraphDlg::OnInitDialog()
{
...
...
...

// TODO: Add extra initialization here

/////////////////////////
// MY CODE STARTS HERE
/////////////////////////

// Install a system timer.
int iInstallResult;

iInstallResult = SetTimer(1,
                         500,
                         NULL);

if (iInstallResult == 0 )
{
```

7

```
    MessageBox ("cannot install timer!");

    }

    // Select the Red radio button
    m_dlg.m_RedRadio = 0;

    m_Radius = 50;
    m_Direction = 1;

    /////////////////////////
    // MY CODE ENDS HERE
    /////////////////////////

    return TRUE;
    // return TRUE  unless you set the focus to a control
    }
```

The code you added initializes the m_Radius and m_Direction variables as follows:

```
m_Radius = 50;
m_Direction = 1;
```

Attaching Code to the Timer Event

At the beginning of this chapter, you installed a timer and verified that the OnTimer() function was executed every 500 milliseconds. You'll now add code to the OnTimer() function:

☐ Add the following code to the OnTimer() function in the GraphDlg.cpp file:

```
    void CGraphDlg::OnTimer(UINT nIDEvent)
    {
    // TODO: Add your message handler code here
    // and/or call default

    /////////////////////////
    // MY CODE STARTS HERE
    /////////////////////////

    //// MessageBeep((WORD)-1);

    m_Radius = m_Radius + m_Direction;

    if (m_Radius >= 100 )
    {
    m_Direction = -1;
    }


    if (m_Radius <=10)
    {
    m_Direction = 1;
    }
```

7

```
// Cause the execution of the OnPaint() function
Invalidate();

////////////////////////
// MY CODE ENDS HERE
////////////////////////

    ...
    ...
    ...
    }
```

The m_Direction variable can be 1 or -1. m_Radius is then increased or decreased by 1:

m_Radius = m_Radius + m_Direction;

A series of two if statements are then executed to determine the value of m_Radius. If m_Radius exceeds 100, the value of m_Direction is set to -1:

```
if (m_Radius >= 100 )
{
m_Direction = -1;
}
```

If m_Radius is less than or equal to 10, the value of m_Direction is set to 1:

```
if (m_Radius <=10)
{
m_Direction = 1;
}
```

Because the OnTimer() function is executed every 500 milliseconds, the values of m_Radius and m_Direction are as follows:

m_Direction	m_Radius
1	50
1	51
1	52
...	...
...	...
...	...
1	100
-1	99
-1	98
-1	97
...	...
...	...
...	...
-1	11

7

m_Direction	m_Radius
-1	10
1	11
1	12
...	...
...	...
...	...

The last statement you typed in the OnTimer() function executes the Invalidate() function:

```
// Cause the execution of the OnPaint() function
Invalidate();
```

The Invalidate() function causes WM_PAINT to occur. Thus, every 500 milliseconds, the WM_PAINT event occurs, which causes the OnPaint() function to be executed.

NOTE

The WM_PAINT event occurs automatically whenever Windows discovers the window needs to be repainted. You can force the generation of the WM_PAINT event by executing the Invalidate() function as follows:

```
// Cause the execution of the OnPaint() function
Invalidate();
```

Modifying the Code Attached to the WM_PAINT Event

You attached code to the WM_PAINT event of the IDD_GRAPH_DIALOG dialog box earlier in this chapter; follow these steps to modify it:

☐ Select ClassWizard from the View menu.

☐ In the Message Maps tab of the ClassWizard window, select the following event:

Class name: CGraphDlg
Object ID: CGraphDlg
Message: WM_PAINT

☐ Click the Edit Code button of ClassWizard.

Visual C++ responds by opening the file GraphDlg.cpp with the function OnPaint() (in the GraphDlg.cpp file) ready for you to edit.

7

☐ Modify the code in the OnPaint() function as follows:

```
void CGraphDlg::OnPaint()
{
    if (IsIconic())
        {
          ...
          ...
          ...
        }
    else
        {

///////////////////////////
// MY CODE STARTS HERE
///////////////////////////


//// MessageBeep((WORD)-1);

//// OnDrawgraphicsButton();


// Create a DC object
CPaintDC dc(this);

// Create a new pen
CPen MyNewPen;

MyNewPen.CreatePen (PS_SOLID,
                    10,
                    RGB(255,0,0) );


// Select the new pen.
CPen*  pOriginalPen;
pOriginalPen = dc.SelectObject(&MyNewPen);


// CRect MyRectangle (20,
//                    10,
//                    120,
//                    110);


CRect MyRectangle (20,
                   10,
                   20+m_Radius*2,
                   10+m_Radius*2);


dc.Ellipse (&MyRectangle);

// Return the original pen
dc.SelectObject(pOriginalPen);
```

7

```
/////////////////////////
// MY CODE ENDS HERE
/////////////////////////
   ...
   ...
   ...
        }
   ...
   ...
   ...
   }
```

The code you typed comments out the statement that defines the rectangle:

```
// CRect MyRectangle (20,
//                    10,
//                    120,
//                    110);
```

New coordinates are defined for the rectangle that will enclose the circle:

```
CRect MyRectangle (20,
                   10,
                   20+m_Radius*2,
                   10+m_Radius*2);
```

The lower-right corner of the rectangle is at `20 + m_Radius * 2` pixels to the right of the window's left edge and `10 + m_Radius * 2` pixels below the top of the window.

Recall that the `OnTimer()` function changes the value of `m_Radius`. For example, when `m_Radius` is equal to `50`, the lower-right corner of the rectangle is 20+50*2=120 pixels to the right of the window's left edge and 10+50*2=110 pixels below the window's top edge. Then `OnTimer()` changes the value of `m_Radius` to 51, which makes the lower-right corner of the rectangle enclosing the circle 20+51*2=122 pixels to the right of the window's left edge and 10+51*2=112 pixels below the window's top edge. In other words, the circle will be drawn with a different radius every time the `OnTimer()` function is executed.

Modifying the Installation Setting of the Timer

You'll now change the timer's setting. When you installed the timer, you set the second parameter of the `SetTimer()` function to `500`, which means that the `OnTimer()` function is executed every 500 milliseconds. To see "fast action" in the Graph program, set the second parameter of `SetTimer()` to `50` to execute the `OnTimer()` function every 50 milliseconds:

☐ Select ClassWizard from the View menu.

☐ In the Message Maps tab of the ClassWizard window, select the following event:

Class name:	CGraphDlg
Object ID:	CGraphDlg
Message:	WM_INITDIALOG

7

☐ Click the Edit Code button of ClassWizard.

Visual C++ responds by opening the file GraphDlg.cpp with the function `OnInitDialog()` *ready for you to edit.*

☐ Modify the code in the `OnInitDialog()` function as follows:

```
BOOL CGraphDlg::OnInitDialog()
{
...
...
// TODO: Add extra initialization here

////////////////////////
// MY CODE STARTS HERE
////////////////////////

// Install a system timer.
int iInstallResult;

iInstallResult = SetTimer(1,
                          50,
                          NULL);

if (iInstallResult == 0 )
{

MessageBox ("cannot install timer!");

}


// Select the Red radio button
m_dlg.m_RedRadio = 0;


m_Radius = 50;
m_Direction = 1;

////////////////////////
// MY CODE ENDS HERE
////////////////////////

return TRUE;
// return TRUE  unless you set the focus to a control
}
```

As you can see, now the second parameter of `SetTimer()` is `50`:

```
iInstallResult = SetTimer(1,
                          50,
                          NULL);
```

☐ Select Save All from the File menu.

☐ Build and execute the Graph program.

Notice that the radius of the circle changes every 50 milliseconds.

Drawing Circles with Different Colors

The Graph program currently draws the circles with a red pen, but the IDD_CUSTOM_DIALOG dialog box was designed so that you can select different colors for the pen that draws the circles. Once you select a radio button, the m_RedRadio variable changes accordingly (m_RedRadio=0 for red, m_RedRadio=1 for green, and m_RedRadio=2 for blue). To change colors according to the value of m_RedRadio, you have to modify the code in the OnPaint() function (in the GraphDlg.cpp file).

Exercise 1 at the end of this chapter instructs you to modify the OnPaint() program so that the circles will be drawn according to the selected color.

Summary

This chapter has shown how drawing programs are created. You have learned about the WM_PAINT event and how to attach drawing code to the OnPaint() function. Various drawing functions have been used in this chapter—(Ellipse(), CreatePen(), SelectObject(), and so on. You have also learned how to install a timer and attach code to the WM_TIMER event, which is executed periodically.

Q&A

Q **I'm confused! I created the new pen as follows:**

```
CClientDC dc(this);
CPen MyNewPen;
MyNewPen.CreatePen (PS_SOLID,
                    10,
                    RGB(255,0,0) );
```

Then I selected it with these statements:

```
CPen*  pOriginalPen;
pOriginalPen = dc.SelectObject(&MyNewPen);
```

But when I selected the original pen, I used SelectObject() as follows:

```
dc.SelectObject(pOriginalPen);
```

Why not use &OriginalPen?

A When you created the new pen, you used the following statement, which created an object of class CPen:

```
CPen MyNewPen;
```

You then selected the new pen as follows:

```
pOriginalPen = dc.SelectObject(&MyNewPen);
```

7

The parameter of SelectObject() is &MyNewPen because SelectObject() expects the address of the new pen as its parameter. The returned value of SelectObject() is the address of the original pen. This is why you declare pOriginalPen as a pointer to CPen:

```
CPen*  pOriginalPen;
```

When you execute SelectObject() as follows, the returned value of SelectObject() (which is a pointer to CPen) matches pOriginalPen:

```
pOriginalPen = dc.SelectObject(&MyNewPen);
```

Finally, when you return the original pen as follows, you supply pOriginalPen as the parameter of SelectObject() because SelectObject() expects the address of the pen as its parameter:

```
dc.SelectObject(pOriginalPen);
```

Q I drew the ellipse with the following statements, but the result is a circle, not an ellipse. Why?

```
// Draw the circle
dc.Ellipse (&MyRectangle);
```

A Before executing the Ellipse() function, you declared MyRectangle as follows:

```
CRect MyRectangle (20,
                   10,
                   120,
                   110);
```

The rectangle is a square with each side being 100 pixels long, so the ellipse enclosed by this rectangle must be a circle. A circle is a special case of an ellipse.

Q Before adding the code in the OnPaint() function, the Graph program did not repaint the window when needed, as shown in Figure 7.8. But guess what? I dragged the Graph window just a little bit on the screen (without hiding any part of the circle), and Windows repainted it. So it looks to me as though Windows does repaint the window sometimes.

A Good observation. When Windows can take care of the required repainting, it does it automatically for you.

Quiz

1. When does the WM_DESTROY event of a dialog box occur?

2. What do the following statements do?

```
CPen MyNewPen;
MyNewPen.CreatePen (PS_SOLID,
                    10,
                    RGB(255,0,0) );
```

Exercises

1. Modify the OnPaint() function (in the GraphDlg.cpp file) so that the circles of the Graph program will be drawn in the selected color specified by the IDD_CUSTOM_DIALOG dialog box.

2. After finishing Exercise 1, when executing the Graph program, you will have to perform the following steps to change the circle's color:

   ☐ Click the Draw Graphics button.

   ☐ Select a color from the IDD_CUSTOM_DIALOG dialog box.

   ☐ Click the OK button of the IDD_CUSTOM_DIALOG dialog box to draw the circle in the selected color.

   Add code to the Graph program so that the program immediately draws the circle with the selected color (without the user having to click the OK button). That is, once the user selects a color in the IDD_CUSTOM_DIALOG dialog box, the program should immediately draw the circle with the selected color.

Quiz Answers

1. The WM_DESTROY event of a dialog box occurs when the dialog box is about to be destroyed.

2. These statements create a red pen whose width is 10 pixels.

Exercise Answers

1. Follow these steps to modify the Graph program so that the circles will be drawn in the selected color as specified by the IDD_CUSTOM_DIALOG dialog box:

   ☐ Modify the OnPaint() function (in the GraphDlg.cpp file) as follows:

```
void CGraphDlg::OnPaint()
{
    if (IsIconic())
     {
       ...
       ...
       ...
     else
     {

/////////////////////////
// MY CODE STARTS HERE
/////////////////////////
```

7

```
//// MessageBeep((WORD)-1);

//// OnDrawgraphicsButton();


// Create a DC object
CPaintDC dc(this);

// Create a new pen
CPen MyNewPen;

//MyNewPen.CreatePen (PS_SOLID,
//                    10,
//                    RGB(255,0,0) );

switch (m_dlg.m_RedRadio)
{
case 0:
MyNewPen.CreatePen (PS_SOLID,
                    10,
                    RGB(255,0,0) );
break;

case 1:
MyNewPen.CreatePen (PS_SOLID,
                    10,
                    RGB(0,255,0) );
break;

case 2:
MyNewPen.CreatePen (PS_SOLID,
                    10,
                    RGB(0,0,255) );
break;
}


// Select the new pen.
CPen*  pOriginalPen;
pOriginalPen = dc.SelectObject(&MyNewPen);


// CRect MyRectangle (20,
//                    10,
//                    120,
//                    110);


CRect MyRectangle (20,
                   10,
                   20+m_Radius*2,
                   10+m_Radius*2);
```

```
dc.Ellipse (&MyRectangle);

// Return the original pen
dc.SelectObject(pOriginalPen);


///////////////////////////
// MY CODE ENDS HERE
///////////////////////////
...
...
...
}
```

A `switch` is created that examines the value of `m_RedRadio`; accordingly, the pen is created with the proper color:

```
switch (m_dlg.m_RedRadio)
{
case 0:
MyNewPen.CreatePen (PS_SOLID,
                    10,
                    RGB(255,0,0) );
break;

case 1:
MyNewPen.CreatePen (PS_SOLID,
                    10,
                    RGB(0,255,0) );
break;

case 2:
MyNewPen.CreatePen (PS_SOLID,
                    10,
                    RGB(0,0,255) );
break;
}
```

Note that the `m_RedRadio` variable is referred to in the `OnPaint()` function as follows:

```
switch (m_dlg.m_RedRadio)
{

}
```

The `m_dlg` object is a data member of the `CGraphDlg` class, so it's accessible from within the member functions of the `CGraphDlg` class. `m_RedRadio` is a member variable of `m_dlg`, so from within the `OnPaint()` function, you refer to this variable as `m_dlg.m_RedRadio`.

☐ Build and execute the Graph program.

☐ Click the Draw Graphics button, select a color from the IDD_CUSTOM_DIALOG dialog box, click the OK button of the IDD_CUSTOM_DIALOG dialog box, and notice that the circle is drawn in the selected color.

7

2. To modify the Graph program again so that the circle is drawn in the selected color without clicking IDD_CUSTOM_DIALOG's OK button, follow these steps:

☐ Select ClassWizard from the View menu.

☐ In the Message Maps tab of ClassWizard, select the following event:

Class name: CSetDlg
Object ID: IDC_RED_RADIO
Message: BN_CLICKED

☐ Click the Add Function button of ClassWizard, name the new function OnRedRadio, then click the Edit Code button.

Visual C++ responds by opening the file SetDlg.cpp with the function OnRedRadio() *ready for you to edit.*

☐ Write the following code in the OnRedRadio() function:

```
void CSetDlg::OnRedRadio()
{
// TODO: Add your control notification handler code here

////////////////////////
// MY CODE STARTS HERE
////////////////////////

UpdateData(TRUE);

////////////////////////
// MY CODE ENDS HERE
////////////////////////

}
```

As soon as you select the Red radio button, the m_RedRadio variable is updated, and the circle is drawn with a red pen.

Now you need to attach code to the BN_CLICKED event of the other radio buttons in a similar manner. Here is the code for the other radio buttons:

```
void CSetDlg::OnBlueRadio()
{
// TODO: Add your control notification handler code here

////////////////////////
// MY CODE STARTS HERE
////////////////////////

UpdateData(TRUE);

////////////////////////
// MY CODE ENDS HERE
////////////////////////

}
```

```
void CSetDlg::OnGreenRadio()
{
// TODO: Add your control notification handler code here

///////////////////////
// MY CODE STARTS HERE
///////////////////////

UpdateData(TRUE);

///////////////////////
// MY CODE ENDS HERE
///////////////////////

}
```

Once you click any radio button, the circle will be drawn in the selected color, without needing to click the OK button first.

7

Week

2

At a Glance

On the first day of Week 2, you'll learn how to display bitmaps from within your Visual C++ programs.

On the second day, you'll learn how to create programs that use different fonts and font sizes.

On the third day, you'll learn how to load BMP files during runtime and display the loaded BMP files. While you're creating today's program, you'll also learn how to display the common Open dialog box, a standard dialog box used for selecting a file from the hard drive.

On the fourth day, you'll learn what a single-document interface (SDI) application is and how to create one with Visual C++.

On the fifth day, you'll learn how to write a Visual C++ program that performs background tasks.

On the sixth day, you'll learn what a multiple-document interface (MDI) application is and how to create one with Visual C++.

On the seventh day, you'll learn how to write code that writes and reads data to and from files by using serialization.

Day **8**

Displaying Bitmaps

In this chapter, you'll learn how to display bitmaps from within your Visual C++ programs.

The MyBMP Program

The MyBMP program demonstrates how you can display bitmap files from within your Visual C++ programs. Before creating the MyBMP program, let's review its specifications:

- When you start the MyBMP program, the window shown in Figure 8.1 appears. As you can see, a BMP picture is displayed in the window.

- You can now resize the window of the MyBMP program, and the BMP picture displayed in the window is resized accordingly. Figure 8.2 shows the window of the MyBMP program at a smaller size.

Figure 8.1.

The window of the MyBMP program.

Figure 8.2.

The BMP picture is resized as you shrink the MyBMP window.

Now that you know what the MyBMP program is supposed to do, you can start creating the project.

Creating the Project of the MyBMP Program

To create the project of the MyBMP program, follow these steps:

☐ Create the C:\TYVCPROG\PROGRAMS\CH08 directory.

☐ Start Visual C++ and select New from the File menu.

Visual C++ responds by displaying the New dialog box.

☐ Select the Projects tab of the New dialog box.

☐ Select MFC AppWizard(exe) from the list of project types.

☐ Type MyBmp in the Project Name box.

☐ Click the button that is located on the right of the Location box and select the C:\TYVCPROG\PROGRAMS\CH08 directory.

☐ Click the OK button.

> *Visual C++ responds by displaying the MFC AppWizard Step 1 window.*

☐ Set the Step 1 window to create a dialog-based application, then click the Next button.

> *Visual C++ responds by displaying the MFC AppWizard - Step 2 of 4 window.*

☐ In the Step 2 window, use the default settings and enter the title MyBMP, then click the Next button.

> *Visual C++ responds by displaying the MFC AppWizard - Step 3 of 4 window.*

☐ In the Step 3 window, use the default settings and click the Next button.

> *Visual C++ responds by displaying the MFC AppWizard Step 4 of 4 window.*

☐ In the Step 4 window, use the default settings, then click the Finish button.

> *Visual C++ responds by displaying the New Project Information window.*

☐ Click the OK button of the New Project Information window.

> *Visual C++ responds by creating the project of the MyBMP program and all its associated files.*

☐ Select Set Active Configuration from the Build menu, select MyBmp - Win32 Release from the Project Default Configuration dialog box, then click the OK button.

That's it—you're ready to start designing the program.

The Visual Design of MyBMP's Main Window

You'll now visually design the main window of the MyBMP program:

☐ In the Project Workspace, click the ResourceView tab and expand the MyBMP resources item, then expand the Dialog item. Finally, double-click the IDD_MYBMP_DIALOG item.

☐ Delete the OK button, Cancel button, and TODO text in the IDD_MYBMP_DIALOG dialog box.

☐ Design the IDD_MYBMP_DIALOG dialog box according to Table 8.1.

Table 8.1. The properties table of the IDD_MYBMP_DIALOG dialog box.

Object	Property	Setting
Dialog Box	**ID**	**IDD_MYBMP_DIALOG**
	Caption	The MyBMP Program
	Font	System, Size 10
	Border	Resizing (Styles tab)

Note

In Table 8.1, you set the Border property of the dialog box to Resizing in the Styles tab, which enables you to enlarge or shrink the area of the MyBMP window by dragging its edges during runtime.

The Visual Design of the Menu

You'll now visually design the menu of the MyBMP program:

☐ In the Project Workspace, select the ResourceView tab and right-click the MyBMP resources item.

Visual C++ responds by displaying a pop-up menu.

☐ Select Insert from the menu, then select Menu from the Insert Resource dialog box that opens. Next, click the New button.

Visual C++ responds by displaying an empty menu in design mode.

☐ Customize the menu so that the File menu has an Exit item and the Help menu has an About item. (See Figures 8.3 and 8.4.)

Figure 8.3.

The File menu of the MyBMP program.

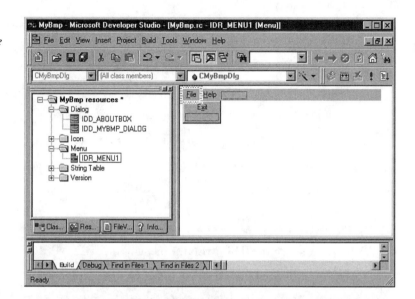

Figure 8.4.

The Help menu of the MyBMP program.

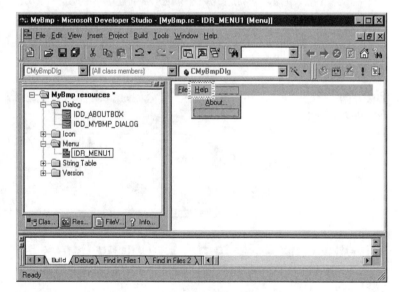

Notice that Visual C++ assigns IDR_MENU1 as the default ID for the new menu. Next, associate the IDR_MENU1 menu with the CMyBMPDlg class. Here is how you do that:

☐ While the menu window of IDR_MENU1 is selected, select ClassWizard from the View menu.

Visual C++ responds by displaying the Adding a Class dialog box.

☐ Make sure the "Select an existing class" radio button is selected, then click the OK button.

Visual C++ responds by displaying the Select Class dialog box.

☐ Select the CMyBmpDlg item, then click the Select button.

Visual C++ responds by displaying the MFC ClassWizard dialog box.

☐ Click the OK button of the MFC ClassWizard dialog box.

Attaching the Menu to the Dialog Box

You'll now attach the IDR_MENU1 menu to the IDD_MYBMP_DIALOG dialog box:

☐ Double-click the IDD_MYBMP_DIALOG item in the Project Workspace window.

Visual C++ responds by displaying the IDD_MYBMP_DIALOG dialog box in design mode.

☐ Set the Menu property (in the General tab) of IDD_MYBMP_DIALOG to IDR_MENU1. (See Figure 8.5.)

Figure 8.5.

Setting the Menu property to IDR_MENU1.

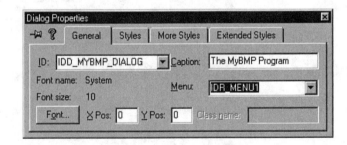

Attaching Code to the Exit Menu Item

You'll now attach code to the COMMAND event of the Exit menu item:

☐ Highlight the IDR_MENU1 item in the Project Workspace window, then select ClassWizard from the View menu.

Visual C++ responds by displaying the MFC ClassWizard dialog box.

8

☐ Select ID_FILE_EXIT in the Object IDs list, select COMMAND in the Message list, then click the Add Function button.

Visual C++ responds by suggesting you name the new function OnFileExit.

☐ Accept OnFileExit as the name of the new function, then click the Edit Code button.

☐ Enter the following code in the OnFileExit() function (in the MyBMPDlg.cpp file):

```
void CMyBMPDlg::OnFileExit()
{
// TODO: Add your command handler code here

/////////////////////////
// MY CODE STARTS HERE
/////////////////////////

OnOK();

/////////////////////////
// MY CODE ENDS HERE
/////////////////////////

}
```

The code you typed is executed when you select Exit from the File menu; it terminates the MyBMP program.

☐ Select Save All from the File menu to save your work.

☐ Build and execute the MyBMP program to make sure it works as expected.

Displaying the About Dialog Box

You'll now add the code that's executed when you select the About item from the Help menu:

☐ Double-click the IDR_MENU1 item in the Project Workspace window to display the menu in design mode.

☐ Select ClassWizard from the View menu.

☐ Select the ID_HELP_ABOUT item from the Object IDs list, select COMMAND from the Messages list, then click the Add Function button.

Visual C++ responds by suggesting you name the function OnHelpAbout.

☐ Click the Edit Code button, then add the following code in the OnHelpAbout() function:

```
void CMyBMPDlg::OnHelpAbout()
{
// TODO: Add your command handler code here
```

```
/////////////////////////
// MY CODE STARTS HERE
/////////////////////////

CAboutDlg dlg;
dlg.DoModal();

/////////////////////////
// MY CODE ENDS HERE
/////////////////////////

}
```

☐ Save your work.

☐ Build and execute the program to make sure the About dialog box is displayed when you click the About item from the Help menu.

☐ Select Exit from the File menu to terminate the MyBMP program.

Inserting a BMP Picture in Your Project

You'll now draw the BMP picture:

☐ Execute the Paint program that comes with Windows 95 (usually in the Accessories folder).

☐ Select Attributes from Paint's Image menu.

Paint responds by displaying the Attributes dialog box.

☐ Set the Width box to 250 pixels and the Height box to 250 pixels. Finally, click the OK button of the Attributes dialog box.

Paint responds by displaying an empty area (250 pixels by 250 pixels) ready for you to paint. (See Figure 8.6.)

☐ Draw something with Paint. Figure 8.7 shows how you can import clip-art to enhance your program.

☐ Select Save As from Paint's File menu and save your drawing as a 256-Color BMP file with the filename MyBMP.BMP in the C:\TYVCPROG\PROGRAMS\CH08\ MyBMP\RES directory.

☐ Terminate the Paint program.

Now add the MyBMP.BMP file to the MyBMP project:

☐ In the Project Workspace, click the ResourceView tab and right-click the MyBMP resources item.

Figure 8.6.

*Ready to paint
with Paint.*

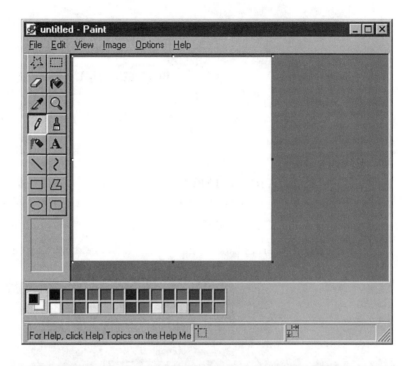

Figure 8.7.

*Importing clip-art
into Paint.*

☐ Click the Import item from the pop-up menu that Visual C++ displays.

> *Visual C++ responds by displaying the Import Resource dialog box.*

☐ Select the C:\TYVCProg\Programs\CH08\MyBMP\Res\MyBMP.BMP file, then click the Import button.

> *Visual C++ responds by adding the MyBMP.BMP picture to the project.*

The ID that Visual C++ assigned to the new picture is IDB_BITMAP1. Change this ID to IDB_MYBMP:

☐ Right-click the IDB_BITMAP1 item in the Project Workspace window, then select Properties from the pop-up menu.

☐ Set the ID to IDB_MYBMP.

The Bitmap Properties window should now look like the one in Figure 8.8.

Figure 8.8.

The Bitmap Properties window.

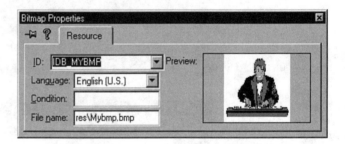

☐ Select Save All from the File menu to save your work.

You can build and execute the MyBMP program to make sure everything is OK. Of course, you won't see your picture because you haven't added the code for displaying the MyBMP.BMP picture.

Displaying the Bitmap Picture

You'll now write code that displays the bitmap:

☐ Select ClassWizard from the view menu.

☐ In the Message Maps tab of the ClassWizard window, select the following event:

Class name:	CMyBMPDlg
Object ID:	CMyBMPDlg
Message:	WM_PAINT

8

☐ Click the Edit Code button of ClassWizard.

Visual C++ responds by opening the file MyBMPDlg.cpp with the function OnPaint() *ready for you to edit.*

☐ Write the following code in the OnPaint() function:

```
void CMyBMPDlg::OnPaint()
{
  if (IsIconic())
      {
...
...
...
      }
      else
      {

////////////////////////
// MY CODE STARTS HERE
////////////////////////

CPaintDC dc(this);

HBITMAP hbitmap =
   ::LoadBitmap(::AfxGetInstanceHandle(),
                MAKEINTRESOURCE(IDB_MYBMP) );

// Create a memory DC
HDC hMemDC = ::CreateCompatibleDC(NULL);

// Select the bitmap in the memory dc.
SelectObject(hMemDC,hbitmap);


// Copy the memory dc into the screen dc
::StretchBlt(dc.m_hDC,    //destination
             50,
             50,
             100,
             100,
             hMemDC,      // Source
             0,
             0,
             250,
             250,
             SRCCOPY);

// Delete the memory DC and the bitmap
::DeleteDC(hMemDC);
::DeleteObject(hbitmap);


////////////////////////
// MY CODE ENDS HERE
////////////////////////
```

8

```
        CDialog::OnPaint();
            }
        }
```

The code you typed creates a device context (dc):

```
CPaintDC dc(this);
```

Then a variable of type HBITMAP is created:

```
HBITMAP hbitmap;
```

The hbitmap variable is assigned the returned value of the LoadBitmap() function:

```
hbitmap =
    ::LoadBitmap(::AfxGetInstanceHandle(),
                 MAKEINTRESOURCE(IDB_MYBMP) );
```

The preceding statement supplies ::AfxGetInstanceHandle() as the first parameter of the LoadBitmap() function. The AfxGetInstanceHandle() function returns the current instance of the application. The current instance of the application is the required value of the first parameter of the LoadBitmap() function.

This is the second parameter:

```
MAKEINTRESOURCE(IDB_MYBMP)
```

During the visual design of the project, you set MyBMP.BMP's ID to IDB_MYBMP. MAKEINTRESOURCE() is a macro that converts IDB_MYBMP to a value as required by the second parameter of LoadBitmap(). Therefore, the LoadBitmap() function loads the picture of MyBMP.BMP.

NOTE   The contents of the MyBMP.BMP file are stored in the MyBMP.rc file. After you build the MyBMP program, its contents become an integral part of the MyBMP.EXE program file, so the LoadBitmap()function "loads" the BMP picture from the MyBMP.EXE file.

NOTE   In this chapter, you're creating a program that has the BMP file embedded in the EXE program, so you have to incorporate the BMP file into the projects during design time. This technique does not let the user select an arbitrary BMP file from the hard drive. In Chapter 10, "Loading and Displaying Picture Files," you'll learn how to create a

> program that uses a different technique for loading and displaying
> BMP files, one that lets the user load and display any BMP file during
> runtime.

Next, you created a memory device context as follows:

```
HDC hMemDC = ::CreateCompatibleDC(NULL);
```

What is a *memory device context?* It is a section in memory that's an exact replica of your screen. In Windows you can't display bitmaps directly in the screen; you have to place them in a memory device context (dc). When everything is ready to be displayed, you transfer the contents of the memory dc to the screen dc.

The :: operator is used in the preceding statement, because the Windows CreateCompatibleDC() SDK function is used. You're indicating to the compiler that you want to use the SDK function (not a member function of the CMyBMPDlg class).

Now that the hMemDC has been created, you can select the bitmap into the memory dc (in plain English, it means "place the BMP picture in the memory device context"):

```
SelectObject(hMemDC,hbitmap);
```

Now that everything is ready, you can transfer the contents of the memory dc into the screen as follows:

```
// Copy the memory dc into the screen dc
::StretchBlt(dc.m_hDC,   //destination
             50,
             50,
             100,
             100,
             hMemDC,   //Source
             0,
             0,
             250,
             250,
             SRCCOPY);
```

The first parameter of the SDK function StretchBlt() is dc.m_hDC, which is the device context of the destination—the screen. The second and third parameters are the x and y coordinates in the IDD_MYBMP_DIALOG dialog box where the upper-left corner of the BMP picture will be displayed.

The fourth and fifth parameters of the StretchBlt() function are the width and height, respectively, of the area where the BMP picture will be displayed. During the visual design, you set the width and height of the picture to 250 pixels for each. Now you've specified that the BMP picture should be enclosed in a rectangle with its upper-left corner at coordinates

50,50. Furthermore, you specify that the width and height of the rectangle holding the BMP picture should be 100 pixels wide and 100 pixels high. This means that the StretchBlt() function will have to shrink the original large BMP picture to fit in the smaller rectangle.

The sixth parameter in the preceding statement is hMemDC, which specifies the source dc. The seventh and eighth parameters of StretchBlt() indicate the upper-left corner of the rectangle at coordinates 0,0 in the source picture; the ninth and tenth parameters indicate the width and height of the rectangle. This rectangle defines the area in the source BMP picture that will be transferred to the destination. The values you supplied mean that the entire BMP picture will be transferred.

The last parameter specifies the operation you want to be performed by the StretchBlt() function. You specified SRCCOPY to copy the picture from the memory dc to the screen dc in the IDD_MYBMP_DIALOG dialog box.

The last two statements added in the OnPaint() function delete hMemDC and hbitmap:

```
// Delete the memory DC and the bitmap
::DeleteDC(hMemDC);
::DeleteObject(hbitmap);
```

☐ Select Save All from the File menu to save your work.

☐ Build and execute the MyBMP program to see your code in action.

The window of the MyBMP program should display the MyBMP.BMP picture as specified by the parameters of the StretchBlt() function. (See Figure 8.9.)

Figure 8.9.

The window of the MyBMP program.

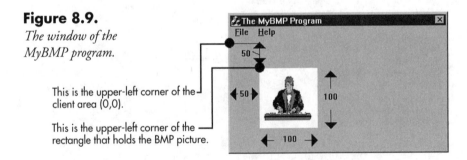

This is the upper-left corner of the client area (0,0).

This is the upper-left corner of the rectangle that holds the BMP picture.

☐ Select Exit from the File menu to terminate the MyBMP program.

8

Enlarging the BMP Picture

In the previous section, you shrank the picture from 250 pixels × 250 pixels to 100 pixels × 100 pixels. For practice, try enlarging the BMP picture:

☐ Modify the parameters of the StretchBlt() function in the OnPaint() function:

```
::StretchBlt(dc.m_hDC,    //destination
            50,
            50,
            300,
            300,
            hMemDC,  // Source
            0,
            0,
            250,
            250,
            SRCCOPY);
```

As you can see, the width and height of the destination picture is now set to 300 pixels × 300 pixels.

☐ Build and execute the MyBMP program.

The MyBMP.BMP picture is so large now that it can't fit in the MyBMP window. (See Figure 8.10.)

Figure 8.10.

Enlarging the MyBMP.BMP picture.

☐ Size the window of the MyBMP program so that it's large enough to contain the picture. The result is shown in Figure 8.11.

☐ Select Exit from MyBMP's File menu to terminate the program.

Figure 8.11.

*After enlarging the
window of the
MyBMP program.*

Adding Two Data Member Variables
to the `CMyBMPDlg` Class

You'll now add two data members to the `CMyBMPDlg` class:

☐ In the Project Workspace, click the FileView tab and expand the MyBMP Files item, then expand the Header Files item. Finally, double-click the MyBMPDlg.h item to display that file.

☐ Add the `m_Width` and `m_Height` data members to the `CMyBMPDlg` class (in the MyBMPDlg.h file). After adding these data members, the class declaration of `CMyBMPDlg` should look like the following:

```
class CMyBMPDlg : public CDialog
{
// Construction
public:
CMyBMPDlg(CWnd* pParent = NULL);   // standard constructor


/////////////////////////////
// MY CODE STARTS HERE
/////////////////////////////

int m_Width;
int m_Height;
```

8

```
/////////////////////////////
// MY CODE ENDS HERE
/////////////////////////////

. . .
. . .
. . .
};
```

Why did you add the m_Width and m_Height data members? Because you want to update these data members with the width and height of the IDD_MYBMP_DIALOG dialog box, and you want every member function of the CMyBMPDlg class to be able to access these variables.

Extracting the Width and Height of the Window

You declared the m_Width and m_Height data members in the previous section; now you'll update them with the width and height of the IDD_MYBMP_DIALOG dialog box:

☐ Select ClassWizard from the View menu.

☐ In the Message Maps tab of ClassWizard, select the following event:

Class name:	CMyBMPDlg
Object ID:	CMyBMPDlg
Message:	WM_SIZE

☐ Click the Add Function button to add the OnSize() function.

☐ Click the Edit Code button of ClassWizard.

> *Visual C++ responds by opening the file MyBMPDlg.cpp with the function* OnSize() *ready for you to edit.*

☐ Write the following code in the OnSize() function:

```
void CMyBMPDlg::OnSize(UINT nType, int cx, int cy)
{
CDialog::OnSize(nType, cx, cy);

// TODO: Add your message handler code here

/////////////////////////
// MY CODE STARTS HERE
/////////////////////////

m_Width = cx;
m_Height = cy;

Invalidate();
```

```
/////////////////////////
// MY CODE ENDS HERE
/////////////////////////

    }
```

The OnSize() function is automatically executed when the size of the IDD_MYBMP_DIALOG dialog box changes, such as when you drag the edges of the MyBMP window. The OnSize() function is also executed when you display the IDD_MYBMP_DIALOG dialog box for the first time.

The second and third parameters of the OnSize() function are cx, the new width of the window, and cy, the new height of the window. Therefore, m_Width and m_Height are updated with values representing the width and height of the IDD_MYBMP_DIALOG window:

```
m_Width = cx;
m_Height = cy;
```

The Invalidate() function is executed to force the execution of the OnPaint() function:

```
Invalidate();
```

Resizing the BMP Picture

You'll now write code that changes the size of the BMP picture to the exact size of the client area of the IDD_MYBMP_DIALOG dialog box. (The *client area* is the window area available for displaying a picture.)

☐ Modify the OnPaint() function (in the MyBMPDlg.cpp file) as follows:

```
void CMyBMPDlg::OnPaint()
{
    if (IsIconic())
        {
...
...
...
        }
    else
        {

/////////////////////////
// MY CODE STARTS HERE
/////////////////////////

CPaintDC dc(this);


HBITMAP hbitmap;

hbitmap =
    ::LoadBitmap(::AfxGetInstanceHandle(),
                    MAKEINTRESOURCE(IDB_MYBMP) );
```

8

```
// Create a new memory DC
HDC hMemDC = ::CreateCompatibleDC(NULL);

SelectObject(hMemDC,hbitmap);


// Copy the memory dc into the screen dc
::StretchBlt(dc.m_hDC,    //destination
             0,
             0,
             m_Width,
             m_Height,
             hMemDC,  // Source
             0,
             0,
             250,
             250,
             SRCCOPY);

// Delete the memory DC and the bitmap
::DeleteDC(hMemDC);
::DeleteObject(hbitmap);


////////////////////////
// MY CODE ENDS HERE
////////////////////////


    CDialog::OnPaint();
    }
}
```

In the preceding code, you modified the parameters of the StretchBlt() function:

```
::StretchBlt(dc.m_hDC,    //destination
             0,
             0,
             m_Width,
             m_Height,
             hMemDC,  // Source
             0,
             0,
             250,
             250,
             SRCCOPY);
```

Now the first and second parameters are set to 0 so that the top-left corner of the BMP picture will be at the top-left corner of the window. Also, now the fourth and fifth parameters of the StretchBlt() function are m_Width and m_Height. This means that the BMP picture will be stretched to fit the entire client area of the IDD_MYBMP_DIALOG dialog box.

☐ Select Save All from the File menu to save your work.

☐ Build and execute the MyBMP program.

☐ Experiment by dragging the window's edges. Notice that as you change the size of the MyBMP's window, the picture shrinks or enlarges to fit the entire size of the dialog box. (See Figures 8.12 and 8.13.)

Figure 8.12.

A smaller window results in a smaller picture.

Figure 8.13.

A larger window results in a larger picture.

Summary

In this chapter, you have learned how to display BMP pictures and stretch them to any size you want.

Q&A

Q Suppose I want to distribute the MyBMP.EXE program. Should I include the MyBMP.BMP file with the distribution disk?

A No. The MyBMP.BMP file is an integral part of the MyBMP.EXE file.

Q **Where can I learn to design programs that let the user load and display any BMP file during runtime?**

A The technique described in Chapter 10, lets the user load and display any BMP file from the hard drive.

Q **The code I typed in the OnSize() function of the MyBMP program uses the cx and cy parameters of the OnSize() function. I noticed that the OnSize() function also has the nType parameter as its first parameter. What is this parameter used for?**

A The nType parameter specifies that the window was resized in some way. For example, if nType is equal to SIZE_MAXIMIZED, it means the window was maximized. The following if statement can be used to detect whether the window was maximized:

```
if ( nType == SIZE_MAXIMIZED )
{

// Write code here that is executed whenever the
// window is maximized.
...
...
...

}
```

Similarly, you can detect whether the window was minimized by using the following if statement:

```
if ( nType == SIZE_MIMIMIZED )
{

// Write here code that is executed whenever the
// window was maximized.
...
...
...

}
```

Quiz

1. What do the cx and cy parameters of the OnSize() function specify?
2. The StretchBlt() function does which of the following?
   a. There is no such function.
   b. Stretches the window as specified in the function's parameters.
   c. Stretches the picture as specified in the function's parameters.

Exercise

Modify the MyBMP program so that the PC beeps when the user maximizes the window of the MyBMP program.

Quiz Answers

1. The cx and cy parameters of the OnSize() function specify the new size of the window.

2. c

Exercise Answer

Use these steps to modify the MyBMP program:

☐ Display the IDD_MYBMP_DIALOG dialog box in design mode.

☐ Check the Maximize check box.

☐ Check the Minimize check box.

Figure 8.14 shows the Properties dialog box with its Styles tab displayed. As you can see, the Maximize and Minimize check boxes are checked.

Figure 8.14.

Selecting the Maximize and Minimize check boxes for the IDD_MYBMP_DIALOG dialog box.

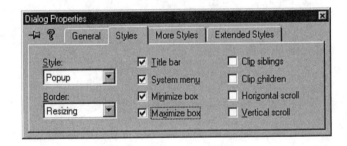

Now that you've checked the Maximize and Minimize check boxes, the MyBMP window will have maximize and minimize icons on its upper-right corner. Also, the program's system menu will include Maximize and Minimize menu items. (The user can display the system menu of the program by clicking the icon on the upper-left corner of the window.)

8

☐ Modify the `OnSize()` function (in the MyBMPDlg.cpp file) as follows:

```
void CMyBMPDlg::OnSize(UINT nType, int cx, int cy)
{
  CDialog::OnSize(nType, cx, cy);

// TODO: Add your message handler code here

////////////////////////////
// MY CODE STARTS HERE
////////////////////////////

if (nType == SIZE_MAXIMIZED)
{
MessageBeep((WORD)-1);
}

m_Width = cx;
m_Height = cy;

Invalidate();

////////////////////////////
// MY CODE ENDS HERE
////////////////////////////

}
```

The code you typed examines the value of `nType`:

```
if (nType == SIZE_MAXIMIZED)
{
MessageBeep((WORD)-1);
}
```

The code under the `if` statement is executed if the user maximizes the window. This code causes the PC to beep.

☐ Save your work.

☐ Build and execute the MyBMP program and make sure the PC beeps when you maximize the MyBMP window.

Day **9**

Displaying Text in Different Fonts

In this chapter, you'll learn how to create programs that use different fonts and font sizes.

The MyFnt Program

The MyFnt program illustrates how you can create programs that use different fonts and different font sizes, but before creating it yourself, let's review its specifications:

- When you start the MyFnt program, the window shown in Figure 9.1 appears.

Figure 9.1.

*The window of the
MyFnt program.*

■ You can then type text in the edit box. Whatever you type in the edit box appears
   in the window of the MyFnt program with the selected font, size, and shadowing
   style.

Figures 9.2 and 9.3 show some samples of text created with the MyFnt program.

Figure 9.2.

*Sample text in
Arial font.*

Figure 9.3.

Sample text in Brush Script MT font.

Creating the Project of the MyFnt Program

To create the project of the MyFnt program, follow these steps:

☐ Create the C:\TYVCPROG\PROGRAMS\CH09 directory.

☐ Start Visual C++ and select New from the File menu.

Visual C++ responds by displaying the New dialog box.

☐ Select the Projects tab of the New dialog box.

☐ Select MFC AppWizard(exe) from the list of project types.

☐ Type MyFnt in the Project Name box.

☐ Click the button that is located on the right of the Location box and select the C:\TYVCPROG\PROGRAMS\CH09 directory.

☐ Click the OK button.

Visual C++ responds by displaying the MFC AppWizard Step 1 window.

☐ Set the Step 1 window to create a dialog-based application, then click the Next button.

☐ In the Step 2 window, use the default settings and enter MyFnt as the dialog box title. When you're done, click the Next button.

☐ In the Step 3 window, accept the default settings and click the Next button.

☐ In the Step 4 window, notice that AppWizard has created the CMyFntApp and CMyFntDlg classes. Click the Finish button, then click the OK button of the New Project Information window.

Visual C++ responds by creating the project and all its associated files.

☐ Select Set Active Configuration from the Build menu and then select MyFnt - Win32 Release from the Set Active Project Configuration dialog box.

The Visual Design of the MyFnt Program

You'll now visually design the IDD_MYFNT_DIALOG dialog box that serves as the main window of the MyFnt program:

☐ In the Project Workspace, click the ResourceView tab, expand the MyFnt resources items, expand the Dialog item, and double-click the IDD_MYFNT_DIALOG dialog box.

Visual C++ responds by displaying the IDD_MYFNT_DIALOG dialog box in design mode.

☐ Delete the OK button, Cancel button, and TODO text of the IDD_MYFNT_DIALOG dialog box.

☐ Design the IDD_MYFNT_DIALOG dialog box according to Table 9.1. When you finish, it should look like the one in Figure 9.4.

Table 9.1. The properties table of the IDD_MYFNT_DIALOG dialog box.

Object	Property	Setting
Dialog Box	**ID**	**IDD_MYFNT_DIALOG**
	Caption	The MyFnt Program
	Font	System, Size 10
Push Button	**ID**	**IDC_EXIT_BUTTON**
	Caption	E&xit
Edit Box	**ID**	**IDC_DATA_EDIT**
	Client edge	Checked (Extended Styles tab)
	Static edge	Checked (Extended Styles tab)
	Modal frame	Checked (Extended Styles tab)

9

Figure 9.4.
*The
IDD_MYFNT_DIALOG
dialog box in design
mode.*

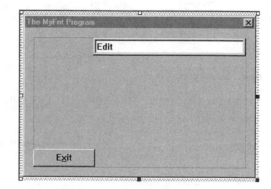

9

Attaching a Variable to the Edit Box

To attach a variable to the IDC_DATA_EDIT edit box control, follow these steps:

☐ Select ClassWizard from the View menu.

☐ In the Member Variables tab of ClassWizard, make the following selections:

> Class name: CMyFntDlg
> Control ID: IDC_DATA_EDIT

☐ Click the Add Variable button and set the variable as follows:

> Variable name: m_DataEdit
> Category: Value
> Variable type: CString

☐ Click the OK button, then click ClassWizard's OK button.

Attaching Code to the BN_CLICKED Event of the Exit Button

You'll now attach code to the BN_CLICKED event of the Exit button:

☐ Select ClassWizard from the View menu.

☐ In the Message Maps tab of ClassWizard, select the following event:

> Class name: CMyFntDlg
> Object ID: IDC_EXIT_BUTTON
> Message: BN_CLICKED

☐ Click the Add Function button, name the new function OnExitButton, and click the Edit Code button.

Visual C++ responds by opening the file MyFntDlg.cpp with the function OnExitButton() *ready for you to edit.*

☐ Write the following code in the OnExitButton() function:

```
void CMyFntDlg::OnExitButton()
{
// TODO: Add your control notification handler code here

/////////////////////////
// MY CODE STARTS HERE
/////////////////////////

OnOK();

/////////////////////////
// MY CODE ENDS HERE
/////////////////////////

}
```

The code you entered, which is executed when you click the Exit button, terminates the MyFnt program.

Attaching Code to the EN_CHANGE Event of the Edit Box

You'll now attach code to the EN_CHANGE event of the edit box, which occurs when you change the edit box's contents:

☐ Select ClassWizard from the View menu.

☐ In the Message Maps tab of the ClassWizard window, select the following event:

Class name:	CMyFntDlg
Object ID:	IDC_DATA_EDIT
Message:	EN_CHANGE

☐ Click the Add Function button, name the new function OnChangeDataEdit, and click the Edit Code button.

Visual C++ responds by opening the file MyFntDlg.cpp with the function OnChangeDataEdit() *ready for you to edit.*

☐ Write the following code in the OnChangeDataEdit() function:

```
void CMyFntDlg::OnChangeDataEdit()
{
// TODO: If this is a RICHEDIT control, the control will not
// send this notification unless you modify CDialog::OnInitDialog()
// function to send the EM_SETEVENTMASK message to the control
// with the ENM_CHANGE flag ORed into the lParam mask.

// TODO: Add your control notification handler code here

//////////////////////////
// MY CODE STARTS HERE
//////////////////////////

Invalidate();

//////////////////////////
// MY CODE ENDS HERE
//////////////////////////

}
```

The code that you typed is made up of the following statement:

```
Invalidate();
```

The Invalidate() function causes the OnPaint() function to be executed. Thus, whenever the user types something in the IDC_DATA_EDIT edit box, the code that you attached to the EN_CHANGE event of the IDC_DATA_EDIT edit box will cause the execution of the OnPaint() function. You'll verify this in the following section.

Attaching Code to the WM_PAINT Event

You'll now attach code to the WM_PAINT event:

☐ Select ClassWizard from the View menu.

☐ In the Message Maps tab of ClassWizard, select the following event:

Class name:	CMyFntDlg
Object ID:	CMyFntDlg
Message:	WM_PAINT

☐ Click the Edit Code button of ClassWizard.

Visual C++ responds by opening the file MyFntDlg.cpp with the function OnPaint() ready for you to edit.

☐ Modify the following code in the `OnPaint()` function:

```
void CMyFntDlg::OnPaint()
{
    if (IsIconic())
        {
...
...
...
        }
    else
        {
/////////////////////////
// MY CODE STARTS HERE
/////////////////////////

MessageBeep((WORD)-1);

/////////////////////////
// MY CODE ENDS HERE
/////////////////////////

CDialog::OnPaint();
    }
}
```

The code you typed causes the PC to beep whenever you change the contents of the edit box.

☐ Select Save All from the File menu.

☐ Build and execute the MyFnt program.

☐ Type something in the edit box and make sure the PC beeps.

☐ Click the Exit button to terminate the program.

Displaying Text

The experiment in the previous section has proved that the `OnPaint()` function is executed when you change the contents of the edit box. `OnPaint()` is executed whenever the edit box is changed because the code you attached earlier to the `EN_CHANGE` event of the edit box calls the `Invalidate()` function.

Now try modifying the `OnPaint()` function to display the contents of the edit box:

☐ Modify the `OnPaint()` function (in the MyFntDlg.cpp file) as follows:

```
void CMyFntDlg::OnPaint()
{
    if (IsIconic())
        {
...
...
...
```

9

```
      }
      else
      {
//////////////////////
// MY CODE STARTS HERE
//////////////////////

/// MessageBeep((WORD)-1);

CPaintDC dc(this); // device context for painting

// Update control's variables
UpdateData(TRUE);

// Set the background mode to transparent.
dc.SetBkMode( TRANSPARENT );

// Create a font object
CFont MyFont;

MyFont.CreateFont (25,
                   0,
                   0,
                   0,
                   400,
                   FALSE,
                   FALSE,
                   0,
                   ANSI_CHARSET,
                   OUT_DEFAULT_PRECIS,
                   CLIP_DEFAULT_PRECIS,
                   DEFAULT_QUALITY,
                   DEFAULT_PITCH | FF_SWISS,
                   "Arial");


// Select the new font object
CFont* pOldFont = dc.SelectObject(&MyFont);


// Draw the text
dc.TextOut (100,
            120,
            m_DataEdit);


// Select the old font
dc.SelectObject(pOldFont);

//////////////////////
// MY CODE ENDS HERE
//////////////////////

CDialog::OnPaint();

      }
```

9

The code you typed comments out the beeping:

```
/// MessageBeep((WORD)-1);
```

Then a device context (dc) is created:

```
CPaintDC dc(this); // device context for painting
```

The control variables are then updated:

```
UpdateData(TRUE);
```

In other words, the OnPaint() function is executed because you changed the contents of the edit box. Earlier, you attached the m_DataEdit variable to the edit box. Therefore, after executing the UpdateData() function with TRUE as its parameter, the m_DataEdit variable is updated with the new contents of the edit box.

You then use the SetBkMode() function to set the background mode to transparent mode:

```
dc.SetBkMode( TRANSPARENT );
```

When you set the background mode to transparent mode, subsequent statements that draw text on the screen will draw the text without changing the original background color.

You then created an object called MyFont of class CFont:

```
CFont MyFont;
```

The CreateFont() function sets its characteristics:

```
MyFont.CreateFont (25,
                   0,
                   0,
                   0,
                   400,
                   FALSE,
                   FALSE,
                   0,
                   ANSI_CHARSET,
                   OUT_DEFAULT_PRECIS,
                   CLIP_DEFAULT_PRECIS,
                   DEFAULT_QUALITY,
                   DEFAULT_PITCH | FF_SWISS,
                   "Arial");
```

There are 14 parameters to the CreateFont() function; they specify how to create the font.

NOTE

One of the nice things about Visual C++ is its ability to give you instant help. No one expects you to remember the meaning of the 14 parameters of the CreateFont() function. You can immediately discover the meaning of each parameter by highlighting the text CreateFont, then pressing F1 on the keyboard.

You've created a font; now you apply this font by executing the SelectObject() function as follows:

```
// Select the new font object
CFont* pOldFont = dc.SelectObject(&MyFont);
```

Note that the returned value of the SelectObject() function is a pointer to the original font (the font replaced by the new MyFont object).

Now that the m_DataEdit variable is updated and the new MyFont is selected, you can finally draw the text:

```
// Draw the text
dc.TextOut (100,
            120,
            m_DataEdit);
```

The first and second parameters specify the location of the upper-left corner of the cell displaying the first character. The first character will be displayed 100 units to the right of the MyFnt window's left edge and 120 units below the window's top edge.

The third parameter of the TextOut() function is the string that will be displayed. You supplied m_DataEdit as the third parameter, so the contents of the edit box will be displayed.

The last statement you executed returns the original font:

```
// Select the old font
dc.SelectObject(pOldFont);
```

☐ Select Save All from the File menu.

☐ Build and execute the MyFnt program.

☐ Type something in the edit box.

The window of the MyFnt program displays the text you typed in the edit box, using the font you set in the OnPaint() function. (See Figure 9.5.)

☐ Experiment with the MyFnt program, then click its Exit button to terminate the program.

Figure 9.5.

Displaying the text in the edit box.

Changing the Font During Runtime

In the following sections, you'll add code that lets the user change the font during runtime. The user will change the font by making a selection from a group of radio buttons.

☐ In the Project Workspace, click the ResourceView tab and expand the MyFnt resources item, then the Dialog item. Finally, double-click the IDD_MYFNT_DIALOG item.

Visual C++ responds by displaying the IDD_MYFNT_DIALOG dialog box in design mode.

☐ Place a group box in the IDD_MYFNT_DIALOG dialog box and set its properties as follows:

ID:	`IDC_SIZE_STATIC`
Caption:	`Size`
Client edge:	Checked (Extended Styles tab)
Static edge:	Checked (Extended Styles tab)
Modal frame:	Checked (Extended Styles tab)

☐ Place four radio buttons in the group box and set their properties according to Table 9.2. When you finish, the IDD_MYFNT_DIALOG dialog box should look like the one in Figure 9.6. Place the radio buttons one after the other so that their ID numbers will be in sequential order.

Table 9.2. The properties table for the four radio buttons.

Object	Property	Setting
Radio Button	**ID**	**IDC_25_RADIO**
	Caption	25
	Group	Checked (General tab)
Radio Button	**ID**	**IDC_50_RADIO**
	Caption	50
	Group	Not Checked (General tab)
Radio Button	**ID**	**IDC_75_RADIO**
	Caption	75
	Group	Not Checked (General tab)
Radio Button	**ID**	**IDC_100_RADIO**
	Caption	100
	Group	Not Checked (General tab)

9

Figure 9.6.
The four radio buttons in design mode.

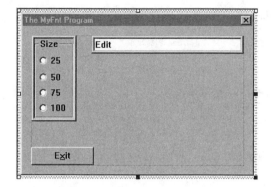

Follow these steps to make sure the radio buttons' ID numbers are in sequential order:

☐ Select Resource Symbols from the View menu.

Visual C++ responds by displaying the Resource Symbol dialog box.

☐ Browse through the IDs in the Resource Symbol dialog box and verify that the radio buttons' IDs have sequential numbers in the following order:

```
IDC_25_RADIO
IDC_50_RADIO
IDC_75_RADIO
IDC_100_RADIO
```

Attaching a Variable to the Radio Buttons

During the visual design of the radio buttons, you checked the Group property for the IDC_25_RADIO radio button, but not for the rest of the radio buttons. This means that the four radio buttons belong to the same group; therefore, a single variable is used to note the status of any of the radio buttons. Here is how you attach a variable to the four radio buttons:

☐ Select ClassWizard from the View menu.

☐ In the Member Variables tab of ClassWizard, make the following selections:

Class name: CMyFntDlg
Control ID: IDC_25_RADIO

☐ Click the Add Variable button and set the variable as follows:

Variable name:	m_SizeRadio
Category:	Value
Variable type:	int

☐ Click the OK button of the Add Member Variable dialog box, then click ClassWizard's OK button.

So when m_SizeRadio is equal to 0, the IDC_25_RADIO radio button is selected. When m_SizeRadio is equal to 1, the IDC_50_RADIO radio button is selected, and so on.

Initializing the Radio Buttons

If you build and execute the MyFnt program now, you'll realize that none of the radio buttons is selected when you start the program. To make the IDC_25_RADIO radio button the selected radio button when the program starts, you need to write code in the OnInitDialog() function as follows:

☐ Select ClassWizard from the View menu.

☐ In the Message Maps tab of ClassWizard, select the following event:

Class name:	CMyFntDlg
Object ID:	MyFntDlg
Message:	WM_INITDIALOG

☐ Click the Edit Code button of ClassWizard.

Visual C++ responds by opening the file MyFntDlg.cpp with the function OnInitDialog() *ready for you to edit.*

☐ Write the following code in the OnInitDialog() function:

```
BOOL CMyFntDlg::OnInitDialog()
{
...
...
...
// TODO: Add extra initialization here

/////////////////////////
// MY CODE STARTS HERE
/////////////////////////

m_SizeRadio = 0;
UpdateData(FALSE);

/////////////////////////
// MY CODE ENDS HERE
/////////////////////////

return TRUE;
```

9

```
// return TRUE  unless you set the focus to a control
}
```

The code you typed sets the m_SizeRadio variable to 0 and calls the UpdateData() function
with its parameter set to FALSE:

```
m_SizeRadio = 0;
UpdateData(FALSE);
```

This means that the IDC_25_RADIO radio button will be selected.

NOTE

Previously, you typed code in the OnPaint() function (in the
MyFntDlg.cpp file) that draws the text as follows:

```
// Draw the text
dc.TextOut (100,
            120,
            m_DataEdit);
```

Text is displayed in imaginary rectangles. The preceding statement
means that the first character will be drawn with the upper-left corner
of its imaginary rectangle 100 units to the right of the window's left
edge and 120 units below the window's top edge.

Depending on the placement of the four radio buttons, you may have
to start drawing the text a little bit more to the right. When the
program executes, if you see that the first character is drawn in the area
of the four radio buttons, change the first parameter of TextOut(). For
example, to draw the first character 150 units to the right of the left
edge, use the following statement:

```
// Draw the text
dc.TextOut (150,
            120,
            m_DataEdit);
```

Changing the Font According to the Size Radio Buttons

You'll now set the font according to the radio buttons' settings:

☐ Modify the OnPaint() function (in the MyFntDlg.cpp file) as follows:

```
void CMyFntDlg::OnPaint()
{
  if (IsIconic())
      {
...
...
...
      }
```

```
    else
        {
/////////////////////
// MY CODE STARTS HERE
/////////////////////

/// MessageBeep((WORD)-1);

CPaintDC dc(this); // device context for painting

// Update the variables of the controls
UpdateData(TRUE);

// Set the background mode to transparent.
dc.SetBkMode( TRANSPARENT );

// Create a font object
CFont MyFont;

MyFont.CreateFont (25+25*m_SizeRadio,
                   0,
                   0,
                   0,
                   400,
                   FALSE,
                   FALSE,
                   0,
                   ANSI_CHARSET,
                   OUT_DEFAULT_PRECIS,
                   CLIP_DEFAULT_PRECIS,
                   DEFAULT_QUALITY,
                   DEFAULT_PITCH | FF_SWISS,
                   "Arial");


// Select the new font object
CFont* pOldFont = dc.SelectObject(&MyFont);



// Draw the text
dc.TextOut (150,
            120,
            m_DataEdit);


// Select the old font
dc.SelectObject(pOldFont);

/////////////////////
// MY CODE ENDS HERE
/////////////////////

CDialog::OnPaint();
        }
    }
```

You modified the first parameter of the CreateFont() function as follows:

```
MyFont.CreateFont (25+25*m_SizeRadio,
                   0,
                   0,
                   0,
                   400,
                   FALSE,
                   FALSE,
                   0,
                   ANSI_CHARSET,
                   OUT_DEFAULT_PRECIS,
                   CLIP_DEFAULT_PRECIS,
                   DEFAULT_QUALITY,
                   DEFAULT_PITCH | FF_SWISS,
                   "Arial");
```

If m_SizeRadio is equal to 0, the first parameter of CreateFont() is 25+25*0=25. If m_SizeRadio is equal to 1, the first parameter is 25+25*1=50, and so on. Therefore, the first parameter of the CreateFont() function is set according to the selected radio button:

Selected Button	First Parameter of CreateFont()
IDC_25_RADIO	25
IDC_50_RADIO	50
IDC_75_RADIO	75
IDC_100_RADIO	100

Attaching Code to the BN_CLICKED Event of the Radio Buttons

You'll now attach code to the BN_CLICKED event of the IDC_25_RADIO radio button:

☐ Select ClassWizard from the View menu.

☐ In the Message Maps tab of ClassWizard, select the following event:

Class name:	CMyFntDlg
Object ID:	IDC_25_RADIO
Message:	BN_CLICKED

☐ Click the Add Function button, name the new function On25Radio, and click the Edit Code button.

Visual C++ responds by opening the file MyFntDlg.cpp with the function On25Radio() ready for you to edit.

☐ Write the following code in the On25Radio() function:

```
void CMyFntDlg::On25Radio()
{
// TODO: Add your control notification handler code here
```

```
//////////////////////////
//  MY CODE STARTS HERE
//////////////////////////

Invalidate();

//////////////////////////
//  MY CODE ENDS HERE
//////////////////////////

    }
```

The code you typed executes the Invalidate() function:

```
Invalidate();
```

This means that when you click the IDC_25_RADIO radio button, the OnPaint() function is executed. For example, if the MyFnt program displays text with its font at size 75, after you click the IDC_25_RADIO radio button, the text will be displayed at size 25.

☐ Use ClassWizard again to attach code to the BN_CLICKED event of the IDC_50_RADIO radio button and name the function On50Radio. Edit the On50Radio() function (in the MyFntDlg.cpp file) as follows:

```
void CMyFntDlg::On50Radio()
{
// TODO: Add your control notification handler code here

//////////////////////////
//  MY CODE STARTS HERE
//////////////////////////

Invalidate();

//////////////////////////
//  MY CODE ENDS HERE
//////////////////////////

    }
```

☐ Follow the same procedure for the IDC_75_RADIO and IDC_100_RADIO radio buttons, substituting the correct object IDs and function names (use the procedure for IDC_50_RADIO if you need help).

As a result of adding this code for the radio buttons, the OnPaint() function is executed when you select any of the radio buttons.

☐ Select Save All from the File menu to save your work.

☐ Build and execute the MyFnt program.

☐ Type something in the edit box, then click the radio buttons.

MyFnt responds by displaying the text at the size corresponding to the radio button you selected. Figures 9.7 and 9.8 show the text displayed at different sizes.

☐ Experiment with the MyFnt program, then click the Exit button to terminate the program.

Figure 9.7.

The font size displayed when the 25 radio button is selected.

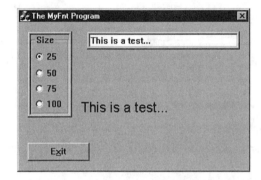

Figure 9.8.

The font size displayed when the 100 radio button is selected.

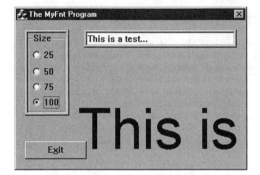

Displaying Shadowed Text

Displaying shadowed text from within your Visual C++ program is easy. *Shadowed text* is composed of two separate texts overlapping each other. For example, the top of Figure 9.9 shows two *A* characters: the dark red A on the left and the light red A on the right.

The middle A in Figure 9.9 is constructed with an *offset*. The light red A is placed over the dark red A slightly below and to the right. The result is an A that looks as though it has a shadow. The bottom A is composed by overlapping the dark red A over the light red A and offsetting the heavy red A slightly.

Figure 9.9.
Displaying shadowed
text.

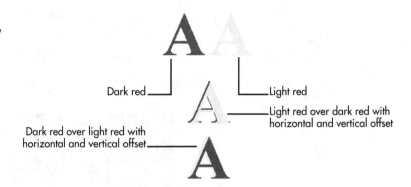

Dark red

Light red

Light red over dark red with
horizontal and vertical offset

Dark red over light red with
horizontal and vertical offset

Other shadow combinations can be generated. For example, you can place the dark red A over
the light red A, but offset the dark red A slightly above and to the left.

You'll now add code to the MyFnt program that displays the text of the edit box as shadowed
text.

Placing a Shadow Check Box in the MyFnt Window

First, add a check box to the IDD_MYFNT_DIALOG dialog box:

☐ Place a check box in the IDD_MYFNT_DIALOG dialog box and set its properties as
follows:

ID:	`IDC_SHADOW_CHECK`
Caption:	`&Shadow`
Client edge:	Checked (Extended Styles tab)
Static edge:	Checked (Extended Styles tab)
Modal frame:	Checked (Extended Styles tab)

Attaching a Variable to the Shadow Check Box

You'll now attach a variable to the Shadow check box:

☐ Select ClassWizard from the View menu.

☐ In the Member Variables tab of ClassWizard, make the following selection:

Class name:	`CMyFntDlg`
Control ID:	`IDC_SHADOW_CHECK`

9

☐ Click the Add Variable button and set the variable as follows:

Variable name:	`m_ShadowCheck`
Category:	`Value`
Variable type:	`BOOL`

☐ Click the OK button of the Add Member Variable dialog box, then click ClassWizard's OK button.

Attaching Code to the Shadow Check Box

You'll now add code that displays the text as a shadowed text:

☐ Select ClassWizard from the View menu.

☐ In the Message Maps tab of ClassWizard, select the following event:

Class name:	`CMyFntDlg`
Object ID:	`IDC_SHADOW_CHECK`
Message:	`BN_CLICKED`

☐ Click the Add Function button, name the new function `OnShadowCheck`, and click the Edit Code button.

Visual C++ responds by opening the file MyFntDlg.cpp with the function `OnShadowCheck()` *ready for you to edit.*

☐ Write the following code in the `OnShadowCheck()` function:

```
void CMyFntDlg::OnShadowCheck()
{
// TODO: Add your control notification handler code here

/////////////////////////
// MY CODE STARTS HERE
/////////////////////////

Invalidate();

/////////////////////////
// MY CODE ENDS HERE
/////////////////////////

}
```

The code you typed causes the execution of the `OnPaint()` function. Thus, whenever the Shadow check box is clicked, the `OnPaint()` function will be executed.

You'll now add the code in the OnPaint() function that draws shadowed text or nonshadowed text, depending on whether the Shadow check box is checked:

☐ Edit the OnPaint() function (in the MyFntDlg.cpp file) as follows:

```
void CMyFntDlg::OnPaint()
{
   if (IsIconic())
      {
...
...
...
      }
   else
      {

///////////////////////
// MY CODE STARTS HERE
///////////////////////


/// MessageBeep((WORD)-1);

CPaintDC dc(this); // device context for painting

// Update the variables of the controls
UpdateData(TRUE);

// Set the background mode to transparent.
dc.SetBkMode( TRANSPARENT );

// Create a font object
CFont MyFont;

MyFont.CreateFont (25+25*m_SizeRadio,
                   0,
                   0,
                   0,
                   400,
                   FALSE,
                   FALSE,
                   0,
                   ANSI_CHARSET,
                   OUT_DEFAULT_PRECIS,
                   CLIP_DEFAULT_PRECIS,
                   DEFAULT_QUALITY,
                   DEFAULT_PITCH | FF_SWISS,
                   "Arial");


// Select the new font object
CFont* pOldFont = dc.SelectObject(&MyFont);


if (m_ShadowCheck == TRUE )
{
```

```
    ///  MessageBeep((WORD)-1);

    // Set the color of the text
    dc.SetTextColor( RGB(255,0,0) );


    // Draw the text
    dc.TextOut (150,
                120,
                m_DataEdit);


    }

    // Set the color of the text
    dc.SetTextColor( RGB(0, 255, 0) );

    // Draw the text
    dc.TextOut (150 + 25,
                120 + 25,
                m_DataEdit);


    // Select the old font
    dc.SelectObject(pOldFont);


    /////////////////////
    // MY CODE ENDS HERE
    /////////////////////

        CDialog::OnPaint();
      }
    }
```

The code in the OnPaint() function first creates the device context:

```
CPaintDC dc(this); // device context for painting
```

Then the variables of the controls are updated:

```
// Update variables of controls
UpdateData(TRUE);
```

Then the background mode is set to transparent mode:

```
// Set the background mode to transparent.
dc.SetBkMode( TRANSPARENT );
```

An object of class CFont is created:

```
CFont MyFont;
MyFont.CreateFont (25+25*m_SizeRadio,
                   0,
                   0,
                   0,
                   400,
```

```
                    FALSE,
                    FALSE,
                    0,
                    ANSI_CHARSET,
                    OUT_DEFAULT_PRECIS,
                    CLIP_DEFAULT_PRECIS,
                    DEFAULT_QUALITY,
                    DEFAULT_PITCH | FF_SWISS,
                    "Arial");
```

Then the new font object is selected:

```
CFont* pOldFont = dc.SelectObject(&MyFont);
```

An `if` statement is then executed to examine the status of the Shadow check box:

```
if (m_ShadowCheck == TRUE )
{
...
...
...
}
```

If the Shadow check box is checked, the code under the `if` statement is executed. When drawing shadowed text, the contents of the edit box are drawn twice. The code under the `if` statement draws the text in red by setting the color as follows:

```
dc.SetTextColor( RGB(255,0,0) );
```

From now on, whenever the `TextOut()` function is executed, the text is drawn with a red pen.

The last statement under the `if` statement draws the text:

```
dc.TextOut (150,
            120,
            m_DataEdit);
```

The statements following the `if` block are executed no matter what the status of the Shadow check box is. However, now the text is drawn with a green pen because the `SetTextColor()` function is executed with `RGB(0,255,0)` as its parameter:

```
dc.SetTextColor( RGB(0, 255, 0) );
```

Then the `TextOut()` function is executed to draw the text:

```
dc.TextOut (150 + 25,
            120 + 25,
            m_DataEdit);
```

Note that when text is drawn for the second time, the first and second parameters of the `TextOut()` function are `150 + 25` and `120 + 25`; the first time `TextOut()` was executed, they were `150` and `120`. Therefore, the second text is drawn with the offset specified by the first and second parameters of `TextOut()`, which specify the upper-left corner of the imaginary rectangle enclosing the characters. (See Figure 9.10.)

Figure 9.10.

*Offsetting the
second text.*

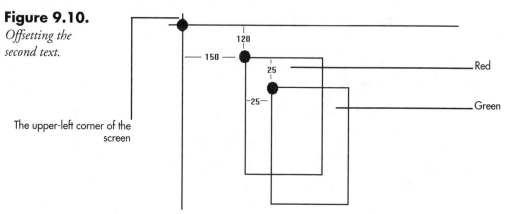

The upper-left corner of the
screen

As shown in Figure 9.10, the green text is offset from the red text by 25 horizontal units and 25 vertical units. Actually, 25 units is too much! In shadowed text, the offset is typically 3 horizontal and 3 vertical units. For demonstration purposes, however, 25 units is used, as explained in the following steps:

☐ Select Save All from the File menu.

☐ Build and execute the MyFnt program.

☐ Type A in the edit box, click the 100 radio button, then check the Shadow check box.

The window of MyFnt now looks like Figure 9.11.

Figure 9.11.

*Offsetting text by 25
horizontal units and
25 vertical units.*

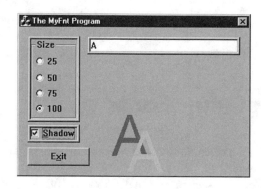

As you can see, the red A was drawn first and then the green A was drawn with an offset of 25 horizontal units and 25 vertical units.

☐ Experiment with the MyFnt program, then click the Exit button to terminate the program.

The MyFnt program is almost ready to display shadowed text; just add a few more modifications:

☐ Modify the second TextOut() function of the OnPaint() function as follows:

```
// Draw the text
dc.TextOut (150 + 3,
            120 + 3,
            m_DataEdit);
```

The offset has been changed to 3 horizontal units and 3 vertical units.

☐ Select Save All from the File menu.

☐ Build and execute the MyFnt program.

☐ Type A in the edit box, select the 100 radio button, and check the Shadow check box.

MyFnt responds by displaying the A character as shadowed text. (See Figure 9.12.)

Figure 9.12.

Displaying shadowed text with the MyFnt program.

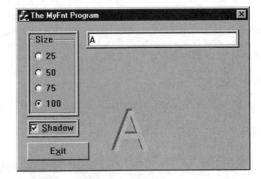

☐ Experiment with the MyFnt program, then click its Exit button to terminate the program.

Using Other Fonts

So far, you have drawn text by setting the last parameter of the CreateFont() function to Arial. What will happen if the PC on which the MyFnt program is executed doesn't have the Arial font installed? If your program includes a font that wasn't installed, Windows will try to substitute a close match for the font you supplied as the last parameter of the CreateFont() function.

9

NOTE

In the exercise at the end of this chapter, you'll experiment by supplying other values for the last parameter of the CreateFont() function. You'll do this by adding a list box to the MyFnt program that lets the user select various fonts.

9

Summary

In this chapter, you have learned how to draw text and how to select its font and other characteristics with the CreateFont() function. You have also learned how to create shadowed text (also called 3-D text) and set different colors for the text foreground.

Q&A

Q What are raised fonts and inset fonts, and how can I generate them?

A The *raised font* looks as though it's raised above the display surface, and the *inset font* looks as though it's embedded in the display surface. You generate them the same way you generate the shadowed font. In fact, you could consider raised and inset fonts as special cases of shadowed fonts.

Although the shadowed font is usually constructed by using two different colors, the raised and inset fonts are typically displayed on a light gray display surface. The raised or inset character is then drawn on the light gray surface as follows:

☐ The background character is displayed.

☐ Then the foreground character is displayed with a horizontal and vertical offset relative to the background character. The character's foreground color is black and its background color is white, or vice versa.

The top of Figure 9.13 shows a black *A* and a white *A* on a light gray background; then several possibilities for placing one *A* over the other are shown.

Figure 9.13.

Raised and inset fonts.

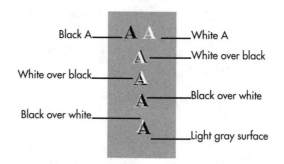

Q **I have some ideas for creating attractive-looking fonts. But it takes too long to create these fonts from within my Visual C++ program. By the time I add the code, I forget my "creative" ideas. Any suggestions?**

A There are many combinations and possibilities for creating attractive fonts—use different sizes, fonts, and colors; offset in different directions; use different surface colors. Before creating a particular font in your Visual C++ program, try using the Paint program that comes with Windows 95. Draw a character, draw another character, and then drag the first character over the second using Paint's tools. When you're satisfied with the font, create it from within your Visual C++ program.

Quiz

1. The EN_CHANGE event of the edit box control occurs when?
   a. Whenever the edit box is enabled
   b. Whenever the edit box is disabled
   c. Whenever the user changes the contents of the edit box

2. What is the CreateFont() function's job?

3. What is the TextOut() function's job?

Exercise

Currently, the MyFnt program draws the font as Arial font (see the last parameter of the CreateFont() function). Modify the MyFnt program so that various fonts can be selected by the user. In particular, let the user select the font from a list box. (To perform this exercise, follow the steps in the solution to this exercise.)

Quiz Answers

1. c

2. The CreateFont() function defines the font that will be used when drawing the text with the TextOut() function.

3. The TextOut() function draws text. The text that's drawn is specified as the third parameter of the TextOut() function.

Exercise Answer

Follow these steps to modify the MyFnt program:

☐ Place a list box control in the IDD_MYFNT_DIALOG dialog box.

☐ Set the properties of the list box as follows:

ID:	IDC_FONT_LIST
Client edge:	Checked (Extended Styles tab)
Static edge:	Checked (Extended Styles tab)
Modal frame:	Checked (Extended Styles tab)

The IDD_MYFNT_DIALOG dialog box should now look like the one in Figure 9.14 (the dialog box was enlarged vertically, and the list box was placed below the Shadow check box).

Figure 9.14.
The
IDD_MYFNT_DIALOG
dialog box with its list
box in design mode.

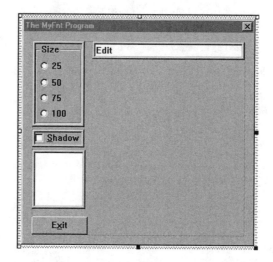

Attach the m_FontList variable to the IDC_FONT_LIST list box as follows:

☐ Select ClassWizard from the View menu.

☐ In the Member Variables tab of ClassWizard, make the following selections:

Class name:	CMyFntDlg
Control ID:	IDC_FONT_LIST

☐ Click the Add Variable button and set the variable as follows:

Variable name:	m_FontList
Category:	Control
Variable type:	CListBox

☐ Click the OK button, then click ClassWizard's OK button.

☐ Edit the OnInitDialog() function (in the MyFntDlg.cpp file) as follows:

```
BOOL CMyFntDlg::OnInitDialog()
{
....
....
....

// TODO: Add extra initialization here

/////////////////////////
// MY CODE STARTS HERE
/////////////////////////

m_SizeRadio = 0;
UpdateData(FALSE);


m_FontList.AddString("Arial");
m_FontList.AddString("System");
m_FontList.AddString("Times New Roman");
m_FontList.AddString("Brush Script MT");

m_FontList.SelectString(0, "Arial");


/////////////////////////
// MY CODE ENDS HERE
/////////////////////////

return TRUE;
// return TRUE  unless you set the focus to a control
}
```

The code you added to the OnInitDialog() function adds three items to the list box:

```
m_FontList.AddString("Arial");
m_FontList.AddString("System");
m_FontList.AddString("Times New Roman");
m_FontList.AddString("Brush Script MT");
```

The list box will have the Arial string as its first item, System as the second item, Times New Roman as the third item, and Brush Script MT as the fourth item.

When you start the program, the list box will highlight the Arial item in the list:

```
m_FontList.SelectString(0, "Arial");
```

☐ Use ClassWizard to create a function for the LBN_SELCHANGE event of the IDC_FONT_LIST list box. Name the function OnSelchangeFontList.

☐ Edit the OnSelchangeFontList() function (in the MyFntDlg.cpp file) as follows:

```
void CMyFntDlg::OnSelchangeFontList()
{
```

```
// TODO: Add your control notification handler code here

/////////////////////////
// MY CODE STARTS HERE
/////////////////////////

Invalidate();

/////////////////////////
// MY CODE ENDS HERE
/////////////////////////

}
```

The OnSelchangeFontList() function is executed whenever the user makes a selection from the IDC_FONT_LIST list box.

The code you typed causes the execution of the OnPaint() function:

```
Invalidate();
```

☐ Modify the OnPaint() function (in the MyFntDlg.cpp file) as follows:

```
void CMyFntDlg::OnPaint()
{
  if (IsIconic())
      {
....
....
....
      }
    else
      {

/////////////////////////
// MY CODE STARTS HERE
/////////////////////////


/// MessageBeep((WORD)-1);

CPaintDC dc(this); // device context for painting

// Update m_DataEdit
UpdateData(TRUE);

// Set the background mode to transparent.
dc.SetBkMode( TRANSPARENT );

CString CurrentSelectedText;
m_FontList.GetText(m_FontList.GetCurSel(),
                   CurrentSelectedText);

// Create a font object
CFont MyFont;
```

```
MyFont.CreateFont (25+25*m_SizeRadio,
                   0,
                   0,
                   0,
                   400,
                   FALSE,
                   FALSE,
                   0,
                   ANSI_CHARSET,
                   OUT_DEFAULT_PRECIS,
                   CLIP_DEFAULT_PRECIS,
                   DEFAULT_QUALITY,
                   DEFAULT_PITCH | FF_SWISS,
                   CurrentSelectedText);


// Select the new font object
CFont* pOldFont = dc.SelectObject(&MyFont);


if (m_ShadowCheck == TRUE )
{

/// MessageBeep((WORD)-1);

// Set the color of the text
dc.SetTextColor( RGB(255,0,0) );

// Draw the text
dc.TextOut (150,
            120,
            m_DataEdit);


}

// Set the color of the text
dc.SetTextColor( RGB(0, 255, 0) );


// Draw the text
dc.TextOut (150 + 3,
            120 + 3,
            m_DataEdit);


// Select the old font
dc.SelectObject(pOldFont);


/////////////////////
// MY CODE ENDS HERE
/////////////////////

CDialog::OnPaint();
    }
}
```

You added the statement that declares the `CurrentSelectedText` variable:

```
CString CurrentSelectedText;
```

The `CurrentSelectedText` variable will hold the text selected from the list box. You assign the selected text from the list box to the `CurrentSelectedText` variable as follows:

```
m_FontList.GetText(m_FontList.GetCurSel(),
                   CurrentSelectedText);
```

The `GetText()` function fills the second parameter of `GetText()` with the text mentioned in the first parameter of the `GetText()` function. This is the first parameter:

```
m_FontList.GetCurSel()
```

`GetCurSel()` returns the index number representing the item currently selected in the list box. For example, if the first item in the list is selected, the `GetCurSel()` function returns 0. If the second item is currently selected, `GetCurSel()` returns 1, and so on.

When 0 is supplied as the first parameter of the `GetText()` function, the second parameter of `GetText()` is filled with the first item of the list box. When 1 is supplied as the second parameter of the `GetText()` function, the second parameter of `GetText()` is filled with the second item of the list box, and so on.

Therefore, the `CurrentSelectedText` variable is filled with the text selected in the list box.

You also change the last parameter of the `CreateFont()` function:

```
MyFont.CreateFont (25+25*m_SizeRadio,
                   0,
                   0,
                   0,
                   400,
                   FALSE,
                   FALSE,
                   0,
                   ANSI_CHARSET,
                   OUT_DEFAULT_PRECIS,
                   CLIP_DEFAULT_PRECIS,
                   DEFAULT_QUALITY,
                   DEFAULT_PITCH | FF_SWISS,
                   CurrentSelectedText);
```

The last parameter of the `CreateFont()` function is now the selected font from the list box.

☐ Select Save All from the File menu.

☐ Build and execute the MyFnt program.

☐ Experiment with the MyFnt program, then click the Exit button to terminate the program.

Figures 9.15 through 9.17 show some of the text fonts drawn with the MyFnt program.

Figure 9.15.

Drawing Arial shadowed text.

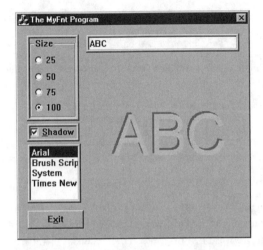

Figure 9.16.

Drawing Brush Script MT shadowed text.

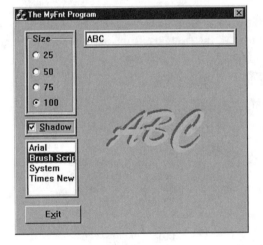

Figure 9.17.

Drawing Brush Script MT nonshadowed text.

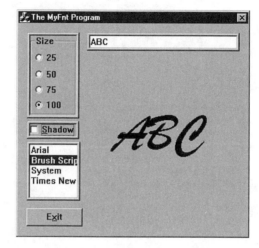

Day 10

Loading and Displaying Picture Files

In this chapter, you'll learn how to load BMP files during runtime and display the loaded BMP files. While you're creating this chapter's program, you'll learn how to display the common Open dialog box, a standard dialog box used for selecting a file from the hard drive.

NOTE

In Chapter 8, "Displaying Bitmaps," you learned how to display BMP pictures embedded in the program's EXE file. The MyBMP.EXE program in Chapter 8 lets you display only BMP pictures incorporated into the project during its visual design. In this chapter, you'll create a program that lets the user load any BMP file from the hard drive during runtime, then display that BMP picture.

NOTE

The program of this chapter uses the TegoSoft BMP ActiveX control—an ActiveX control that enables you to write programs that display and animate BMP picture files. Thus, in this chapter you'll be instructed to download the TegoSoft BMP ActiveX control from the TegoSoft Internet Web site.

Note that even if you currently do not have access to the Internet, it is recommended that you at least browse through this chapter. This way you'll see how easy it is to write programs that use an ActiveX control to load and display BMP pictures during runtime.

Downloading the BMP ActiveX Control from the Internet and Installing the BMP ActiveX Control

To download the BMP ActiveX control from the Internet, follow these steps:

☐ Use your Internet connection to connect to the Internet.

☐ Use your Internet browser program to log into the following Internet URL address:

```
http://www.tegosoft.com/BkVcBmpSamp.htm
```

☐ Follow the directions on the preceding HTML page to download a sample program that includes the BMP ActiveX control.

☐ Follow the directions given on the preceding HTML page to install the sample program that you downloaded.

That's it! You now have the BMP ActiveX control installed in your PC. In the following sections, you'll write a Visual C++ program that uses this ActiveX control.

NOTE

Now that you have the BMP ActiveX control installed in your system, you can write programs that utilize this control for displaying BMP files.

In the following sections you'll write a Visual C++ program, called MyPic, that uses the BMP ActiveX control to load and display BMP files. The MyPic program is Copyright TegoSoft Inc.

The MyPic Program

Before creating the MyPic program yourself, let's review its specifications:

■ When you start the MyPic program, the window shown in Figure 10.1 appears.

Figure 10.1.

The window of the MyPic program.

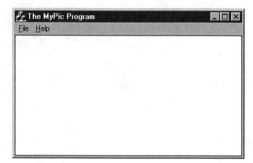

■ You can then select Open from MyPic's File menu to display the Open BMP File dialog box shown in Figure 10.2.

■ Once you select a BMP file, the MyPic program displays the picture of the BMP file, and the window's caption displays the name of the BMP file.

■ You can drag the edges of the window to shrink or enlarge its size; the picture displayed in the window shrinks or increases accordingly. The BMP picture is always displayed over the entire client area of the program's window. (See Figures 10.3 and 10.4, which show an example of an open BMP file.)

Figure 10.2.

The Open BMP File dialog box.

Figure 10.3.

Enlarging the window size increases the picture's size.

Figure 10.4.

Shrinking the window size shrinks the picture's size.

10

Creating the Project of the MyPic Program

To create the project of the MyPic program, follow these steps:

☐ Create the C:\TYVCPROG\PROGRAMS\CH10 directory.

☐ Start Visual C++ and select New from the File menu.

   Visual C++ responds by displaying the New dialog box.

☐ Select the Projects tab of the New dialog box.

☐ Select MFC AppWizard(exe) from the list of project types.

☐ Type MyPic in the Project Name box.

☐ Click the button that is located on the right of the Location box and select the C:\TYVCPROG\PROGRAMS\CH10 directory.

☐ Click the OK button.

   Visual C++ responds by displaying the MFC AppWizard Step 1 window.

☐ In Step 1, select the dialog-based option to create a dialog-based application, then click the Next button.

☐ In Step 2, use the default settings and enter MyPic for the dialog box's title. When you're done, click the Next button.

☐ In Step 3, use the default settings, then click Next.

☐ In Step 4, use the default settings, and notice that AppWizard has created the CMyPicApp and CMyPicDlg classes. Click the Finish button.

   Visual C++ responds by displaying the New Project Information window.

☐ Click the OK button of the New Project Information window.

   Visual C++ responds by creating the project of the MyPic program and all its associated files.

☐ Select Set Active Configuration from the Build menu, then select MyPic - Win32 Release and click the OK button.

That's it—you're ready to start designing the program.

10

The Visual Design of MyPic's Main Window

You'll now visually design the IDD_MYPIC_DIALOG dialog box that serves as the main window of the MyPic program.

NOTE

> In the visual design of the IDD_MYPIC_DIALOG dialog box, you will use the TegoSoft BMP ActiveX control. Thus, it is assumed that you already downloaded and installed the BMP ActiveX control as described earlier in this chapter. You will not be able to perform the steps of this section unless you have already downloaded and installed the BMP ActiveX control.

Follow these steps to visually design the IDD_MYPIC_DIALOG dialog box:

☐ In the Project Workspace, click the ResourceView tab and expand the MyPic resources item, then the Dialog item. Finally, double-click the IDD_MYPIC_DIALOG item.

Visual C++ responds by displaying the IDD_MYPIC_DIALOG dialog box in design mode.

☐ Delete the TODO text, OK button, and Cancel button of the IDD_MYPIC_DIALOG dialog box.

Next, you need to place the TegoSoft BMP ActiveX control in the IDD_MYPIC_DIALOG dialog box. But before you can place a BMP control in the IDD_MYPIC_DIALOG dialog box, you first have to add the BMP ActiveX control to the MyPic project. Here is how you do that:

☐ Select Add to Project from the Project menu.

Visual C++ responds by opening the Add to Project submenu next to the Project menu.

☐ Select Components and Controls from the Add to Project submenu (See Figure 10.5.)

Visual C++ responds by displaying the Components and Controls Gallery dialog box. (See Figure 10.6.)

Figure 10.5.

Selecting Components and Controls from the Add to Project submenu.

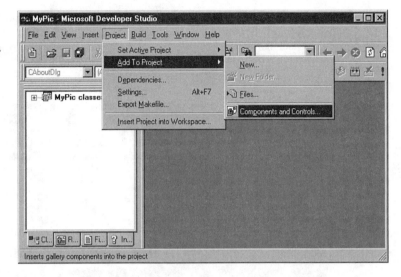

Figure 10.6.

The Components and Controls Gallery dialog box.

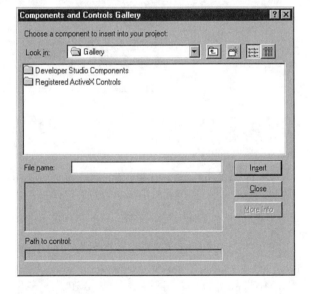

☐ In the Components and Controls Gallery dialog box, double-click the Registered ActiveX Controls item.

Visual C++ responds by displaying all the registered ActiveX controls in your system. (See Figure 10.7.)

Figure 10.7.

Displaying all the registered ActiveX controls in the Components and Controls Gallery dialog box.

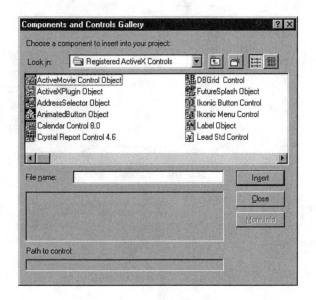

☐ Use the scroll bar of the Components and Controls Gallery dialog box to find the TegoSoft BMP ActiveX Control item, select the TegoSoft BMP ActiveX Control item by clicking it, and then click the Insert button of the Components and Controls Gallery dialog box.

Visual C++ responds by displaying a small confirmation message box asking you whether you want to insert the component that you selected to the project.

☐ Click the OK button of the confirmation message box.

Visual C++ responds by displaying the Confirm Classes dialog box. (See Figure 10.8.)

The Confirm Classes dialog box displays the names of the classes that Visual C++ will add to the MyPic project in order to add the BMP ActiveX control.

☐ Click the OK button of the Confirm Classes dialog box.

Visual C++ responds by adding the BMP ActiveX control to the MyPic project and by redisplaying the Components and Controls Gallery dialog box.

☐ Click the Close button of the Components and Controls Gallery dialog box.

10

Figure 10.8.

The Confirm Classes
dialog box.

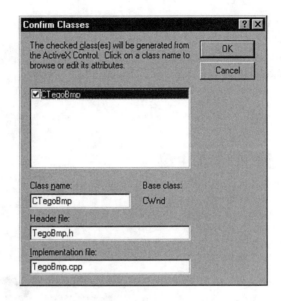

That's it! You completed adding the BMP ActiveX control to the MyPic project. From now on, you can use the BMP ActiveX control in the MyPic project just as you use standard Visual C++ controls. That is, you can place the BMP ActiveX control in the IDD_MYPIC_DIALOG box, you can set the properties of the BMP ActiveX control, and you can attach code to the events of the BMP ActiveX control.

Take a look at your Controls toolbar. As shown in Figure 10.9, your Controls toolbar now contains the tool of the BMP ActiveX control.

NOTE

If you don't see the Controls toolbar on your Visual C++ desktop, select Customize from the Tools menu, select the Toolbars tab of the Customize dialog box, and place a check mark in the Controls check box.

You'll now place a BMP ActiveX control in the IDD_MYPIC_DIALOG dialog box:

☐ Click the tool of the BMP ActiveX control in the Controls toolbar and then click in the IDD_MYPIC_DIALOG dialog box.

The Missing License dialog box appears. (See Figure 10.10.)

Figure 10.9.

The tool of the BMP ActiveX control in the Controls toolbar.

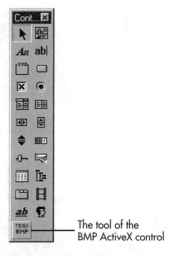

The tool of the BMP ActiveX control

Figure 10.10.

The Missing License dialog box of the BMP ActiveX control.

NOTE

The Missing License dialog box serves as a reminder that you are using the Learning Edition of the BMP ActiveX control. This means that you can use the BMP ActiveX control for learning purposes only. You are not allowed to distribute the control to others, and you are not allowed to incorporate this ActiveX control in your HTML pages. To learn how to obtain the Professional Licensed edition of the BMP ActiveX control and other powerful ActiveX controls, you can visit the TegoSoft Web site at http://www.tegosoft.com.

10

☐ Click the OK button of the Missing License dialog box.

Visual C++ responds by placing the BMP ActiveX control in the IDD_MYPIC_DIALOG dialog box at the point where you clicked the mouse. (See Figure 10.11.)

NOTE Remember, for your convenience, you can display the IDD_MYPIC_DIALOG dialog box in full-screen mode by selecting Full Screen from the View menu. To cancel the full-screen mode, press the Esc key.

Figure 10.11.
The BMP ActiveX control in the IDD_MYPIC_DIALOG dialog box.

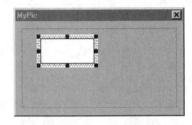

10

You can now treat the BMP ActiveX control just as you treat a standard Visual C++ control. You can drag it with the mouse to move it, you can size it by dragging its handles, and you can set its properties by right-clicking the control and selecting Properties from the pop-up menu.

☐ Design the IDD_MYPIC_DIALOG dialog box according to Table 10.1. When you finish, it should look like the one in Figure 10.12.

Table 10.1. The properties table of the IDD_MYPIC_DIALOG dialog box.

Object	Property	Setting
Dialog Box	**ID**	**IDD_MYPIC_DIALOG**
	Caption	The MyPic Program
	Font	System, size 10
	Border	Resizing (Styles tab)
	Minimize box	Checked (Styles tab)
	Maximize box	Checked (Styles tab)
BMP Control	**ID**	**IDC_BMP_CONTROL**

Figure 10.12.
The
IDD_MYPIC_DIALOG
dialog box in design
mode.

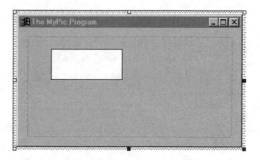

NOTE

Table 10.1 specifies setting the Border property of the dialog box to Resizing. The Border list box is in the Styles tab of IDD_MYPIC_DIALOG's Properties window. Setting the Border property to Resizing enables you to enlarge or shrink the program's window by dragging its edges during runtime.

The Maximize and Minimize check boxes in the Styles tab should also be checked so that the IDD_MYPIC_DIALOG dialog box can be maximized and minimized during runtime.

Table 10.1 specifies to set the ID property of the BMP ActiveX control to IDC_BMP_CONTROL. Besides the ID property, the BMP ActiveX control has other properties that you can set. However, in the MyPic program, you will set these other properties from within your code.

The Visual Design of the Menu

You'll now visually design the menu of the MyPic program:

☐ In the Project Workspace window, select the ResourceView tab and right-click the MyPic resources item.

Visual C++ responds by displaying a pop-up menu.

☐ Select Insert from the menu.

Visual C++ responds by displaying the Insert Resource dialog box.

☐ Select the Menu item from the Insert Resource dialog box, then click the New button.

Visual C++ responds by displaying an empty menu in design mode.

10

☐ Customize the menu as shown in Figures 10.13 and 10.14. As shown in Figures 10.13 and 10.14, you have to add the Open BMP and Exit items to the File menu and the About item to the Help menu.

Figure 10.13.

The File menu of the MyPic program.

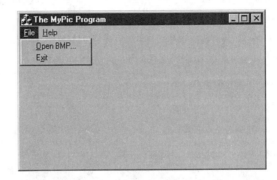

Figure 10.14.

The Help menu of the MyPic program.

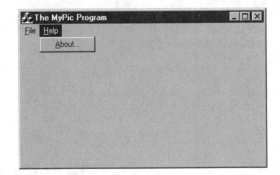

The default ID that Visual C++ assigns to the new menu is IDR_MENU1. Change the ID to IDR_MYPIC_MENU:

☐ Set the ID property of the menu to `IDR_MYPIC_MENU` by right-clicking the IDR_MENU1 item in the Project Workspace window, selecting Properties, then setting the ID property in the Properties window that pops up.

Next, you have to associate the menu with the `CMyPicDlg` class. Here is how you do that:

☐ While the menu window is selected, select ClassWizard from the View menu.

Visual C++ responds by displaying the Adding a Class dialog box.

☐ Make sure that the "Select an existing class" radio button is selected, then click the OK button.

Visual C++ responds by displaying the Select Class dialog box.

☐ Select the CMyPicDlg item, then click the Select button.

Visual C++ responds by displaying the MFC ClassWizard dialog box.

☐ Click the OK button of the MFC ClassWizard dialog box.

Attaching the Menu to the Dialog Box

You'll now attach the IDR_MYPIC_MENU menu to the IDD_MYPIC_DIALOG dialog box:

☐ Double-click the IDD_MYPIC_DIALOG item in the Project Workspace window.

Visual C++ responds by displaying IDD_MYPIC_DIALOG in design mode.

☐ Set the Menu property (in the General tab) of IDD_MYPIC_DIALOG to IDR_MYPIC_MENU. (To display the Properties window, right-click a free area of the dialog box and select Properties from the menu that pops up.)

You've finished the visual design of the IDD_MYPIC_DIALOG dialog box and the visual design of the program's menu. To see your design in action, follow these steps:

☐ Select Build MyPic.EXE from the Build menu.

☐ Select Execute MyPic.EXE from the Build menu.

Visual C++ responds by executing the MyPic.EXE program. The main window of MyPic.EXE appears, as shown in Figure 10.15.

Figure 10.15.

The main window of the MyPic.EXE program.

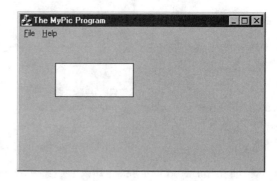

As you can see, the main window of the MyPic.EXE program (the IDD_MYPIC_DIALOG dialog box) looks just as you designed it. It has a blank BMP ActiveX control in it, and it has a menu bar with two menus: File and Help.

☐ Experiment with the MyPic.EXE program and make sure that the File and Help menus look as shown in Figures 10.13 and 10.14.

10

☐ Terminate the MyPic.EXE program by clicking the × icon at the upper-right corner of the program's window.

Attaching a Variable to the BMP ActiveX Control

You'll now attach a variable to the BMP control, so you can use the variable later to write code that accesses the properties of the BMP control. Follow these steps to attach a variable to the IDC_BMP_CONTROL control:

☐ Select ClassWizard from the View menu.

Visual C++ responds by displaying the MFC ClassWizard dialog box.

☐ Select the Member Variables tab of the MFC ClassWizard dialog box. (See Figure 10.16.)

Figure 10.16.

Selecting the Member Variables tab of ClassWizard.

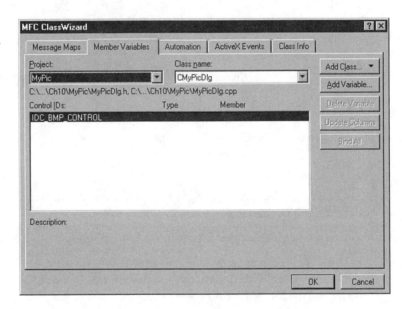

☐ Make sure that the Class name list box is set to CMyPicDlg.

The CMyPicDlg class is associated with the IDD_MYPIC_DIALOG dialog box (the main window of the MyPic program). Because you're going to attach a variable to a control in the IDD_MYPIC_DIALOG dialog box, the Class name list box should be set to CMyPicDlg. As a result, the variable that you'll attach to the control will be a data member of the CMyPicDlg class.

☐ Select IDC_BMP_CONTROL in the Object IDs list to attach a variable to the IDC_BMP_CONTROL control, then click the Add Variable button.

Visual C++ responds by displaying the Add Member Variable dialog box shown in Figure 10.17.

Figure 10.17.

The Add Member Variable dialog box.

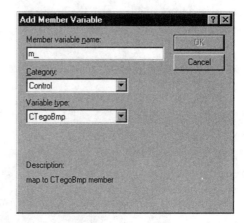

☐ Set the Add Member Variable dialog box as follows:

Member variable name:	`m_bmp`
Category:	`Control`
Variable type:	`CTegoBmp`

☐ Click the OK button of the Add Member Variable dialog box, then click the OK button of the ClassWizard dialog box.

You've finished attaching a variable to the IDC_BMP_CONTROL control!

Putting it all together, you have attached a variable of type `CTegoBmp` to the IDC_BMP_CONTROL control and named it `m_bmp`. In the following sections, you'll write the code of the MyPic.EXE program and use the `m_bmp` variable to access the properties of the BMP control.

Writing the Code That Initializes the Size of the BMP Control

As shown in Figure 10.15, currently when the MyPic.EXE program starts, the BMP control appears in the program's window at the same size and location as it was when you visually designed the IDD_MYPIC_DIALOG dialog box.

You'll now write initialization code that sets the location and size of the BMP control so that it would fit exactly in the program's window. This way, upon starting the program, the BMP control will be exactly the same size as the program's window. You'll attach this initialization code to the WM_INITDIALOG event of the IDD_MYPIC_DIALOG dialog box (because the WM_INITDIALOG event occurs upon starting the program).

Follow these steps to attach code to the WM_INITDIALOG event of the IDD_MYPIC_DIALOG dialog box:

☐ Select ClassWizard from the View menu, select the Message Maps tab, and use the ClassWizard dialog box to select the following event:

Class name:	CMyPicDlg
Object ID:	CMyPicDlg
Message:	WM_INITDIALOG

Your MFC ClassWizard dialog box should now look like the one shown in Figure 10.18.

Figure 10.18.

Selecting the WM_INITDIALOG event.

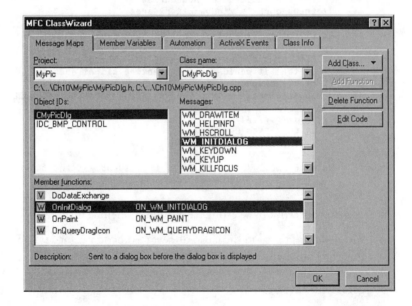

☐ Click the Edit Code button of ClassWizard.

Visual C++ responds by opening the file MyPicDlg.cpp with the function OnInitDialog() *ready for you to edit. Remember, you can view and edit code in full-screen mode (select Full Screen from the View menu and press Esc to cancel the full-screen mode).*

The OnInitDialog() function already has some code written by Visual C++. You'll type your own code below this comment line:

```
// TODO: Add extra initialization here
```

☐ Write the following code in the OnInitDialog() function:

```
BOOL CMyPicDlg::OnInitDialog()
{
CDialog::OnInitDialog();
...
...
...

// TODO: Add extra initialization here

/////////////////////////
// MY CODE STARTS HERE
/////////////////////////

// Get the rectangular boundaries of
// the program's window client area.
CRect rect;
GetClientRect(&rect);

// Set the position and size of the BMP control
// so that it would cover the entire client area
// of the program's window.
m_bmp.SetWindowPos(NULL,0,0,rect.right,rect.bottom,NULL);

/////////////////////////
// MY CODE ENDS HERE
/////////////////////////

return TRUE;   // return TRUE  unless you set the focus
               // to a control
}
```

☐ Save your work by selecting Save All from the File menu.

The code you typed in the OnInitDialog() function is made up of three statements. The following are the first two statements:

```
CRect rect;
GetClientRect(&rect);
```

The first statement declares an object of class CRect called rect:

```
CRect rect;
```

The CRect class is used for storing the coordinates and size of rectangles. The second statement uses the GetClientRect() function to store the rectangular area of the program's client area in the rect object:

```
GetClientRect(&rect);
```

The client area of the program's window is the area of the window where you can display the bitmap. For example, the menu bar area is not part of the client area. So at this point, the rect object holds the rectangular area of the program's window client area. In particular, the right data member of rect (rect.right) holds the width of the program's client area, and the data member bottom (rect.bottom) holds the height of the program's client area.

Finally, the last statement that you typed in the OnInitDialog() function uses the SetWindowPos() function to set the size and coordinates of the IDC_BMP_CONTROL control to be the same as the rectangular area of the program's window:

```
m_bmp.SetWindowPos(NULL,0,0,rect.right,rect.bottom,NULL);
```

The preceding statement executes the SetWindowPos() function on the m_bmp variable you attached to the IDC_BMP_CONTROL control. The SetWindowPos() function sets the coordinates of the control according to the second, third, fourth, and fifth parameters of the function. The second and third parameters specify the x and y coordinates of the top-left corner of the control. In the preceding statement, the second and third parameters are both 0 because you want the top-left corner of the control to be at the top-left corner of the program's window. The fourth and fifth parameters specify the width and height of the control. In the preceding statement, the fourth parameter is set to rect.right and the fifth parameter is set to rect.bottom. As discussed earlier, rect.right holds the width of the program's client area, and rect.bottom holds the height of the program's client area.

Because the OnInitDialog() function is automatically executed whenever the program starts, from now on, upon starting the program, the BMP control will cover the entire client area of the program's window.

To see the initialization code you typed in the OnInitDialog() function in action, follow these steps:

☐ Select Build MyPic.EXE from the Build menu.

☐ Select Execute MyPic.EXE from the Build menu.

> *Visual C++ responds by executing the MyPic.EXE program. As expected, now the BMP control covers the entire client area of the program's window. (See Figure 10.19.)*

So as you have just verified, upon starting the program, the BMP control covers the entire client area of the program's window. However, if you now change the size of the program's window, the BMP control will not resize itself to the new window size. To see this, try the following:

☐ Increase the width of the program's window by dragging the right edge of the program's window toward the right. (See Figure 10.20.)

10

Figure 10.19.

The BMP control now covers the entire client area of the program's window.

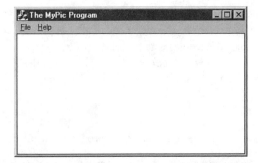

Figure 10.20.

Increasing the program's window width.

As you can see, after increasing the program's window width, the BMP control remains at its original width. In the following section, you'll write code so that whenever the program's window size is changed, the BMP control will be automatically resized to the new window's size.

☐ Terminate the MyPic.EXE program by clicking the × icon at the upper-right corner of the program's window.

Attaching Code to the WM_SIZE Event of the IDD_MYPIC_DIALOG Dialog Box

As shown in Figure 10.20, currently after the program's window is resized, the BMP control remains at its original size.

You'll now write code that is responsible for automatically resizing the BMP control to the new window size. You'll attach this code to the WM_SIZE event of the IDD_MYPIC_DIALOG dialog box (because the WM_SIZE event occurs whenever the program's window is resized).

Follow these steps to attach code to the WM_SIZE event of the IDD_MYPIC_DIALOG dialog box:

☐ Select ClassWizard from the View menu, select the Message Maps tab, and use the ClassWizard dialog box to select the following event:

Class name:	CMyPicDlg
Object ID:	CMyPicDlg
Message:	WM_SIZE

Your MFC ClassWizard dialog box should now look like the one shown in Figure 10.21.

Figure 10.21.

Selecting the WM_SIZE *event.*

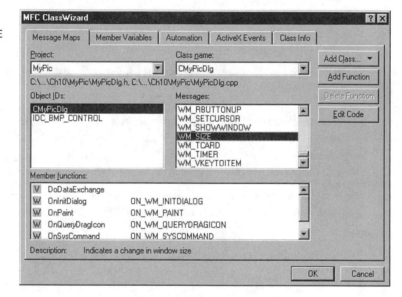

☐ Click the Add Function button.

Visual C++ responds by adding the OnSize() *function.*

☐ Click the Edit Code button of ClassWizard.

Visual C++ responds by opening the file MyPicDlg.cpp with the function OnSize() *ready for you to edit. Remember, you can view and edit code in full-screen mode (select Full Screen from the View menu and press Esc to cancel the full-screen mode).*

☐ Write the following code in the OnSize() function:

```
BOOL CMyPicDlg::OnSize(UINT nType, int cx, int cy)
{
CDialog::OnSize(nType, cx, cy);

// TODO: Add your message handler code here
```

```
/////////////////////////
// MY CODE STARTS HERE
/////////////////////////

// Set the size of the BMP control to the
// new size of the program's window.
m_bmp.SetWindowPos(NULL,0,0,cx,cy,NULL);

/////////////////////////
// MY CODE ENDS HERE
/////////////////////////

}
```

☐ Save your work by selecting Save All from the File menu.

The code you typed in the OnInitDialog() function is made up of a single statement:

```
m_bmp.SetWindowPos(NULL,0,0,cx,cy,NULL);
```

This statement executes the SetWindowPos() function on the BMP control to set the size of the control to the new size of the program's window. The new size of the program's window is provided by the parameters cx and cy of the OnSize() function. That's why in the preceding statement, the fourth and fifth parameters of SetWindowPos() are cx and cy.

Because the OnSize() function is automatically executed whenever the program's window size is changed, from now on, whenever the program's window is resized, the BMP control size will be resized according to the new size of the program's window.

To see the code you typed in the OnSize() function in action, follow these steps:

☐ Select Build MyPic.EXE from the Build menu.

☐ Select Execute MyPic.EXE from the Build menu.

   Visual C++ responds by executing the MyPic.EXE program.

☐ Increase the width of the program's window by dragging the right edge of the program's window towards the right.

As you can see, the size of the BMP control adjusts itself to the new size of the program's window. The code that you wrote in the OnSize() function is working!

☐ Terminate the MyPic.EXE program by clicking the × icon at the upper-right corner of the program's window.

Attaching Code to the Exit Menu Item

You'll now attach code to the COMMAND event of the Exit menu item:

☐ Highlight the IDR_MYPIC_MENU item in the Project Workspace window, then select ClassWizard from the View menu.

   Visual C++ responds by displaying the MFC ClassWizard dialog box.

☐ Select ID_FILE_EXIT in the Object IDs list, select COMMAND in the Message list, then click the Add Function button.

   Visual C++ responds by suggesting OnFileExit *as the new function's name.*

☐ Accept OnFileExit as the name of the new function, then click the Edit Code button.

☐ Enter code in the OnFileExit() function (in the MyPicDlg.cpp file) as follows:

```
void CMyPicDlg::OnFileExit()
{
// TODO: Add your command handler code here

/////////////////////////
// MY CODE STARTS HERE
/////////////////////////

OnOK();

/////////////////////////
// MY CODE ENDS HERE
/////////////////////////


}
```

This code, which terminates the MyPic program, is executed whenever you select Exit from the File menu.

☐ Save your work.

☐ Build and execute MyPic.EXE to make sure the Exit menu item works as expected.

Attaching Code to the About Menu Item

You'll now add the code that's executed when you select the About item from the Help menu:

☐ Select the IDR_MYPIC_MENU item in the Project Workspace window.

☐ Select ClassWizard from the View menu.

10

☐ Select the ID_HELP_ABOUT item from the Object IDs list, select COMMAND in the Messages list, then click the Add Function button.

   Visual C++ responds by suggesting OnHelpAbout *as the new function's name.*

☐ Accept the function name that Visual C++ suggests, then click the Edit Code button.

☐ Enter code in the OnHelpAbout() function as follows:

```
void CMyPicDlg::OnHelpAbout()
{
// TODO: Add your command handler code here

/////////////////////////
// MY CODE STARTS HERE
/////////////////////////

CAboutDlg dlg;
dlg.DoModal();

/////////////////////////
// MY CODE ENDS HERE
/////////////////////////


}
```

This code creates an object dlg of class CAboutDlg, the class associated with the About dialog box IDD_ABOUTBOX:

```
CAboutDlg dlg;
```

Then the About dialog box is displayed as a modal dialog box:

```
dlg.DoModal();
```

☐ Save your work.

☐ Build and execute the program to make sure the About dialog box is displayed when you select the About item from the Help menu.

☐ Experiment with the program, then select Exit from the File menu to terminate the MyPic program.

Attaching Code to the Open Menu Item

You'll now attach code to the Open menu item of the File menu. This code will let the user select a BMP file from the hard drive and then display the selected BMP file in the BMP control.

☐ Highlight the IDR_MYPIC_MENU item in the Project Workspace window, then select ClassWizard from the View menu.

Visual C++ responds by displaying the MFC ClassWizard dialog box.

☐ Select ID_FILE_OPENBMP in the Object IDs list, select COMMAND in the Message list, then click the Add Function button.

Visual C++ responds by suggesting OnFileOpenbmp *as the new function's name.*

☐ Accept OnFileOpenbmp as the name of the new function, then click the Edit Code button.

☐ Enter code in the OnFileOpenbmp() function as follows:

```
void CMyPicDlg::OnFileOpenbmp()
{
// TODO: Add your command handler code here

/////////////////////////////
// MY CODE STARTS HERE
/////////////////////////////

m_bmp.SetBmpFilename("C:\\Movie.BMP");

/////////////////////////////
// MY CODE ENDS HERE
/////////////////////////////

}
```

☐ Save your work.

The code you typed uses the SetBmpFilename() function of the BMP ActiveX control to display the BMP file C:\Movie.BMP in the BMP control:

```
m_bmp.SetBmpFilename("C:\\Movie.BMP");
```

The SetBmpFilename() function of the BMP ActiveX control is responsible for loading the specified BMP file from the hard drive and displaying the BMP file in the BMP control. As you can see, the SetBmpFilename() function is very simple to use—it has a single parameter that contains the name and path of the BMP file you want to display. In the preceding statement, the parameter you supplied specifies the Movie.BMP file from the root directory of your C: drive, so in the following steps you'll use the Paint program of Windows to draw a picture and save it as Movie.BMP in the C:\ directory.

NOTE

Don't forget to use the two backslash characters (\\) required by C/C++ when specifying the path of a file:

```
m_bmp.SetBmpFilename("C:\\Movie.BMP");
```

If you use only one backslash, the function will not find the BMP file.

Follow these steps to draw the Movie.BMP picture:

☐ Execute the Windows Paint program in the Accessories folder.

☐ Select Attributes from Paint's Image menu.

Paint responds by displaying the Attributes dialog box.

☐ Set the Width box to 250 pixels and the Height box to 90 pixels. Finally, click the OK button of the Attributes dialog box.

Paint responds by displaying an empty area (250 pixels × 90 pixels) ready for you to paint.

☐ Draw something with Paint. (See Figure 10.22 for an example; this image shows how you can import clip-art to enhance your program.)

Figure 10.22.

Using the Paint program.

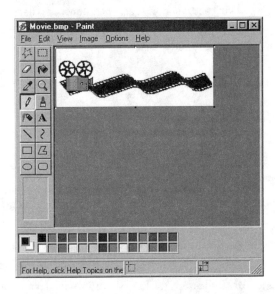

☐ Select Save As from Paint's File menu and save your drawing as a BMP file with the filename Movie.BMP in the C:\ directory (in the root directory of C:).

☐ Terminate the Paint program.

To see the code that you attached to the Open menu item in action, follow these steps:

☐ Build and execute the MyPic.EXE program.

☐ Select Open from the File menu.

The window of the MyPic program appears with the picture of the C:\Movie.BMP file in it. (See Figure 10.23.)

Figure 10.23.
*The Movie.BMP
picture displayed in
the program's
window.*

☐ Use the mouse to enlarge MyPic's window by dragging its edges.

*As you enlarge MyPic's window, the BMP picture is enlarged accordingly. (See Figures
10.24 and 10.25.)*

10

Figure 10.24.
*Enlarging MyPic's
window to enlarge the
BMP picture.*

Figure 10.25.
*Shrinking MyPic's
window to shrink the
BMP picture.*

☐ Experiment with the MyPic program, then select Exit from the File menu to terminate the program.

Loading and Displaying a BMP Picture During Runtime

The code you typed in the OnFileOpenbmp() function loads and displays the C:\Movie.BMP file as follows:

```
m_bmp.SetBmpFilename("C:\\Movie.BMP");
```

The BMP filename is *hard-coded* (specified in the program's code). You'll now add code that does the following: When you select Open BMP from MyPic's File menu, an Open BMP File dialog box appears. You can then select the BMP picture from the hard drive, and the MyPic program will display it.

☐ Modify the code in the OnFileOpenbmp() function (in the MyPicDlg.cpp file) as follows:

```
void CMyPicDlg::OnFileOpenbmp()
{
// TODO: Add your command handler code here

/////////////////////////////
// MY CODE STARTS HERE
/////////////////////////////

char FileName[500];
char FileTitle[100];

OPENFILENAME ofn;
memset(&ofn, 0, sizeof(ofn));
ofn.lStructSize = sizeof(OPENFILENAME);
ofn.hwndOwner=NULL;
ofn.hInstance =NULL;

ofn.lpstrFilter  =
TEXT("Bitmap picture files *.bmp\0*.bmp\0All Files *.*\0*.*\0\0");

ofn.lpstrCustomFilter = NULL;
ofn.nMaxCustFilter = 0;
ofn.nFilterIndex = 1;
ofn.lpstrFile = FileName;
ofn.nMaxFile = 500;
ofn.lpstrFileTitle = FileTitle;
ofn.nMaxFileTitle = 99;
ofn.lpstrInitialDir = NULL;
ofn.lpstrTitle = "Open BMP File";
ofn.Flags = OFN_FILEMUSTEXIST;
ofn.lpstrDefExt = "BMP";
ofn.lCustData =NULL;
ofn.lpfnHook = NULL;
ofn.lpTemplateName =NULL;
```

10

```
FileName[0]='\0';

GetOpenFileName(&ofn);

if (FileName[0]=='\0')
{
return;
}

m_bmp.SetBmpFilename(FileName);

/////////////////////////
// MY CODE ENDS HERE
/////////////////////////

}
```

The code you typed declares two variables:

```
char FileName[500];
char FileTitle[100];
```

The FileName variable is declared as a string that can contain a maximum of 500 characters; FileTitle is declared as a string that can contain a maximum of 100 characters. FileName will store the filename and path of the selected BMP file, and FileTitle will store the filename of the loaded BMP file without the path.

Next, the ofn structure of type OPENFILENAME is declared:

```
OPENFILENAME ofn;
```

The OPENFILENAME structure has various structure members. The next block of code sets the values of the data members of the ofn structure.

The FileName string is set to null:

```
FileName[0]='\0';
```

Then the GetOpenFileName() function is executed:

```
GetOpenFileName(&ofn);
```

GetOpenFileName() displays a common dialog box. Note that it has a single parameter. Previously, you set the values of the data members of the ofn structure, so the GetOpenFileName() function will display the common dialog box according to the setting of the ofn structure.

When you set the values of the data members of the ofn structure, you set the lpstrFile data member to FileName as follows:

```
ofn.lpstrFile = FileName;
```

The preceding statement means that GetOpenFileName() will fill the FileName string with the path and filename of the selected file.

An `if` statement is then executed to examine the value of `FileName`:

```
if (FileName[0]=='\0')
{
return;
}
```

If you don't select a file when the common dialog box is displayed, the `FileName` variable is not modified by the `GetOpenFileName()` function. In this case, the code under the `if` statement will be executed, which terminates the `OnFileOpenbmp()` function. If you do select a file, the `FileName` variable is updated with the path and filename of the selected file, and the code under the `if` statement is not executed.

At this point in the program, the `FileName` variable stores the filename and path of the BMP file that was selected. So you can actually load and display the selected BMP file as follows:

```
m_bmp.SetBmpFilename(FileName);
```

That is, now the parameter of the `SetBmpFilename()` function is set to the variable `FileName`.

NOTE

The `GetOpenFileName()` function simply lets the user select a file from the hard drive; it doesn't actually load the selected file. To load and display the selected file, use the `SetBmpFilename()` function of the BMP ActiveX control as follows:

```
m_bmp.SetBmpFilename(FileName);
```

where *FileName* is the name of the string variable that holds the filename of the BMP file to be displayed.

☐ Save your work, then build and execute the MyPic program.

☐ Select Open BMP from the File menu.

MyPic responds by displaying the dialog box shown in Figure 10.26.

The dialog box shown in Figure 10.26 is displayed according to the parameter you supplied to the `GetOpenFileName()` function—namely, the setting of the `ofn` data structure.

☐ Select a BMP file with the dialog box, then click the Open button.

MyPic responds by loading and displaying the selected BMP file.

☐ Experiment with the MyPic program, then terminate it.

Figure 10.26.
The Open BMP File dialog box.

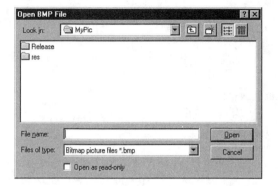

NOTE

There's something wrong with the MyPic program! Can you tell what it is? Try the following:

☐ Select Open BMP from the File menu of MyPic.

MyPic responds by displaying the Open BMP File dialog box.

☐ While the dialog box is displayed, select Open BMP from the File menu again.

Oops! Another Open BMP File dialog box appears! The Exercise at the end of this chapter shows how this problem can be easily fixed.

☐ Close the two Open BMP File dialog boxes and then terminate the MyPic.EXE program.

Changing the Window's Caption

Currently, the caption of the MyPic window is The MyPic Program. (See, for example, Figure 10.24.) You'll now add code that displays the name of the loaded file in the window's caption.

☐ Add the following statement at the end of the OnFileOpenbmp() function (in the MyPicDlg.cpp file):

```
SetWindowText(FileTitle);
```

After adding this statement, the OnFileOpenbmp() function looks as follows:

```
void CMyPicDlg::OnFileOpenbmp()
{
// TODO: Add your command handler code here
```

```
/////////////////////////
// MY CODE STARTS HERE
/////////////////////////

char FileName[500];
char FileTitle[100];

OPENFILENAME ofn;
memset(&ofn, 0, sizeof(ofn));
ofn.lStructSize = sizeof(OPENFILENAME);
ofn.hwndOwner=NULL;
ofn.hInstance =NULL;

ofn.lpstrFilter  =
TEXT("Bitmap picture files *.bmp\0*.bmp\0All Files *.*\0*.*\0\0");

ofn.lpstrCustomFilter = NULL;
ofn.nMaxCustFilter = 0;
ofn.nFilterIndex = 1;
ofn.lpstrFile = FileName;
ofn.nMaxFile = 500;
ofn.lpstrFileTitle = FileTitle;
ofn.nMaxFileTitle = 99;
ofn.lpstrInitialDir = NULL;
ofn.lpstrTitle = "Open BMP File";
ofn.Flags = OFN_FILEMUSTEXIST;
ofn.lpstrDefExt = "BMP";
ofn.lCustData =NULL;
ofn.lpfnHook = NULL;
ofn.lpTemplateName =NULL;

FileName[0]='\0';

GetOpenFileName(&ofn);

if (FileName[0]=='\0')
{
return;
}

m_bmp.SetBmpFilename(FileName);

SetWindowText(FileTitle);

/////////////////////////
// MY CODE ENDS HERE
/////////////////////////

}
```

You set the caption of the window as follows:

```
SetWindowText(FileTitle);
```

The GetOpenFileName() function updates the FileTitle variable with the filename (without the path) of the selected file. You supplied FileTitle as the parameter of the SetWindowText() function.

☐ Save your work, then build and execute the MyPic program.

☐ Select Open BMP from the File menu.

MyPic responds by displaying the Open dialog box that lets you select a file.

☐ Select a BMP file with the common dialog box, then click the Open button.

MyPic responds by loading and displaying the selected BMP file. However, now the caption of MyPic's window shows the name of the loaded file. (See Figure 10.27.)

Figure 10.27.
The window's caption displays the name of the displayed file.

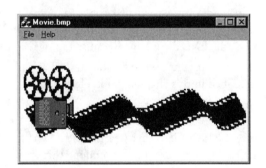

☐ Experiment with the MyPic program, then terminate it.

Summary

In this chapter, you learned how to load and display BMP pictures during runtime. You can select any file from the hard drive and display the picture during the program's execution.

While creating the MyPic program, you learned how to use the GetOpenFileName() function to set up a common dialog box for selecting a file from the hard drive. You also learned how to set the caption of the window to the name of the selected file.

Q&A

Q In this chapter I wrote a program that uses the BMP ActiveX control to open and display BMP files. Is it possible to use the BMP ActiveX control for writing a program that performs animation?

A Yes. The BMP ActiveX control has additional functions that enable you to write a program that displays an animation show. In Chapter 21, "Sound, Animation, and

DirectX," you'll learn how to use the BMP ActiveX control for writing a program that displays an animation show. The animation program of Chapter 21 displays an animation show that is synchronized with sound.

Q Writing a program as described in this chapter means I supply the program file as well as the BMP files to my end-user. Can I create a program with the BMP file embedded in the EXE program file?

A Yes. The MyBMP.EXE program you created in Chapter 8 is an example of a program in which the BMP file is an integral part of the EXE program file.

Q In Chapter 8, I learned how to create a program with an embedded BMP file. In this chapter, the BMP file wasn't embedded in the EXE file. Which method is better?

A It depends on the particular application you're developing. Naturally, if you embed the BMP file in your EXE file, the user can't load whatever file he or she wants. Also, the EXE file is larger because the BMP file is added.

If you want your user to be able to load any file he or she wants, the technique described in this chapter is suitable.

In general, if you want to display a certain BMP picture in your application without letting the user choose the BMP file, it is better to embed the BMP file into the EXE file. Why? Because the BMP file will never be separated from the EXE file. If you use the technique in this chapter, you'll have to give your user the BMP file as well as the EXE file. You then run the risk of the user losing the BMP file or accidentally deleting or altering it.

Quiz

When specifying a path of a file in C/C++, you must use two backslash characters (\\), as in the following statement:

```
C:\\MyDir\\MyFile.TXT
```

   a. True

   b. False

Exercise

Currently, if the user selects Open BMP from MyPic's File menu, the Open BMP File dialog box is displayed. If the user again selects Open BMP from the File menu, another Open BMP File dialog box is displayed. Now there are two dialog boxes onscreen.

Modify the program so that the user can't open more than one dialog box at any given time. (To perform this exercise, follow the steps outlined in the solution of this exercise.)

Quiz Answer

    a. True

Exercise Answer

Follow these steps to solve the exercise:

☐ Modify the OnFileOpenbmp() function (in the MyPicDlg.cpp file) as follows:

```
void CMyPicDlg::OnFileOpenbmp()
{
// TODO: Add your command handler code here

/////////////////////////////
// MY CODE STARTS HERE
/////////////////////////////

char FileName[500];
char FileTitle[100];


OPENFILENAME ofn;
memset(&ofn, 0, sizeof(ofn));
ofn.lStructSize = sizeof(OPENFILENAME);

//ofn.hwndOwner=NULL;

ofn.hwndOwner=m_hWnd;

ofn.hInstance =NULL;

ofn.lpstrFilter =
TEXT("Bitmap picture files *.bmp\0*.bmp\0All Files *.*\0*.*\0\0");

ofn.lpstrCustomFilter = NULL;
ofn.nMaxCustFilter = 0;
ofn.nFilterIndex = 1;
ofn.lpstrFile = FileName;
ofn.nMaxFile = 500;
ofn.lpstrFileTitle = FileTitle;
ofn.nMaxFileTitle = 99;
ofn.lpstrInitialDir = NULL;
ofn.lpstrTitle = "Open BMP File";
ofn.Flags = OFN_FILEMUSTEXIST;
ofn.lpstrDefExt = "BMP";
ofn.lCustData =NULL;
```

10

```
ofn.lpfnHook = NULL;
ofn.lpTemplateName =NULL;

FileName[0]='\0';

GetOpenFileName(&ofn);

if (FileName[0]=='\0')
{
return;
}

m_bmp.SetBmpFilename(FileName);

SetWindowText(FileTitle);

/////////////////////////////
// MY CODE ENDS HERE
/////////////////////////////

}
```

The code you typed comments out this statement:

```
//ofn.hwndOwner=NULL;
```

Instead, the following statement is used:

```
ofn.hwndOwner=m_hWnd;
```

In other words, the structure member hwndOwner of the ofn structure is updated with the value of the m_hWnd data member of the CMyPicDlg class. Therefore, the dialog box displayed by GetOpenFileName() is displayed so that the IDD_MYPIC_DIALOG dialog box is the "owner" of the common dialog box.

☐ Save your work, then build and execute the MyPic program.

☐ Select Open BMP from MyPic's File menu. While the Open BMP File dialog box is displayed, try to click in the main window of the MyPic program.

As you can see, you cannot switch to the main window of the MyPic program while the dialog box is displayed.

Day 11

Writing Single-Document Interface (SDI) Applications

In this chapter, you'll learn what a single-document interface application is and how to create one with Visual C++.

What Is an SDI Application?

As its name implies, a *single-document interface* (SDI) application lets you work with a single document. The document is where the program's data is stored. The program allows you to save the document into a file and open previously saved documents from files. For example, in a text editor SDI program, the document you work on is text. You can save text into text files and load text from previously saved text files. Similarly, in a sound editor SDI program, you can save sound into sound files and load sound from previously saved sound files.

In an SDI program, you can work on only one document at any time; you can't open several documents simultaneously. An example of an SDI program is the Notepad program shipped with Windows. You can view and edit text files with Notepad. However, you can view and edit only one file at a time, not several files simultaneously. Figure 11.1 shows the Notepad program with an open file.

Figure 11.1.

The Windows Notepad program (an SDI program).

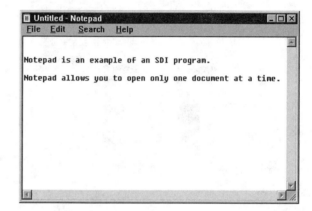

A multiple-document interface (MDI) program also works with documents, but you can work on several documents simultaneously. An example of an MDI program is the Word for Windows program. Chapter 13, "Writing Multiple-Document Interface (MDI) Applications," will cover this topic in more detail.

The Circle.EXE Program

In this chapter, you'll write a Visual C++ program called Circle.EXE, an example of an SDI program. Before you start writing the Circle program, let's first specify what it should look like and what it should do:

- When you start the Circle program, its window should display a circle in the middle. (See Figure 11.2.)

- The Circle program is a simple SDI program; its document is a circle. You can place the circle anywhere in the window and then save the circle into a file. Later, you can open the previously saved file, and the circle will appear onscreen.

- You can draw a circle anywhere in Circle's window by simply clicking the mouse at the desired point. Figure 11.3 shows the window of the Circle program after clicking the mouse at the upper-right corner of the program's window.

Figure 11.2.

The main window of the Circle program.

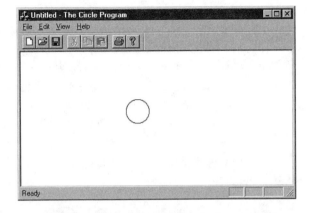

Figure 11.3.

Drawing a circle at the upper-right corner of the window.

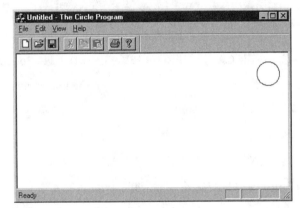

■ You can save the circle into a file by selecting Save (or Save As) from the File menu of the Circle program. (See Figure 11.4.)

Figure 11.4.

The File menu of the Circle program.

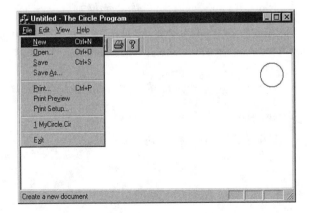

■ You can load a previously saved circle by selecting Open from the File menu of the Circle program. Once you select Open from the File menu, the Circle program displays an Open dialog box for selecting the saved file.

■ You can print the currently displayed circle by selecting Print from the File menu.

■ The Circle program includes a toolbar displayed at the top of the program's window. Click the desired tool on the toolbar to perform the operation you want. For example, clicking the Save tool (the one with a disk icon) is equivalent to selecting Save from the File menu.

Now that you know what the Circle program should do, let's start by creating the project of the Circle program.

Creating the Project of the Circle Program

Follow these steps to create the project and skeleton files of the Circle program:

☐ Create the C:\TYVCPROG\PROGRAMS\CH11 directory.

☐ Start Visual C++ and select New from the File menu.

Visual C++ responds by displaying the New dialog box.

☐ Select the Projects tab of the New dialog box.

☐ Select MFC AppWizard(exe) from the list of project types.

☐ Type Circle in the Project Name box.

☐ Click the button that is located on the right of the Location box and select the C:\TYVCPROG\PROGRAMS\CH11 directory.

☐ Click the OK button.

Visual C++ responds by displaying the MFC AppWizard - Step 1 window.

☐ Set the Step 1 window as shown in Figure 11.5 to create a single-document–type application, then click the Next button. Note that the "Single document" radio button is selected.

Visual C++ responds by displaying the MFC AppWizard - Step 2 of 6 window.

☐ Set the Step 2 window as shown in Figure 11.6, then click the Next button.

Visual C++ responds by displaying the MFC AppWizard - Step 3 of 6 window.

Figure 11.5.

*Creating an SDI
application.*

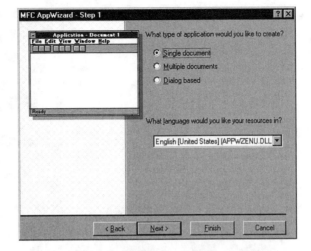

Figure 11.6.

*Choosing the option
for no database
support.*

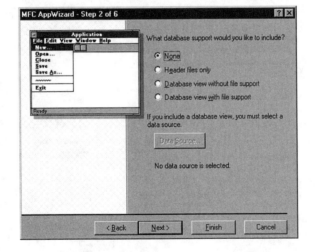

☐ Set the Step 3 window as shown in Figure 11.7, then click the Next button.

Visual C++ responds by displaying the MFC AppWizard - Step 4 of 6 window.

Figure 11.7.

*Setting the Step 3
window of
App Wizard.*

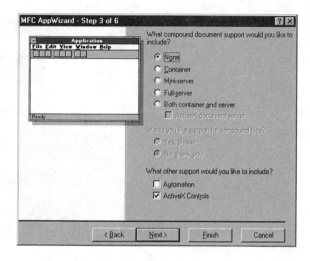

☐ Set the Step 4 window as shown in Figure 11.8. You want the program to support these features: docking toolbar, initial status bar, printing and print preview, and 3-D controls. Leave the combo box specifying the number of files on the recent file list at the default setting of 4. When you're done, click the Next button.

Visual C++ responds by displaying the MFC App Wizard - Step 5 of 6 window.

Figure 11.8.

*Selecting which
features to include.*

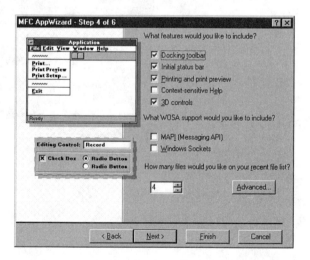

☐ In the Step 5 window, use the default settings and click the Next button. (See Figure 11.9.)

Visual C++ responds by displaying the MFC App Wizard - Step 6 of 6 window.

Figure 11.9.

The Step 5 window of AppWizard.

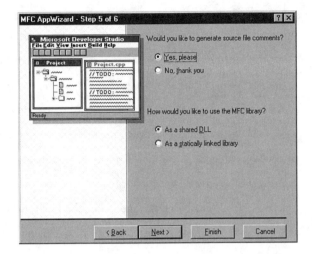

In the Step 6 window, notice that AppWizard has created the following classes for you: CCircleApp, CMainFrame, CCircleDoc, CCircleView. (See Figure 11.10.)

Figure 11.10.

Checking the classes created by AppWizard.

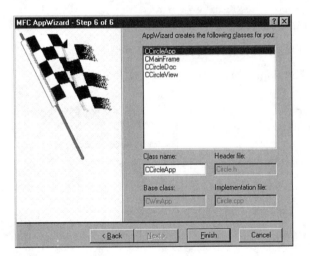

The two most important classes are CCircleView and CCircleDoc. In the following sections, you will write code in the member functions of these two classes only. The CCircleView class is the Circle program's *view class,* which is responsible for what you see onscreen. The CCircleDoc class is the Circle program's *document class,* which is responsible for storing the document (the data) of the program. The code you write in the document class will be responsible for saving your circle drawing into a file and loading previously saved files.

☐ Click the Finish button of the Step 6 of 6 window.

Visual C++ responds by displaying the New Project Information window.

☐ Click the OK button of the New Project Information window.

Visual C++ responds by creating the project and all its associated files.

☐ Select Set Active Configuration from the Build menu.

Visual C++ responds by displaying the Set Active Project Configuration dialog box.

☐ Select Circle - Win32 Release, then click the OK button.

That's it! You've finished creating the project and skeleton files of the Circle program.

Running the Circle Program Before Customization

Before you start customizing the Circle program, first build and execute it. You'll see that the skeleton files Visual C++ created for you yield an SDI program that already performs some functions.

☐ Build and execute the Circle.EXE program.

The main window of the Circle program appears, as shown in Figure 11.11.

Figure 11.11.

The main window of the Circle program before customization.

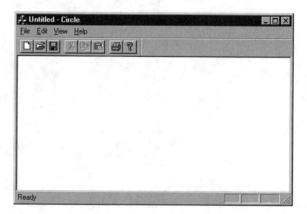

As you can see, the skeleton code yielded a nice-looking SDI program. The program includes a standard SDI menu system and toolbar. Of course, at this point the Circle program won't do what you want it to do. In the following sections, you'll write code that customizes the

11

Circle program so you can draw a circle, save the circle drawing into a file, and load previously saved files.

☐ Terminate the Circle program by selecting Exit from its File menu.

As you can see, although you haven't written a single line of code yet, the Exit menu item does what it's supposed to do—terminate the program.

Declaring the Data Members of the Document Class

As discussed earlier, the code you write in the document class is responsible for storing the document (the program's data). This code will enable you to save the program's data into a file and to load data from previously saved files. You'll now add data members to CCircleDoc, the document class of the Circle program, for storing Circle's document data:

☐ Select the FileView tab of the Project Workspace window, expand the Circle Files item, expand the Header Files item, and finally double-click the CircleDoc.h item.

Visual C++ responds by opening the CircleDoc.h file. The CircleDoc.h file is where the document class of the Circle program (the CCircleDoc *class) is declared.*

You'll now declare two data members in the CCircleDoc class:

☐ Modify the declaration of the CCircleDoc class as follows:

```
class CCircleDoc : public CDocument
{
protected: // create from serialization only
     CCircleDoc();
     DECLARE_DYNCREATE(CCircleDoc)

// Attributes
public:

//////////////////////////
// MY CODE STARTS HERE
//////////////////////////

int m_PosX;
int m_PosY;

//////////////////////////
// MY CODE ENDS HERE
//////////////////////////

// Operations
public:

...
...
};
```

11

☐ Save your work.

The code you added to the declaration of the CCircleDoc class declares two int data members, m_PosX and m_PosY:

```
int m_PosX;
int m_PosY;
```

The m_PosX data member will be used for storing the x coordinate of the circle you draw, and the m_PosY data member will be used for storing the y coordinate of the circle.

If you wish, you can add additional data members that define the drawn circle, such as the radius or color of the circle. However, for simplicity's sake, in the Circle program you can specify only the x-y coordinate of the circle, the point at which the circle will be drawn. All other aspects of the circle will be fixed.

The document class of the Circle program now has two data members: m_PosX and m_PosY. These data members make up the document of the Circle program. Later, you will write code for saving m_PosX and m_PosY into a file and loading data from previously saved files into m_PosX and m_PosY.

Declaring the Data Members of the View Class

As discussed earlier, the code you write in the view class is responsible for what you see onscreen. The data members you're adding to the view class are a mirror image of the data members you declared in the document class, because the code of the view class is supposed to display onscreen whatever the document specifies. For example, if the document specifies that the circle should be displayed at a certain x-y coordinate, the code of the view class will display the circle at the specified coordinate. You'll now add data members to CCircleView, the view class of the Circle program, for drawing a circle in the program's window:

☐ Open the file CircleView.h, where the view class of the Circle program is declared. You'll now declare two data members in the CCircleView class:

☐ Modify the declaration of the CCircleView class as follows:

```
class CCircleView : public CView
{
protected: // create from serialization only
    CCircleView();
    DECLARE_DYNCREATE(CCircleView)

// Attributes
public:
    CCircleDoc* GetDocument();

/////////////////////////
// MY CODE STARTS HERE
/////////////////////////
```

```
int m_PosX;
int m_PosY;

////////////////////////
// MY CODE ENDS HERE
////////////////////////


// Operations
public:

...
...
};
```

☐ Save your work.

The code you added to the declaration of the CCircleView class is identical to the code you added for the CCircleDoc class. This code declares two int data members, m_PosX and m_PosY, used for holding the x-y coordinates of the circle:

```
int m_PosX;
int m_PosY;
```

At this point, the document class and the view class have the same two data members: m_PosX and m_PosY. The values of these data members should always be the same in each class, so that the values stored in the document are the same as the values you see onscreen. Therefore, the code you write in the following sections will ensure that the document class data members always have the same values as their corresponding view class data members.

Initializing the Data Members of the Document Class

You'll now write the code that initializes the data members of the document class in the OnNewDocument() member function of the CCircleDoc class.

☐ Open the file CircleDoc.cpp and locate the OnNewDocument() function.

☐ Write the following code in the OnNewDocument() function:

```
BOOL CCircleDoc::OnNewDocument()
{
if (!CDocument::OnNewDocument())
    return FALSE;

// TODO: add reinitialization code here
// (SDI documents will reuse this document)
```

```
/////////////////////////
// MY CODE STARTS HERE
/////////////////////////

// Initialize the data members of the document.
m_PosX = 200;
m_PosY = 100;

/////////////////////////
// MY CODE ENDS HERE
/////////////////////////

return TRUE;

}
```

☐ Save your work.

As its name implies, the OnNewDocument() member function of the document class is automatically executed whenever a new document is created—when you start the program and when you select New from the File menu.

The code you wrote in the OnNewDocument() function initializes the value of the m_PosX data member to 200 and the m_PosY data member to 100:

```
m_PosX = 200;
m_PosY = 100;
```

When a new document is created, the m_PosX document data member will be set to a value of 200 and the m_PosY document data member will be set to a value of 100.

Initializing the Data Members of the View Class

In the preceding section, you initialized the data members of the document class. They represent the values that will be stored in a document file. You'll now write the code that initializes the data members of the view class, which are just as important as the data members of the document class. They represent what you see onscreen.

Follow these steps to write the code that initializes the view class data members in the OnInitialUpdate() member function of the CCircleView class:

☐ Select ClassWizard from the View menu.

☐ In the Message Maps tab of ClassWizard, select the following event:

Class name:	CCircleView
Object ID:	CCircleView
Message:	OnInitialUpdate

☐ Click the Add Function button.

Visual C++ responds by adding the OnInitialUpdate() *function.*

☐ Click the Edit Code button.

Visual C++ responds by opening the file Circle View.cpp with the function OnInitialUpdate() *ready for you to edit.*

☐ Write the following code in the OnInitialUpdate() function:

```
void CCircleView::OnInitialUpdate()
{
CView::OnInitialUpdate();

// TODO: Add your specialized code here and/or call
//       the base class

/////////////////////////
// MY CODE STARTS HERE
/////////////////////////

// Get a pointer to the document
CCircleDoc* pDoc = GetDocument();

// Update data members of the view with the
// corresponding document values.
m_PosX  = pDoc->m_PosX;
m_PosY  = pDoc->m_PosY;

/////////////////////////
// MY CODE ENDS HERE
/////////////////////////
```

☐ Save your work.

As its name implies, the OnInitialUpdate() member function of the CCircleView class is responsible for initializing the data members of the view class. The code you just attached to the OnInitalUpdate() function updates the view class data members with the current values of the document class data members.

The first statement you typed uses the GetDocument() function to extract a pointer, pDoc, to the document:

```
CCircleDoc* pDoc = GetDocument();
```

The remaining statements you typed use the pDoc pointer to initialize the view class data members with the current values of the document class data members:

```
m_PosX  = pDoc->m_PosX;
m_PosY  = pDoc->m_PosY;
```

These statements update the m_PosX and m_PosY data members of the view class with the corresponding document data members.

Writing the Code That Displays the Circle

You'll now write the code that displays the circle onscreen. In which class will you write this code? You guessed it! In the view class, because it's responsible for what you see onscreen. You'll write the drawing code in the OnDraw() member function of the CCircleView class. The OnDraw() function of the view class is automatically executed whenever the program's window needs to be drawn.

☐ Open the file CircleView.cpp and locate the OnDraw() function.

☐ Write the following code in the OnDraw() function:

```
void CCircleView::OnDraw(CDC* pDC)
{
CCircleDoc* pDoc = GetDocument();
ASSERT_VALID(pDoc);

// TODO: add draw code for native data here

////////////////////////
// MY CODE STARTS HERE
////////////////////////

// Define the rectangular boundaries of the
// circle to be drawn.
RECT  rect;
rect.left = m_PosX - 20;
rect.top = m_PosY -20;
rect.bottom = m_PosY + 20;
rect.right = m_PosX +20;

// Draw the circle.
pDC->Ellipse(&rect);

////////////////////////
// MY CODE ENDS HERE
////////////////////////

}
```

☐ Save your work.

The code you typed in the OnDraw() function draws a circle in the program's window at the position specified by the m_PosX and m_PosY data members of the view class.

11

The first five statements you typed define the coordinates and dimensions of a rectangle called rect:

```
RECT  rect;
rect.left = m_PosX - 20;
rect.top = m_PosY -20;
rect.bottom = m_PosY + 20;
rect.right = m_PosX +20;
```

These statements define the rectangle so that its center is at the x-y coordinate specified by the m_PosX and m_PosY data members. The width of the rectangle is 40 pixels, and the height is also 40 pixels, so rect is defined as a square.

The last statement you typed uses the Ellipse() function to draw an ellipse:

```
pDC->Ellipse(&rect);
```

pDC, the parameter of the OnDraw() function, is the pointer to the dc (device context). By executing the Ellipse() function on the pDC pointer, you are drawing an ellipse in the program's window.

As you can see, the parameter of the Ellipse() function in the preceding statement is &rect. Therefore, the ellipse will be drawn within the boundaries of the rectangle you defined. Because rect is a square, the ellipse will be drawn as a circle.

Putting it all together, the code you wrote in the OnDraw() function draws a circle in the program's window at the x-y coordinate specified by the m_PosX and m_PosY data members of the view class.

☐ Build and execute the Circle program to see your code in action.

Visual C++ responds by executing the Circle program. The main window of the Circle program appears, as shown in Figure 11.12.

Figure 11.12.

The main window of the Circle program after customization.

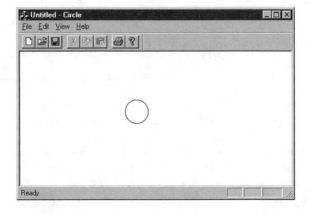

As you can see, the drawing code you wrote in the OnDraw() function is working—a circle is drawn in the program's window at the x-y coordinate x=200, y=100. That's because the code you wrote in OnNewDocument() initialized the document class data members m_PosX and m_PosY to m_PosX=200 and m_PosY=100, and the code you wrote in OnInitialupdate() updated the m_PosX and m_PosY view class data members with the values of the document class data members.

The drawing code you wrote in the OnDraw() member function of the view class is executed when the screen needs to be redrawn and when you select Print from the File menu. The code in OnDraw() is responsible for both what you see onscreen and what is printed when you select Print from the File menu. To see the Print menu item in action, do the following:

☐ Select Print from the File menu of the Circle program.

The Circle program responds by displaying the Print dialog box. (See Figure 11.13.)

Figure 11.13.

The Print dialog box.

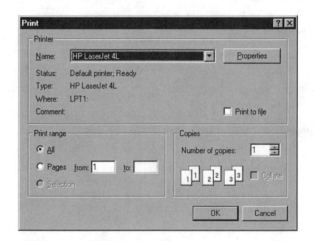

☐ Click the OK button.

The Circle program responds by printing a page with a circle drawn on it.

☐ Terminate the Circle program by selecting Exit from its File menu.

Drawing the Circle at Any Point Onscreen

At this point, when you start the Circle program, it displays a circle at the x-y coordinate x=200, y=100. You'll now write code that enables you to draw the circle anywhere in the program's window by simply clicking the mouse at the desired point. Because this code involves what you see onscreen, you'll write it in the view class.

☐ Select ClassWizard from the View menu.

☐ In the Message Maps tab of ClassWizard, select the following event:

Class name:	CCircleView
Object ID:	CCircleView
Message:	WM_LBUTTONDOWN

☐ Click the Add Function button.

Visual C++ responds by adding the OnLButtonDown() *function.*

☐ Click the Edit Code button.

Visual C++ responds by opening the file CircleView.cpp with the function OnLButtonDown() *ready for you to edit.*

☐ Write the following code in the OnLButtonDown() function:

```
void CCircleView::OnLButtonDown(UINT nFlags, CPoint point)
{

// TODO: Add your message handler code here
// and/or call default

/////////////////////////
// MY CODE STARTS HERE
/////////////////////////

// Update the m_PosX and m_PosY data members of
// the view class with the x-y coordinate of the
// point where the mouse was clicked.
m_PosX = point.x;
m_PosY = point.y;

// Trigger a call to the OnDraw() function.
Invalidate();

// Get a pointer to the document
CCircleDoc* pDoc = GetDocument();

// Update data members of the document with the
// new values of the view class data members.
pDoc->m_PosX = m_PosX;
pDoc->m_PosY = m_PosY ;

// Signal that the document has been modified.
pDoc->SetModifiedFlag(TRUE);

/////////////////////////
// MY CODE ENDS HERE
/////////////////////////

CView::OnLButtonDown(nFlags, point);

}
```

11

☐ Save your work.

The OnLButtonDown() member function of the view class is automatically executed when you click the left mouse button on the program's window.

The second parameter of the OnLButtonDown() function, point, specifies the point onscreen where you clicked the mouse button: point.x holds the x-coordinate of the point, and point.y holds the y-coordinate.

The first two statements you typed update the m_PosX and m_PosY data members of the view class with the x-y coordinates of the point where the mouse was clicked:

```
m_PosX = point.x;
m_PosY = point.y;
```

The next statement calls the Invalidate() function to execute the OnDraw() function:

```
Invalidate();
```

Recall that the code you wrote in the OnDraw() function draws a circle at the point specified by m_PosX and m_PosY. Therefore, the preceding statements will draw a circle at the point where the mouse was clicked.

The next statement uses the GetDocument() function to extract a pointer, pDoc, to the document:

```
CCircleDoc* pDoc = GetDocument();
```

The next two statements use the pDoc pointer to update the data members of the document class with the new values of the view class data members:

```
pDoc->m_PosX = m_PosX;
pDoc->m_PosY = m_PosY ;
```

Now the data members of the document class have the same values as their corresponding data members in the view class. When you change the values of data members in the view class, you should change the corresponding data members in the document class to the same values. This is necessary because you always want the data stored in the program's document to be the same as the data viewed onscreen.

The last statement you typed calls the SetModifiedFlag() function:

```
pDoc->SetModifiedFlag();
```

Note that the SetModified() function is executed on the pDoc document pointer, because it's a member function of the document class (not the view class). What does the SetModifiedFlag() function do? It raises a flag in the document to indicate that the data has been changed. If you try to exit the program without first saving the currently open document, the program will display a warning message box to give you a chance to save the changes made in the document. You should always call the SetModifiedFlag() function after changing the values of the document class data members.

☐ Build and execute the Circle program to see the code you wrote in the OnLButtonDown() function in action.

Visual C++ responds by executing the Circle program. The main window of the Circle program appears, as shown in Figure 11.12.

☐ Click the mouse at the upper-right corner of the program's window.

The Circle program responds by drawing a circle at the point where you clicked the mouse. (See Figure 11.14.)

Figure 11.14.

Drawing a circle at the upper-right corner of the program's window.

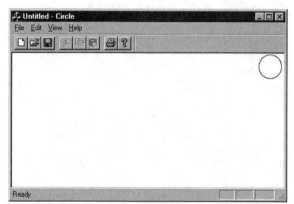

☐ Try clicking the mouse at various points in the program's window to see how the circle is drawn.

☐ Terminate the Circle program by selecting Exit from its File menu.

Writing Code That Saves and Loads Files

You'll now write the code responsible for saving the document into a file and loading previously saved files. You'll write this code in the document class.

☐ Open the file CircleDoc.cpp and locate the Serialize() function.

The Serialize() function is automatically executed when you select Save, Save As, or Open from the File menu of the program:

```
void CCircleDoc::Serialize(CArchive& ar)
{
```

```
if (ar.IsStoring())
    {
    // TODO: add storing code here

    }
    else
    {
    // TODO: add loading code here

    }
}
```

The code in the Serialize() function is made up of a simple if...else statement:

```
if (ar.IsStoring())
    {
    // TODO: add storing code here
    ..........................................
    ... This code is automatically executed ...
    ... whenever the user selects Save or   ...
    ... Save As from the File menu.         ...
    ..........................................
    }
    else
    {
    // TODO: add loading code here
    ..........................................
    ... This code is automatically executed ...
    ... whenever the user selects Open      ...
    ... from the File menu.                 ...
    ..........................................

    }
```

This is the if condition of the if...else statement:

```
if (ar.IsStoring())
```

In this code, ar is the parameter of the Serialize() function and represents the archive (the file) you're trying to read or write. If you select Save or Save As from the File menu, the condition of the preceding if statement is satisfied and the code under the if is executed. If you select Open from the File menu, the code under the else is executed.

Therefore, your job is to do the following:

1. Write code under the if statement that writes data to the file.
2. Write code under the else statement that reads data from the file.

The code for writing and reading data to and from the file is easy. Follow these steps:

☐ Write the following code in the Serialize() function:

```
void CCircleDoc::Serialize(CArchive& ar)
    {
```

```
if (ar.IsStoring())
   {
   // TODO: add storing code here

   ////////////////////////
   // MY CODE STARTS HERE
   ////////////////////////

   // Save m_PosX and m_PosY into the file.
   ar << m_PosX;
   ar << m_PosY;

   ////////////////////////
   // MY CODE ENDS HERE
   ////////////////////////

   }
   else
   {
   // TODO: add loading code here

   ////////////////////////
   // MY CODE STARTS HERE
   ////////////////////////

   // Fill m_PosX and m_PosY with data from the file.
   ar >> m_PosX;
   ar >> m_PosY;

   ////////////////////////
   // MY CODE ENDS HERE
   ////////////////////////

   }
}
```

☐ Save your work.

The code responsible for saving data into the file (the code under the if statement) is this:

```
ar << m_PosX;
ar << m_PosY;
```

The insertion operator (<<) indicates that you want to save data into the file. For example, this statement stores the data member m_PosX of the document class into the file:

```
ar << m_PosX;
```

Into what file? It depends on what file the user is trying to save. If, for example, the user selected Save As from the File menu and selected the file MyFile.TRY from the Save As dialog box, the statement ar<<m_PosX; will store the m_PosX variable in the MyFile.TRY file. You can think of ar as the file the user selected.

NOTE

> ar is the archive object (an object of class CArchive) corresponding to the file the user selected. Therefore, the following statement literally means "Save the variable m_PosX into the file that the user selected":
>
> ```
> ar << m_PosX;
> ```
>
> The CArchive class is discussed in Chapter 14, "File Access and Serialization."

The code responsible for loading the data from the file into the variables (the code under the else statement in the Serialize() function) is this:

```
ar >> m_PosX;
ar >> m_PosY;
```

The extraction operator (>>) indicates that you want to load data from the file into the variable. For example, the following statement fills the data member m_PosX with data from the file:

```
ar >> m_PosX;
```

From which file? Again, it depends on what you did. If, for example, you selected Open from the File menu, then selected the file MyFile.TRY from the Open File dialog box, the statement ar>>m_PosX will fill the m_PosX variable with data from the MyFile.TRY file.

The order in which you extract the data must be the same order used for saving the data. For example, if you save data to the file with these statements:

```
ar << Var1;
ar << Var2;
ar << Var3;
```

when you extract the data from the file into the variables, you must use the same order:

```
ar >> Var1;
ar >> Var2;
ar >> Var3;
```

NOTE

> In the previous code, you used the insertion (<<) and extraction (>>) operators on several lines. You can also use these operators on a single line. For example, these three statements:
>
> ```
> ar << Var1;
> ar << Var2;
> ar << Var3;
> ```

are equivalent to this single statement:

```
ar << Var1 << Var2 << Var3;
```

Similarly, these three statements:

```
ar >> Var1;
ar >> Var2;
ar >> Var3;
```

are equivalent to this single statement:

```
ar >> Var1 >> Var2 >> Var3;
```

You have finished writing the code for the Circle program!

☐ Build and execute the Circle program to see your code in action.

Visual C++ responds by executing the Circle program. The main window of the Circle program appears, as shown back in Figure 11.12.

The title of the program's window is currently Untitled - Circle. The Untitled means you just started the program and haven't saved the document into a file.

To test the saving and loading code you wrote in the Serialize() function of the document class, do the following:

☐ Click the mouse at the lower-left corner of the program's window.

The Circle program responds by drawing the circle at the lower-left corner of the program's window. (See Figure 11.15.)

Figure 11.15.

Drawing a circle at the lower-left corner of the window.

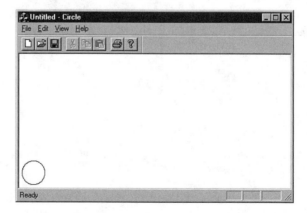

11

Now save the document into a file as follows:

☐ Select Save As from the File menu of the Circle program.

The Circle program responds by displaying the Save As dialog box. (See Figure 11.16.)

Figure 11.16.

*The Save As
dialog box.*

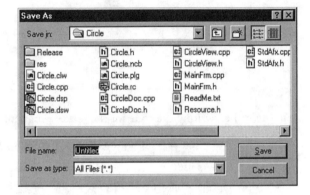

☐ Type MyCircle.Cir in the File name edit box, then click the Save button.

The Circle program responds by creating the MyCircle.Cir file and saving the document into this file.

Because you saved the document in the file MyCircle.Cir, the title of the program's window is now MyCircle.Cir - Circle. (See Figure 11.17.)

Figure 11.17.

*Changing the title
of the program's
window.*

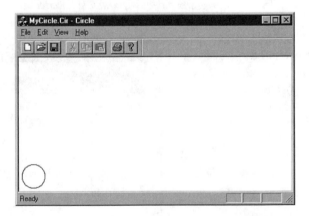

To make sure your document is saved in the MyCircle.Cir file, do the following:

☐ Select New from the File menu of the Circle program.

The Circle program responds by closing the MyCircle.Cir document and opening a new document.

The window of your Circle program should now look like the one back in Figure 11.12— the title of the program's window is Untitled - Circle, and there is a circle in the center of the window.

Now open the MyCircle.Cir document as follows:

☐ Select Open from the File menu of the Circle program.

The Circle program responds by displaying the Open dialog box. (See Figure 11.18.)

Figure 11.18.

The Open dialog box.

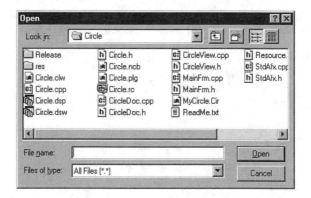

☐ Use the Open dialog box to select the MyCircle.Cir file you saved earlier, then click the Open button.

The Circle program responds by opening the MyCircle.Cir file.

The window of your Circle program should now look like the one back in Figure 11.17— the title of the program's window is MyCircle.Cir - Circle, and the circle is drawn in the lower-left corner.

The code you wrote in the Serialize() member function of the document class is working! You can save documents into files and load previously saved files.

Keep experimenting with the Circle program. For example, place the circle at different places in the window and save the document under different filenames. As you experiment with the Circle program, notice that the File menu of the program maintains a most recently used (MRU) file list. (See Figure 11.19.)

Figure 11.19.

*The MRU file list of
Circle's File menu.*

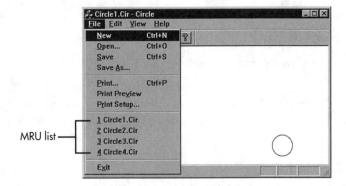

MRU list

The MRU list in the File menu lists the last four files you've worked with. When you click one of the files in the MRU list, the file is opened. Why four? Recall that when you created the project of the Circle program, in Step 4 of the AppWizard you accepted the default setting of 4 for the number of files in your MRU list. (Refer to Figure 11.8.)

NOTE

The Circle program includes a toolbar displayed at the top of the window. You can perform operations by clicking the tool you want on the toolbar. For example, clicking the Save tool on the toolbar (the one with a disk icon) is equivalent to selecting Save from the File menu; clicking the About tool (the one with a question mark icon) is the same as selecting About from the Help menu.

The tools were created for you by Visual C++ when you created the project and skeleton files of the program. In Chapter 15, "Toolbars and Status Bars," you'll learn how to create your own custom tools in the program's toolbar.

☐ Terminate the Circle program by selecting Exit from its File menu.

Enhancing the Circle Program

You will now enhance the Circle program in two ways:

☐ Change the caption in the title of the application's window from Circle to The Circle Program.

☐ Change the default file type displayed in the Save As and Open dialog boxes from *.* to *.cir. This means that whenever you select Open or Save As from the dialog box, the default files displayed in the File list box will have a .cir file extension.

Follow these steps to perform the enhancements:

☐ In the Project Workspace window, select the ResourceView tab, expand the Circle resources item, then expand the String Table item.

After you expand the String Table item, a second String Table item appears underneath it. (See Figure 11.20.)

Figure 11.20.

Expanding the String Table item in the Project Workspace window.

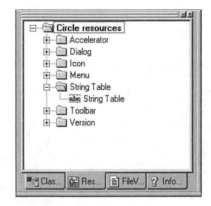

☐ Double-click the second String Table item in the Project Workspace window.

Visual C++ responds by displaying the String Table dialog box of the Circle project. (See Figure 11.21.)

Figure 11.21.

The String Table dialog box.

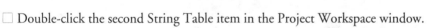

ID	Value	Caption
IDR_MAINFRAME	128	Circle\n\nCircle\n\n\nCircle.Document
AFX_IDS_APP_TITLE	57344	Circle
AFX_IDS_IDLEMESSAGE	57345	Ready
ID_FILE_NEW	57600	Create a new document\nNew
ID_FILE_OPEN	57601	Open an existing document\nOpen
ID_FILE_CLOSE	57602	Close the active document\nClose
ID_FILE_SAVE	57603	Save the active document\nSave
ID_FILE_SAVE_AS	57604	Save the active document with a new r
ID_FILE_PAGE_SETUP	57605	Change the printing options\nPage Setu
ID_FILE_PRINT_SETUP	57606	Change the printer and printing options\
ID_FILE_PRINT	57607	Print the active document\nPrint
ID_FILE_PRINT_PREVIEW	57609	Display full pages\nPrint Preview
ID_FILE_MRU_FILE1	57616	Open this document
ID_FILE_MRU_FILE2	57617	Open this document
ID_FILE_MRU_FILE3	57618	Open this document

You use the String Table dialog box to view and edit various strings used by the program. As you can see in Figure 11.21, the string whose ID is IDR_MAINFRAME is currently highlighted. This is the current value of the string:

```
Circle\n\nCircle\n\n\nCircle.Document\nCircle Document
```

The \n serves as a separator between substrings. Therefore, the preceding string is made of the following seven substrings:

```
Circle
Null
Circle
Null
Null
Circle.Document
Circle Document
```

The substrings you need to work with are the first, fourth, and fifth substrings. The first substring specifies the title in the program's main window. Your objective is to make the program's main window title The Circle Program. Therefore, you need to change the first substring from Circle to The Circle Program.

The fourth and fifth substrings specify the default document type displayed in the Save As dialog box and Open dialog box. For example, if you set the fourth substring to

```
CIR Files (*.cir)
```

and the fifth substring to

```
.cir
```

when you select Save As or Open from the File menu, the files listed in the File list box will have the .cir file extension, and the text in the file type box will be CIR Files (*.cir).

Figure 11.22 shows the Open dialog box, listing files with the .cir extension. The text CIR Files (*.cir) appears in the file type box.

Now change the IDR_MAINFRAME string so that the first substring will be The Circle Program, the fourth substring will be CIR Files (*.cir), and the fifth substring will be .cir. All the rest of the substrings will remain the same. Here is how you do that:

☐ Double-click the IDR_MAINFRAME string.

Visual C++ responds by displaying the String Properties window for the IDR_MAINFRAME *string. (See Figure 11.23.)*

Figure 11.22.

The Open dialog box, listing files with the .cir extension.

Figure 11.23.

The String Properties window for the **IDR_MAINFRAME** *string.*

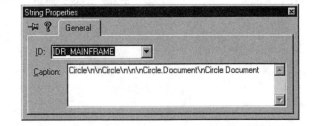

The value of the string is displayed in the Caption box.

☐ Change the value of the string to this:

```
The Circle Program\n\nCircle\nCIR Files (*.
cir)\n.cir\nCircle.Document\nCircle Document
```

NOTE

The preceding text should be typed on a single line; don't press the Enter key. Visual C++ will wrap the line when it's too long.

Your String Properties window for the **IDR_MAINFRAME** string should now look like the one shown in Figure 11.24.

Figure 11.24.

Changing the string value in the String Properties window.

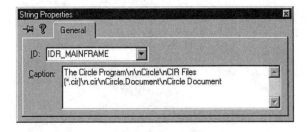

11

☐ Close the String Properties window and Save your work by selecting Save All from the File menu.

☐ Build and execute the Circle.EXE program to see the effects of the changes you made to the IDR_MAINFRAME string.

Visual C++ responds by executing the Circle program. The main window of the Circle program appears, as shown in Figure 11.25.

Figure 11.25.

The main window of the Circle program.

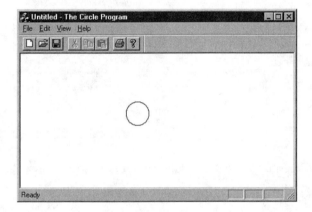

As shown in Figure 11.25, the title of the program's window includes the text The Circle Program, because you set the first substring of the IDR_MAINFRAME string to The Circle Program.

☐ Select Save As from the File menu of the Circle program.

The Circle program responds by displaying the Save As dialog box. (See Figure 11.26.)

Figure 11.26.

The Save As dialog box listing files with the .cir extension.

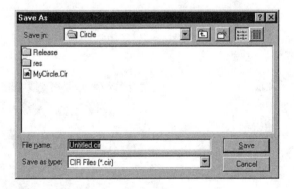

As shown in Figure 11.26, now the Save As dialog box lists files with the .cir file extension and the text in the file type box is CIR Files (*.cir). That's because you set the fourth substring of the IDR_MAINFRAME string to CIR Files (*.cir), and the fifth substring to .cir.

Summary

In this chapter, you have written an SDI (single-document interface) program called Circle.EXE that behaves like a standard Windows SDI program—it lets you view a document, store the document in a file, and load previously saved files. The steps you took to create the Circle program are the same steps you'll take when you design other SDI programs.

Q&A

Q In this chapter, I learned how to write an SDI program. How do I write a multiple-document interface (MDI) program?

A In Chapter 13, "Writing Multiple-Document Interface (MDI) Applications," you'll learn how to create MDI programs.

Quiz

1. What does SDI stand for?
2. What is the purpose of the code you write in the view class of an SDI program?
3. What is the purpose of the code you write in the document class of an SDI program?
4. What code do you write in the Serialize() member function of the document class?

Exercise

The title of the Circle program's window currently displays the text The Circle Program. Enhance the Circle program so that the title will include the text The SDI Circle Program instead of The Circle Program.

Quiz Answers

1. SDI stands for *single-document interface.* The word "single" in single-document interface means that you can work on only one document at a time (unlike multiple-document interface, in which multiple documents are used).

2. The code you write in the member functions of the view class is responsible for what you see onscreen.

3. The code you write in the member functions of the document class is responsible for maintaining the program's data, particularly saving documents and loading previously saved files.

4. The code you write in the `Serialize()` member function of the document class is responsible for saving data into files and loading previously saved files.

Exercise Answer

To make the title of the program's window display the text The SDI Circle Program, you have to change the IDR_MAINFRAME string so that its first substring will be The SDI Circle Program. The rest of the substrings remain the same. Here is how you do that:

☐ In the Project Workspace, select the ResourceView tab and expand the Circle resources item and the String Table item. Finally, double-click the second String Table item.

Visual C++ responds by displaying the String Table dialog box of the Circle project.

☐ Double-click the IDR_MAINFRAME string.

Visual C++ responds by displaying the String Properties window for the IDR_MAINFRAME *string.*

☐ Change the value of the string to this (remember to type this code on a single line):

```
The SDI Circle Program\n\nCircle\nCIR Files
➥(*.cir)\n.cir\nCircle.Document\nCircle Document
```

☐ Save your work.

That's it! If you build and execute the Circle program, you'll see that the text The SDI Circle Program appears in the title of the program's window.

Day **12**

Multitasking

In this chapter, you'll learn how to create a Visual C++ program that performs background tasks. *Multitasking* is the ability to work on other tasks within the same program or run other programs while your program performs background tasks.

The Tasks Program

To illustrate how to write a Visual C++ program that performs several background tasks, you'll write a program called Tasks. Before you start writing the program, first review what it should look like and what it should do:

■ When you start the Tasks program, the program's window contains two Task edit boxes: Task 1 (50 ms), and Task 2 (500 ms). (See Figure 12.1.)

Figure 12.1.

The window of the Tasks program.

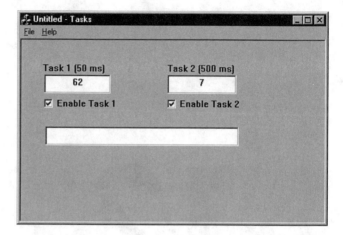

- The Tasks program performs two background tasks. The first increments the number in the Task 1 edit box every 50 milliseconds, and the second increments the number in the Task 2 edit box every 500 milliseconds.

- The two tasks are performed in the background. For example, while you type in the edit box at the bottom of the program's window, the two tasks will keep running. You can also switch to another Windows program, and the two tasks will keep on running.

NOTE

The two background tasks of the Tasks program are performed only when Windows is idle—when all the currently running applications aren't receiving any messages from Windows.

Because a typical Windows program has a lot of idle time, from your point of view, it seems as though the tasks are running simultaneously with other programs. However, in reality, the Tasks program performs its tasks only when the system is idle.

- Each of the two Task edit boxes has a check box below it. You can disable a task by removing the check mark from its corresponding check box. For example, to disable Task 1, remove the check mark from the Enable Task 1 check box.

- To terminate the Tasks program, select Exit from the program's File menu.

Now that you know what the Tasks program should do, you can start by creating the project.

12

Creating the Project of the Tasks Program

The Tasks program is an SDI-type (single-document interface) program, like the one you created in Chapter 11, "Writing Single-Document Interface (SDI) Applications." Follow these steps to create the project and skeleton files of the Tasks program:

☐ Create the directory C:\TYVCPROG\PROGRAMS\CH12.

☐ Start Visual C++ and select New from the File menu.

　　Visual C++ responds by displaying the New dialog box.

☐ Select the Projects tab of the New dialog box.

☐ Select MFC AppWizard(exe) from the list of project types.

☐ Type Tasks in the Project Name box.

☐ Click the button that is located on the right of the Location box and select the C:\TYVCPROG\PROGRAMS\CH12 directory.

☐ Click the OK button.

　　Visual C++ responds by displaying the MFC AppWizard - Step 1 window.

☐ Set the Step 1 window as you did in Chapter 11 by choosing the "Single document" radio button to create an SDI program. When you're done, click the Next button.

☐ In the Step 2 window, choose "None" because you don't want the program to support any database features. Then click the Next button.

☐ In the Step 3 window, leave the options at the default settings and click the Next button.

☐ Set the Step 4 window as shown in Figure 12.2. That is, remove the check marks from all the check boxes except the 3-D controls check box.

☐ In the Step 5 window, select the "Yes, please" and "As a shared DLL" radio buttons, as you've done in previous chapters, then click the Next button.

☐ Set the Step 6 window as follows: Select the CTasksView class in the list box at the top and set the Base class drop-down list to CFormView. (See Figure 12.3.) When you're done, click the Finish button.

　　Visual C++ responds by displaying the New Project Information window.

12

Figure 12.2.

Setting the Step 4 window.

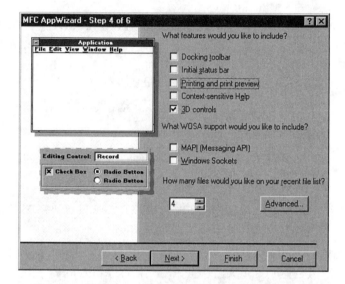

Figure 12.3.

Specifying the Base class for the Tasks program's view class.

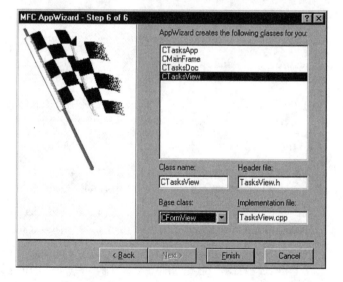

☐ Click the OK button.

Visual C++ responds by creating the project and skeleton files of the Tasks program.

☐ Select Set Active Configuration from the Build menu.

Visual C++ responds by displaying the Set Active Project Configuration dialog box.

12

☐ Select Tasks - Win32 Release, then click the OK button.

That's it! You've finished creating the project and skeleton files of the Tasks program.

Customizing the Menu of the Tasks Program

You'll now customize the menu of the Tasks program:

☐ In the Project Workspace window, select the ResourceView tab and expand the Tasks resources item, then expand the Menu item. Finally, double-click the IDR_MAINFRAME item under the Menu item.

Visual C++ responds by displaying the IDR_MAINFRAME menu in design mode ready for you to customize.

☐ Open the File pop-up menu of the IDR_MAINFRAME menu (by clicking the File menu title) and delete all its menu items except Exit. (To delete a menu item, select it, then press the Delete key.)

☐ Delete the entire Edit pop-up menu of the IDR_MAINFRAME menu by clicking the Edit menu title, then pressing the Delete key.

☐ Do not customize the Help pop-up menu.

☐ Build and execute the Tasks.EXE program to see your customization of the IDR_MAINFRAME menu in action.

☐ Make sure the menu looks just as you customized it—the File menu has only one menu item (Exit), there is no Edit menu, and the Help menu has the About Tasks menu item. (See Figures 12.4 and 12.5.)

12

Figure 12.4.

The File menu of the Tasks program.

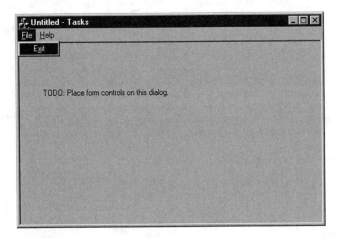

Figure 12.5.

The Help menu of the Tasks program.

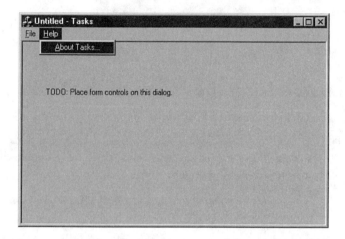

Although you removed the Open, Save, and Save As menu items of the File menu, their accelerator keys still work. To verify this, do the following:

☐ Press Ctrl+O on the keyboard.

> *The Tasks program responds by displaying the Open dialog box, just as though you selected Open from the File menu.*

☐ Close the Open dialog box by clicking its Cancel button.

☐ Press Ctrl+S on the keyboard.

> *The Tasks program responds by displaying the Save As dialog box, just as though you selected Save As from the File menu.*

☐ Close the Save As dialog box by clicking its Cancel button.

☐ Terminate the Tasks program by selecting Exit from its File menu.

To remove the accelerator keys, follow these steps:

☐ Select the ResourceView tab in the Project Workspace, expand the Accelerator item, and double-click the IDR_MAINFRAME item.

> *Visual C++ responds by displaying a list of all the accelerators in the Tasks program. (See Figure 12.6.)*

12

Figure 12.6.

Listing the program's accelerator keys.

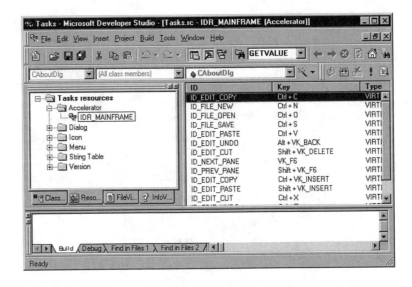

☐ Delete all the accelerators by pressing the Delete key again and again until all the accelerator keys are removed.

☐ Save your work.

☐ Now build and execute the Tasks.EXE program to make sure the accelerators are no longer working.

☐ Press Ctrl+O and Ctrl+S and make sure nothing happens.

☐ Terminate the Tasks program by selecting Exit from its File menu.

The Visual Design of the Program's Form

When you created the project of the Tasks program, you specified CFormView as the base class of the program's view class. (Refer to Figure 12.3.) Visual C++ created a form (a dialog box) that's attached to the program's view class. This dialog box serves as the main window of the program. Visual C++ named this dialog box IDD_TASKS_FORM. You'll now customize the IDD_TASKS_FORM dialog box until it looks like the window shown back in Figure 12.1:

☐ In the Project Workspace window, select the ResourceView tab, expand the Dialog item, and double-click the IDD_TASKS_FORM item.

Visual C++ responds by displaying the IDD_TASKS_FORM dialog box in design mode.

12

☐ Delete the static text control displaying the text TODO: Place form controls on this dialog.

☐ Set up the IDD_TASKS_FORM dialog box according to Table 12.1. When you finish, it should look like Figure 12.7.

Table 12.1. The properties table of the IDD_TASKS_FORM dialog box.

Object	Property	Setting
Dialog Box	**ID**	**IDD_TASKS_FORM**
	Font	System, Size 10
Static Text	**ID**	**IDC_STATIC**
	Caption	Task 1 (50 ms)
Edit Box	**ID**	**IDC_TASK1_EDIT**
	Multi-line	Checked (Styles tab)
	Align text	Centered (Styles tab)
Check Box	**ID**	**IDC_ENABLE_TASK1_CHECK**
	Caption	Enable Task 1
Static Text	**ID**	**IDC_STATIC**
	Caption	Task 2 (500 ms)
Edit Box	**ID**	**IDC_TASK2_EDIT**
	Multi-line	Checked (Styles tab)
	Align text	Centered (Styles tab)
Check Box	**ID**	**IDC_ENABLE_TASK2_CHECK**
	Caption	Enable Task 2
Edit Box	**ID**	**IDC_TEST_EDIT**

Figure 12.7.

The IDD_TASKS_FORM dialog box in design mode.

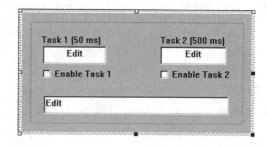

NOTE

It's OK to assign the same ID to more than one control if your code won't be using those controls. For example, in Table 12.1, the two static text controls have the same IDs because the ID IDC_STATIC is never used from within the code.

☐ Save your work, then build and execute the program to see your visual design in action.

Visual C++ responds by executing the Tasks program. The main window of the Tasks program looks like Figure 12.8, just as you designed it.

Figure 12.8.
The main window of the Tasks program.

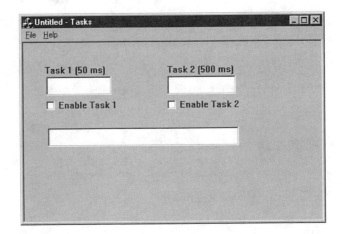

12

☐ Terminate the Tasks program by selecting Exit from its File menu.

Attaching Variables to Controls in IDD_TASKS_FORM

You'll now attach variables to the Task 1 edit box, Enable Task 1 check box, Task 2 edit box, and Enable Task 2 check box. When you write the program's code, you'll use these variables to access the controls.

☐ Select ClassWizard from the View menu.

☐ In the Member Variables tab of ClassWizard, make sure that the Class name is set to CTasksView and attach variables to the controls as follows:

Object ID	Variable Name	Variable Type
IDC_ENABLE_TASK1_CHECK	m_EnableTask1Check	BOOL
IDC_ENABLE_TASK2_CHECK	m_EnableTask2Check	BOOL
IDC_TASK1_EDIT	m_Task1Edit	long
IDC_TASK2_EDIT	m_Task2Edit	long

You set the variables of the IDC_TASK1_EDIT and IDC_TASK2_EDIT edit boxes to type long because your code will display numbers in these dialog boxes. You don't have to attach a variable to the IDC_TEST_EDIT edit box, because the code you write won't have to access this edit box. It's included in the Tasks program only to illustrate that you can type in it while the two tasks are running in the background.

Initializing the Two Check Box Controls

You'll now write code that initializes the two check box controls (IDC_ENABLE_TASK1_CHECK and IDC_ENABLE_TASK2_CHECK) so that when you start the program, they will have check marks in them. You'll write this initialization code in the OnInitialUpdate() member function of the program's view class:

☐ Select ClassWizard from the View menu.

☐ In the Message Maps tab of ClassWizard, select the following event:

> Class name: CTasksView
> Object ID: CTasksView
> Message: OnInitialUpdate

☐ Click the Add Function button.

> *Visual C++ responds by adding the function* OnInitialUpdate().

☐ Click the Edit Code button.

> *Visual C++ responds by opening the file TasksView.cpp with the function* OnInitialUpdate() *ready for you to edit.*

☐ Write the following code in the OnInitialUpdate() function:

```
void CTasksView::OnInitialUpdate()
{

CFormView::OnInitialUpdate();

// TODO: Add your specialized code here and/or call the
//       base class

////////////////////////////
// MY CODE STARTS HERE
////////////////////////////

// Place check marks in the IDC_ENABLE_TASK1_CHECK
// and IDC_ENABLE_TASK2_CHECK check boxes.
m_EnableTask1Check = TRUE;
m_EnableTask2Check = TRUE;
UpdateData(FALSE);
```

```
///////////////////////
// MY CODE ENDS HERE
///////////////////////

    }
```

☐ Save your work.

The first two statements you wrote in the OnInitialUpdate() function set the variables of the two check box controls to values of TRUE:

```
m_EnableTask1Check = TRUE;
m_EnableTask2Check = TRUE;
```

The third statement transfers the new values of the variables to the screen:

```
UpdateData(FALSE);
```

Therefore, when you start the program, the two check box controls will have check marks in them.

☐ Build and execute the program to see your initialization code in action.

Visual C++ responds by executing the Tasks program. The main window of the Tasks program appears with check marks in the two check box controls. (See Figure 12.9.)

Figure 12.9.

The main window of the Tasks program.

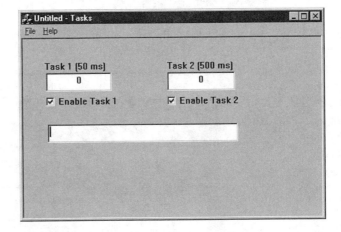

12

☐ Terminate the Tasks program.

Writing the Code That Performs the Background Tasks

Recall that the Tasks program should perform two background tasks: incrementing a counter in the Task 1 edit box and incrementing another counter in the Task 2 edit box. To write code that accomplishes these background tasks, you need to attach code to the `OnIdle` event of the program's application class (`CTasksApp`). This event occurs whenever the system is idle and no other tasks are being performed.

Follow these steps to attach code to the `OnIdle` event of the program's application class:

☐ In the Message Maps tab of ClassWizard, select the following event:

Class name:	`CTasksApp`
Object ID:	`CTasksApp`
Message:	`OnIdle`

NOTE

In the preceding step, you are instructed to attach code to the program's application class (`CTasksApp`), not to the program's view class. Make sure the correct class is entered in ClassWizard's Class name box.

After selecting the `OnIdle` event of the `CTasksApp` class, your ClassWizard window should look like Figure 12.10.

Figure 12.10.

Selecting the `OnIdle` *event with ClassWizard.*

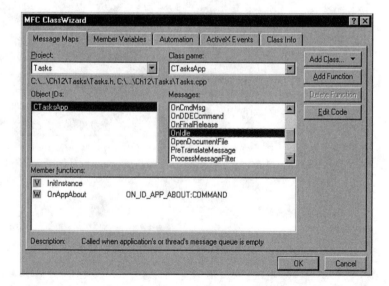

☐ Click the Add Function button of ClassWizard.

Visual C++ responds by adding the OnIdle() *member function to the* CTasksApp *class.*

☐ Click the Edit Code button.

Visual C++ responds by opening the file Tasks.cpp with the function OnIdle() *ready for you to edit.*

The code you write in the OnIdle() function will be automatically executed whenever the system is idle (no other tasks are being performed). To verify this, first write some simple code in the OnIdle() function that causes the PC to beep:

☐ Write the following code in the OnIdle() function:

```
BOOL CTasksApp::OnIdle(LONG lCount)
{

// TODO: Add your specialized code here and/or call the
// base class

/////////////////////////
// MY CODE STARTS HERE
/////////////////////////

// Call the base class CWinApp::OnIdle() function to
// finish its overhead tasks.
CWinApp::OnIdle(lCount);

// Beep.
MessageBeep((WORD)-1);

// Return TRUE so that OnIdle() will be called again.
return TRUE;

/////////////////////////
// MY CODE ENDS HERE
/////////////////////////

}
```

☐ Save your work.

The first statement you typed calls the OnIdle() member function of the base class CWinApp:

```
CWinApp::OnIdle(lCount);
```

CWinApp is the base class of the CTasksApp class (the application class of the Tasks program). It's necessary to call the OnIdle() member function of the base class because it performs overhead tasks needed for the normal operation of the program.

The next statement you typed in the OnIdle() function causes the PC to beep:

```
MessageBeep((WORD)-1);
```

12

The last statement terminates the OnIdle() function and returns a value of TRUE:

```
return TRUE;
```

When you terminate the OnIdle() function by returning a value of TRUE, the OnIdle() function will be executed again and again for as long as the system is idle.

☐ Build and execute the program to see (or rather, hear) the code you wrote in the OnIdle() function in action.

As you can hear, the code you wrote causes continuous beeping through the PC speaker. The code you typed in the OnIdle() function is being executed again and again for as long as the system is idle.

☐ Try to type something in the edit boxes of the Tasks program.

As you can hear, even while you are typing in the edit boxes, your PC keeps on beeping. That's because when you type characters in an edit box, there is some idle time between typing each character. During the idle time, the OnIdle() function is automatically executed and the code you wrote causes the PC to beep.

The OnIdle() function is executed even when other programs are currently active. To verify this, do the following:

☐ Leave the Tasks program running and start another Windows program, such as Paint.

As you can hear, the PC keeps beeping even while the other program is active. As long as the system is idle, the OnIdle() function of the Tasks program is executed.

☐ Switch back to the Tasks program.

☐ Open the File menu of the Tasks program.

The PC stops beeping because the OnIdle() function stops executing when you open a menu of the Tasks program. However, when you open a menu of another program, the OnIdle() function of the Tasks program will keep on executing.

☐ Terminate the Tasks program.

Now that you've verified the OnIdle() function is executed whenever the system is idle, change the code in the OnIdle() function so that it will perform two tasks (instead of beeping): the first to increment a counter in the Task 1 edit box and the second to increment a counter in the Task 2 edit box. You will write the code so that the first task will be executed every 50 milliseconds and the second task will be executed every 500 milliseconds.

☐ Change the code of the OnIdle() function in the Tasks.cpp file:

```
BOOL CTasksApp::OnIdle(LONG lCount)
{

// TODO: Add your specialized code here and/or call the
// base class

/////////////////////////
// MY CODE STARTS HERE
/////////////////////////

// Call the base class CWinApp::OnIdle() function to
// finish its overhead tasks.
CWinApp::OnIdle(lCount);

// Get a pointer to the document template.
POSITION pos = GetFirstDocTemplatePosition();
CDocTemplate* pDocTemplate = GetNextDocTemplate(pos);

// Get a pointer to the document.
pos = pDocTemplate->GetFirstDocPosition();
CDocument* pDoc = pDocTemplate->GetNextDoc(pos);

// Get a pointer to the view.
pos = pDoc->GetFirstViewPosition();
CTasksView* pView =(CTasksView*) pDoc->GetNextView(pos);

// Declare and initialize two static
// variables: PrevTimeTask1 and PrevTimeTask2.
static DWORD PrevTimeTask1 = 0;
static DWORD PrevTimeTask2 = 0;

// Get the current time.
DWORD CurrentTime = GetTickCount();

// Update the variables of the controls.
pView->UpdateData(TRUE);

// If more than 50 milliseconds have elapsed since task 1
// was last performed and the Enable Task 1 check box is
// checked, perform task 1.
if (CurrentTime > PrevTimeTask1+50 &&
    pView->m_EnableTask1Check )
    {
    pView->m_Task1Edit = pView->m_Task1Edit+1;
    pView->UpdateData(FALSE);
    PrevTimeTask1 = CurrentTime;
    }

// If more than 500 milliseconds have elapsed since task 2
// was last performed and the Enable Task 2 check box is
// checked, perform task 2.
if (CurrentTime > PrevTimeTask2+500 &&
pView->m_EnableTask2Check )
```

12

```
        {
        pView->m_Task2Edit = pView->m_Task2Edit+1;
        pView->UpdateData(FALSE);
        PrevTimeTask2 = CurrentTime;
        }

// Return TRUE so that OnIdle() will be called again.
return TRUE;

/////////////////////////
// MY CODE ENDS HERE
/////////////////////////

        }
```

☐ Save your work.

The first statement you wrote calls the OnIdle() member function of the base class CWinApp:

```
CWinApp::OnIdle(lCount);
```

Remember that this is necessary because the OnIdle() member function of the base class performs overhead tasks needed for the program's normal operation.

The next six statements extract a pointer to the view of the program:

```
// Get a pointer to the document template.
POSITION pos = GetFirstDocTemplatePosition();
CDocTemplate* pDocTemplate = GetNextDocTemplate(pos);

// Get a pointer to the document.
pos = pDocTemplate->GetFirstDocPosition();
CDocument* pDoc = pDocTemplate->GetNextDoc(pos);

// Get a pointer to the view.
pos = pDoc->GetFirstViewPosition();
CTasksView* pView =(CTasksView*) pDoc->GetNextView(pos);
```

You do this because subsequent statements in the OnIdle() function need to access data members and member functions of the view class. Because the OnIdle() function is not a member of the program's view class, the preceding statements extract a pointer to the view of the program.

After the preceding six statements are executed, the pointer pView points to the view of the program. Subsequent statements in the OnIdle() function will use the pView pointer to access data members and member functions of the program's view class.

The next two statements declare and initialize to 0 two numeric static variables, PrevTimeTask1 and PrevTimeTask2:

```
static DWORD PrevTimeTask1 = 0;
static DWORD PrevTimeTask2 = 0;
```

Because you are declaring these variables as static, they won't lose their values once the OnIdle() function is terminated. On the next execution of the OnIdle() function, PrevTimeTask1 and PrevTimeTask2 will hold the same values they had when the previous iteration of OnIdle() terminated.

In the preceding statements, PrevTimeTask1 and PrevTimeTask2 are initialized to 0 so that on the first execution of the OnIdle() function, each of these variables will have a value of 0. The PrevTimeTask1 variable holds a number indicating the last time Task 1 was executed; the PrevTimeTask2 variable holds a number indicating the last time Task 2 was executed.

The next statement fills the variable CurrentTime with the returned value of the GetTickCount() function:

```
DWORD CurrentTime = GetTickCount();
```

The GetTickCount() function returns the number of milliseconds that have elapsed since Windows was started. The variable CurrentTime now holds the number of milliseconds elapsed since you started Windows.

The next statement updates the data members of the view class with the current contents of the controls onscreen:

```
pView->UpdateData(TRUE);
```

Recall that earlier statements in the OnIdle() function extracted pView—a pointer to the program's view. Therefore, after the preceding statement is executed, the two variables attached to the Enable Task 1 and Enable Task 2 check boxes are updated according to their states.

The next block of code uses an if statement to determine whether more than 50 milliseconds have elapsed since Task 1 was executed and whether the Enable Task 1 check box is checked:

```
if (CurrentTime > PrevTimeTask1+50 &&
    pView->m_EnableTask1Check )
    {
    pView->m_Task1Edit = pView->m_Task1Edit+1;
    pView->UpdateData(FALSE);
    PrevTimeTask1 = CurrentTime;
    }
```

If this is the case, the preceding if condition is satisfied, and these three statements under the if are executed:

```
pView->m_Task1Edit = pView->m_Task1Edit+1;
pView->UpdateData(FALSE);
PrevTimeTask1 = CurrentTime;
```

These statements increment the value in the Task 1 edit box and update the PrevTimeTask1 static variable with the value of CurrentTime.

12

The next block of code uses an `if` statement to determine whether more than 500 milliseconds have elapsed since Task 2 was executed and whether the Enable Task 2 check box is checked:

```
if (CurrentTime > PrevTimeTask2+500 &&
pView->m_EnableTask2Check )
    {
    pView->m_Task2Edit = pView->m_Task2Edit+1;
    pView->UpdateData(FALSE);
    PrevTimeTask2 = CurrentTime;
    }
```

If this is the case, the preceding `if` condition is satisfied, and these three statements under the `if` are executed:

```
pView->m_Task2Edit = pView->m_Task2Edit+1;
pView->UpdateData(FALSE);
PrevTimeTask2 = CurrentTime;
```

These statements increment the value in the Task 2 edit box and update the `PrevTimeTask2` static variable with the value of `CurrentTime`.

The last statement terminates the `OnIdle()` function and returns a value of `TRUE`:

```
return TRUE;
```

As discussed earlier, if you terminate the `OnIdle()` function by returning a value of `TRUE`, the `OnIdle()` function will be executed again and again for as long as the system is idle.

The Tasks program is now finished. To see the code you wrote in the `OnIdle()` function in action, do the following:

☐ Build and execute the Tasks.EXE program.

   Visual C++ responds by executing the Tasks program.

As expected, the code you attached to the `OnIdle()` function performs two tasks. One task keeps incrementing a counter in the IDC_TASK1_EDIT edit box every 50 milliseconds, and the second task keeps incrementing a counter in the IDC_TASK2_EDIT box every 500 milliseconds.

☐ Leave the Tasks program running, start another Windows program, make the window of the other program the active window, and verify that the Tasks program keeps performing the two tasks.

☐ Terminate the Tasks program.

Summary

In this chapter, you learned how to write code that performs background tasks; this ability to perform background tasks while working on other tasks is called multitasking. As you have seen, adding a background task to your Visual C++ program is quite simple—just attach code to the OnIdle event of the program's application class. The code you attach to the OnIdle event will be automatically executed whenever the system is idle.

Q&A

Q **In the code I wrote in the OnIdle() function of the Tasks program, the Task 1 edit box is updated as follows:**

```
pView->m_Task1Edit = pView->m_Task1Edit + 1;
pView->UpdateData(FALSE);
```

Why can't I use simpler code (without using the pView pointer), such as the following?

```
m_Task1Edit = m_Task1Edit + 1;
UpdateData(FALSE);
```

A The variable m_Task1Edit and the function UpdateData() are both members of the program's view class (CTasksView). The OnIdle() function is a member function of the program's application class (CTasksApp). Therefore, to access m_Task1Edit and UpdateData() from the OnIdle() function, you first have to extract a pointer to the program's view (pView), then use this pointer to access m_Task1Edit and UpdateData().

Quiz

1. When does the OnIdle event occur?
2. The OnIdle() function is a member function of which class?

Exercise

Enhance the Tasks program as follows:

Add an additional edit box to the program's main window and add a third background task that keeps on incrementing a counter in this edit box every 1000 milliseconds, or every second.

Quiz Answers

1. The OnIdle event occurs when the system is idle.
2. The OnIdle() function is a member function of the program's application class.

Exercise Answer

To add a third edit box and a task that increments a counter every 1000 milliseconds, follow these steps:

☐ Add a third edit box to the IDD_TASKS_FORM dialog box. Set the ID of this edit box to IDC_TASK3_EDIT.

☐ Attach a variable of type long to the IDC_TASK3_EDIT edit box and name this variable m_Task3Edit.

☐ Modify the code of the OnIdle() function as follows:

```
BOOL CTasksApp::OnIdle(LONG lCount)
{

// TODO: Add your specialized code here and/or call the
// base class

//////////////////////////
// MY CODE STARTS HERE
//////////////////////////

// Call the base class CWinApp::OnIdle() function to
// finish its overhead tasks.
CWinApp::OnIdle(lCount);

// Get a pointer to the document template.
POSITION pos = GetFirstDocTemplatePosition();
CDocTemplate* pDocTemplate = GetNextDocTemplate(pos);

// Get a pointer to the document.
pos = pDocTemplate->GetFirstDocPosition();
CDocument* pDoc = pDocTemplate->GetNextDoc(pos);

// Get a pointer to the view.
pos = pDoc->GetFirstViewPosition();
CTasksView* pView =(CTasksView*) pDoc->GetNextView(pos);

// Declare and initialize three static
// variables: PrevTimeTask1, PrevTimeTask2, and PrevTimeTask3.
static DWORD PrevTimeTask1 = 0;
static DWORD PrevTimeTask2 = 0;
static DWORD PrevTimeTask3 = 0;
```

12

```
// Get the current time.
DWORD CurrentTime = GetTickCount();

// Update the variables of the controls.
pView->UpdateData(TRUE);

// If more than 50 milliseconds have elapsed since task 1
// was last performed and the Enable Task 1 check box is
// checked, perform task 1.
if (CurrentTime > PrevTimeTask1+50 &&
pView->m_EnableTask1Check )
   {
   pView->m_Task1Edit = pView->m_Task1Edit+1;
   pView->UpdateData(FALSE);
   PrevTimeTask1 = CurrentTime;
   }

// If more than 500 milliseconds have elapsed since task 2
// was last performed and the Enable Task 2 check box is
// checked, perform task 2.
if (CurrentTime > PrevTimeTask2+500 &&
pView->m_EnableTask2Check )
   {
   pView->m_Task2Edit = pView->m_Task2Edit+1;
   pView->UpdateData(FALSE);
   PrevTimeTask2 = CurrentTime;
   }

// If more than 1000 milliseconds have elapsed since task 3
// was last performed, perform task 3.
if (CurrentTime > PrevTimeTask3+1000)
{
   pView->m_Task3Edit = pView->m_Task3Edit+1;
   pView->UpdateData(FALSE);
   PrevTimeTask3 = CurrentTime;
   }

// Return TRUE so that OnIdle() will be called again.
return TRUE;

/////////////////////////
// MY CODE ENDS HERE
/////////////////////////

}
```

12

Day 13

Writing Multiple-Document Interface (MDI) Applications

In this chapter, you'll learn what a multiple-document interface (MDI) application is and how to create one with Visual C++.

What Is a Multiple-Document Interface (MDI) Application?

Recall from Chapter 11, "Writing Single-Document Interface (SDI) Applications," that an SDI program lets you work with documents, but only one document at a time. You can create a document, save the document into a file, and load previously saved files.

A multiple-document interface program (an MDI program) also enables you to work with documents. However, an MDI program lets you work on and open several documents simultaneously. Microsoft Word is an example of an MDI program. Figure 13.1 shows Microsoft Word with several documents open.

Figure 13.1.

An example of an MDI program.

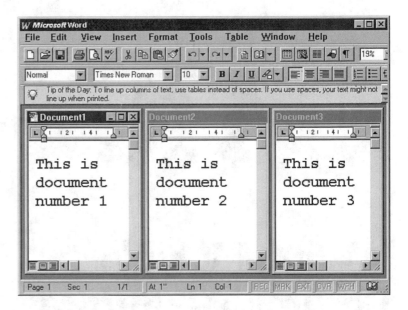

 NOTE

In this chapter, you'll learn how to write a multiple-document interface program. As you'll soon see, the steps you need to take to create a multiple-document interface program are not much different than the steps you took when you created a single-document interface program in Chapter 11. However, an MDI program is much more powerful and impressive than an SDI program.

Even if you haven't read Chapter 11, or haven't read it recently, you can still follow this chapter's material. This chapter does not assume any know-how from Chapter 11.

The MCircle.EXE Program

In this chapter, you'll write a Visual C++ program called MCircle.EXE, an example of an MDI program. Before you start writing the MCircle program, first review what it should look like and what it should do.

13

The MCircle.EXE program is very similar to the Circle.EXE program you wrote in Chapter 11. The only difference is that the MCircle.EXE program will be an MDI program, so you can open several documents simultaneously:

■ When you start the MCircle program, the window of the program should look like Figure 13.2.

Figure 13.2.

The window of the MCircle program at startup.

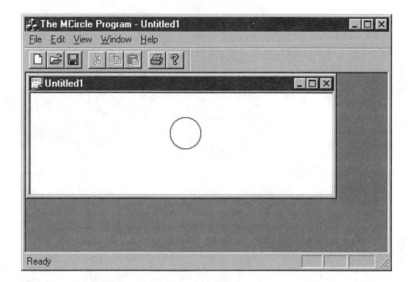

■ When you start the MCircle program, it creates a new circle document and displays the window (or view) of this document. As shown in Figure 13.2, the title of the new document is Untitled1. It contains the word "Untitled" because the document has just been created and hasn't been saved into a file. When you save it, the title Untitled1 will be replaced with the name of the saved file.

■ The MCircle program is a simple MDI program in which the document is a circle. You can place the circle anywhere in the window by simply clicking the mouse at the desired point, then save the circle into a file. At a later time, you can open a previously saved file, and the saved circle will appear onscreen.

■ You can save the drawn circle into a file by selecting Save (or Save As) from the File menu of the MCircle program. (See Figure 13.3.)

You can load a previously saved circle by selecting Open from the File menu of the MCircle program. Once you select Open from the File menu, the MCircle program displays an Open dialog box for selecting the previously saved circle file.

■ You can print the currently displayed document by selecting Print from the File menu.

13

Figure 13.3.

The File menu of the MCircle program.

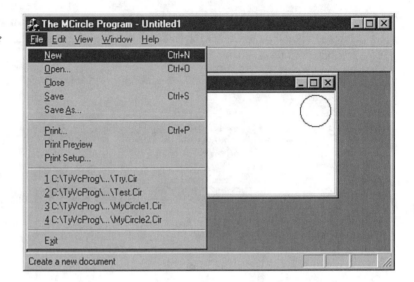

■ In the MCircle program, you can open several documents simultaneously because it's an MDI program. Figure 13.4 shows the desktop of the MCircle program with three circle documents open.

Figure 13.4.

Opening three circle documents simultaneously.

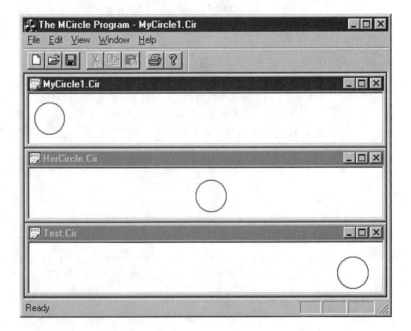

You can minimize any of the windows of the currently open documents. Figure 13.5 shows the desktop of the MCircle program with three windows minimized.

Figure 13.5.
Minimizing the windows of three circle documents.

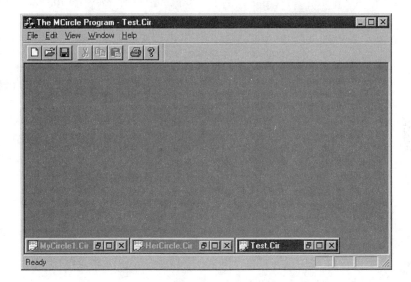

- You can use the Window menu of the MCircle program to move from one window to another. At any given time, the Window menu lists the names of all the currently open windows on the desktop. (See Figure 13.6.)

Figure 13.6.
The Window menu of the MCircle program.

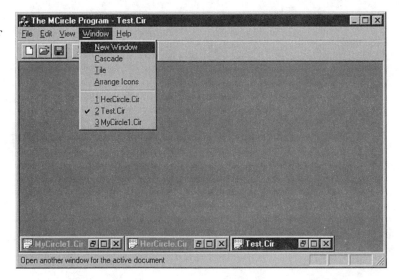

The New Window item of the Window menu enables you to display several views (windows) of the same document. When you select New Window, the MCircle program responds by opening another window for the current document. For example, Figure 13.7 shows two windows for the same document—both of these windows display the circle of the Test.Cir document. When you change one view of the document, the other view is automatically updated.

Figure 13.7.

Opening two views of the same document.

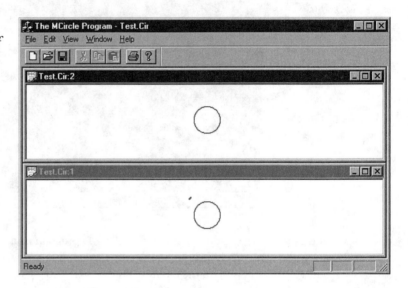

Why is seeing several views of the same document useful? If you have an MDI program with an extremely long document, such as a long text document or a large picture, you may need to work on several sections of the same document at a time. In such cases, you can open several views (windows) of the same document and display a different section of the document in each window. When you change one view of the document, all the other views of the document are automatically updated.

■ The MCircle program includes a toolbar displayed at the top of the program's window. You can perform various operations by clicking the tool you need. For example, clicking the Save tool on the toolbar (the one with a disk icon) is equivalent to selecting Save from the File menu; clicking the About tool (the one with the question mark icon) is the same as selecting About from the Help menu.

Now that you know what the MCircle program should do, start creating this program.

13

Creating the Project of the MCircle Program

Follow these steps to create the project and skeleton files of the MCircle program:

☐ Create the directory C:\TYVCPROG\PROGRAMS\CH13.

☐ Start Visual C++ and select New from the File menu.

Visual C++ responds by displaying the New dialog box.

☐ Select the Projects tab of the New dialog box.

☐ Select MFC AppWizard(exe) from the list of project types.

☐ Type MCircle in the Project Name box.

☐ Click the button that is located on the right of the Location box and select the C:\TYVCPROG\PROGRAMS\CH13 directory.

☐ Click the OK button.

Visual C++ responds by displaying the MFC AppWizard - Step 1 window.

☐ In the Step 1 window, choose the "Multiple documents" radio button to create an MDI program. (See Figure 13.8.) When you're done, click the Next button.

Figure 13.8.

Creating an MDI program.

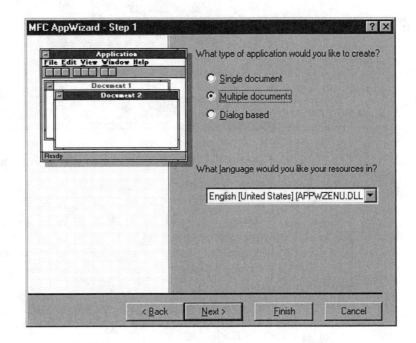

☐ In the Step 2 window, select the "None" option because you don't want the program to support any database features. Click the Next button.

☐ In the Step 3 window, leave the options at their default settings and click the Next button.

☐ Set the Step 4 window as shown in Figure 13.9. You want the program to support these features: docking toolbar, initial status bar, printing and print preview, and 3-D controls. Leave the number of files for the MRU (most recently used) list at the default setting of 4. When you're done, click the Next button.

Figure 13.9.

Choosing features to include in your MDI program.

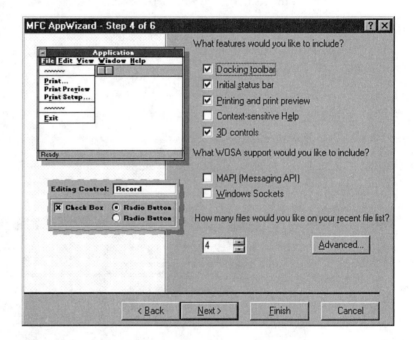

☐ In the Step 5 window, use the default settings and click the Next button.

☐ In the Step 6 window, notice that Visual C++ has created the following classes for you: CMCircleApp, CMainFrame, CChildFrame, CMCircleDoc, and CMCircleView. (See Figure 13.10.) Remember from Chapter 11 that the document class, CMCircleDoc, is where you write code for maintaining the program's data, and the view class, CMCircleView, is where you write code concerning what you see onscreen. You'll write code in the member functions of these two classes only. When you're done reviewing the classes, click the Finish button.

Visual C++ responds by displaying the New Project Information window.

Figure 13.10.

The classes created for the MCircle program.

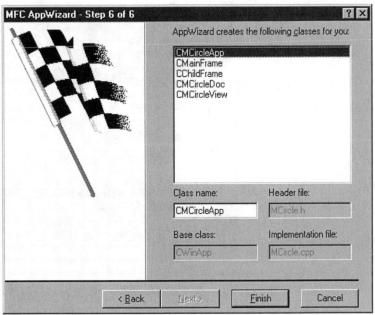

☐ Click the OK button of the New Project Information window.

Visual C++ responds by creating the project file and associated files of the MCircle program.

☐ Select Set Active Configuration from the Build menu.

Visual C++ responds by displaying the Set Active Project Configuration dialog box.

☐ Select MCircle - Win32 Release in the Set Active Project Configuration dialog box, then click the OK button.

That's it! You've finished creating the project file and skeleton files of the MCircle program.

Running the MCircle Program Before Customization

Before you start customizing the MCircle program, first build and execute it at this stage. As you'll see, the skeleton files Visual C++ created for you yield an MDI program that already performs some functions.

☐ Build and execute the MCircle.EXE program.

Visual C++ responds by executing the MCircle.EXE program. The main window of the MCircle program appears, as shown in Figure 13.11.

Figure 13.11.

The main window of the MCircle program.

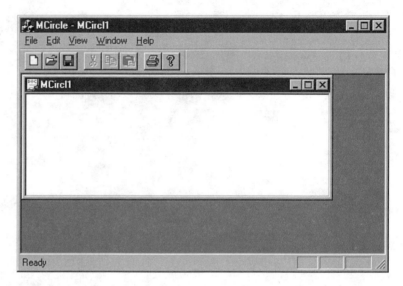

At this early stage, you already have a working MDI program! The skeleton code that Visual C++ wrote for you yielded an impressive MDI program that includes a standard MDI menu system and toolbar.

Of course, at this point the MCircle program doesn't do what you want it to, so in the following sections, you'll write code to customize the MCircle project. The code will enable you to create circle documents, save circle documents, and load previously saved documents. You will also be able to work on multiple circle documents simultaneously.

☐ Terminate the MCircle program by selecting Exit from its File menu.

Declaring the Data Members of the Document Class

The code you'll write in the document class, CMCircleDoc, of the MCircle program is responsible for storing the document (the program's data). This code will enable you to save the program's data into a file and load data from previously saved files. You'll now add data members to the document class that will be used for storing MCircle's document data:

☐ Select the FileView tab of the Project Workspace window, expand the MCircle Files item, expand the Header Files item, and finally double-click the MCircleDoc.h item.

Visual C++ responds by opening the MCircleDoc.h file. The MCircleDoc.h file is where the document class of the MCircle program (the CMCircleDoc *class) is declared.*

13

You'll now declare two data members in the CMCircleDoc class:

☐ Modify the declaration of the CMCircleDoc class as follows:

```
class CMCircleDoc : public CDocument
{
protected: // create from serialization only
     CMCircleDoc();
     DECLARE_DYNCREATE(CMCircleDoc)

// Attributes
public:

/////////////////////////
// MY CODE STARTS HERE
/////////////////////////

int m_PosX;
int m_PosY;

/////////////////////////
// MY CODE ENDS HERE
/////////////////////////

// Operations
...
...
...

};
```

☐ Save your work.

The code you added to the declaration of the CMCircleDoc class declares two int data members, m_PosX and m_PosY:

```
int m_PosX;
int m_PosY;
```

The m_PosX data member will be used for storing the x coordinate of the circle you draw, and the m_PosY data member will be used for storing the y coordinate of the circle. You can add other data members that define the drawn circle, such as its radius or color. However, to keep it simple, in the MCircle program you'll specify only the x-y coordinate of the circle—the point where the circle will be drawn. All other aspects will be fixed.

The document class of the MCircle program now has two data members: m_PosX and m_PosY. These data members are the data composing the document of the MCircle program. Later, you will write code for saving m_PosX and m_PosY into a file and loading data from previously saved files into the m_PosX and m_PosY data members.

13

Declaring the Data Members of the View Class

The code you write in the view class, CMCircleView, of the MCircle program is responsible for what you see onscreen. You'll now add data members to the view class so that when you write code later, you can use these data members to draw a circle in the documents' windows.

The view class data members are a mirror image of the data members you added to the document class. This is necessary because the code of the view class is supposed to display onscreen whatever the document specifies. For example, if the document specifies that the circle should be displayed at a certain x-y coordinate, the code of the view class will display the circle at the specified coordinate.

☐ Open the file MCircleView.h, where the view class, CMCircleView, is declared. (Select the FileView tab of the Project Workspace window, expand the MCircle Files item, expand the Header Files item, and double-click the MCircleView.h item.)

You'll now declare two data members (with the same names as the document class data members) in the CMCircleView class:

☐ Modify the declaration of the CMCircleView class as follows:

```
class CMCircleView : public CView
{
protected: // create from serialization only
    CMCircleView();
    DECLARE_DYNCREATE(CMCircleView)

// Attributes
public:
    CMCircleDoc* GetDocument();

/////////////////////////
// MY CODE STARTS HERE
/////////////////////////

int m_PosX;
int m_PosY;

/////////////////////////
// MY CODE ENDS HERE
/////////////////////////

// Operations
...
...
...


};
```

☐ Save your work.

13

The code you added to the declaration of the CMCircleView class is identical to the code you added for the CMCircleDoc class. This code declares two int data members, m_PosX and m_PosY:

```
int m_PosX;
int m_PosY;
```

The m_PosX data member will hold the x coordinate of the circle, and the m_PosY data member will hold the y coordinate of the circle. Now the document class and the view class have the same two data members: m_PosX and m_PosY.

The code you write later to draw the circle will be written in the view class of the program. This code will draw the circle according to the values of the m_PosX and m_PosY view class data members. The code you write later for saving and loading circles will be written in the document class of the program. This code will use the m_PosX and m_PosY document class data members.

As you will see in the following sections, the values of the view class data members should always be the same as the values of the document class data members. You want the values stored in the document to be the same as the values that you see onscreen. Therefore, the code you write in the following sections will ensure that the data members of these two classes always have the same values.

Initializing the Data Members of the Document Class

You'll now write the code that initializes the data members of the document class in the OnNewDocument() member function of the document class:

☐ Open the file MCircleDoc.cpp and locate the OnNewDocument() function.

☐ Write the following code in the OnNewDocument() function:

```
BOOL CMCircleDoc::OnNewDocument()
{
if (!CDocument::OnNewDocument())
   return FALSE;

// TODO: add reinitialization code here
// (SDI documents will reuse this document)

////////////////////////
// MY CODE STARTS HERE
////////////////////////

// Initialize the data members of the document.
m_PosX = 200;
m_PosY = 50;
```

13

```
/////////////////////////
// MY CODE ENDS HERE
/////////////////////////

return TRUE;
}
```

☐ Save your work.

The `OnNewDocument()` member function of the document class is automatically executed whenever a new document is created by starting the program or selecting New from the File menu.

The code you wrote in the `OnNewDocument()` function initializes the value of the `m_PosX` data member to `200` and initializes the `m_PosY` data member to `50`:

```
m_PosX = 200;
m_PosY = 50;
```

Therefore, whenever a new document is created, the `m_PosX` document data member will be set to a value of `200` and the `m_PosY` document data member will be set to a value of `50`.

Initializing the Data Members of the View Class

In the preceding section, you initialized the data members of the document class, which represent the values stored in a document file. You'll now write the code that initializes the data members of the view class, which represent what you see onscreen. This code is written in the `OnInitialUpdate()` member function of the view class.

☐ Select ClassWizard from the View menu. In the Message Maps tab of the ClassWizard window, select the following event:

Class name:	CMCircleView
Object ID:	CMCircleView
Message:	OnInitialUpdate

☐ Click the Add Function button of ClassWizard.

Visual C++ responds by adding the `OnInitialUpdate()` *function.*

☐ Click the Edit Code button of ClassWizard.

Visual C++ responds by opening the file MCircleView.cpp with the function `OnInitialUpdate()` *ready for you to edit.*

☐ Write the following code in the `OnInitialUpdate()` function:

```
void CMCircleView::OnInitialUpdate()
{
CView::OnInitialUpdate();
```

```
    // TODO: Add your specialized code here and/or call the base
    //       class

    /////////////////////////////
    // MY CODE STARTS HERE
    /////////////////////////////

    // Get a pointer to the  document
    CMCircleDoc* pDoc = GetDocument();

    // Update data members of the view with the
    // corresponding document values.
    m_PosX  = pDoc->m_PosX;
    m_PosY  = pDoc->m_PosY;

    /////////////////////////////
    // MY CODE ENDS HERE
    /////////////////////////////

    }
```

☐ Save your work.

The `OnInitialUpdate()` member function of the view class initializes the view class data members. The code you just attached to the `OnInitialUpdate()` function updates the view class data members with the current values of the document class data members.

The first statement you typed uses the `GetDocument()` function to extract a pointer, `pDoc`, to the document:

```
CMCircleDoc* pDoc = GetDocument();
```

The remaining statements use the `pDoc` pointer to initialize the view class data members with the current values of the document data members:

```
m_PosX  = pDoc->m_PosX;
m_PosY  = pDoc->m_PosY;
```

These statements update the `m_PosX` and `m_PosY` data members of the view class with the corresponding document class data members.

Writing the Code That Displays the Circle

You'll now write the code in the view class that displays the circle onscreen. As discussed earlier, the view class is responsible for whatever you see onscreen, so you'll write the drawing code in the `OnDraw()` member function of the `CMCircleView` class. The `OnDraw()` function of the view class is automatically executed whenever there is a need to draw the document's window.

☐ Open the file MCircleView.cpp and locate the `OnDraw()` function.

13

☐ Write the following code in the OnDraw() function:

```
void CMCircleView::OnDraw(CDC* pDC)
{
CMCircleDoc* pDoc = GetDocument();
ASSERT_VALID(pDoc);

// TODO: add draw code for native data here

/////////////////////////
// MY CODE STARTS HERE
/////////////////////////

// Define the rectangular boundaries of the
// circle to be drawn.
RECT  rect;
rect.left = m_PosX - 20;
rect.top = m_PosY -20;
rect.bottom = m_PosY + 20;
rect.right = m_PosX +20;

// Draw the circle.
pDC->Ellipse(&rect);

/////////////////////////
// MY CODE ENDS HERE
/////////////////////////

}
```

☐ Save your work.

The code you typed in the OnDraw() function draws a circle at the position specified by the m_PosX and m_PosY data members of the view class.

The first five statements you typed define the coordinates and dimensions of a rectangle called rect:

```
RECT  rect;
rect.left = m_PosX - 20;
rect.top = m_PosY -20;
rect.bottom = m_PosY + 20;
rect.right = m_PosX +20;
```

These statements define the rectangle's center at the x-y coordinate specified by the m_PosX and m_PosY data members. The width and height of the rectangle are both 40 pixels, so the rect rectangle is defined as a square.

The last statement you typed uses the Ellipse() function to draw an ellipse:

```
pDC->Ellipse(&rect);
```

pDC, the parameter of the OnDraw() function, is the pointer to the dc (device context). By executing the Ellipse() function on the pDC pointer, you are drawing an ellipse in the window. The parameter of the Ellipse() function in the preceding statement is &rect.

13

Therefore, the ellipse will be drawn within the boundaries of the rectangle you defined. Because the rect rectangle is a square, the ellipse will be drawn as a circle.

Putting it all together, the code you wrote in the OnDraw() function draws a circle at the x-y coordinate specified by the m_PosX and m_PosY view class data members.

☐ Build and execute the MCircle.EXE program to see your drawing code in action.

Visual C++ responds by executing the MCircle program. The main window of the MCircle program appears, as shown in Figure 13.12.

Figure 13.12.

The main window of the MCircle program with a circle document.

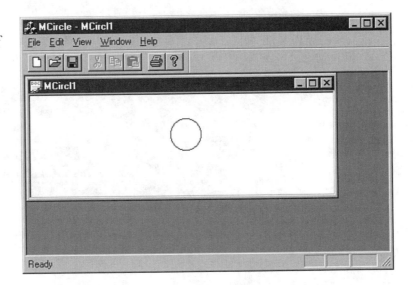

As you can see, the drawing code you wrote in the OnDraw() function is working—when you start the MCircle program, a new document called MCircl1 is created and a circle is drawn at the x-y coordinate x=200, y=50. That's because the code you wrote in the OnNewDocument() member function of the document class initialized the document class data members m_PosX and m_PosY to m_PosX=200 and m_PosY=50, and the code you wrote in the OnInitialUpdate() member function of the view class updated the m_PosX and m_PosY view class data members with the values of the document class data members.

13

Exploring the MDI Features of the MCircle Program

As you can see, the SDI Circle program in Chapter 11 and the MDI MCircle program in this chapter are very similar. However, MCircle is an MDI program, so the focus of this chapter is on exploring the MDI features of the program that let you create and work on several

documents simultaneously. To see some of the MDI features of the MCircle program, create
two additional documents:

☐ Select New from the File menu of the MCircle program.

*The MCircle program responds by creating a second new document called MCircl2 and
displaying the window (view) of this document on the desktop.*

☐ Select New from the File menu of the MCircle program again.

*The MCircle program responds by creating a new document called MCircl3 and displaying
the window (view) of this document on the desktop.*

The desktop of your MCircle program should now look like the one shown in Figure 13.13—
three windows (views) of three documents are open on the desktop.

Figure 13.13.

*Opening three
windows (views) of
three documents.*

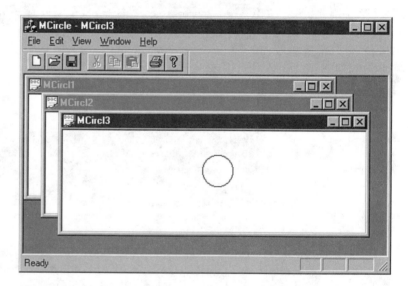

The MCircle program automatically assigns these names to the three documents: MCircl1,
MCircl2, and MCircl3. If you create a fourth document, the MCircle program will
automatically assign the name MCircl4 to it. Later in the chapter, you'll write code that
enables you to save a document into a file. When you save a document, the name of the
document will be the filename under which you saved the document.

NOTE

In the Exercise section at the end of this chapter, you'll learn how to
enhance the MCircle program so that the default names of new
documents will be Untitled1, Untitled2, Untitled3, and so on.

Now experiment with some of the MDI features of the MCircle program:

☐ Select Tile from the Window menu of the MCircle program.

The MCircle program responds by displaying the three windows of the documents in tile format. (See Figure 13.14.)

Figure 13.14.

Viewing the documents in tile format.

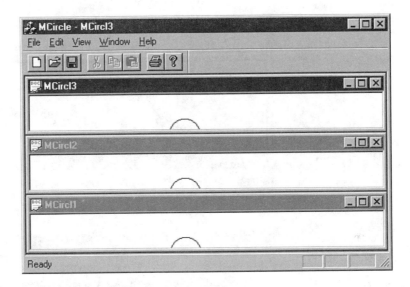

As shown in Figure 13.14, you can see only half a circle in each of the three windows because the main window is too small. Increase the height of the window as follows:

☐ Increase the height of the MCircle program's main window by dragging the bottom edge of the main window downward.

☐ Select Tile from the Window menu of the MCircle program.

The desktop of your MCircle program should now look like Figure 13.15—you can see a whole circle in each of the windows.

To view the windows of the three documents in cascading format, do the following:

☐ Select Cascade from the Window menu of the MCircle program.

The MCircle program responds by displaying the three documents in cascading format. (See Figure 13.16.)

13

Figure 13.15.

Increasing the height of the main window for viewing tiled documents.

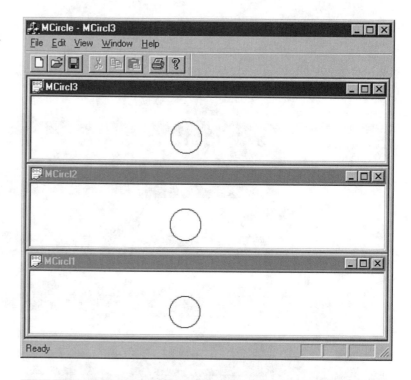

Figure 13.16.

Viewing the documents in cascading format.

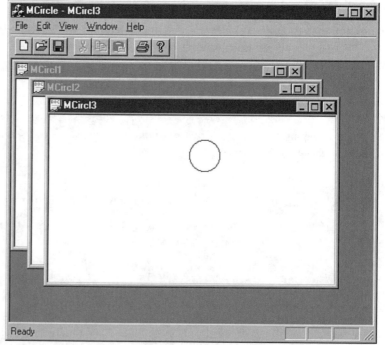

You can minimize the windows of the three documents as follows:

- Minimize the MCircl1 window by clicking its Minimize button, the small icon with an underscore mark (_) at the upper-right corner.
- Minimize the MCircl2 window.
- Minimize the MCircl3 window.

The desktop of the MCircle program with the windows of the three documents minimized is shown in Figure 13.17.

Figure 13.17.
Minimizing the windows of the three cascaded documents.

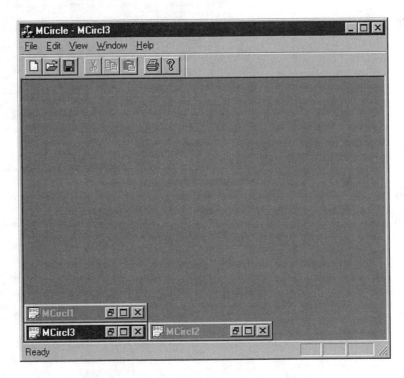

You can move any minimized window to any location on the desktop by dragging it.

☐ Move the three minimized windows to different locations in the desktop.

You can now arrange the three minimized windows in an orderly manner:

☐ Select Arrange Icons from the Window menu of the MCircle program.

The MCircle program responds by rearranging the minimized windows as shown back in Figure 13.17.

The Window menu of the MCircle program has one additional menu item you have not experimented with yet—the New Window menu item. You'll get a chance to experiment with this menu item later in the chapter.

The Window menu of the MCircle program also lists all the windows' names of the currently open documents. You currently have three open windows on the desktop—MCircl1, MCircl2, and MCircl3—so their names are listed in the Window menu. (See Figure 13.18.)

Figure 13.18.

Listing currently open documents in the Window menu.

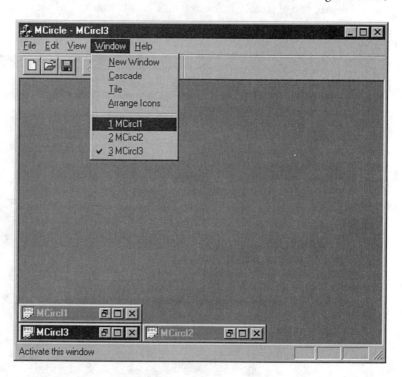

The drawing code you wrote in the OnDraw() member function of the view class is executed when there is a need to redraw the screen and when you select Print from the File menu. The code you wrote is responsible both for what you see onscreen and what is printed when you select Print from the File menu. To see the Print menu item of the MCircle program in action, print the MCircl1 document:

☐ Select MCircl1 from the Window menu of the MCircle program.

☐ Select Print from the File menu of the MCircle program.

The MCircle program responds by displaying the Print dialog box. (See Figure 13.19.)

13

Figure 13.19.
The Print dialog box.

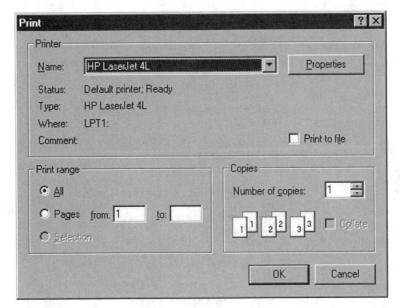

☐ Click the OK button of the Print dialog box.

The MCircle program responds by printing the MCircl1 document on your printer.

☐ Terminate the MCircle program by selecting Exit from its File menu.

Writing Code That Draws the Circle at Any Location

At this point, when you create a new document, the window displays a circle at the x-y coordinate x=200, y=50. You'll now write code that enables you to draw the circle anywhere in the document's window by simply clicking the mouse at the desired point. You'll write this code in the view class because it concerns what you see onscreen.

☐ Select ClassWizard from the View menu. In the Message Maps tab of the ClassWizard window, select the following event:

Class name:	CMCircleView
Object ID:	CMCircleView
Message:	WM_LBUTTONDOWN

☐ Click the Add Function button of ClassWizard.

Visual C++ responds by adding the OnLButtonDown() *function.*

☐ Click the Edit Code button of ClassWizard.

Visual C++ responds by opening the file MCircleView.cpp with the function OnLButtonDown() *ready for you to edit.*

☐ Write the following code in the OnLButtonDown() function:

```
void CMCircleView::OnLButtonDown(UINT nFlags, CPoint point)
{
// TODO: Add your message handler code here and/or call
//          default

/////////////////////////
// MY CODE STARTS HERE
/////////////////////////

// Update the m_PosX and m_PosY data members of
// the view class with the x-y coordinate of the
// point where the mouse was clicked.
m_PosX = point.x;
m_PosY = point.y;

// Trigger a call to the OnDraw() function.
Invalidate();

// Get a pointer to the document
CMCircleDoc* pDoc = GetDocument();

// Update data members of the document with the
// new values of the view class data members.
pDoc->m_PosX = m_PosX;
pDoc->m_PosY = m_PosY ;

// Signal that the document has been modified.
pDoc->SetModifiedFlag(TRUE);

/////////////////////////
// MY CODE ENDS HERE
/////////////////////////

CView::OnLButtonDown(nFlags, point);

}
```

☐ Save your work.

The OnLButtonDown() member function of the view class is automatically executed when you press the left mouse button down over the document's window.

The second parameter of the OnLButtonDown() function, point, specifies the point onscreen where you pressed the mouse button; point.x holds the x coordinate, and point.y holds the y coordinate of the point.

The first two statements you typed update the m_PosX and m_PosY view class data members with the x and y coordinates of the point where you clicked the mouse:

```
m_PosX = point.x;
m_PosY = point.y;
```

The next statement calls the `Invalidate()` function, which causes the execution of the `OnDraw()` function:

```
Invalidate();
```

Recall that the code you wrote in the `OnDraw()` function draws a circle at the point specified by `m_PosX` and `m_PosY`, so the preceding statements will draw a circle at the point where you clicked the mouse.

The next statement uses the `GetDocument()` function to extract a pointer, `pDoc`, to the document:

```
CMCircleDoc* pDoc = GetDocument();
```

The next two statements use the `pDoc` pointer to update the document class data members with the new values of the view class data members:

```
pDoc->m_PosX = m_PosX;
pDoc->m_PosY = m_PosY ;
```

Now the document class data members have the same values as their corresponding data members in the view class. When you change the values of data members in the view class, you should change the corresponding data members in the document class to the same values so that the data stored in the document of the program is the same as the data you view onscreen.

The last statement you typed calls the `SetModifiedFlag()` function:

```
pDoc->SetModifiedFlag();
```

In the preceding statement, the `SetModified()` function is executed on the `pDoc` document pointer, because `SetModifiedFlag()` is a member function of the document class (not the view class). As its name implies, the `SetModifiedFlag()` function raises a flag in the document to indicate that the document's data has been changed. If you try to exit the program without saving the modified document first, the program will display a warning message box to give you a chance to save the changes made in the document. You should always call the `SetModifiedFlag()` function after changing the values of the document class data members.

☐ Build and execute the MCircle.EXE program to see the code you wrote in the `OnLButtonDown()` function in action.

Visual C++ responds by executing the MCircle program. The desktop of the MCircle program appears with a new document titled MCircl1. (Refer to Figure 13.12.)

☐ Click the mouse at the upper-right corner of the program's window.

The MCircle program responds by drawing a circle at the point where you clicked the mouse.

☐ Try clicking the mouse at various points in the document's window and notice how a circle is drawn at each point where you click the mouse.

13

☐ Create new documents (by selecting New from the File menu) and verify that clicking the mouse produces the same results.

☐ Terminate the MCircle program by selecting Exit from its File menu.

When you terminate the program, the MCircle program displays a message box asking whether you would like to save changes you have made to the documents. Click the No button of the message box because you don't want to save any changes. In the following section, you'll write the code responsible for saving the documents into files.

Writing Code That Saves and Loads Documents

You'll now write the code responsible for saving the documents into files and loading previously saved document files. You'll write this code in the document class.

☐ Open the file MCircleDoc.cpp and locate the `Serialize()` function. It should look like this:

```
void CMCircleDoc::Serialize(CArchive& ar)
{
if (ar.IsStoring())
    {
    // TODO: add storing code here
    }
else
    {
    // TODO: add loading code here
    }
}
```

The `Serialize()` function is automatically executed when you select Save, Save As, or Open from the File menu of the program. As you can see, the code in the `Serialize()` function is made up of a simple `if...else` statement:

```
if (ar.IsStoring())
    {
    // TODO: add storing code here
    ...........................................
    ... This code is automatically executed ...
    ... whenever the user selects Save or   ...
    ... Save As from the File menu.         ...
    ...........................................
    }
else
    {
    // TODO: add loading code here
    ...........................................
    ... This code is automatically executed ...
    ... whenever the user selects Open      ...
    ... from the File menu.                  ...
    ...........................................
    }
```

13

This is the `if` condition of the `if...else` statement:

```
if (ar.IsStoring())
```

In this code, the parameter of the `Serialize()` function, `ar`, represents the archive (the file) you are trying to read or write. If you select Save or Save As from the File menu, the condition of the preceding `if` statement is satisfied and the code under the `if` is executed. If you select Open from the File menu, the code under the `else` is executed.

Therefore, your job is to do the following:

1. Write code under the `if` statement that writes data to the file.
2. Write code under the `else` statement that reads data from the file.

Follow these steps to write this code:

☐ Write the following code in the `Serialize()` function:

```
void CMCircleDoc::Serialize(CArchive& ar)
{
if (ar.IsStoring())
    {
    // TODO: add storing code here

    ///////////////////////
    // MY CODE STARTS HERE
    ///////////////////////

    // Save m_PosX and m_PosY into the file.
    ar << m_PosX;
    ar << m_PosY;

    ///////////////////////
    // MY CODE ENDS HERE
    ///////////////////////

    }
    else
    {
    // TODO: add loading code here

    ///////////////////////
    // MY CODE STARTS HERE
    ///////////////////////

    // Fill m_PosX and m_PosY with data from the file.
    ar >> m_PosX;
    ar >> m_PosY;

    ///////////////////////
    // MY CODE ENDS HERE
    ///////////////////////

    }
}
```

13

☐ Save your work.

The code you wrote under the `if` statement is responsible for saving data into the file:

```
ar << m_PosX;
ar << m_PosY;
```

The insertion operator (<<) indicates you want to save data into the file. For example, this statement stores the data member `m_PosX` of the document class into the file:

```
ar << m_PosX;
```

Into what file? It depends on what you did. If you select Save As, then select the file MyFile.TRY from the Save As dialog box, the statement `ar << m_PosX;` will store the `m_PosX` variable in the MyFile.TRY file. You can think of `ar` as the file that you selected.

NOTE

> `ar` is the archive object (an object of class `CArchive`) that corresponds to the file you selected. Therefore, the statement `ar << m_PosX;` literally means "save the variable `m_PosX` into the file you selected."
>
> The `CArchive` class is discussed in Chapter 14, "File Access and Serialization."

The code you wrote under the `else` statement in the `Serialize()` function is responsible for loading the data from the file into the variables:

```
ar >> m_PosX;
ar >> m_PosY;
```

The extractor operator (>>) indicates you want to load data from the file into the variable. For example, this statement fills the data member `m_PosX` with data from the file:

```
ar >> m_PosX;
```

Again, the file depends on what you did. If you select Open from the File menu, then select the file MyFile.TRY from the Open File dialog box, the statement `ar >> m_PosX` will fill the `m_PosX` variable with data from MyFile.TRY.

Note that the order in which you extract the data must be the same order used for saving the data. For example, if you save data to the file with these statements:

```
ar << Var1;
ar << Var2;
ar << Var3;
```

when you extract the data from the file into the variables, you must use the same order:

```
ar >> Var1;
ar >> Var2;
ar >> Var3;
```

In the previous code you used the insertion (<<) and extractor (>>) operators on several lines. You can also use these operators on a single line. For example, these three statements:

```
ar << Var1;
ar << Var2;
ar << Var3;
```

are equivalent to this single statement:

```
ar << Var1 << Var2 << Var3;
```

☐ Build and execute the MCircle.EXE program to see your code in action.

Visual C++ responds by executing the MCircle program, which creates a new document called MCircl1. The main window of the MCircle program looks like the one shown in Figure 13.12.

To test the saving and loading code you wrote in the `Serialize()` function of the document class, do the following:

☐ Click the mouse at the lower-left corner of the MCircl1 window.

The MCircle program responds by drawing the circle at the lower-left corner of the MCircl1 window.

Now, save the document into a file as follows:

☐ Select Save As from the File menu of the MCircle program.

The MCircle program responds by displaying the Save As dialog box. (See Figure 13.20.)

Figure 13.20.
The Save As dialog box.

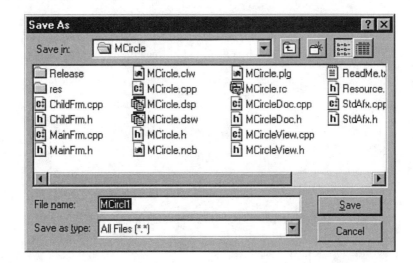

13

☐ Delete the name MCircl1 in the File name edit box and enter MyCircle.Cir, then click the Save button.

The MCircle program responds by creating the MyCircle.Cir file and saving the document into this file.

Because you saved the document in the file MyCircle.Cir, the title of the document's window is now MyCircle. (See Figure 13.21.)

Figure 13.21.

The window's title changes to the filename of the saved document.

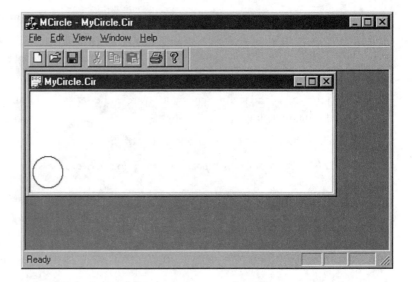

To verify your document is indeed saved in the MyCircle.Cir file, do the following:

☐ Select Close from the File menu of the MCircle program.

The MCircle program responds by closing the MyCircle document.

☐ Select Open from the File menu of the MCircle program.

The MCircle program responds by displaying the Open dialog box. (See Figure 13.22.)

☐ Use the Open dialog box to select the MyCircle.Cir file you saved earlier, then click the Open button.

The MCircle program responds by opening the MyCircle.Cir file.

The window of your MCircle program should now look like the one shown in Figure 13.21—the window of the MyCircle.Cir document is open on the desktop with a circle drawn in the lower-left corner.

13

Figure 13.22.

The Open dialog box.

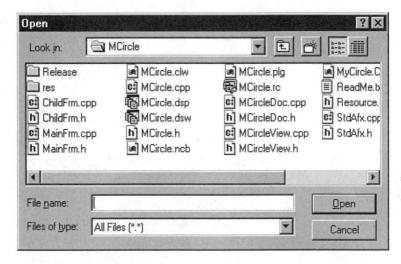

You have just verified that the code you wrote in the `Serialize()` member function of the document class is working! You are able to save documents into files and load previously saved files.

☐ Keep experimenting with the MCircle program. For example, create new documents (by selecting New from the File menu), place the circle at different places in their windows, and save the documents under different filenames.

As you experiment with the MCircle program, notice that the File menu of the program maintains a most recently used file list—an MRU list. (See Figure 13.23.)

Figure 13.23.

The MRU list in MCircle's File menu.

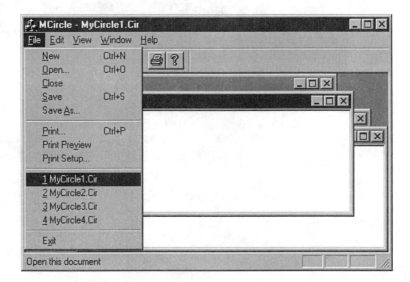

13

The MRU list of the MCircle program lists the four most recent files you've worked on. When you click one of the files in the list, the file is opened. Recall that when you created the project of the MCircle program, you accepted the default setting of 4 for the MRU list in Step 4 of the AppWizard. (Refer to Figure 13.9.)

 NOTE

> The tools on the toolbar of the MCircle program were created for you by Visual C++ when you created the project and skeleton files of the project. In Chapter 15, "Toolbars and Status Bars," you'll learn how to create your own custom tools in the program's toolbar.

Notice that the main window of the MCircle program displays this title:

```
MCircle - filename
```

where *filename* is the name of the currently active window. For example, in Figure 13.24, the title of the program's main window is MCircle - MyCircle1.Cir because the MyCircle1.Cir document is the currently active window.

Figure 13.24.

The title of the program's main window reflects the filename of the active window.

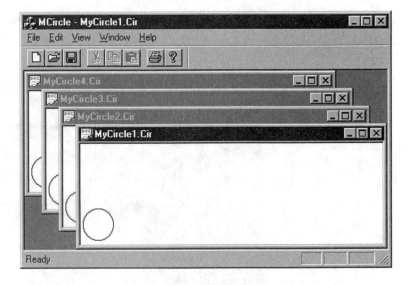

☐ Terminate the MCircle program by selecting Exit from its File menu.

Multiple Views of the Same Document

The MCircle program doesn't currently support multiple views of the same document—being able to open several windows for the same document. In a program that supports multiple views of the same document, when you change the data in one of the windows, the data in the rest of the windows (of the same document) is updated automatically. To verify that currently the MCircle program does not support multiple views, try the following experiment:

☐ Execute the MCircle program by selecting Execute MCircle.EXE from the Build menu.

The main window of the MCircle program appears with a new document called MCircl1 (its default name).

☐ Select Save from the File menu and save the new document as Test.Cir.

☐ Select New Window from the Window menu.

The MCircle program responds by opening another view (another window) for the Test.Cir document.

☐ Select Tile from the Window menu.

Your MCircle program should now look like Figure 13.25.

Figure 13.25.
Two views of the Test.Cir document.

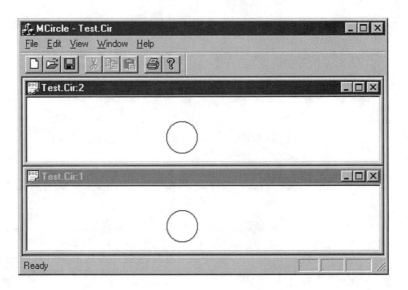

13

As you can see, the Test.Cir document has two views (windows): one with the title Test.Cir:1 and the other with the title Test.Cir:2.

☐ Click the mouse at the upper-right corner of the Test.Cir:2 window.

The MCircle program responds by drawing the circle at the point where you clicked the mouse. However, the Test.Cir:1 window is not updated. (See Figure 13.26.)

Figure 13.26.

After changing the Test.Cir:2 window, the Test.Cir:1 window is not updated.

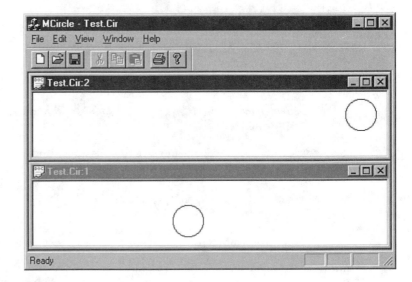

When you change one view of a document, the other view of the same document is not updated! This means that the MCircle program does not currently support multiple views of the same document.

In the following sections, you'll add code to the MCircle program so that when you change one view of a document, all the other views of the same document will be updated automatically.

☐ Terminate the MCircle program by selecting Exit from its File menu.

The UpdateAllViews() and OnUpdate() Functions

When you change a certain view by drawing the circle at a new point, you want to update all the views of the particular document you're changing. You do that by calling the UpdateAllViews() member function of the document class, which notifies all the views of the modified document that they need to be updated. The UpdateAllViews() function does this by calling the OnUpdate() member function of the view class for each view that should be updated.

13

So, your job is is to do the following:

1. Write the code that calls UpdateAllViews() whenever a view is changed by drawing a circle.

2. Write the OnUpdate() member function of the view class.

Calling the UpdateAllViews() **Function**

As stated, when you change a view by drawing a circle, you need to call the UpdateAllViews() member function of the document class. Follow these steps to add the statement that calls this function:

☐ Open the file MCircleView.cpp and locate the OnLButtonDown() function. (You wrote the code of the OnLButtonDown() function earlier; it draws a circle at the point where you clicked the mouse.)

☐ Add the following statement to the end of the OnLButtonDown() function:

```
// Update all the other views of the same document.
pDoc->UpdateAllViews(this);
```

After you add this statement, your OnLButtonDown() function should look like this:

```
void CMCircleView::OnLButtonDown(UINT nFlags, CPoint point)
{
// TODO: Add your message handler code here and/or call
//       default

/////////////////////////
// MY CODE STARTS HERE
/////////////////////////

// Update the m_PosX and m_PosY data members of
// the view class with the x-y coordinate of the
// point where the mouse was clicked.
m_PosX = point.x;
m_PosY = point.y;

// Trigger a call to the OnDraw() function.
Invalidate();

// Get a pointer to the document
CMCircleDoc* pDoc = GetDocument();

// Update data members of the document with the
// new values of the view class data members.
pDoc->m_PosX = m_PosX;
pDoc->m_PosY = m_PosY ;

// Signal that the document has been modified.
pDoc->SetModifiedFlag(TRUE);
```

13

```
// Update all the other views of the same document.
pDoc->UpdateAllViews(this);

/////////////////////////
// MY CODE ENDS HERE
/////////////////////////

CView::OnLButtonDown(nFlags, point);

}
```

The statement you just added to the `OnLButtonDown()` function calls the `UpdateAllViews()` member function of the document class:

```
pDoc->UpdateAllViews(this);
```

The parameter `this` is passed to tell `UpdateAllViews()` which is the current view (the `this` keyword is a pointer to the current view object). This way, `UpdateAllViews()` will update all the views of the current document except the current view.

For example, if you clicked the mouse at the upper-right corner in a certain view (window) of the document Test.Cir, `UpdateAllViews()` will update all the other views of Test.Cir. There is no need for `UpdateAllViews()` to update the current view, because it's already been updated.

The `OnUpdate()` Member Function of the View Class

At this point, when you draw a circle in any view of a particular document, the `UpdateAllViews()` member function of the document class is executed. The `UpdateAllViews()` function will update the contents of the other views of the same document by calling the `OnUpdate()` member function of the view class. Therefore, you need to write the `OnUpdate()` function. Here is how you do that:

☐ Select ClassWizard from the View menu. In the Message Maps tab of ClassWizard, select the following event:

Class name:	CMCircleView
Object ID:	CMCircleView
Message:	OnUpdate

☐ Click the Add Function button of ClassWizard.

Visual C++ responds by adding the `OnUpdate()` *function.*

☐ Click the Edit Code button of ClassWizard.

Visual C++ responds by opening the file MCircleView.cpp with the function `OnUpdate()` *ready for you to edit.*

☐ Write the following code in the OnUpdate() function:

```
void CMCircleView::OnUpdate(CView* pSender, LPARAM lHint,
                           CObject* pHint)
{
// TODO: Add your specialized code here and/or call the base
//       class

/////////////////////////
// MY CODE STARTS HERE
/////////////////////////

// Get a pointer to the document
CMCircleDoc* pDoc = GetDocument();

// Update the view with the current document values.
m_PosX = pDoc->m_PosX;
m_PosY = pDoc->m_PosY;

// Trigger a call to the OnDraw() function.
Invalidate();

/////////////////////////
// MY CODE ENDS HERE
/////////////////////////

}
```

☐ Save your work.

The first statement you typed in the OnUpdate() function extracts pDoc (the pointer for the document class):

```
CMCircleDoc* pDoc = GetDocument();
```

Then the data members of the view class are updated with the current values of the document:

```
m_PosX = pDoc->m_PosX;
m_PosY = pDoc->m_PosY;
```

Finally, the Invalidate() function is used to trigger a call to the OnDraw() function so that the circle will be drawn at the new location specified by m_PosX and m_PosY:

```
Invalidate();
```

That's it! You have finished writing all the necessary code for multiple viewing of the same document.

To verify that the MCircle program supports multiple viewing of the same document, do the following:

☐ Execute the MCircle program by selecting Execute MCircle.EXE from the Build menu.

The main window of the MCircle program appears with a new document.

13

☐ Select Save from the File menu and save the new document as Try.Cir.

☐ Select New Window from the Window menu.

> *The MCircle program responds by opening another view (another window) for the Try.Cir document.*

☐ Select Tile from the Window menu.

As you can see, the document Try.Cir has two views (windows): one with the title Try.Cir:1 and the other with the title Try.Cir:2.

☐ Click the mouse at the upper-right corner of the Try.Cir:2 window.

> *The MCircle program responds by drawing the circle at the point where you clicked the mouse in the Try.Cir:2 window; the Try.Cir:1 window is automatically updated. (See Figure 13.27.)*

Figure 13.27.

After changing the Try.Cir:2 window, the Try.Cir:1 window is automatically updated.

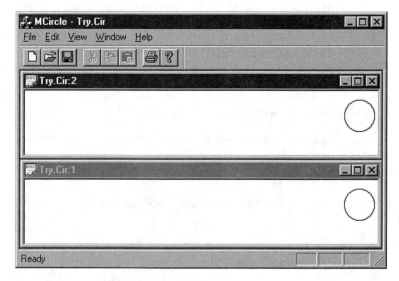

☐ Keep drawing the circle in one window of the Try.Cir document at different locations and notice how the other window of the Try.Cir document is automatically updated.

You can now add as many views as you want for the Try.Cir document by selecting New Window from the Window menu. You'll see that when you change one view of Try.Cir, all the other views are updated automatically.

☐ Terminate the MCircle program by selecting Exit from its File menu.

13

Enhancing the MCircle Program

You will now enhance the MCircle program in two ways:

1. Change the caption in the title of the program's main window from

   `MCircle - `*`filename`*

   to

   `The MCircle Program - `*`filename`*

   (where *`filename`* is the name of the currently active window).

2. Change the default file type displayed in the Save As and Open dialog boxes from `*.*` to `*.cir`. When you select Open or Save As from the File menu, the default files displayed in the Files of type list box will have a .cir file extension.

Follow these steps to perform these enhancements:

☐ Select the ResourceView tab of the Project Workspace window, expand the MCircle resources item, then expand the String Table item.

After you expand the String Table item, a second String Table item appears under the first. (See Figure 13.28.)

Figure 13.28.

Expanding the String Table item in the Project Workspace window.

13

☐ Double-click the second String Table item in the Project Workspace window.

Visual C++ responds by displaying the String Table dialog box of the MCircle project. (See Figure 13.29.)

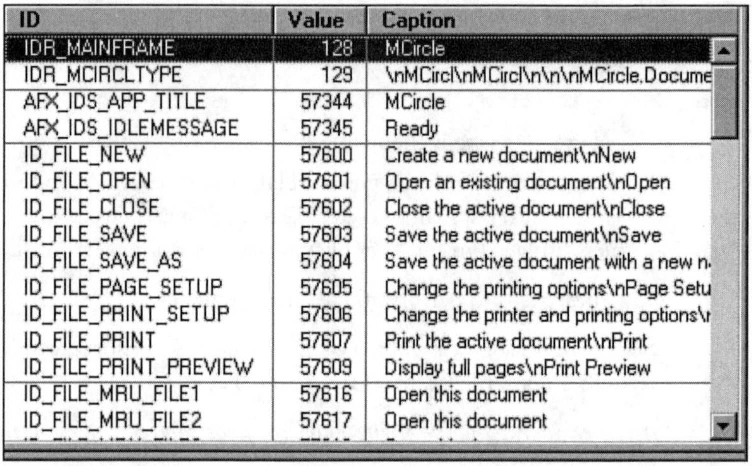

Figure 13.29.

The String Table dialog box.

ID	Value	Caption
IDR_MAINFRAME	128	MCircle
IDR_MCIRCLTYPE	129	\nMCircl\nMCircl\n\n\nMCircle.Docume
AFX_IDS_APP_TITLE	57344	MCircle
AFX_IDS_IDLEMESSAGE	57345	Ready
ID_FILE_NEW	57600	Create a new document\nNew
ID_FILE_OPEN	57601	Open an existing document\nOpen
ID_FILE_CLOSE	57602	Close the active document\nClose
ID_FILE_SAVE	57603	Save the active document\nSave
ID_FILE_SAVE_AS	57604	Save the active document with a new n
ID_FILE_PAGE_SETUP	57605	Change the printing options\nPage Setu
ID_FILE_PRINT_SETUP	57606	Change the printer and printing options\r
ID_FILE_PRINT	57607	Print the active document\nPrint
ID_FILE_PRINT_PREVIEW	57609	Display full pages\nPrint Preview
ID_FILE_MRU_FILE1	57616	Open this document
ID_FILE_MRU_FILE2	57617	Open this document

The String Table dialog box lets you view and edit various strings used by the program. As you can see from Figure 13.29, the string whose ID is IDR_MAINFRAME is currently highlighted. The current value of this string is MCircle. In an MDI program, the IDR_MAINFRAME string specifies the text in the title of the program's main window. You'll now change the value of the IDR_MAINFRAME string from MCircle to The MCircle Program. Here is how you do that:

☐ Double-click the IDR_MAINFRAME string.

Visual C++ responds by displaying the String Properties window for the IDR_MAINFRAME string.

The value of the string is displayed in the Caption box.

☐ Change the value of the string to The MCircle Program.

Your String Properties window for the IDR_MAINFRAME string should now look like Figure 13.30.

The string listed below the IDR_MAINFRAME string in the String Table dialog box (refer to Figure 13.29) is the IDR_MCIRCLTYPE string. The current value of the IDR_MCIRCLTYPE string is this:

\nMCircl\nMCircl\n\n\nMCircle.Document\nMCircl Document

13

Figure 13.30.

Entering a new string value for the IDR_MAINFRAME string.

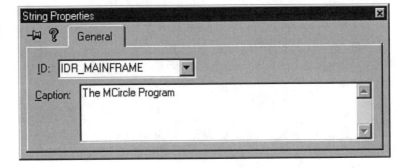

The \n in the string serves as a separator between substrings. Therefore, the preceding string is made of the following seven substrings:

```
Null
MCircl
MCircl
Null
Null
MCircle.Document
MCircl Document
```

The fourth and fifth substrings specify the default document type displayed in the Save As dialog box and Open dialog box of the program. For example, if you set the fourth substring to CIR Files (*.cir) and the fifth substring to .cir, when you select Save As or Open from the File menu, the files listed in the File name list box will have the .cir file extension and the text in the Files of type box will be CIR Files (*.cir). (See Figure 13.31.)

Figure 13.31.

The Open dialog box, listing files with the .cir extension.

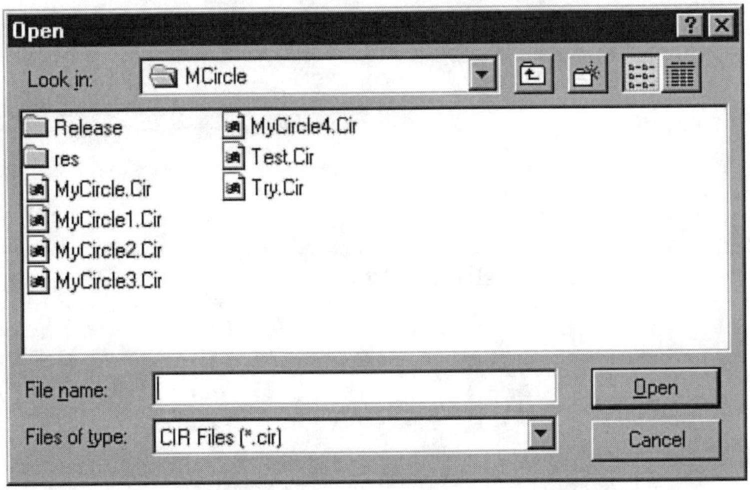

13

You'll now change the IDR_MCIRCLTYPE string so that the fourth substring will be CIR Files (*.cir), and the fifth substring will be .cir. All the rest of the substrings will remain as they are now. Here is how you do that:

☐ Double-click the IDR_MCIRCLTYPE string in the String Table dialog box.

   Visual C++ responds by displaying the String Properties window for the IDR_MCIRCLTYPE string.

The value of the string is displayed in the Caption box.

☐ Change the value of the string to this:

```
\nMCircl\nMCircl\nCIR Files (*.cir)\n.cir\nMCircle.Document\nMCircl
Document
```

 NOTE   The preceding text should be typed on a single line without pressing the Enter key. Visual C++ will wrap the line when it's too long.

Your String Properties window for the IDR_MCIRCLTYPE string should now look like the one shown in Figure 13.32.

Figure 13.32.

Entering a new string value for the IDR_MCIRCLTYPE string.

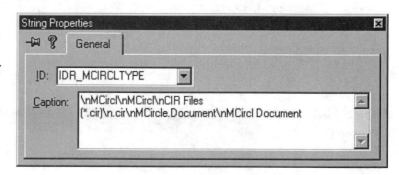

☐ Save your work.

☐ Build and execute the MCircle.EXE program to see the effects of the changes you made to the IDR_MAINFRAME and IDR_MCIRCLTYPE strings.

   Visual C++ responds by executing the MCircle program. The main window of the MCircle program appears, as shown in Figure 13.33.

13

Figure 13.33.

The title of the program's main window now includes the text The MCircle Program.

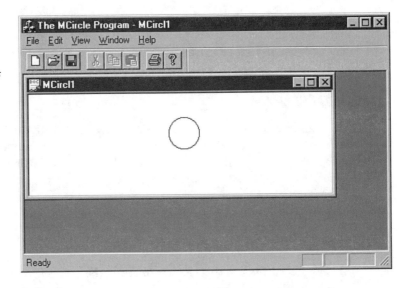

As shown in Figure 13.33, the title of the program's main window now includes the text The MCircle Program because you set the value of the IDR_MAINFRAME string to The MCircle Program.

☐ Select Save As from the File menu of the MCircle program.

The MCircle program responds by displaying the Save As dialog box. (See Figure 13.34.)

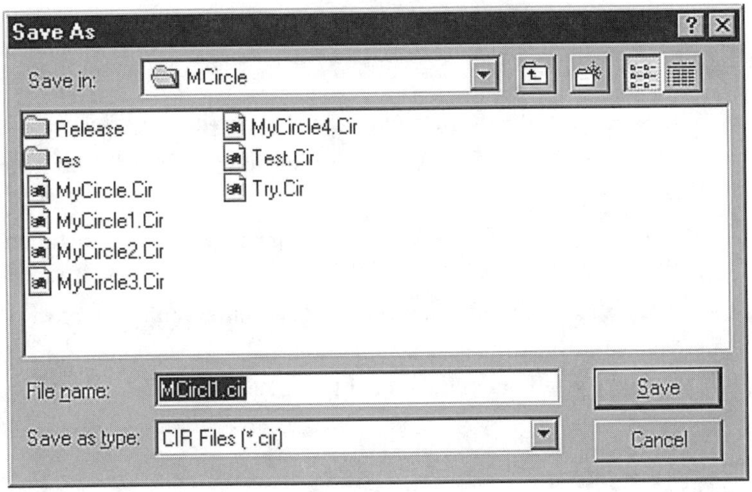

Figure 13.34.

The Save As dialog box, listing files with the .cir file extension.

13

As shown in Figure 13.34, now the Save As dialog box lists files with the .cir file extension and the text in the Save as type box is CIR Files (*.cir) because you set the fourth substring of the IDR_MCIRCLTYPE string to CIR Files (*.cir) and the fifth substring to .cir.

Summary

In this chapter, you wrote an MDI program called MCircle.EXE that behaves like a standard Windows MDI program—it lets you view several documents, save the documents into files, and load previously saved files. The steps you took to create the MCircle program are the same steps for designing other MDI programs. You can use these steps as template steps for your future MDI projects.

Q&A

Q **The steps I took in this chapter to create the MCircle MDI program are not much different from the steps I took in Chapter 11 to create the Circle SDI program, yet the MCircle MDI program is much more impressive. So why would I ever want to write an SDI program when writing the MDI version of the same program doesn't require much more effort?**

A In most cases, you'll probably find it best to write MDI programs. However, you may find it useful sometimes to write SDI programs, in which the user is forced to work on only one document at a time, to save space, resources, or time.

Quiz

1. What is the purpose of the code you write in the view class of an MDI program?
2. What is the purpose of the code you write in the document class of an MDI program?
3. What code do you write in the Serialize() member function of the document class of an MDI program?
4. What does the UpdateAllViews() member function of the document class do?
5. How does the UpdateAllViews() member function of the document class notify all the views of the document that they need to be updated?

Exercise

Currently, whenever you create a new document, the default name assigned to the new document is MCirclX (where X is an integer). For example, the default name of the first new document is MCircl1, the next will be MCircl2, and so on.

Modify the MCircle program so that the default name assigned to the new document is Untitled*X* (where *X* is an integer). For example, the default name of the first new document will be Untitled1, the next will be Untitled2, and so on.

Hint: To set the default name that MCircle assigns to new documents, change the value of the second substring of the IDR_MCIRCLTYPE from `MCircl` to `Untitled`.

Quiz Answers

1. The code you write in the member functions of the view class of an MDI program is responsible for what you see onscreen.

2. The code you write in the member functions of the document class of an MDI program is responsible for maintaining the program's data. In particular, this code is responsible for saving documents into files and loading previously saved files.

3. The code you write in the `Serialize()` member function of the document class is responsible for saving data into files and loading previously saved files.

4. The `UpdateAllViews()` member function of the document class notifies all the views of the document that they need to be updated.

5. The `UpdateAllViews()` function notifies all the views of the document that they need to be updated by calling the `OnUpdate()` member function of the view class for each view that should be updated.

Exercise Answer

To make the default name that the MCircle program assigns to new documents Untitled*X* (where *X* is an integer), change the value of the second substring of the IDR_MCIRCLTYPE from `MCircl` to `Untitled`. All the rest of the substrings will remain as they are now. Here is how you do that:

☐ In the ResourceView tab of the Project Workspace window, expand the MCircle resources item, then expand the String Table item.

After you expand the String Table item, a second String Table item appears under the first.

☐ Double-click the second String Table item in the Project Workspace window.

Visual C++ responds by displaying the String Table dialog box of the MCircle project.

☐ Double-click the IDR_MCIRCLTYPE string.

Visual C++ responds by displaying the String Properties window for the IDR_MCIRCLTYPE string.

13

☐ Change the value of the string to the following (remember to type this on a single line without pressing Enter):

```
\nUntitled\nMCircl\nCIR Files (*.cir)\n.cir\nMCircle.Document\nMCircl
Document
```

☐ Save your work.

That's it! If you build and execute the MCircle program now, you'll see that whenever it creates a new document, the default name assigned to the new document is Untitled$X$ (for example, Untitled1, Untitled2, and so on).

13

Day 14

File Access and Serialization

In this chapter, you'll learn how to write code that writes and reads data to and from files by using *serialization,* which is a process that lets you save data to the hard drive.

The CArchive Class

Recall from Chapter 11, "Writing Single-Document Interface (SDI) Applications," and from Chapter 13, "Writing Multiple-Document Interface (MDI) Applications," that the parameter of the Serialize() member function of the document class is an object of class CArchive. For example, a typical Serialize() function of the document class looks like this:

```
void CTryDoc::Serialize(CArchive& ar)
{
```

```
if (ar.IsStoring())
  {

  ///////////////////////
  // MY CODE STARTS HERE
  ///////////////////////

  ar << m_Var1 << m_Var2 << m_Var3;

  ///////////////////////
  // MY CODE ENDS HERE
  ///////////////////////

  }
else
  {

  ///////////////////////
  // MY CODE STARTS HERE
  ///////////////////////

  ar >> m_Var1 >> m_Var2 >> m_Var3;

  ///////////////////////
  // MY CODE ENDS HERE
  ///////////////////////

  }

}
```

The parameter of the `Serialize()` function (`ar`) is an archive object (an object of class `CArchive`) and corresponds to a file. In the case of the `Serialize()` function of the document class, `ar` corresponds to the file you select from the File menu. For example, if you select Open from the File menu and then select the file MyFile.TXT, the `Serialize()` function is automatically executed and the parameter `ar` corresponds to the file MyFile.TXT.

Sometimes you'll find it useful to create and customize a `CArchive` object yourself, such as when you don't want the user to select the file, but you want to serialize data to or from a specific file. In the following sections, you'll learn how to write code that serializes data to and from a file. This code uses the `CArchive` class to save data into a particular file and load data from a previously saved file.

The Arch Program

You'll now write the Arch program. The code you'll write creates an object of class `CArchive` and uses this object to write and read data to and from a file. Before you start writing the Arch program, let's first review what the program should look like and what it should do:

■ When you start the Arch program, the main window of the program appears, as shown in Figure 14.1.

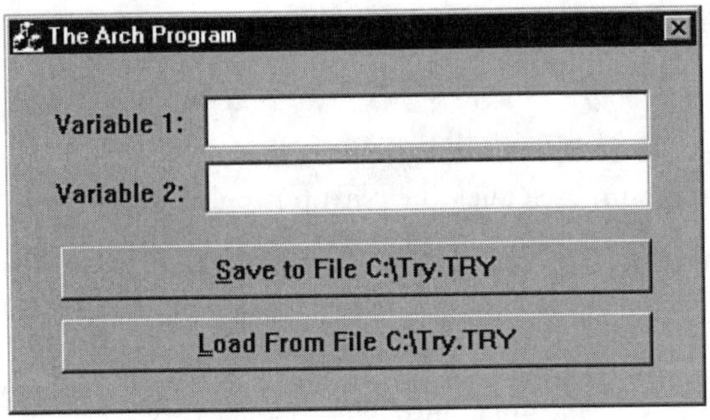

Figure 14.1.

The main window of the Arch program.

As you can see from Figure 14.1, the main window of the program displays a blank form with two fields, Variable 1 and Variable 2, and two pushbuttons, Save to File C:\Try.TRY and Load From File C:\Try.TRY.

■ You can set the Variable 1 and Variable 2 fields to any string value and then click the Save to File C:\Try.TRY button. The Arch program will respond by saving the two string values into the file C:\Try.TRY.

■ You can then type different values in the fields and click the Load From File C:\Try.TRY button. The Arch program will respond by loading the values previously stored in the C:\Try.TRY file and displaying them in the Variable 1 and Variable 2 fields.

Now that you know what the Arch program is supposed to do, you can start writing it.

Creating the Project of the Arch Program

Follow these steps to create the project and skeleton files of the Arch program:

☐ Create the C:\TYVCPROG\PROGRAMS\CH14 directory.

☐ Start Visual C++ and select New from the File menu.

Visual C++ responds by displaying the New dialog box.

☐ Select the Projects tab of the New dialog box.

☐ Select MFC AppWizard (exe) from the list of project types.

☐ Type Arch in the Project Name box.

☐ Click the button that is located on the right of the Location box and select the C:\TYVCPROG\PROGRAMS\CH14 directory.

14

☐ Click the OK button.

Visual C++ responds by displaying the MFC AppWizard - Step 1 window.

☐ In the Step 1 window, select the "Dialog based" radio button to create a dialog-based program, then click the Next button.

☐ Set the Step 2 window as follows, then click the Next button:

About Box:	Checked
Context-sensitive Help:	Not Checked
3D Controls:	Checked
Automation:	Not Checked
ActiveX Controls:	Checked
Windows Sockets:	Not Checked
Dialog title:	`The Arch Program`

☐ In the Step 3 window, use the default settings and click the Next button.

☐ Click the Finish button of the Step 4 window.

Visual C++ responds by displaying the New Project Information window.

☐ Click the OK button of the New Project Information window.

Visual C++ responds by creating the project file and associated files of the Arch program.

☐ Select Set Active Configuration from the Build menu.

Visual C++ responds by displaying the Set Active Project Configuration dialog box.

☐ Select Arch - Win32 Release in the Set Active Project Configuration dialog box, then click the OK button.

That's it! You've finished creating the project file and skeleton files of the Arch program.

The Visual Design of the Arch Program

You'll now visually design the dialog box that serves as the main window of the Arch program (the IDD_ARCH_DIALOG dialog box):

☐ In the ResourceView tab of the Project Workspace window, expand the Arch resources item, expand the Dialog item, and double-click the IDD_ARCH_DIALOG item.

Visual C++ responds by displaying the IDD_ARCH_DIALOG dialog box in design mode.

☐ Delete the OK button, Cancel button, and text in the IDD_ARCH_DIALOG dialog box.

☐ Set up the IDD_ARCH_DIALOG dialog box according to Table 14.1. When you finish, it should look like Figure 14.2.

Table 14.1. The properties table of the IDD_ARCH_DIALOG dialog box.

Object	Property	Setting
Dialog Box	**ID**	**IDD_ARCH_DIALOG**
	Caption	The Arch Program
	Font	System, Size 10
Static Text	**ID**	**IDC_STATIC**
	Caption	Variable 1:
Edit Box	**ID**	**IDC_VAR1_EDIT**
Static Text	**ID**	**IDC_STATIC**
	Caption	Variable 2:
Edit Box	**ID**	**IDC_VAR2_EDIT**
Push Button	**ID**	**IDC_SAVE_BUTTON**
	Caption	&Save to File C:\\Try.TRY
Push Button	**ID**	**IDC_LOAD_BUTTON**
	Caption	&Load From File C:\\Try.TRY

NOTE

Note that in Table 14.1, these are the captions of the pushbuttons:

```
&Save to File C:\\Try.TRY
&Load From File C:\\Try.TRY
```

You typed a double-backslash (\\), because in Visual C/C++, when you want to use the \ character in a string, you have to precede it with another \ character.

☐ Build and execute the Arch.EXE program to see your visual design in action.

Visual C++ responds by executing the Arch.EXE program. The main window of Arch.EXE appears, as shown back in Figure 14.1.

As you can see, the main window of the Arch.EXE program (the IDD_ARCH_DIALOG dialog box) appears just as you designed it.

14

Figure 14.2.

The IDD_ARCH_DIALOG dialog box in design mode (after customization).

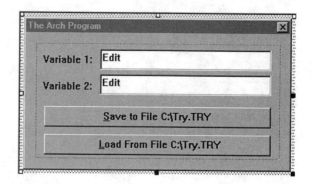

☐ Terminate the Arch.EXE program by clicking the × icon located at the top-right corner of the program's window.

Attaching Variables to the Two Edit Boxes

You'll now attach variables to the two edit box controls of the IDD_ARCH_DIALOG dialog box, because when you write the program's code, you'll use these variables to read the contents of the edit box controls.

Follow these steps to attach a variable to the IDC_VAR1_EDIT edit box control:

☐ Select ClassWizard from the View menu. In the Member Variables tab, make the following selection:

Class name:	CArchDlg
Control ID:	IDC_VAR1_EDIT

☐ Click the Add Variable button of ClassWizard and set the variable as follows:

Variable name:	m_Var1Edit
Category:	Value
Variable type:	CString

☐ Click the OK button of the Add Member Variable dialog box.

Next, attach a variable to the IDC_VAR2_EDIT edit box control:

☐ Use the ClassWizard dialog box to make the following selection:

Class name:	CArchDlg
Control ID:	IDC_VAR2_EDIT

14

☐ Click the Add Variable button of ClassWizard and set the variable as follows:

Variable name:	`m_Var2Edit`
Category:	`Value`
Variable type:	`CString`

☐ Click the OK button of the Add Member Variable dialog box.

☐ Click the OK button of ClassWizard.

Attaching Code to the Save Button

When you click the Save to File C:\Try.TRY button, the contents of the two edit boxes (IDC_VAR1_EDIT and IDC_VAR2_EDIT) should be serialized into the file C:\Try.TRY.

Follow these steps to attach code to the Save button:

☐ Select ClassWizard from the View menu. In the Message Maps tab of ClassWizard, select the following event:

Class name:	`CArchDlg`
Object ID:	`IDC_SAVE_BUTTON`
Message:	`BN_CLICKED`

☐ Click the Add Function button, name the new function `OnSaveButton`, then click the Edit Code button.

Visual C++ responds by opening the file ArchDlg.cpp with the function `OnSaveButton()` *ready for you to edit.*

☐ Write the following code in the `OnSaveButton()` function:

```
void CArchDlg::OnSaveButton()
{

// TODO: Add your control notification handler code here

/////////////////////////
// MY CODE STARTS HERE
/////////////////////////

// Update m_Var1Edit and m_Var2Edit with the
// screen contents.
UpdateData(TRUE);

// Create the file C:\Try.TRY.
CFile f;
f.Open("C:\\Try.TRY",
       CFile::modeCreate | CFile::modeWrite );
```

14

```
    // Create an archive object.
    CArchive ar( &f, CArchive::store );

    // Serialize m_Var1Edit and m_Var2Edit into the archive.
    ar << m_Var1Edit << m_Var2Edit;

    // Close the archive
    ar.Close();

    // Close the file.
    f.Close();

    ////////////////////////
    // MY CODE ENDS HERE
    ////////////////////////

    }
```

☐ Save your work.

The first statement you typed updates the variables of the edit boxes (m_Var1Edit and m_Var2Edit) with the current values displayed in the edit boxes:

```
UpdateData(TRUE);
```

The next two statements create the file C:\\Try.TRY:

```
CFile f;
f.Open("C:\\Try.TRY",
       CFile::modeCreate ¦ CFile::modeWrite );
```

The first statement creates an object of class CFile, called f, and the second statement uses the Open() member function of the CFile class to create the C:\Try.TRY file.

The next statement creates an object, called ar, of class CArchive:

```
CArchive ar( &f, CArchive::store );
```

As you can see, this statement passes two parameters to the constructor function of CArchive. The first parameter is the address of the CFile object associated with the archive. In this statement, the first parameter is &f, the address of the CFile object of the C:\Try.TRY file. Therefore, the archive object ar will be associated with the file C:\Try.TRY.

The second parameter in this statement specifies the mode of the archive object. An archive object can be created for storage purposes (to save variables into the archive) or for loading purposes (to load data from the archive into variables). This is the second parameter:

```
CArchive::store
```

Therefore, the archive object ar will be used for storage purposes, because you want the m_Var1Edit and m_Var2Edit variables to be saved into the archive whenever you click the Save button.

Now that you have an archive object associated with the file C:\Try.TRY, and this archive object is in a storage mode, you can serialize variables into the file Try.TRY. The next statement in the function serializes the two data members, m_Var1Edit and m_Var2Edit, into Try.TRY:

```
ar << m_Var1Edit << m_Var2Edit;
```

The next statement uses the Close() member function of the CArchive class to close the ar archive:

```
ar.Close();
```

The last statement uses the Close() member function of the CFile class to close the file associated with the f object (Try.TRY):

```
f.Close();
```

Attaching Code to the Load Button

When you click the Load From File C:\Try.TRY button, the contents of the two edit boxes (IDC_VAR1_EDIT and IDC_VAR2_EDIT) should be filled with the values stored in the file Try.TRY.

Follow these steps to attach code to the Load button:

☐ Select ClassWizard from the View menu. In the Message Maps tab of ClassWizard, select the following event:

Class name:	CArchDlg
Object ID:	IDC_LOAD_BUTTON
Message:	BN_CLICKED

☐ Click the Add Function button, name the new function OnLoadButton, then click the Edit Code button.

Visual C++ responds by opening the file ArchDlg.cpp with the function OnLoadButton() *ready for you to edit.*

☐ Write the following code in the OnLoadButton() function:

```
void CArchDlg::OnLoadButton()
{

// TODO: Add your control notification handler code here

//////////////////////////
// MY CODE STARTS HERE
//////////////////////////
```

14

```
// Open the file C:\Try.TRY.
CFile f;
if ( f.Open("C:\\Try.TRY", CFile::modeRead)== FALSE )
   return;

// Create an archive object.
CArchive ar( &f, CArchive::load );

// Serialize data from the archive into m_Var1Edit and
// m_Var2Edit.
ar >> m_Var1Edit >> m_Var2Edit;

// Close the archive
ar.Close();

// Close the file.
f.Close();

// Update screen with the new values of m_Var1Edit and
// m_Var2Edit.
UpdateData(FALSE);

/////////////////////
// MY CODE ENDS HERE
/////////////////////

}
```

☐ Save your work.

The first two statements you typed open the file C:\Try.TRY in read mode:

```
CFile f;
if ( f.Open("C:\\Try.TRY", CFile::modeRead)== FALSE )
   return;
```

The first statement creates an object of class CFile, called f:

```
CFile f;
```

The second statement is an if statement that uses the Open() member function of the CFile class to open the C:\Try.TRY file in read mode:

```
if ( f.Open("C:\\Try.TRY", CFile::modeRead)== FALSE )
   return;
```

If the returned value of the Open() function is FALSE, you know that the file cannot be opened, in which case the if condition is satisfied and the function is terminated with the return statement.

The next statement creates an object of class CArchive called ar:

```
CArchive ar( &f, CArchive::load );
```

As you can see, this statement passes two parameters to the constructor function of CArchive.

14

The first parameter is the address of the CFile object associated with the archive. In this statement, the first parameter is &f, the address of the CFile object of the C:\Try.TRY file. Therefore, the archive object ar will be associated with the file Try.TRY.

The second parameter specifies the mode of the archive object. As stated before, an archive object can be created for storage purposes or for loading purposes. This is the second parameter, so the archive object ar will be used for loading purposes:

```
CArchive::load
```

You want to use ar for loading purposes because you want to load data from the archive into the m_Var1Edit and m_Var2Edit variables whenever you click the Load button.

Now that you have an archive object associated with the file Try.TRY, and this archive object is in a loading mode, you can serialize data from Try.TRY into variables.

The next statement in the function serializes data from Try.TRY into the two data members, m_Var1Edit and m_Var2Edit:

```
ar >> m_Var1Edit >> m_Var2Edit;
```

The next statement uses the Close() member function of the CArchive class to close the ar archive:

```
ar.Close();
```

The next statement uses the Close() member function of the CFile class to close the file associated with the f object (Try.TRY):

```
f.Close();
```

The last statement in the OnLoadButton() function updates the screen (the two edit boxes) with the new values of m_Var1Edit and m_Var2Edit:

```
UpdateData(FALSE);
```

You've finished writing the code for the Arch program!

☐ Build and execute the Arch.EXE program to test your code.

   Visual C++ responds by executing the program.

Experiment with the Save and Load buttons as follows:

☐ Type something in the two edit boxes.

☐ Click the Save button.

   The Arch program responds by saving the contents of the two edit boxes into the C:\Try.TRY file.

14

☐ Change the contents of the two edit boxes.

☐ Click the Load button.

> *The Arch program responds by loading the contents of the C:\Try.TRY file. The two edit box controls now display the original text you typed.*

As you can see, when you click the Save button, the contents of the two edit boxes are saved; when you click the Load button, the edit boxes are filled with the saved data.

Summary

In this chapter, you learned how to serialize data to and from a file, which requires very little code. You can use this code in all your future programs when you need to save and load data to and from files.

Q&A

Q In the Arch.EXE program I wrote in this chapter, I serialized string variables to and from a file. Can I serialize other types of variables?

A Yes. You can serialize other types of variables (just as you serialized the CString variables of the Arch.EXE program).

Quiz

1. Describe what the following code does:

```
CFile f;
f.Open("C:\\Try.TRY",
        CFile::modeCreate | CFile::modeWrite );

CArchive ar( &f, CArchive::store );

long MyNumber = 100;
CString MyString = "Test";

ar << MyNumber << MyString;

ar.Close();

f.Close();
```

2. Describe what the following code does:

```
// Open the file C:\Try.TRY.
CFile f;
f.Open("C:\\Try.TRY", CFile::modeRead);
```

```
// Create an archive object.
CArchive ar( &f, CArchive::load );

// Declare two variables.
long MyNumber;
CString MyString;

// Serialize data from the archive into the MyNumber
// and MyString variables.
ar >> MyNumber >> MyString;

// Close the archive
ar.Close();

// Close the file.
f.Close();
```

Exercise

Write code that serializes the text THIS IS A TEST into the file C:\Test.TRY.

Quiz Answers

1. Here is the code for Question 1 with explanatory comments:

```
// Create the file C:\Try.TRY.
CFile f;
f.Open("C:\\Try.TRY",
        CFile::modeCreate | CFile::modeWrite );

// Create an archive object.
CArchive ar( &f, CArchive::store );

// Declare and initialize two variables.
long MyNumber = 100;
CString MyString = "Test";

// Serialize the two variables MyNumber and MyString into
// the archive.
ar << MyNumber << MyString;

// Close the archive
ar.Close();

// Close the file.
f.Close();
```

2. Here is the code for Question 2 with explanatory comments:

```
// Open the file C:\Try.TRY.
CFile f;
f.Open("C:\\Try.TRY", CFile::modeRead);
```

14

```
// Create an archive object.
CArchive ar( &f, CArchive::load );

// Declare two variables.
long MyNumber;
CString MyString;

// Serialize data from the archive into the MyNumber
// and MyString variables.
ar >> MyNumber >> MyString;

// Close the archive
ar.Close();

// Close the file.
f.Close();
```

Exercise Answer

The following code serializes the string THIS IS A TEST into the file C:\Test.TRY:

```
// Create the file C:\Test.TRY.
CFile f;
f.Open("C:\\Test.TRY",
       CFile::modeCreate | CFile::modeWrite );

// Create an archive object.
CArchive ar( &f, CArchive::store );

// Declare and initialize a string variable.
CString MyString = "THIS IS A TEST";

// Serialize the variable MyString into the archive.
ar << MyString;

// Close the archive
ar.Close();

// Close the file.
f.Close();
```

Week

3

15

16

17

18

19

20

21

At a Glance

This is the third and final week! On the first day of this week, you'll learn how to incorporate toolbars and status bars into your Visual C++ programs. As you'll see, with Visual C++ it is very easy.

On the second day, you'll learn how to write your own software library (.LIB file) that contains your own classes. Typically, you design your own software libraries to distribute and sell or to distribute within your organization.

On the third day, you'll learn about DLLs. You'll learn what a DLL is, how to create a DLL with Visual C++, and how to use a DLL in Visual C++.

On the fourth day, you'll learn how to create an ActiveX control with Visual C++.

On the fifth and sixth day, you'll learn how to customize the ActiveX control you created on the fourth day.

On the seventh day, you'll learn how to write a program that includes animation and sound. You'll write a Visual C++ program that includes animation, playback of a WAV sound file, and playback of a MIDI sound file. At the end of the seventh day, you'll also learn about the DirectX technology.

Day 15

Toolbars and Status Bars

In this chapter, you'll learn how to incorporate toolbars and status bars into your Visual C++ programs. As you'll see, it's very easy with Visual C++.

The Shp Program

You'll now create the Shp program, a program that illustrates how the toolbar and status bar are incorporated into a Visual C++ program.

The Shp program has a Circle icon and a Rectangle icon on its toolbar. When you click the Circle icon on the toolbar, you can then click the mouse in the window of the Shp program to draw a circle. The circle will be drawn with its center at the point where the mouse was clicked. When you click the Rectangle icon on the toolbar, you can then click the mouse in the window of the Shp program to draw a rectangle. The rectangle will be drawn at the point where the mouse was clicked. (See Figure 15.1.)

Figure 15.1.

Drawing a rectangle with the Shp program.

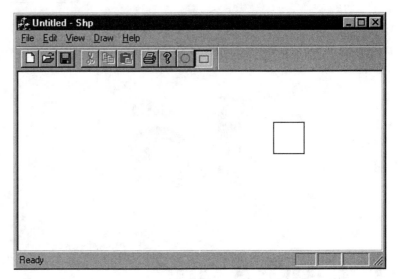

Creating the Project of the Shp Program

You'll now create the project of the Shp program:

☐ Create the C:\TYVCPROG\PROGRAMS\CH15 directory and start Visual C++.

☐ Select New from the File menu.

Visual C++ responds by displaying the New dialog box.

☐ Select the Projects tab of the New dialog box.

☐ Select MFC AppWizard(exe) from the list of project types.

☐ Type Shp in the Project Name box.

☐ Click the button that is located on the right of the Location box and select the C:\TYVCPROG\PROGRAMS\CH15 directory.

☐ Click the OK button.

Visual C++ responds by displaying the MFC AppWizard Step 1 window.

☐ In the Step 1 window, select the "Single document" radio button, then click the Next button.

15

☐ In the Step 2 window, leave the default settings, then click the Next button.

☐ In the Step 3 window, leave the default settings, then click the Next button.

☐ Set the Step 4 window to include a docking toolbar, an initial status bar, printing and print preview, and 3-D controls. (See Figure 15.2.) When you're done, click the Next button.

Figure 15.2.

Selecting features to include in the Shp program.

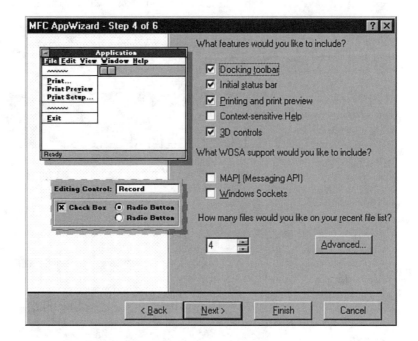

☐ In the Step 5 window, use the default settings, then click the Next button.

☐ Leave the default settings as they are in the Step 6 window, then click the Finish button.

Visual C++ responds by displaying the New Project Information window.

☐ Click the OK button of the New Project Information window.

Visual C++ responds by creating the project of the Shp program and all its associated files.

☐ Select Set Active Configuration from the Build menu, then select Shp - Win32 Release from the Set Active Project Configuration dialog box and click the OK button.

That's it—you are now ready to start designing the Shp program.

The Default Toolbar

Before you start writing the code of the Shp program, review what the Shp program can do at this point in developing the program. The Shp program already has several features—consider them gifts from Microsoft.

☐ Build and execute the Shp.EXE program to see what features it already has.

Visual C++ responds by executing the Shp.EXE program, and the window shown in Figure 15.3 appears. As you can see, the Shp.EXE program includes a toolbar (below the menu bar). The toolbar displays icons of several tools.

Figure 15.3.

The window of the Shp program.

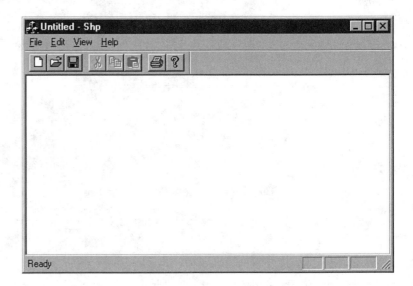

The toolbar serves as a visual menu. Try displaying the About dialog box:

☐ Select About Shp from the Help menu.

The Shp program responds by displaying the About dialog box.

☐ Click the OK button to close the About dialog box.

Instead of using the menu to display the About dialog box, you can use the toolbar:

☐ Click the Help tool, the rightmost icon on the toolbar (the one with a question mark icon). Note that you can program the tool names to be anything you want; in Chapter 13, "Writing Multiple-Document Interface (MDI) Applications," this tool was referred to as the About tool.

Shp responds by displaying the About dialog box.

The Help tool serves the same purpose as the About item of the Help menu.

The Print Tool

To the left of the Help tool, you see the Print tool, which serves the same purpose as the Print item of the File menu.

☐ Prepare your printer for printing.

☐ Click the Print tool on the toolbar.

> *The Shp program responds by letting you print the contents of its window. If you send the contents of Shp's window to the printer, a blank page will be printed at this point in the program's development.*

Later in this chapter, you'll write code that displays a circle and a rectangle in Shp's window. You'll then be able to click the Print tool to send the contents of Shp's window to the printer.

The Save Tool

The third tool from the left is the Save tool (the one with a disk icon), which serves the same purpose as the Save item of the File menu.

☐ Click the Save tool.

> *Shp responds by displaying the Save As dialog box.*

☐ Click the Cancel button of the Save As dialog box.

For now, you have nothing to save, but later you'll add code to the Shp program that saves files to the hard drive.

The New and Open Tools

The first and second tools from the left on the toolbar are the New and Open tools. The New tool looks like a blank page, and the Open tool looks like an open folder. These tools serve the same purpose as the New and Open items of the File menu. Later, you'll add code to the Shp program that makes use of the New and Open tools.

NOTE

As you have just seen, the toolbar of the Shp program has several useful tools, a gift from Microsoft. Later, you'll enhance the Shp program so that the toolbar will include your own custom-made tools. In particular, you'll add the Circle tool and the Rectangle tool.

The Default Status Bar

The Shp program includes a status bar that displays various status messages to the user.

☐ Place (but do not click) the mouse cursor on the Help tool.

As shown in Figure 15.4, the status bar displays text to describe the purpose of the Help tool. In a similar manner, the status bar displays descriptions of other tools on the toolbar.

Figure 15.4.

The status bar message for the Help tool.

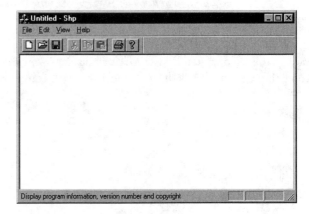

☐ Place the mouse cursor on other tools and observe the messages that the status bar displays.

The status bar also displays messages corresponding to the menu items. To see this in action, do the following:

☐ Open the File menu, then use the arrow keys to highlight the Exit menu item.

As shown in Figure 15.5, the status bar displays a message describing the action of the Exit menu item.

The View Menu

The View menu of the Shp program, shown in Figure 15.6, has two menu items: Toolbar and Status Bar. Currently, both these menu items have check marks in them, which means the Shp program is displaying the toolbar and status bar.

☐ Select the Toolbar item from the View menu to remove the check mark.

Shp responds by removing the toolbar. (See Figure 15.7.)

15

Figure 15.5.

The status bar's message about the Exit menu item.

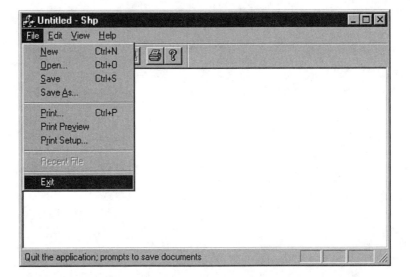

Figure 15.6.

The View menu of the Shp program.

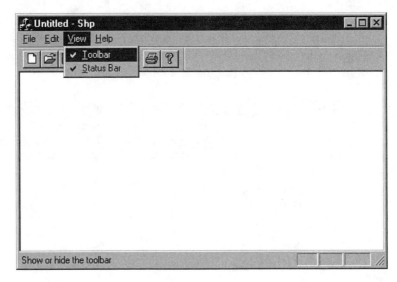

☐ Open the View menu of the Shp program; notice that the Toolbar item of the View menu does not have a check mark.

☐ Select the Toolbar item from the View menu to place a check mark next to it.

> *Shp responds by including the toolbar in Shp's window; now, a check mark appears in the Toolbar menu item.*

Figure 15.7.

The Shp program without its toolbar.

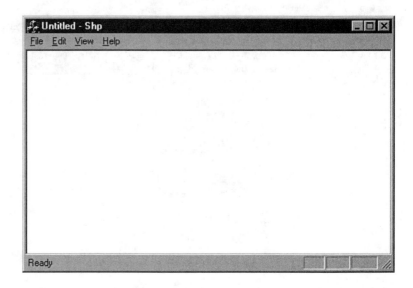

The Toolbar menu item toggles; selecting it places or removes the check mark from the menu item. The Status Bar menu item of the View menu also toggles. When there's a check mark next to the Status Bar menu item, the status bar appears in Shp's window; no check mark means there's no status bar in Shp's window. (See Figure 15.8.)

Figure 15.8.

The window of the Shp program without its status bar.

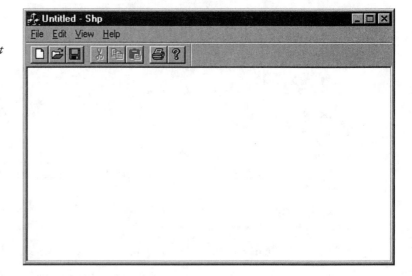

15

Displaying the Toolbar in Different Formats

So far, you have displayed the toolbar horizontally below the menu bar, as shown in Figure 15.3. However, the Shp program lets you display the toolbar in other locations and other formats.

15

☐ Double-click the space to the left of the Print tool on the toolbar.

Shp responds by displaying the toolbar as a floating toolbar. (See Figure 15.9.)

Figure 15.9.

The floating toolbar.

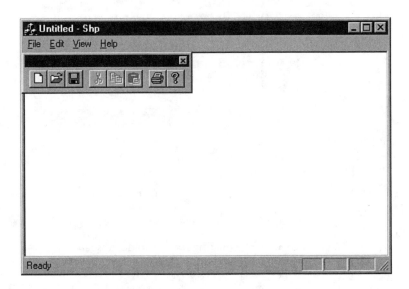

You can now drag the caption of the floating toolbar to any location onscreen. You can move the toolbar both within and outside the window of the Shp program.

☐ Drag the toolbar (by dragging its caption) to a different location on the screen.

You can place the toolbar as a fixed (non-floating) vertical toolbar as follows:

☐ Drag the toolbar toward the left edge of the Shp's window. While you drag the toolbar, you'll see a rectangle the size of the toolbar following the mouse movements. When the mouse cursor is near the inner left edge of the window, you'll see that the rectangle becomes a vertical rectangle. At that point, release the mouse.

Shp responds by displaying the toolbar as a fixed vertical toolbar. (See Figure 15.10).

Figure 15.10.

Displaying the toolbar as a fixed vertical toolbar.

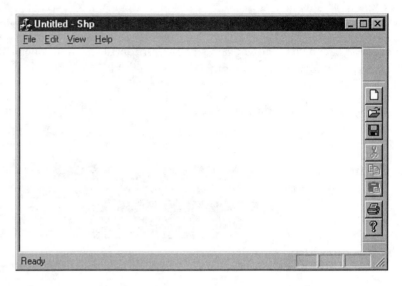

The toolbar can also be placed on the right edge of the screen or even horizontally along the bottom of the window above the status bar.

☐ Double-click the space underneath the Save tool on the toolbar.

   Shp responds by displaying the toolbar as a floating toolbar.

☐ Drag the edges of the floating toolbar to decrease its width.

As shown in Figure 15.11, you can also display the toolbar with more than one row of icons.

Figure 15.11.

Displaying the toolbar with two rows of icons.

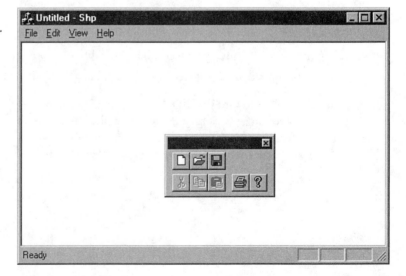

15

☐ Drag the toolbar upward. When the rectangle representing the toolbar becomes a narrow horizontal rectangle, release the mouse.

The toolbar is now attached to the upper edge of the window (below the menu bar).

Status Keys on the Status Bar

Look at the status bar again. The right side includes space for displaying the status of the Caps Lock, Num Lock, and Scroll Lock keys.

☐ Press the Num Lock key several times. As you can see, the status bar displays the text Num when the Num Lock key is on.

☐ Experiment with the Caps Lock, Num Lock, and Scroll Lock keys. Figure 15.12 shows the status bar when these keys are on.

Figure 15.12.

Indicating the status of the Caps Lock, Num Lock, and Scroll Lock keys.

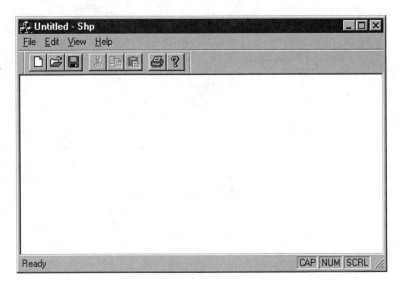

NOTE

As you have seen, all the toolbar and status bar features that the Shp program includes are incorporated without having to write any code.

☐ Experiment with the Shp program, then select Exit from the File menu to terminate the program.

Adding the Circle Tool

You'll now add the Circle tool to the toolbar:

☐ In the Project Workspace window, select the ResourceView tab, expand the Shp resources item, then expand the Toolbar item.

The Project Workspace should now look like Figure 15.13. As you can see, the ID of the toolbar is IDR_MAINFRAME.

Figure 15.13.

The IDR_MAINFRAME of the Toolbar item.

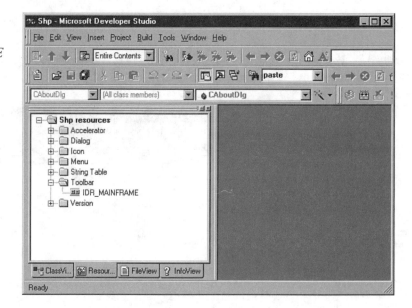

☐ Double-click the IDR_MAINFRAME item.

Visual C++ responds by displaying the toolbar in design mode. (See Figure 15.14.)

If you click the New tool (the leftmost icon) on the toolbar shown in Figure 15.14, the New icon (the one that looks like a blank page) is displayed in design mode. Similarly, if you click the Open tool, the Open icon is displayed in design mode. (See Figure 15.15.)

The toolbar has an empty icon to the right of the question mark icon. This is where you'll add the new icon.

☐ Click the rightmost icon on the toolbar.

Visual C++ responds by displaying the new empty icon ready for you to design. (See Figure 15.16.)

15

Figure 15.14.

The icon of the New tool in design mode.

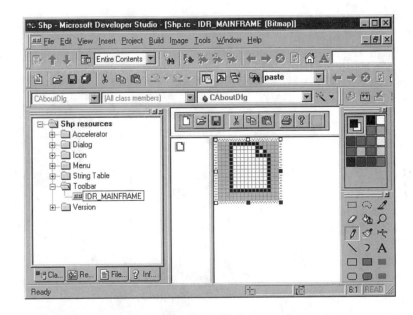

Figure 15.15.

The icon of the Open tool in design mode.

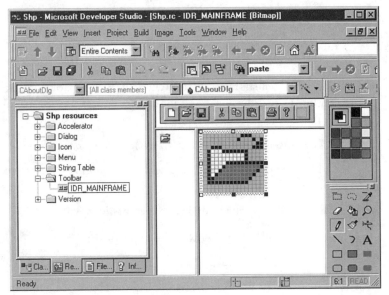

Figure 15.16.

The new icon of the toolbar ready for you to design.

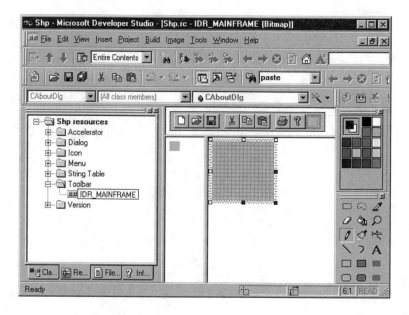

You'll now draw in the new empty icon with a red drawing pen:

☐ Select Customize from the Tools menu.

   Visual C++ responds by displaying the Toolbars dialog box.

☐ Select the Toolbars tab and place a check mark in the Colors check box, then click the Close button. (Depending on the setting of your Visual C++, you may already have a check mark in the Colors check box.)

   Visual C++ responds by displaying the Colors palette shown in Figure 15.17.

☐ Click the Select Color tool in the rightmost column on the first row of the Graphics Tools window.

☐ Click the Red palette to draw in the empty icon with a red pen.

☐ Click the Ellipse tool in the leftmost column on the last row of the Graphics Tools window.

NOTE

To examine the nature and purpose of each tool in the Graphics Tools window, hold the mouse cursor without clicking over the tool you want to examine. Visual C++ responds by displaying a yellow rectangle—called a *tool tip*—showing the tool's name.

15

Figure 15.17.
The Colors palette.

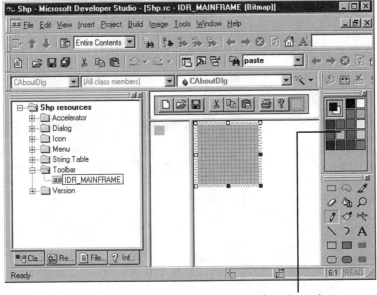

The Colors palette

Now you are ready to draw a red circle:

☐ Click in the new icon and drag the mouse while holding the left mouse button down.

Visual C++ responds by drawing a circle, as shown in Figure 15.18.

Figure 15.18.
Drawing a circle in the new icon.

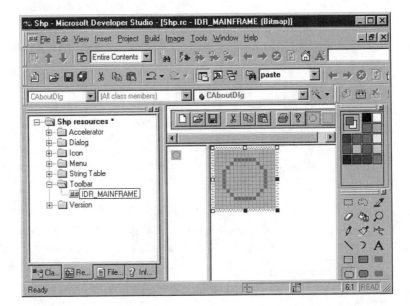

☐ Although you haven't finished designing the Shp program, build and execute it to check your progress.

Visual C++ responds by executing the Shp.EXE program, and the window shown in Figure 15.19 appears.

Figure 15.19.

The window of the Shp program with its new Circle tool.

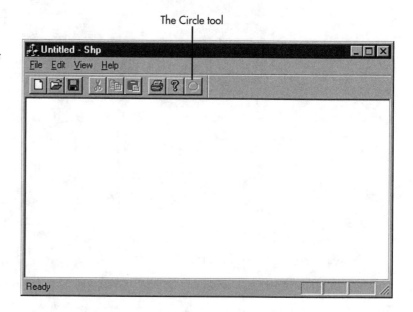

Of course, the Circle tool isn't working yet because you haven't added code for it. Furthermore, the Circle tool is disabled (dimmed).

☐ Select Exit from the File menu of the Shp program to terminate the program.

Adding the Rectangle Tool

You'll now add the Rectangle tool to the toolbar:

☐ Display the IDR_MAINFRAME toolbar in design mode and click the empty icon to the right of the Circle tool. Visual C++ placed a new empty icon on the toolbar after you drew the icon for the Circle tool.

Visual C++ responds by displaying the new empty icon, ready for you to design.

☐ Repeat the same steps you used to draw the Circle icon, but now draw a rectangle instead of a circle. In Figure 15.20, the Rectangle tool is shown two rows above the Circle tool.

After drawing the new icon, it should look like Figure 15.20.

☐ Save your work.

15

Figure 15.20.

The new icon for the Rectangle tool.

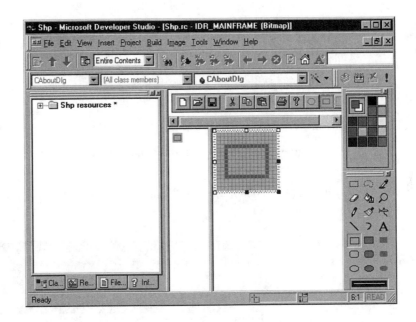

☐ Build and execute the Shp.EXE program to check your progress.

The window of the Shp program appears, as shown in Figure 15.21. The toolbar now contains the Circle tool and the Rectangle tool; both are disabled (dimmed) at this stage.

☐ Select Exit from the File menu of the Shp program to terminate the program.

Figure 15.21.

The Circle tool and the Rectangle tool in Shp's toolbar.

The Rectangle tool

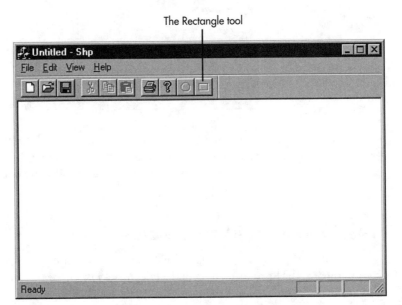

Creating the Menu of the Shp Program

You'll now create the Draw menu of the Shp program:

☐ In the ResourceView tab of the Project Workspace window, expand the Shp resources item, expand the Menu item and then double-click the IDR_MAINFRAME item.

Visual C++ responds by displaying the menu of the Shp program in design mode.

☐ Drag the title of the Help menu to the right to make space for a new menu between the Help menu and the View menu.

☐ Create the Draw menu, shown in Figure 15.22, with two items in it: the Circle item and the Rectangle item.

Figure 15.22.

The Draw menu of the Shp program.

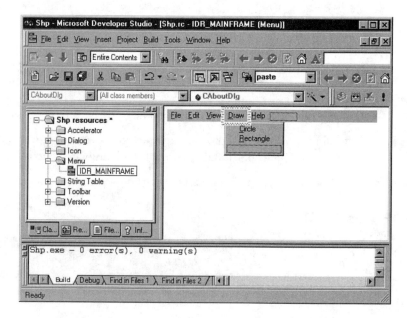

☐ Make sure the ID of the Circle menu item is ID_DRAW_CIRCLE and the ID of the Rectangle menu item is ID_DRAW_RECTANGLE. To do this, double-click the Circle or Rectangle menu item to display its Properties window and examine the ID box in the General tab.

Assigning an ID to the New Tools

As stated, the toolbar serves as a visual menu. For example, the Print tool serves the same purpose as the Print menu item of the File menu. Likewise, you want the Circle tool to have the same function as the Circle item of the Draw menu and the Rectangle tool to have the same function as the Rectangle item of the Draw menu. Here is how you accomplish this:

☐ Display the toolbar in design mode (double-click the IDR_MAINFRAME item under the Toolbar item in the Project Workspace window).

☐ Double-click the Circle icon of the toolbar in the window of the IDR_MAINFRAME toolbar window. Do not double-click the big Circle icon in the window; instead, double-click the small icon on the toolbar.

   Visual C++ responds by displaying the Toolbar Button Properties window of the Circle tool.

☐ Set the ID box in the Toolbar Button Properties window of the Circle icon to ID_DRAW_CIRCLE.

In the preceding step, you set the ID of the Circle tool to the same ID used by the Circle menu item of the Draw menu; therefore, the Circle tool will perform the same function as the Circle menu item.

☐ Set the Prompt box in the Toolbar Button Properties window to Draw circle with the mouse.

During the execution of the Shp program, when the Circle menu item is highlighted, the text Draw circle with the mouse will be displayed in the status bar. This text will also be displayed on the status bar when the mouse cursor is placed on the Circle tool of the toolbar.

☐ Double-click the small Rectangle tool of the toolbar (not the big Rectangle icon in the window) in the window of the IDR_MAINFRAME toolbar window.

   Visual C++ responds by displaying the Toolbar Button Properties window of the Rectangle tool.

☐ Set the ID box in the Properties window of the Rectangle tool to ID_DRAW_RECTANGLE.

In the preceding step, you set the ID of the Rectangle tool to the same ID used by the Rectangle menu item of the Draw menu. From now on, the Rectangle tool will perform the same function as the Rectangle menu item.

☐ Set the Prompt box in the Toolbar Button Properties window to Draw rectangle with the mouse.

Now the text Draw rectangle with the mouse will be displayed in the status bar when the Rectangle item is highlighted in the Draw menu. This text will also be displayed in the status bar when the mouse cursor is placed on the Rectangle tool.

☐ Save your work.

☐ Build and execute the Shp.EXE program to make sure you performed the preceding steps correctly.

The Circle and Rectangle tools are currently disabled. Now check to see whether the corresponding menu items for the Circle and Rectangle tools are disabled, too:

☐ Open the Draw menu.

Yes, the Circle and Rectangle menu items are disabled because you haven't attached any code to them yet.

☐ Select Exit from the File menu of the Shp program to terminate the program.

Attaching Code to the Circle Menu Item

You'll now attach code to the Circle menu item of the Draw menu:

☐ Click the ResourceView tab of the Project Workspace window, expand the Shp Resources item, expand the Menu item, highlight the IDR_MAINFRAME item, then select ClassWizard from the View menu.

Visual C++ responds by displaying the MFC ClassWizard dialog box.

☐ In the Message Maps tab of ClassWizard, make sure the Class name box is set to `CShpView` and select the following event:

Class name:	`CShpView`
Object ID:	`ID_DRAW_CIRCLE`
Message:	`COMMAND`

NOTE

> You must set the Class name box in the preceding step to `CShpView`. (The default setting that ClassWizard set for the Class name is `CMainFrame`.) If you are new to Visual C++, probably the most common error you'll make while creating this book's programs is not setting the Class name box of the MFC ClassWizard window as instructed.

☐ Click the Add Function button, name the new function `OnDrawCircle`, and click the Edit Code button.

Visual C++ responds by opening the file ShpView.cpp with the function `OnDrawCircle()` *ready for you to edit.*

☐ Write the following code in the `OnDrawCircle()` function:

```
void CShpView::OnDrawCircle()
{
// TODO: Add your command handler code here
```

```
////////////////////////
// MY CODE STARTS HERE
////////////////////////

// Good old MessageBeep()
::MessageBeep((WORD)-1);

////////////////////////
// MY CODE ENDS HERE
////////////////////////


    }
```

The code you typed is executed when you click the Circle tool or select Circle from the Draw menu.

The code you typed causes the PC to beep:

```
// Good old MessageBeep()
::MessageBeep((WORD)-1);
```

Yes, the good old `MessageBeep()` function is used to verify that the code is executed when you click the Circle tool or select Circle from the Draw menu.

☐ Save your work.

☐ Build and execute the Shp.EXE program.

The window of the Shp program appears, as shown in Figure 15.23.

Figure 15.23.

The toolbar of the Shp program with its Circle tool enabled.

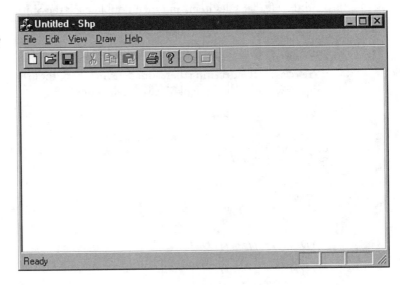

As you can see, now the Circle tool is enabled. The Rectangle tool is still disabled because you haven't attached code for it yet.

☐ Click the Circle tool on the toolbar.

The Shp program responds by causing the PC to beep.

☐ Select the Circle item of the Draw menu.

The Shp program responds by causing the PC to beep.

☐ Place the mouse cursor (without clicking) on the Circle tool.

The status bar displays the text Draw circle with the mouse.

☐ Highlight the Circle menu item of the Draw menu.

The status bar displays the text Draw circle with the mouse.

☐ Experiment with the Shp program, then select Exit from the File menu to terminate the program.

Declaring the Data Members of the View Class

You'll now declare four data members, m_XPos, m_YPos, m_Shape, and m_SelectedShapeOnToolbar, in the view class (CShpView):

☐ In the Project Workspace window, click the FileView tab, expand the Shp files item, expand the Header Files item, and then double-click the ShpView.h item.

Visual C++ responds by opening the ShpView.h file.

☐ Declare m_XPos, m_YPos, m_Shape, and m_SelectedShapeOnToolbar as data members of the CShpView class. After declaring these four data members, the CShpView class declaration (in the ShpView.h file) should look like the following:

```
class CShpView : public CView
{
protected: // create from serialization only
CShpView();
DECLARE_DYNCREATE(CShpView)

// Attributes
public:
  CShpDoc* GetDocument();


/////////////////////////
// MY CODE STARTS HERE
/////////////////////////
```

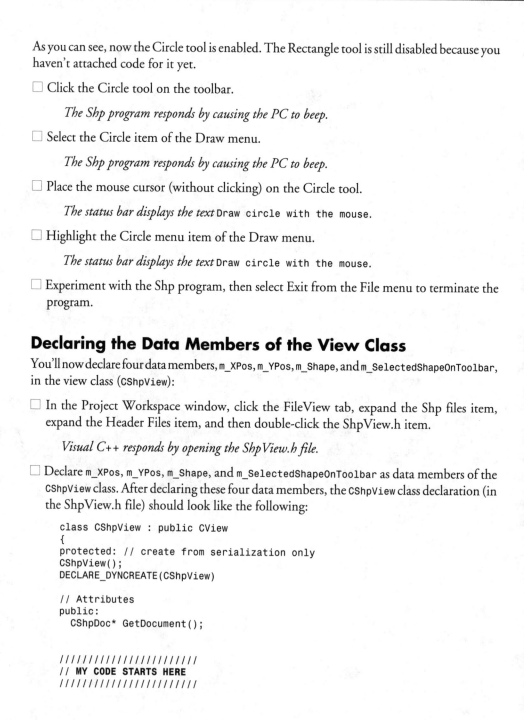

```
int       m_XPos;
int       m_YPos;
CString   m_Shape;
CString   m_SelectedShapeOnToolbar;

/////////////////////////
// MY CODE ENDS HERE
/////////////////////////
...
...
...
};
```

Now the CShpView class has the m_XPos, m_YPos, m_Shape, and m_SelectedShapeOnToolbar data members. The data members m_XPos and m_YPos will store the x-y coordinates of the currently displayed shape (a circle or a rectangle). m_Shape will store the string indicating which shape is currently being displayed (CIRCLE or RECTANGLE). m_SelectedShapeOnToolbar will store the currently selected icon on the toolbar (CIRCLE or RECTANGLE).

Declaring the Data Members of the Document Class

In the previous section, you declared four data members in the view class (CShpView): m_XPos, m_YPos, m_Shape, and m_SelectedShapeOnToolbar. The document class (CShpDoc) should have a mirror image of three of these view class data members. You'll now declare the following three data members in the document class: m_XPos, m_YPos, and m_Shape.

☐ Open the ShpDoc.h file and add the declarations of these data members as follows:

```
class CShpDoc : public CDocument
{
protected: // create from serialization only
CShpDoc();
DECLARE_DYNCREATE(CShpDoc)

// Attributes
public:

/////////////////////////
// MY CODE STARTS HERE
/////////////////////////

int     m_XPos;
int     m_YPos;
CString m_Shape;

/////////////////////////
// MY CODE ENDS HERE
/////////////////////////
...
...
...
};
```

Now the view class (CShpView) has four data members—m_XPos, m_YPos, m_Shape, and m_SelectedShapeOnToolbar—and the document class (CShpDoc) has three data members—m_XPos, m_YPos, and m_Shape. You'll set the data members of the document class to be mirror images of the view class data members.

During the execution of the Shp program, you can change the view. For example, when you select a certain shape from the toolbar (Circle or Rectangle) and then click the mouse to draw the shape, the code you write will update the m_XPos, m_YPos, and m_Shape view class data members. You will also write code that updates the m_XPos, m_YPos, and m_Shape data members of the document class with the same values as the view class data members.

These values must be the same because you want to save the drawing into a file, and the file you'll save will contain the values of m_XPos, m_YPos, and m_Shape. There is no reason to have the m_SelectedShapeOnToolbar as a data member of the document class, because when you save the file to the hard drive, there is no need to save the status of the Circle and Rectangle icons of the toolbar.

Attaching Code to the UPDATE_COMMAND_UI Message of the Circle Menu Item

You'll now attach code to the UPDATE_COMMAND_UI message of the Circle menu item:

☐ Select ClassWizard from the View menu.

  Visual C++ responds by displaying the MFC ClassWizard dialog box.

☐ In the Message Maps tab of ClassWizard, make sure the Class name box is set to CShpView and select the following event:

Class name:	CShpView
Object ID:	ID_DRAW_CIRCLE
Message:	UPDATE_COMMAND_UI

☐ Click the Add Function button, name the new function OnUpdateDrawCircle, then click the Edit Code button.

  Visual C++ responds by opening the file ShpView.cpp with the function OnUpdateDrawCircle() ready for you to edit.

☐ Write the following code in the OnUpdateDrawCircle() function:

```
void CShpView::OnUpdateDrawCircle(CCmdUI* pCmdUI)
{
// TODO: Add your command update UI handler code here

/////////////////////////
// MY CODE STARTS HERE
/////////////////////////
```

15

```
        if (m_SelectedShapeOnToolbar == "CIRCLE" )
        {
            // Place check mark to the left of the menu item
            pCmdUI->SetCheck(1);
        }
        else
        {
            // Remove check mark from menu item
            pCmdUI->SetCheck(0);
        }

        /////////////////////////
        // MY CODE ENDS HERE
        /////////////////////////

    }
```

The UPDATE_COMMAND_UI event occurs before the Draw menu is displayed. As you know, the Draw menu contains two items: Circle and Rectangle. When you open the Draw menu, the menu items will be displayed. Before the menu is opened, however, the UPDATE_COMMAND_UI event occurs. This is your chance to have code executed before displaying the menu.

What code would you want to execute before displaying the items of the Draw menu? You want to place a check mark next to the item selected last; in other words, you want to maintain the m_SelectedShapeOnToolbar data member with data containing either the string "CIRCLE" or the string "RECTANGLE". When you select the Circle tool or the Circle item from the Draw menu, the m_SelectedShapeOnToolbar string should be filled with the string "CIRCLE". When you select the Rectangle tool or the Rectangle item from the Draw menu, the m_SelectedShapeOnToolbar string should be filled with the string "RECTANGLE".

Now when you open the Draw menu, the UPDATE_COMMAND_UI event occurs. The code you typed examines the value of the m_SelectedShapeOnToolbar data member, and accordingly, a check mark is placed or removed from the Circle menu item.

The code you typed in the OnUpdateDrawCircle() function takes care of the Circle menu item. The parameter of the OnUpdateDrawCircle() function is pCmdUI:

```
void CMainFrame::OnUpdateDrawCircle(CCmdUI* pCmdUI)
{
...
...
...
}
```

pCmdUI is a pointer that represents the Circle menu item.

The code under the if statement is executed when m_SelectedShapeOnToolbar is equal to "CIRCLE":

```
if (m_SelectedShapeOnToolbar == "CIRCLE" )
{
    // Place check mark to the left of menu item
    pCmdUI->SetCheck(1);
```

```
}
else
{
    // Remove check mark from menu item
    pCmdUI->SetCheck(0);
}
```

The code under the `if` statement places a check mark next to the Circle menu item:

```
pCmdUI->SetCheck(1);
```

The code under the `else` is executed if `m_SelectedShapeOnToolbar` is not equal to `"CIRCLE"`. This code removes the check mark from the Circle menu item:

```
pCmdUI->SetCheck(0);
```

NOTE

> To place a check mark next to a menu item, use the `SetCheck()` function as follows:
>
> ```
> pCmdUI->SetCheck(1);
> ```
>
> The preceding statement assumes that `pCmdUI` is a pointer to the menu item.
>
> To remove a check mark from a menu item, use the `SetCheck()` function as follows:
>
> ```
> pCmdUI->SetCheck(0);
> ```
>
> The preceding statement again assumes that `pCmdUI` is a pointer to the menu item.
>
> There's no harm done if you try to place a check mark next to a menu item that's already checked or try to remove a check mark from a menu item with no check mark.

Attaching Code to the UPDATE_COMMAND_UI Message of the Rectangle Menu Item

You'll now attach code to the `UPDATE_COMMAND_UI` message of the Rectangle menu item:

☐ Select ClassWizard from the View menu.

Visual C++ responds by displaying the MFC ClassWizard dialog box.

15

15

☐ In the Message Maps tab of ClassWizard, select the following event:

Class name:	CShpView
Object ID:	ID_DRAW_RECTANGLE
Message:	UPDATE_COMMAND_UI

☐ Click the Add Function button, name the new function OnUpdateDrawRectangle, then click the Edit Code button.

Visual C++ responds by opening the file ShpView.cpp with the function OnUpdateDrawRectangle() *ready for you to edit.*

☐ Write the following code in the OnUpdateDrawRectangle() function:

```
void CShpView::OnUpdateDrawRectangle(CCmdUI* pCmdUI)
{
// TODO: Add your command update UI handler code here

////////////////////////
// MY CODE STARTS HERE
////////////////////////

if (m_SelectedShapeOnToolbar == "RECTANGLE" )
{
    // Place check mark to the left of menu item
    pCmdUI->SetCheck(1);
}
else
{
    // Remove check mark from menu item
    pCmdUI->SetCheck(0);
}

////////////////////////
// MY CODE ENDS HERE
////////////////////////


}
```

The code you typed in the OnUpdateDrawRectangle() function is very similar to the code in the OnUpdateDrawCircle() function. However, now pCmdUI represents the pointer to the Rectangle menu item because you attached code to the UPDATE_COMMAND_UI event of the Rectangle menu item.

☐ Save your work.

☐ Build and execute the Shp program.

☐ Open the Draw menu.

As you can see, the Rectangle menu item is still disabled because you haven't attached code to it yet. Also, note that the Circle menu item does not have a check mark next to it. Why? Because you haven't set the value of m_SelectedShapeOnToolbar to either CIRCLE or RECTANGLE. In the next section, you'll initialize the value of m_SelectedShapeOnToolbar to CIRCLE so that the Circle menu item will have a check mark next to it.

☐ Terminate the Shp program.

Initializing the m_SelectedShapeOnToolbar **Data Member**

You'll now write code that initializes the m_SelectedShapeOnToolbar data member of the view class:

☐ Add code in the constructor function of the CShpView class (in the ShpView.cpp file) as follows:

```
/////////////////////////////////////////////////////
// CShpView construction/destruction

CShpView::CShpView()
{
// TODO: add construction code here

///////////////////////////
/// MY CODE STARTS HERE
///////////////////////////

m_SelectedShapeOnToolbar = "CIRCLE";

///////////////////////////
/// MY CODE ENDS HERE
///////////////////////////

}
```

The code you typed sets the value of the m_Selected ShapeOnToolbar data member to CIRCLE:

```
m_SelectedShapeOnToolbar ="CIRCLE";
```

When you start the Shp program, an object of class CShpView is created, which means that the constructor function of the CShpView class is executed. This causes the m_SelectedShapeOnToolbar data variable to be equal to CIRCLE.

☐ Save your work.

☐ Build and execute the Shp program.

☐ Open the Draw menu of the Shp program.

As you can see in Figure 15.24, the Circle menu item of the Draw item has a check mark.

Figure 15.24.

The Circle menu item
with a check mark.

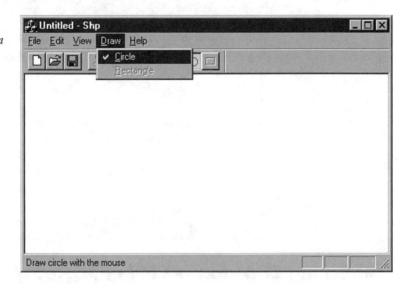

 NOTE

The check mark next to the Circle item, shown in Figure 15.24, also tells you that Circle was the last menu item selected from the Draw menu. Because the toolbar is the visual representation of the menu, how does it indicate that the Circle menu item was the last item selected from the Draw menu?

Figure 15.25 shows the icon of the Circle tool in its "pushed-down" position. The beauty of this feature is that you do not have to write any code to draw the icon to display it in this pushed-down position. All you have to do is set the ID of the Circle tool to the ID of the Circle menu item.

☐ Terminate the Shp program.

Figure 15.25.

The icon of the Circle tool in its pushed-down position.

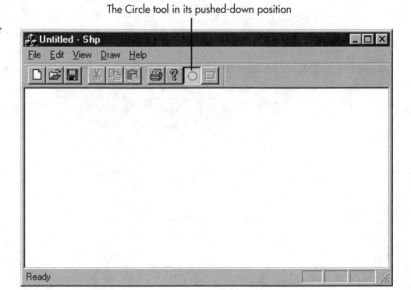

The Circle tool in its pushed-down position

Attaching Code to the Circle and Rectangle Menu Items

You'll now attach code to the Circle and Rectangle menu items of the Draw menu:

☐ Select ClassWizard from the View menu.

Visual C++ responds by displaying the MFC ClassWizard dialog box.

☐ In the Message Maps tab of ClassWizard, select the following event (remember to check the class name carefully):

Class name:	CShpView
Object ID:	ID_DRAW_CIRCLE
Message:	COMMAND

☐ Click the Edit Code button of ClassWizard.

Visual C++ responds by opening the file ShpView.cpp with the function OnDrawCircle() *ready for you to edit.*

☐ Edit the code in the OnDrawCircle() function (in the ShpView.cpp file) as follows:

```
void CShpView::OnDrawCircle()
{
// TODO: Add your command handler code here
```

15

15

```
/////////////////////////
// MY CODE STARTS HERE
/////////////////////////

// Good old MessageBeep()
//::MessageBeep((WORD)-1);

m_SelectedShapeOnToolbar = "CIRCLE";

/////////////////////////
// MY CODE ENDS HERE
/////////////////////////

}
```

The code you typed is executed when you select Circle from the Draw menu or click the Circle tool. This code sets the m_SelectedShapeOnToolbar data member to CIRCLE:

```
m_SelectedShapeOnToolbar = "CIRCLE";
```

Next, attach code to the Rectangle menu item:

☐ Select ClassWizard from the View menu.

Visual C++ responds by displaying the MFC ClassWizard dialog box.

☐ In the Message Maps tab of ClassWizard, select the following event:

Class name:	CShpView
Object ID:	ID_DRAW_RECTANGLE
Message:	COMMAND

☐ Click the Add Function button, name the new function OnDrawRectangle, then click the Edit Code button.

Visual C++ responds by opening the file ShpView.cpp with the function OnDrawRectangle() ready for you to edit.

☐ Edit the code in the OnDrawRectangle() function (in the ShpView.cpp file) as follows:

```
void CShpView::OnDrawRectangle()
{
// TODO: Add your command handler code here

/////////////////////////
// MY CODE STARTS HERE
/////////////////////////

m_SelectedShapeOnToolbar = "RECTANGLE";

/////////////////////////
// MY CODE ENDS HERE
/////////////////////////

}
```

The code you typed is executed when you select Rectangle from the Draw menu or click the Rectangle tool. This code sets the `m_SelectedShapeOnToolbar` data member to `RECTANGLE`:

```
m_SelectedShapeOnToolbar = "RECTANGLE";
```

☐ Save your work.

☐ Build and execute the Shp.EXE program.

   Visual C++ responds by executing the Shp.EXE program.

☐ Click the Rectangle tool.

   Visual C++ responds by displaying the Rectangle tool in its pushed-down position.

☐ Open the Draw menu.

As you can see, the Rectangle menu item has a check mark.

☐ Experiment with the Shp program, and note that whenever the Circle menu item has a check mark, the Circle tool is displayed in its pushed-down state. Likewise, whenever the Rectangle menu item has a check mark, the Rectangle tool is displayed in its pushed-down state.

☐ Terminate the program.

Attaching Code to the `WM_LBUTTONDOWN` Event of the View Class

Whenever you press the mouse's left button, the `WM_LBUTTONDOWN` event of the view class occurs. You'll now attach code to the `WM_LBUTTONDOWN` event of the view class:

☐ Select ClassWizard from the View menu.

   Visual C++ responds by displaying the MFC ClassWizard dialog box.

☐ In the Message Maps tab of ClassWizard, select the following event:

Class name:	CShpView
Object ID:	CShpView
Message:	WM_LBUTTONDOWN

☐ Click the Add Function button, then click the Edit Code button.

   Visual C++ responds by opening the file ShpView.cpp with the function `OnLButtonDown()` function ready for you to edit.

15

15

☐ Write the following code in the OnLButtonDown() function:

```
void CShpView::OnLButtonDown(UINT nFlags, CPoint point)
{
// TODO: Add your message handler code here and/or call default

/////////////////////////
// MY CODE STARTS HERE
/////////////////////////

// Update the data members of the view
m_XPos    = point.x;
m_YPos    = point.y;
m_Shape   = m_SelectedShapeOnToolbar;


// Update the data member of the document
// with the new value of the view.

CShpDoc* pDoc = GetDocument();

pDoc->m_Shape = m_Shape;
pDoc->m_XPos  = m_XPos;
pDoc->m_YPos  = m_YPos;

// Trigger a call to the OnDraw function.
Invalidate();

/////////////////////////
// MY CODE ENDS HERE
/////////////////////////

CView::OnLButtonDown(nFlags, point);
}
```

The second parameter of the OnLButtonDown() function is point:

```
void CShpView::OnLButtonDown(UINT nFlags, CPoint point)
{
...
...
...
}
```

point represents the coordinates of the mouse at the time the left mouse button was pressed.

The code you typed sets the value of the two view class data members to the x-y coordinates of the mouse at the time you pressed the left mouse button:

```
m_XPos    = point.x;
m_YPos    = point.y;
```

Then the m_Shape data member is updated with the current selected tool on the toolbar:

```
m_Shape   = m_SelectedShapeOnToolbar;
```

So, what have you accomplished so far? You've updated the view class data members with the data of the shape that will be drawn. To draw the shape, you have to know where to draw the shape (m_XPos and m_YPos), and you need to know what to draw (m_Shape can be CIRCLE or RECTANGLE). Next, you are going to update the corresponding data members of the document class.

You extract a pointer to the document:

```
CShpDoc* pDoc = GetDocument();
```

Then you update the data members of the document with the new values of the view:

```
pDoc->m_Shape = m_Shape;
pDoc->m_XPos  = m_XPos;
pDoc->m_YPos  = m_YPos;
```

Again, you update the data members of the document because later you'll write code that saves to the hard drive a file containing the data members m_XPos, m_YPos, and m_Shape of the document class.

Then the Invalidate() function is executed to cause the execution of the OnDraw() function:

```
Invalidate();
```

The actual drawing of the shape will be accomplished in the OnDraw() function. The shape will be drawn based on the values of m_XPos, m_YPos, and m_Shape.

Drawing the Circle and the Rectangle

You'll now type the code that causes the Shp program to draw a circle or a rectangle at the point where you click the mouse:

☐ Open the ShpView.cpp file and modify the OnDraw() function as follows:

```
void CShpView::OnDraw(CDC* pDC)
{
    CShpDoc* pDoc = GetDocument();
    ASSERT_VALID(pDoc);

// TODO: add draw code for native data here

/////////////////////////////
// MY CODE STARTS HERE
/////////////////////////////

RECT  MyRect;
MyRect.left = m_XPos - 20;
MyRect.top = m_YPos -20;
MyRect.bottom = m_YPos + 20;
MyRect.right = m_XPos +20;
```

```
if (m_Shape == "CIRCLE")
{
pDC->Ellipse(&MyRect);
}

if (m_Shape == "RECTANGLE")
{

pDC->Rectangle(&MyRect);

}

////////////////////////////
// MY CODE ENDS HERE
////////////////////////////

}
```

The code you typed declares a rectangle:

```
RECT MyRect;
MyRect.left = m_XPos - 20;
MyRect.top = m_YPos -20;
MyRect.bottom = m_YPos + 20;
MyRect.right = m_XPos +20;
```

Note that the circle you'll draw is enclosed by this rectangle. The center of the rectangle serves as the center of the circle. (See Figure 15.26.)

Figure 15.26.

Declaring the rectangle to enclose a circle with a radius of 20.

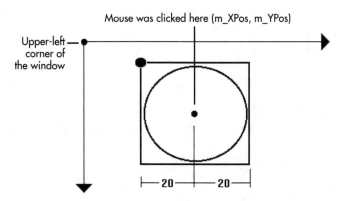

An if statement is then executed to examine the value of m_Shape:

```
if (m_Shape == "CIRCLE")
{

pDC->Ellipse(&MyRect);

}
```

If m_Shape is equal to CIRCLE, a circle is drawn.

The second `if` statement also examines the value of `m_Shape`; if `m_Shape` is equal to `RECTANGLE`, a rectangle is drawn:

```
if (m_Shape == "RECTANGLE")
{

pDC->Rectangle(&MyRect);

}
```

☐ Save your work.

☐ Build and execute the Shp.EXE program.

☐ Click the Circle tool, then click in the window of the Shp program.

Shp responds by drawing a circle. (See Figure 15.27.)

Figure 15.27.

Drawing a circle with the Shp program.

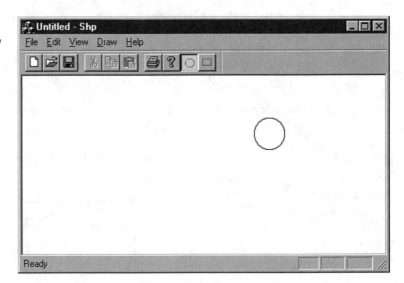

☐ Click the Rectangle tool, then click in the window of the Shp program.

Shp responds by drawing a rectangle, as shown back in Figure 15.1.

☐ Experiment with the Shp program, then terminate the program.

Initializing the Data Members of the Document Class

Whenever a new document is created by starting the program or selecting New from the File menu, the data members of the document class should be initialized to some value. You'll now write the code that does this:

☐ Open the ShpDoc.cpp file, search for the OnNewDocument() function in the ShpDoc.cpp file, then add code to the OnNewDocument() function as follows:

```
BOOL CShpDoc::OnNewDocument()
{
    if (!CDocument::OnNewDocument())
        return FALSE;

    // TODO: add reinitialization code here
    // (SDI documents will reuse this document)

///////////////////////////
// MY CODE STARTS HERE
///////////////////////////

m_XPos  = 10;
m_YPos  = 10;
m_Shape = "CIRCLE";

///////////////////////////
// MY CODE ENDS HERE
///////////////////////////

    return TRUE;
}
```

The OnNewDocument() function is executed when you start the Shp program or select New from the File menu of the Shp program.

The code you typed sets the values of the data members of the document class:

```
m_XPos  = 10;
m_YPos  = 10;
m_Shape = "CIRCLE";
```

☐ Save your work.

☐ Build and execute the Shp.EXE program.

The window of the Shp program appears without any circle or rectangle. In the OnNewDocument() function, you initialized the data members as follows:

```
m_XPos  = 10;
m_YPos  = 10;
m_Shape = "CIRCLE";
```

Why doesn't the window of the Shp program have a circle according to the preceding data? Because the OnDraw() function (in the ShpView.cpp file) draws the shape according to the data members of the view class (not the data members of the document class). This means you have to initialize the data members of the view class according to the data members of the document class. You'll accomplish this in the next section.

Initializing the Data Members of the View Class

You'll now initialize the data members of the view class to the values of the document class data members:

☐ Select ClassWizard from the View menu. In the Message Maps tab of ClassWizard, select the following event:

> Class name: CShpView
> Object ID: CShpView
>   Message: OnInitialUpdate

☐ Click the Add Function button, then click the Edit Code button.

> *Visual C++ responds by opening the file ShpView.cpp with the function* OnInitialUpdate() *ready for you to edit.*

☐ Write the following code in the OnInitialUpdate() function(in the ShpView.cpp file) as follows:

```
void CShpView::OnInitialUpdate()
{
    CView::OnInitialUpdate();

// TODO: Add your specialized code here and/or
// call the base class

///////////////////////////
// MY CODE STARTS HERE
///////////////////////////

// get a pointer to the  document
CShpDoc* pDoc = GetDocument();

// update data members of view with the
// corresponding document values
m_XPos  = pDoc->m_XPos;
m_YPos  = pDoc->m_YPos;
m_Shape = pDoc->m_Shape;

///////////////////////////
// MY CODE ENDS HERE
///////////////////////////

}
```

The OnInitialUpdate() function is automatically executed when you start the Shp program or select New from the File menu. The OnInitialUpdate() function is executed after the document has already been created and initialized.

A pointer to the document is extracted:

15

15

```
CShpDoc* pView = GetDocument();
```

Then the data members of the view class are updated with the values of the data members of the document:

```
m_XPos  = pDoc->m_XPos;
m_YPos  = pDoc->m_YPos;
m_Shape = pDoc->m_Shape;
```

☐ Save your work.

☐ Build and execute the Shp.EXE program.

The window of the Shp program appears with a circle in it. (See Figure 15.28.)

As you can see in Figure 15.28, the shape is a circle whose center is 10 units to the right of the window's left edge and 10 units below the window's top edge.

Figure 15.28.

The circle in the Shp window when you start the Shp program.

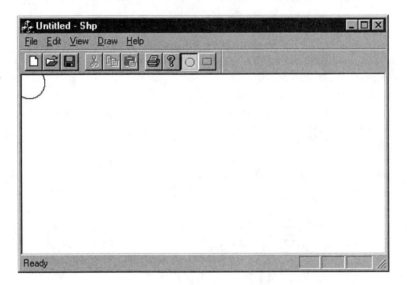

☐ Click in the window of the Shp program.

Shp responds by drawing a circle at the point where you clicked.

☐ Select New from the File menu of the Shp program.

Shp responds by opening a new document, and a circle at point x=10, y=10 appears in the window.

☐ Experiment with the Shp program, then terminate the program.

The Preparing to Save Flag

In the OnLButtonDown() function of the view class (in the ShpView.cpp file), you wrote code that sets the document class data members to the values of the view class data members. Later, you'll write code that saves the document class data members to the hard drive.

When you terminate the Shp program, it should display a message box asking whether the document should be saved. Also, when you select New from the File menu of the Shp program, the program should display a message asking whether the data of the previous document should be saved. To accomplish this, you have to call the SetModifiedFlag() function whenever the document is modified.

☐ Open the ShpView.cpp file and search for the OnLButtonDown() function.

☐ Modify the OnLButtonDown() function (in the ShpView.cpp file) as follows:

```
void CShpView::OnLButtonDown(UINT nFlags, CPoint point)
{
// TODO: Add your message handler code here and/or call default

/////////////////////////
// MY CODE STARTS HERE
/////////////////////////

m_XPos     = point.x;
m_YPos     = point.y;
m_Shape    = m_SelectedShapeOnToolbar;


// Update the data member of the document
// with the new value of the view.
CShpDoc* pDoc = GetDocument();

pDoc->m_Shape = m_Shape;
pDoc->m_XPos  = m_XPos;
pDoc->m_YPos  = m_YPos;

// Set the Modify flag of the document class to TRUE
pDoc->SetModifiedFlag();


Invalidate();

/////////////////////////
// MY CODE ENDS HERE
/////////////////////////

CView::OnLButtonDown(nFlags, point);
}
```

The statement you added to the OnLButtonDown() function calls the SetModifiedFlag() member function of the document class:

15

15

```
// Set the Modify flag of the document class to TRUE
pDoc->SetModifiedFlag();
```

☐ Save your work.

☐ Select Build Shp.EXE from the Build menu.

☐ Execute the Shp.EXE program.

☐ Click in the window of the Shp program.

Shp responds by drawing the shape at the point where you clicked.

☐ Select New from the File menu of the Shp program.

Shp responds by displaying a message box asking whether you want to save the document.

☐ Click the No button (at this point, you don't want to save the document).

☐ Experiment with the Shp program, then select Exit from its File menu.

Shp responds by displaying a message box asking whether you want to save the document.

☐ Click the No button (at this point, you don't want to save the document).

Writing and Reading Data to a File

The last thing to add to the Shp program is the code that saves the data members of the document to a file and loads previously saved files:

☐ Open the ShpDoc.cpp file, search for the Serialize() function, then add code to the Serialize() function (in the ShpDoc.cpp file) as follows:

```
/////////////////////////////////////////////////////////
// CShpDoc serialization

void CShpDoc::Serialize(CArchive& ar)
{
  if (ar.IsStoring())
    {
    // TODO: add storing code here

/////////////////////////
// MY CODE STARTS HERE
/////////////////////////

ar<<m_XPos;
ar<<m_YPos;
ar<<m_Shape;

/////////////////////////
// MY CODE ENDS HERE
/////////////////////////
```

```
          }
          else
          {
          // TODO: add loading code here

//////////////////////////
// MY CODE STARTS HERE
//////////////////////////

ar>>m_XPos;
ar>>m_YPos;
ar>>m_Shape;

//////////////////////////
// MY CODE ENDS HERE
//////////////////////////

          }
}
```

The code you typed under the `if` statement saves the data members of the document to the file. The code you typed under the `else` statement updates the data members of the document from a previously saved file.

☐ Save your work.

☐ Build and execute the Shp.EXE program.

The window of the Shp program appears with a circle in its upper-left corner.

☐ Click the mouse in the upper-right corner of the Shp program.

Shp responds by displaying a circle at the point where you clicked.

☐ Select Save As from the File menu of the Shp program and save the file as `MyCircle.Shp`.

Now the MyCircle.Shp file contains the data members `m_XPos`, `m_YPos`, and `m_Shape` of the document class. The values of these data members correspond to the circle you drew in the upper-right corner of the window.

☐ Select New from the File menu of the Shp program.

A new document is created, and the Shp program displays the initial circle in the upper-left corner of the window.

☐ Select Open from the File menu of the Shp program and select the MyCircle.Shp file you previously saved.

Shp responds by displaying the circle you previously saved. The circle will appear in the upper-right corner of the window.

15

☐ Click the Rectangle tool and draw a rectangle by clicking the mouse.

☐ Select Save as from the File menu of the Shp program and save the file as `MyRect.Shp`.

☐ Select New from the File menu of the Shp program.

> *The initial circle in the upper-left corner of Shp's program appears.*

☐ Select Open from the File menu of the Shp program and load the MyRect.Shp file.

> *The rectangle you previously saved appears.*

☐ Experiment with the Shp program by saving additional files and make sure the Save As and Open features work as expected.

☐ Select Exit from the File menu of the Shp program to terminate the program.

NOTE

> Experiment with the other features of the Shp program, such as the Print tool, Help tool, Print Preview, and so on. These features were created for you by Visual C++ without you having to write any code.

Summary

In this chapter, you learned how to create and use a toolbar and a status bar. As you've seen, the toolbar serves as a visual menu.

Typically, you do not place icons for each of the menu items, because too many icons on the toolbar makes it difficult to locate a tool during runtime. Instead, place icons on the toolbar that correspond to the most frequently used menu items.

Q&A

Q When I place the mouse cursor on the icons of the toolbar, a tool tip is displayed. For example, when I place the mouse cursor on the New icon, the tool tip displays the text New. I would like to add tool tips for the Circle and Rectangle icons as well. Can it be done?

A Yes, it can be done. In the Exercise section of this chapter, you'll learn how to do this.

Q I saved the `m_XPos`, `m_YPos`, and `m_Shape` data members to a file, but the data member `m_SelectedShapeOnToolbar` of the view class was not saved. I did not declare the data member `m_SelectedShapeOnToolbar` in the document class. Why?

A The `m_SelectedShapeOnToolbar` data member indicates which icon (Circle or Rectangle) is currently selected on the toolbar. However, to draw a shape, you don't need to know which icon is currently selected. All that's needed to draw the shape is its location (`m_XPos` and `m_YPos`) and shape (`m_Shape`, which can be `CIRCLE` or `RECTANGLE`).

Q During the course of this chapter, I was instructed to save the data files of the Shp program with the file extension `*.shp` (for example, MyCircle.Shp). Does the file extension have to be Shp?

A No. You can save the data files by any name and any file extension (for example, OurDrawing.drw).

Quiz

1. The ID of the icons on the toolbar are set to the ID of what?

2. What is the reason for setting the ID of the toolbar's icons to the IDs of the menu items?

3. When a menu item has a check mark next to it, how will the corresponding icon on the toolbar be shown?

4. When a menu item is disabled, how will the corresponding icon on the toolbar be shown?

Exercise

Add tool tips to the Circle and Rectangle tools of the toolbar.

Quiz Answers

1. The IDs of the icons on the toolbar are set to the IDs of the corresponding menu items.

2. You want the effects of clicking the toolbar's icon to be identical to the effects of selecting the corresponding menu items.

3. When a menu item has a check mark next to it, the corresponding icon on the toolbar is shown in its pushed-down state.

15

15

4. When a menu item is disabled, the corresponding icon on the toolbar will be shown dimmed.

Exercise Answer

Follow these steps to add tool tips to the Circle and Rectangle tools:

☐ Display the toolbar in design mode (select the ResourceView tab of the Project Workspace window, expand the Shp resources item, expand the Toolbar item, and finally double-click the IDR_MAINFRAME item).

Visual C++ responds by displaying the toolbar in design mode.

☐ Double-click the Circle icon on the toolbar.

Visual C++ responds by displaying the Toolbar Button Properties window.

☐ Modify the contents of the Prompt box as follows:

```
Draw circle with the mouse\nDraw Circle
```

During runtime, when you place the mouse cursor on the Circle icon, the text `Draw circle with the mouse` *will appear in the status bar. The text* `Draw Circle` *will appear in a tool tip next to the Circle icon.*

☐ Double-click the Rectangle icon on the toolbar.

Visual C++ responds by displaying the Toolbar Button Properties window.

☐ Modify the contents of the Prompt box as follows:

```
Draw rectangle with the mouse\nDraw Rectangle
```

During runtime, when you place the mouse cursor on the Rectangle icon, the text `Draw rectangle with the mouse` *will appear in the status bar. The text* `Draw Rectangle` *will appear in a tool tip next to the Rectangle icon.*

Day **16**

Creating Your Own Classes and Modules

As you have probably noticed in this book, Visual C++ is a highly *modular* programming language. This means you can create applications by "plugging in" software modules created by others. Classic examples of such software modules are the Microsoft classes you have used throughout this book (the MFC).

In this chapter, you'll learn how to write your own software modules that contain your own classes. Typically, you design your own software modules to distribute and sell them or to distribute them in your organization.

Why Create Professional Software Modules?

Typically, you design a *software module* to perform a task that's not otherwise available in Visual C++ and that's not easy to create. For example, you can design a software module that enables programmers to display 3-D graphs.

Sure, programmers could probably design such 3-D programs by themselves, but most programmers prefer to purchase an off-the-shelf software module that performs the task. Therefore, the programmer can concentrate on his or her own program. When the application requires displaying 3-D graphs, the programmer can plug in your software module rather then spend time designing one.

NOTE

In this book, the term *programmer* usually means you, the reader, and the term *end-user* means the person who uses your application.

In this chapter, however, you'll learn how to write software modules and how to distribute them to other programmers. Therefore, the term *programmer* means another programmer who uses your software modules, and the term *end-user* means a person (a Visual C++ programmer) who purchases and uses your software modules.

Why not create a function or set of functions that perform the particular task, then distribute the C++ source code to your end-users? There are several reasons for not distributing your software as a set of C++ functions:

■ The person who receives your code might accidentally (or even not accidentally) mess up the code.

■ You don't want your end-user to know how you created the task; you only want your user to know how to use your software.

■ Your end-user expects a "finished product" that can be easily plugged into his or her projects.

Different Formats for Software Modules

The current trend is to sell and distribute software in the form of software modules. Naturally, the format of the software module depends on the particular software package and programming language your user uses. For example, you can create ActiveX controls (OCX

16

files) or DLL files. The advantage of creating an ActiveX control or a DLL file is that programmers of many different languages can use your software module because DLL files and ActiveX controls are supported by a variety of Windows programming languages. You'll learn how to create DLL files in Chapter 17, "Creating Your Own DLLs," and ActiveX controls in Chapter 18, "Creating Your Own ActiveX Control (Part I)," and Chapter 19, "Creating Your Own ActiveX Control (Part II)."

You can also distribute software modules exclusively to Visual C++ programmers by creating a Visual C++ library file (.LIB file). For example, you can create and distribute a file called Circle.LIB that lets your users perform operations related to a circle (for example, calculate the circle's area). Instead of writing functions that calculate the circle's area, your user simply plugs the Circle.LIB file into his or her application. Your responsibility is only to supply information to your users, telling them how they can apply your library to calculate circles' areas. In the following sections, you'll create the Circle.LIB library. Its code is simple; the point is to teach you how a library is prepared with Visual C++ and how to prepare the library for distribution.

Creating the Project of the Circle.LIB Library

Follow these steps to create the project for the Circle.LIB library:

☐ Create the directory C:\TYVCPROG\PROGRAMS\CH16 and start Visual C++.

☐ Select New from the File menu.

   Visual C++ responds by displaying the New dialog box.

☐ Select the Projects tab of the New dialog box.

☐ Select Win32 Static Library from the list of project types. (See Figure 16.1.)

☐ Type Circle in the Project Name box.

☐ Click the button that is located on the right of the Location box and select the C:\TYVCPROG\PROGRAMS\CH16 directory.

☐ Click the OK button.

☐ Select Set Active Configuration from the Build menu, select Circle - Win32 Release in the Set Active Project Configuration dialog box, then click the OK button.

That's it! You've finished creating the project file of the Circle.LIB library.

Figure 16.1.

Selecting Win32 Static Library in the New Projects dialog box.

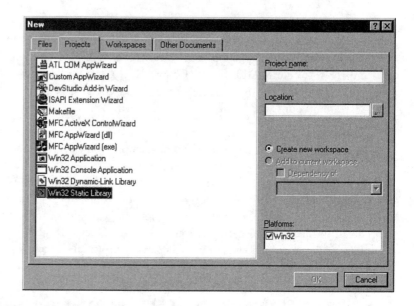

Creating the Circle.cpp and Circle.h Files

The Circle.LIB file you create will be generated from the Circle.cpp and Circle.h files. You'll now create the Circle.cpp and Circle.h files. First create the Circle.CPP file as follows:

☐ Select New from the File menu.

> *Visual C++ responds by displaying the New dialog box.*

☐ Make sure that the Files tab of the New dialog box is selected and then select the C++ Source File item (because you are now creating a C++ source file).

☐ In the File Name box, type `Circle.cpp`.

☐ Click the OK button of the New dialog box.

> *Visual C++ responds by creating the Circle.cpp file and displaying its window where you can type code.*

☐ Type the following code in the Circle.CPP file:

```
//////////////////
// Circle.CPP
//////////////////

// Copyright (C)
```

16

```
// This file is used for generating the Circle.LIB file

#include "Circle.h"
```

☐ Save your work by selecting Save All from the File menu.

Next, create the Circle.h header file as follows:

☐ Select New from the File menu.

> *Visual C++ responds by displaying the New dialog box.*

☐ Make sure that the Files tab of the New dialog box is selected and then select the `C/C++ Header File` item (because you are now creating a C++ header file).

☐ In the File Name box, type `Circle.h`.

☐ Click the OK button of the New dialog box.

> *Visual C++ responds by creating the Circle.h file and displaying its window where you can type code.*

☐ Type the following code in the Circle.h file:

```
/////////////////
// Circle.H
/////////////////

// Copyright (C)
```

☐ Save your work by selecting Save All from the File menu.

You now have the Circle.cpp and Circle.h files used for generating the Circle.LIB library. (Of course, later you'll write more code in these files.)

To make sure you've successfully added the Circle.cpp and Circle.h files to the project, do the following:

☐ Select the FileView tab of the Project Workspace window.

☐ Expand the Circle files item and make sure that the Circle.CPP file and Circle.h file are listed.

Your Project Workspace window should now look like Figure 16.2. As shown, the Circle.cpp file and the Circle.h file are part of the project.

You have performed all the overhead tasks needed for telling Visual C++ to generate the Circle.LIB library. It's now time to start writing the code of the project.

16

Figure 16.2.
*Listing the files of the
Circle project.*

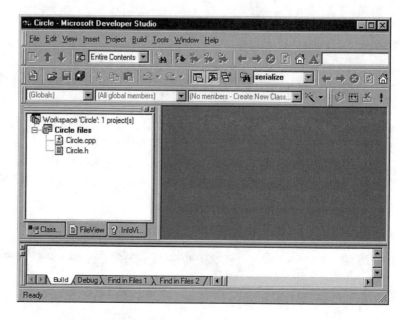

Declaring the `CCircle` Class

You'll now write the code that declares a class called `CCircle`:

☐ Select Open from the File menu and select the Circle.h file.

Visual C++ responds by opening the Circle.h file.

☐ Add code to the Circle.h file as follows:

```
////////////////
// Circle.h
////////////////

// Copyright (C)

// Class declaration

class CCircle
{
public:

 CCircle();  // Constructor

 void  SetRadius   ( int r );
 int   GetRadius   ( void );
 void  DisplayArea ( void );

 ~CCircle();  // Destructor
```

```
    private:
     int m_radius;
     float CalcArea    ( void  );


    };
```

The code you typed in Circle.h declares the CCircle class:

```
class CCircle
{
...
...
...
};
```

The public section of the class contains the constructor, destructor, and three member functions:

```
public:

 CCircle();  // Constructor

 void  SetRadius  ( int r );
 int   GetRadius  ( void );
 void  DisplayArea ( void );

 ~CCircle();  // Destructor
```

The private section of the class contains one data member and one member function:

```
private:
 int m_radius;
 float CalcArea    ( void );
```

☐ Select Save from the File menu to save the Circle.h file.

Writing Code in the Circle.cpp File

You'll now write code in the Circle.cpp file:

☐ Select Open from the File menu and open the Circle.cpp file.

☐ Add code to the Circle.cpp file as follows:

```
/////////////////
// Circle.cpp
/////////////////

// Copyright (C)

// This file is used for generating the Circle.LIB file

#include "Circle.h"

#include <windows.h>
```

```c
#include <stdio.h>
#include <stdlib.h>
#include <string.h>

/////////////////////////////
// The constructor function
/////////////////////////////
CCircle::CCircle()
{


}

/////////////////////////////
// The destructor function
/////////////////////////////
CCircle::~CCircle()
{


}

/////////////////////////////
// The SetRadius() function
/////////////////////////////
void  CCircle::SetRadius   ( int r )
{

m_radius = r;

}

/////////////////////////////
// The GetRadius() function
/////////////////////////////
int   CCircle::GetRadius   ( void )
{

return m_radius;

}


/////////////////////////////
// The CalcArea() function
/////////////////////////////
float CCircle::CalcArea ( void )
{

return float(3.14 * m_radius * m_radius);

}


/////////////////////////////
// The DisplayArea() function
/////////////////////////////
void  CCircle::DisplayArea ( void )
{
```

```
float   fArea;
char    sArea[100];

fArea = CalcArea ();


sprintf ( sArea, "Area is:%f", fArea );


MessageBox ( NULL,
             sArea,
             "Circle Area",
             0 );

}
```

16

☐ Save your work by selecting Save All from the File menu.

The code you typed starts with several #include statements:

```
#include "Circle.h"

#include <windows.h>

#include <stdio.h>
#include <stdlib.h>
#include <string.h>
```

The constructor and destructor functions of CCircle have no code:

```
/////////////////////////////
// The constructor function
/////////////////////////////
CCircle::CCircle()
{


}
/////////////////////////////
// The destructor function
/////////////////////////////
CCircle::~CCircle()
{


}
```

The SetRadius() member function sets the m_radius data member:

```
/////////////////////////////
// The SetRadius() function
/////////////////////////////
void  CCircle::SetRadius   ( int r )
{

m_radius = r;

}
```

The `GetRadius()` member function returns the `m_radius` data member:

```
/////////////////////////////////
// The GetRadius() function
/////////////////////////////////
int   CCircle::GetRadius   ( void  )
{

return m_radius;

}
```

The `CalcArea()` member function calculates the circle's area:

```
/////////////////////////////////
// The CalcArea() function
/////////////////////////////////
float CCircle::CalcArea ( void )
{

return float(3.14 * m_radius * m_radius);

}
```

The `DisplayArea()` function displays the calculated area:

```
/////////////////////////////////
// The DisplayArea() function
/////////////////////////////////
void  CCircle::DisplayArea ( void  )
{

float  fArea;
char   sArea[100];

fArea = CalcArea ();

sprintf ( sArea, "Area is:%f", fArea );

MessageBox ( NULL,
             sArea,
             "Circle Area",
             0 );

}V
```

Making the Circle.LIB Library

You are now ready to generate the Circle.LIB file:

☐ Select Build Circle.LIB from the Build menu.

Visual C++ responds by creating the Circle.LIB file.

Take a look in your \TYVCPROG\PROGRAMS\CH16\CIRCLE\RELEASE directory.
This directory now contains the Circle.LIB file!

Testing the Library: The Test1.EXE Program

You'll now write a program called Test1.EXE that uses the Circle.LIB library:

☐ Close the Circle project and all its associated files by selecting Close Workspace from the File menu.

☐ When Visual C++ displays a message box asking you whether you wish to close all the document windows, click the Yes button of the message box.

☐ Select New from the File menu.

Visual C++ responds by displaying the New dialog box.

☐ Select the Projects tab of the New dialog box.

☐ Select MFC AppWizard(exe) from the list of project types.

☐ Type Test1 in the Project Name box.

☐ Click the button that is located on the right of the Location box and select the C:\TYVCPROG\PROGRAMS\CH16 directory.

☐ Click the OK button.

Visual C++ responds by displaying the MFC AppWizard - Step 1 window.

☐ In the Step 1 window, select the option to create a dialog-based application, then click the Next button.

☐ In the Step 2 window, leave all the check boxes at their default settings and set the title of the dialog to The Test1 Program. When you're done, click the Next button.

☐ In the Step 3 window, use the default settings and click the Next button.

☐ In the Step 4 window, notice that AppWizard has created the classes CTest1App and CTest1Dlg. Click the Finish button.

Visual C++ responds by displaying the New Project Information window.

☐ Click the OK button of the New Project Information window.

Visual C++ responds by creating the project file and skeleton files of the Test1 program.

☐ Select Set Active Configuration from the Build menu.

Visual C++ responds by displaying the Set Active Project Configuration dialog box.

☐ Select Test1 - Win32 Release in the Set Active Project Configuration dialog box, then click the OK button.

That's it! You've finished creating the project of the Test1 program.

16

The Visual Design of the Test1 Program's Main Window

You'll now visually design the main window of the Test1 program:

☐ In the Project Workspace window, select the ResourceView tab, expand the Test1 resources item, expand the Dialog item, then double-click the IDD_TEST1_DIALOG item.

Visual C++ responds by displaying the IDD_TEST1_DIALOG dialog box in design mode.

☐ Delete the OK button, Cancel button, and text in the IDD_TEST1_DIALOG dialog box.

☐ Set up the IDD_TEST1_DIALOG dialog box according to Table 16.1. When you finish, it should look like Figure 16.3.

Table 16.1. The properties table of the IDD_TEST1_DIALOG dialog box.

Object	Property	Setting
Dialog Box	**ID**	**IDD_TEST1_DIALOG**
	Caption	The Test1 Program
	Font	System, Size 10
Static Text	**ID**	**IDC_STATIC**
	Caption	Testing the Circle.LIB Library
Push Button	**ID**	**IDC_MYCIRCLE_BUTTON**
	Caption	&My Circle
	Client edge	Checked (Extended Styles tab)
	Static edge	Checked (Extended Styles tab)
	Modal frame	Checked (Extended Styles tab)
Push Button	**ID**	**IDC_HERCIRCLE_BUTTON**
	Caption	He&r Circle
	Client edge	Checked (Extended Styles tab)
	Static edge	Checked (Extended Styles tab)
	Modal frame	Checked (Extended Styles tab)
Push Button	**ID**	**IDC_HISCIRCLE_BUTTON**
	Caption	&His Circle
	Client edge	Checked (Extended Styles tab)
	Static edge	Checked (Extended Styles tab)
	Modal frame	Checked (Extended Styles tab)

16

Object	Property	Setting
Push Button	**ID**	**IDC_OURCIRCLE_BUTTON**
	Caption	&Our Circle
	Client edge	Checked (Extended Styles tab)
	Static edge	Checked (Extended Styles tab)
	Modal frame	Checked (Extended Styles tab)

16

Figure 16.3.
The
IDD_TEST1_DIALOG
dialog box in design
mode (after
customization).

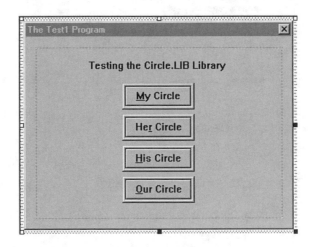

Attaching Code to the My Circle Button

You'll now attach code to the My Circle button of the IDD_TEST1_DIALOG dialog box:

☐ Select ClassWizard from the View menu. In the Message Maps tab of ClassWizard, select
the following event:

Class name:	CTest1Dlg
Object ID:	IDC_MYCIRCLE_BUTTON
Message:	BN_CLICKED

☐ Click the Add Function button, name the new function OnMycircleButton, then click the
Edit Code button.

Visual C++ responds by opening the file Test1Dlg.cpp with the function OnMycircleButton()
ready for you to edit.

☐ Write the following code in the `OnMycircleButton()` function:

```
void CTest1Dlg::OnMycircleButton()
{

// TODO: Add your control notification handler code here

////////////////////////////
// MY CODE STARTS HERE
////////////////////////////

// Create the object
CCircle MyCircle;

// Set the radius of the circle
MyCircle.SetRadius(1);

// Display the area
MyCircle.DisplayArea();

////////////////////////////
// MY CODE ENDS HERE
////////////////////////////

}
```

The code you typed creates the `MyCircle` object of class `CCircle`:

`CCircle MyCircle;`

The radius of `MyCircle` is set to 1:

`MyCircle.SetRadius(1);`

Finally, the area of `MyCircle` is displayed:

`MyCircle.DisplayArea();`

Attaching Code to the His Circle Button

You'll now attach code to the His Circle button of the IDD_TEST1_DIALOG dialog box:

☐ Select ClassWizard from the View menu. In the Message Maps tab of ClassWizard, select the following event:

Class name:	CTest1Dlg
Object ID:	IDC_HISCIRCLE_BUTTON
Message:	BN_CLICKED

☐ Click the Add Function button, name the new function `OnHiscircleButton`, then click the Edit Code button.

16

Visual C++ responds by opening the file Test1Dlg.cpp with the function OnHiscircleButton() *ready for you to edit.*

☐ Write the following code in the OnHiscircleButton() function:

```
void CTest1Dlg::OnHiscircleButton()
{

// TODO: Add your control notification handler code here

////////////////////////
// MY CODE STARTS HERE
////////////////////////

// Create the object
CCircle HisCircle;

// Set the radius of the circle
HisCircle.SetRadius(2);

// Display the area
HisCircle.DisplayArea();

////////////////////////
// MY CODE ENDS HERE
////////////////////////

}
```

The code you typed is similar to the code you typed in the OnMycircleButton() function, except that now you have created the HisCircle object and set the radius to 2.

Attaching Code to the Her Circle Button

You'll now attach code to the Her Circle button of the IDD_TEST1_DIALOG dialog box:

☐ Select ClassWizard from the View menu. In the Message Maps tab of ClassWizard, select the following event:

Class name:	CTest1Dlg
Object ID:	IDC_HERCIRCLE_BUTTON
Message:	BN_CLICKED

☐ Click the Add Function button, name the new function OnHercircleButton, then click the Edit Code button.

Visual C++ responds by opening the file Test1Dlg.cpp with the function OnHercircleButton() *ready for you to edit.*

☐ Write the following code in the `OnHercircleButton()` function:

```
void CTest1Dlg::OnHercircleButton()
{

// TODO: Add your control notification handler code here

/////////////////////////
// MY CODE STARTS HERE
/////////////////////////

// Create the object
CCircle HerCircle;

// Set the radius of the circle
HerCircle.SetRadius(3);

// Display the area
HerCircle.DisplayArea();

/////////////////////////
// MY CODE ENDS HERE
/////////////////////////

}
```

The code you typed is similar to the code you typed in the `OnMycircleButton()` and the `OnHiscircleButton()` functions, except that now you have created the `HerCircle` object and set the radius to 3.

Attaching Code to the Our Circle Button

You'll now attach code to the Our Circle button of the IDD_TEST1_DIALOG dialog box:

☐ Select ClassWizard from the View menu. In the Message Maps tab of ClassWizard, select the following event:

Class name:	CTest1Dlg
Object ID:	IDC_OURCIRCLE_BUTTON
Message:	BN_CLICKED

☐ Click the Add Function button, name the new function `OnOurcircleButton`, then click the Edit Code button.

Visual C++ responds by opening the file Test1Dlg.cpp with the function `OnOurcircleButton()` *ready for you to edit.*

☐ Write the following code in the `OnOurcircleButton()` function:

```
void CTest1Dlg::OnOurcircleButton()
{

// TODO: Add your control notification handler code here
```

16

```
///////////////////////
// MY CODE STARTS HERE
///////////////////////

// Create the object
CCircle OurCircle;

// Set the radius of the circle
OurCircle.SetRadius(4);

// Display the area
OurCircle.DisplayArea();

///////////////////////
// MY CODE ENDS HERE
///////////////////////

}
```

☐ Save your work.

The code you typed is similar to the code you attached to the other buttons of the IDD_TEST1_DIALOG dialog box, except that now you have created the OurCircle object and set the radius to 4.

Plugging in the Circle.LIB Library

If you try to build the Test1 project now, you'll get plenty of errors! Why? Because the Test1 project knows nothing about the CCircle class. Therefore, you must use the #include statement on the Circle.h file at the beginning of the Test1Dlg.h file:

☐ Open the Test1Dlg.h file and use an #include statement on the Circle.h file as follows:

```
// Test1Dlg.h : header file
//

/////////////////////////////////////////////////////
// CTest1Dlg dialog

///////////////////////
// MY CODE STARTS HERE
///////////////////////

#include "C:\TyVcProg\Programs\Ch16\Circle\Circle.H"

///////////////////////
// MY CODE ENDS HERE
///////////////////////
...
...
...
```

Because you used the #include statement on the Circle.h file, the prototypes of the CCircle class member function will be known to the compiler. However, the linker needs to use the actual code of these member functions, which is in the Circle.LIB file. In the following steps, you'll plug the Circle.LIB file into the Test1 project:

☐ Select Add To Project from the Project menu and then select Files from the submenu that pops up.

Visual C++ responds by displaying the Insert Files into Project dialog box. (See Figure 16.4.)

Figure 16.4.

The Insert Files into Project dialog box.

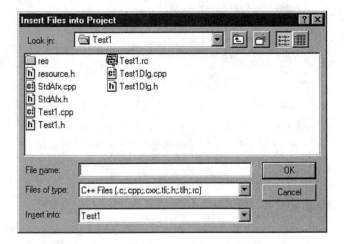

You'll now add the \TYVCPROG\PROGRAMS\CH16\CIRCLE\RELEASE\Circle.LIB file to the project:

☐ Set the Files of Type drop-down list to Library files (.lib).

☐ Select the \TYVCPROG\PROGRAMS\CH16\CIRCLE\RELEASE\Circle.LIB file, then click the OK button.

Visual C++ responds by adding the \TYVCPROG\PROGRAMS\CH16\CIRCLE\RELEASE\Circle.LIB file to the Test1 project.

☐ Save your work.

16

Building and Executing the Test1 Program

You'll now build and execute the Test1 program:

☐ Select Build Test1.EXE from the Project menu.

> *Visual C++ responds by compiling and linking the Test1 program.*

☐ Select Execute Test1.EXE from the Project menu.

> *Visual C++ responds by executing the Test1.EXE program and displaying the window shown in Figure 16.5.*

16

Figure 16.5.
The window of the Test1.EXE program.

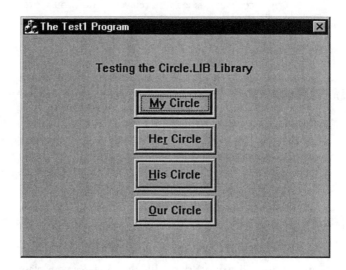

☐ Experiment with the four buttons of the Test1 program and verify that the program operates properly.

☐ Terminate the Test1 program by clicking the × icon at the upper-right corner of the program's window.

Distributing Your Software Modules

In the preceding section you proved that the Circle.LIB library works as expected. So what will you distribute to your users? You have to distribute to the following:

■ The Circle.LIB file.
■ The Circle.h file.

■ Documentation showing how to use Circle.LIB. (It is a good idea to distribute the Test1 program as part of your documentation because your user can see how the Circle.LIB library is used.)

NOTE

Note that your CCircle class calculates the area of the circle by using the formula Area=3.14*radius*radius, but because you did not supply the source code, the "secret" of calculating the circle's area remains with you. Your user doesn't know how you performed the calculations! Of course, this is more relevant when you write code that accomplishes a more complicated task.

Summary

In this chapter, you learned how to create a library file (.LIB file) that contains your own class. As you have seen, creating a library file with Visual C++ is quite simple. Once you finish your library file, you can distribute it to other Visual C++ programmers who can incorporate it into their projects.

Q&A

Q Why do I have to distribute the .h file that declares my class with my .LIB file?

A You must distribute the .h file that declares your class with your .LIB file so that your end-user's project will know about your class (the names and types of your class data members and the prototypes of your class member functions).

Quiz

1. When you distribute your library file to your end-user you have to distribute the source code of your library.
    a. True
    b. False
2. To use your library file, your end-user needs to add your .LIB file to his or her project and then build the project.
    a. True
    b. False

16

Exercise

Describe the steps needed to create a project for a library file.

Quiz Answers

1. b
2. a

Exercise Answer

To create a project for a library file, use the following steps:

☐ Select New from the File menu.

Visual C++ responds by displaying the New dialog box.

☐ Select the Projects tab of the New dialog box.

☐ Select Win32 Static Library from the list of project types.

☐ Type the name of the library that you want to create in the Project Name box.

☐ Click the button that is located on the right of the Location box and select the directory where you want to create the project.

☐ Click the OK button.

Day 17

Creating Your Own DLLs

In this chapter, you'll learn what a *DLL* (dynamic link library) is, how to create a DLL with Visual C++, and how to use a DLL in Visual C++.

What Is a DLL?

A DLL is a library file that contains functions. A programmer can integrate a DLL file into his or her program and use the DLL's functions. For example, you can create a DLL called CIRCLE.DLL containing functions that pertain to circles, such as `DrawCircle()`, `CalculateCircleArea()`, and so on. You can then distribute the CIRCLE.DLL file to other programmers, and they can use these functions in their programs.

As its name implies, a DLL is a library linked dynamically to the program that uses it. This means that when you create the EXE file of your program, you don't link the DLL file to your program. The DLL file will be dynamically linked to your program during runtime. So when you write a program that uses a DLL, you must distribute the DLL file with the EXE file of your program.

NOTE

For a program that uses a DLL file to work, the DLL file must reside in any of the following directories:

- The \WINDOWS\SYSTEM directory
- Any directory within the DOS path
- The directory where the program resides

Typically, the INSTALL program copies the DLL file into the user's \WINDOWS\SYSTEM directory so that other programs can use the DLL file and your program won't depend on the current setting of the user's DOS path.

A DLL file can be used by any programming language that supports DLLs (for example, Visual C++ and Visual Basic). In the following sections, you'll create a simple DLL file and write a Visual C++ program that uses this file.

Creating a DLL

In the following sections, you'll create a DLL file called MyDLL.DLL and you'll write a program that uses its functions.

Creating the Project of MyDLL.DLL

Follow these steps to create the project for MyDLL.DLL:

☐ Create the directory C:\TYVCPROG\PROGRAMS\CH17 and start Visual C++.

☐ Select New from the File menu.

   Visual C++ responds by displaying the New dialog box.

☐ Select the Projects tab of the New dialog box.

☐ Select Win32 Dynamic-Link Library from the list of project types. (See Figure 17.1.)

17

Figure 17.1.

*Selecting Win32
Dynamic-Link
Library in the New
Projects dialog box.*

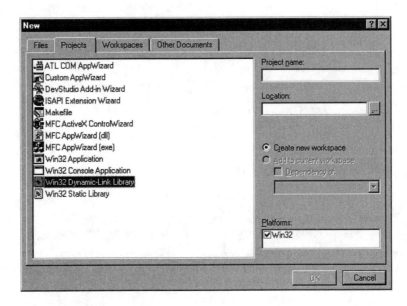

☐ Type MyDLL in the Project name box.

☐ Click the button that is located on the right of the Location box and select the C:\TYVCPROG\PROGRAMS\CH17 directory.

☐ Click the OK button.

☐ Select Set Active Configuration from the Build menu, select MyDLL - Win32 Release in the Set Active Project Configuration dialog box, then click the OK button.

That's it! You've finished creating the project file of the MyDLL.DLL library.

Writing the Overhead Code of the DLL

Writing the code of a DLL involves writing some overhead code that's the same for all DLLs. In the following steps, you'll write this overhead code in two files: MyDLL.cpp and MyDLL.def.

Follow these steps to create the MyDLL.cpp file:

☐ Select New from the File menu.

Visual C++ responds by displaying the New dialog box.

☐ Make sure that the Files tab of the New dialog box is selected and then select the C++ Source File item (because you are now creating a C++ source file).

☐ In the File Name box, type MyDLL.cpp.

☐ Click the OK button of the New dialog box.

Visual C++ responds by creating the MyDLL.cpp file and displaying its window where you can type code.

☐ Type the following code in the MyDLL.CPP file:

```
/////////////////////////////////////////////
// MyDLL.cpp
//
// A sample DLL.
//
/////////////////////////////////////////////

#include <windows.h>

/////////////////////////////////////////////
// DllEntryPoint(): The entry point of the DLL
//
/////////////////////////////////////////////
BOOL WINAPI DllEntryPoint (HINSTANCE hDLL, DWORD dwReason,
                           LPVOID Reserved)
{

switch (dwReason)
   {

   case DLL_PROCESS_ATTACH:
       {


       break;
       }


   case DLL_PROCESS_DETACH:
       {

       break;
       }
   }

return TRUE;

}
```

☐ Save your work by selecting Save All from the File menu.

Follow these steps to create the MyDLL.def file:

☐ Select New from the File menu.

Visual C++ responds by displaying the New dialog box.

☐ Make sure that the Files tab of the New dialog box is selected and then select the Text File item.

☐ In the File Name box, type MyDLL.def.

☐ Click the OK button of the New dialog box.

Visual C++ responds by creating the MyDLL.def file and displaying its window where you can type code.

☐ Type the following in the MyDLL.def file (note that in .def files, the semicolon is used for indicating a comment):

```
;;;;;;;;;;;;;;;;;;;;;;;;;;;;;;;;;;
; MyDLL.def
;
; The DEF file for the MyDLL.DLL DLL.
;

LIBRARY    mydll

CODE       PRELOAD MOVEABLE DISCARDABLE
DATA       PRELOAD SINGLE

EXPORTS
   ; The names of the DLL functions
```

☐ Save your work by selecting Save All from the File menu.

You now have the MyDLL.cpp and MyDLL.def files used for generating MyDLL.DLL. (Of course, later you'll write more code in these files.)

To make sure you've successfully added the MyDLL.cpp and MyDLL.def files to the project, do the following:

☐ Select the FileView tab of the Project Workspace window and expand the MyDLL Files item.

Your Project Workspace window should now look like Figure 17.2—the MyDLL.cpp and MyDLL.def files are part of the project.

You have performed all the overhead tasks needed for telling Visual C++ to generate MyDLL.DLL. It's now time to start writing the code.

17

Figure 17.2.

Listing the files of the MyDLL project.

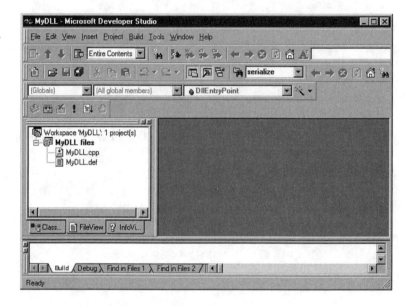

Customizing the MyDLL.cpp File

First, you'll customize the MyDLL.cpp file, which currently looks like this:

```
/////////////////////////////////////////
// MyDLL.cpp
//
// A sample DLL.
//
/////////////////////////////////////////

#include <windows.h>

/////////////////////////////////////////
// DllEntryPoint(): The entry point of the DLL
//
/////////////////////////////////////////
BOOL WINAPI DllEntryPoint (HINSTANCE hDLL, DWORD dwReason,
                           LPVOID Reserved)
{

switch (dwReason)
   {

   case DLL_PROCESS_ATTACH:
       {

       break;
       }
```

17

```
    case DLL_PROCESS_DETACH:
        {

        break;
        }
    }

return TRUE;

}
```

As you can see, the code you wrote earlier in the MyDLL.cpp file has one function: DllEntryPoint(), which is the entry point of the DLL. When an EXE program that uses a DLL loads the DLL, the DllEntryPoint() function is automatically executed. (You'll write an EXE program that loads MyDLL.DLL and uses its functions later in this chapter.)

The DllEntryPoint() function is made up of a switch statement:

```
BOOL WINAPI DllEntryPoint (HINSTANCE hDLL, DWORD dwReason,
                           LPVOID Reserved)
{

switch (dwReason)
    {

    case DLL_PROCESS_ATTACH:
        {

        break;
        }

    case DLL_PROCESS_DETACH:
        {

        break;
        }
    }

return TRUE;

}
```

The switch statement evaluates dwReason (the second parameter of the DllEntryPoint() function).

The code under the DLL_PROCESS_ATTACH case is executed when the DLL is attached to the EXE file (when the EXE file loads the DLL). Therefore, you can write initialization code under the DLL_PROCESS_ATTACH case.

The code under the DLL_PROCESS_DETACH case is executed when the DLL is detached from the EXE file. For example, when the EXE that uses the DLL terminates, the code under the

17

`DLL_PROCESS_DETACH` case is executed. Therefore, you can write clean-up code under the `DLL_PROCESS_DETACH` case.

Now you'll add two simple functions to the MyDll.cpp file. Later in the chapter, you will create an EXE file that will use these functions:

☐ Add a function called `MyBeep()` to the end of the MyDLL.cpp file as follows:

```
int MyBeep(void)
{

// Beep
MessageBeep( (WORD) -1 );

return 1;

}
```

☐ Add another function called `MyDelay()` to the end of the MyDLL.cpp file as follows:

```
int MyDelay( long wait )
{

// Delay.
Sleep(wait);

return 1;

}
```

NOTE   As you can see, the two functions you added to MyDLL.DLL are very simple; their only purpose is to illustrate how to add functions to a DLL. Later in the chapter you'll write an EXE program that loads MyDLL.DLL and uses the `MyBeep()` and `MyDelay()` functions.

You now have to declare the prototypes of the `MyBeep()` and `MyDelay()` functions:

☐ Add the prototype declarations of these functions to the beginning of the MyDLL.cpp file as follows:

```
///////////////////////////////////////////
// MyDLL.cpp
//
// A sample DLL.
//
///////////////////////////////////////////

#include <windows.h>

// Declare the DLL functions prototypes.
int MyBeep ( void );
int MyDelay ( long wait );
```

☐ Save your work by selecting Save All from the File menu.

The code in your MyDLL.cpp file should now look like this:

```cpp
///////////////////////////////////////////
// MyDLL.cpp
//
// A sample DLL.
//
///////////////////////////////////////////

#include <windows.h>

// Declare the DLL functions prototypes.
int MyBeep  ( void );
int MyDelay ( long wait );


///////////////////////////////////////////////
// DllEntryPoint(): The entry point of the DLL
//
///////////////////////////////////////////////
BOOL WINAPI DllEntryPoint (HINSTANCE hDLL, DWORD dwReason,
                            LPVOID Reserved)
{
switch (dwReason)
    {
    case DLL_PROCESS_ATTACH:
        {
        break;
        }
    case DLL_PROCESS_DETACH:
        {
        break;
        }
    }

return TRUE;
}

int MyBeep(void)
{
// Beep
MessageBeep( (WORD) -1 );
return 1;
}

int MyDelay( long wait )
{
// Delay.
Sleep(wait);
return 1;
}
```

17

Customizing the MyDLL.def File

The last thing you have to do is customize the MyDLL.def file:

☐ Open the MyDLL.def file and modify it as follows:

```
;;;;;;;;;;;;;;;;;;;;;;;;;;;;;;;;;;;;;;
; MyDLL.def
;
; The DEF file for the MyDLL.DLL DLL.
;

LIBRARY    mydll

CODE       PRELOAD MOVEABLE DISCARDABLE
DATA       PRELOAD SINGLE

EXPORTS
    ; The names of the DLL functions
    MyBeep
    MyDelay
```

☐ Save your work by selecting Save All from the File menu.

The def file defines various characteristics of the DLL. Notice that the comment lines are preceded with the semicolon character (;) (not the // characters).

In the preceding code, you set the library name with the LIBRARY statement because you're creating MyDLL.DLL:

```
LIBRARY    mydll
```

In the preceding code, you also added the two function names MyBeep and MyDelay under the EXPORTS statement:

```
EXPORTS
    ; The names of the DLL functions
    MyBeep
    MyDelay
```

Therefore, an EXE program that loads MyDLL.DLL will be able to use the two functions MyBeep() and MyDelay().

That's it! You have finished writing all the necessary code for creating MyDLL.DLL. To create the MyDLL.DLL file, do the following:

☐ Select Build MyDLL.DLL from the Build menu.

Visual C++ responds by creating the MyDLL.DLL file.

You can verify that Visual C++ created the MYDLL.DLL file by examining your C:\TYVCPROG\PROGRAMS\CH17\MYDLL\RELEASE directory.

17

NOTE

Visual C++ created the MyDLL.DLL file in the C:\TYVCPROG\ PROGRAMS\CH17\MYDLL\RELEASE directory, because when you created the project of MyDLL.DLL, you set the Default Project Configuration to `MyDLL - Win32 Release`.

Had you left the Default Project Configuration at the default setting `MyDLL - Win32 Debug`, Visual C++ would have created the MyDLL.DLL file in the C:\TYVCPROG\PROGRAMS\CH17\ MYDLL\DEBUG directory.

You now have a DLL file called MyDLL.DLL with two functions: `MyBeep()` and `MyDelay()`. You can now distribute this DLL file to any programmer of a language that supports DLLs (for example, Visual C++ or Visual Basic); this programmer will be able to use the functions of your DLL.

When you distribute the DLL, you should also supply documentation that specifies the prototypes of the `MyBeep()` and `MyDelay()` functions.

In the following section, you'll write a Visual C++ program that loads MyDLL.DLL and uses its two functions.

Writing a Visual C++ Program That Uses MyDLL.DLL

In the following sections, you'll write a Visual C++ program called Test2.EXE that uses the DLL you created. The Test2.EXE program will load MyDLL.DLL and use its two functions, `MyBeep()` and `MyDelay()`.

Creating the Project of the Test2 Program

To create the project of the Test2 program, do the following:

☐ Close the MyDLL project and all its associated files by selecting Close Workspace from the File menu.

☐ When Visual C++ displays a message box asking you whether you want to close all the document windows, click the Yes button of the message box.

☐ Select New from the File menu.

Visual C++ responds by displaying the New dialog box.

17

☐ Select the Projects tab of the New dialog box.

☐ Select MFC AppWizard (exe) from the list of project types.

☐ Type Test2 in the Project Name box.

☐ Click the button that is located on the right of the Location box and select the C:\TYVCPROG\PROGRAMS\CH17 directory.

☐ Click the OK button.

> *Visual C++ responds by displaying the MFC AppWizard - Step 1 window.*

☐ Set the Step 1 window to create a dialog-based application, then click the Next button.

☐ In the Step 2 window, leave all the check boxes at their default settings and set the title of the dialog to The Test2 Program. When you're done, click the Next button.

☐ In the Step 3 window, use the default settings and click the Next button.

☐ Notice that AppWizard has created the CTest2App and CTest2Dlg classes, then click the Finish button of the Step 4 window.

> *Visual C++ responds by displaying the New Project Information window.*

☐ Click the OK button of the New Project Information window.

> *Visual C++ responds by creating the project file and skeleton files of the Test2 program.*

☐ Select Set Active Configuration from the Build menu.

> *Visual C++ responds by displaying the Set Active Project Configuration dialog box.*

☐ Select Test2 - Win32 Release in the Set Active Project Configuration dialog box, then click the OK button.

That's it! You've finished creating the project of the Test2 program.

The Visual Design of the Test2 Main Window

You'll now visually design the main window of the Test2 program:

☐ In the ResourceView tab of the Project Workspace window, expand the Test2 resources item, expand the Dialog item and double-click the IDD_TEST2_DIALOG item.

> *Visual C++ responds by displaying the IDD_TEST2_DIALOG dialog box in design mode.*

☐ Delete the OK button, Cancel button, and text in the IDD_TEST2_DIALOG dialog box.

17

☐ Set up the IDD_TEST2_DIALOG dialog box according to Table 17.1. When you finish, the dialog box should look like Figure 17.3.

Table 17.1. The properties table of the IDD_TEST2_DIALOG dialog box.

Object	Property	Setting
Dialog Box	**ID**	**IDD_TEST2_DIALOG**
	Caption	The Test2 Program
	Font	System, Size 10
Static Text	**ID**	**IDC_STATIC**
	Caption	Testing the MyDLL.DLL DLL
Push Button	**ID**	**IDC_LOAD_BUTTON**
	Caption	&Load MyDLL.DLL
Push Button	**ID**	**IDC_TEST_BUTTON**
	Caption	&Test MyDLL.DLL

Figure 17.3.
*The
IDD_TEST2_DIALOG
dialog box in design
mode (after
customization).*

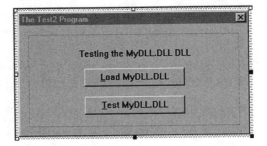

Declaring Global Variables

As you'll soon see, the code that loads and uses MyDLL.DLL uses global variables. You'll now declare these global variables:

☐ Open the file Test2Dlg.cpp and add code to its beginning, as follows:

```
// Test2Dlg.cpp : implementation file
//

#include "stdafx.h"
#include "Test2.h"
#include "Test2Dlg.h"
```

```
#ifdef _DEBUG
#define new DEBUG_NEW
#undef THIS_FILE
static char THIS_FILE□ = __FILE__;
#endif

////////////////////////
// MY CODE STARTS HERE
////////////////////////

// The instance of the MyDLL.DLL library.
HINSTANCE gLibMyDLL = NULL;

// Declare the MyBeep() function of the MyDLL.DLL library.
typedef int (*MYBEEP)(void);
MYBEEP MyBeep;

// Declare the MyDelay() function of
// the MyDLL.DLL library.
typedef int (*MYDELAY)(long);
MYDELAY MyDelay;

////////////////////////
// MY CODE ENDS HERE
////////////////////////
```

☐ Save your work.

The statements you've just added to the beginning of the Test2Dlg.cpp file declare several global variables.

The first statement declares the gLibMyDLL variable and initializes it to NULL:

```
HINSTANCE gLibMyDLL = NULL;
```

The code that loads MyDLL.DLL uses gLibMyDLL for storing the handle of the DLL.

The next two statements declare the MyBeep() function of the MyDLL.DLL library. The first statement declares a variable type called MYBEEP that holds a pointer (address) of a function that returns int and takes no parameters:

```
typedef int (*MYBEEP)(void);
```

The second statement declares a variable MyBeep of type MYBEEP:

```
MYBEEP MyBeep;
```

From now on, the variable MyBeep can be considered a regular function that returns an int and takes no parameters.

Similarly, the last two statements you typed declare the MyDelay() function of MyDLL.DLL:

```
typedef int (*MYDELAY)(long);
MYDELAY MyDelay;
```

17

Notice that these statements declare `MyDelay()` as a function that returns an `int` type and takes one parameter of type `long`.

Loading MyDLL.DLL

Before you can use the functions of MyDLL.DLL, you must first load MyDLL.DLL. You'll attach the code that accomplishes this to the Load pushbutton so that the DLL will be loaded when the user clicks the Load button. Normally, you would want the DLL to be loaded automatically without the user having to click anything, so you would write the code that loads a DLL library at the entry point of the program. For example, in the Test2.EXE program, you could attach the code that loads a DLL to the `OnInitDialog()` member function of the `CTest2Dlg` class (in the Test2Dlg.cpp file).

Follow these steps to attach code to the Load button:

☐ Select ClassWizard from the View menu. In the Message Maps tab of ClassWizard, select the following event:

Class name:	CTest2Dlg
Object ID:	IDC_LOAD_BUTTON
Message:	BN_CLICKED

☐ Click the Add Function button, name the new function `OnLoadButton`, and click the Edit Code button.

Visual C++ responds by opening the file Test2Dlg.cpp with the function `OnLoadButton()` *ready for you to edit.*

☐ Write the following code in the `OnLoadButton()` function:

```
void CTest2Dlg::OnLoadButton()
{

// TODO: Add your control notification handler code here

/////////////////////////
// MY CODE STARTS HERE
/////////////////////////

// If the MyDLL.DLL has already been loaded,
// tell the user and terminate this function.
if ( gLibMyDLL != NULL )
    {
    MessageBox("The MyDLL.DLL DLL has already been loaded.");
    return;
    }

// Load the MyDLL.DLL DLL.
gLibMyDLL = LoadLibrary("MYDLL.DLL");
```

17

```
// If the DLL was not loaded successfully, display
// an error message box.
if ( gLibMyDLL == NULL )
    {
    char msg[300];
    strcpy (msg, "Cannot load the MYDLL.DLL DLL. ");
    strcat (msg, "Make sure that the file MYDLL.DLL ");
    strcat (msg, "is in your \\WINDOWS\\SYSTEM directory.");
    MessageBox( msg );
    }

// Get the address of the MyBeep() function
// of the MyDLL.DLL library.
MyBeep = (MYBEEP)GetProcAddress(gLibMyDLL, "MyBeep");

// Get the address of the MyDelay() function
// of the MyDLL.DLL library.
MyDelay = (MYDELAY)GetProcAddress(gLibMyDLL, "MyDelay");

/////////////////////
// MY CODE ENDS HERE
/////////////////////

}
```

☐ Save your work by selecting Save All from the file menu.

The first statement you typed in the OnLoadButton() function is an if statement:

```
if ( gLibMyDLL != NULL )
    {
    MessageBox("The MyDLL.DLL DLL has already been loaded.");
    return;
    }
```

This if statement determines whether MyDLL.DLL has already been loaded by evaluating the gLibMyDLL global variable. If gLibMyDLL is not equal to NULL, MyDLL.DLL has already been loaded (the user clicked the Load button previously). If this is the case, the if condition is satisfied and the code under the if displays a message box telling the user that MyDLL.DLL has already been loaded; the function is terminated with the return statement.

If, however, gLibMyDLL is equal to NULL, the MyDLL.DLL has not been loaded yet, and the rest of the statements in the function are executed. (Recall that when you declared the global variable gLibMyDLL you initialized it to NULL. Therefore, when the user clicks the Load button for the first time, gLibMyDLL is NULL.)

The next statement uses the LoadLibrary() function to load MyDLL.DLL and assign the handle of the DLL to the gLibMyDLL variable:

```
gLibMyDLL = LoadLibrary("MYDLL.DLL");
```

Note that the name of the DLL file—MyDLL.DLL—is specified without the full pathname. The `LoadLibrary()` function will search for the DLL file in the current directory, in all the directories within the DOS path, and in the \WINDOWS\SYSTEM directory. If the `LoadLibrary()` function fails in loading the DLL, `LoadLibrary()` will return NULL.

The next statement is an `if` statement that evaluates the returned value of the `LoadLibrary()` function:

```
if ( gLibMyDLL == NULL )
   {
   char msg[300];
   strcpy (msg, "Cannot load the MYDLL.DLL DLL. ");
   strcat (msg, "Make sure that the file MYDLL.DLL ");
   strcat (msg, "is in your \\WINDOWS\\SYSTEM directory.");
   MessageBox( msg );
   }
```

If the returned value of `LoadLibrary()` was NULL, the DLL was not loaded successfully. If this is the case, the statements under the `if` display a message box telling the user that MyDLL.DLL cannot be loaded. The message box also tells the user to make sure that MyDLL.DLL is in the \WINDOWS\SYSTEM directory.

The next statement uses the `GetProcAddress()` function to fill the variable `MyBeep` with the address of the `MyBeep()` function of MyDLL.DLL:

```
MyBeep = (MYBEEP)GetProcAddress(gLibMyDLL, "MyBeep");
```

As you can see, the first parameter of the `GetProcAddress()` function is the handle of the DLL, and the second parameter is the name of the function whose address you want to retrieve.

At this point, the global variable `MyBeep` is filled with the address of the `MyBeep()` function of MyDLL.DLL. This means that from now on you can use the `MyBeep` variable as if it were the `MyBeep()` function. You can call the `MyBeep()` function just the way you call any other function.

Similarly, the last statement in the `OnLoadButton()` function fills the `MyDelay` global variable with the address of the `MyDelay()` function of MyDLL.DLL:

```
MyDelay = (MYDELAY)GetProcAddress(gLibMyDLL, "MyDelay");
```

From now on, you can call the `MyDelay()` function of MyDLL.DLL just as you call any other function.

Attaching Code to the Test MyDLL.DLL Button

You'll now attach code to the Test MyDLL.DLL button. This code will test MyDLL.DLL by calling its two functions `MyBeep()` and `MyDelay()`.

Follow these steps to attach code to the Test MyDLL.DLL button:

☐ Select ClassWizard from the View menu. In the Message Maps tab of ClassWizard, select the following event:

Class name:	CTest2Dlg
Object ID:	IDC_TEST_BUTTON
Message:	BN_CLICKED

☐ Click the Add Function button, name the new function OnTestButton, then click the Edit Code button.

Visual C++ responds by opening the file Test2Dlg.cpp with the function OnTestButton() *ready for you to edit.*

☐ Write the following code in the OnTestButton() function:

```
void CTest2Dlg::OnTestButton()
{

// TODO: Add your control notification handler code here

/////////////////////////
// MY CODE STARTS HERE
/////////////////////////

// If the MyDLL.DLL has not been loaded yet, tell
// the user and terminate this function.
if ( gLibMyDLL == NULL )
   {
   MessageBox ("You must first load the MyDLL.DLL DLL.");
   return;
   }

// Call the MyBeep() function of the MyDLL.DLL DLL.
MyBeep();

// Call the MyDelay() function of the MyDLL.DLL DLL.
MyDelay(500);

// Call the MyBeep() function of the MyDLL.DLL DLL.
MyBeep();

/////////////////////////
// MY CODE ENDS HERE
/////////////////////////

}
```

☐ Save your work by selecting Save All from the File menu.

The first statement you typed in the `OnTestButton()` function is an `if` statement:

```
if ( gLibMyDLL == NULL )
   {
   MessageBox ("You must first load the MyDLL.DLL DLL.");
   return;
   }
```

This `if` statement checks whether the `gLibMyDLL` variable is `NULL`. If it is, MyDLL.DLL has not been loaded yet. If this is the case, the code under the `if` displays a message box telling the user that MyDLL.DLL must be loaded, and the function is terminated with the `return` statement.

If, however, the `gLibMyDLL` variable is not `NULL` because MyDLL.DLL has been loaded, the rest of the statements in the function are executed:

```
// Call the MyBeep() function of the MyDLL.DLL DLL.
MyBeep();
```

```
// Call the MyDelay() function of the MyDLL.DLL DLL.
MyDelay(500);
```

```
// Call the MyBeep() function of the MyDLL.DLL DLL.
MyBeep();
```

These statements simply call the `MyBeep()` and `MyDelay()` functions of MyDLL.DLL. Therefore, when the user clicks the Test MyDLL.DLL button, the program will beep once, delay for 500 milliseconds (half a second), then beep again.

To see the code you wrote in action, do the following:

☐ Build and execute the Test2.EXE program to see your code in action.

> *Visual C++ responds by executing the Test2.EXE program and displaying the window shown in Figure 17.4.*

☐ Click the Load MyDLL.DLL button.

> *The Test2.EXE program responds by displaying a message box telling you that MyDLL.DLL could not be loaded.*

Test2.EXE could not load the MyDLL.DLL library because you haven't copied the MyDLL.DLL file to any directory within the DOS path, the directory where the Test2.EXE file resides, or the \WINDOWS\SYSTEM directory.

☐ Use the Windows Explorer to copy the MyDLL.DLL file you created earlier from the \TYVCPROG\PROGRAMS\CH17\MYDLL\RELEASE directory to your \WINDOWS\SYSTEM directory. (Note: if you are using Windows NT then you should copy the MyDLL.DLL file to your \WINNT\SYSTEM32 directory.)

Figure 17.4.

The window of the Test2.EXE program.

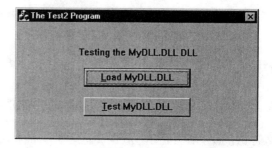

☐ Switch back to the Test2.EXE program and click the Load MyDLL.DLL button again.

This time, the Test2.EXE program loads MyDLL.DLL successfully (no error message is displayed).

☐ Click the Test MyDLL.DLL button.

As expected, the Test2.EXE program responds by beeping twice, with a 500-millisecond delay between the beeps.

NOTE

If for some reason your PC speaker (or sound card) does not beep, you can modify the code of MyDLL.DLL so that the MyBeep() function of MyDLL.DLL displays a message box instead of beeping. After you modify and build the project of MyDLL.DLL, don't forget to copy the new version of the MyDLL.DLL file to your \WINDOWS\SYSTEM directory (or to your \WINNT\SYSTEM32 directory if you are using Windows NT).

☐ Terminate the Test2.EXE program by clicking the × icon at the upper-right corner of the program's window.

As you have just seen, the Test2.EXE program successfully loads the MyDLL.DLL file and uses its functions.

Summary

In this chapter, you learned how to create a dynamic link library (a DLL file) that contains your own functions. As you have seen, creating a DLL file with Visual C++ is quite simple.

Once you finish your DLL file, you can distribute it to other Visual C++ programmers who can incorporate it into their projects. Your DLL could also be used by programmers of any programming language that supports DLLs (for example, Visual Basic).

Q&A

Q **The Test2.EXE program I wrote in this chapter uses the MyDLL.DLL file I created in this chapter, but I didn't have to add the MyDLL.DLL file to the project of the Test2.EXE program. Why?**

A You did not have to add MyDLL.DLL to the project of the Test2.EXE program because the Test2.EXE program loads MyDLL.DLL in runtime—the MyDLL.DLL file is a dynamic link library, so it's linked to the program that uses it during runtime.

Quiz

1. When you distribute your DLL file to your end-user, you must distribute the source code of your library.

    a. True

    b. False

2. To use your DLL file, your end-user needs to add your DLL file to his or her project and then build the project.

    a. True

    b. False

Exercise

Describe the steps you take to create a project for a DLL file.

Quiz Answers

1. b

2. b

Exercise Answer

To create a project for a DLL file, use the following steps:

☐ Select New from the File menu.

   Visual C++ responds by displaying the New dialog box.

☐ Select the Projects tab of the New dialog box.

☐ Select Win32 Dynamic-Link Library from the list of project types.

☐ Type the name of the project in the Project Name box.

☐ Click the button that is located on the right of the Location box and select the directory in which you want to create the project.

☐ Click the OK button.

Day 18

Creating Your Own ActiveX Control (Part I)

In this chapter and the following two chapters, you'll learn how to create your own ActiveX control by using Visual C++.

Reviewing ActiveX Controls

Before you start learning how to create an ActiveX control, first review what an ActiveX control is. In Chapter 3, "Using ActiveX Controls," you learned that an ActiveX control is a file with an OCX extension (for example, MyButton.OCX) that you can use in your Visual C++ applications. Visual C++ and other visual programming languages enable you to incorporate an ActiveX control into your program and use it just as you use standard Visual C++ controls. You place an ActiveX control in a dialog box, set its properties, and attach code to its events. Once you create your own ActiveX control, you can distribute it to other programmers who can plug your ActiveX control into their programs.

Because the file extension of ActiveX controls is .OCX, ActiveX controls are sometimes referred to as OCX controls. In this chapter and the next two chapters, the term *ActiveX control* is used.

The MyClock ActiveX Control

In this chapter and the following two chapters, you'll develop and test your own ActiveX control, called MyClock.OCX. As its name implies, the MyClock.OCX control will be used for displaying the current time. When a programmer places a MyClock.OCX control in a form or dialog box, the MyClock.OCX control will keep displaying the current time.

Creating the Project of the MyClock.OCX Control

Follow these steps to create the project for the MyClock.OCX control:

☐ Create the directory C:\TYVCPROG\PROGRAMS\CH18 and start Visual C++.

☐ Select New from the File menu.

   Visual C++ responds by displaying the New dialog box.

☐ Select the Projects tab of the New dialog box.

☐ Select MFC ActiveX ControlWizard from the list of project types. (See Figure 18.1.)

☐ Type MyClock in the Project Name box.

☐ Click the button that is located on the right of the Location box and select the C:\TYVCPROG\PROGRAMS\CH18 directory.

☐ Click the OK button.

   Visual C++ responds by displaying the MFC ActiveX ControlWizard - Step 1 of 2 dialog box. (See Figure 18.2.)

☐ Leave the ActiveX ControlWizard Step 1 window at its default settings, as shown in Figure 18.2, then click the Next button.

   Visual C++ responds by displaying the ActiveX ControlWizard - Step 2 of 2 dialog box. (See Figure 18.3.)

☐ Leave the ActiveX ControlWizard Step 2 window at its default settings, as shown in Figure 18.3, then click the Finish button.

   Visual C++ responds by displaying the New Project Information dialog box.

18

Figure 18.1.

Selecting MFC ActiveX ControlWizard in the New Projects dialog box.

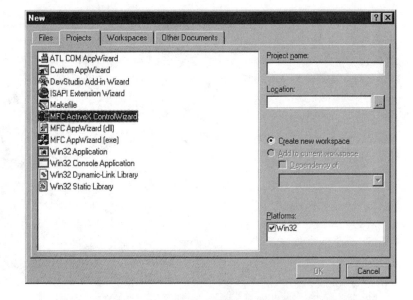

Figure 18.2.

Step 1 of the MFC ActiveX ControlWizard.

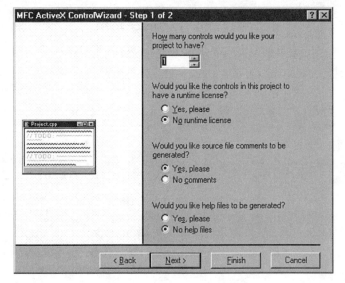

18

Figure 18.3.

*Step 2 of the
MFC ActiveX
ControlWizard.*

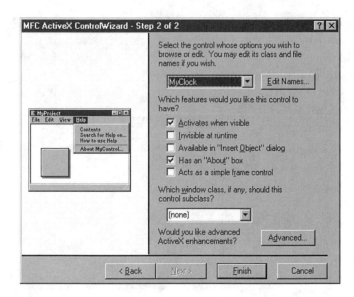

☐ Click the OK button of the New Project Information dialog box, then select Set Active
Configuration from the Build menu.

   Visual C++ responds by displaying the Set Active Project Configuration dialog box.

☐ Select MyClock - Win32 Release in the Set Active Project Configuration dialog box, then
click the OK button.

That's it! You've finished creating the project file and skeleton files of the MyClock.OCX
ActiveX control.

Checking the MyClock Control Before Customization

In the preceding section, you created the project and skeleton files of the MyClock control.
Your job, with the help of Visual C++, is to customize these files so that the MyClock control
will look and behave the way you want it to.

Before you start customizing the files of the MyClock control, first build and test the
MyClock control in its current state. As you'll see, the skeleton files you created in the
preceding section already have code that actually produces a working ActiveX control.

18

To build the MyClock control, do the following:

☐ Select Build MyClock.OCX from the Build menu.

> *Visual C++ responds by compiling and linking the files of the MyClock control and creating the file MyClock.OCX.*

Although you haven't written a single line of code, you have a working ActiveX control in your hands—MyClock.OCX. In the following section, you'll test the MyClock.OCX control.

Testing the MyClock Control with Test Container

The ultimate way to test an ActiveX control is to use a visual programming language that lets the programmer add the ActiveX control to the Tools window. Once you add the ActiveX control to the Tools window, you can test it by placing it in forms (dialog boxes), by changing its properties, and by attaching code to its events. For example, to test the MyClock.OCX control, you can write a Visual C++ program that uses the MyClock.OCX control. (You learned how to write a Visual C++ program that uses an ActiveX control in Chapter 3.)

Another way to test an ActiveX control is to use the Test Container program that comes with Visual C++, which lets you test an ActiveX control by placing it in the window of the Test Container program.

Follow these steps to test the MyClock control with the Test Container program:

☐ Select ActiveX Control Test Container from the Tools menu.

> *Visual C++ responds by executing the Test Container program. (See Figure 18.4.)*

Figure 18.4.
The Test Container program.

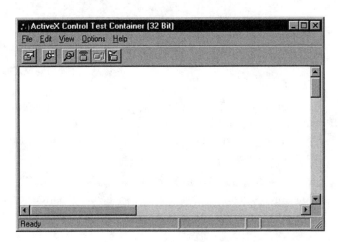

NOTE

If you have problems starting the Test Container program from Visual C++, you can start it directly from Windows:

☐ Click the Start button of Windows, select Programs, select Microsoft Visual C++ 5, and finally select ActiveX Control Test Container.

☐ Select Insert OLE Control from Test Container's Edit menu.

Test Container responds by displaying the Insert OLE Control dialog box.

☐ Select MyClock Control from the list displayed in the dialog box, then click the OK button.

Test Container responds by inserting the MyClock control. (See Figure 18.5.)

Figure 18.5.

The Test Container program after you insert the MyClock control.

The tool of the MyClock control

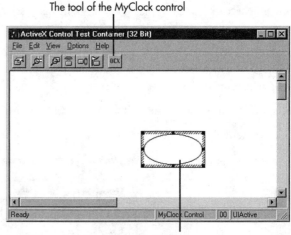

The MyClock control

As shown in Figure 18.5, the MyClock control now appears in the window of Test Container, and its tool icon appears in the toolbar of Test Container. Notice that the tool icon of the MyClock control displays the letters *OCX.* Later, you'll customize the MyClock control so that the tool icon will display a more appropriate picture of a clock.

Notice also that the MyClock control displays an ellipse. The skeleton code that Visual C++ wrote for you is displaying this ellipse. Later, you'll customize the code of the MyClock control so that it will do what it's supposed to—display the current time.

18

The MyClock control is surrounded by a frame with handles you can use to size the MyClock control. For example, to make the control taller, do the following:

☐ Drag any of the handles at the bottom of the control's frame downward, then release the mouse.

Once you release the mouse, the control changes its size, and the size of the ellipse in the control changes accordingly. (See Figure 18.6.)

Figure 18.6.
Increasing the size of the MyClock control.

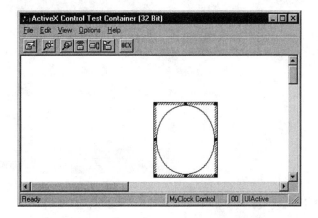

Besides sizing the control, Test Container also allows you to move the control:

☐ Drag the frame of the control to the point where you want to place the control. Drag any point of the control's frame except where the handles are.

Once you release the mouse, the control moves to that point. Figure 18.7 shows the window of Test Container after you move the MyClock control to the upper-left corner.

Figure 18.7.
Moving the MyClock control to the upper-left corner of the window.

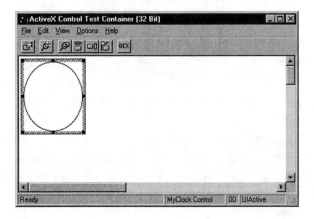

18

You can also place several MyClock controls in the window of Test Container:

☐ Click the tool of the MyClock control on Test Container's toolbar, shown in Figure 18.5.

Test Container responds by placing another MyClock control in its window. (See Figure 18.8.)

Figure 18.8.

Placing another MyClock control in the window of Test Container.

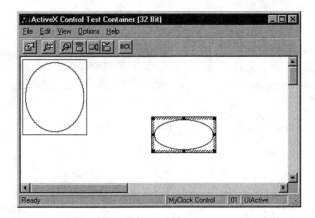

☐ Place several more MyClock controls by clicking the tool of the MyClock control.

In the preceding steps, you used Test Container to test the visual aspects of the MyClock control: placing the control in the window of Test Container, sizing the control, moving the control, and placing several controls in the window.

Test Container also lets you test the events and properties of the control. However, at this point the MyClock control does not have any events or properties, because Visual C++ couldn't guess which ones you wanted. Later, when you add properties and events to the MyClock control, you'll use Test Container to test them.

You have just verified, with Test Container's help, that the skeleton code Visual C++ wrote for you produces a functional ActiveX control. Of course, the code doesn't make the MyClock control behave and look the way you want it to, so you'll customize its files throughout this chapter and the next.

☐ Terminate Test Container by selecting Exit from the File menu.

Customizing the Picture of the MyClock Control Tool

As shown in Figure 18.5, the icon of the MyClock control tool displays a picture of the letters *OCX*. You'll now customize the MyClock control so that its tool will display a picture of a clock.

18

To customize the icon of the MyClock control tool, you need to work on the bitmap IDB_MYCLOCK. This bitmap was created by Visual C++.

To display the IDB_MYCLOCK bitmap in design mode, do the following:

☐ In the Project Workspace window, select the ResourceView tab, expand the MyClock resources item, expand the Bitmap item, then double-click the IDB_MYCLOCK item.

Visual C++ responds by displaying the IDB_MYCLOCK bitmap in design mode.

☐ Use the visual tools of Visual C++ to change the picture of the IDB_MYCLOCK bitmap from the letters *OCX* to a picture of a simple clock—a circle with two lines, the clock's hands, in it.

Figure 18.9 shows the IDB_MYCLOCK bitmap before customization, and Figure 18.10 shows the IDB_MYCLOCK bitmap after customization.

Figure 18.9.
The IDB_MYCLOCK bitmap before customization.

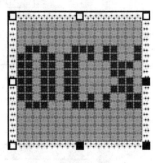

Figure 18.10.
The IDB_MYCLOCK bitmap after customization.

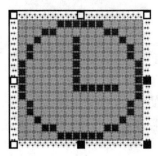

☐ Save your work.

To see your work in action, do the following:

☐ Select Build MyClock.OCX from the Project menu.

Visual C++ responds by compiling and linking the MyClock control.

   ☐ Select ActiveX Control Test Container from the Tools menu.

      Visual C++ responds by running the Test Container program.

   ☐ Select Insert OLE Control from Test Container's Edit menu.

      Test Container responds by displaying the Insert OLE Control dialog box.

   ☐ Select MyClock Control from the list displayed in the dialog box, then click the OK button.

      Test Container responds by inserting the MyClock control and displaying its tool on Test Container's toolbar. (See Figure 18.11.)

Figure 18.11.
The new tool icon of the MyClock control.

The tool of the MyClock control ──────

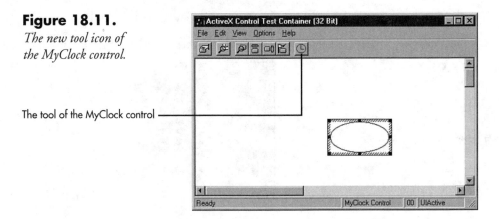

The tool icon of the MyClock tool now displays your picture of a clock!

   ☐ Terminate Test Container by selecting Exit from the File menu.

Summary

In this chapter, you used Visual C++ to create the skeleton files for the MyClock.OCX ActiveX control. As you have seen, even though you haven't written any code yet, the skeleton code Visual C++ writes for you produces a working control that displays an ellipse in it.

You also customized the icon of the MyClock control tool to display a picture of a clock.

In the next two chapters, you will further customize the MyClock control by writing the code responsible for displaying the current time, adding properties to the MyClock control, and adding events to the MyClock control.

18

Q&A

Q Can I test the MyClock ActiveX control with Visual Basic?

A Yes. Just like Visual C++, Visual Basic supports ActiveX controls, so you can use the MyClock.OCX control in your Visual Basic programs just as you can use other ActiveX controls.

Q Suppose I write a Visual C++ program called MyProg.EXE that uses the MyClock.OCX control. Do I have to distribute the MyClock.OCX file with the MyProg.EXE file to my users?

A Yes. You have to distribute both the MyProg.EXE file and the MyClock.OCX file to your user. You have to instruct your user to copy the MyClock.OCX file to his or her \WINDOWS\SYSTEM directory (or you can write an Install program that will automatically copy the MyClock.OCX to the user's \WINDOWS\SYSTEM directory).

Quiz

1. When you distribute your .OCX file to your end-user, you have to distribute the source code of your ActiveX control.

    a. True
    b. False

2. How can you test your ActiveX control?

Exercise

Describe the steps you take to create a project for an ActiveX control.

Quiz Answers

1. b

2. You can test your ActiveX control by writing a program that uses it (using Visual C++, Visual Basic, or any other programming language that supports ActiveX controls) or by using the Test Container program of Visual C++.

Exercise Answer

To create a project for an ActiveX control, take the following steps:

☐ Select New from the File menu.

☐ Select the Projects tab of the New dialog box.

☐ Select MFC ActiveX ControlWizard from the list of project types.

☐ Type the project name in the Project Name box.

☐ Click the button that is located on the right of the Location box and select the directory in which you want to create the project.

☐ Click the OK button.

☐ Click the Next button in the ActiveX ControlWizard Step 1 dialog box, click the Finish button in the ActiveX ControlWizard Step 2 dialog box, and finally click the OK button of the New Project Information dialog box.

Day **19**

Creating Your Own ActiveX Control (Part II)

In this chapter, you'll continue developing the MyClock control that you created in the previous chapter—you'll write the code that makes the control continuously display the current time, you'll add properties to the control, and you'll write the code that sets the control's initial size.

NOTE Because you'll continue working on the previous chapter's project, this chapter assumes that you have read and performed all the steps in Chapter 18, "Creating Your Own ActiveX Control (Part I)."

Drawing in the MyClock Control

Currently, the MyClock control displays an ellipse. However, you want the MyClock control to display the current time, so you need to write code that does this. First, you'll write code that draws text in the MyClock control:

☐ Start Visual C++.

☐ Open the project workspace file (.DSW file) of the MyClock control you created in the previous chapter (if it's not open) by selecting Open Workspace from the File menu, then selecting the C:\TYVCProg\Programs\CH18\MyClock\MyClock.DSW file.

☐ Open the file MyClockCtl.cpp.

MyClockCtl.cpp is the implementation file of the MyClock control created for you by Visual C++; it's where you'll write your own code for customizing the MyClock control:

☐ Locate the function OnDraw() in the MyClockCtl.cpp file.

The OnDraw() function currently looks like this:

```
/////////////////////////////////////////////////////////
// CMyClockCtrl::OnDraw - Drawing function

void CMyClockCtrl::OnDraw(
    CDC* pdc, const CRect& rcBounds, const CRect& rcInvalid)
{

// TODO: Replace the following code with your own drawing code.
pdc->FillRect(rcBounds,
    CBrush::FromHandle((HBRUSH)GetStockObject(WHITE_BRUSH)));
pdc->Ellipse(rcBounds);

}
```

The OnDraw() function is automatically executed whenever there is a need to draw the control (for example, when the control is placed in a dialog box for the first time). The code currently in the OnDraw() function draws an ellipse in the control. Change the code in the OnDraw() function so that the control will display your own text:

☐ Delete the code currently in the OnDraw() function and replace it with your own custom code as follows:

```
void CMyClockCtrl::OnDraw(
    CDC* pdc, const CRect& rcBounds, const CRect& rcInvalid)
{

///////////////////////////
// MY CODE STARTS HERE
///////////////////////////

// Fill the control with white color.
pdc->FillRect(rcBounds,
    CBrush::FromHandle((HBRUSH)GetStockObject(WHITE_BRUSH)));

// Draw text in the control.
pdc->ExtTextOut(rcBounds.left,
                rcBounds.top,
                ETO_CLIPPED,
                rcBounds,
                "This is my first OCX control",
                28,
                NULL);

///////////////////////////
// MY CODE ENDS HERE
///////////////////////////

}
```

☐ Save your work.

The code you typed in the OnDraw() function is made up of two statements. The following is the first statement:

```
pdc->FillRect(rcBounds,
    CBrush::FromHandle((HBRUSH)GetStockObject(WHITE_BRUSH)));
```

This statement executes the FillRect() function on the pdc object to fill the control with white color. pdc (the first parameter of the OnDraw() function) is a pointer to an object of class CDC and holds the dc (device context) of the control. Therefore, after the preceding statement is executed, the entire area of the control will be filled with a white color. The first parameter of the FillRect() function specifies the rectangular area to be filled, and the second parameter of the FillRect() function specifies the color with which the rectangular area will be filled.

Notice that the preceding statement uses the variable rcBounds (an object of class CRect), which is the second parameter of the OnDraw() function. It specifies the rectangular dimensions (boundaries) of the control. For example, rcBounds.left is the x coordinate of the upper-left corner of the control.

The second statement is the following:

```
pdc->ExtTextOut(rcBounds.left,
                rcBounds.top,
                ETO_CLIPPED,
```

19

```
rcBounds,
"This is my first OCX control",
28,
NULL);
```

This statement executes the ExtTextOut() function on the pdc object to display text in the control. As stated, pdc (the first parameter of the OnDraw() function) is a pointer to an object of class CDC and holds the dc (device context) of the control. Therefore, after the preceding statement is executed, the text This is my first OCX control will be displayed in the MyClock control.

Notice that the preceding statement also uses the variable rcBounds (an object of class CRect), which is the second parameter of the OnDraw() function. As stated, rcBounds specifies the rectangular dimensions (boundaries) of the control.

NOTE

Use the ExtTextOut() member function of the MFC CDC class to display text in the control. The first two parameters of the ExtTextOut() function are the x-y coordinates of the text to be displayed. The third parameter specifies how the text will be displayed. When the third parameter is set to ETO_CLIPPED, the text will be clipped to a rectangle. The fourth parameter specifies the rectangle area in which the text will be displayed. The fifth parameter is a string that holds the text to be displayed, and the sixth parameter is the length of the string to be displayed. The seventh parameter specifies the spacing between the displayed characters. When the seventh parameter is set to NULL, the characters will be displayed with the default spacing.

To see your drawing code in action, follow these steps:

☐ Build MyClock.OCX by selecting Build MyClock.ocx from the Build menu.

Visual C++ responds by compiling and linking the files of the MyClock control.

☐ Start the Test Container program by selecting ActiveX Control Test Container from the Tools menu. (If you have problems starting the Test Container program from Visual C++, you can start it directly from Windows by clicking the Start button of Windows, then selecting Programs, then Microsoft Visual C++ 5, and finally ActiveX Control Test Container.)

Visual C++ responds by running the Test Container program.

☐ Select Insert OLE control from Test Container's Edit menu.

Test Container responds by displaying the Insert OLE control dialog box.

☐ Select MyClock Control from the list displayed in the dialog box, then click the OK button.

> *Test Container responds by inserting the MyClock control. As shown in Figure 19.1, the text* `This is my first` *is displayed in the control.*

☐ Increase the width of the MyClock control by dragging the handle on the control's right edge to the right. (See Figure 19.2.)

Figure 19.1.
The MyClock control displaying the text `This is my first.`

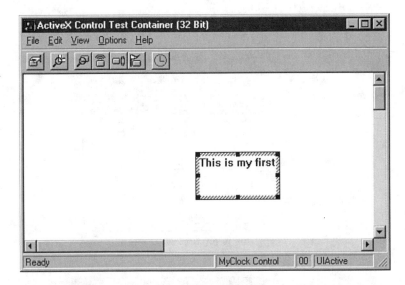

Figure 19.2.
The MyClock control after increasing its width.

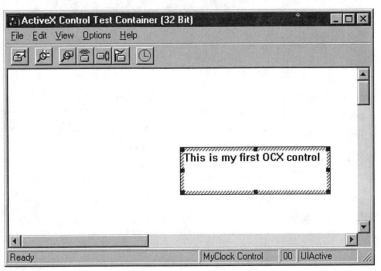

19

The code that you wrote in the OnDraw() function is working! Whenever the MyClock control needs to be redrawn, such as when you resize the control, the OnDraw() function is automatically executed and the code you wrote displays the text This is my first OCX control in the control.

☐ Place several more controls in the window of Test Container by clicking the tool of the MyClock control in the Test Container toolbar. Move each of the controls to a different place in the window by dragging any point on the control's frame except the points where the control's handles are located. Each control displays the text This is my first OCX control. (See Figure 19.3.)

Figure 19.3.

Displaying several MyClock controls.

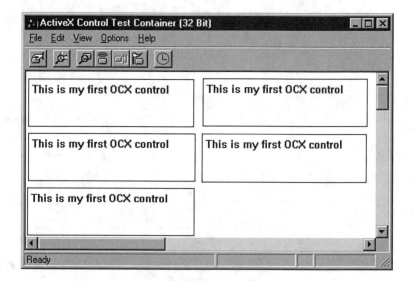

☐ Terminate Test Container by selecting Exit from the File menu.

NOTE

It's necessary to terminate the Test Container program, because the Visual C++ linker will fail to link the MyClock project if any program is using the MyClock.OCX control.

Displaying the Current Time in the MyClock Control

The code of the MyClock control currently displays the text This is my first OCX control. You'll now change the code so that it will display the current time:

☐ Open the file MyClockCtl.cpp (if it's not open).

☐ Modify the OnDraw() function as follows:

```
void CMyClockCtrl::OnDraw(
     CDC* pdc, const CRect& rcBounds, const CRect& rcInvalid)
{

// TODO: Replace the following code with your own drawing
//       code.

/////////////////////////
// MY CODE STARTS HERE
/////////////////////////

// Fill the control with white color.
pdc->FillRect(rcBounds,
     CBrush::FromHandle((HBRUSH)GetStockObject(WHITE_BRUSH)));

char CurrentTime[30];
struct tm *newtime;
long lTime;

// Get the current time
time(&lTime);
newtime=localtime(&lTime);

// Convert the time into a string.
strcpy(CurrentTime, asctime(newtime));

// Pad the string with 1 blank.
CurrentTime[24]=' ';

// Terminate the string.
CurrentTime[25] = 0;

// Display the current time
pdc->ExtTextOut(rcBounds.left,
                rcBounds.top,
                ETO_CLIPPED,
                rcBounds,
                CurrentTime,
                strlen(CurrentTime),
                NULL);

/////////////////////////
// MY CODE ENDS HERE
/////////////////////////

}
```

19

☐ Save your work.

The first statement in the `OnDraw()` function remains the same as before:

```
pdc->FillRect(rcBounds,
      CBrush::FromHandle((HBRUSH)GetStockObject(WHITE_BRUSH)));
```

This statement fills the control with white color.

The next three statements you typed in the `OnDraw()` function declare three local variables:

```
char CurrentTime[30];
struct tm *newtime;
long lTime;
```

The rest of the code uses these three variables to get the current time and display it.

This statement uses the `time()` function to store in the variable `lTime` the number of seconds elapsed since midnight of January 1, 1970:

```
time(&lTime);
```

Of course, this number is not "friendly" enough, so you use the next statement to convert the number stored in `lTime` into a friendlier representation of time:

```
newtime=localtime(&lTime);
```

This statement uses the `localtime()` function to convert `lTime` into a structure of type `tm` and assigns the result to the structure `newtime`. Now the fields of the structure `newtime` store the current time.

The next statement uses the `asctime()` function to convert the current time stored in `newtime` into a string:

```
strcpy(CurrentTime, asctime(newtime));
```

The resulting string is assigned to the `CurrentTime` string, which now contains a string with 24 characters representing the current time. This string includes the day of the week, month, time, and year.

The next statement fills the 24th character at the end of the `CurrentTime` string with a blank for cosmetic reasons:

```
CurrentTime[24]=' ';
```

The next statement terminates the `CurrentTime` string:

```
CurrentTime[25]=0;
```

Finally, the last statement you typed in the `OnDraw()` function uses the `ExtTextOut()` function to display the `CurrentTime` string in the control:

```
pdc->ExtTextOut(rcBounds.left,
                rcBounds.top,
                ETO_CLIPPED,
                rcBounds,
                CurrentTime,
                strlen(CurrentTime),
                NULL);
```

☐ Build MyClock.OCX to see the code you added to OnDraw() in action.

Visual C++ responds by compiling and linking the files of the MyClock control.

☐ Select ActiveX Control Test Container from the Tools menu.

Visual C++ responds by running the Test Container program.

☐ Select Insert OLE control from Test Container's Edit menu.

Test Container responds by displaying the Insert OLE control dialog box.

☐ Select the MyClock control, then click the OK button.

Test Container responds by inserting the MyClock control.

☐ Increase the width of the MyClock control. (See Figure 19.4.)

Figure 19.4.

The MyClock control displaying the current time.

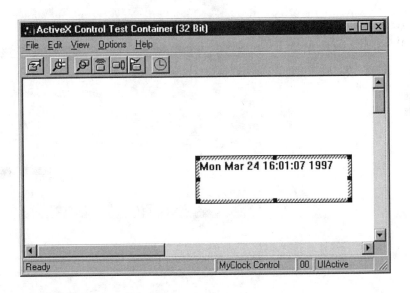

As you can see, the code you wrote in the OnDraw() function displays the current time in the control. However, the time is not updated continuously. In the following section, you will enhance the code so that the control will keep displaying the current time continuously.

☐ Terminate Test Container by selecting Exit from the File menu.

Displaying the Current Time Continuously

To display the time continuously, you need to do the following:

☐ Write code that installs a timer for the MyClock control with a 1000-millisecond interval.

☐ Attach code to the WM_TIMER event of the MyClock control.

After you install such a timer, Windows sends a WM_TIMER message every 1000 milliseconds (every second) to the MyClock control, and the code you attach to the WM_TIMER event of the MyClock control is executed. The code you attach to the WM_TIMER event will simply display the current time, so the current time will be displayed continuously.

You want to install the timer when the control is first created, so you need to attach the code that installs the timer to the WM_CREATE event of the control:

☐ Display the ClassWizard dialog box by selecting ClassWizard from the View menu. In the Message Maps tab of ClassWizard, select the following event:

Class Name:	CMyClockCtrl
Object ID:	CMyClockCtrl
Message:	WM_CREATE

Your ClassWizard dialog box should now look like the one shown in Figure 19.5.

Figure 19.5.

Selecting the
WM_CREATE event in
ClassWizard.

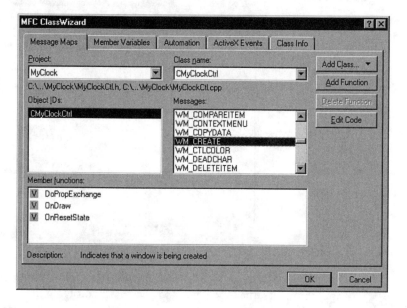

☐ Click the Add Function button.

Visual C++ responds by adding the `OnCreate()` *member function to the* `CMyClockCtrl` *class.*

☐ Click the Edit Code button of ClassWizard.

ClassWizard responds by opening the file MyClockCtrl.cpp, with the function `OnCreate()` *ready for you to edit.*

☐ Write the following code in the `OnCreate()` function:

```
int CMyClockCtrl::OnCreate(LPCREATESTRUCT lpCreateStruct)
{

if (COleControl::OnCreate(lpCreateStruct) == -1)
   return -1;

// TODO: Add your specialized creation code here

//////////////////////////
// MY CODE STARTS HERE
//////////////////////////

// Install a timer.
SetTimer(1, 1000, NULL);

//////////////////////////
// MY CODE ENDS HERE
//////////////////////////

return 0;

}
```

☐ Save your work.

The code you wrote is composed of one statement that uses the `SetTimer()` function to install a timer with a 1000-millisecond interval:

```
SetTimer(1, 1000, NULL);
```

From now on, Windows will send a `WM_TIMER` message to the control every 1000 milliseconds.

Now you need to attach code to the `WM_TIMER` event of the control:

☐ Select ClassWizard from the View menu. In the Message Maps tab of ClassWizard, select the following event:

Class Name:	CMyClockCtrl
Object ID:	CMyClockCtrl
Message:	WM_TIMER

☐ Click the Add Function button.

Visual C++ responds by adding the `OnTimer()` *member function to the* `CMyClockCtrl` *class.*

19

☐ Click the Edit Code button of ClassWizard.

ClassWizard responds by opening the file MyClockCtl.cpp, with the function `OnTimer()` *ready for you to edit.*

☐ Write the following code in the `OnTimer()` function:

```
void CMyClockCtrl::OnTimer(UINT nIDEvent)
{

// TODO: Add your message handler code here and/or call
//       default

/////////////////////////
// MY CODE STARTS HERE
/////////////////////////

// Trigger a call to the OnDraw() function.
InvalidateControl();

/////////////////////////
// MY CODE ENDS HERE
/////////////////////////

COleControl::OnTimer(nIDEvent);

}
```

☐ Save your work.

The code you wrote has one statement that uses the `InvalidateControl()` function to trigger a call to the `OnDraw()` function you wrote earlier:

`InvalidateControl();`

Calling the `InvalidateControl()` function causes the control to redraw itself.

The code you wrote in the `OnCreate()` function installs a timer with a 1000-millisecond interval. As a result, the code you wrote in the `OnTimer()` function is automatically executed every 1000 milliseconds. This code causes the execution of the `OnDraw()` function by calling the `InvalidateControl()` function. The code you wrote in the `OnDraw()` function displays the current time; therefore, every 1000 milliseconds the displayed time is updated.

To see your timer code in action follow these steps:

☐ Build MyClock.OCX.

Visual C++ responds by compiling and linking the files of the MyClock control.

☐ Select ActiveX control Test Container from the Tools menu.

Visual C++ responds by running the Test Container program.

19

☐ Select Insert OLE control from Test Container's Edit menu.

Test Container responds by displaying the Insert OLE control dialog box.

☐ Select the MyClock control, then click the OK button.

Test Container responds by inserting the MyClock control.

☐ Increase the width of the MyClock control so you can see the seconds portion of the time.

As you can see, now the MyClock control displays the current time continuously—the seconds portion of the time keeps changing.

☐ Terminate Test Container by selecting Exit from the File menu.

Adding Stock Properties to the MyClock Control

Stock properties (or standard properties) are predefined. As you'll see, adding a stock property to a control is very easy. Table 19.1 lists all the stock properties you can add to an ActiveX control.

Table 19.1. Stock properties.

Property	Stored Value
Appearance	The control's appearance (for example, 3-D or flat)
BackColor	The control's background color
BorderStyle	The control's border style
Caption	The control's caption
Enabled	The control's enabled/disabled status
Font	The control's font for drawing text
ForeColor	The control's foreground color
hWnd	The control's window handle
ReadyState	The control's readiness state
Text	The control's text

For practice, you'll now add two stock properties to the MyClock control, BackColor and ForeColor. Follow these steps to add the BackColor property to the MyClock control:

☐ Select ClassWizard from the View menu. In the Automation tab of ClassWizard, make sure the Class name list box is set to CMyClockCtrl. (See Figure 19.6.)

19

Figure 19.6.

Selecting the Automation tab of ClassWizard.

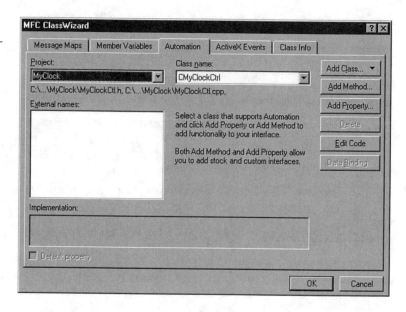

☐ Click the Add Property button.

Visual C++ responds by displaying the Add Property dialog box.

☐ Click the down arrow of the External names combo box and select BackColor from the list.

Your Add Property dialog box should now look like the one shown in Figure 19.7.

☐ Click the OK button of the Add Property dialog box.

The ClassWizard dialog box reappears, as shown in Figure 19.8.

As shown in Figure 19.8, the External names list now contains the property BackColor preceded by the letter S, which indicates that BackColor is a stock property.

Now add the ForeColor property:

☐ Click the Add Property button.

Visual C++ responds by displaying the Add Property dialog box.

☐ Click the down arrow of the External names combo box and select ForeColor from the list.

☐ Click the OK button of the Add Property dialog box.

The ClassWizard dialog box reappears, as shown in Figure 19.9.

19

Figure 19.7.

Selecting BackColor in the Add Property dialog box.

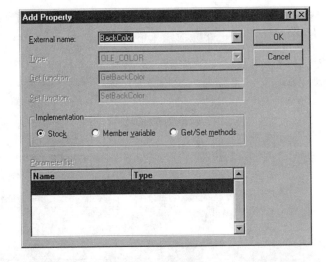

Figure 19.8.

The ClassWizard dialog box after you add the BackColor stock property.

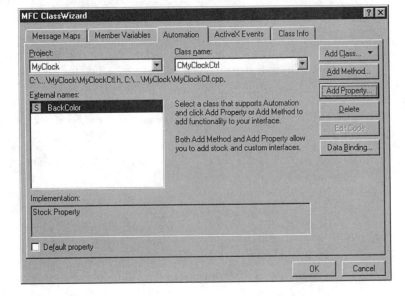

Figure 19.9.

The ClassWizard dialog box after you add the ForeColor stock property.

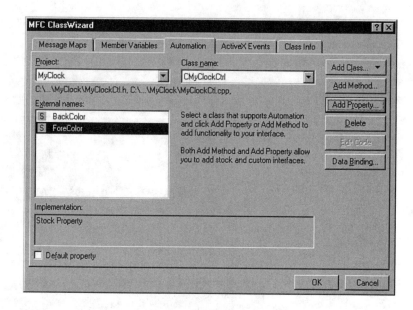

As shown in Figure 19.9, the External names list now contains both the BackColor property and ForeColor property preceded by the letter S, because both are stock properties.

☐ Click the OK button of ClassWizard.

That's it! You have finished adding the BackColor and ForeColor properties to the MyClock control.

To verify that the MyClock control now has the BackColor and ForeColor properties, do the following:

☐ Build MyClock.OCX.

Visual C++ responds by compiling and linking the files of the MyClock control.

☐ Select ActiveX control Test Container from the Tools menu.

Visual C++ responds by running the Test Container program.

☐ Select Insert OLE control from Test Container's Edit menu.

Test Container responds by displaying the Insert OLE control dialog box.

☐ Select the Myclock control, then click the OK button.

Test Container responds by inserting the MyClock control.

☐ Increase the width of the MyClock control so you can see the entire text of the current time.

☐ Select Properties from the View menu of Test Container.

Test Container responds by displaying the Properties dialog box. (See Figure 19.10.)

Figure 19.10.

The Properties dialog box of Test Container.

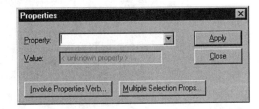

☐ Click the down arrow of the Property combo box.

Test Container responds by popping up a list with the properties of the MyClock control. (See Figure 19.11.) The only properties listed are the BackColor and ForeColor properties.

Figure 19.11.

Listing the properties of the MyClock control.

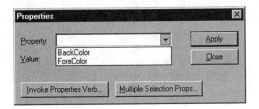

☐ Select the BackColor property.

Your Properties dialog box should now look like Figure 19.12.

19

Figure 19.12.

Selecting the BackColor property.

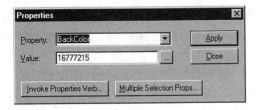

The Properties dialog box displays the current value of the BackColor property and enables you to change this value. You can specify a color by typing its corresponding value, or you can select the color visually by clicking the three-dots button to the right of the Value edit box.

☐ Click the three-dots button to the right of the Value edit box.

The Colors dialog box appears. (See Figure 19.13.)

Figure 19.13.

The Colors dialog box.

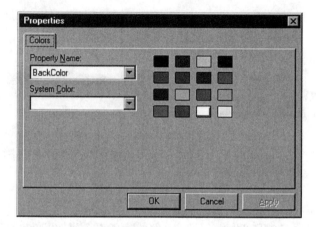

If you try to set the BackColor property of the MyClock control to any color, you'll see that the background color of the control doesn't change to the color you selected. Why not? Because you've only added the BackColor property to the MyClock control—you haven't written the code that makes the BackColor property functional.

In the following section, you'll write code that makes the BackColor and ForeColor properties functional. When you set the BackColor or ForeColor property to a certain value, your code will change the background or foreground color of the control to the color you selected.

☐ Terminate Test Container by selecting Exit from the File menu.

Making the BackColor and ForeColor Properties Functional

The MyClock control currently has the BackColor and ForeColor properties, but does not make use of the values stored in these properties. You'll now write the code that accomplishes that in the OnDraw() function:

☐ Open the file MyClockCtl.cpp (if it's not open).

☐ Delete the first statement at the beginning of the OnDraw() function (the statement that fills the control with white color).

19

☐ Add code at the beginning of the `OnDraw()` function so it looks like the following:

```
void CMyClockCtrl::OnDraw(
  CDC* pdc, const CRect& rcBounds, const CRect& rcInvalid)
{

// TODO: Replace the following code with your own drawing
//       code.

///////////////////////////
// MY CODE STARTS HERE
///////////////////////////

// Set the foreground color (i.e. the text color)
// according to the ForeColor property.
pdc->SetTextColor(TranslateColor(GetForeColor()));

// Set the background mode to transparent mode.
pdc->SetBkMode(TRANSPARENT);

// Create a brush based on the BackColor property.
CBrush bkBrush(TranslateColor(GetBackColor()));

// Paint the background using the BackColor property
pdc->FillRect(rcBounds, &bkBrush);

char CurrentTime[30];
struct tm *newtime;
long lTime;

// Get the current time
time(&lTime);
newtime=localtime(&lTime);

// Convert the time into a string.
strcpy(CurrentTime, asctime(newtime));

// Pad the string with 1 blank.
CurrentTime[24]=' ';

// Terminate the string.
CurrentTime[25] = 0;

// Display the current time
pdc->ExtTextOut(rcBounds.left,
                rcBounds.top,
                ETO_CLIPPED,
                rcBounds,
                CurrentTime,
                strlen(CurrentTime),
                NULL);

///////////////////////////
// MY CODE ENDS HERE
///////////////////////////

}
```

19

☐ Save your work.

The statements you added to the beginning of the OnDraw() function change the background color and foreground color of the MyClock control according to the current values of the BackColor and ForeColor properties. Therefore, whenever there is a need to redraw the control (whenever the OnDraw() function is executed), the control will be painted with the background and foreground colors currently stored in the BackColor and ForeColor properties.

The first statement you added to the the OnDraw() function sets the text color (the foreground color) of the control according to the current value of the ForeColor property:

```
pdc->SetTextColor(TranslateColor(GetForeColor()));
```

Notice that the value of the ForeColor property is retrieved with the GetForeColor() function.

The next statement sets the background mode to transparent mode:

```
pdc->SetBkMode(TRANSPARENT);
```

The next statement creates a brush (bkBrush) based on the current value of the BackColor property:

```
// Create a brush based on the BackColor property.
CBrush bkBrush(TranslateColor(GetBackColor()));
```

Notice that you retrieve the BackColor property by using the GetBackColor() function.

The last statement you added fills the control with the color of the bkBrush brush (the color of the BackColor property):

```
// Paint the background using the BackColor property
pdc->FillRect(rcBounds, &bkBrush);
```

Notice that the first parameter of the FillRect() function is rcBounds. rcBounds (an object of class CRect) is the second parameter of the OnDraw() function. It specifies the rectangular dimensions (boundaries) of the control.

To see the code that you added to the OnDraw() function in action, do the following:

☐ Select Build MyClock.OCX from the Build menu.

Visual C++ responds by compiling and linking the files of the MyClock control.

☐ Start Test Container, select Insert OLE control from its Edit menu, select the MyClock control, then click the OK button.

Test Container responds by inserting the MyClock control.

19

☐ Increase the width of the MyClock control so that you can see the entire text of the current time.

☐ Select Properties from the View menu of Test Container.

Test Container responds by displaying the Properties dialog box.

☐ Click the down arrow of the Property combo box.

Test Container responds by popping up a list with the properties of the MyClock control.

☐ Select the BackColor property.

☐ Click the three-dots button to the right of the Value edit box.

A Colors dialog box appears, shown in Figure 19.13.

☐ Select the red color by clicking the rectangle painted red, then click the Apply button.

☐ Click the OK button of the Colors dialog box, then click the Close button of the Properties dialog box.

As you can see, the control changed its background color to red. The code you added to the OnDraw() *function is working!*

Similarly, you can experiment with the ForeColor property. You will see that after you set the ForeColor property to a certain color, the foreground color of the control (the color of the text) changes accordingly.

☐ Terminate Test Container by selecting Exit from the File menu.

Setting the Initial Size of the MyClock Control

As you have seen in the preceding steps, when you place the MyClock control in the window of Test Container, its initial size is not wide enough. To see the seconds portion of the displayed time, you have to make the control wider.

You'll now add code that sets the initial size of the MyClock control so that the control will be wide enough when you place it in a window.

☐ Open the file MyClockCtl.cpp (if it's not open).

☐ Locate the constructor function of the CMyclockCtrl class in the MyClockCtl.cpp file and add the following code:

```
CMyclockCtrl::CMyClockCtrl()
{
InitializeIIDs(&IID_DMyClock, &IID_DMyClockEvents);

// TODO: Initialize your control's instance data here.
```

19

```
////////////////////////
// MY CODE STARTS HERE
////////////////////////

// Set initial size of control to width=200, height=15.
SetInitialSize(200, 15);

////////////////////////
// MY CODE ENDS HERE
////////////////////////

}
```

☐ Save your work.

The code you typed in the constructor function has one statement that uses the `SetInitialSize()` function to set the initial width of the control to 200 and the initial height to 15:

```
SetInitialSize(200, 15);
```

To see your code in action, do the following:

☐ Compile and link the MyClock control's files by selecting Build MyClock.ocx from the Build menu.

☐ Start Test Container, select Insert OLE control from its Edit menu, select the MyClock control, then click the OK button.

Test Container responds by inserting the MyClock control.

As you can see, the MyClock control is now wide enough! You don't have to widen it to see the seconds portion of the time.

☐ Terminate Test Container by selecting Exit from the File menu.

Adding a Custom Property to the MyClock Control

In many cases, you will have to add a property to your ActiveX control that's not a standard property. Such a property is called a *custom property*—a property custom-made by you.

In the following steps, you'll add an additional property to the MyClock control called UpdateInterval, which is used for storing numbers. You will use this property later in the chapter, but now all you want to do is add it to the MyClock control:

☐ Select ClassWizard from the View menu. In the Automation tab of ClassWizard, make sure the Class name box is set to `CMyClockCtrl`.

☐ Click the Add Property button.

Visual C++ responds by displaying the Add Property dialog box.

☐ Type UpdateInterval in the External name combo box and set the Type list box to long.

☐ Make sure the Member variable radio button is selected in the Implementation frame.

Your Add Property dialog box should now look like Figure 19.14.

Figure 19.14.

Adding the UpdateInterval property in the Add Property dialog box.

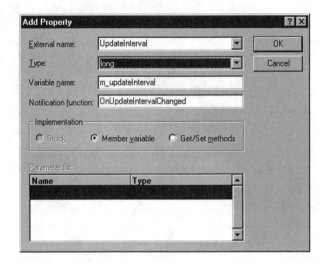

By setting the Add Property dialog box as shown in Figure 19.14, you are specifying that the name of the new property should be UpdateInterval and that this property will be used to hold numbers of type long. Figure 19.14 also shows the Variable name box set to m_updateInterval. This means that the variable associated with the UpdateInterval property will be m_updateInterval, a data member of the CMyClockCtrl class.

In Figure 19.14, the Notification function box is set to OnUpdateIntervalChange. Whenever the value of the UpdateInterval property is changed, the function OnUpdateIntervalChange() will be executed automatically. You'll write the code of the OnUpdateIntervalChange() function later.

☐ Click the OK button of the Add Property dialog box.

The ClassWizard dialog box reappears, as shown in Figure 19.15.

Figure 19.15.

Listing the UpdateInterval custom property in ClassWizard.

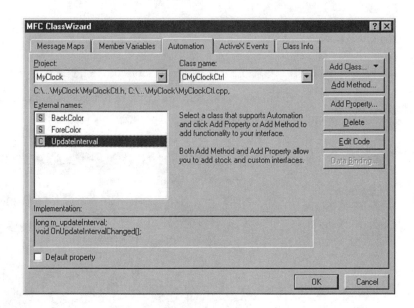

As shown in Figure 19.15, the Name list now contains the property UpdateInterval preceded by the letter c to indicate that UpdateInterval is a custom property.

☐ Click the OK button of ClassWizard.

That's it! You've finished adding the UpdateInterval custom property to the MyClock control. To verify that the MyClock control now has the UpdateInterval property, do the following:

☐ Select Build MyClock.ocx from the Build menu.

☐ Start Test Container, select Insert OLE control from its Edit menu, select the MyClock control, then click the OK button.

Test Container responds by inserting the MyClock control.

☐ Select Properties from the View menu of Test Container.

☐ Click the down arrow of the Property combo box.

Test Container responds by popping up a list with the properties of the MyClock control. (See Figure 19.16.) The UpdateInterval property you added to the control is in the list.

Figure 19.16.

Checking listed properties in the Properties dialog box.

□ Select the UpdateInterval property.

Your Properties dialog box should now look like Figure 19.17.

Figure 19.17.

The Properties dialog box after you select the UpdateInterval property.

As you can see from Figure 19.17, the Properties dialog box displays the current value of the UpdateInterval property and enables you to change this value. You can specify a new value for the UpdateInterval property by entering it in the Value edit box, then clicking the Apply button.

If you try to set the UpdateInterval property of the MyClock control to a value, the UpdateInterval property will be changed to the new value, but nothing will happen to the control. Why not? Because you haven't written the code that makes the UpdateInterval property functional. You'll do that later in this chapter.

□ Terminate Test Container by selecting Exit from the File menu.

Initializing the UpdateInterval Property

At this point, when you place the MyClock control in a dialog box or form, the UpdateInterval property is not initialized to any specific value. You'll now write code that initializes the UpdateInterval property to 1000.

To write code that initializes the UpdateInterval property to 1000, do the following:

□ Open the file MyClockCtl.cpp (if it's not open).

☐ Locate the function DoPropExchange() in the MyClockCtl.cpp file and add code as follows:

```
void CMyClockCtrl::DoPropExchange(CPropExchange* pPX)
{
ExchangeVersion(pPX, MAKELONG(_wVerMinor, _wVerMajor));
COleControl::DoPropExchange(pPX);

// TODO: Call PX_ functions for each persistent custom
//       property.

/////////////////////////
// MY CODE STARTS HERE
/////////////////////////

// Initialize the UpdateInterval property to 1000.
PX_Long(pPX, _T("UpdateInterval"), m_updateInterval, 1000);

/////////////////////////
// MY CODE ENDS HERE
/////////////////////////

}
```

☐ Save your work.

The code you wrote in the DoPropExchange() has one statement that uses the PX_Long() function to initialize the value of the UpdateInterval property to 1000:

```
PX_Long(pPX, _T("UpdateInterval"), m_updateInterval, 1000);
```

The PX_Long() function is used because the UpdateInterval property is of type long. To initialize other types of properties, you can use other PX_ functions, such as PX_Bool(), PX_Short, and PX_String().

NOTE

> Be careful when you type this statement:
>
> ```
> PX_Long(pPX,_T("UpdateInterval"),m_updateInterval,1000);
> ```
>
> The second parameter is _T("UpdateInterval") because UpdateInterval is the property you are initializing.
>
> The third parameter is m_updateInterval (with a lowercase u in update) because m_updateInterval is the variable associated with the UpdateInterval property. As you saw in Figure 19.14, when you added the UpdateInterval property, you specified the name of the variable as m_updateInterval (not m_UpdateInterval).

To see your initialization code in action, do the following:

☐ Select Build MyClock.ocx from the Build menu.

☐ Start Test Container, select Insert OLE control from its Edit menu, select the MyClock control, then click the OK button.

☐ Select Properties from Test Container's View menu, click the down arrow of the Property combo box and select the UpdateInterval property.

Your Properties dialog box should now look like the one shown in Figure 19.18. As expected, the initial value of the UpdateInterval property is 1000. The code you wrote in the DoPropExchange() function is working!

Figure 19.18.

The Properties dialog box after you select the UpdateInterval property.

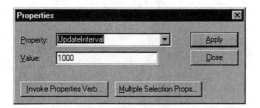

☐ Terminate Test Container by selecting Exit from the File menu.

Making the UpdateInterval Property Functional

At this point, the MyClock control has the UpdateInterval property, which has been initialized to 1000. You'll now add code to the MyClock control that makes the UpdateInterval property functional.

What should the UpdateInterval property do? This property should determine the interval at which the MyClock control updates itself. Currently, the MyClock control updates the displayed time every 1000 milliseconds, because you installed the timer of the control in the OnCreate() function with a 1000-millisecond interval. You'll now enhance the code of the MyClock control, so that it will update the displayed time every X milliseconds, where X is the current value of the UpdateInterval property. Here is how you do that:

☐ Open the file MyClockCtl.cpp (if it's not open).

☐ Locate the function OnUpdateIntervalChanged() in the MyClockCtl.cpp file. ClassWizard wrote this function for you when you added the UpdateInterval property; it's automatically executed when the value of the UpdateInterval property is changed.

☐ Add code to the `OnUpdateIntervalChanged()` function as follows:

```
void CMyClockCtrl::OnUpdateIntervalChanged()
{

// TODO: Add notification handler code

/////////////////////////
// MY CODE STARTS HERE
/////////////////////////

// Reinstall the timer with interval set
// to the current value of the UpdateInterval
// property.
SetTimer(1, (UINT)m_updateInterval, NULL);

/////////////////////////
// MY CODE ENDS HERE
/////////////////////////

SetModifiedFlag();

}
```

☐ Save your work.

The code you added is a single statement that reinstalls the timer and sets the timer's interval to the value of the variable `m_updateInterval`:

```
SetTimer(1, (UINT)m_updateInterval, NULL);
```

Recall that `m_updateInterval` is the variable of the UpdateInterval property. Therefore, whenever someone changes the value of the UpdateInterval property, the interval of the timer changes accordingly. Note that in the preceding statement the cast `(UINT)` is used, because the `SetTimer()` function expects its second parameter to be of type `UINT`, and the UpdateInterval property is defined as type `long`.

NOTE

> Be careful when you type this statement:
>
> ```
> SetTimer(1, (UINT)m_updateInterval, NULL);
> ```
>
> The second parameter is `m_updateInterval`, not `m_UpdateInterval`.

Recall that in the `OnCreate()` function you set the interval of the timer to 1000 milliseconds with this statement:

```
SetTimer(1, 1000, NULL);
```

Now change the `OnCreate()` function so that it will use the current value of the UpdateInterval property, not the hard-coded value of `1000`. This way, whenever a MyClock control is created, the initial value of the timer interval will be the same as the current value of the UpdateInterval property.

☐ Locate the OnCreate() function in the MyClockCtl.cpp file and change it as follows:

```
int CMyClockCtrl::OnCreate(LPCREATESTRUCT lpCreateStruct)
{

if (COleControl::OnCreate(lpCreateStruct) == -1)
   return -1;

// TODO: Add your specialized creation code here

////////////////////////
// MY CODE STARTS HERE
////////////////////////

// Install a timer.
SetTimer(1, (UINT)m_updateInterval, NULL);

////////////////////////
// MY CODE ENDS HERE
////////////////////////

return 0;

}
```

Again, when you type the preceding code, make sure you type m_updateInterval (not m_UpdateInterval).

☐ Save your work.

To see the code you attached to the OnUpdateIntervalChanged() function in action, do the following:

☐ Select Build MyClock.ocx from the Build menu.

☐ Start Test Container, select Insert OLE control from its Edit menu, select the MyClock control, then click the OK button.

☐ Select Properties from Test Container's View menu, click the down arrow of the Property combo box, and select the UpdateInterval property.

As you can see, the initial value of the UpdateInterval property is 1000, because earlier you wrote code in the DoPropExchange() function that initializes the UpdateInterval property to 1000.

☐ Observe the seconds portion of the displayed time in the MyClock control and make sure the time is updated every 1000 milliseconds.

☐ Change the value of the UpdateInterval property to 5000 and click the Apply button.

19

☐ Observe the MyClock control again and notice that now the time is updated every 5000 milliseconds.

As soon as you changed the UpdateInterval property to 5000, the code you wrote in the OnUpdateIntervalChanged() function was automatically executed; this code set the timer's interval to the new value of the UpdateInterval property.

☐ Terminate Test Container by selecting Exit from the File menu.

Validating the Value of the UpdateInterval Property

You can write code that validates the value entered for the UpdateInterval property. Suppose, for example, that you don't want the user to enter negative values for the UpdateInterval property. Your validation code will prompt the user with a message box and set the UpdateInterval property to a valid value. To write this validation code, follow these steps:

☐ Open the file MyClockCtl.cpp (if it's not open).

☐ Locate the function OnUpdateIntervalChanged() in the MyClockCtl.cpp file and add code as follows:

```
void CMyClockCtrl::OnUpdateIntervalChanged()
{

// TODO: Add notification handler code

/////////////////////////
// MY CODE STARTS HERE
/////////////////////////

// Make sure the user did not set the property to a
// negative value.
if (m_updateInterval < 0)
   {
   MessageBox("This property cannot be negative!");
   m_updateInterval = 1000;
   }

// Reinstall the timer with interval set
// to the current value of the UpdateInterval
// property.
SetTimer(1, (UINT)m_updateInterval, NULL);

/////////////////////////
// MY CODE ENDS HERE
/////////////////////////

SetModifiedFlag();

}
```

19

☐ Save your work.

The validation code you added to the `OnUpdateIntervalChanged()` function is made up of a single `if` statement:

```
if (m_updateInterval < 0)
   {
   MessageBox("This property cannot be negative!");
   m_updateInterval = 1000;
   }
```

This `if` statement evaluates the value of the UpdateInterval property (`m_updateInterval`) to see whether it's less than `0`. If `m_updateInterval` is less than `0`, the code under the `if` displays an error message box and sets the value of `m_updateInterval` to a valid value (`1000`).

To see your validation code in action, follow these steps:

☐ Select Build MyClock.ocx from the Build menu.

☐ Start Test Container, select Insert OLE control from its Edit menu, select the MyClock control, then click the OK button.

☐ Select Properties from Test Container's View menu and set the Property combo box to UpdateInterval.

☐ Change the value of the UpdateInterval property to a negative value (for example, `-1000`) and click the Apply button.

As expected, the message box shown in Figure 19.19 appears.

Figure 19.19.

The message box that appears after you set the UpdateInterval property to a negative value.

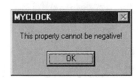

☐ Click the OK button of the message box.

☐ Observe the value of the UpdateInterval. It should be `1000`.

The validation code that you wrote in the `OnUpdateIntervalChanged()` function is working. When someone tries to set the UpdateInterval property to a negative value, your validation code displays a message box and sets the UpdateInterval property to `1000`.

☐ Terminate Test Container by selecting Exit from the File menu.

Summary

In this chapter, you customized the MyClock ActiveX control you created in the previous chapter. You have added to the control stock properties and a custom property.

In the next chapter, you'll further customize the MyClock ActiveX control—you'll add to the control a stock event, a custom event, a stock method, and a custom method.

Q&A

Q In this chapter and the previous chapter, I tested the MyClock.OCX control by using the Test Container program that comes with Visual C++. How else can I test the MyClock.OCX control?

A You can test the MyClock.OCX control by writing a Visual C++ program that uses it. Refer to Chapter 3, "Using ActiveX Controls," to review how to write a Visual C++ program that uses an ActiveX control.

Quiz

1. What is a stock property?
2. Give an example of a stock property.
3. After adding a stock property to an ActiveX control, you need to write the code that makes the stock property functional.
    a. True
    b. False
4. What is a custom property?

Exercise

Write a dialog-based Visual C++ program that uses the MyClock ActiveX control.

Quiz Answers

1. Stock properties (or standard properties) are predefined by Visual C++. Table 19.1 lists all the stock properties you can add to an ActiveX control.
2. Any of the properties listed in Table 19.1, such as BackColor, is a stock property.

3. a. After you add a stock property to an ActiveX control, you need to write code that makes it functional. For example, after you added the two stock properties BackColor and ForeColor to the MyClock control, you wrote code in the OnDraw() function that uses these properties.

4. A custom property is a property custom-made by you. Any property that's not a stock property is a custom property. For example, the UpdateInterval property of the MyClock.OCX control is a custom property.

Exercise Answer

To write a dialog-based Visual C++ program that uses the MyClock ActiveX control refer to Chapter 3, which shows you how to add an ActiveX control to your Visual C++ project and how to use the ActiveX control from within your Visual C++ program.

19

Day 20

Creating Your Own
ActiveX Control (Part III)

In this chapter, you'll continue developing the MyClock control that you created and customized in the previous two chapters—you'll add to the control a Properties page, events, and methods.

NOTE   Because you'll continue working on the previous two chapters' project, this chapter assumes that you have read and performed all the steps in Chapters 18 and 19.

Adding a Properties Page to the MyClock Control

So far, you have accessed the properties of the MyClock control by selecting Properties from Test Container's View menu and then using the Properties dialog box to view and set values of properties.

Another way to view or set properties during design time is with *properties pages,* which let you view or change properties in a friendly visual manner. Each properties page lets you view or set related properties. For example, you can view or select color properties in the Colors properties page and font properties in the Fonts properties page.

To illustrate what a properties page is and how to add it to a control, you'll add a Colors properties page to the MyClock control for viewing or setting the BackColor and ForeColor properties.

Before you write the code that adds the Colors properties page, first run the Test Container program and verify that the MyClock control does not have the Colors properties page:

☐ Start Test Container, select Insert OLE Control from its Edit menu, select the MyClock control, then click the OK button.

Test Container responds by inserting the MyClock control.

☐ Double-click the thin frame surrounding the MyClock control.

The MyClock Control Properties dialog box appears, as shown in Figure 20.1.

Figure 20.1.

The MyClock Control Properties dialog box.

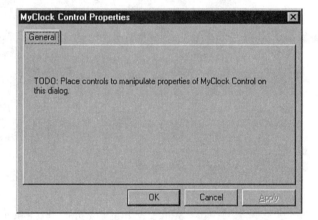

As shown in Figure 20.1, the MyClock Control Properties dialog box includes only one tab—the General tab—because the MyClock control has only the General properties page. After you write code adding the Colors properties page, the MyClock Properties dialog box will have another tab called Colors.

NOTE The preceding step instructs you to display the MyClock Control Properties dialog box by double-clicking the frame surrounding the MyClock control. You can also click the MyClock control, then select Properties MyClock Control Object from Test Container's Edit menu.

The General tab (the General properties page) currently includes this text:

```
TODO: Place controls to manipulate properties of MyClock Control on this dialog.
```

The General properties page should contain general properties that don't belong to any other properties page. Later in this chapter, you'll customize the General properties page.

☐ Close the MyClock Control Properties dialog box by clicking its OK button.

☐ Terminate the Test Container program by selecting Exit from the File menu.

To write the code that adds the Colors properties page to the MyClock control, follow these steps:

☐ Open the file MyClockCtl.cpp (if it's not open) and locate the Property Pages table in the MyClockCtl.cpp file. The Property Pages table currently looks like this:

```
/////////////////////////////////////////////
// Property pages

// TODO: Add more property pages as needed.
//       Remember to increase the count!
BEGIN_PROPPAGEIDS(CMyClockCtrl, 1)
    PROPPAGEID(CMyClockPropPage::guid)
END_PROPPAGEIDS(CMyClockCtrl)
```

☐ Modify the Property Pages table as follows (the statements you change or add are shown in boldface type):

```
/////////////////////////////////////////////
// Property pages

// TODO: Add more property pages as needed.
//       Remember to increase the count!
BEGIN_PROPPAGEIDS(CMyClockCtrl, 2)
    PROPPAGEID(CMyClockPropPage::guid)
    PROPPAGEID(CLSID_CColorPropPage)
END_PROPPAGEIDS(CMyClockCtrl)
```

First, you modified the second parameter in this statement from 1 to 2:

```
BEGIN_PROPPAGEIDS(CMyclockCtrl, 2)
```

You also added this statement:

```
PROPPAGEID(CLSID_CColorPropPage)
```

☐ Save your work.

Now take a close look at how the Property Pages table is constructed. The first statement begins the table:

```
BEGIN_PROPPAGEIDS(CMyclockCtrl, 2)
```

20

The first parameter, CMyClockCtrl, is the class name of the MyClock control. The second parameter, 2, specifies the total number of property pages. As you add more property pages to the control, you have to change this parameter accordingly.

The next two statements list the IDs of the property pages. The first statement lists the ID of the General properties page:

```
PROPPAGEID(CMyclockPropPage::guid)
```

This statement was written for you by Visual C++ when you created the project of the MyClock project. That's why the MyClock control already has a General properties page.

The second ID statement lists the ID of the Colors properties page:

```
PROPPAGEID(CLSID_CColorPropPage)
```

The last statement of the Property Pages table ends the table:

```
END_PROPPAGEIDS(CMyClockCtrl)
```

By adding the ID of the Colors properties page to the Property Pages table, you added the Colors properties page to the MyClock control. You don't have to write any additional code!

To make sure the MyClock control now has the Colors properties page, follow these steps:

☐ Select Build MyClock.ocx from the Build menu.

☐ Start Test Container, select Insert OLE Control from its Edit menu, select the MyClock control, then click the OK button.

☐ Double-click the frame of the MyClock control (or click the MyClock control and select Properties MyClock Control Object from the Edit menu of Test Container).

The MyClock Control Properties dialog box appears, as shown in Figure 20.2.

Figure 20.2.

The MyClock Control Properties dialog box with the Colors properties page.

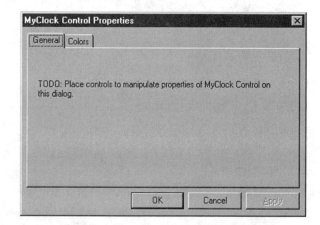

The MyClock Control Properties dialog box now includes two property pages: General and Colors.

☐ Select the Colors Properties page. (See Figure 20.3.)

Figure 20.3.

The Colors Properties page of the MyClock Control.

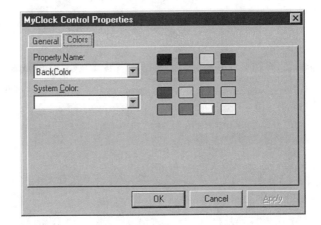

As you can see, the Colors Properties page gives you an easy and user-friendly interface to view and set the color properties of the MyClock control. You can select the desired Color property from the Property Name combo box and set its value by clicking the desired color.

After you click the down arrow of the Property Name combo box, it lists only the color properties of the MyClock control so you can concentrate on the color aspect of the control. (See Figure 20.4.)

Figure 20.4.

The Property Name combo box lists only the Colors properties.

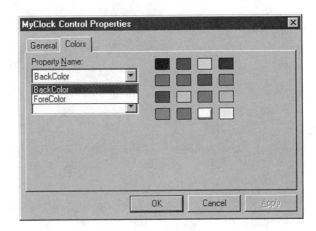

20

☐ Experiment with the Colors properties page and notice how easy it is to use. Make sure the MyClock control changes its foreground and background colors according to your selections after you click the OK button of the dialog box.

☐ Close the MyClock Control Properties dialog box by clicking its OK button.

☐ Terminate the Test Container program by selecting Exit from the File menu.

Customizing the General Properties Page

As you have seen in the previous steps, the MyClock control now has two properties pages: General and Colors. The Colors properties page is fully functional. However, the General properties page does not include any properties. You'll now customize the General properties page so that you can view and set the value of the UpdateInterval property.

To customize the General properties page, you need to work on the IDD_PROPPAGE_ MYCLOCK dialog box, created for you by Visual C++. To display the IDD_PROPPAGE_ MYCLOCK dialog box, do the following:

☐ In the ResourceView tab of the Project Workspace window, expand the MyClock resources item, expand the Dialog item, and double-click the IDD_PROPPAGE_MYCLOCK item.

Visual C++ responds by displaying the IDD_PROPPAGE_MYCLOCK dialog box in design mode ready for you to edit. (See Figure 20.5.) (Remember, for your convenience you can view the dialog box in full-screen mode by selecting Full Screen from the View menu. To cancel the Full-screen mode, press the Esc key.)

Figure 20.5.

The IDD_PROPPAGE_ MYCLOCK dialog box before customization.

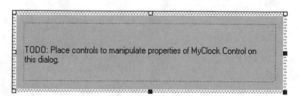

☐ Delete the TODO text in the IDD_PROPPAGE_MYCLOCK dialog box.

☐ Place a static text control in the dialog box, right-click it, select Properties from the pop-up menu that pops up, and set the Caption property of the static text control to UpdateInterval:.

☐ Place an edit box control in the dialog box, right-click it, select Properties from the pop-up menu that pops up, and set the ID property of the edit box control to IDC_UPDATE_INTERVAL.

☐ Close the Properties box of the edit box control and save your work by selecting Save All from the File menu.

Your IDD_PROPPAGE_MYCLOCK dialog box should now look like the one shown in Figure 20.6.

Figure 20.6.

The IDD_PROPPAGE_MYCLOCK dialog box after customization.

Now you have to attach a variable to the IDC_UPDATE_INTERVAL edit box and associate this variable with the UpdateInterval property. Here is how you do that:

☐ Select ClassWizard from the View menu. In the Member Variables tab, set the Class Name box to `CMyClockPropPage`.

Your ClassWizard dialog box should now look like Figure 20.7.

Figure 20.7.

The Member Variables tab after you select the `CMyClockPropPage` class.

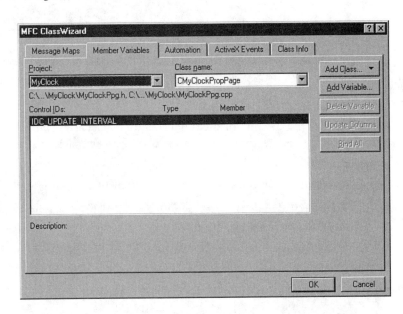

☐ Make sure that IDC_UPDATE_INTERVAL is selected in the Control IDs list, then click the Add Variable button and make the following selections in the Add Member Variable dialog box:

Variable name: `m_updateInterval`
Category: `Value`

Variable type: long
Optional Property name: UpdateInterval

Your Add Member Variable dialog box should now look like Figure 20.8.

Figure 20.8.

Attaching a variable to the IDC_ UPDATE_INTERVAL edit box.

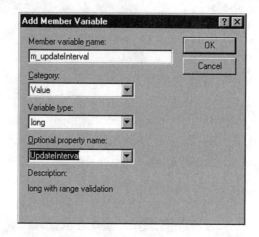

☐ Click the OK button of the Add Member Variable dialog box, then click the OK button of ClassWizard.

☐ Save your work.

That's it! You have finished customizing the General properties page. To make sure the General properties page is no longer blank and it enables the user to view and set the UpdateInterval property, follow these steps:

☐ Select Build MyClock.ocx from the Build menu.

☐ Start Test Container, select Insert OLE Control from its Edit menu, select the MyClock control, then click the OK button.

☐ Double-click the frame of the MyClock control (or click the MyClock control and select Properties MyClock Control Object from the Edit menu of Test Container).

The MyClock Control Properties dialog box appears, as shown in Figure 20.9.

As shown in Figure 20.9, the General properties page looks just the way you designed it. The edit box contains the value 1000 because this is the current value of the UpdateInterval property. The edit box contains the value of the UpdateInterval property because when you created it with ClassWizard, you set the Optional Property Name combo box to UpdateInterval.

Figure 20.9.
The General proper-ties page now includes the UpdateInterval property.

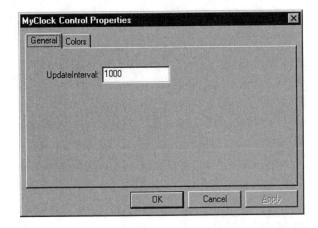

☐ Try to set the UpdateInterval property to various values, then click the OK button and make sure the MyClock control updates itself accordingly. For example, if you set the UpdateInterval to 5000, the seconds portion of the clock should change once every 5 seconds.

☐ Terminate the Test Container program by selecting Exit from the File menu.

What Have You Accomplished So Far?

So far, you have written the code that makes the MyClock control display the current time, added two stock properties (BackColor and ForeColor) and one custom property (UpdateInterval), written validation code for the UpdateInterval property, added a Colors properties page to the MyClock control, and customized the General properties page of the MyClock control.

In the following sections, you'll further customize the MyClock control by adding a stock event, a custom event, and a method.

Adding Stock Events to the MyClock Control

Now you'll learn how to add a stock event to the control. As you'll see, the steps to add a stock event are as easy as the steps you took when you added a stock property. *Stock events,* such as Click (mouse click) and DblClick (mouse double-click), are predefined. You can add any of the following stock events to an ActiveX control:

- Click
- DblClick
- Error
- KeyDown
- KeyPress
- KeyUp
- MouseDown
- MouseMove
- MouseUp
- ReadyStateChanged

The names of these events describe when they occur: The Click event occurs when you click the control, the DblClick event occurs when you double-click the control, the Error event occurs when there's an error within the control, the KeyDown event occurs when you press a key while the control has the keyboard focus, and so on. The mouse events apply to any of the mouse buttons: left, middle, or right. For practice, let's add two stock events to the MyClock control: Click and DblClick.

Follow these steps to add the Click event to the MyClock control:

☐ Select ClassWizard from the View menu. In the ActiveX Events tab of ClassWizard, set the Class name box to CMyClockCtrl.

Your ClassWizard dialog box should now look like Figure 20.10.

☐ Click the Add Event button.

   Visual C++ responds by displaying the Add Event dialog box.

☐ Click the down arrow of the External name combo box and select Click from the list that pops up.

Your Add Event dialog box should now look like Figure 20.11.

☐ Click the OK button of the Add Event dialog box.

The ClassWizard dialog box reappears, as shown in Figure 20.12.

Figure 20.10.

Setting the class name to CMyClockCtrl *in the ActiveX Events tab.*

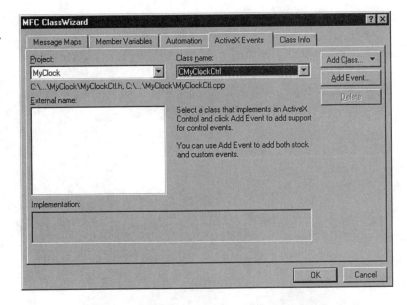

Figure 20.11.

Setting the External name combo box to Click.

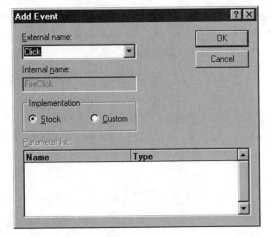

As shown in Figure 20.12, the External name list now contains the event Click preceded by the letter S to indicate that this is a stock event.

Now use the same steps to add the DblClick event:

☐ Click the Add Event button, click the down arrow of the External name combo box, select DblClick from the pop-up list, and click the OK button of the Add Event dialog box.

The ClassWizard dialog box reappears, as shown in Figure 20.13.

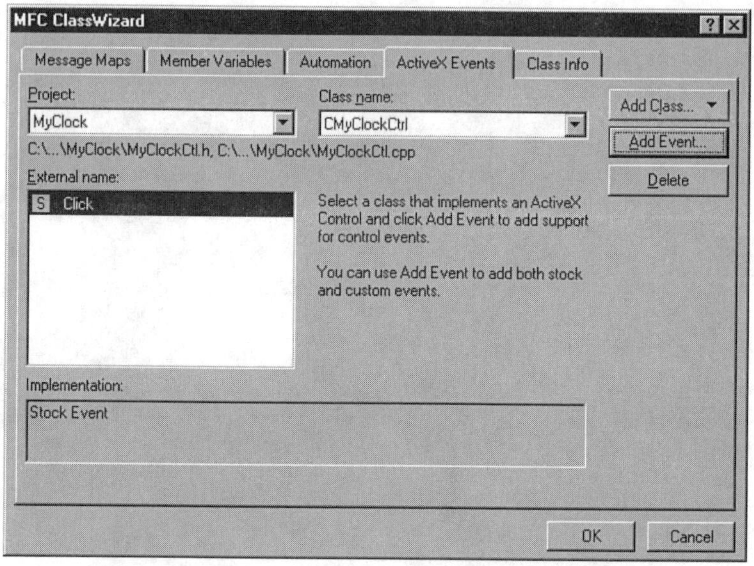

Figure 20.12.

The ClassWizard dialog box after you add the Click *stock event.*

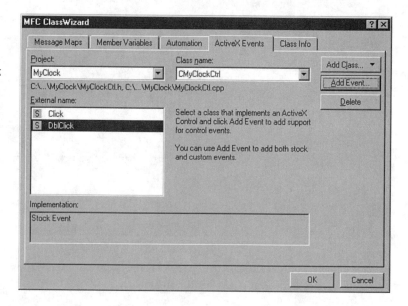

Figure 20.13.

The ClassWizard dialog box after adding the DblClick *stock event.*

Now the External name list contains both the Click event and DblClick event preceded by the letter S to indicate they're stock events.

☐ Click the OK button of ClassWizard.

That's it! You've finished adding the Click and DblClick events to the MyClock control. This means that programmers who use your MyClock control in their programs will be able to attach code to these events.

To make sure the MyClock control now has the Click and DblClick events, do the following:

☐ Select Build MyClock.ocx from the Build menu.

☐ Start Test Container, select Insert OLE Control from its Edit menu, select the MyClock control, then click the OK button.

☐ Select Event Log from the View menu of Test Container.

Test Container responds by displaying the Event Log dialog box. (See Figure 20.14.)

Figure 20.14.

The Event Log dialog box of Test Container.

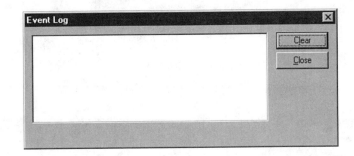

The Event Log dialog box displays a log of events as they occur. To verify that the MyClock control has a Click event, do the following:

☐ Leave the Event Log dialog box open.

☐ Click in the MyClock control. (Don't click on the frame of the control; click inside the control.)

The Event Log dialog box logs a Click event. (See Figure 20.15.)

Figure 20.15.

Logging a Click event in the Event Log dialog box.

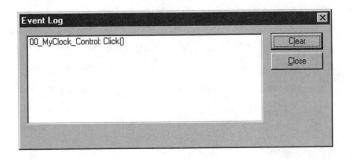

20

☐ Click the MyClock control several more times, and notice how the Event Log dialog box logs a Click event each time you click the MyClock control. (See Figure 20.16.) Notice that it doesn't matter which mouse button you use to click the MyClock control.

Figure 20.16.

Logging four Click *events.*

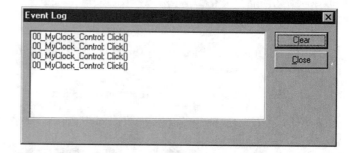

To verify that the MyClock control has a DblClick event, do the following:

☐ Double-click in the MyClock control.

The Event Log dialog box logs a DblClick event. (See Figure 20.17.)

Figure 20.17.

Logging a DblClick *event in the Event Log dialog box.*

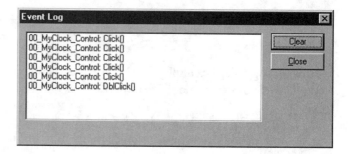

☐ Double-click the MyClock control several more times, and notice how the Event Log dialog box logs a DblClick event and a Click event each time you click the MyClock control. That's because every time you double-click the control, two events occur: a regular click and a double-click. The first click of a double-click is a regular click. Notice, too, that the DblClick event occurs whether you use the left, middle, or right mouse button.

☐ Terminate Test Container by selecting Exit from the File menu.

20

Adding a Custom Event to the MyClock Control

In many cases, you'll have to add a custom-made event to your ActiveX control, called a *custom event*. You'll now add a custom event to the MyClock control called NewMinute. Later you will make this event functional, but now all you want to do is add it to the MyClock control.

Follow these steps to add the NewMinute custom event to the MyClock control:

☐ Select ClassWizard from the View menu.

☐ In the ActiveX Events tab of ClassWizard, make sure that the Class name box is set to CMyClockCtrl.

Your ClassWizard dialog box should now look like Figure 20.18.

Figure 20.18.

The ActiveX Events tab.

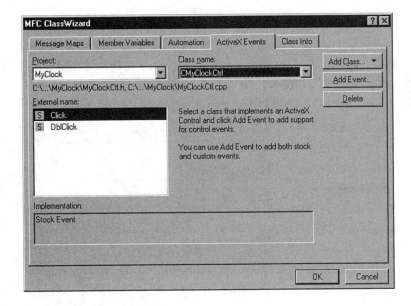

☐ Click the Add Event button.

Visual C++ responds by displaying the Add Event dialog box.

☐ Enter NewMinute in the External name combo box.

Notice that as you type NewMinute in the External name combo box, Visual C++ automatically fills the Internal name edit box with the text FireNewMinute.

Your Add Event dialog box should now look like Figure 20.19.

Figure 20.19.

Entering NewMinute *in the Add Event dialog box.*

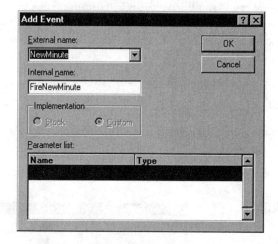

☐ Click the OK button of the Add Event dialog box.

The ClassWizard dialog box reappears, as shown in Figure 20.20.

Figure 20.20.

The ClassWizard dialog box after you add the NewMinute *custom event.*

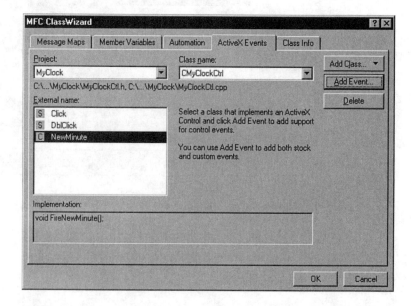

As shown in Figure 20.20, the External name list now contains the event NewMinute preceded by the letter C to indicate that this is a custom event.

☐ Close the ClassWizard dialog box by clicking its OK button.

NOTE

When you add a custom event to a control, you can add parameters to the event by clicking the empty item in the Parameter list. (Refer to Figure 20.19.) In the preceding steps, you were not instructed to add a parameter in the Add Event dialog box, because you don't want the NewMinute event to have any parameters.

In your future ActiveX control projects, you may need to add parameters to a certain event. When an event has parameters, whoever receives the event can make use of these parameters to get more information about the event.

That's it! You have finished adding the NewMinute custom event to the MyClock control. To verify that the MyClock control now has the NewMinute event, do the following:

☐ Select Build MyClock.ocx from the Build menu.

☐ Start Test Container, select Insert OLE Control from its Edit menu, select the MyClock control, then click the OK button.

To see a list of all the events of the MyClock control, do the following:

☐ Select View Event List from the Edit menu of Test Container.

Test Container responds by displaying the Events for MyClock Control dialog box. (See Figure 20.21.)

Figure 20.21.

The Events for MyClock Control dialog box.

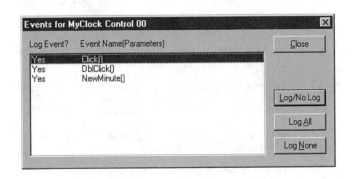

20

As you can see, the NewMinute event is listed! The MyClock control has three events: Click, DblClick, and NewMinute.

☐ Close the dialog box by clicking its Close button.

☐ Terminate Test Container by selecting Exit from the File menu.

Firing the NewMinute Event

As you have just verified, the MyClock control has the NewMinute event you added. However, to make the NewMinute event occur, you need to write some code.

When you add a stock event to a control, such as the DblClick event you added earlier, it already includes built-in code that makes the event happen. In the case of the DblClick event, it occurs automatically whenever you double-click the MyClock control.

However, when you add a custom event to a control, you need to write code that makes the event happen. Your code needs to recognize that the event has occurred and then use the Fire function of the event to fire the event—to make the event happen. The Fire function of the NewMinute event is FireNewMinute(). To make the NewMinute event happen, your code needs to detect when it occurs, then call the FireNewMinute() function.

When should the NewMinute event occur? Whenever a new minute begins. Follow these steps to write the code that fires the NewMinute event:

☐ Open the file MyClockCtl.cpp (if it's not open).

☐ Locate the function OnDraw() in the MyClockCtl.cpp file and add an if statement to the end of the OnDraw() function as follows:

```
void CMyClockCtrl::OnDraw(
  CDC* pdc,const CRect& rcBounds,const CRect& rcInvalid)
{
// TODO: Replace the following code with your own drawing
//       code.

/////////////////////////////
// MY CODE STARTS HERE //
/////////////////////////////

// Set the foreground color (i.e. the text color)
// according to the ForeColor property.
pdc->SetTextColor(TranslateColor(GetForeColor()));

// Set the background mode to transparent mode.
pdc->SetBkMode(TRANSPARENT);

// Create a brush based on the BackColor property.
CBrush bkBrush(TranslateColor(GetBackColor()));
```

20

```
// Paint the background using the BackColor property
pdc->FillRect(rcBounds, &bkBrush);

char CurrentTime[30];
struct tm *newtime;
long lTime;

// Get the current time
time(&lTime);
newtime=localtime(&lTime);

// Convert the time into a string.
strcpy(CurrentTime, asctime(newtime));

// Pad the string with 1 blank.
CurrentTime[24]=' ';

// Terminate the string.
CurrentTime[25] = 0;

// Display the current time
pdc->ExtTextOut(rcBounds.left,
                rcBounds.top,
                ETO_CLIPPED,
                rcBounds,
                CurrentTime,
                strlen(CurrentTime),
                NULL);

// If new minute has just begun, fire a NewMinute event.
if (newtime->tm_sec==0)
    FireNewMinute();

////////////////////////
// MY CODE ENDS HERE //
////////////////////////

}
```

The code you just added to the OnDraw() function is one if statement:

```
if (newtime->tm_sec==0)
    FireNewMinute();
```

This if statement checks whether the tm_sec field of the newtime structure is currently 0. If it is, a new minute has just begun, and the FireNewMinute() function is executed to fire the NewMinute event:

```
FireNewMinute();
```

Note that the FireNewMinute() event is called without any parameters because you didn't specify any when you added the NewMinute event to the control.

You have finished writing the code that fires the NewMinute event! Now whenever a new minute begins, the code you wrote will fire a NewMinute event, and the code attached to the NewMinute event will be executed automatically.

20

The code you wrote for detecting the NewMinute event is not perfect. This code is executed whenever the OnDraw() function is executed, which is determined by the value of the UpdateInterval property. If the UpdateInterval property is ever set to a value greater than 1000 milliseconds, a new minute might begin without your code detecting it.

To verify that the code you wrote actually fires the NewMinute event, do the following:

☐ Select Build MyClock.ocx from the Build menu.

☐ Start Test Container, select Insert OLE Control from its Edit menu, select the MyClock control, then click the OK button.

☐ Select Event Log from the View menu of Test Container.

   Test Container responds by displaying the Event Log dialog box.

☐ Leave the Event Log dialog box open.

☐ Observe the time that the MyClock control displays and wait for a new minute to begin.

As expected, as soon as a new minute begins, the Event Log dialog box logs the NewMinute event! (See Figure 20.22.)

Figure 20.22.

The Event Log dialog box after a new minute has begun.

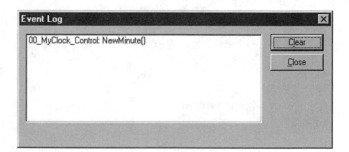

You have just verified that the NewMinute event is working. Whenever a new minute begins, the code you wrote in the OnDraw() function detects that a new minute has begun, and your code fires the NewMinute event by calling the FireNewMinute() function.

☐ Terminate Test Container by selecting Exit from the File menu.

Adding Methods to the MyClock Control

Besides adding properties and events to an ActiveX control, you can also add *methods*, which are like C++ member functions. After you add a method to your control, programmers who use your control can use your method in their programs. For example, suppose you add a method called `MyMethod()` to the MyClock control. Then, if a programmer adds a MyClock control in his or her program and names it `Clock1`, the programmer can use a statement such as the following:

```
Clock1.MyMethod()
```

This statement would execute the `MyMethod()` method on the Clock1 control.

The `AboutBox()` Method: A Gift from Visual C++

Although you haven't written any code to add a method to the MyClock control, it already has a method called `AboutBox()` created by Visual C++ when you created the MyClock's project. As its name implies, the `AboutBox()` method displays an About dialog box for the MyClock control. When programmers who use your MyClock control call the `AboutBox()` method from their programs, an About dialog box appears.

Before you add your own methods to the MyClock control, let's test the `AboutBox()` method that Visual C++ created for you:

☐ Start Test Container, select Insert OLE Control from its Edit menu, select the MyClock control, then click the OK button.

☐ Select Invoke Methods from the Edit menu of Test Container.

Test Container responds by displaying the Invoke Control Method dialog box. (See Figure 20.23.)

Figure 20.23.

The Invoke Control Method dialog box.

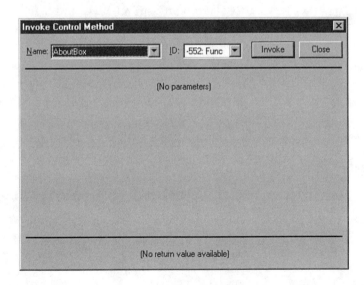

As shown in Figure 20.23, the Name list box of the Invoke Control Method dialog box is set to `AboutBox`. If you click the Invoke button, Test Container will execute the `AboutBox()` method of the MyClock control.

☐ Click the Invoke button.

> *Test Container responds by executing the* `AboutBox()` *method of the MyClock control. The* `AboutBox()` *method displays an About dialog box, shown in Figure 20.24.*

Figure 20.24.

The About dialog box displayed by the `AboutBox()` *method.*

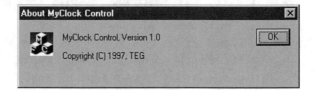

☐ Close the About dialog box by clicking its OK button.

☐ Close the Invoke Control Method dialog box by clicking its Close button.

☐ Terminate Test Container by selecting Exit from the File menu.

In the following sections, you'll add more methods to the MyClock control.

NOTE

> If you wish, you can customize the About dialog box shown in Figure 20.24. To customize it, you need to work on the IDD_ABOUTBOX_MYCLOCK dialog box created by Visual C++.
>
> To display the IDD_ABOUTBOX_MYCLOCK dialog box, do the following:
>
> ☐ In the ResourceView tab of the Project Workspace window, expand the MyClock resources item, then expand the Dialog item.
>
> ☐ Double-click the IDD_ABOUTBOX_MYCLOCK item.

Adding a Stock Method to the MyClock Control

Stock methods are predefined. Visual C++ supports two stock methods: `DoClick()` and `Refresh()`. The `DoClick()` method simulates a clicking of the control. In other words, executing the `DoClick()` method has the same effect as clicking the control. The `Refresh()`

method causes the control to redraw itself by triggering a call to the OnDraw() function of the control.

For practice, add the Refresh() stock method to the MyClock control by following these steps:

☐ Select ClassWizard from the View menu. In the OLE Automation tab of ClassWizard, make sure the Class name box is set to CMyClockCtrl.

☐ Click the Add Method button.

   Visual C++ responds by displaying the Add Method dialog box.

☐ Click the down arrow of the External name combo box and select Refresh from the list that pops up.

Your Add Method dialog box should now look like Figure 20.25.

Figure 20.25.

The Add Method dialog box after setting the External name combo box to Refresh.

☐ Click the OK button of the Add Method dialog box.

The ClassWizard dialog box reappears, as shown in Figure 20.26.

As shown in Figure 20.26, the External names list now contains the method Refresh preceded by the letter M to indicate that Refresh is a method.

☐ Close the ClassWizard dialog box by clicking its OK button.

20

Figure 20.26.

The ClassWizard dialog box after you add the Refresh() *stock method.*

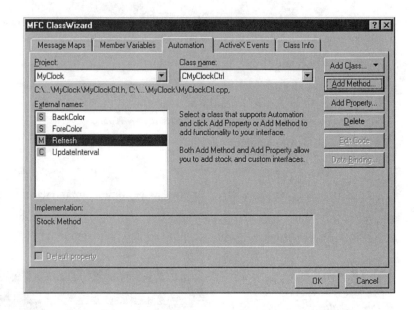

That's it! You have finished adding the Refresh() stock method to the MyClock control. To verify that the MyClock control now has the Refresh() method and to see it in action, do the following:

☐ Select Build MyClock.ocx from the Build menu.

☐ Start Test Container, select Insert OLE Control from its Edit menu, select the MyClock control, then click the OK button.

To see the Refresh() method in action, you first have to increase the value of the UpdateInterval property. Currently, the UpdateInterval property is set to 1000 milliseconds (1 second), so the MyClock control keeps updating itself every second. Therefore, when you invoke the Refresh() method, you can't see the effects of the Refresh() method.

Increase the value of the UpdateInterval property as follows:

☐ Select Properties from Test Container's View menu, click the down arrow of the Property combo box, and select the UpdateInterval property.

☐ Change the value of the UpdateInterval property to 15000, click the Apply button, then click the Close button.

☐ Observe the MyClock control and verify that the displayed time is refreshed every 15000 milliseconds (15 seconds).

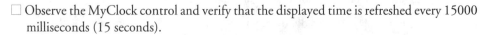

NOTE

In the preceding steps, you changed the UpdateInterval property of the MyClock control by selecting Properties from the View menu of Test Container. You can also double-click the frame of the MyClock control, then set the UpdateInterval property in the General properties page.

Now test the `Refresh()` method as follows:

☐ Select Invoke Methods from the Edit menu of Test Container.

Test Container responds by displaying the Invoke Control Method dialog box.

☐ Make sure the Name list box of the Invoke Control Method dialog box is set to Refresh, as shown in Figure 20.27, because you want to test the `Refresh()` method.

Figure 20.27.

The Invoke Control Method dialog box.

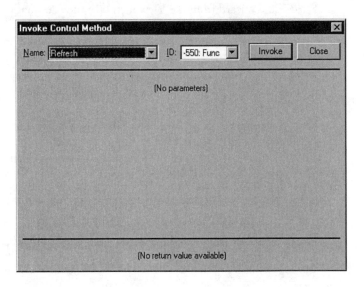

☐ Move the Invoke Control Method dialog box by dragging its title so that you can see the MyClock control.

☐ Click the Invoke button.

Test Container responds by executing the `Refresh()` method of the MyClock control. As soon as you click the Invoke button, the MyClock control redraws itself. The `Refresh()` method you added to the MyClock control is working!

☐ Click the Invoke button several more times, and notice that after each click, the MyClock control redraws itself.

☐ Close the Invoke Control Method dialog box by clicking its Close button.

☐ Terminate Test Container by selecting Exit from the File menu.

Adding a Custom Method to the MyClock Control

In many cases, you'll want to add your own method, which isn't a standard method, to your ActiveX control. Such a method is called a *custom method*. In this section, you'll add a simple custom method, called Beep(), to the MyClock control. Calling this method will generate a beep.

Follow these steps to add the Beep() custom method to the MyClock control:

☐ Select ClassWizard from the View menu. In the Automation tab of ClassWizard, make sure the Class name box is set to CMyClockCtrl.

☐ Click the Add Method button.

> *Visual C++ responds by displaying the Add Method dialog box.*

☐ Type Beep in the External name combo box.

As you type Beep in the External name combo box, Visual C++ automatically fills the Internal name edit box with the text Beep. The Internal name edit box specifies the function name of the MyClock control that will be executed when anyone executes the Beep() method. You'll write the code of the Beep() function soon.

☐ Set the Return type list box to void because you don't want the Beep() method to return any value.

Your Add Method dialog box should now look like Figure 20.28.

☐ Click the OK button of the Add Method dialog box.

The ClassWizard dialog box reappears, as shown in Figure 20.29.

As shown in Figure 20.29, the External names list now contains the method Beep preceded by the letter M to indicate that Beep is a method.

20

Figure 20.28.

Adding the Beep()
method to the
MyClock control.

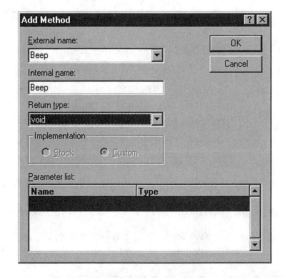

Figure 20.29.

The ClassWizard
dialog box after you
add the Beep()
custom method.

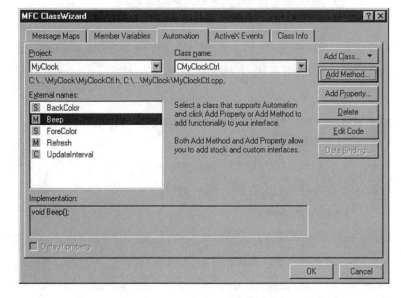

20

NOTE

When you add a custom method to a control, you can add parameters by clicking the empty item in the Parameter list of the Add Method dialog box. (Refer to Figure 20.28.)

In the preceding steps, you weren't instructed to add any parameters, but you might want to do this in future ActiveX projects. When a method has parameters, whoever calls the method needs to pass these parameters to the method.

☐ Close the ClassWizard dialog box by clicking its OK button.

To write the code of the Beep() method, do the following:

☐ Open the file MyClockCtl.cpp (if it's not open) and locate the function Beep(). (Visual C++ wrote the skeleton of this function when you added the Beep() method.)

☐ Write the following code in the Beep() function:

```
void CMyClockCtrl::Beep()
{
// TODO: Add your dispatch handler code here

/////////////////////////
// MY CODE STARTS HERE
/////////////////////////

MessageBeep((WORD)-1);

/////////////////////////
// MY CODE ENDS HERE
/////////////////////////

}
```

☐ Save your work.

The code you just typed in the Beep() function uses the MessageBeep() function to beep:

```
MessageBeep((WORD)-1);
```

That's it! You have finished adding the Beep() custom method to the MyClock control. To verify that the MyClock control now has the Beep() method and to see (or rather, hear) the Beep() method in action, do the following:

☐ Select Build MyClock.ocx from the Build menu.

☐ Start Test Container, select Insert OLE Control from its Edit menu, select the MyClock control, then click the OK button.

Now test the Beep() method as follows:

☐ Select Invoke Methods from the Edit menu of Test Container.

Test Container responds by displaying the Invoke Control Method dialog box.

☐ Set the Name list box of the Invoke Control Method dialog box to Beep, as shown in Figure 20.30, because you want to test the Beep() method.

Figure 20.30.

Testing the Beep()
method with the
Invoke Control
Method dialog box.

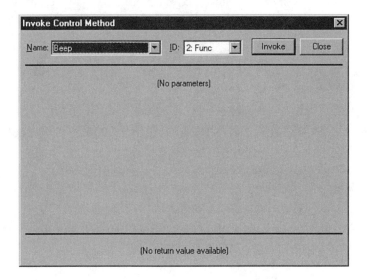

☐ Click the Invoke button several times.

As you can hear, each time you click the Invoke button, your PC beeps. The Beep() custom method you added to the MyClock control is working!

☐ Close the Invoke Control Method dialog box by clicking its Close button.

☐ Terminate Test Container by selecting Exit from the File menu.

Summary

In this chapter, you completed customizing the MyClock ActiveX control you created in the previous two chapters. You have added to the control a Properties page, a stock event, a custom event, a stock method, and a custom method. As you have seen, developing an ActiveX control with Visual C++ is easy.

Q&A

Q **What other programming language, besides Visual C++, supports ActiveX controls?**

A ActiveX controls are becoming very popular. Almost all modern visual programming languages support ActiveX controls (for example, Visual Basic). Once you finish developing an ActiveX control, programmers of all languages that support ActiveX controls, such as Visual C++ and Visual Basic, can use your ActiveX control.

Quiz

1. What is a stock event?
2. After adding a stock event to an ActiveX control, you need to write the code that makes the stock event occur.

   a. True
   b. False

3. What is a custom event?
4. After adding a custom event to an ActiveX control, you need to write the code that makes the custom event occur.

   a. True
   b. False

Exercise

Add a new method to the MyClock.OCX control called SayHello() that will display a Hello message box.

Quiz Answers

1. Stock events (or standard events) are predefined by Visual C++. For example, the Click event is a stock event.
2. b. After you add a stock event to an ActiveX control, you do *not* need to write code that makes the event occur. For example, after you added the two stock events Click and DblClick to the MyClock control, you did not have to write any code to make these events occur.

20

3. A custom event is an event custom-made by you. Any event that's not a stock event is a custom event. For example, the NewMinute event of the MyClock.OCX control is a custom event.

4. a. After you add a custom event to an ActiveX control, you need to write code that makes the event occur. You do that by calling the Fire() function of the event. For example, after you added the custom event NewMinute, you had to write code that detects when it occurs. This code fired the NewMinute event by calling the FireNewMinute() function.

Exercise Answer

To add the SayHello() method to the MyClock ActiveX control, follow these steps:

☐ Open the project workspace file (.DSW file) of the MyClock control (if it's not open) by selecting Open Workspace from the File menu, then selecting the C:\TYVCPROG\ PROGRAMS\CH18\MYCLOCK\MyClock.DSW file.

☐ Select ClassWizard from the View menu. In the Automation tab of ClassWizard, make sure the Class name box is set to CMyClockCtrl and click the Add Method button.

Visual C++ responds by displaying the Add Method dialog box.

☐ Type SayHello in the External name combo box. Visual C++ automatically fills the Internal name edit box with the text SayHello.

☐ Set the Return type list box to void because you don't want the SayHello() method to return any value.

☐ Click the OK button of the Add Method dialog box.

☐ Close the ClassWizard dialog box by clicking its OK button.

To write the code of the SayHello() method, do the following:

☐ Open the file MyClockCtl.cpp and locate the function SayHello(). (Visual C++ wrote the skeleton of this function when you added the SayHello() method.)

☐ Write the following code in the SayHello() function:

```
void CMyClockCtrl::SayHello()
{
// TODO: Add your dispatch handler code here

//////////////////////////
// MY CODE STARTS HERE
//////////////////////////
```

20

```
MessageBox("Hello!");

/////////////////////
// MY CODE ENDS HERE
/////////////////////

}
```

☐ Save your work.

That's it! You have finished adding the SayHello() custom method to the MyClock control.

To verify that the MyClock control now has the SayHello() method and to see the SayHello() method in action, do the following:

☐ Select Build MyClock.ocx from the Build menu.

☐ Start Test Container, select Insert OLE Control from its Edit menu, select the MyClock control, then click the OK button.

   Test Container responds by inserting the MyClock control.

Now test the SayHello() method as follows:

☐ Select Invoke Methods from the Edit menu of Test Container.

   Test Container responds by displaying the Invoke Control Method dialog box.

☐ Set the Name list box of the Invoke Control Method dialog box to SayHello and click the Invoke button.

As you can see, a Hello message box is displayed. The SayHello() custom method you added to the MyClock control is working!

Day 21

Sound, Animation, and DirectX

In this chapter, you'll learn how to write a Visual C++ program that displays an animation show with synchronized background sound. The animation program of this chapter will display BMP picture files, play a WAV sound file, and play a MIDI sound file.

In this chapter, you'll also learn about a new graphics and sound technology called DirectX. You'll learn what DirectX is all about and the advantages of using this new technology.

NOTE

The program of this chapter uses the TegoSoft BMP ActiveX control and the TegoSoft Sound ActiveX control. The BMP ActiveX control enables you to write programs that display and animate BMP picture files, and the Sound ActiveX control enables you to write programs that play WAV and MIDI sound files.

Thus, in this chapter you'll be instructed to download the TegoSoft BMP ActiveX control and the TegoSoft Sound ActiveX control from the TegoSoft Internet Web site.

Note that even if you currently do not have access to the Internet, it is recommended that you at least browse through this chapter. This way you'll see how easy it is to write programs that use ActiveX controls for the purpose of displaying an animation show that includes synchronized sound and background sound.

Downloading and Installing the BMP ActiveX Control and the Sound ActiveX Control

You'll now download the BMP ActiveX control and the Sound ActiveX control from the Internet, and you'll install these controls in your system.

NOTE

In Chapter 10, "Loading and Displaying Picture Files," you were instructed to download and install a sample program from the Internet. If you have already downloaded and installed the sample program as instructed in Chapter 10, you can skip the following download steps.

To download the BMP and Sound ActiveX controls from the Internet, follow these steps:

☐ Use your Internet connection to connect to the Internet.

☐ Use your Internet browser program to log into the following Internet URL address:

```
http://www.tegosoft.com/BkVcBmpSamp.htm
```

☐ Follow the directions on the preceding HTML page to download a sample program that includes the BMP and Sound ActiveX controls.

☐ Follow the directions given on the preceding HTML page to install the sample program that you downloaded.

That's it! You now have the BMP and Sound ActiveX controls installed in your system.

NOTE

> Now that you have the BMP and Sound ActiveX controls installed in your system, you can write programs that utilize these controls for displaying animation, playing WAV sound files, and playing MIDI sound files.
>
> In the following sections, you'll write a Visual C++ program, called MyAnim, that uses the Sound and BMP ActiveX controls to display an animation and to play a WAV sound file and a MIDI sound file in the background. The MyAnim program is copyright TegoSoft, Inc..

The MyAnim Program

Before creating the MyAnim program yourself, review its specifications:

■ When you start the MyAnim program, the window shown in Figure 21.1 appears.

■ The window of the MyAnim program displays an animation show of a man dribbling a basketball. Figure 21.1 shows the first frame of the animation show. Figures 21.2 and 21.3 show two other frames of the animation show. You can drag the edges of the window to shrink or enlarge its size; the picture displayed in the window shrinks or increases accordingly. The BMP picture is always displayed over the entire client area of the program's window.

■ While the animation show is displayed, the user can choose to include sound by using the program's Sound menu. (See Figure 21.4.) When the Music menu item is checked, MIDI music is played in the background. And when the Basketball menu item is checked, sound of a basketball hitting the floor is played when the basketball hits the floor. (See Figure 21.3.) The Sound menu with its two options checked is shown in Figure 21.5.

Now that you know what the MyAnim.EXE program is supposed to do, let's start writing this program.

21

Figure 21.1.

The window of the MyAnim program displaying the first frame of the animation show.

Figure 21.2.

The window of the MyAnim program displaying another frame of the animation show.

Figure 21.3.

The window of the MyAnim program displaying the last frame of the animation show (the basketball is hitting the floor).

Figure 21.4.
The Sound menu of the MyAnim.EXE program.

Figure 21.5.
The Sound menu of the MyAnim program with the Music and Basketball options checked.

Creating the Project of the MyAnim Program

To create the project of the MyAnim program, follow these steps:

☐ Create the C:\TYVCPROG\PROGRAMS\CH21 directory.

☐ Start Visual C++ and select New from the File menu.

Visual C++ responds by displaying the New dialog box.

☐ Select the Projects tab of the New dialog box.

☐ Select MFC AppWizard(exe) from the list of project types.

☐ Type MyAnim in the Project Name box.

☐ Click the button that is located on the right of the Location box and select the C:\TYVCPROG\PROGRAMS\CH21 directory.

21

☐ Click the OK button.

Visual C++ responds by displaying the MFC AppWizard Step 1 window.

☐ In Step 1, select the Dialog based option to create a dialog-based application, then click the Next button.

☐ In Step 2, use the default settings and enter MyAnim for the dialog box's title. When you're done, click the Next button.

☐ In Step 3, use the default settings, then click Next.

☐ In Step 4, use the default settings and notice that AppWizard has created the CMyAnimApp and CMyAnimDlg classes. Click the Finish button.

Visual C++ responds by displaying the New Project Information window.

☐ Click the OK button of the New Project Information window.

Visual C++ responds by creating the project of the MyAnim program and all its associated files.

☐ Select Set Active Configuration from the Build menu, then select MyAnim - Win32 Release and click the OK button.

That's it—you're ready to start designing the program.

The Visual Design of MyAnim's Main Window

You'll now visually design the IDD_MYANIM_DIALOG dialog box that serves as the main window of the MyAnim program.

NOTE
In the visual design of the IDD_MYANIM_DIALOG dialog box, you will use the TegoSoft BMP and Sound ActiveX controls. Thus, it is assumed that you already downloaded and installed the BMP and Sound ActiveX controls as described earlier in this chapter. You will not be able to perform the steps of this section unless you have already downloaded and installed the BMP and Sound ActiveX controls.

Follow these steps to visually design the IDD_MYANIM_DIALOG dialog box:

☐ In the Project Workspace, click the ResourceView tab and expand the MyAnim resources item, then the Dialog item. Finally, double-click the IDD_MYANIM_DIALOG item.

Visual C++ responds by displaying the IDD_MYANIM_DIALOG dialog box in design mode.

☐ Delete the TODO text, OK button, and Cancel button of the IDD_MYANIM_DIALOG dialog box.

Next, you need to place the BMP and Sound ActiveX controls in the IDD_MYANIM_DIALOG dialog box. But before you can place these controls in the IDD_MYANIM_DIALOG dialog box, you first have to add these ActiveX controls to the MyAnim project. Here is how you do that:

☐ Select Add to Project from the Project menu.

Visual C++ responds by opening the Add to Project submenu next to the Project menu.

☐ Select Components and Controls from the Add to Project submenu.

Visual C++ responds by displaying the Components and Controls Gallery dialog box.

☐ In the Components and Controls Gallery dialog box, double-click the Registered ActiveX Controls item.

Visual C++ responds by displaying all the registered ActiveX controls in your system.

☐ Use the scroll bar of the Components and Controls Gallery dialog box to find the TegoSoft BMP ActiveX Control item, select the TegoSoft BMP ActiveX Control item by clicking it, and then click the Insert button of the Components and Controls Gallery dialog box.

Visual C++ responds by displaying a small confirmation message box asking you whether you want to insert the component that you selected to the project.

☐ Click the OK button of the confirmation message box.

Visual C++ responds by displaying the Confirm Classes dialog box.

Visual C++ will add to the MyAnim project in order to add the BMP ActiveX control.

☐ Click the OK button of the Confirm Classes dialog box.

Visual C++ responds by adding the BMP ActiveX control to the MyAnim project and by redisplaying the Components and Controls Gallery dialog box.

Next, add the TegoSoft Sound ActiveX control to the project:

☐ Use the scroll bar of the Components and Controls Gallery dialog box to find the TegoSoft Sound ActiveX Control item, select the TegoSoft Sound ActiveX Control item by clicking it, and then click the Insert button of the Components and Controls Gallery dialog box.

Visual C++ responds by displaying a small confirmation message box asking you whether you want to insert the component that you selected to the project.

☐ Click the OK button of the confirmation message box.

Visual C++ responds by displaying the Confirm Classes dialog box.

21

The Confirm Classes dialog box displays the names of the classes that Visual C++ will add to the MyAnim project in order to add the Sound ActiveX control.

☐ Click the OK button of the Confirm Classes dialog box.

> *Visual C++ responds by adding the Sound ActiveX control to the MyAnim project and by redisplaying the Components and Controls Gallery dialog box.*

☐ Click the Close button of the Components and Controls Gallery dialog box.

That's it! You completed adding the BMP and Sound ActiveX controls to the MyAnim project. From now on, you can use the BMP and Sound ActiveX controls in the MyAnim project just as you use standard Visual C++ controls. That is, you can place these controls in the IDD_MYANIM_DIALOG box, you can set the properties of the ActiveX controls, and you can attach code to the events of the ActiveX controls.

Take a look at your Controls toolbar. As shown in Figure 21.6, your Controls toolbar now contains the tools of the BMP and Sound ActiveX controls.

 NOTE

> If you don't see the Controls toolbar on your Visual C++ desktop, select Customize from the Tools menu, select the Toolbars tab of the Customize dialog box, and place a check mark in the Controls check box.

Figure 21.6.

The tools of the BMP and Sound ActiveX controls in the Controls toolbar.

The tool of the BMP ActiveX control

The tool of the Sound ActiveX control

You'll now place a BMP ActiveX control in the IDD_MYANIM_DIALOG dialog box:

☐ Click the tool of the BMP ActiveX control in the Controls toolbar and then click in the IDD_MYANIM_DIALOG dialog box.

The Missing License dialog box appears. (See Figure 21.7.)

Figure 21.7.

The Missing License dialog box of the BMP ActiveX control.

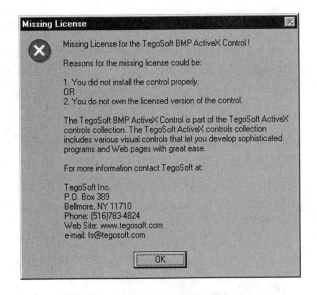

NOTE

The Missing License dialog box serves as a reminder that you are using the Learning Edition of the BMP ActiveX control. This means that you can use the BMP ActiveX control for learning purposes only. You are not allowed to distribute the control to others, and you are not allowed to incorporate this ActiveX control in your HTML pages. To learn how to obtain the Professional Licensed edition of the BMP ActiveX control, you can visit the TegoSoft Web site at `http://www.tegosoft.com`. To learn how to obtain other TegoSoft ActiveX controls, see the Special Disk Offer at the end of this book.

☐ Click the OK button of the Missing License dialog box.

Visual C++ responds by placing the BMP ActiveX control in the IDD_MYANIM_DIALOG dialog box at the point where you clicked the mouse. (See Figure 21.8.)

NOTE

Remember, for your convenience you can display the IDD_MYANIM_DIALOG dialog box in full-screen mode by selecting Full Screen from the View menu. To cancel the full-screen mode, press the Esc key.

21

Figure 21.8.

The BMP ActiveX
control in the
IDD_MYANIM_DIALOG
dialog box.

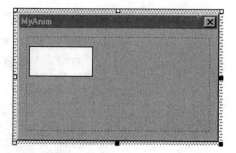

Next, place a Sound ActiveX control in the IDD_MYANIM_DIALOG dialog box:

☐ Click the tool of the Sound ActiveX control in the Controls toolbar and then click in the
IDD_MYANIM_DIALOG dialog box.

The Missing License dialog box of the Sound ActiveX control appears.

☐ Click the OK button of the Missing License dialog box.

Visual C++ responds by placing a Sound ActiveX control in the IDD_MYANIM_DIALOG
dialog box at the point where you clicked the mouse. (See Figure 21.9.)

Figure 21.9.

The
IDD_MYANIM_DIALOG
dialog box with a
BMP ActiveX control
and a Sound ActiveX
control in it.

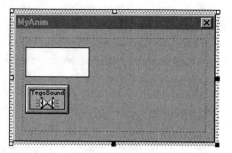

You can now treat the BMP ActiveX control and Sound ActiveX control just as you treat a
standard Visual C++ control. You can drag them with the mouse to move them, you can size
them by dragging their handles, and you can set their properties by right-clicking the desired
control and selecting Properties from the pop-up menu.

☐ Design the IDD_MYANIM_DIALOG dialog box according to Table 21.1. When you
finish, it should look like the one in Figure 21.10.

21

Table 21.1. The properties table of the IDD_MYANIM_DIALOG dialog box.

Object	Property	Setting
Dialog Box	ID	IDD_MYANIM_DIALOG
	Caption	The MyAnim Program
	Font	System, size 10
	Border	Resizing (Styles tab)
	Minimize box	Checked (Styles tab)
	Maximize box	Checked (Styles tab)
BMP Control	ID	IDC_BMP_CONTROL
Sound Control	ID	IDC_SOUND_CONTROL

Figure 21.10.

*The
IDD_MYANIM_DIALOG
dialog box in design
mode.*

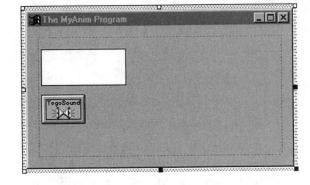

NOTE

Table 21.1 specifies setting the Border property of the dialog box to Resizing. The Border list box is in the Styles tab of IDD_MYANIM_DIALOG's Properties window. Setting the Border property to Resizing enables you to enlarge or shrink the program's window by dragging its edges during runtime.

The Maximize and Minimize check boxes in the Styles tab should also be checked so that the IDD_MYANIM_DIALOG dialog box can be maximized and minimized during runtime.

21

> Table 21.1 specifies to set the ID property of the BMP ActiveX control to IDC_BMP_CONTROL and to set the ID of the Sound ActiveX control to IDC_SOUND_CONTROL. Besides the ID property, the BMP and Sound ActiveX controls have other properties that you can set. However, in the MyAnim program, you will set these other properties from within your code.

The Visual Design of the Menu

You'll now visually design the menu of the MyAnim program:

☐ In the Project Workspace window, select the ResourceView tab and right-click the MyAnim resources item.

Visual C++ responds by displaying a pop-up menu.

☐ Select Insert from the menu.

Visual C++ responds by displaying the Insert Resource dialog box.

☐ Select the Menu item from the Insert Resource dialog box, then click the New button.

Visual C++ responds by displaying an empty menu in design mode.

☐ Customize the menu, as shown in Figures 21.11, 21.12, and 21.13. As shown in these figures, you have to add the Exit item to the File menu, the Basketball and Music items to the Sound menu, and the About item to the Help menu.

Figure 21.11.

The File menu of the MyAnim program.

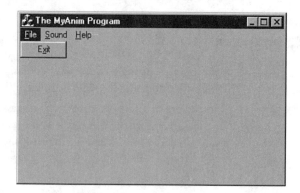

Figure 21.12.

The Sound menu of
the MyAnim program.

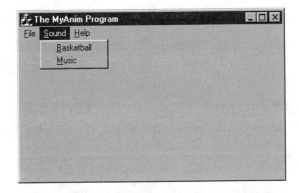

Figure 21.13.

The Help menu of the
MyAnim program.

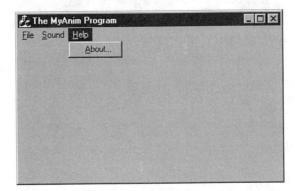

The default ID that Visual C++ assigns to the new menu is `IDR_MENU1`. Change the ID to
`IDR_MYANIM_MENU`:

☐ Set the ID property of the menu to IDR_MYANIM_MENU by right-clicking the
  IDR_MENU1 item in the Project Workspace window, selecting Properties, then setting
  the ID property in the Properties window that pops up.

Next, you have to associate the menu with the `CMyAnimDlg` class. Here is how you do that:

☐ While the menu window is selected, select ClassWizard from the View menu.

  Visual C++ responds by displaying the Adding a Class dialog box.

☐ Make sure that the "Select an existing class" radio button is selected, then click the OK
  button.

  Visual C++ responds by displaying the Select Class dialog box.

21

☐ Select the CMyAnimDlg item, then click the Select button.

Visual C++ responds by displaying the MFC ClassWizard dialog box.

☐ Click the OK button of the MFC ClassWizard dialog box.

Attaching the Menu to the Dialog Box

You'll now attach the IDR_MYANIM_MENU menu to the IDD_MYANIM_DIALOG dialog box:

☐ Double-click the IDD_MYANIM_DIALOG item in the Project Workspace window.

Visual C++ responds by displaying IDD_MYANIM_DIALOG in design mode.

☐ Set the Menu property (in the General tab) of IDD_MYANIM_DIALOG to IDR_MYANIM_MENU. (To display the Properties window, right-click a free area of the dialog box and select Properties from the menu that pops up.)

You've finished the visual design of the IDD_MYANIM_DIALOG dialog box and the visual design of the program's menu. To see your design in action, follow these steps:

☐ Select Build MyAnim.EXE from the Build menu.

☐ Select Execute MyAnim.EXE from the Build menu.

Visual C++ responds by executing the MyAnim.EXE program. The main window of MyAnim.EXE appears, as shown in Figure 21.14.

Figure 21.14.

The main window of the MyAnim.EXE program.

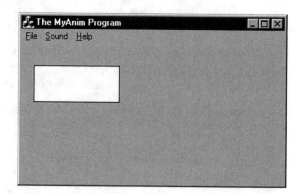

As you can see, the main window of the MyAnim.EXE program (the IDD_MYANIM_DIALOG dialog box) has a blank BMP ActiveX control in it, and it has a menu bar with three menus: File, Sound, and Help.

NOTE

As you can see in Figure 21.14, the BMP ActiveX control appears in the dialog box. However, the Sound ActiveX control does not appear in the dialog box. Why not? The Sound ActiveX control is an example of an ActiveX control that is invisible at runtime. That is, when you place it in the dialog box in design-time, you see it in the dialog box (refer to Figure 21.10). However, when you run the program, the control is invisible.

As you will see later in this chapter, although the Sound ActiveX control is invisible during runtime, you still work with its properties, functions, and events as you do with other controls.

☐ Experiment with the MyAnim.EXE program and make sure that the File and Help menus look as shown in Figures 21.11, 21.12, and 21.13.

☐ Terminate the MyAnim.EXE program by clicking the × icon at the upper-right corner of the program's window.

Attaching Variables to the BMP and Sound ActiveX Controls

You'll now attach variables to the BMP and Sound controls, so you can use these variables later to write code that accesses the properties of these controls. Follow these steps to attach a variable to the IDC_BMP_CONTROL control:

☐ Select ClassWizard from the View menu.

Visual C++ responds by displaying the MFC ClassWizard dialog box.

☐ Select the Member Variables tab of the MFC ClassWizard dialog box.

☐ Make sure that the Class name list box is set to CMyAnimDlg.

The CMyAnimDlg class is associated with the IDD_MYANIM_DIALOG dialog box (the main window of the MyAnim program). Because you're going to attach a variable to a control in the IDD_MYANIM_DIALOG dialog box, the Class name list box should be set to CMyAnimDlg. As a result, the variable that you'll attach to the control will be a data member of the CMyAnimDlg class.

☐ Select IDC_BMP_CONTROL in the Object IDs list to attach a variable to the IDC_BMP_CONTROL control, then click the Add Variable button.

Visual C++ responds by displaying the Add Member Variable dialog box.

21

☐ Set the Add Member Variable dialog box as follows:

Member variable name:	m_bmp
Category:	Control
Variable type:	CTegoBmp

Now, attach a variable to the IDC_SOUND_CONTROL control:

☐ Select IDC_SOUND_CONTROL in the Object IDs list to attach a variable to the IDC_SOUND_CONTROL control, then click the Add Variable button.

Visual C++ responds by displaying the Add Member Variable dialog box.

☐ Set the Add Member Variable dialog box as follows:

Member variable name:	m_snd
Category:	Control
Variable type:	CTegoSnd

☐ Click the OK button of the Add Member Variable dialog box, then click the OK button of the ClassWizard dialog box.

You've finished attaching variables to the IDC_BMP_CONTROL and IDC_SOUND_CONTROL controls!

Putting it all together, you have attached a variable of type CTegoBmp to the IDC_BMP_CONTROL control and named it m_bmp, and you have attached a variable of type CTegoSnd to the IDC_SOUND_CONTROL control and named it m_snd. In the following sections, you'll write the code of the MyAnim.EXE program and use the m_bmp and m_snd variables to access the properties of the BMP and Sound controls.

Copying the Multimedia Files to the Directory Where the MyAnim.EXE Program Resides

The MyAnim.EXE program that you are writing needs to use the following multimedia files for its operation:

■ Basket.WAV (a WAV sound file that contains the sound of a basketball hitting the floor)

■ MyMidi.MID (a MIDI sound file that contains music)

■ Basket1.BMP (the picture used for frame 1 of the animation show)

■ Basket2.BMP (the picture used for frame 2 of the animation show)

■ Basket3.BMP (the picture used for frame 3 of the animation show)

- Basket4.BMP (the picture used for frame 4 of the animation show)
- Basket5.BMP (the picture used for frame 5 of the animation show)

Earlier in this chapter when you downloaded and installed the sample program from the TegoSoft Internet Web site, these multimedia files were installed in your hard drive in the same directory where the sample program was installed. For example, if you installed the sample program in your C:\PROGRAMFILES\TEGOSOFT\ TEGOBMPSAMPLEPROGRAM directory, you'll find these multimedia files in the C:\PROGRAMFILES\TEGOSOFT\TEGOBMPSAMPLEPROGRAM directory.

The MyAnim.EXE that you are now writing resides in the C:\TYVCPROG\PROGRAMS\ CH21\MYANIM\RELEASE directory. So you'll now copy all the preceding multimedia files into the C:\TYVCPROG\PROGRAMS\CH21\MYANIM\RELEASE:

☐ Copy the files Basket.WAV, MyMidi.MID, Basket1.BMP, Basket2.BMP, Basket3.BMP, Basket4.BMP, and Basket5.BMP from the directory where you installed the Tegosoft sample program into your C:\TYVCPROG\PROGRAMS\CH21\MYANIM\RELEASE directory.

NOTE

> The MyAnim.EXE program that you are now developing resides in your C:\TYVCPROG\PROGRAMS\CH21\MYANIM\RELEASE directory. That's because when you started the project you set the Project Active Configuration to MyAnim - Win32 Release. Had you left the Project Active Configuration at the default of MyAnim - Win32 Debug, Visual C++ would have created the MyAnim.EXE program in the C:\TYVCPROG\PROGRAMS\CH21\MYANIM\ DEBUG directory.
>
> Of course, once you complete the design of the MyAnim.EXE program, you can place the MyAnim.EXE file in any desired directory. And because the code of the MyAnim.EXE program (code that you'll write later in this chapter) assumes that the multimedia files used by the program reside in the same directory where the program resides, you have to place the multimedia files in the same directory where you place the MyAnim.EXE file.

In addition to copying the multimedia files to the \RELEASE subdirectory of the MyAnim project, you also need to copy the multimedia files to the directory where the project file of the MyAnim program resides. The project file of the MYANIM program is MyAnim.dsw, and it resides in your C:\TYVCPROG\PROGRAMS\CH21\MYANIM directory.

The next section explains why you need to copy the multimedia files also to the directory where the program's project file resides.

21

☐ Copy the files Basket.WAV, MyMidi.MID, Basket1.BMP, Basket2.BMP, Basket3.BMP, Basket4.BMP, and Basket5.BMP from the directory where you installed the TegoSoft sample program into your C:\TYVCPROG\PROGRAMS\CH21\MYANIM directory.

NOTE

Before continuing to the next section, make sure that *both* your C:\TYVCPROG\PROGRAMS\CH21\MYANIM\RELEASE directory and your C:\TYVCPROG\PROGRAMS\CH21\MYANIM directory now contain these files: Basket.WAV, MyMidi.MID, Basket1.BMP, Basket2.BMP, Basket3.BMP, Basket4.BMP, and Basket5.BMP.

As explained in the next section, it is important that both these directories contain the multimedia files.

Writing the Initialization Code of the MyAnim.EXE Program

You'll now write the initialization code of the MyAnim.EXE program. As usual in a dialog-based program, you'll attach this code to the WM_INITDIALOG event of the dialog box that serves as the program's main window.

Follow these steps to attach code to the WM_INITDIALOG event of the IDD_MYANIM_DIALOG dialog box:

☐ Select ClassWizard from the View menu, select the Message Maps tab, and use the ClassWizard dialog box to select the following event:

Class name:	CMyAnimDlg
Object ID:	CMyAnimDlg
Message:	WM_INITDIALOG

☐ Click the Edit Code button of ClassWizard.

Visual C++ responds by opening the file MyAnimDlg.cpp with the function OnInitDialog() *ready for you to edit. Remember, you can view and edit code in full-screen mode (select Full Screen from the View menu and press Esc to cancel the full-screen mode).*

The OnInitDialog() function already has some code written by Visual C++. You'll type your own code below this comment line:

```
// TODO: Add extra initialization here
```

21

☐ Write the following code in the `OnInitDialog()` function:

```
BOOL CMyAnimDlg::OnInitDialog()
{
CDialog::OnInitDialog();
...
...
...

// TODO: Add extra initialization here

//////////////////////////
// MY CODE STARTS HERE
//////////////////////////

// Initialize the program's window width and
// height to 300 X 220.
SetWindowPos(NULL,NULL,NULL,300,220,SWP_NOMOVE);

// Load the BMP control with the 5 frames of the animation show.
m_bmp.SetFrame(0,"Basket1.BMP");
m_bmp.SetFrame(1,"Basket2.BMP");
m_bmp.SetFrame(2,"Basket3.BMP");
m_bmp.SetFrame(3,"Basket4.BMP");
m_bmp.SetFrame(4,"Basket5.BMP");

//////////////////////
// MY CODE ENDS HERE
//////////////////////

return TRUE;  // return TRUE  unless you set the focus
              // to a control
}
```

☐ Save your work by selecting Save All from the File menu.

The following is the first statement that you typed in the `OnInitDialog()` function:

```
SetWindowPos(NULL,NULL,NULL,300,220,SWP_NOMOVE);
```

This statement uses the `SetWindowPos()` function to set the program's window width to 300 and height to 220 (in units of pixels). The fourth parameter of the `SetWindowPos()` function specifies the window's width, and the fifth parameter specifies the window's height. The sixth parameter, `SWP_NOMOVE`, specifies that you don't want to move the window (you only want to size the window).

The remaining five statements that you typed in the `OnInitDialog()` function are the following:

```
m_bmp.SetFrame(0,"Basket1.BMP");
m_bmp.SetFrame(1,"Basket2.BMP");
m_bmp.SetFrame(2,"Basket3.BMP");
m_bmp.SetFrame(3,"Basket4.BMP");
m_bmp.SetFrame(4,"Basket5.BMP");
```

21

These statements execute the SetFrame() function of the BMP ActiveX control on the m_bmp control. The first parameter of the SetFrame() method specifies the frame number to be set, and the second parameter specifies the BMP filename of the BMP picture that you want to put in the frame. As you can see, the first frame is frame number 0, the second frame is frame number 1, the third frame is frame number 2, and so on.

Notice that in the preceding code, only the name of the BMP filename is specified. The full directory pathname of the BMP filename is not specified. When the full directory pathname of the BMP file is not specified, the program assumes that the BMP file resides in the current directory. What is the current directory? It depends. If you are executing the MyAnim.EXE program from Windows (by using the Explorer program or by using the Run option from the Start menu), the current directory is the directory where the MyAnim.EXE program resides. However, if you are running the MyAnim.EXE program by selecting Execute MyAnim.EXE from the Build menu of Visual C++, the current directory is the directory where the project file of the MyAnim program resides. This is why, in the previous section, you were instructed to copy the multimedia files to both the \RELEASE subdirectory of the MyAnim program and to the directory where the project file of the program resides. This way, the MyAnim.EXE program will work as expected both when you run it from within Visual C++ and when you run it directly from Windows.

Putting it all together, the code that you wrote in the OnInitDialog() function fills five frames of the BMP Active control with five BMP files: Basket1.BMP, Basket2.BMP, Basket3.BMP, Basket4.BMP, and Basket5.BMP. Because the full pathnames of these directories is not specified, the program assumes that these BMP files reside on the current directory.

Attaching Code to the WM_SIZE Event of the IDD_MYANIM_DIALOG Dialog Box

When the user changes the size of the program's window, you want the BMP control to adjust itself to the new size of the program's window. This way, the pictures of the animation show will always be the same size as the program's window.

You'll now write code that is responsible for automatically resizing the BMP control to the new window size. You'll attach this code to the WM_SIZE event of the IDD_MYANIM_DIALOG dialog box (because the WM_SIZE event occurs when the program's window is resized).

Follow these steps to attach code to the WM_SIZE event of the IDD_MYANIM_DIALOG dialog box:

☐ Select ClassWizard from the View menu, select the Message Maps tab, and use the ClassWizard dialog box to select the following event:

21

Class name:	CMyAnimDlg
Object ID:	CMyAnimDlg
Message:	WM_SIZE

☐ Click the Add Function button.

Visual C++ responds by adding the OnSize() *function.*

☐ Click the Edit Code button of ClassWizard.

Visual C++ responds by opening the file MyAnimDlg.cpp with the function OnSize() *ready for you to edit. Remember, you can view and edit code in full-screen mode (select Full Screen from the View menu and press Esc to cancel the full-screen mode).*

☐ Write the following code in the OnSize() function:

```
BOOL CMyAnimDlg::OnSize(UINT nType, int cx, int cy)
{
CDialog::OnSize(nType, cx, cy);

// TODO: Add your message handler code here

/////////////////////////
// MY CODE STARTS HERE
/////////////////////////

// Set the size of the BMP control to the
// new size of the program's window.
m_bmp.SetWindowPos(NULL,0,0,cx,cy,NULL);

/////////////////////////
// MY CODE ENDS HERE
/////////////////////////

}
```

☐ Save your work by selecting Save All from the File menu.

The code you typed in the OnSize() function is made up of a single statement:

```
m_bmp.SetWindowPos(NULL,0,0,cx,cy,NULL);
```

This statement executes the SetWindowPos() function on the BMP control to set the size of the control to the new size of the program's window. The new size of the program's window is provided by the parameters cx and cy of the OnSize() function. That's why in the preceding statement, the fourth and fifth parameters of SetWindowPos() are cx and cy.

Because the OnSize() function is automatically executed when the program's window size is changed, from now on, when the program's window is resized, the BMP control size will be resized according to the new size of the program's window.

21

To see the code you typed in the OnSize() function in action, follow these steps:

☐ Select Build MyAnim.EXE from the Build menu.

☐ Select Execute MyAnim.EXE from the Build menu.

Visual C++ responds by executing the MyAnim.EXE program. The main window of the program appears as shown in Figure 21.15.

Figure 21.15.

The main window of the MyAnim.EXE program.

☐ Increase the width and height of the program's window by dragging the right edge of the program's window toward the right and dragging the bottom edge of the program's window downward.

As you can see, the size of the BMP control adjusts itself to the new size of the program's window. (See Figure 21.16.) The code that you wrote in the OnSize() function is working!

As you can see, at this point, the MyAnim.EXE program displays only the first frame (frame number 0) of the animation. Later you will write the code that is responsible for displaying the other frames of the animation—one after the other. This will create the illusion that the basketball player is dribbling the basketball.

☐ Terminate the MyAnim.EXE program by clicking the × icon at the upper-right corner of the program's window.

Attaching Code to the Exit Menu Item

You'll now attach code to the COMMAND event of the Exit menu item:

☐ Highlight the IDR_MYANIM_MENU item in the Project Workspace window, then select ClassWizard from the View menu.

Visual C++ responds by displaying the MFC ClassWizard dialog box.

21

Figure 21.16.

The main window of the MyAnim.EXE program after increasing the program window's width and height.

☐ Select ID_FILE_EXIT in the Object IDs list, select COMMAND in the Message list, then click the Add Function button.

Visual C++ responds by suggesting OnFileExit *as the new function's name.*

☐ Accept OnFileExit as the name of the new function, then click the Edit Code button.

☐ Enter code in the OnFileExit() function (in the MyAnimDlg.cpp file) as follows:

```
void CMyAnimDlg::OnFileExit()
{
// TODO: Add your command handler code here

/////////////////////////
// MY CODE STARTS HERE
/////////////////////////

OnOK();

/////////////////////////
// MY CODE ENDS HERE
/////////////////////////


}
```

This code, which terminates the MyAnim program, is executed when you select Exit from the File menu.

21

☐ Save your work.

☐ Build and execute MyAnim.EXE to make sure the Exit menu item works as expected.

Attaching Code to the About Menu Item

You'll now add the code that's executed when you select the About item from the Help menu:

☐ Select the IDR_MYANIM_MENU item in the Project Workspace window.

☐ Select ClassWizard from the View menu.

☐ Select the ID_HELP_ABOUT item from the Object IDs list, select COMMAND in the Messages list, then click the Add Function button.

> *Visual C++ responds by suggesting* `OnHelpAbout` *as the new function's name.*

☐ Accept the function name that Visual C++ suggests, then click the Edit Code button.

☐ Enter code in the `OnHelpAbout()` function as follows:

```
void CMyAnimDlg::OnHelpAbout()
{
// TODO: Add your command handler code here

//////////////////////////
// MY CODE STARTS HERE
//////////////////////////

CAboutDlg dlg;
dlg.DoModal();

//////////////////////////
// MY CODE ENDS HERE
//////////////////////////


}
```

This code creates an object `dlg` of class `CAboutDlg`, the class associated with the About dialog box IDD_ABOUTBOX:

```
CAboutDlg dlg;
```

Then the About dialog box is displayed as a modal dialog box:

```
dlg.DoModal();
```

☐ Save your work.

☐ Build and execute the program to make sure the About dialog box is displayed when you select the About item from the Help menu.

21

☐ Experiment with the program, then select Exit from the File menu to terminate the MyAnim program.

Installing a Timer

At this point, the MyAnim.EXE program displays only frame number 0 of the animation. However, you want to write animation code to display all the frames of the animation show, one frame after the other, to create the illusion that the man is dribbling the basketball.

To write this animation code, you need to write code that installs a timer and then you need to write code that displays a different frame in each iteration of the timer.

To write the code that installs the timer, follow these steps:

☐ Add the following statement to the OnInitDialog() function in the MyAnimDlg.CPP file:

```
// Install a 50 milliseconds timer.
SetTimer(1, 50, NULL);
```

After adding this statement to the OnInitDialog() function, your OnInitDialog() function should look as follows:

```
BOOL CMyAnimDlg::OnInitDialog()
{
CDialog::OnInitDialog();
...
...
...

// TODO: Add extra initialization here

/////////////////////////
// MY CODE STARTS HERE
/////////////////////////

// Initialize the program's window width and
// height to 300 X 220.
SetWindowPos(NULL,NULL,NULL,300,220,SWP_NOMOVE);

// Load the BMP control with the 5 frames of the animation show.
m_bmp.SetFrame(0,"Basket1.BMP");
m_bmp.SetFrame(1,"Basket2.BMP");
m_bmp.SetFrame(2,"Basket3.BMP");
m_bmp.SetFrame(3,"Basket4.BMP");
m_bmp.SetFrame(4,"Basket5.BMP");

// Install a 50 milliseconds timer.
SetTimer(1, 50, NULL);

/////////////////////////
// MY CODE ENDS HERE
/////////////////////////
```

21

```
return TRUE;   // return TRUE  unless you set the focus
               // to a control
}
```

☐ Save your work.

The statement that you added to the `OnInitDialog()` function installs a timer with a 50 milliseconds interval:

```
SetTimer(1, 50, NULL);
```

From now on, a `WM_TIMER` event will occur every 50 milliseconds. In the following section, you'll attach code to the `WM_TIMER` event.

Attaching Code to the `WM_TIMER` Event of the IDD_MYANIM_DIALOG Dialog Box

You'll now write code that is responsible for the animation. You'll attach this code to the `WM_TIMER` event of the IDD_MYANIM_DIALOG dialog box.

Follow these steps to attach code to the `WM_TIMER` event of the IDD_MYANIM_DIALOG dialog box:

☐ Select ClassWizard from the View menu, select the Message Maps tab, and use the ClassWizard dialog box to select the following event:

Class name:	CMyAnimDlg
Object ID:	CMyAnimDlg
Message:	WM_TIMER

☐ Click the Add Function button.

Visual C++ responds by adding the `OnTimer()` *function.*

☐ Click the Edit Code button of ClassWizard.

Visual C++ responds by opening the file MyAnimDlg.cpp with the function `OnTimer()` *ready for you to edit.*

☐ Write the following code in the `OnTimer()` function:

```
void CMyAnimDlg::OnTimer(UINT nIDEvent)
{
// TODO: Add your message handler code here and/or call default

/////////////////////////
// MY CODE STARTS HERE
/////////////////////////
```

```
// Display the next frame of the animation.
long CurrentFrame = m_bmp.GetCurrentFrame();
CurrentFrame = CurrentFrame + 1;
m_bmp.SetCurrentFrame(CurrentFrame);

////////////////////////
// MY CODE ENDS HERE
////////////////////////

CDialog::OnTimer(nIDEvent);
}
```

☐ Save your work.

The code that you typed in the OnTimer() function is made up of three statements. The first statement is the following:

```
long CurrentFrame = m_bmp.GetCurrentFrame();
```

This statement declares the variable CurrentFrame and uses the GetCurrentFrame() function of the BMP ActiveX control to fill the CurrentFrame variable with the number of the currently displayed frame.

The second statement increments CurrentFrame by one:

```
CurrentFrame = CurrentFrame + 1;
```

Finally, the last statement uses the SetFrame() function of the BMP ActiveX control to set the currently displayed frame to the new number of CurrentFrame.

So putting it all together, on each iteration of OnTimer(), a new frame will be displayed in the BMP control—first, frame number 0, then frame number 1, then frame number 2, and so on. Note that after the last frame is displayed, the BMP ActiveX control automatically resets its current frame to the first frame (frame number 0).

To see your animation code in action, follow these steps:

☐ Build and execute the program.

As expected, the program displays an animation show of a man dribbling a basketball.

☐ Increase the width and height of the program's window and verify that the animation show pictures increase accordingly.

☐ Experiment with the program, then select Exit from the File menu to terminate the MyAnim program.

At this point, the MyAnim.EXE program displays an animation show. However, the animation show is silent. In the following sections, you'll write code that adds sound to the

21

animation. In particular, when the basketball is shown hitting the floor, your code will play sound of a basketball hitting the floor. In addition, your code will play background music.

Attaching Code to the Basketball Menu Item of the Sound Menu

You'll now add the code that's executed when the user selects Basketball from the Sound menu:

☐ Select the IDR_MYANIM_MENU item in the Project Workspace window.

☐ Select ClassWizard from the View menu.

☐ Select the ID_SOUND_BASKETBALL item from the Object IDs list, select COM-MAND in the Messages list, then click the Add Function button.

Visual C++ responds by suggesting OnSoundBasketball *as the new function's name.*

☐ Accept the function name that Visual C++ suggests, then click the Edit Code button.

☐ Enter code in the OnSoundBasketball() function as follows:

```
void CMyAnimDlg::OnSoundBasketball()
{
// TODO: Add your command handler code here

////////////////////////
// MY CODE STARTS HERE
////////////////////////

// Toggle the state of the Basketball menu item.
CMenu* pMenu = GetMenu();
UINT MenuState = pMenu->GetMenuState(ID_SOUND_BASKETBALL,0);
if (MenuState==MF_CHECKED)
   MenuState=MF_UNCHECKED;
else
   MenuState=MF_CHECKED;
pMenu->CheckMenuItem(ID_SOUND_BASKETBALL,MenuState);

////////////////////////
// MY CODE ENDS HERE
////////////////////////

}
```

☐ Save your work.

The code that you typed toggles the state of the Basketball menu item. If the Basketball menu item currently has a check mark next to it, then after the user selects Basketball from the Sound menu, the check mark will be removed. And if the Basketball menu item currently does not have a check mark next to it, then after the user selects Basketball from the Sound menu, a check mark will be placed next to the Basketball menu item.

Playing the Sound of a Basketball Hitting the Floor

In the previous section, you wrote the code that lets the user place and remove a check mark from the Basketball item of the Sound menu. You'll now write the code that actually plays the sound of a basketball hitting the floor. This code will play the sound, provided that the Basketball menu item currently has a check mark next to it.

☐ Add the following statements at the end of the OnTimer() function in the MyAnimDlg.CPP file:

```
// If the current displayed frame is
// frame #4, and the Basketball menu
// item is checked, play the Basket.WAV
// sound file.
if (CurrentFrame==4)
   {
   CMenu* pMenu = GetMenu();
   UINT MenuState = pMenu->GetMenuState(ID_SOUND_BASKETBALL,0);
   if (MenuState==MF_CHECKED)
       m_snd.PlayWavFile("Basket.WAV",0,-1);
   }
```

After adding these statements to the OnTimer() function, your OnTimer() function should look as follows:

```
void CMyAnimDlg::OnTimer(UINT nIDEvent)
{
// TODO: Add your message handler code here and/or call default

//////////////////////////
// MY CODE STARTS HERE
//////////////////////////

// Display the next frame of the animation.
long CurrentFrame = m_bmp.GetCurrentFrame();
CurrentFrame = CurrentFrame + 1;
m_bmp.SetCurrentFrame(CurrentFrame);

// If the current displayed frame is
// frame #4, and the Basketball menu
// item is checked, play the Basket.WAV
// sound file.
if (CurrentFrame==4)
   {
   CMenu* pMenu = GetMenu();
   UINT MenuState = pMenu->GetMenuState(ID_SOUND_BASKETBALL,0);
   if (MenuState==MF_CHECKED)
       m_snd.PlayWavFile("Basket.WAV",0,-1);
   }

//////////////////////
// MY CODE ENDS HERE
//////////////////////

CDialog::OnTimer(nIDEvent);
}
```

21

☐ Save your work.

The code that you typed uses if statements to determine whether the currently displayed frame is frame number 4 and the Basketball menu item has a check mark next to it. If this is the case, the WAV file Basket.WAV is played using the following statement:

```
m_snd.PlayWavFile("Basket.WAV",0,-1);
```

This statement executes the PlayWavFile() method of the Sound ActiveX control to play the WAV file Basket.WAV. The first parameter of the PlayWavFile() function specifies the filename of the WAV file to be played. When the WAV filename is specified without the full directory pathname, the WAV file is assumed to reside on the current directory. As discussed earlier in this chapter, when you execute the program from within Visual C++, the current directory is the directory where the program's project resides. And when you run the program from Windows, the current directory is the directory where the program's EXE file resides.

The second parameter of the PlayWavFile() method specifies the starting point of the section to be played in units of milliseconds. The third parameter of the PlayWavFile() method specifies the end point of the section to be played in units of milliseconds. When the third parameter is set to -1, as in the preceding code, the WAV file will be played in its entirety. When the third parameter is set to -2, the WAV file will be played in a continuous loop. That is, once the playback reaches the end of the file, the playback starts all over again.

Attaching Code to the Music Menu Item of the Sound Menu

You'll now add the code that's executed when the user selects Music from the Sound menu:

☐ Select the IDR_MYANIM_MENU item in the Project Workspace window.

☐ Select ClassWizard from the View menu.

☐ Select the ID_SOUND_MUSIC item from the Object IDs list, select COMMAND in the Messages list, then click the Add Function button.

Visual C++ responds by suggesting OnSoundMusic *as the new function's name.*

☐ Accept the function name that Visual C++ suggests, then click the Edit Code button.

☐ Enter code in the OnSoundMusic() function as follows:

```
void CMyAnimDlg::OnSoundMusic()
{
// TODO: Add your command handler code here

/////////////////////////
// MY CODE STARTS HERE
/////////////////////////
```

21

```
    // Toggle the state of the Music menu item,
    CMenu* pMenu = GetMenu();
    UINT MenuState = pMenu->GetMenuState(ID_SOUND_MUSIC,0);
    if (MenuState==MF_CHECKED)
       MenuState=MF_UNCHECKED;
    else
       MenuState=MF_CHECKED;
    pMenu->CheckMenuItem(ID_SOUND_MUSIC,MenuState);

    // Play or stop playing the MyMidi MIDI file
    // according to the new state of the Music
    // menu item.
    if (MenuState==MF_CHECKED)
       m_snd.PlayMidiFile("MyMidi.MID",0,-2);
    else
       m_snd.StopMidi();

    //////////////////////
    // MY CODE ENDS HERE
    //////////////////////
    }
```

☐ Save your work.

The first block of code that you typed in the OnSoundMusic() function is

```
CMenu* pMenu = GetMenu();
UINT MenuState = pMenu->GetMenuState(ID_SOUND_MUSIC,0);
if (MenuState==MF_CHECKED)
   MenuState=MF_UNCHECKED;
else
   MenuState=MF_CHECKED;
pMenu->CheckMenuItem(ID_SOUND_MUSIC,MenuState);
```

This code toggles the state of the Music menu item. If the Music menu item currently has a check mark next to it, then after the user selects Music from the Sound menu, the check mark will be removed. And if the Music menu item currently does not have a check mark next to it, then after the user selects Music from the Sound menu, a check mark will be placed next to the Music menu item.

The second block of code that you typed in the OnSoundMusic() function is the following:

```
if (MenuState==MF_CHECKED)
   m_snd.PlayMidiFile("MyMidi.MID",0,-2);
else
   m_snd.StopMidi();
```

If the Music menu item now has a check mark next to it, this code plays the MyMidi.MID file using the following statement:

```
m_snd.PlayMidiFile("MyMidi.MID",0,-2);
```

21

This statement executes the PlayMidiFile() function of the Sound ActiveX control to play the MIDI file MyMidi.MID. The PlayMidi() function is similar to the PlayWavFile() function that was discussed in the previous section. The only difference is that the PlayMidiFile() function is used for playing a MIDI file (not a WAV file). Notice that in the preceding statement, the third parameter of the PlayMidiFile() function is set to -2. When the third parameter is set to -2, the MIDI file will be played in a continuous loop. That is, once the playback reaches the end of the file, the playback starts all over again.

If the Music menu item does not have a check mark next to it, the preceding code stops the MIDI file playback using the following statement:

```
m_snd.StopMidi();
```

This statement uses the StopMidi() function of the Sound ActiveX control to stop the MIDI playback.

The MyAnim.EXE program is now completed. To see (or rather hear) your sound code in action, follow these steps:

☐ Build and execute the program.

☐ Experiment with the Sound menu and make sure that it works as expected.

☐ Terminate the program by selecting Exit from the File menu.

DirectSound Technology

The MyAnim program that you implemented in this chapter demonstrates how your Visual C++ programs can play WAV and MIDI sound files using the Sound ActiveX control.

Sound cards are very popular, and today many PCs have sound cards installed in them. In fact, sound cards became so popular that a new technology called DirectSound evolved. You will not be instructed to implement a DirectSound program in this chapter, but you should be aware of this fascinating and powerful technology.

DirectSound Features

When using DirectSound technology, you can play WAV sound files (just as you can play WAV files with the standard multimedia technology). However, when using DirectSound, you have the following important additional features:

■ *You can play several WAV files simultaneously.* You simply specify the names of the WAV files that you want to play, and the sound card plays the sound files simultaneously.

21

■ *Volume control.* With DirectSound, you can adjust the volume of the sound files. When you play several sound files simultaneously, you can adjust the volume of the individual sound files. As you can imagine, you can create some amazing sound special effects with this feature. For example, you can display images that make sounds. As the user gets closer to the image that makes the sound, the volume becomes louder, and as the user gets away from the image that makes the sound, the sound becomes weaker.

■ *Panning control.* You can distribute different amounts of sound to the left and right speakers of the sound card. For example, you can play 30 percent of the volume through the left speaker and 70 percent of the volume through the right speaker. This volume distribution is called *panning.* As you can imagine, you can create some amazing sound effects with the panning feature. For example, you can display pictures of several images that make sound. As the user gets farther away from one image and gets closer to another image, the volume from one object becomes weaker and the sound from the other object becomes louder. Furthermore, depending on the user's current position, the sound that the left and right speakers produce can be made weaker or stronger in relation to the user's current position. For example, if the user's current position is to the left of an object that produces sound, the right speaker plays the sound. If the user is to the right of the object, the left speaker produces sound.

With the volume control and panning features of DirectSound, you can create some additional amazing sound effects. Consider, for example, displaying a projectile traveling from left to right on your screen. You can add synchronized sound to the animation that makes the sound of projectiles flying from left to right by first playing 100 percent of the volume through the left speaker. As the projectile flies to the right, you weaken the sound through the left speaker and start making the sound through the right speaker louder.

■ *Playback speed.* You can change the playback speed of the sound. When playing several sound files, you can change the playback speed of the individual sound files.

When using an ActiveX control, you can implement DirectSound technology in your program with great ease. It is recommended that you execute some DirectSound demo programs by loading them from the following Internet URL addresses. This way, you'll be able to hear DirectSound in action:

☐ Use your Internet connection to connect to the Internet.

☐ Use your Internet browser program to log into the following Internet URL address:

```
http://www.tegosoft.com/bkinstdx.html
```

21

☐ Follow the directions given on the preceding HTML page to download the MixerDX2.EXE file and save it on your hard drive.

☐ Follow the directions given on the preceding HTML page to install the MixerDX2.EXE file.

 NOTE

To be able to see DirectSound in action, you have to install DirectX. Follow the directions in the preceding HTML page to install DirectX. DirectX is discussed later in this chapter.

That's it. You now have the mixer program installed in your PC.

☐ Execute the mixer program that you downloaded and installed.

The window of the mixer program is shown in Figure 21.17.

☐ Experiment with the mixer program. In particular, load several WAV files, play them simultaneously, change the playback speed of the WAV files, change the volume of the WAV sound files, and pan the sound files to the right and left speakers. (All these operations are accomplished by using the scroll bars of the mixer program, as shown in Figure 21.17.)

Figure 21.17.

A mixer program that illustrates the power of DirectSound to play several sound files simultaneously.

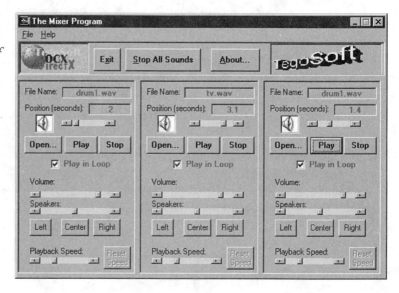

DirectX Technology

DirectSound is actually a part of a technology called DirectX. The two main components of DirectX are

- DirectSound
- DirectDraw

You already saw the power of DirectSound in action. Just as DirectSound lets you use the sound card in the most powerful manner, DirectDraw lets you use the video card in the most powerful manner. To understand the importance of DirectDraw, let's review the device independence feature of Windows.

The Device Independence Feature of Windows

One of the main features that made Windows so popular is its device independence. When you write a Windows program (such as with Visual C++), you, the programmer, do not have to worry about things such as which video card is used, which printer is used, which sound card is used, or any of the other peripherals of the PC. For example, when your program issues a print command to the printer, the printer should print no matter who is the manufacturer of the printer. Windows converts the print command of your program to a print command that is understood by the printer. This conversion is performed with the help of the driver program of the printer. How does Windows know to perform this conversion? When the owner of the PC installed the printer, Windows either accepted or rejected the printer (together with the driver of the printer). Thereafter, Windows knows which printer to use and can convert any print command from any Windows program to a command understood by the printer. The same goes for other peripherals. There are many types of mouse devices in the market, but your program does not care which particular mouse device is installed in the PC. As long as the mouse was accepted by Windows, Windows will respect mouse move events, mouse clicks, and so on.

When it comes to a device such as the printer, the extra time that it takes to convert print commands from the program to commands understood by the printer is insignificant. A printer (even a laser printer) is a mechanical device. The time it takes to rotate mechanical wheels and to push papers is much larger than the time it takes to convert software commands. However, when it comes to a device such as the video card, it's a different story. Typically, you want your video card to react immediately to video commands from the program. When your program moves pictures on the screen, Windows first has to convert the commands to commands understood by the video card. However, due to the fact that Windows has to "consult" the driver of the video card and convert the commands to commands understood

21

by the video card, a lot of time is spent during the conversion. This causes annoying flickering and delays when moving graphic objects on the screen.

The old DOS operating system does a much better job when it comes to video cards. In DOS programs, the programs can access the memory of the video card *directly*. That is, the video card has memory cells, where each memory cell corresponds to one pixel on the screen. This memory cell determines the location and color of the pixel. (Depending on the particular video card, the number of memory cells that correspond to a single pixel vary—the more colors the video card supports, the more memory cells are needed to describe one pixel.) In any case, in DOS, the DOS program can access the memory of the video card directly. The moment the program changes the contents of a memory cell on the video card, the pixel that corresponds to the memory cell changes almost instantaneously. This is why some powerful game programs are DOS programs, not Windows programs. (The problem with DOS, however, is that this operating system is device-dependent. A program that works for one video card does not work on another video card from a different manufacturer or even a different model from the same manufacturer.)

Microsoft realized the limitation of Windows and released the DirectX technology. As implied by its name, DirectDraw (which is that portion of DirectX that is responsible for accessing the video card) performs an almost direct access of the video card. In essence, DirectX includes a large collection of video card drivers. When the program draws something into the screen, due to DirectDraw, the commands are "converted" very fast and the drawing accomplished immediately, without flickering.

Windows is also called a Graphical Operating System. Graphical Operating System means that the operating system uses graphic objects such as command buttons, scroll bars, check boxes, and so on. It does not mean that Windows was designed to perform fast graphical operations such as moving graphic objects. Rather, it means that the operating system uses graphic objects. In fact, as previously discussed, Windows is not the right operating system for performing fast graphics operations.

The graphics limitation of Windows was removed after the introduction of DirectX. Combining Windows and DirectX gives one of the most powerful tools for performing fast graphic operations. With the help of DirectX ActiveX controls, you can develop amazing Visual C++ programs with great ease.

21

Take a look at some DirectX programs in action:

☐ Use your Internet connection to connect to the Internet.

☐ Use your Internet browser program to log into the following Internet URL address:

    http://www.tegosoft.com/bk3dsound.html

☐ Follow the directions given on the preceding HTML page to download the 3DSnd.EXE file and save it on your hard drive.

☐ Follow the directions given on the preceding HTML page to install the 3DSnd.EXE file.

The 3-D Sound program that you installed in the previous step utilizes both DirectSound and DirectDraw technologies. The 3-D Sound lets the user use the mouse and the keyboard to travel in a 3-D picture, encountering various animated objects. (See Figures 21.18, 21.19, and 21.20.) As the user gets closer or farther away from the object, the sound that the objects make gets louder and stronger. For example, when the user is between the elephant and the horse, the user hears both animal sounds. Similarly, when the user gets closer to the belly dancer, the dancer's music gets louder. The program gives a very realistic feeling of traveling in a real world that has animated objected and real sound in it. This type of program is therefore appropriately referred to as *virtual reality*.

Figure 21.18.

When traveling in the 3-D picture, the user encounters an animated elephant.

21

Figure 21.19.
When traveling in the 3-D picture, the user encounters a belly dancer.

Figure 21.20.
When traveling in the 3-D picture, the user encounters an animated horse.

3-D Virtual Reality Programs

As stated, a program that lets users feel as if they are moving in a real world is called a 3-D virtual reality program. Typically, the user uses the mouse or the keyboard to move in the 3-D picture. Often, a 3-D virtual reality program also enables the user to use various tools (for example, a gun to shoot bad creatures, a pencil to write, and so on).

It is obvious from the description of the 3-D virtual reality program that a DirectX technology is needed. Note the huge amount of graphic operations that are performed during the execution of the program: The program has to display new 3-D pictures for each movement of the mouse or the keyboard. That is, the PC has to compute the next 3-D picture to be displayed, which is a small deviation from the current picture being displayed. This must be performed very fast so that the user will get the feeling of smooth moving. Furthermore, the user can encounter animated objects, the user can interact with the objects (using tools such a gun or pencil), and the PC also has to take care of sound playback (which, in the case of DirectSound, means that several sounds are played simultaneously). The walls of the 3-D pictures can be made of any material (wood, marble, and so on). This adds additional graphic burden on the PC, which has to display these textured walls. Don't forget that as the user gets closer or farther away from an object, the object is displayed differently (smaller or larger depending on the user's distance from the object). The volume of the sound depends on the distance of the user from the object that makes the sound. No doubt, the PC has to work hard and fast to perform all these operations. Indeed, Windows DirectX is the perfect tool to accomplish this.

To see such a 3-D virtual reality program that uses DirectX in action:

☐ Use your Internet connection to connect to the Internet.

☐ Use your Internet browser program to log into the following Internet URL address:

    `http://www.tegosoft.com/bkdown3dvr.html`

☐ Follow the directions given on the preceding HTML page to download the Teg3D.exe file and save it on your hard drive.

☐ Follow the directions given on the preceding HTML page to install the Teg3D.exe file.

Figures 21.21 through 21.24 show some of the things that the user encounters while traveling in the 3-D world.

Figure 21.21.

A waving flag in one of the rooms of the 3-D virtual reality program. The user can see what is going on in the adjacent room through the window.

21

Figure 21.22.

One of the rooms of the 3-D virtual reality program has a TV in it. The TV displays a sport show (pictures and sound).

Figure 21.23.

One of the rooms of the 3-D virtual reality program shows a basketball player dribbling a basketball.

NOTE

There are many applications where DirectSound and 3-D virtual reality are applicable. Of course, the first application that comes to mind is game applications. However, the popularity of DirectX is increasing, and many programmers apply this technology for many other types of programming. For example, this technology is frequently used in business applications for demonstrating products (hardware products where the "real" product can be displayed as well as software products). A virtual showroom can be easily implemented with DirectX technology. DirectX is, of course, helpful in education applications, advertising applications, and many other types of applications.

21

Figure 21.24.

The Presidents room has pictures of presidents on the walls.

Summary

In this chapter, you have learned how to use the BMP ActiveX control to display an animation show. You also learned how to use the Sound ActiveX control for adding WAV file playback and MIDI file playback to your program.

At the end of this chapter you learned about the DirectX technology.

Q&A

Q In the MyAnim.EXE program that I wrote in this chapter, I wrote code that installs a timer with a 50 milliseconds interval. Why was 50 chosen as the timer interval?

A Depending on the animation show that you are displaying, you may choose a different value for the timer interval. You can determine which interval is the most realistic by trial and error. You can also write a program that includes a scroll bar that enables the user to set the timer interval.

Quiz

1. Assuming you attached the variable m_bmp to a BMP ActiveX control, what does the following code do?

```
m_bmp.SetFrame(0,"MyPic1.BMP");
m_bmp.SetFrame(1,"MyPic2.BMP");
m_bmp.SetFrame(2,"MyPic3.BMP");
```

21

2. Assuming you attached the variable m_snd to a Sound ActiveX control, what does the following statement do?

```
m_snd.PlayWavFile("MyWav.WAV",0,-2);
```

3. Assuming you attached the variable m_snd to a Sound ActiveX control, what does the following statement do?

```
m_snd.PlayMidiFile("MyMidi.MID",0,-1);
```

4. Assuming you attached the variable m_snd to a Sound ActiveX control, what does the following statement do?

```
m_snd.PlayWavFile("MyWav.WAV",0,3000);
```

Exercise

Currently, upon starting the MyAnim.EXE program, the Basketball menu item of the Sound menu does not have a check mark next to it. Enhance the MyAnim.EXE program so that upon starting the program, the Basketball menu item will have a check mark next to it. To solve this Exercise, follow the steps in the Exercise Answer.

Quiz Answers

1. These statements fill three frames of the BMP control with pictures of three BMP files: MyPic1.BMP, MyPic2.BMP, and MyPic3.BMP. Because the full pathnames of these BMP files are not specified, the program assumes that these BMP files reside in the current directory.

2. This statement plays the WAV file MyWav.WAV in a continuous loop.

3. This statement plays the MIDI file MyMidi.MID from beginning to end.

4. This statement plays the first 3000 milliseconds (3 seconds) of the WAV file MyWav.WAV.

Exercise Answer

Follow these steps to solve the exercise:

☐ Add the following statements at the end of the OnInitDialog() function in the MyAnimDlg.CPP file:

```
// Place check mark next to the Basketball
// menu item of the Sound menu.
CMenu* pMenu = GetMenu();
pMenu->CheckMenuItem(ID_SOUND_BASKETBALL,MF_CHECKED);
```

After adding these statements to the OnInitDialog() function, your OnInitDialog() function should look as follows:

```
BOOL CMyAnimDlg::OnInitDialog()
{
CDialog::OnInitDialog();
…
…
…

// TODO: Add extra initialization here

/////////////////////////
// MY CODE STARTS HERE
/////////////////////////

// Initialize the program's window width and
// height to 300 X 220.
SetWindowPos(NULL,NULL,NULL,300,220,SWP_NOMOVE);

// Load the BMP control with the 5 frames of the animation show.
m_bmp.SetFrame(0,"Basket1.BMP");
m_bmp.SetFrame(1,"Basket2.BMP");
m_bmp.SetFrame(2,"Basket3.BMP");
m_bmp.SetFrame(3,"Basket4.BMP");
m_bmp.SetFrame(4,"Basket5.BMP");

// Install a 50 milliseconds timer.
SetTimer(1, 50, NULL);

// Place a check mark next to the Basketball
// menu item of the Sound menu.
CMenu* pMenu = GetMenu();
pMenu->CheckMenuItem(ID_SOUND_BASKETBALL,MF_CHECKED);

/////////////////////////
// MY CODE ENDS HERE
/////////////////////////

return TRUE;  // return TRUE  unless you set the focus
              // to a control
}
```

☐ Save your work, then build and execute the MyAnim program, and verify that upon starting the program, the Basketball menu item has a check mark next to it.

21

APPENDIX

A

Learning C/C++ Quickly (Part I)

Appendixes A, B, and C assume that you have no previous experience with the C/C++ programming language, but you'll learn C/C++ quickly in these appendixes. This book teaches you how to use Visual C++ for designing and using Windows programs. Naturally, you need some knowledge of C/C++ programming to use the Visual C++ package. The appendixes teach you everything you need to know about C/C++ for this book. Here is the bottom line: If you have never used C/C++ before, these appendixes are for you. After reading Appendixes A, B, and C, you'll have all the know-how needed for this book's chapters.

NOTE   Additional C/C++ topics are presented during the course of this book on a need-to-know-basis as you work through the book's programs.

Creating Console Applications

Visual C++ has the capability of creating *console applications,* which are basically DOS programs executed in a Windows shell. The objective of this book is to teach you how to write C++ Windows applications with the Visual C++ package. Why, then, does this tutorial cover console applications? As you know, PC vendors are shipping their PCs with Windows 95 already installed. So why would anybody want to learn about console applications?

To use Visual C++ to write Windows applications, you need to know some basic C/C++ topics. However, even the simplest Windows program is long and contains several overhead files. Therefore, it is much easier to learn the basics of C/C++ by writing simple console applications than by writing Windows programs.

Writing a Simple Console Application with Visual C++

In this tutorial, you'll write a simple C++ DOS (console) program with Visual C++. You'll save the program you develop in this tutorial in the C:\TYVCPROG\PROGRAMS\APPENDA directory. Follow these steps to begin:

☐ Create the C:\TYVCPROG\PROGRAMS\APPENDA directory.

☐ Start Visual C++. (See Figure A.1.)

> *Windows responds by running the Visual C++ program, and the desktop of Visual C++ is displayed, as shown in Figure A.2.*

Figure A.1.

*The Visual C++
program icon.*

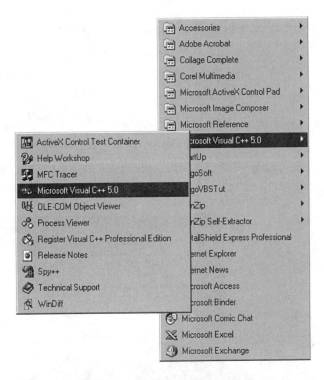

Figure A.2.

*The Microsoft Visual
C++ window.*

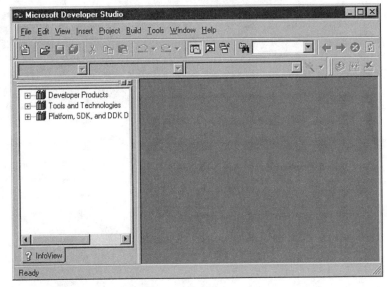

Depending on the setting of your Visual C++, the desktop you see on your PC may look a little different from the one shown in Figure A.2. For now, don't worry about this.

Here is how you create a new project for a console application with Visual C++:

☐ Select New from the File menu of Visual C++.

Visual C++ responds by displaying the New dialog box.

☐ Make sure that the Projects tab of the New dialog box is selected.

☐ Select the Win32 Console Application item in the list of project types, because you're creating a project for a console application. (See Figure A.3.)

Figure A.3.

Creating a new project for a console application.

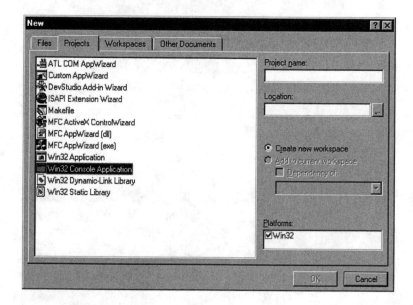

☐ Type MyHello in the Project name box.

☐ Click the button that is located on the right of the Location box and select the C:\TYVCPROG\PROGRAMS\APPENDA directory.

☐ Click the OK button of the New dialog box.

Visual C++ responds by creating the project for your new console application. As shown in Figure A.4, the Project Workspace window for the project (the MyHello project) appears.

Figure A.4.

The Project Workspace window for the MyHello project.

The Project Workspace window ———

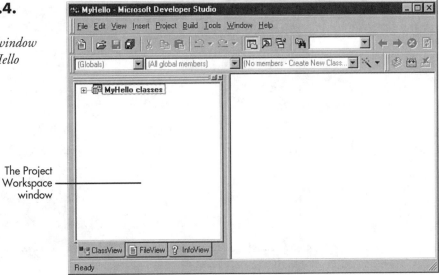

As you can see, the Project Workspace window has three tabs: ClassView, FileView, and InfoView. You'll use the Project Workspace window throughout this book.

As yet, you did not add any files to the MyHello project. Thus, the MyHello project is currently empty. You'll now add a new file to the MyHello project:

☐ Select New from the File menu.

Visual C++ responds by displaying the New dialog box.

☐ Make sure that the Files tab of the New dialog box is selected and select C++ Source File in the list of file types.

☐ Type MyHello.cpp in the File Name edit box. That is, the name of the new file that you are adding to the project is MyHello.cpp. The file extension .cpp is used for source code files in Visual C++. You write the source code of your Visual C++ programs in a file whose extension is .cpp.

Your New dialog box should now look as shown in Figure A.5.

☐ Click the OK button of the new dialog box.

Visual C++ responds by adding the new file MyHello.cpp to the MyHello project and diplaying the window of the MyHello.cpp file so that you'll be able to write code inside it. (See Figure A.6.)

You'll write the code of the MyHello program in the MyHello.cpp file.

Figure A.5.
Adding a new file to the project.

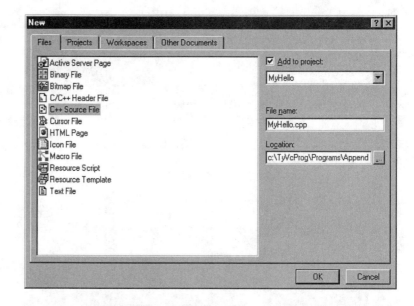

Figure A.6.
The MyHello.cpp file, ready to be edited by you.

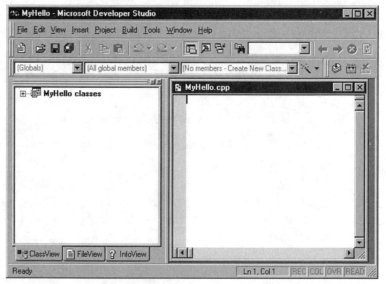

Writing the Code of the MyHello.cpp Program

Now you are ready to write the C++ code of the program, which you will type in the MyHello.cpp window:

A

☐ Type the following code in the MyHello.cpp file:

```
// Program Name: MyHello.cpp

#include <iostream.h>

void main()
{

cout << "Hello, this is my first C++ program \n";

}
```

The MyHello.cpp window should now look like the one shown in Figure A.7.

Figure A.7.
The MyHello.cpp window with code in it.

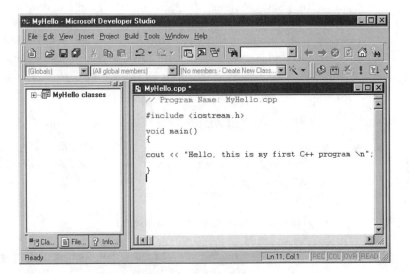

If you have never written C/C++ code before, the code you typed may look as if it came from outer space. But don't worry; the code will be explained later in this chapter. For now, save your work:

☐ Make sure that MyHello.cpp window is selected and choose Save All from the File menu of Visual C++.

Compiling and Linking the MyHello.cpp Program

You'll now compile and link the MyHello program. What does it mean to compile and link? Take a look at Figure A.8, which is a pictorial representation of the compiling and linking process.

Figure A.8.

*Compiling and
linking the MyHello
program.*

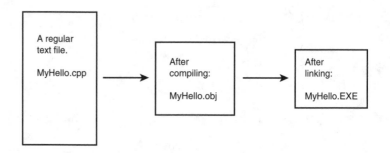

The compiler is a program that comes with Visual C++. It processes the MyHello.cpp text
file to create a new file called MyHello.obj. What can you do with the MyHello.obj file?
Practically nothing! The MyHello.obj file is an intermediate file used by another program
called the linker program, which also comes with Visual C++. The linker program processes
the MyHello.obj file to create a new file called MyHello.EXE—the final program file. You
execute the MyHello.EXE program like any other program.

Try compiling and linking the MyHello program:

☐ Select Build MyHello.EXE from the Build menu of Visual C++.

*Visual C++ responds by compiling the MyHello.cpp file (to create the MyHello.obj file),
then linking the MyHello program (to create the MyHello.EXE file). If you typed the code
of the MyHello.cpp file exactly as you were instructed, Visual C++ displays the following
message (see Figure A.9):*

```
MyHello.exe - 0 error(s). 0 warnings)
```

Figure A.9.

*After compiling and
linking the
MyHello.EXE
program.*

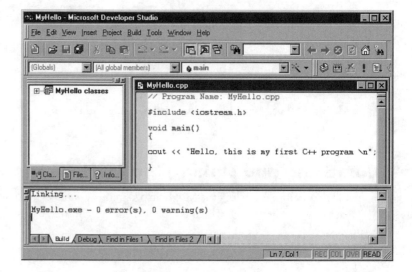

If you didn't type the code exactly as you were instructed, Visual C++ will tell you that errors occurred during the process of compiling and linking the program. In this case, make the appropriate corrections in the MyHello.cpp window, then select Build MyHello.EXE from the Build menu again.

NOTE

C/C++ is case-sensitive. For example, you were instructed to type the following line in the MyHello.cpp file:

```
void main()
```

If you typed `void Main()` instead of `void main()`, or `Void main()` instead of `void main()`, you got errors.

Don't forget to type the semicolon (;) at the end of the line that starts with the word `cout`.

The window at the bottom of the desktop, shown in Figure A.9, is called the *output window*. This window displays the results of the compiling and linking process. When the output window contains the message `0 error(s)`, `0 warning(s)`, this window is referred to as the "happy window" because you are supposed to be happy when you receive 0 errors.

NOTE

When you want to display the output window, select Output from the View menu.

You can enlarge the output window by placing the mouse cursor on its upper edge and dragging the mouse upward. Notice that the output window has several tabs: Build, Debug, Find in Files 1, and Find in Files 2. To view the results of the compiling and linking, make sure that the Build tab is selected, as it is in Figure A.9.

If you did not get the `0 error(s)` message, display the MyHello.cpp file and make sure you typed everything without any syntax errors:

☐ Select Windows from the Window menu to display the Windows dialog box, then select the MyHello.cpp item and click the Activate button.

Executing the MyHello.EXE Program

Once you compile and link the MyHello program without any errors, you can execute the MyHello.EXE program.

☐ Select Execute MyHello.EXE from the Build menu.

Visual C++ responds by executing the MyHello.EXE program, and the window shown in Figure A.10 appears.

Figure A.10.
Executing the MyHello.EXE program.

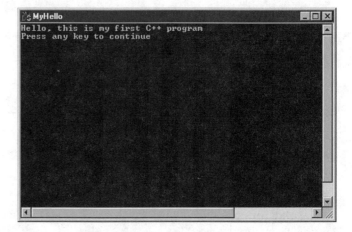

☐ Press any key on your keyboard to terminate the MyHello program.

As you can see from Figure A.10, the MyHello.EXE program displays this message:

```
Hello, this is my first C++ program
```

Examining the MyHello.cpp Program's Code

In reviewing the code of the MyHello.cpp program, you'll notice that the code contains // (backslash) characters. Comments in C++ start with the // characters. For example, the following is a valid C++ comment:

```
// This is my comment.
```

When the compiler "works" on the MyHello.cpp text file, it ignores every line that starts with the // characters.

Here is another example of four comment lines in C++:

```
/////////////////////////////////////
//    This is my comment.
//    I can write here whatever I want.
/////////////////////////////////////
```

Why Use C/C++?

In the beginning, there was the C programming language, invented about two decades ago. It became the most popular programming language for generating professional applications; as a matter of fact, a big portion of the Windows operating system was written with the C programming language. So, if Microsoft chose C to be the programming language for its major product, there must be something good about C. C is successful for several reasons:

- C generates standalone .EXE files. Once you finish creating a program with a C compiler/linker, the result is a file with an .EXE file extension. The .EXE file is the file you distribute to your users; you don't need to distribute any other file with your .EXE file.
- The .EXE file that C generates is a small file.
- C has proved to be a reliable, easy-to-use programming language.
- C compiler/linkers are available at reasonable prices from major software vendors.
- The EXE programs generated by a C compiler/linker are executed quickly by the computer.
- The processes of compiling a .cpp file into an .obj file and linking an .obj file to an .EXE file go very fast.

OK, C is a successful product! But during the past two decades, C programmers accumulated much experience and started to demand more from C. Committees were established to consider suggestions, recommendations, and comments from C users. Eventually, a new programming language was conceived—the C++ programming language.

You could think of C++ as the second version of C. As you'll learn during the course of this tutorial, C++ lets you write *object-oriented programs,* which deal with classes and objects. You'll learn about these topics later in this tutorial.

The #include Statement

The first line you typed in the MyHello.cpp file is a comment line. This is the second line:

```
#include <iostream.h>
```

This statement tells the compiler to do the following:

```
"As you compile the MyHello.cpp file, make use of the iostream.h file."
```

The iostream.h file came with your Visual C++ program. (Later in this chapter, you'll see why you need to tell the compiler to use the iostream.h file.) You then typed the following code:

```
void main()
{

cout << "Hello, this is my first C++ program \n";

}
```

The first line includes the `main()` function:

```
void main()
```

A *function* is a block of code enclosed by curly brackets. The following is an example of a function called `MyFunction`:

```
void MyFunction()
{

// You type the code of the MyFunction() function here

}
```

Later in this tutorial, you'll learn about the `void` word and the parentheses `()` that come after the function name.

Why did we choose to name the function `main()`? Because in C/C++ programs, you must include a function called `main()`. When you execute the MyHello.cpp program, the `main()` function is executed first.

The Code in the `main()` Function

A function's code is typed between the curly brackets. In the MyHello program, you typed the following statement in the `main()` function:

```
cout << "Hello, this is my first C++ program \n";
```

The most important thing you should know about the preceding statement is that it must end with the semicolon character (;). Every C++ statement must end with a semicolon.

The word `cout` causes the PC to display the text appearing after the `<<` characters, so the preceding statement causes the PC to display this text:

```
Hello, this is my first C++ program
```

The `\n` characters are the carriage-return/line-feed characters. By including the `\n` characters, you are telling the PC to advance to the next line on the screen after displaying the text `Hello, this is my first C++ program`. Also, notice that the text you typed (including the `\n` characters) must be enclosed in double quotes (`" "`).

`cout` causes the PC to display characters on the screen, so you could think of `cout` as a function that performs something. But where is the code of `cout`? Who wrote the code that actually sends characters to the screen? Well, it all came with Visual C++, but you have to tell the compiler that `cout` is a preprepared function. In fact, all the information about the exact nature of `cout` is stored in a file called iostream.h. This is why you included the following statement at the beginning of the program:

```
#include <iostream.h>
```

A

NOTE

You can exit Visual C++ now and continue with the project at a later time. Here is how you reload the project:

☐ Start Visual C++.

☐ Select Open Workspace from the File menu and select MyHello.dsw from the C:\TYVCPROG\PROGRAMS\APPENDA\MYHELLO directory.

Visual C++ responds by loading the MyHello project so you can continue with the development of the project.

☐ Click the FileView tab on the bottom of the Project Workspace window.

☐ Click the + icon to the left of the MyHello Files item in the Project Workspace window.

Visual C++ responds by expanding the MyHello files item. Because there is only one file in this project (the MyHello.cpp file), only the MyHello.cpp item appears below the MyHello files item.

☐ Double-click the MyHello.cpp item to display the MyHello.cpp file.

Modifying the MyHello Program

You'll now modify the MyHello program so that it will display the following lines:

```
Hi, this is my first line!
Hi again, this is my second line!!
Hi again, this is my third line!!!
```

☐ Modify the code in the MyHello.cpp file as follows:

```cpp
// Program Name: MyHello.cpp

#include <iostream.h>

void main()
{

//cout << "Hello, this is my first C++ program \n";

cout << "Hi, this is my first line! \n";
cout <<  "Hi again, this is my second line!! \n";
cout << "Hi again, this is my third line!!! \n";

}
```

You commented out the first cout statement:

```
//cout << "Hello, this is my first C++ program \n";
```

Then three cout statements are executed. Each cout statement displays a different message:

```
cout << "Hi, this is my first line! \n";
cout <<  "Hi again, this is my second line!! \n";
cout << "Hi again, this is my third line!!! \n";
```

Again, note that each statement is terminated with the semicolon character.

☐ Select Save All from the File menu to save your work.

☐ Select Build MyHello.EXE from the Build menu.

☐ If you got 0 errors, select Execute MyHello.EXE from the Build menu. (If you got errors in the previous step, make sure you typed the code exactly as you were instructed, and try to build the program again.)

After executing the MyHello program, the window shown in Figure A.11 appears. As you can see, the three messages appear as dictated by the cout statements. Note that the last line, Press any key to continue, is inserted automatically for you; you didn't have to write any code to display that message.

Figure A.11.
The output window of the MyHello program.

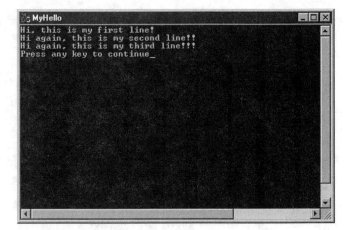

☐ Press any key to terminate the program.

Performing Addition with the MyHello Program

You'll now further modify the MyHello program. In particular, you'll type code that performs addition with two numbers.

☐ Modify the MyHello.cpp file so that it will look like the following:

```
// Program Name: MyHello.cpp

#include <iostream.h>

void main()
{

int iNum1;
int iNum2;
int iResult;

iNum1 = 2;
iNum2 = 3;
iResult = iNum1 + iNum2;

cout << "The result is: \n";
cout << iResult;
cout << "\n";

}
```

First, you deleted the previous code in the main() function, so now it starts with the following statement:

```
int iNum1;
```

The preceding statement defines a variable called iNum1. In C++, you must define the variables before using them. A *variable* contains data, and the iNum1 variable is used for storing the number 2. When defining the variable, you must tell the compiler the name of the variable—in this case iNum1—as well as the type of variable. That is, will the iNum1 variable store text? integers? floating numbers (numbers with fractions)? You preceded the name of the variable with the word int, which means you're telling the compiler that the iNum1 number is defined as an integer.

NOTE

You defined the variable as int and named it iNum1. Another data type in C/C++ is char. A char variable stores a character. For example, the following statement defines the cMyCharacter variable:

```
char cMyCharacter;
```

Note that the name of the cMyCharacter variable is preceded with the letter c and the variable iNum1 is preceded with the letter i. Why? So that it will be easy to read the program. The prefix letters will tell you that iNum1 is a variable declared as int (integer) or that cMyCharacter is a variable declared as char (character).

C++ doesn't require you to precede the names of the variables with letters, but it does make your program easier to read and understand.

You then declared two more variables, iNum2 and iResult:

```
int iNum2;
int iResult;
```

At this point in your program, you have declared three integer variables: iNum1, iNum2, and iResult. You then set the value of iNum1 as follows:

```
iNum1 = 2;
```

From now on, iNum1 is equal to 2.

NOTE

> You set the value of the iNum1 variable as follows:
>
> ```
> iNum1 = 2;
> ```
>
> C++ does not care if you use extra spaces or even spread the statements over two or more lines. Therefore, the following statements all have the same result:
>
> ```
> iNum1      = 2;
> ```
>
> ```
> iNum1=    2;
> ```
>
> ```
> iNum1 =
>           2;
> ```
>
> However, you must not spread text that's enclosed in double quotation marks (""). For example, the following statement is not allowed:
>
> ```
> // Never do this!!!
> cout << " This is
>             not allowed";
> ```

The next statement you typed sets the value of iNum2 to 3:

```
iNum2 = 3;
```

At this point in the program, iNum1 is equal to 2 and iNum2 is equal to 3. Then you set the value of iResult as follows:

```
iResult = iNum1 + iNum2;
```

In essence, you set the value of iResult to 2+3=5.

You display the text The result is: as follows:

```
cout << "The result is: \n";
```

You then execute cout again to display the value of iResult:

```
cout << iResult;
```

Because iResult is not enclosed in double quotes, the cout statement won't display the text iResult. Rather, the cout statement will display the value of iResult, which is 5.

☐ Select Build MyHello.EXE from the Build menu.

☐ Select Execute MyHello.EXE from the Build menu and verify that the MyHello program displays the expected results, shown in Figure A.12.

☐ Press any key to terminate the program.

Figure A.12.
The MyHello program displays the value of iResult.

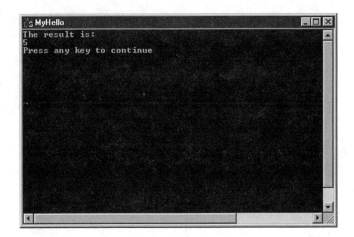

Functions in C++

The MyHello program currently has one function in it, the main() function. You'll now add a second function called AddIt():

☐ Modify the MyHello.cpp file so that it will look like the following:

```
// Program Name: MyHello.cpp

#include <iostream.h>

void main()
{
int iNum1;
int iNum2;
int iResult;

iNum1 = 2;
iNum2 = 3;
```

```
    iResult = AddIt(iNum1, iNum2);

    cout << "The result is: \n";
    cout << iResult;
    cout << "\n";

    }
```

You deleted this statement:

```
iResult = iNum1 + iNum2;
```

and replaced it with the following statement:

```
iResult = AddIt(iNum1, iNum2);
```

AddIt() is the name of a function you'll write in the following sections. The text typed within the parentheses of the AddIt() function is called the *parameters* of the function. The parameters of the function are separated with commas. Therefore, you supplied two parameters to the AddIt() function: iNum1 and iNum2.

What will the AddIt() function do? AddIt() will perform an operation on the parameters iNum1 and iNum2: adding iNum1 to iNum2. Then AddIt() will return the value of the result of the addition. When you execute this statement:

```
iResult = AddIt(iNum1, iNum2);
```

you are telling the compiler to do the following:

```
"Set the value of iResult to the returned value of the AddIt() function".
```

Because you set the parameters of AddIt() to iNum1 and iNum2, the AddIt() function should return the value iNum1+iNum2=2+3=5.

Will the MyHello program work now? The answer is no! C++ is kind enough to supply you with the cout function, as well as many other preprepared functions, but C++ does not come with a function called AddIt() that performs the task described in the preceding paragraphs. The bottom line is that you have to write the AddIt() function yourself.

Declaring the Prototype of the AddIt() Function

When the compiler encounters the words AddIt(iNum1,iNum2) in main(), it doesn't know what they mean. You have to tell the compiler that these words mean a function called AddIt. You also have to tell the compiler that AddIt() takes two parameters and that each of the parameters is a variable of the type integer. Furthermore, you have to tell the compiler that

AddIt() returns an integer. Telling all these things to the compiler means that you have to write the prototype of the AddIt() function:

```
int AddIt( int, int);
```

The prototype declares the AddIt() function as one that returns an integer and takes two parameters, each of which is an integer.

☐ Type the prototype of the AddIt() function at the beginning of the MyHello.cpp file as follows:

```
// Program Name: MyHello.cpp

#include <iostream.h>

// Prototypes
int AddIt( int, int);

void main()
{

int iNum1;
int iNum2;
int iResult;

iNum1 = 2;
iNum2 = 3;

iResult = AddIt(iNum1, iNum2);

cout << "The result is: \n";
cout << iResult;
cout << "\n";

}
```

Now when the compiler encounters AddIt, it will know you're talking about a function called AddIt, and its description is declared in the prototype section at the beginning of the file. In the next section, you'll write the code of the AddIt() function.

NOTE

Every function must have a prototype, so where is the prototype of main()? As it turns out, main() is the only function that does not need a prototype.

Writing the Code of the AddIt() Function

You'll now write the code of the AddIt() function:

☐ In the MyHello.cpp file, add the code of the AddIt() function as follows:

```cpp
// Program Name: MyHello.cpp

#include <iostream.h>

// Prototypes
int AddIt( int, int);

void main()
{

int iNum1;
int iNum2;
int iResult;

iNum1 = 2;
iNum2 = 3;

iResult = AddIt(iNum1, iNum2);

cout << "The result is: \n";
cout << iResult;
cout << "\n";


}

int AddIt(int iNumber1, int iNumber2)
{

int iTheResult;

iTheResult = iNumber1 + iNumber2;

return iTheResult;

}
```

☐ Select Save All from the File menu to save your work.

The AddIt() function looks like this:

```cpp
int AddIt(int iNumber1, int iNumber2)
{

// The code of the AddIt() function
// is typed here

}
```

The body of the function is enclosed in curly brackets. Take a look at the first line of the AddIt() function:

```
int AddIt(int iNumber1, int iNumber2)
```

It's almost the same as the statement of the AddIt() prototype, but the first line of the function does't have a semicolon at the end as the prototype does. Also, the prototype does not have to specify the names of the two integer parameters passed to the AddIt() function, but the first line of the function must include the variables' names.

Passing Parameters to a Function

As you saw in the previous section, the first line of the AddIt() function contains the names of the two integers that main() passes to AddIt(). Therefore, main() includes this statement:

```
iResult = AddIt(iNum1, iNum2);
```

The first line of the AddIt() function means that the code in AddIt() has two variables, iNumber1 and iNumber2, that are integers:

```
int AddIt(int iNumber1, int iNumber2)
```

The value of iNumber1 is the same as the value of iNum1, and the value of iNumber2 is the same as the value of iNum2. This is because the parameters are passed to the AddIt() function in this order: iNumber1, then iNumber2.

Now the code in AddIt() has two variables: iNumber1 and iNumber2. You can write code that performs addition with these two numbers, beginning with this statement:

```
int iTheResult;
```

You declared another variable called iTheResult as an integer. Now AddIt() has three variables: iNumber1, iNumber2, and iTheResult. The next statement sets the value of iTheResult to the result of adding iNumber1 to iNumber2:

```
iTheResult = iNumber1 + iNumber2;
```

Now iTheResult is equal to iNumber1+iNumber2. Because main() executes AddIt(iNum1, iNum2) while iNum1 is equal to 2 and iNum2 is equal to 3, it is as though main() executed AddIt(2,3). So when AddIt() is executed, iNumber1 is assigned the number 2, and iNumber2 is assigned the number 3. Now iTheResult is equal to 2+3=5.

The last statement in the AddIt() function returns the iTheResult variable:

```
return iTheResult;
```

This is the same as saying the following:

```
return 5;
```

because iTheResult is currently equal to 5.

Now look back at this statement in main():

```
iResult = AddIt (iNum1, iNum2);
```

This statement assigns the value 5 to iResult.

☐ Select Build MyHello.EXE from the Build menu.

☐ Select Execute MyHello.EXE from the Build menu and verify that the MyHello program is working as expected.

☐ Press any key to terminate the program.

Scope of Variables

One of the most important things to know about C++ is the scope of the variables. iNum1 is declared in main(), so only main() knows about this variable. If you try to use the iNum1 variable from within AddIt(), you'll get a compiling error. Why? Because the iNum1 variable was declared in main(); therefore, you can use iNum1 only from within the code of main(). The same goes for iNum2 and iResult.

The AddIt() function has three variables: iNumber1, iNumber2, and iTheResult. You can use these variables only from within the code of AddIt(). If you try to use any of these variables from within main(), you'll get a compiling error, because main() doesn't know about these three variables.

Therefore, the scope of the iNum1 variable, as well as iNum2 and iResult, is in main(), but the scope of iNumber1, iNumber2, and iTheResult is in AddIt().

NOTE

In the first line of AddIt(), the first word is int:

```
int AddIt(int iNumber1, int iNumber2)
```

This means that AddIt() returns an integer. Indeed, the last statement in AddIt() is the following:

```
return iTheResult;
```

iTheResult was defined as type integer, so you are indeed returning an integer.

Sometimes, a function doesn't return any value. In this case, the first word on the first line of the function is void. For example, in the

> MyHello program, `main()` does not return any value, so the first word
> on the first line is `void`:
>
> ```
> void main()
> ```
>
> Also, when a function does not have any parameters, you simply use
> parentheses with no text enclosed, as in the first line of `main()`.

Performing Multiplication with the MyHello Program

Modify the MyHello program so that it will multiply two numbers, rather than add them:

☐ Add the prototype of the `DoMultiplication()` function to the beginning of the MyHello.cpp file:

```
// Program Name: MyHello.cpp

#include <iostream.h>

// Prototypes
int AddIt( int, int);
int DoMultiplication( int, int);
```

☐ Modify the `main()` function as follows:

```
void main()
{

int iNum1;
int iNum2;
int iResult;

iNum1 = 2;
iNum2 = 3;

/// iResult = AddIt(iNum1, iNum2);
iResult = DoMultiplication ( iNum1, iNum2 );

cout << "The result is: \n";
cout << iResult;
cout << "\n";

}
```

The code you typed comments out the statement that executes the `AddIt()` function:

```
/// iResult = AddIt(iNum1, iNum2);
```

Then `iResult` is set to the returned value of the `DoMultiplication()` function:

```
iResult = DoMultiplication ( iNum1, iNum2 );
```

In other words, you are passing two parameters, `iNum1` and `iNum2`, to the `DoMultiplication()` function. Because `iNum1` is equal to 2 and `iNum2` is equal to 3, `DoMultiplication` will have to return the number 6 (2*3=6). In C/C++, the multiplication sign is the * (asterisk) character found on your keyboard's 8 key.

☐ Add the `DoMultiplication()` function to the MyHello.cpp file (after the last line of the `AddIt()` function). Here is the code of the complete MyHello.cpp file:

```
// Program Name: MyHello.cpp

#include <iostream.h>

// Prototypes
int AddIt( int, int);
int DoMultiplication( int, int);

void main()
{

int iNum1;
int iNum2;
int iResult;

iNum1 = 2;
iNum2 = 3;

/// iResult = AddIt(iNum1, iNum2);
iResult = DoMultiplication ( iNum1, iNum2 );

cout << "The result is: \n";
cout << iResult;
cout << "\n";


}


int AddIt(int iNumber1, int iNumber2)
{

int iTheResult;

iTheResult = iNumber1 + iNumber2;

return iTheResult;

}
```

A

```
int DoMultiplication( int iNumber1, int iNumber2)
{

int iResultOfMultiply;

iResultOfMultiply = iNumber1 * iNumber2;

return iResultOfMultiply;

}
```

The first line of the `DoMultiplication()` function means that the function returns an integer and that two integers are passed to the function:

```
int DoMultiplication( int iNumber1, int iNumber2)
```

The two parameters that are passed are `iNumber1` and `iNumber2`. It is important to understand that `iNumber1` and `iNumber2` of the `DoMultiplication()` function have absolutely nothing to do with the `iNumber1` and `iNumber2` variables of the `AddIt()` function. In the `AddIt()` function, the `iNumber1` and `iNumber2` variables have their scope in the `AddIt()` function, and in the `DoMultiplication()` function, the scope of `iNumber1` and `iNumber2` is within the `DoMultiplication()` function.

☐ Select Save All from the File menu.

☐ Select Build MyHello.cpp from the Build menu.

☐ Select Execute MyHello.EXE from the Build menu and verify that the MyHello program works as expected—the program should report that 2*3 is 6.

☐ Press any key to terminate the program.

Passing Parameters by Value

Take a look at how `main()` executes the `AddIt()` function:

```
iResult = AddIt( iNum1, iNum2)
```

Now take a look at the first line of the `AddIt()` function:

```
int AddIt( int iNumber1, int iNumber2 )
{

}
```

Every variable is stored in a memory cell in the PC's RAM. So `iNum1` and `iNum2` have their own memory cells. But what about `iNumber1` and `iNumber2` of the `AddIt()` function? Because of the way you wrote the AddIt() function, iNumber1 and iNumber2 have their own memory cells. The value 2 was copied from the memory cell of iNum1 to the memory cell of iNumber1, and the number 3 was copied from the memory cell of iNum2 to the memory cell of iNumber2. But the important thing to note is that iNum1 uses a completely different memory cell from the one used by iNumber1. The same goes for the variables of the DoMultiplication() function. This is illustrated in Figure A.13. Note that this method of passing variables is called *passing the variables by value*.

Figure A.13.

Passing variables by value.

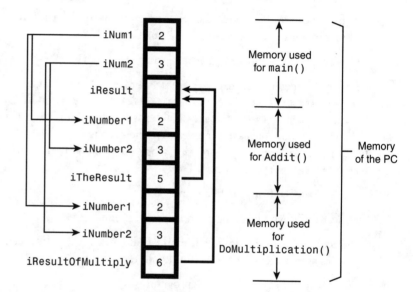

NOTE

A memory cell is called a *byte*. For simplicity, Figure A.13 (as well as subsequent figures) shows that iNum1 occupies one memory cell and iNum2 occupies one memory cell. However, the number of cells that a variable occupies depends on how the variable was defined. For example, when you declare a variable as char, the cMyChar variable occupies a single byte:

```
char cMyChar;
```

However, when a variable is declared as an integer, iNum1 uses four bytes of memory:

```
int iNum1;
```

NOTE

From the previous discussion, you can see that instead of defining the iResultOfMultiply variable in the DoMultiplication() function, you could use a variable called iResult. The DoMultiplication() function could be written as follows:

```
int DoMultiplication( int iNumber1, int iNumber2)
{

int iResult;

iResultOfMultiply = iNumber1 * iNumber2;

return iResult;

}
```

The variable iResult in main() occupies completely different memory cells than the iResult variable in DoMultiplication(). Likewise, you can use iResult in the AddIt() function instead of the iTheResult variable.

You'll now change the names of the parameters of the AddIt() function from iNumber1 and iNumber2 to iX and iY:

☐ Modify the MyHello program so that instead of using iNumber1 and iNumber2 as the variables of AddIt(), the iX and iY variables are used:

```
int AddIt(int iX, int iY)
{

int iTheResult;

iTheResult = iX + iY;

return iTheResult;

}
```

Using the variables iX and iY instead of iNumber1 and iNumber2 does not change what the function does. The function still adds the values of its two parameters and returns the result of the addition.

Using Global Variables

Take a look at Figure A.13. iNum1 is called a *local variable* of main() because its scope is only within main(). Likewise, iNumber1 and iNumber2 in Figure A.13 are local variables to AddIt().

In C, you can use *global variables,* which are variables whose memory cells are shared by all the functions of the program. You don't have to pass the variable to the function, because the function can already use the variable. Follow these steps to see a global variable in action:

☐ At the beginning of the MyHello.cpp file, type the following statement:

```
int I_am_global;
```

The beginning of the MyHello.cpp file should now look like this:

```
// Program Name: MyHello.cpp

#include <iostream.h>

// Prototypes
int AddIt( int, int);
int DoMultiplication( int, int);

// Global variables
int I_am_global;
```

☐ Add the following prototype at the beginning of the MyHello.cpp file:

```
void SquareIt(int);
```

The beginning of the MyHello.cpp file should now look like the following:

```
// Program Name: MyHello.cpp

#include <iostream.h>

// Prototypes
int AddIt( int, int);
int DoMultiplication( int, int);
void SquareIt(int);

// Global variables
int I_am_global;
```

As you can see, you added the prototype of a function called SquareIt(). The SquareIt() function returns void, which means that the function doesn't return any value. The SquareIt() function has one parameter, which is an integer.

☐ Modify the code of the main() function:

```
void main()
{
```

```
        int iNum1;
        int iNum2;
        int iResult;

        iNum1 = 2;
        iNum2 = 3;

        //// iResult = AddIt(iNum1, iNum2);
        //// iResult = DoMultiplication ( iNum1, iNum2 );
        SquareIt(iNum1);
        iResult = I_am_global;

        cout << "The result is: \n";
        cout << iResult;
        cout << "\n";
        }
```

The code you typed in `main()` executes the `SquareIt()` function:

```
SquareIt(iNum1);
```

`SquareIt()` multiplies `iNum1` by `iNum1` and assigns the result to `I_am_global`, the square of `iNum1`.

The next statement you typed sets the value of `iResult` to `I_am_global`:

```
iResult = I_am_global;
```

☐ Add the code of the `SquareIt()` function to the end of the MyHello.cpp file. When you finish, the complete MyHello.cpp file should look like the following:

```
// Program Name: MyHello.cpp

#include <iostream.h>

// Prototypes
int AddIt( int, int);
int DoMultiplication( int, int);
void SquareIt(int);

// Global variables
int I_am_global;


void main()
{

int iNum1;
int iNum2;
int iResult;

iNum1 = 2;
iNum2 = 3;
```

```
//// iResult = AddIt(iNum1, iNum2);
//// iResult = DoMultiplication ( iNum1, iNum2 );
SquareIt(iNum1);
iResult = I_am_global;

cout << "The result is: \n";
cout << iResult;
cout << "\n";

}


int AddIt(int iNumber1, int iNumber2)
{

int iTheResult;

iTheResult = iNumber1 + iNumber2;

return iTheResult;

}


int DoMultiplication( int iNumber1, int iNumber2)
{

int iResultOfMultiply;

iResultOfMultiply = iNumber1 * iNumber2;

return iResultOfMultiply;

}


void SquareIt( int iS )
{

I_am_global = iS * iS;

}
```

The code you typed in the SquareIt() function multiplies iS by iS, and the result is assigned to the I_am_global variable:

```
I_am_global = iS * iS;
```

Because iNum1 is equal to 2, iS is equal to 2, and you set I_am_global to 2*2=4. The important thing to note is that every function has access to I_am_global, because it was declared at the beginning of the MyHello.cpp file and not inside any function. Therefore, both main() and SquareIt() can use this variable.

☐ Select Save All from the File menu to save your work.

☐ Select Build MyHello.EXE from the Build menu.

☐ Select Execute MyHello.EXE from the Build menu and make sure the displayed result is 4 (because 2*2=4).

☐ Terminate the program by pressing any key.

Now here is the interesting part: Avoid using global variables as you avoid the plague! When your project becomes more complex, like including hundreds of functions in the program, it would be very easy to change the value of a global variable by mistake. In other words, it's too easy to change the value of a global variable, because you can set its value from within any function of the program.

Take, for example, the `iTheResult` variable in the `AddIt()` function. This variable is known only in `AddIt()`; no other function can touch this variable. Even if your project contained hundreds of functions, you know that the `AddIt()` function is a completely independent module. No matter what your project does, the `AddIt()` function has a specific purpose (to add two numbers), and it does this regardless of what other functions in your project are doing.

From `main()`, you can execute the `AddIt()` function as follows:

```
iResult = AddIt(iNum1, iNum2);
```

Using the preceding function sets `iResult` to a number that's the result of adding `iNum1` and `iNum2`. However, if you are updating a global variable in `SquareIt()`, and `main()` uses the `SquareIt()` function as in the following:

```
SquareIt( iNum1);

iResult = I_am_global;
```

you are opening the door for the possibility of making silly mistakes. For example, suppose that after a year, you come back to the project and make some modifications to the code. As you are doing your modifications, you insert code between the statements, as follows:

```
SquareIt( iNum1);
...
... // Additional code is inserted here
...
iResult = I_am_global;
```

Here is the problem: Suppose one of the statements you inserted executes another function that also makes use of the `I_am_global` variable. For example, some of the code you inserted between the two statement sets the value of `I_am_global` to 10. Now you have a bug in your program, because you expect `iResult` to be the square of `iNum1`.

You might say: Well, I'll be careful when inserting additional code. However, experience shows that no matter how careful you are, sooner or later you'll make the mistake of changing the value of a global variable as described previously. By the way, such mistakes are very difficult to debug when a program contains thousands of lines of code.

Addresses in C/C++

Take a look at Figure A.13. This figure shows that one of the memory cells is iNum1 and it contains the value 2. As a programmer, you call this memory cell iNum1, but the PC refers to this memory cell by a number. A PC's memory cells are numbered in sequential order: 1,2,3,4, and so on. These numbers are called the *addresses* of the memory cells. As a programmer, you'll probably never need to know the address of the memory cell, which isn't always the same. Depending on what was executed first, what is already stored in memory, and other factors, the address used for storing iNum1 is different even on the same computer. Nevertheless, you can extract the address used for the cell by using the & operator. Follow these steps to see this in action:

☐ Modify the code in main():

```
void main()
{

int iNum1;
int iNum2;
int iResult;

iNum1 = 2;
iNum2 = 3;


cout << "Address of iNum1 is: \n";
cout <<   &iNum1;
cout << "\n";


cout << "Address of iNum2 is: \n";
cout <<   &iNum2;
cout << "\n";


//// iResult = AddIt(iNum1, iNum2);
//// iResult = DoMultiplication ( iNum1, iNum2 );
SquareIt(iNum1);
iResult = I_am_global;


cout << "The result is: \n";
cout << iResult;
cout << "\n";


}
```

The following block of code you added displays the address used for the memory cell of iNum1:

```
cout << "Address of iNum1 is: \n";
cout <<   &iNum1;
cout << "\n";
```

You then used the following code to display the address of the iNum2 variable:

```
cout << "Address of iNum2 is: \n";
cout <<   &iNum2;
cout << "\n";
```

☐ Save your work, compile and link the program, then execute the program.

As shown in Figure A.14, the MyHello program displays the addresses of the memory cells used by iNum1 and iNum2.

Figure A.14.

Displaying the addresses of iNum1 *and* iNum2.

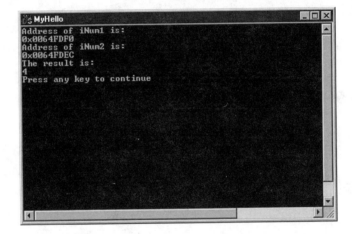

NOTE

In Figure A.14, the address of iNum1 is 0x0064FDF0, and the address of iNum2 is 0x0064FDEC. On your computer, you may see different values for the addresses, but the odd-looking number used for the address isn't important, because you'll never use it in your programs. However, the discussion of addresses leads to the subject of pointers, which is what makes C famous. In fact, if C/C++ did not have the capability of using pointers, it would never have gained the popularity it has.

Figure A.15 shows a pictorial representation of the memory cells. As you can see, I_am_global can be accessed from any function of the program.

Figure A.15.

A pictorial representation of the memory cells.

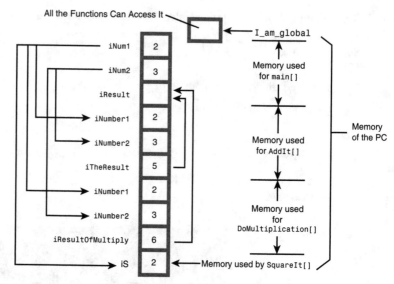

Using Pointers

An integer occupies four bytes in memory, so the left side of Figure A.16 is a more accurate representation of the memory map that shows iNum1 and iNum2.

Figure A.16.

Pointers to iNum1 *and* iNum2.

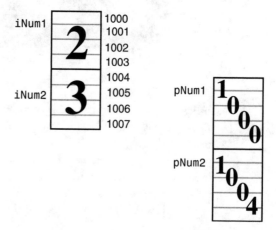

Suppose that iNum1 is equal to 2 and the address of iNum1 is 1000. iNum1 will occupy the bytes at locations 1000, 1001, 1002, and 1003. If iNum2 were equal to 3, iNum2 would occupy the cells at addresses 1004, 1005, 1006, and 1007. Therefore, iNum1 starts at address 1000, and iNum2 starts at address 1004. However, even though iNum1 occupies four addresses, in C/C++ the address of iNum1 is called 1000 and the address of iNum2 is called 1004.

Now declare two variables, pNum1 and pNum2, as pointers. Your objective is to store the number 1000 (the address of iNum1) in pNum1 and the number 1004 (the address of iNum2) in pNum2. This is illustrated on the right side of Figure A.16.

☐ Modify main() so that it will look like the following:

```
void main()
{

int iNum1;
int iNum2;
int iResult;


int* pNum1;
int* pNum2;


iNum1 = 2;
iNum2 = 3;

pNum1 = &iNum1;
pNum2 = &iNum2;


iResult = *pNum1 + *pNum2;

cout << "The result is: \n";
cout << iResult;
cout << "\n";

}
```

The code you typed declares three integers:

```
int iNum1;
int iNum2;
int iResult;
```

Then two additional variables are declared:

```
int* pNum1;
int* pNum2;
```

Note that int* is used in the declarations. So what type of a variable is pNum1? Can you store integers in pNum1? The answer is no. You can store the address of a variable of type integer in pNum1. According to Figure A.16, you should store 1000 in pNum1 because 1000 is the address of iNum1. Similarly, you want to store the address of an integer in pNum2. Then you set the values of iNum1 and iNum2:

```
iNum1 = 2;
iNum2 = 3;
```

Next, you update the values of pNum1 and pNum2 variables:

```
pNum1 = &iNum1;
pNum2 = &iNum2;
```

The preceding two statements store the address of iNum1 into pNum1 and the address of iNum2 into pNum2.

NOTE

pNum1 is called the pointer of iNum1, and pNum2 is called the pointer of iNum2. Although it isn't a C/C++ requirement, pointer names have been preceded with the letter p so that it will be easy to tell that pNum1 is a pointer.

Next, you want to calculate the result of adding iNum1 to iNum2. You could easily use the following statement:

```
iResult = iNum1 + iNum2;
```

However, try performing the calculations by using pointers rather than variables. For example, you use the following statement to calculate the result of adding iNum1 and iNum2:

```
iResult = *pNum1 + *pNum2;
```

When you precede the pointer with the * character, you are extracting the value stored in the address. *pNum1 is the same as *1000 (because pNum1 is equal to 1000 in Figure A.16), so the program checks for the value stored in address 1000. Because pNum1 was declared as int*, (and the program knows that an integer occupies four memory cells), the program looks at addresses 1000, 1001, 1002, and 1003. The program finds the value 2 in these addresses, so *pNum1 is equal to 2. Similarly, *pNum2 is equal to 3 because pNum2 is equal to 1004, and memory cells 1004, 1005, 1006, and 1007 contain an integer with a value of 3.

Finally, cout is executed to display the value of iResult:

```
cout << "The result is: \n";
cout << iResult;
cout << "\n";
```

☐ Save your work, compile and link the MyHello program, then execute the program. Make sure that iResult is 5 (2+3=5).

☐ Terminate the program by pressing any key.

It might seem as though pointers are a lot of trouble and were invented for the sole purpose of confusing a new C/C++ programmer, but this is not the case at all. To see why pointers are so important, suppose a certain function wants another function to be able to change its

A

variable. For example, `main()` has a variable called `iToBeChanged`, and `main()` requires the `ChangeIt()` function to change the value of `iToBeChanged`. You could declare the `iToBeChanged` variable as a global variable, but if you do that, any function will be able to change `iToBeChanged`. You need to find a way to allow only the `ChangeIt()` function to change the `iToBeChanged` variable. You'll perform this task in the following steps:

☐ Declare the following prototype at the beginning of the MyHello.cpp file:

```
void ChangeIt(int*);
```

In other words, you are declaring a function that doesn't return anything. The parameter of the `ChangeIt()` function is a pointer to an integer.

☐ Modify the code of the `main()` function:

```
void main()
{

int iToBeChanged;

int* pToBeChanged;


iToBeChanged = 2;


pToBeChanged = &iToBeChanged;

ChangeIt( pToBeChanged);

cout << "iToBeChanged = \n";
cout << iToBeChanged;
cout << "\n";

}
```

The code you typed declares an integer variable:

```
int iToBeChanged;
```

Then the code declares a pointer to an integer variable:

```
int* pToBeChanged;
```

The `iToBeChanged` variable is then set to 2:

```
iToBeChanged = 2;
```

The pointer is then updated with the address of the `iToBeChanged` variable:

```
pToBeChanged = &iToBeChanged;
```

Next, the ChangeIt() function is executed:

```
ChangeIt( pToBeChanged);
```

You'll write the code of the ChangeIt() function later, but for now, assume that the ChangeIt() function changes the value of iToBeChanged.

Finally, the value of the iToBeChanged variable is displayed:

```
cout << "iToBeChanged = \n";
cout << iToBeChanged;
cout << "\n";
```

☐ Add the ChangeIt() function to the end of the MyHello.cpp file:

```
void ChangeIt(int* pMyVariable)
{

*pMyVariable = *pMyVariable + 1;

}
```

Recall that main() executes ChangeIt() as follows:

```
ChangeIt(pToBeChanged);
```

So, the parameter of ChangeIt() is the address of the iToBeChanged integer. As you know by now, *pToBeChanged is the value stored in iToBeChanged (which is 2). The code in the ChangeIt() function changes the value of the parameter that was passed to it:

```
*iMyVariable = *iMyVariable + 1;
```

Therefore, if *iMyVariable was passed to ChangeIt() as 2, the code in the ChangeIt() function changes 2 to 3 (2+1=3).

☐ Save your work.

☐ Compile and link the program.

☐ Execute the MyHello program and verify that the result is 3.

☐ Terminate the program by pressing any key.

Keep in mind that main() enables the ChangeIt() function to touch the iToBeChanged variable. No other function in the program can touch the iToBeChanged variable, because main() passes the address of iToBeChanged to the ChangeIt() function.

if **Statements**

You'll now learn about the if statement in C/C++. An if statement examines the value of a variable. Based on the result, certain code is executed. To see the if statement in action, follow these steps:

☐ Modify the main() function:

```
void main()
{

int iMyVariable;
int iHerVariable;

iMyVariable = 20;
iHerVariable = 30;

if (iMyVariable == 20 )
    {
    cout << "Yes, it is 20! \n";
    }

if ( iHerVariable == 50 )
    {
    cout << "It's 50! \n";
    }
else
    {
    cout << "It's not 50! \n";
    }

}
```

The code you typed declares two variables:

```
int iMyVariable;
int iHerVariable;
```

Then you set the values of the two variables:

```
iMyVariable = 20;
iHerVariable = 30;
```

An if statement is then executed:

```
if (iMyVariable == 20 )
    {
    cout << "Yes, it is 20! \n";
    }
```

The code under the if is executed if iMyVariable is equal to 20. This code displays the following message:

```
Yes, it is 20!
```

Another if statement is then executed:

```
if ( iHerVariable == 50 )
   {
   cout << "It's 50! \n";
   }
else
   {
   cout << "It's not 50! \n";
   }
```

The code under the if statement is executed if iHerVariable is equal to 50. The code under the else is executed if iHerVariable is not equal to 50.

NOTE

Note that two equal signs (==) are used in the if statement. For example, if iOurVariable is equal to 100, the code under the following if statement is executed:

```
if ( iOurVariable == 100 )
   {
   // This code is executed provided
   // that iOurVariable is equal to 100.
   }
```

Again, make sure to use two equal signs when you're using if statements.

☐ Save your work.

☐ Compile and link the program.

☐ Execute the program.

As shown in Figure A.17, the program displays the corresponding messages.

☐ Terminate the program by pressing any key.

Figure A.17.

The messages displayed when the if *and* if...else *statements are executed.*

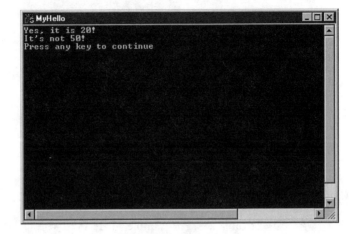

You can use other comparing statements with the if statement, as shown in the following example:

```
if ( i< 0 )
    {
    // This code is executed provided
    // that i is less than 0
    }


if ( i< = 0 )
    {
    // This code is executed provided
    // that i is less than or equal to 0
    }


if ( I > 0 )
    {
    // This code is executed provided
    // that I is greater than 0
    }

if ( I >=0 )
    {
    // This code is executed provided
    // that I is greater than or equal to 0
    }

if ( i != 3 )
    {
    // This code is executed provided
    // that i is not equal to 3
    }
```

```
if ( i == 3 && j == 4 )
   {
   // This code is executed provided
   // that i is equal to 3
   // and (&&) j is equal to 4
   }

if ( i == 3 ¦¦ j == 4 )
   {
   // This code is executed provided
   // that i is equal to 3
   // or (¦¦) j is equal to 4
   }
```

Strings

Strings are used to hold text. For example, "This is my string" is a string. C/C++ has a variety of data types: int, long, char, and so on. But in C/C++, there is no data type of the type string. So, how do you handle strings? You actually build the string character-by-character, as demonstrated in the following steps:

☐ Modify main() so that it will look like the following:

```
void main()
{

char sMyString[100];

strcpy(sMyString, "ABC");

cout << sMyString;
cout << "\n";

}
```

The code you typed declares a variable called sMyString of type char:

```
char sMyString[100];
```

The square brackets are used to declare arrays in C/C++. sMyString is a variable capable of holding 100 characters. You then execute the strcpy() function:

```
strcpy(sMyString, "ABC");
```

The strcpy() function works as follows:

The first parameter of strcpy() is the destination string; the second parameter is the source string. The strcpy() function copies the contents of the source string to the destination string. In the preceding statement, the string "ABC" is copied into the sMyString string.

A

If you were able to examine the characters of the sMyString variable at this point, you'd see the following:

- The first character of sMyString is A.
- The second character of sMyString is B.
- The third character of sMySTring is C.

Also, the fourth character of sMyString contains the value 0. The strcpy() function automatically inserts 0 for the fourth character of sMyString. In C/C++, when the last character of a string is 0, it means this is the end of the string.

Finally, you display the contents of sMyString:

```
cout << sMyString;
cout << "\n";
```

As you have seen, main() uses the strcpy() function. However, you don't have to write the strcpy() function yourself. Why? Because C/C++ is good enough to include the strcpy() function. C/C++ comes with many useful functions you can use from within your programs. You don't have to write the code of the strcpy() function yourself, but you do have to include its prototype. As it turns out, the file string.h (a file that comes with the C/C++ compiler) has the prototype of the strcpy() function. So all you have to do is simply use the #include statement at the beginning of the MyHello.cpp file:

Type the following statement at the beginning of the MyHello.cpp file:

```
#include <string.h>
```

Now the beginning of the MyHello.cpp file should look like this:

```
// Program Name: MyHello.cpp

#include <iostream.h>
#include <string.h>
```

☐ Save your work.

☐ Compile and link the program.

☐ Execute the MyHello program and verify that it displays the string ABC, as shown in Figure A.18.

Figure A.18.

Displaying strings.

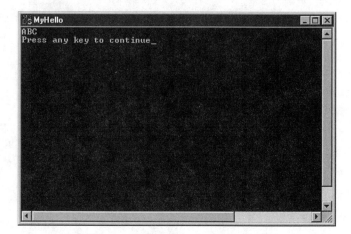

Summary

This is the end of Part I of the tutorial. Do you know the essentials of C/C++? To *really know* C/C++, you would have to program with it daily for at least several years. C/C++ is such a powerful, rich language that knowing everything about it is a long process, requiring years of experience. However, because technology is changing so rapidly, you often may be asked to start writing sophisticated Windows programs in a very short time. Most programmers cannot afford to spend too long on the study of C/C++, and reality dictates that you'll start designing and developing Visual C++ Windows programs immediately. You'll learn about additional C/C++ topics during the course of this book, but on a need-to-know basis. During the development of the programs, when a new C/C++ topic is used, it will be discussed at that point.

In Part II of this tutorial (Appendix B), you'll start learning about the C/C++ topics of classes and objects.

APPENDIX

B

Learning C/C++ Quickly (Part II)

In this part of the tutorial, you'll learn about topics such as structures, classes, and objects.

C/C++ Structures

As you saw, in C/C++ you can declare variables as follows:

```
int iMyVariable;
```

In the preceding statement, you declared iMyVariable as an integer. Here is a declaration of a variable of type char:

```
char cMyCar;
```

Data types such as int, float, char, and long are an integral part of C/C++, so you don't have to write any code that tells the compiler what these words mean. However, C/C++ also lets you declare your own custom-made data types. In the following section, you'll learn how to declare *structures*, which can be considered custom-made data types.

The MyStruct Program

The MyStruct program illustrates the use of structures in C/C++. Follow these steps to create the program:

☐ Create the C:\TYVCPROG\PROGRAMS\APPENDB directory. You'll save all the programs of Appendix B into this directory.

☐ Start Visual C++.

   Windows responds by running the Visual C++ program, and the desktop of Visual C++ is displayed.

☐ If you currently have an open project, select Close Workspace from the File menu of Visual C++.

☐ Select New from the File menu of Visual C++.

   Visual C++ responds by displaying the New dialog box.

☐ Make sure that the Projects tab of the New dialog box is selected.

☐ Select the Win32 Console Application item in the list of project types.

☐ Type MyStruct in the Project Name box.

☐ Click the button that is located on the right of the Location box and select the C:\TYVCPROG\PROGRAMS\APPENDB directory.

☐ Click the OK button of the New dialog box.

Visual C++ responds by creating the MyStruct project.

You'll now add a new file called MyStruct.cpp to the MyStruct project:

☐ Select New from the File menu.

Visual C++ responds by displaying the New dialog box.

☐ Make sure that the Files tab of the New dialog box is selected and select C++ Source File in the list of file types.

☐ Type MyStruct.cpp in the File Name edit box.

☐ Click the OK button of the new dialog box.

Visual C++ responds by adding the new file MyStruct.cpp to the MyStruct project and opening the window of the MyStruct.cpp file so that you'll be able to write code inside it.

☐ Type the following code in the MyStruct.cpp file:

```
// The MyStruct.CPP Program

#include <iostream.h>
#include <string.h>

// Declaring the structure.
struct MYSTRUCTURE
      {
      char sName[100];
      int  iAge;
      };


void main()
{

MYSTRUCTURE MyStructure;

strcpy( MyStructure.sName, "David" );
MyStructure.iAge = 13;

cout << "My name is ";
cout << MyStructure.sName;
cout << " and I am ";
cout << MyStructure.iAge;
cout << " years old.";
cout << "\n";


}
```

The code you typed uses two #include statements:

```
#include <iostream.h>
#include <string.h>
```

You include the file iostream.h because the code in main() uses cout, and the file string.h because the code in main() uses the strcpy() function (declared in the string.h file). You then declare a structure:

```
struct MYSTRUCTURE
     {
     char sName[100];
     int  iAge;
     };
```

Note the syntax for declaring a structure. The struct word appears first, followed by the name of the structure type. In this program, the structure type is called MYSTRUCTURE. Then the actual definition of the structure is declared in curly brackets. Don't forget to type the semicolon after the last curly bracket. Now take a look at the code in the curly brackets:

```
char sName[100];
int  iAge;
```

This means that MYSTRUCTURE is composed of a string called sName and an integer called iAge. sName and iAge are called the structure's *data members;* you've now declared the "inside" of the MYSTRUCTURE structure.

The code in main() declares a variable called MyStructure of type MYSTRUCTURE:

```
MYSTRUCTURE MyStructure;
```

Remember that in Appendix A you declared the iNum1 variable as follows:

```
int iNum1;
```

When you declare MyStructure to be a structure of type MYSTRUCTURE, think of MyStructure just as you think of iNum1. MyStructure is the name of the variable, and it's of type MYSTRUCTURE, just as iNum1 is of type int. (Note that, traditionally, the name of the structure is composed of lowercase or mixed-case characters, as in MyStructure, while the name of the structure type is all uppercase characters, as in MYSTRUCTURE.)

The next statement you typed in main() copies the string David into the MyStructure.sName data member:

```
strcpy ( MyStructure.sName, "David" );
```

The preceding statement refers to the sName data member as the following:

```
MyStructure.sName
```

The next statement updates the iAge data member of the structure:

```
MyStructure.iAge = 13;
```

Then a series of cout statements are executed:

```
cout << "My name is ";
cout << MyStructure.sName;
cout << " and I am ";
cout << MyStructure.iAge;
cout << " years old.";
cout << "\n";
```

To put it all together, the MyStruct program displays the message:

```
My name is David and I am 13 years old.
```

☐ Select Save All from the File menu to save your work.

☐ Select Build MyStruct.EXE from the Build menu.

☐ Select Execute MyStruct.EXE from the Build menu.

> *Visual C++ responds by executing the MyStruct program. As you can see, the MyStruct program displays this message:*

```
My name is David and I am 13 years old.
```

☐ Terminate the program by pressing any key.

Creating More Variables of Type MYSTRUCTURE

In the previous section, you created the variable MyStructure of type MYSTRUCTURE. You'll now create more variables of type MYSTRUCTURE:

☐ Modify the code in main() so that the MyStruct.cpp file will look like the following:

```
// The MyStruct.CPP Program

#include <iostream.h>
#include <string.h>

// Declaring the structure.
struct MYSTRUCTURE
      {
      char sName[100];
      int  iAge;
      };


void main()
{

MYSTRUCTURE MyStructure;

MYSTRUCTURE HerStructure;
```

B

```
        strcpy(MyStructure.sName,"David");
        MyStructure.iAge = 13;

        cout << "My name is ";
        cout << MyStructure.sName;
        cout << " and I am ";
        cout << MyStructure.iAge;
        cout << " years old.";
        cout << "\n";

        strcpy(HerStructure.sName,"Kim");
        HerStructure.iAge = 12;

        cout << "My name is ";
        cout << HerStructure.sName;
        cout << " and I am ";
        cout << HerStructure.iAge;
        cout << " years old.";
        cout << "\n";

    }
```

The main() function declares two variables, MyStructure and HerStructure:

```
MYSTRUCTURE MyStructure;

MYSTRUCTURE HerStructure;
```

MyStructure has two members: MyStructure.sName and MyStructure.iAge. HerStructure also has two members: HerStructure.sName and HerStructure.iAge.

You updated the data members of MyStructure as you did in the previous version of the MyStruct program:

```
strcpy(MyStructure.sName,"David");
MyStructure.iAge = 13;
```

Then the message is displayed:

```
cout << "My name is ";
cout << MyStructure.sName;
cout << " and I am ";
cout << MyStructure.iAge;
cout << " years old.";
cout << "\n";
```

The preceding statements display this message:

```
My name is David and I am 13 years old.
```

Next, the data members of HerStructure are updated:

```
strcpy(HerStructure.sName,"Kim");
HerStructure.iAge = 12;
```

The sName data member of HerStructure is set to Kim, and the iAge data member is set to 12.

Then a message is displayed:

```
cout << "My name is ";
cout << HerStructure.sName;
cout << " and I am ";
cout << HerStructure.iAge;
cout << " years old.";
cout << "\n";
```

The preceding statements display this message:

```
My name is Kim and I am 12 years old.
```

☐ Select Save All from the File menu.

☐ Select Build MyStruct.EXE from the Build menu.

☐ Select Execute MyStruct.EXE from the Build menu.

> *The MyStruct program responds by displaying these messages:*
>
> ```
> My name is David and I am 13 years old.
> My name is Kim and I am 12 years old.
> ```

☐ Terminate the program by pressing any key.

Classes

One of the main features of C++ that doesn't exist in C is the concept of *classes*. In fact, they're the most important concept in C++. C++ classes are similar to C structures. A C structure, however, defines only the data associated with the structure. The following example is a C structure:

```
struct CIRCLE
{
int radius;
int color;
};
```

After you declare the structure, you can use it from within your main() statement, as follows:

```
void main()
{
CIRCLE MyCircle;
...
...
...

MyCircle.radius = 10;
MyCircle.color = 255;  // 255 represents a color
...
...
...
}
```

The `MyCircle` structure has data associated with it (`radius` and `color`). A class in C++, on the other hand, has both data and functions associated with it. The data of the class is called *data members,* and the functions of the class are called *member functions.* In a program that uses classes, therefore, the following code is allowed:

```
MyCircle.radius = 20;
MyCircle.color = 255;
MyCircle.DisplayCircle();
```

The first two statements update the `radius` and `color` data members of `MyCircle`; the third statement uses the member function `DisplayCircle()` to display the `MyCircle` circle. `MyCircle` is called an *object* of class `CIRCLE`. Your program can declare another object called `HerCircle` of class `CIRCLE` as follows:

```
CIRCLE HerCircle;
```

The `radius` and `color` data members of `HerCircle` can be updated as follows:

```
HerCircle.radius = 30;
HerCircle.color = 0;
```

You can then use the `DisplayCircle()` member function to display the `HerCircle` circle:

```
HerCircle.DisplayCircle();
```

Declaring a Class

Before you can do anything with the class, your program must declare the class (just as before using the `MYSTRUCTURE` structure you have to declare its data members). In this section, you learn about the syntax used to declare a class. For practice, you'll declare a class called `Circle`:

```
class Circle
{
public:
    Circle();
    void SetRadius(void);
    void GetRadius(void);
    ~Circle();
private:
    void CalculateArea(void);
    int radius;
    int color;
};
```

The class declaration has the following skeleton:

```
class Circle
{
...
...
...
Here you type the declaration of the class
```

```
...
...
...
};
```

The `class` keyword is an indication to the compiler that whatever is typed between the curly brackets ({}) belongs to the class declaration. (Don't forget to include the semicolon at the end of the declaration.) The class declaration contains the declarations of data members (for example, `int radius`) and prototypes of the member functions of the class. In the `Circle` class declaration, there are two data members:

```
int radius;
int color;
```

The declaration also contains five prototypes of member functions:

```
Circle();
void SetRadius(void);
void GetRadius(void);
~CCircle();
void CalculateArea(void);
```

The first and fourth prototypes look strange. The first one is the prototype of the *constructor* function:

```
Circle();
```

You'll learn about the role of the constructor function later in this chapter; for now, examine the syntax that C++ uses for the prototype of the constructor function. When you write the prototype of the constructor function, you must follow these rules:

■ Every class declaration must include the prototype of the constructor function.

■ The name of the constructor function must be the same as the class name, followed by (). If you declare a class called `Rectangle`, for example, it must include the declaration of its constructor function, which must be `Rectangle()`. The declaration of the `Rectangle` class, therefore, looks like the following:

```
class Rectangle
{
public:
  Rectangle(); // The constructor
...
...
...
private:
...
...
...
};
```

■ Don't mention any returned value for the constructor function. (The constructor function must be of type `void`, but do not mention it.)

■ The constructor function must be under the `public` keyword.

NOTE

> At this point, you are probably asking yourself: What are the `public` and `private` keywords mentioned in the class declaration? These keywords indicate the visibility (accessibility) of the class's data members and member functions. You'll learn about these keywords later in the section "The `public` and `private` Keywords." For now, just remember that the constructor function must be under the `public` keyword.

The constructor function always has a return value of type `void` (even though you should not mention it in the prototype). As you'll soon see, the constructor function usually has one or more parameters.

The Destructor Function

The destructor function is mentioned in the class declaration as follows:

```
class Circle
{
public:
...
...
...
~Circle(); // The destructor
private:
...
...
...
};
```

Notice the tilde character (~) that precedes the prototype of the destructor function. (On most keyboards, you'll find the tilde character to the left of the 1 key.) When you write the prototype of the destructor function, observe the following rules:

■ The name of the destructor function must be the same as the class name, preceded by the ~ character. If you declare a class called `Rectangle`, for example, the name of the destructor function must be `~Rectangle`. The declaration of the `Rectangle` class, therefore, looks like this:

```
class Rectangle
{
public:
    Rectangle();  // The constructor
    ...
    ...
    ...
    ~Rectangle(); // The destructor
private:
```

```
      . . .
      . . .
      . . .
   };
```

■ Don't mention any returned value for the destructor function. (The destructor function must be of type void, but do not mention it.)

■ The destructor function does not have any parameters.

The public and private Keywords

You include the prototype of the functions and the declaration of the data members under the public or private section of the class declaration. The public and private keywords tell the compiler the accessibility of the functions and the data members. For example, the SetRadius() function is defined under the public section, which means that any function in the program can call the SetRadius() function. However, because the CalculateArea() function is declared under the private section, only code in the member functions of the Circle class can call the CalculateArea() function.

Similarly, because the radius data member is declared under the private section, only code in the member functions of the Circle class can update or read the value of this data member directly. Had you declared the radius data member under the public section, however, any function in the program could access (read and update) the radius data member.

NOTE   The class declaration defines the accessibility of its member functions and its data members with the public and private keywords.

The Circle Program

So far, you've learned about some important syntax topics of class declaration in C++. Now you're ready to write a program that makes use of a class. The program you'll write is called Circle.cpp.

Writing the Code of the Circle.cpp Program

Follow these steps to write the Circle.cpp program:

☐ Select Close Workspace from the File menu to close any opened project.

☐ When Visual C++ displays a message box asking you if you want to close all document windows, click the Yes button.

☐ Select New from the File menu of Visual C++.

   Visual C++ responds by displaying the New dialog box.

☐ Make sure that the Projects tab of the New dialog box is selected.

☐ Select the Win32 Console Application item in the list of project types.

☐ Type `Circle` in the Project Name box.

☐ Click the button that is located on the right of the Location box and select the C:\TYVCPROG\PROGRAMS\APPENDB directory.

☐ Click the OK button of the New dialog box.

   Visual C++ responds by creating the Circle project.

You'll now add a new file called Circle.cpp to the Circle project:

☐ Select New from the File menu.

   Visual C++ responds by displaying the New dialog box.

☐ Make sure that the Files tab of the New dialog box is selected and select C++ Source File in the list of file types.

☐ Type `Circle.cpp` in the File Name edit box.

☐ Click the OK button of the new dialog box.

   Visual C++ responds by adding the new file Circle.cpp to the Circle project and opening the window of the Circle.cpp file so that you'll be able to write code inside it.

☐ Type the Circle program's code in Listing B.1 in the Circle.cpp file.

Listing B.1. The Circle.cpp program.

```
// Program Name: Circle.CPP

// #include files
#include <iostream.h>

// Declare the CCircle class
class CCircle
{
public:
CCircle( int r);    // Constructor
void   SetRadius(int r);
void   DisplayArea(void);
~CCircle();         // Destructor
private:
float CalculateArea(void);
```

```
int m_Radius;
int m_Color;
};

// The constructor function
CCircle::CCircle ( int r )
{

// Set the radius
m_Radius = r;

}

// The destructor function
CCircle::~CCircle ()
{


}

// Function Name: DisplayArea()
void CCircle::DisplayArea ( void )
{

float fArea;

fArea = CalculateArea ( );

// Print the area
cout << "The area of the circle is: " << fArea;
cout << "\n";

}

// Function Name: CalculateArea()
float CCircle::CalculateArea ( void )
{

float f;

f = (float) (3.14 * m_Radius * m_Radius);

return f;

}

void main(void)
{
// Create an object of class Circle with
// radius equal to 10.
CCircle MyCircle ( 10 );

// Display the area of the circle
MyCircle.DisplayArea();

}
```

NOTE

Class names usually start with the letter C (the CCircle class, the CRectangle class, and so on). Data-member names usually start with the characters m_ (m_Radius, m_Colors, and so on).

These naming conventions aren't requirements in Visual C++, but they help you identify the names of classes and data members.

You haven't been instructed to type the code of the SetRadius() member function yet; you'll do that later in this appendix.

Examining the Circle Program's Code

In this section, you'll go over the code of the Circle.cpp program. First, the code must include the iostream.h file because the cout statement is used in this program:

```
#include <iostream.h>
```

The Circle.cpp program then declares the CCircle class:

```
class CCircle
{
public:
CCircle( int r);        // Constructor
void    SetRadius(int r);
void    DisplayArea(void);
~CCircle();             // Destructor
private:
float CalculateArea(void);
int m_Radius;
int m_Color;
};
```

The public section contains four prototypes. The first is the prototype of the constructor function:

```
CCircle( int r);        // Constructor
```

As always, the prototype of the constructor function doesn't mention that the function is of type void. Notice that the constructor function has the parameter int r.

Next are two more prototypes:

```
void    SetRadius(int r);
void    DisplayArea(void);
```

Remember, you'll be able to access these functions from any function in the program because they're public member functions. The fourth prototype under the public section is the prototype of the destructor function:

```
~CCircle();
```

Again, the prototype of the destructor function doesn't mention that this function is of type void. Notice that the ~ character precedes the name of the destructor function.

The `private` section of the `CCircle` class declaration contains the prototype of one function and the declaration of two data members:

```
private:
float CalculateArea(void);
int m_Radius;
int m_Color;
```

Because `CalculateArea()` is declared under the `private` section of the `CCircle` class declaration, you can call the `CalculateArea()` function only from within member functions of the `CCircle` class.

Now look at the `main()` function:

```
void main(void)
{

// Create an object of class CCircle with radius
// equal to 10.
CCircle MyCircle ( 10 );

// Display the area of the circle
MyCircle.DisplayArea();

}
```

The first statement in `main()` creates an object called `MyCircle` of class `CCircle`:

```
CCircle MyCircle ( 10 );
```

This statement causes the execution of the constructor function. At first glance, the notation for executing the constructor function may look strange. However, this notation makes sense: As stated earlier, the statement creates an object called `MyCircle` of class `CCircle`. The `MyCircle` object is created with a radius equal to 10 because the constructor function `CCircle()` has radius as its parameter.

Before continuing to examine the `main()` function, look at the constructor function:

```
// The constructor function
CCircle::CCircle ( int r )
{

// Set the radius
m_Radius = r;

}
```

The constructor function has one parameter, `int r`, as specified in its prototype. In the first line of the function, the function name is preceded by the text `CCircle::`, which means that the `CCircle()` function is a member function of the `CCircle` class:

B

```
CCircle::CCircle ( int r )
{
...
...
...
}
```

The code in the constructor function consists of a single statement:

```
m_Radius = r;
```

The parameter r is passed to the constructor function. Because you created MyCircle in main(), 10 is passed to the constructor function:

```
CCircle MyCircle ( 10 );
```

The statement in the constructor function sets the value of m_Radius to r:

```
m_Radius = r;
```

In short, the constructor function sets the value of m_Radius to 10. Recall that m_Radius was declared as a data member of the CCircle class, so any member function (public or private) of the CCircle class can read or update m_Radius.

At this point, the object MyCircle of class CCircle has been created, and its data member m_Radius has been set to 10. The next statement in main() executes the DisplayArea() member function:

```
MyCircle.DisplayArea();
```

You declared the DisplayArea() function in the public section of the CCircle class declaration; therefore, main() can access the DisplayArea() function. The dot (.) operator separates the name of the object MyCircle and the DisplayArea() function, giving the following instruction to the compiler:

```
"Execute the DisplayArea() function on the MyCircle object."
```

The DisplayArea() function displays the area of the MyCircle object.

Look at the code of the DisplayArea() function:

```
void CCircle::DisplayArea ( void )
{

float fArea;

fArea = CalculateArea ( );

// Print the area
cout << "The area of the circle is: " << fArea;
cout << "\n";

}
```

Again, the compiler knows that this function is a member function of the CCircle class, because the first line uses the CCircle:: notation. The function declares a local float variable called fArea:

```
float fArea;
```

Then the CalculateArea() function is executed:

```
fArea = CalculateArea ( );
```

CalculateArea() is a member function of the CCircle class; therefore, DisplayArea() can call the CalculateArea() function. The CalculateArea() function returns the area of the circle as a float number. The next statement in DisplayArea() uses cout to display the value of fArea:

```
cout << "The area of the circle is: " << fArea;
cout << "\n";
```

This statement streams the value of fArea and the string The area of the circle is: onto the screen.

NOTE

> You can use a single cout statement to display more than one string, as shown in this example:
> ```
> cout << "The area of the circle is: " << fArea;
> ```
> The preceding statement produces the same result as the following two statements:
> ```
> cout << "The area of the circle is: ";
> cout << fArea;
> ```

Now examine the CalculateArea() function. The first line of the CalculateArea() function uses the CCircle:: text to indicate that this function is a member function of the CCircle class:

```
float CCircle::CalculateArea ( void )
{

float f;

f = (float) (3.14 * m_Radius * m_Radius);

return f;

}
```

The CalculateArea() function declares a local variable called f:

```
float f;
```

Then the area of the circle is calculated and assigned to the f variable:

```
f = (float) (3.14 * m_Radius * m_Radius);
```

The text (float) is called *cast*. The number 3.14 is a float number (number with fractions), and m_Radius is an integer. The preceding statement multiplies an integer by an integer, then the result is multiplied by the float number 3.14. What is the data type of the result? You must assign a float number to f, because f was declared as float. Therefore, you cast the result of the multiplication with the (float) text. *Casting* is the process of converting the result to the desired data type.

CalculateArea() does not have any parameters. How, then, does this function know to substitute 10 for m_Radius? During the execution of the Circle program, the history of executing functions is traced. First, main() creates the MyCircle object:

```
Circle MyCircle ( 10 );
```

This code causes the execution of the constructor function, which causes the m_Radius variable of the MyCircle object to be equal to 10. Then main() executes the DisplayArea() function on the MyCircle object:

```
MyCircle.DisplayArea();
```

DisplayArea() executes the CalculateArea() function:

```
fArea = CalculateArea ( );
```

CalculateArea() knows to use 10 for the value of m_Radius since CalculateArea() is executed because DisplayArea() was executed on the MyCircle object. CalculateArea() can access m_Radius because CalculateArea() is a member function of the CCircle class and m_Radius is a data member of the CCircle class.

The last statement in CalculateArea() returns the calculated area:

```
return f;
```

The destructor function looks like this:

```
CCircle::~CCircle ()
{

}
```

The first line of the destructor function starts with the CCircle:: text, an indication that this function is a member function of the CCircle class. No further code is used in the destructor function. You should know, however, that the destructor function is executed automatically whenever the MyCircle object is destroyed—in this program, it's destroyed when the program terminates.

Notice that the SetRadius() function was not used in the program.

Compiling and Linking the Circle Program

You'll now compile and link the Circle.cpp program.

☐ Select Build Circle.EXE from the Build menu.

Visual C++ responds by compiling and linking the Circle.cpp program.

☐ Execute the Circle.EXE program.

The Circle.EXE program displays this message:

```
The area of the circle is: 314.
```

☐ Terminate the program by pressing any key.

The Circle2 Program

So far, you have declared a class called CCircle, you have created the object MyCircle of class CCircle, and you have calculated and displayed the area of the MyCircle object.

Although main() looks very elegant and short, it doesn't demonstrate the object-oriented nature of C++. The Circle2 program shows how you can create more than one object of class CCircle.

Writing the Code of the Circle2 Program

You'll now write the code of the Circle2.cpp program by following these steps:

☐ Select Close Workspace from the File menu to close any opened project.

☐ When Visual C++ displays a message box asking you if you want to close all document windows, click the Yes button.

☐ Select New from the File menu of Visual C++.

Visual C++ responds by displaying the New dialog box.

☐ Make sure that the Projects tab of the New dialog box is selected.

☐ Select the Win32 Console Application item in the list of project types.

☐ Type Circle2 in the Project Name box.

☐ Click the button that is located on the right of the Location box and select the C:\TYVCPROG\PROGRAMS\APPENDB directory.

☐ Click the OK button of the New dialog box.

Visual C++ responds by creating the Circle2 project.

You'll now add a new file called Circle2.cpp to the Circle2 project:

☐ Select New from the File menu.

    Visual C++ responds by displaying the New dialog box.

☐ Make sure that the Files tab of the New dialog box is selected, and select C++ Source File in the list of file types.

☐ Type `Circle2.cpp` in the File Name edit box.

☐ Click the OK button of the new dialog box.

    Visual C++ responds by adding the new file Circle2.cpp to the Circle2 project and opening the window of the Circle2.cpp file so that you'll be able to write code inside it.

☐ Type the code of the Circle2.cpp program as it appears in Listing B.2.

Listing B.2. The code of the Circle2.cpp program.

```cpp
// Program Name: Circle2.CPP

// #include files
#include <iostream.h>

// Declare the Circle class
class CCircle
{
public:
CCircle( int r);    // Constructor
void    SetRadius(int r);
void    DisplayArea(void);
~CCircle();          // Destructor
private:
float CalculateArea(void);
int m_Radius;
int m_Color;
};

// The constructor function
CCircle::CCircle ( int r )
{

// Set the radius
m_Radius = r;

}

// The destructor function
CCircle::~CCircle ()
{

}
```

B

```
// Function Name: DisplayArea()
void CCircle::DisplayArea ( void )
{

float fArea;

fArea = CalculateArea ( );

// Print the area
cout << "The area of the circle is: " << fArea;

}
// Function Name: CalculateArea()
float CCircle::CalculateArea ( void )
{

float f;

f = (float) (3.14 * m_Radius * m_Radius);

return f;

}

void main(void)
{
// Create an object of class CCircle with
// radius equal to 10.
CCircle MyCircle ( 10 );

// Create an object of class CCircle with
// radius equal to 20.
CCircle HerCircle ( 20 );

// Create an object of class CCircle with
// radius equal to 30.
CCircle HisCircle ( 30 );

// Display the area of the circles
MyCircle.DisplayArea();
cout << "\n";
HerCircle.DisplayArea();
cout << "\n";
HisCircle.DisplayArea();
cout << "\n";

}
```

Examining the Code of the Circle2 Program

In this section, you'll examine the code of the Circle2.cpp program. First, because the Circle2 program uses cout, you need to include the iostream.h file:

```
#include <iostream.h>
```

Then the class declaration of the CCircle class appears:

```
class CCircle
{
public:
    CCircle( int r);      // Constructor
    void    SetRadius(int r);
    void    DisplayArea(void);
    ~CCircle();             // Destructor
private:
    float CalculateArea(void);
    int m_Radius;
    int m_Color;
};
```

This class declaration is identical to the one in the Circle.cpp program. The constructor function of the CCircle class, the destructor function, the DisplayArea() function, and the CalculateArea() function are also the same as those for the Circle.cpp program. The code in the main() function is the only difference in the Circle2.cpp program:

```
void main(void)
{

// Create an object of class Circle with
// radius equal to 10.
CCircle MyCircle ( 10 );

// Create an object of class Circle with
// radius equal to 20.
CCircle HerCircle ( 20 );

// Create an object of class Circle with
// radius equal to 30.
CCircle HisCircle ( 30 );

// Display the area of the circles
MyCircle.DisplayArea();
cout << "\n";
HerCircle.DisplayArea();
cout << "\n";
HisCircle.DisplayArea();
cout << "\n";

}
```

The first statement in main() creates an object called MyCircle of class CCircle with its m_Radius data member equal to 10:

```
CCircle MyCircle ( 10 );
```

The next two statements create two more objects:

```
CCircle HerCircle ( 20 );
CCircle HisCircle ( 30 );
```

The HerCircle object is created with its m_Radius data member equal to 20, and the HisCircle object is created with its m_Radius data member equal to 30.

NOTE

> C++ is known as an OOP (object-oriented programming) language because it deals with objects.

Now that these three objects have been created, main() displays the circles' areas by using the DisplayArea() member function on the corresponding circle objects:

```
MyCircle.DisplayArea();
cout << "\n";
HerCircle.DisplayArea();
cout << "\n";
HisCircle.DisplayArea();
cout << "\n";
```

Between the execution of the DisplayArea() functions, cout is used to print a carriage-return/line-feed character (\n) so that an empty line will appear between the messages.

When the first DisplayArea() function is executed, its code executes the CalculateArea() function:

```
MyCircle.DisplayArea();
```

CalculateArea() makes use of the m_Radius data member, but which m_Radius will be used? The m_Radius of the MyCircle object is used because DisplayArea() works on the MyCircle object.

Similarly, when the CalculateArea() function is executed from within the DisplayArea() function, the m_Radius of the HerCircle object is used:

```
HerCircle.DisplayArea();
```

When the area of the HisCircle object is displayed, the m_Radius of HisCircle is used to calculate the area.

Compiling, Linking, and Executing the Circle2 Program

To see your code in action, follow these steps:

☐ Select Save All from the File menu to save your work.

☐ Select Build Circle2.EXE from the Build menu.

> *Visual C++ responds by compiling and linking the Circle2 program.*

☐ Select Execute Circle2.EXE from the Build menu.

Visual C++ responds by executing the Circle2.EXE program.

The Circle2 program should report the areas corresponding to the three circle objects: MyCircle has an area of 3.14*10*10=314, HerCircle has an area of 3.14*20*20=1256, and HisCircle has an area of 3.14*30*30=2826.

☐ Terminate the program by pressing any key.

In the preceding section, you entered the code of the Circle2.cpp program from Listing B.2; however, most of the code had been typed already in the Circle.cpp file. As you're probably starting to realize, that's the idea of object-oriented programming. You created the class during the development of the Circle.cpp program. From now on, you can develop other programs (such as the Circle2.cpp program) with a minimum of typing because you did most of the work during the development of the Circle.cpp program. In fact, the only thing you have to do to the Circle.cpp program to convert it to the Circle2.cpp program is to modify its main() function.

Reusing the CCircle **Class**

Notice how short and elegant the main() function of the Circle2 program is. This function is easy to read and, more important, easy to maintain. If you decide you need more accuracy in calculating the circle areas, you can simply change the code of the CalculateArea() member function. (You can change 3.14 to 3.1415, for example.)

If you type the class declaration in a file called CCircle.h, you can remove the CCircle class declaration from the Circle.cpp and Circle2.cpp files, then add the following statement at the beginning of the Circle.cpp and Circle2.cpp files:

```
#include "CCircle.h"
```

NOTE

Notice that in both Circle.cpp and Circle2.cpp, m_Radius was set by the constructor function. You cannot change the value of m_Radius from within main(), because m_Radius was declared in the private section of the class declaration.

Follow these steps to see the advantage of using classes in action:

☐ While the Circle2 project is open, select New from the File menu.

Visual C++ responds by displaying the New dialog box.

☐ Make sure that the Files tab of the New dialog box is selected.

☐ Select C/C++ Header File from the list of file types.

☐ Type CCircle.h in the File Name box.

☐ Click the OK button of the New dialog box.

> *Visual C++ responds by adding the new header file CCircle.h to the Circle2 project and displaying the CCircle.h file so that you'll be able to write code inside it.*

☐ Type the CCircle class declaration and its member functions in the CCircle.h file. (You can use Copy and Paste from the Edit menu to copy the CCircle class declaration from the Circle2.cpp file into the CCircle.h file.) Make sure the CCircle.h file looks like the one in Listing B.3.

☐ Select Save All from the File menu.

Listing B.3. The listing of the CCircle.h file.

```
// CCircle.h

// Declare the CCircle class
class CCircle
{
public:
CCircle( int r);     // Constructor
void    SetRadius(int r);
void    DisplayArea(void);
~CCircle();          // Destructor
private:
float CalculateArea(void);
int m_Radius;
int m_Color;
};

// The constructor function
CCircle::CCircle ( int r )
{

// Set the radius
m_Radius = r;

}

// The destructor function
CCircle::~CCircle ()
{

}

// Function Name: DisplayArea()
```

continues

Listing B.3. continued

```cpp
void CCircle::DisplayArea ( void )
{

float fArea;

fArea = CalculateArea ( );

// Print the area
cout << "The area of the circle is: " << fArea;
cout << "\n";

}

// Function Name: CalculateArea()
float CCircle::CalculateArea ( void )
{

float f;

f = (float) (3.14 * m_Radius * m_Radius);

return f;

}
```

☐ Modify the code in the Circle2.cpp file as follows:

```cpp
// Program Name: Circle2.CPP

// #include files
#include <iostream.h>
#include "CCircle.h"

void main(void)
{
// Create an object of class CCircle with
// radius equal to 10.
CCircle MyCircle ( 10 );

// Create an object of class CCircle with
// radius equal to 20.
CCircle HerCircle ( 20 );

// Create an object of class CCircle with
// radius equal to 30.
CCircle HisCircle ( 30 );

// Display the area of the circles
MyCircle.DisplayArea();
cout << "\n";
HerCircle.DisplayArea();
cout << "\n";
```

```
HisCircle.DisplayArea();
cout << "\n";

}
```

Note that you deleted the `CCircle` class declaration from the Circle2.cpp file. Instead, you included the `CCircle` class declaration by including the CCircle.h file.

NOTE

When you included the iostream.h file, you used the following statement:

`#include <iostream.h>`

When you included the CCircle.h file, you used the following statement:

`#include "CCircle.h"`

One h file is enclosed with the < > characters, and the other h file is enclosed with the " " characters.

One of the settings of Visual C++ is the Include path, which sets a path to the directory where several h files reside. iostream.h resides in the directory mentioned in the Include path of Visual C++; therefore, you can enclose the filename with the < > characters. Specifically, the iostream.h file resides in the \INCLUDE directory of Visual C++, which is also the default setting of the Include path.

On the other hand, the CCircle.h file resides in the C:\TYVCPROG\PROGRAMS\APPENDB\CIRCLE2 directory, which isn't mentioned in the Include path. This means you have to enclose the filename CCircle.h with the " " characters so the compiler will know to look for the CCircle.h file in the current directory of the project.

☐ Save your work by selecting Save All from the File menu.

☐ Select Build Circle2.cpp from the Build menu.

Visual C++ responds by compiling and linking the Circle2 program.

☐ Select Execute Circle2.EXE from the Build menu.

Visual C++ responds by executing the Circle2.EXE program. Check that the areas reported by the Circle2 program are correct.

☐ Terminate the program by pressing any key.

In a similar manner, you can modify the Circle.cpp program so that it will look like the following:

```
// Program Name: Circle.CPP

// #include files
#include <iostream.h>
#include "CCircle.h"


void main(void)
{
// Create an object of class Circle with
// radius equal to 10.
CCircle MyCircle ( 10 );

// Display the area of the circle
MyCircle.DisplayArea();

}
```

In the preceding code, you deleted the class declaration of CCircle from the Circle.cpp file. Instead, you included this statement:

```
#include "CCircle.h"
```

Overloaded Functions

In C++ (but not in C), you can use the same function name for more than one function. For example, you can declare two SetRadius() functions in the class declaration of the CCircle class. Such functions are called *overloaded functions*. Modify the CCircle class declaration to include an overloaded function:

☐ Select Open from the File menu and load the CCircle.h file from the C:\TYVCPROG\PROGRAMS\APPENDB\CIRCLE2 directory.

☐ Modify CCircle.h file so that it will look as follows:

```
// CCircle.h

// Declare the CCircle class
class CCircle
{
public:
CCircle( int r);     // Constructor

void    SetRadius(int r);          // Overloaded
void    SetRadius(int r, int c );  // Overloaded

void    DisplayArea(void);
~CCircle();            // Destructor

int m_Color;
```

```
    int m_Radius;

    private:
    float CalculateArea(void);
    //int m_Radius;
    // int Color;
    };

    // The constructor function
    CCircle::CCircle ( int r )
    {

    // Set the radius
    m_Radius = r;

    }

    // The destructor function
    CCircle::~CCircle ()
    {

    }

    // Function Name: DisplayArea()
    void CCircle::DisplayArea ( void )
    {

    float fArea;

    fArea = CalculateArea ( );

    // Print the area
    cout << "The area of the circle is: " << fArea;
    cout << "\n";

    }

    // Function Name: CalculateArea()
    float CCircle::CalculateArea ( void )
    {

    float f;

    f = (float) (3.14 * m_Radius * m_Radius);

    return f;

    }
```

This modified CCircle class is similar to the original CCircle class. However, now the int
m_Radius and int m_Color data members have been moved from the private section to the
public section so you could access m_Color from main(). As you can see, now the CCircle class
has two SetRadius() member functions:

```
void    SetRadius(int r);            // Overloaded
void    SetRadius(int r, int c );    // Overloaded
```

The first SetRadius() member function has one parameter, and the second SetRadius() has two parameters.

☐ Add the following code to the end of the CCircle.h file:

```
// Function Name: SetRadius()
void CCircle::SetRadius ( int r)
{

m_Radius = r;
m_Color = 255;

}
```

The code of the SetRadius() function sets the m_Radius data member to r, the parameter that was passed to SetRadius(). The code also sets the m_Color data member to 255.

☐ Add the following code to the end of the CCircle.h file:

```
// Function Name: SetRadius()
void CCircle::SetRadius ( int r, int c)
{

m_Radius = r;
m_Color = c;

}
```

The code of this second SetRadius() function sets the m_Radius data member to r. The code also sets the m_Color data member to c, the second parameter that was passed to SetRadius().

☐ Select Save All from the File menu to save your work.

☐ Open the Circle.cpp file and modify the code of the main() function as follows:

```
// Program Name: Circle2.CPP

// #include files
#include <iostream.h>
#include "CCircle.h"

void main ( void)
{
// Create the MyCircle object with radius equal to 10
CCircle MyCircle (10);

// Display the radius of the circle
cout << "The Radius is: " << MyCircle.m_Radius;
cout << "\n";

//Set the radius of MyCircle to 20.
MyCircle.SetRadius (20);

// Display the radius of the circle
cout << "The Radius is: " << MyCircle.m_Radius;
cout << "\n";
```

```
            // Display the color of the circle
            cout << "The Color of the circle is: " << MyCircle.m_Color;
            cout << "\n";


            // Use the other SetRadius() function
            MyCircle.SetRadius (40, 100);

            // Display the radius of the circle
            cout << "The Radius is: " << MyCircle.m_Radius;
            cout << "\n";

            // Display the color of the circle
            cout << "The Color of the circle is: " << MyCircle.m_Color;
            cout << "\n";


      }
```

☐ Select Save All from the File menu to save your work.

Examining the Modified `main()` Function of the Circle2 Program

This CCircle class is similar to the CCircle class used in the previous programs, except that the int m_Color data member has been moved from the private section to the public section. Also, the CCircle class declaration now has the following set of overloaded functions:

```
void    SetRadius(int r);              // Overloaded
void    SetRadius(int r, int c );      // Overloaded
```

The CCircle class has two SetRadius() functions: one with a single parameter (int r) and the other with two parameters (int r and int c). The first SetRadius() member function sets m_Radius to the value that was passed to it and also sets m_Color to 255:

```
void CCircle::SetRadius ( int r)
{

m_Radius = r;
m_Color = 255;

}
```

The second SetRadius() member function sets m_Radius and m_Color to the values that were passed to them:

```
void CCircle::SetRadius ( int r, int c)
{

m_Radius = r;
m_Color = c;

}
```

The `main()` function starts by creating the `MyCircle` object:

```
CCircle MyCircle (10);
```

The radius of `MyCircle` is then displayed:

```
// Display the radius of the circle
cout << "The Radius is: " << MyCircle.m_Radius;
cout << "\n";
```

The radius of `MyCircle` is changed to `20`:

```
//Set the Radius of MyCircle to 20.
MyCircle.SetRadius (20);
```

And the new radius is displayed:

```
// Display the radius of the circle
cout << "The Radius is: " << MyCircle.m_Radius;
cout << "\n";
```

In the preceding statements, the first `SetRadius()` was used. This means that only one parameter was passed to `SetRadius()`, which set `m_Color` to `255`. The value of `m_Color` is then displayed:

```
// Display the color of the circle
cout << "The Color of the circle is: " << MyCircle.m_Color;
cout << "\n";
```

Next, you used the second `SetRadius()` function:

```
// Use the other SetRadius() function
MyCircle.SetRadius (40, 100);
```

In the preceding statement, you set the radius to `40` and the color to `100`. Next, you display the radius and the color:

```
// Display the radius of the circle
cout << "The Radius is: " << MyCircle.m_Radius;
cout << "\n";
```

```
// Display the color of the circle
cout << "The Color of the circle is: " << MyCircle.m_Color;
cout << "\n";
```

☐ Select Build Circle2.cpp from the Build menu.

☐ Select Execute Circle2.EXE from the Build menu.

Check that the Circle2 program reports the radius and color of the `MyCircle` object as dictated in `main()`.

☐ Terminate the program by pressing any key.

How does the program know which `SetRadius()` function to use? By noticing the number of parameters you supplied to the function.

NOTE

The Circle2.cpp program illustrates how to set up and use overloaded functions, but it doesn't demonstrate how overloaded functions are used in practice. To understand the practical use of overloaded functions, consider a program that calculates the area of a circle and the area of a rectangle. As you know, the area of a circle is calculated in the following way:

```
Circle Area = Radius * Radius * 3.14
```

You also know that the area of a rectangle is calculated like this:

```
Rectangle Area = SideA * SideB
```

One way to write a program that calculates the area for both the circle and the rectangle is to write the following two functions:

```
CalculateCircleArea(Radius)
CalculateRectangleArea(SideA, SideB)
```

With overloaded functions, however, you can use a single function from within your program: `CalculateArea()`. The `CalculateArea()` function is an overloaded function. When only one parameter is supplied to the `CalculateArea()` function, the program calculates the circle's area; when two parameters are supplied to the `CalculateArea()` function, the program calculates the rectangle's area.

At first glance, this business of overloaded functions seems to be no help at all. After all, you have to write two separate functions; one function calculates the circle's area, and the other function calculates the rectangle's area. So what's the big deal about overloaded functions?

Consider what your main program looks like. Instead of remembering that the program has one function for calculating the circle's area and another function for calculating the rectangle's area, all you have to remember is that the program has one function—`CalculateArea()`—that takes care of both the circle and the rectangle. You have to know how to use the function, of course, which means you have to know what parameters, and how many, you should supply to the function.

Still, you may not agree that overloaded functions really help when it comes to calculating the areas of circles and rectangles. You'll learn to appreciate overloaded functions, however, when you create Windows applications. As you'll see in this book, Visual C++ comes with hundreds of useful Windows functions, many of which are overloaded functions. When you use these functions, your programs are easy to write, easy to read, and easy to maintain.

B

Declaring Variables in C++ Versus C

In C, you declare your variables at the beginning of the function. The following `main()` function declares the variable `i` at its beginning; then, `1,000` lines later, it uses the variable `i`:

```
void main(void)
{
i = 3;
...
...
...
// 1,000 lines of code
...
...
...

i =i + 1;
...
...
...
}

}
```

In C++, however, you don't have to declare your variables at the beginning of the function. The preceding C `main()` function can be written in C++:

```
void main(void)
{
...
...
...
// 1,000 lines of code
...
...
...
int i = 3;
i = i + 1;
...
...
...
}

}
```

Therefore, the variable `i` is declared closer to the code that uses it. Don't try to use the `i` variable before it's declared, of course.

Default Parameters

Another convenient feature of C++ that doesn't exist in C is default parameters. In C, you can declare the following function prototype:

```
int MyFunction (int a,
                int b,
                int c,
                int d);
```

The actual function may look like this:

```
int MyFunction (int a,
                int b,
                int c,
                int d)
{
...
...
...
}
```

If you execute MyFunction() from within main(), you must supply four parameters, because that's what you specified in the prototype of the function. So from within main(), you can execute MyFunction() as follows:

```
MyFunction (int 1,
            int 4,
            int 3,
            int 7);
```

C++ is more liberal than C. The designers of C++ knew that although you specified four parameters for MyFunction(), in most cases, you'll use the same values for some of the parameters of the function. Therefore, C++ enables you to specify default parameters in the prototype of MyFunction(), as in the following example:

```
MyFunction ( int a = 10,
             int b = 20,
             int c = 30,
             int d = 40 );
```

From main(), you can execute MyFunction():

```
main()
{
...
...
...
int iResult;
iResult = MyFunction();
...
...
...
}
```

Because you did not supply any parameters for MyFunction(), the compiler automatically interprets your statement this way:

```
main()
{
...
...
...
int iResult;
iResult = MyFunction(10,
                     20,
                     30,
                     40);
...
...
...
}
```

In addition, you can override some of the default parameters as follows:

```
main()
{
...
...
...
int iResult;
iResult = MyFunction(100, 200);
...
...
...
}
```

Because you didn't supply any third and fourth parameters to MyFunction(), the compiler automatically interprets your statement in the following way:

```
main()
{
...
...
...
int iResult;
iResult = MyFunction(100, 200, 30, 40);
...
...
...
}
```

In other words, you overrode the first and second parameters, and the compiler automatically substituted the third and fourth parameters (as indicated in the prototype of the function).

NOTE

When using a default parameter, you must use all the default parameters that appear after that parameter. For example, the following is not allowed:

```
void main(void)
{
...
...
...
int iResult;
iResult = MyFunction(100,
                     ,   // Not allowed
                 300
                 400);
...
...
...
}
```

Because you overrode the first parameter, you must specify a value for the second parameter as well.

B

Summary

In this chapter, you learned about classes and objects in C++ and the major differences between C and C++. C++ concepts are not difficult; they represent the natural evolution of the C programming language. C++ enables you to write complex programs that are easy to read and understand.

Consider the following declaration of the CPersonGoToWork class:

```
class CPersonGoToWork
{
public:
CPersonGoToWork(); // The constructor
void WakeUp(void);
void Wash(void);
void Dress(void);
void Eat(void);
void TakeBus(void);
void TakeCar(void);
void TakeSubway(void);
void TurnPCon(void);
void TurnIrrigationOn(void);
void CalibrateRadar(void);
~CPersonGoToWork(); // The destructor

private:
...
...
...
}
```

This class contains member functions that display cartoon characters doing something during the course of going to work. The TakeCar() function displays a person getting into a car, for example, and the TakeSubway() function displays a person taking a subway to work.

Consider the following main() program:

```
void main(void)
{
// Create an object called Jim
// for Mr. Jim Smart the programmer.
CPersonGoToWork Jim;

// Show Jim going to work.
Jim.WakeUp(void);
Jim.Wash(void);
Jim.Dress(void);
Jim.Eat(void);
Jim.TakeCar(void);
Jim.TurnPCon(void);

// Create an object called Jill
// for Ms. Jill Officer the policewoman.
CPersonGoToWork Jill;

// Show Jill going to work.
Jill.WakeUp(void);
Jill.Wash(void);
Jill.Dress(void);
Jill.Eat(void);
Jill.TakeCar(void);
Jill.CalibrateRadar();

// Create an object called Don
// for Mr. Don Farmer the farmer.
CPersonGoToWork Don;

// Show Don going to work.
Don.WakeUp(void);
Don.Wash(void);
Don.Dress(void);
Don.Eat(void);
Don.TurnIrrigationOn(void);

}
```

As you can see, main() can be written in a matter of minutes and can be easily understood and maintained. The real work of writing such a program, of course, is writing the member functions of the CPersonGoToWork class. When the class is ready, however, writing main() is very easy—this is the main advantage of using Visual C++ for writing Windows applications.

MFC is a group of C++ classes supplied with the Visual C++ package. As you'll see during the course of this book, most of your program is written already! All you have to do is understand the powerful member functions that exist in the MFC and apply them to your Windows applications.

In the next appendix (the third and last part of the tutorial), you'll learn about the inheritance topic of C++.

NOTE

As you'll see during the course of this book, writing Visual C++ Windows programs is actually very easy. Why? Because during the creation of your Visual C++ programs, you'll use C++ functions that were supplied with the Visual C++ package. You could say that knowing Visual C++ amounts to knowing how to use the C++ member functions and classes supplied with Visual C++.

B

APPENDIX C

Learning C/C++ Quickly (Part III)

In this part of the tutorial, you'll learn about the important topics of inheritance and hierarchy in C++.

The Rect Program

You'll begin by writing the Rect.cpp program:

☐ Create the C:\TYVCPROG\PROGRAMS\APPENDC directory (you'll save the programs of this appendix in this directory).

☐ Start Visual C++.

☐ If you currently have an open project, select Close Workspace from the File menu of Visual C++.

☐ Select New from the File menu of Visual C++.

   Visual C++ responds by displaying the New dialog box.

☐ Make sure that the Projects tab of the New dialog box is selected.

☐ Select the Win32 Console Application item in the list of project types.

☐ Type Rect in the Project Name box.

☐ Click the button that is located on the right of the Location box and select the C:\TYVCPROG\PROGRAMS\APPENDC directory.

☐ Click the OK button of the New dialog box.

   Visual C++ responds by creating the Rect project.

You'll now add a new file called Rect.cpp to the Rect project:

☐ Select New from the File menu.

   Visual C++ responds by displaying the New dialog box.

☐ Make sure that the Files tab of the New dialog box is selected, and select C++ Source File in the list of file types.

☐ Type Rect.cpp in the File Name edit box.

☐ Click the OK button of the new dialog box.

   Visual C++ responds by adding the new file Rect.cpp to the Rect project and opening the window of the Rect.cpp file so that you'll be able to write code inside it.

☐ In the Rect.cpp window, type the code shown in Listing C.1.

☐ Select Build Rect.Exe from the Build menu.

  Visual C++ responds by compiling and linking the Rect program.

☐ Select Execute Rect.EXE from the Build menu.

  As you can see, the Rect.EXE program displays a message that tells you the area of a rectangle.

☐ Terminate the program by pressing any key.

Listing C.1. The Rect.cpp program.

```
// Program Name: Rect.CPP

// #include
#include <iostream.h>

// The CRectangle class declaration

class CRectangle
{
public:
CRectangle(int w, int h);  // Constructor

void DisplayArea (void);    // Member function

~CRectangle();              // Destructor

int m_Width;   // Data member
int m_Height;  // Data member

};

// The constructor function

CRectangle::CRectangle( int w, int h)
{

m_Width = w;
m_Height = h;

}

// The destructor function
CRectangle::~CRectangle()
{

}

// Function Name: DisplayArea()

void CRectangle::DisplayArea(void)
{
```

continues

Listing C.1. continued

```
int iArea;

iArea = m_Width * m_Height;

cout << "The area is: " << iArea << "\n";

}

void main(void)
{

CRectangle MyRectangle ( 10, 5 );

MyRectangle.DisplayArea();

}
```

The Rect Program's Code

In this section, you'll go over the code of the Rect.cpp program. The program starts by including the iostream.h file because the cout statement is used:

```
#include <iostream.h>
```

Then the program declares the CRectangle class:

```
class CRectangle
{
public:
CRectangle(int w, int h);  // Constructor

void DisplayArea (void);   // Member function

~CRectangle();             // Destructor

int m_Width;   // Data member
int m_Height;  // Data member

};
```

The CRectangle class declaration contains the constructor function, the destructor function, the DisplayArea() member function, and two data members. The constructor function simply initializes the data members:

```
CRectangle::CRectangle( int w, int h)
{

m_Width = w;
m_Height = h;

}
```

No code appears in the destructor function, and the `DisplayArea()` function calculates the area of the rectangle and then displays it:

```
void CRectangle::DisplayArea(void)
{

int iArea;

iArea = m_Width * m_Height;

cout << "The area is: " << iArea << "\n";

}
```

The `main()` function creates an object called `MyRectangle` of class `CRectangle`:

```
CRectangle MyRectangle ( 10, 5 );
```

Because (`10`, `5`) is passed to the constructor function, the `MyRectangle` object has its width equal to `10` and height equal to `5`.

`main()` then displays the area of `MyRectangle`:

```
MyRectangle.DisplayArea();
```

As you can see, the `CRectangle` class enables you to calculate the area of the rectangle. Suppose you want to calculate the area of a rectangle with its width equal to `20` and height equal to `5`. What would you do? You could add `SetWidth()` and `SetHeight()` member functions that set the values of `m_Width` and `m_Height`. Therefore, the `CRectangle` class declaration would look like this:

```
// The CRectangle class declaration

class CRectangle
{
public:
CRectangle(int w, int h);   // Constructor

void DisplayArea (void);

void SetWidth  ( int w );
void SetHeight ( int h );

~CRectangle();              // Destructor

int m_Width;
int m_Height;
};
```

The `SetWidth()` and `SetHeight()` member functions would look like this:

```
// Function Name: SetWidth()

void CRectangle::SetWidth(int w)
{
```

```
m_Width = w;

}


// Function Name: SetHeight()

void CRectangle::SetHeight(int h)
{

m_Height = h;

}
```

Your main() function would look like this:

```
void main(void)
{

// Create the MyRectangle with width equal to 10
// and height equal to 5
CRectangle MyRectangle (10,5);

// Display the area
MyRectangle.DisplayArea();

// Change the width and height
MyRectangle.SetWidth(20);
MyRectangle.SetHeight(5);

// Display the area
MyRectangle.DisplayArea();

}
```

Adding Member Functions

There is nothing wrong with the preceding program's design, but it assumes you own the source code of the CRectangle class and therefore can modify it at any time. In many cases, software vendors don't give you the source code of the class; for one thing, they don't want you to have the source code because they worked hard to develop it. Also, they don't want you to mess with the source code of the class, because you could accidentally damage the class.

Nevertheless, in many cases you need to add some of your own member functions, just as you needed to add the SetWidth() and SetHeight() functions to the CRectangle class.

Class Hierarchy

To solve the problem of adding member functions, you can use the *class hierarchy* concept of C++, which enables you to create a new class from the original class. The original class is called the *base class*, and the class you create is called the *derived class*. The derived class inherits data members and member functions from its base class. When you create the derived class, you can add member functions and data members to it.

In this section, you create a class called CNewRectangle from the CRectangle class. The base class is CRectangle, and the derived class is CNewRectangle. Listing C.2 shows the code of the Rect2.cpp program that creates the derived class. Don't write the code of the Rect2.cpp program yet. You'll be instructed to type this code later in this chapter.

Listing C.2. The Rect2.cpp program.

```
// Program Name: Rect2.CPP

// #include
#include <iostream.h>

// The CRectangle class declaration (base class)
class CRectangle
{
public:
CRectangle(int w, int h);   // Constructor

void DisplayArea (void);

~CRectangle();            // Destructor

int m_Width;
int m_Height;

};

// The declaration of the derived class CNewRectangle
class CNewRectangle : public CRectangle
{

public:
CNewRectangle(int w, int h);  // Constructor

void SetWidth (int w);
void SetHeight (int h);

~CNewRectangle();            // Destructor

};

// The constructor function of CRectangle (base)
CRectangle::CRectangle( int w, int h)
{

cout << "In the constructor of the base class" << "\n";
```

continues

Listing C.2. continued

```
m_Width = w;
m_Height = h;

}

// The destructor function of CRectangle (base)

CRectangle::~CRectangle()
{

cout << "In the destructor of the base class" << "\n";

}

// Function Name: DisplayArea() (base)
void CRectangle::DisplayArea(void)
{

int iArea;

iArea = m_Width * m_Height;

cout << "The area is: " << iArea << "\n";

}

// The constructor function of CNewRectangle (derived)
CNewRectangle::CNewRectangle( int w,int h):CRectangle( w, h)
{

cout << "In the constructor of the derived class" << "\n";

}

// The destructor function of CNewRectangle (derived)
CNewRectangle::~CNewRectangle()
{

cout << "In the destructor of the derived class" << "\n";

}

// Function Name: SetWidth() (derived)
void CNewRectangle::SetWidth(int w)
{

m_Width = w;

}

// Function Name: SetHeight() (derived)
void CNewRectangle::SetHeight(int h)
{
```

```
m_Height = h;

}

void main(void)
{

CNewRectangle MyRectangle (10, 5);

MyRectangle.DisplayArea();

MyRectangle.SetWidth (100);
MyRectangle.SetHeight (20);

MyRectangle.DisplayArea();

}
```

The Rect2 Program's Code

The Rect2.cpp program declares the CRectangle class exactly as it was declared in the Rect.cpp program:

```
class CRectangle
{
public:
CRectangle(int w, int h);  // Constructor

void DisplayArea (void);

~CRectangle();            // Destructor

int m_Width;
int m_Height;

};
```

The Rect2.cpp program then declares a class called CNewRectangle, which is derived from the CRectangle class:

```
// The declaration of the derived class CNewRectangle
class CNewRectangle : public CRectangle
{

public:
CNewRectangle(int w, int h);  // Constructor

void SetWidth (int w);
void SetHeight (int h);

~CNewRectangle();             // Destructor

};
```

In the first line of the declaration of the derived class, the text : `public CRectangle` indicates that `CNewRectangle` is derived from `CRectangle`:

```
class CNewRectangle : public CRectangle
{
...
...
...
};
```

The derived class has a constructor function, a destructor function, the `SetWidth()` function, and the `SetHeight()` function. As you'll see, the `CNewRectangle` class has all the features of the `CRectangle` class. For example, even though the data members `m_Width` and `m_Height` don't appear as data members of `CNewRectangle`, `CNewRectangle` inherited these data members from `CRectangle`. Also, even though `CNewRectangle` doesn't have `DisplayArea()` as one of its member functions, for all practical purposes, it does because `CNewRectangle` inherited the `DisplayArea()` function from its base class.

The constructor function of the base class simply sets the values for the data members of the class:

```
CRectangle::CRectangle( int w, int h )
{

cout << "In the constructor of the base class" << "\n";

m_Width = w;
m_Height = h;

}
```

The cout statement is used in the preceding constructor function so you can tell during the program's execution that this constructor function was executed.

Following is the destructor function of the base class:

```
CRectangle::~CRectangle()
{

cout << "In the destructor of the base class" << "\n";

}
```

Again, the cout statement is used so you'll be able to tell this function was executed.

The `DisplayArea()` function of the base class calculates and displays the area:

```
void CRectangle::DisplayArea(void)
{

int iArea;

iArea = m_Width * m_Height;
```

```
cout << "The area is: " << iArea << "\n";
}
```

Now look at the constructor function of the derived class:

```
CNewRectangle::CNewRectangle(int w,int h):CRectangle(w,h)
{
cout << "In the constructor of the derived class" << "\n";
}
```

The first line of the preceding function includes this text:

```
:CRectangle(w,h)
```

This code means that when an object of class CNewRectangle is created, the constructor function of the base class is executed and the parameters (w and h) are passed to the constructor function of the base class.

The code in the constructor function of the derived class uses the cout statement so that during the program's execution you'll be able to tell that this function was executed.

Following is the destructor function of the derived class:

```
CNewRectangle::~CNewRectangle()
{
cout << "In the destructor of the derived class" << "\n";
}
```

Again, the cout statement is used so you'll be able to tell when this function is executed.

Following are the SetWidth() and SetHeight() functions of the derived class:

```
void CNewRectangle::SetWidth(int w)
{
m_Width = w;
}
void CNewRectangle::SetHeight(int h)
{
m_Height = h;
}
```

main() starts by creating an object of class CNewRectangle:

```
CNewRectangle MyRectangle (10, 5);
```

The preceding statement creates the `MyRectangle` object of class `CNewRectangle`. Because `CNewRectangle` is derived from `CRectangle`, however, you can use member functions from the base class:

```
MyRectangle.DisplayArea();
```

The preceding statement executes the `DisplayArea()` member function on the `MyRectangle` object. Even though the `CNewRectangle` class doesn't have the `DisplayArea()` member function in its class declaration, `CNewRectangle` inherited the `DisplayArea()` member function of the base class `CRectangle`.

The `main()` function then uses the `SetWidth()` and `SetHeight()` member functions to set new values for `m_Width` and `m_Height`:

```
MyRectangle.SetWidth (100);
MyRectangle.SetHeight (20);
```

Finally, `main()` uses the `DisplayArea()` function to display the area of the rectangle:

```
MyRectangle.DisplayArea();
```

Now that you understand the code of the Rect2.cpp program, you're ready to see it in action.

☐ Select Close Workspace from the File menu.

☐ When Visual C++ displays a message box asking you whether you want to close all document windows, click the Yes button.

☐ Select New from the File menu of Visual C++.

   Visual C++ responds by displaying the New dialog box.

☐ Make sure that the Projects tab of the New dialog box is selected.

☐ Select the Win32 Console Application item in the list of project types.

☐ Type Rect2 in the Project Name box.

☐ Click the button that is located on the right of the Location box and select the C:\TYVCPROG\PROGRAMS\APPENDC directory.

☐ Click the OK button of the New dialog box.

   Visual C++ responds by creating the Rect2 project.

You'll now add a new file called Circle.cpp to the Circle project:

☐ Select New from the File menu.

   Visual C++ responds by displaying the New dialog box.

☐ Make sure that the Files tab of the New dialog box is selected and select C++ Source File in the list of file types.

☐ Type `Rect2.cpp` in the File Name edit box.

☐ Click the OK button of the new dialog box.

> *Visual C++ responds by adding the new file Rect2.cpp to the Rect2 project and opening the window of the Rect2.cpp file so that you'll be able to write code inside it.*

☐ In the Rect2.cpp window, type the code shown in Listing C.2 earlier in this chapter.

You now can compile, link, and execute the Rect2.cpp program, as follows:

☐ Select Build Rect2.exe from the Build menu.

☐ Select Execute Rect2.EXE from the Build menu.

The Rect2.cpp program first executes the constructor function of the base class, then executes the constructor function of the derived class because of the following statement in `main()`:

```
CNewRectangle MyRectangle(10, 5);
```

The Rect2.cpp program then displays the area of a rectangle with its width equal to `10` and height equal to `5`. Next, the program displays the area of a rectangle with its width equal to `100` and height equal to `20`.

Finally, when the `main()` function is done, the `MyRectangle` object is destroyed. The destructor function of the derived class was executed, then the destructor function of the base class was executed.

When the object was created, the constructor function of the base class was executed, then the constructor function of the derived class was executed. When the object was destroyed, the destructor function of the derived class was executed, then the destructor function of the base class was executed.

Illustrating Class Hierarchy

Figure C.1 shows the class hierarchy relationship between `CRectangle` and `CNewRectangle`.

Figure C.1.
The class hierarchy of `CRectangle` *and* `CNewRectangle`.

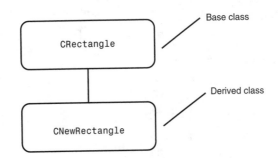

The relationship shown in Figure C.1 is simple, but the class hierarchy can be as complex as you want it to be. For example, you may want to construct another derived class, called CNewNewRectangle, derived from the CNewRectangle class. Its class declaration would look like this:

```
class CNewNewRectangle: public CNewRectangle
{
...
...
...
};
```

In the preceding declaration, CNewNewRectangle serves as the derived class and CNewRectangle serves as the base class. You can now declare another derived class for which CNewNewRectangle serves as the base class.

Figure C.2 shows a complex class hierarchy, which isn't shown just for educational purposes. In fact, as you'll see later in this book, the class hierarchy of MFC is far more complex than the one shown in the figure.

How can you use this illustration of a class hierarchy? You can tell which member functions you can execute. By looking at Figure C.2, you can tell that you can execute a member function that exists in class A on objects of class B, C, D, E, F, G, and H. You also can execute a member function in class F on an object of class G, E, and H, but you cannot execute a member function in class F on objects of class A, B, C, D, and E.

Figure C.2.

A complex class hierarchy.

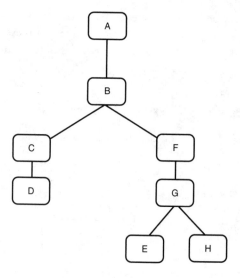

Overriding a Member Function

Sometimes, you may find it necessary to override a particular member function. Suppose you purchase the CRectangle class; you like this class, and you want to use it in your applications. The only problem is you don't like the way the author of the CRectangle class wrote the DisplayArea() function. Can you override that function? Sure. You'll now demonstrate how to do this by modifying the Rect2.cpp program. Follow these steps to modify the Rect2.cpp program:

☐ Add another prototype function to the declaration of the CNewRectangle class in the Rect2.cpp file as follows:

```
// The declaration of the derived class CNewRectangle
class CNewRectangle : public CRectangle
{

public:
CNewRectangle(int w, int h);  // Constructor

void SetWidth (int w);
void SetHeight (int h);

void DisplayArea();

~CNewRectangle(); // Destructor

};
```

In the preceding example, the prototype of the DisplayArea() function was added to the class declaration of the CNewRectangle derived class.

☐ Add the code of the DisplayArea() function of the derived class to the Rect2.cpp file:

```
// Function Name: DisplayArea() (derived)
void CNewRectangle::DisplayArea(void)
{

int iArea;

iArea = m_Width * m_Height;

cout << "================= \n";
cout << "The area is: " << iArea << "\n";
cout << "================= \n";

}
```

As you can see, the Rect2.cpp program now has two DisplayArea() functions. One is a member function of the CRectangle class (the base class), and the other is a member function of the CNewRectangle class (the derived class).

The `main()` function remains exactly as it was before:

```
void main(void)
{

CNewRectangle MyRectangle (10, 5);

MyRectangle.DisplayArea();

MyRectangle.SetWidth (100);
MyRectangle.SetHeight (20);

MyRectangle.DisplayArea();

}
```

☐ Save your work by selecting Save All from the File menu.

☐ Select Build Rect2.exe from the Build menu.

Visual C++ responds by compiling and linking the Rect2.cpp program.

☐ Select Execute Rect2.EXE from the Build menu.

The output of Rect2.cpp is the same as before, except that now the areas are displayed with the `DisplayArea()` function of the derived class. This means that when the following statement is executed, the `DisplayArea()` of the derived class, not the base class, is executed:

```
MyRectangle.DisplayArea();
```

☐ Terminate the program by pressing any key.

Using Pointers to Objects

In many cases, it is convenient to use pointers to objects. You'll now add code to the Rect2.cpp program that demonstrates this concept.

☐ Modify the `main()` function of Rect2.cpp as follows:

```
void main(void)
{

CNewRectangle MyRectangle (10, 5);

CNewRectangle* pMyRectangle = &MyRectangle;

pMyRectangle->DisplayArea();


pMyRectangle->SetWidth (100);
pMyRectangle->SetHeight (20);


pMyRectangle->DisplayArea();

}
```

As you can see, `main()` creates an object `MyRectangle` of class `CNewRectangle`:

```
CNewRectangle MyRectangle (10, 5);
```

Then `main()` declares a pointer `pMyRectangle` of type `CNewRectangle`:

```
CNewRectangle* pMyRectangle = &MyRectangle;
```

In the preceding statement, the address of the `MyRectangle` object is assigned to `pMyRectangle`.

The rest of the statements in `main()` are similar to the original code of `main()`. However, unlike the original code of `main()`, now `main()` uses the pointer of the `MyRectangle` object to execute the member function.

The `DisplayArea()` function is executed as follows:

```
pMyRectangle->DisplayArea();
```

You execute the `SetWidth()` and `SetHeight()` functions this way:

```
pMyRectangle->SetWidth (100);
pMyRectangle->SetHeight (20);
```

The name of the member function is separated from the pointer of the object with the `->` characters.

☐ Compile and link the Rect2.cpp program by selecting Build Rect2.exe from the Build menu.

☐ Execute the Rect2.EXE program by selecting Execute Rect2.exe from the Build menu.

☐ Check that the results of the Rect2.EXE program are the same as before.

☐ Terminate the program by pressing any key.

The new and delete Operators

You created the `MyRectangle` object in `main()` as follows:

```
void main(void)
{

CNewRectangle MyRectangle (10, 5);

CNewRectangle* pMyRectangle = &MyRectangle;

pMyRectangle->DisplayArea();

...
...
...

}
```

In the preceding `main()` function, the object is destroyed when `main()` terminates. Similarly, if you create the object from within a function called `MyFunction()`, the memory used for storing the `MyRectangle` object is freed automatically when `MyFunction()` terminates:

```
void MyFunction(void)
{

CNewRectangle MyRectangle (10, 5);

CNewRectangle* pMyRectangle = &MyRectangle;

pMyRectangle->DisplayArea();

...
...
...

}
```

The object is created with the following statement:

```
CNewRectangle MyRectangle (10, 5);
```

Then the pointer to the object is created:

```
CNewRectangle* pMyRectangle = &MyRectangle;
```

You can also use the `new` operator, which is equivalent to C's `malloc()` function. (The `malloc()` function allocates memory.) You'll now add code to the Rect2.cpp program that demonstrates how you can use the `new` operator.

☐ Modify the `main()` function of Rect2.cpp as follows:

```
void main(void)
{

CNewRectangle* pMyRectangle;
pMyRectangle = new CNewRectangle(10,5);

pMyRectangle->DisplayArea();


pMyRectangle->SetWidth (100);
pMyRectangle->SetHeight (20);


pMyRectangle->DisplayArea();

delete pMyRectangle;
}
```

☐ Select Save All from the File menu to save your work.

☐ Select Build Rect2.exe from the Build menu.

☐ Select Execute Rect2.EXE from the Build menu.

As you can see, the output of Rect2.EXE is the same as before.

☐ Terminate the program by pressing any key.

Now look at the code of the `main()` function of the Rect2.cpp program. The pointer `pMyRectangle` is declared. This pointer is declared as a pointer to an object of class `CNewRectangle`:

```
CNewRectangle* pMyRectangle;
```

Then the `new` operator is used to create a new object of class `CNewRectangle`. The address of this new object is stored in the pointer `pMyRectangle`:

```
pMyRectangle = new CNewRectangle(10,5);
```

The rest of the code in `main()` remains the same as it was before. To execute the `DisplayArea()` member function on the object, for example, you use this statement:

```
pMyRectangle->DisplayArea();
```

The last thing `main()` does is free the memory occupied by the object:

```
delete pMyRectangle;
```

The `delete` operator must be used to free objects created with the `new` operator.

NOTE

If you use the `new` operator from within a function, the memory occupied by the pointer is freed automatically when the function terminates (because the pointer is just a local variable to the function). The pointer holds a memory address where the actual object is stored; that memory is not freed when the function terminates. You must use the `delete` operator to free the memory occupied by the object.

NOTE

In the Rect2.cpp program, you created the object by using two statements in `main()`:

```
CNewRectangle* pMyRectangle;
pMyRectangle = new CNewRectangle(10,5);
```

In Visual C++, you typically see these statements combined in one statement:

```
CNewRectangle* pMyRectangle = new CNewRectangle(10,5);
```

This statement is identical to the preceding two statements.

Summary

Congratulations! You've finished the quick C++ tutorial. Starting in Chapter 1, "Writing Your First Visual C++ Application," you'll write true C++ Windows applications. Visual C++ enables you to write professional applications in a very short time. This is possible because Microsoft ships Visual C++ with a set of powerful classes called the MFC library. Learning Visual C++ amounts to knowing how to use the member functions of the MFC.

Visual C++ enables you to design your windows, dialog boxes, menus, bitmaps, and icons visually—you use the mouse and the visual tools to design these objects. Visual C++ also includes a wizard program called AppWizard, which writes the overhead code for you. A Windows application usually requires several overhead files; they appear in every Windows application you'll write. Instead of typing these repetitive, boring overhead files yourself, you can use AppWizard to generate and write them for you. You'll learn how to use AppWizard throughout this book.

Finally, Visual C++ is equipped with a wizard program called ClassWizard. As you learned in this appendix, when you know that a certain class is available, you can derive other classes that inherit the data members and member functions of the base class.

Unlike the `CRectangle` and `CNewRectangle` classes discussed in this appendix, the MFC classes are very powerful. Deriving classes from the MFC requires a great deal of typing. Don't worry, though—ClassWizard takes care of this task. ClassWizard inserts the prototypes of the member functions into the declaration of the derived classes and even starts writing the function for you. All you have to do is type your own specific code in the functions ClassWizard prepares for you.

These wizards are what Visual C++ is all about. Throughout this book, you'll use these wizards extensively.

INDEX

MACMILLAN COMPUTER PUBLISHING USA

A VIACOM COMPANY

Technical

Support:

If you need assistance with the information in this book or with a CD/Disk accompanying the book, please access the Knowledge Base on our Web site at **http://www.superlibrary.com/general/support**. Our most Frequently Asked Questions are answered there. If you do not find the answer to your questions on our Web site, you may contact Macmillan Technical Support **(317) 581-3833** or e-mail us at **support@mcp.com**.

Teach Yourself Microsoft Visual InterDev in 21 Days

Michael Van Hoozer

Using the familiar, day-by-day format of the best-selling *Teach Yourself* series, this easy-to-follow tutorial will provide users with a solid understanding of Visual InterDev, Microsoft's new Web application development environment. In no time, they will learn how to perform a variety of tasks, including front-end scripting, database and query design, content creation, server-side scripting, and more.

CD-ROM contains Internet Explorer 3.0, Microsoft ActiveX and HTML development tools, plus additional ready-to-use templates, graphics, scripts, Java applets, and ActiveX controls.

Price: $39.99 USA/$56.95 CDN
ISBN: 1-57521-093-2   800 pp.

User level: New-Casual-Accomplished
Internet-Web Publishing

Teach Yourself Visual Basic 5 in 21 Days, Fourth Edition

Nathan Gurewich & Ori Gurewich

Using a logical, easy-to-follow approach, this international bestseller teaches readers the fundamentals of developing programs. It starts with the basics of writing a program and then moves on to adding voice, music, sound, and graphics.

Price: $29.99 USA/$42.95 CDN
ISBN: 0-672-30978-5   1,000 pp.

User level: New-Casual
Programming

Teach Yourself Database Programming with Visual Basic 5 in 21 Days, Second Edition

Michael Amundsen & Curtis Smith

Visual Basic, the 32-bit programming language from Microsoft, is used by programmers to create Windows and Windows 95 applications. It can also be used to program applications for the Web. This book shows those programmers how to design, develop, and deploy Visual Basic applications for the World Wide Web.

Written by a Microsoft Certified Visual Basic Professional. CD-ROM includes sample code and third-party utilities.

Price: $45.00 USA/$63.95 CDN
ISBN: 0-672-31018-X   1,000 pp.

User level: New-Casual-Accomplished
Programming

Visual Basic for Applications Unleashed

Paul McFedries

Combining both power and ease of use, Visual Basic for Applications (VBA) is the common language for developing macros and applications across all Microsoft Office components. Using the format of the best-selling *Unleashed* series, users will master the intricacies of this popular language and exploit the full power of VBA.

CD-ROM is packed with author's sample code, sample spreadsheets, databases, projects, templates, utilities, and evaluation copies of third-party tools and applications.

Price: $49.99 USA/$70.95 CDN
ISBN: 0-672-31046-5   800 pp.

User level: Accomplished-Expert
Programming

VBScript Unleashed

Brian Johnson

In *VBScript Unleashed*, Web programming techniques are presented in a logical and easy-to-follow sequence that helps readers understand the principles involved in developing programs. The reader begins with learning the basics to writing a first program and then builds on that to add interactivity, multimedia, and more to Web page designs.

CD-ROM includes valuable source code and powerful utilities.

Price: $39.99 USA/$56.95 CDN   *User level: Casual-Accomplished-Expert*
ISBN: 1-57521-124-6   *650 pp.*   *Internet-Programming*

Teach Yourself Visual J++ in 21 Days

Laura Lemay, Patrick Winters, and David Blankenbeckler

Readers will learn how to use Visual J++, Microsoft's Windows version of Java, to design and create Java applets for the World Wide Web. Visual J++ includes many new features to Java including visual resource editing tools, source code control, syntax coloring, visual project management, and integrated bills. All those tools are covered in detail, giving readers the information they need to write professional Java applets for the Web.

CD-ROM includes all the source code from the book and all the examples.

Price: $39.99 USA/$56.95 CDN   *User level: Casual-Accomplished*
ISBN: 1-57521-158-0   *800pp.*   *Internet-Programming*

Visual J++ Unleashed

Bryan Morgan, et al.

Java is the hottest programming language being learned today. And Microsoft's Windows version of Java, code-named Visual J++, may prove to be even hotter. Microsoft has added several new development features, such as graphic designing, to the Java language. *Visual J++ Unleashed* shows readers how to exploit the Java development potential of Visual J++.

CD-ROM includes source code from the book and powerful utilities.

Price: $49.99 USA/$70.95 CDN   *User level: Accomplished-Expert*
ISBN: 1-57521-161-0   *1,000 pp.*   *Internet-Programming*

Tom Swan's Mastering Java with Visual J++

Tom Swan

Microsoft anticipates that its Visual J++ will fast become the leading Java development tool. This book, written by a leading industry expert and best-selling author includes chapter summaries, tips, hints, and warnings to teach readers how to program Java applications with Visual J++.

CD-ROM includes source code and Java utilities.

Price: $49.99 USA/$70.95 CAN   *User level: Casual-Accomplished*
ISBN: 1-57521-210-2   *750 pp.*   *Internet-Programming*

Add to Your Sams Library Today with the Best Books for Programming, Operating Systems, and New Technologies

The easiest way to order is to pick up the phone and call

1-800-428-5331

between 9:00 a.m. and 5:00 p.m. EST.
For faster service please have your credit card available.

ISBN	Quantity	Description of Item	Unit Cost	Total Cost
1-57521-093-2		Teach Yourself Microsoft Visual InterDev in 21 Days (Book/CD-ROM)	$39.99	
0-672-30978-5		Teach Yourself Visual Basic 5 in 21 Days, Fourth Edition	$29.99	
0-672-31018-x		Teach Yourself Database Programming with Visual Basic 5 in 21 Days, Second Edition (Book/CD-ROM)	$45.00	
0-672-31046-5		Visual Basic for Applications Unleashed (Book/CD-ROM)	$49.99	
1-57521-124-6		VBScript Unleashed (Book/CD-ROM)	$39.99	
1-57521-158-0		Teach Yourself Visual J++ in 21 Days (Book/CD-ROM)	$39.99	
1-57521-161-0		Visual J++ Unleashed (Book/CD-ROM)	$49.99	
1-57521-210-2		Tom Swan's Mastering Java with Visual J++ (Book/CD-ROM)	$49.99	
		Shipping and Handling: See information below.		
		TOTAL		

Shipping and Handling: $4.00 for the first book, and $1.75 for each additional book. Floppy disk: add $1.75 for shipping and handling. If you need to have it NOW, we can ship product to you in 24 hours for an additional charge of approximately $18.00, and you will receive your item overnight or in two days. Overseas shipping and handling adds $2.00 per book and $8.00 for up to three disks. Prices subject to change. Call for availability and pricing information on latest editions.

201 W. 103rd Street, Indianapolis, Indiana 46290

1-800-428-5331 — Orders   1-800-835-3202 — FAX   1-800-858-7674 — Customer Service

Special Disk Offer
The Full Version of the
TegoSoft OCX Control Kit

You can order the full version of the TegoSoft OCX Control Kit directly from TegoSoft, Inc.

The TegoSoft OCX Control Kit includes a variety of powerful OCX controls (ActiveX controls) for Visual C++ (as well as many other programming languages that support OCX controls).

Here are some of the OCX ActiveX controls that are included in the TegoSoft OCX Control Kit:

- An advanced multimedia OCX control (to play WAV, MIDI, CD audio, and movie files)
- An advanced animation OCX control
- 3-D button controls (for example, 3-D buttons, 3-D spin)
- A spy OCX control (which lets you intercept Windows messages of other applications)
- Gadget OCX controls
- A PC speaker OCX control (which enables you to play WAV files through the PC speaker without a sound card and without any drivers)
- Other powerful OCX controls

The price of the TegoSoft OCX Control Kit is $29.95. Please add $5.00 for shipping and handling. New York State residents, please add appropriate sales tax.

When ordering from outside the U.S.A., your check or money order must be in U.S. dollars and drawn from a U.S. bank.

To order by mail, send check or money order to

TegoSoft, Inc.
Attn.: OCX-Kit-VC521
Box 389
Bellmore, NY 11710

Phone: (516)783-4824
Web Site: http://www.tegosoft.com
E-mail: ts@tegosoft.com

You can also order the Download version of the product with a credit card (see details on how to order in the TegoSoft Web Site http://www.tegosoft.com). *Note:* Download version is identical in contents to the Disk version.

Visual C++ Environment and Tools Gallery

Learn how to write Visual C++ programs that use ActiveX (OCX) controls.

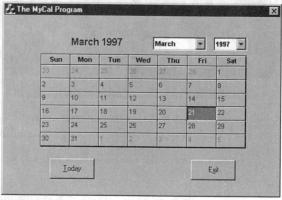

Learn to write programs that display images.

Write MDI (multiple document interface) programs.